Membership in International Organizations

Gerd Droesse

Membership in International Organizations

Paradigms of Membership Structures, Legal Implications of Membership and the Concept of International Organization

ASSER PRESS

Springer

Gerd Droesse
Vienna, Austria

ISBN 978-94-6265-326-9 ISBN 978-94-6265-327-6 (eBook)
https://doi.org/10.1007/978-94-6265-327-6

Published by T.M.C. ASSER PRESS, The Hague, The Netherlands www.asserpress.nl
Produced and distributed for T.M.C. ASSER PRESS by Springer-Verlag Berlin Heidelberg

This T.M.C. ASSER PRESS imprint is published by the registered company Springer-Verlag GmbH, DE part of Springer Nature.
The registered company address is: Heidelberger Platz 3, 14197 Berlin, Germany

Für Alessia

Preface

The idea to write a book on *Membership in International Organizations* came to me when I worked on the book *Funds for Development: Multilateral Channels of Concessional Financing* (2011), of which I am the editor and main contributor. While working on that book, I analyzed in detail the membership frameworks of international financial institutions. At the time, I noticed many issues regarding the traditional concept of membership that, in my view, required amplification and revision.

While traditional concepts of membership are still relevant for international organizations with treaty foundation, they do not take into sufficient account the evolution of public international law and the emergence of new paradigms of organizational structures and institutional frameworks, not established by a treaty, and with membership structures which do not only, or predominantly, comprise states as members, or those without any formal membership structures. Considering these new paradigms, a wider definition of international organization and subject of international law is warranted.

It is also necessary for international organizations to open themselves to the outside by promoting institutionalized participation of a wide range of transnational actors. International organizations should become open and multi-level and multi-actor institutions that give a voice to a wide variety of stakeholders, which may include, in addition to states, sub-state actors, technical government agencies and regulatory agencies, private sector entities, and philanthropy and civil society.

This book, which is based on a doctoral thesis submitted at Hamburg University, seeks to address these issues in a holistic manner by highlighting the many links that exist between membership and concepts such as constitution and constitutionalization, subject of international law and international legal personality, as well as with organizations' institutional, capital and governance structures, representation arrangements and operational and funding modalities, and with the very concepts of "intergovernmental organization" and "international organization".

Vienna, Austria Gerd Droesse

Acknowledgements

First and foremost, I wish to thank Prof. Dr. Armin Hatje for his support and his valuable suggestions, and Prof. Dr. Stefan Oeter and Prof. Dr. Markus Kotzur for their comments. I also wish to express my appreciation to Damien Eastwood, Assistant General Counsel; May Yap, Advisor (Finance); and Christopher L. Damandl, Senior Counsel, Asian Development Bank; Lisa Tabassi, Head, Legal Services, Organization for Security and Co-operation in Europe; and Samy Ben-Jaffar, formerly Director, Private Sector Facility, Green Climate Fund, and currently, Chief Executive Officer, Dubai Green Fund, for their comments and suggestions. The advice of Doo-Sik Kim, Senior Partner and Haneul Jung, Senior Foreign Attorney of the Shin and Kim law firm in Seoul on matters of Korean law was much appreciated.

I also wish to thank Maricris Jan Tobias, Ruby Vitto, and Romina Grace B. Rosellon for their help in finalizing the book, and Janette Husmillo and the staff of the Max Planck Institute for Comparative Public Law and International Law in Heidelberg for their support.

Contents

About the Author

Gerd Droesse is a recognized specialist in institutional law, international administrative law, complex institutional and financial policy matters, and corporate governance issues, with more than 30 years of experience in working for international organizations. Dr. Droesse helped in facilitating the transition of the World Green Economy Organization to a new type of intergovernmental organization with treaty foundation.

Previously, he contributed to setting up the legal and institutional framework of the Green Climate Fund where he served as the Legal Counsel of the Interim Secretariat, Acting General Counsel, and Senior Advisor of the GCF. With the Asian Development Bank (ADB) he worked as Lead Specialist, Institution and Coordination (Director) in the Office of The Secretary, as the Legal Adviser of the Asian Development Bank Institute, and as Head of the Special Practice Group: Institutional and Administrative in the Office of the General Counsel.

With extensive experience in resource mobilization issues, funding mechanisms and innovative modalities of financing, and ability to conduct comprehensive reviews of Human Resources policies, he also contributed to the work of Food and Agriculture Organization (FAO) of the United Nations as legal adviser to the Director of Personnel.

Dr. Droesse is qualified as a lawyer in Germany. He studied law and history at the universities of Würzburg (Germany) and Lausanne (Switzerland) and international relations at the Johns Hopkins SAIS Bologna Center in Italy and holds a Doctor of Law degree (*summa cum laude*) of Hamburg University. Dr. Droesse is the editor and main contributor of the book "Funds for Development: Multilateral Channels of Concessional Financing" which was launched in 2011 at the National University of Singapore and has contributed chapters to four books. Currently, he teaches "Law of International Organizations" at the Paris School of International Affairs (SciencesPo).

Abbreviations

ADB	Asian Development Bank
AfDB	African Development Bank
AIIB	Asian Infrastructure Investment Bank
AMRO	ASEAN+3 Macroeconomic Research Office
ASEAN	Association of Southeast Asian Nations
ASEAN+3	ASEAN + China, Japan, South Korea (ASEAN+3)
BCIE	Central American Bank for Economic Integration
BIS	Bank for International Settlements
CAF	Corporación Andina de Fomento
CDB	Caribbean Development Bank
CDM	Clean Development Mechanism
CEDARE	Programme for the Arab Region and Europe
CER	Certified Emission Reductions
CGIAR	Consultative Group for International Agricultural Research
CGIF	Credit Guarantee and Investment Facility
CoE	Council of Europe
COP	Conference of the Parties
CPISA	Convention on the Privileges and Immunities of the Specialized Agencies
CSCE	Conference for Security and Co-operation in Europe
CTBT	Comprehensive Nuclear-Test-Ban Treaty
CTBTO	Comprehensive Nuclear-Test-Ban Treaty Organization
DAC	Development Assistance Committee
EADB	East African Development Bank
EBRD	European Bank for Reconstruction and Development
ECAFE	UN Economic Commission for Asia and the Far East
ECB	European Central Bank
ECHR	European Court of Human Rights
ECLA	UN Economic Commission for Latin America
ECOSOC	Economic and Social Council of the United Nations

EDB	Eurasian Development Bank
EEC	European Economic Union
EIB	European Investment Bank
ESCWA	UN Economic and Social Commission for Western Asia
ESMA	European Securities and Markets Authority
EU	European Union
EURATOM	European Atomic Energy Community Treaty
EuroLat	Euro-Latin American Parliamentary Assembly
FAO	Food and Agriculture Organization
FOPREL	Forum of the Presidents of the Legislative Powers of Central America
FSB	Financial Stability Board
FSF	Financial Stability Forum
GATT	General Agreement on Tariffs and Trade
Gavi Alliance	Global Alliance for Vaccines and Immunization
GCF	Green Climate Fund
GEF	Global Environment Facility
General Convention	Convention on the Privileges and Immunities of the United Nations
GET	Global Environment Trust
GIZ	Gesellschaft für Internationale Zusammenarbeit
Global Fund	Global Fund to Fight Aids, Tuberculosis and Malaria
GMBH	Gesellschaft mit beschränkter Haftung
HIPC	Heavily Indebted Poor Countries
HRC	Human Rights Committee
IADB	Inter-American Development Bank
IAEA	International Atomic Energy Agency
IAIS	International Association of Insurance Supervisors
IANA	Internet Assigned Numbers Authority
IATA	International Air Transport Association
IAU	International Administrative Unions
IBRD	International Bank for Reconstruction and Development
ICANN	Internet Corporation for Assigned Names and Numbers
ICAO	International Civil Aviation Organization
ICC	International Criminal Court
ICJ	International Court of Justice
ICPC	International Criminal Police Commission
ICRC	International Committee of the Red Cross
IDA	International Development Association
IFAD	International Fund for Agricultural Development
IFFIm	International Finance Facility for Immunisation
IFI	International Financial Institutions
IGO	Intergovernmental Organizations
ILA	International Law Association
ILC	International Law Commission

ILO	International Labour Organization
IMF	International Monetary Fund
IMO	International Maritime Organization
INGO	International Nongovernmental Organization
INMARSAT	International Maritime Satellite Organization
INTELSAT	International Telecommunications Satellite Organization
INTERPOL	International Criminal Police Origination
IO	International Organization
IOIA	International Organizations Immunity Act
IOM	International Organization for Migration
IOSCO	International Organization of Securities Commissions
IPPC	International Plant Protection Convention
IPU	Inter-Parliamentary Union
IRENA	International Renewable Energy Agency
IRO	International Refugee Organization
IRRI	International Rice Research Institute
ISDB	Islamic Development Bank
ISFD	Islamic Solidarity Fund for Development
ISO	International Organization for Standardization
ISSB	International Standard-Setting Bodies
ITC	International Tin Council
ITO	International Trade Organization
ITU	International Telecommunication Union
IUOTO	International Union for Official Tourism Organizations
KFW	Kreditanstalt für Wiederaufbau
MDB	Multilateral Development Bank
MOU	Memorandum of Understanding
NDB	New Development Bank
NDF	Nordic Development Fund
NGO	Nongovernmental Organization
OAS	Organization of American States
ODA	Official Development Assistance
OECD	Organisation for Economic Co-operation and Development
OIE	World Organisation for Animal Health
OLA	United Nations Office of Legal Affairs
OPCW	Organization for the Prohibition of Chemical Weapons
OPEC	Organization of the Petroleum Exporting Countries
OSCE	Organization for Security and Co-operation in Europe
PAIGH	Pan American Institute for Geography and History
PCT	Patent Cooperation Treaty
PRC	People's Republic of China
QAB	Quasi-autonomous Bodies
REIO	Regional Economic Integration Organization
SBI	Subsidiary Body of Implementation
SCPI	South Caucasus Parliamentary Initiative

SITA	Societé Internationale de Telecommunications Aeronautiques
TEU	Treaty on European Union
TFEU	Treaty on the Functioning of the European Union
TNC	Transnational Corporations
UN	United Nations
UNCCD	United Nations Convention to Combat Desertification
UNCTAD	United Nations Conference on Trade and Development
UNDP	United Nations Development Programme
UNESCAP	UN Economic Commission for Asia and the Pacific
UNFCCC	United Nations Framework Agreement on Climate Change
UN-HABITAT	United Nations Human Settlement Programme
UNHCR	UN High Commissioner for Refugees
UNICEF	United Nations Children Fund
UNIDO	United Nations Industrial Development Organization
UNIFEM	United Nations Development Fund for Women
UNMIK	United Nations Interim Administration Mission in Kosovo
UNPF	United Nations Population Fund
UNRWA	United Nations Relief and Works Agency for Palestine Refugees in the Near East
UNU	United Nations University
UNWTO	World Tourism Organization
UPU	Universal Postal Union
VCLT	Vienna Convention on the Law of Treaties
VCLTIO	Vienna Convention on the Law of Treaties between States and International Organizations or Between International Organizations
WADB	West African Development Bank
WCO	World Customs Organization
WFP	World Food Programme
WHO	World Health Organization
WIPO	World Intellectual Property Organization
WMO	World Meteorological Organization
WTO	World Trade Organization

Chapter 1
Introduction

Contents

1.1 Traditional Concepts of International Organization

Traditional concepts of international organization are largely based on the state-centric concepts developed after the Peace of Westphalia of 1648. These concepts are predicated on the distinction between the public and private sphere and the corresponding distinction between governmental and nongovernmental organizations, the traditional paradigm of an international organization with a treaty foundation, restrictive concepts of "subject of international law" and "international legal personality", and the mantra that there cannot be an international organization without members.

The term "international organization", "which was probably first used by the Scottish jurist James Lorimer,[1] is used with many connotations". It is defined under certain conventions to mean, and was largely understood in the past, as being synonymous with the term "intergovernmental organization". Moreover, the term is often used with the additional connotation of "public international organization". Traditional theories of international law also emphasize the establishment of international organizations by a treaty or other international agreement and sometimes also require that an organization be endowed with international legal per-

[1] See Potter 1945, p. 805.

All weblinks are updated as of 28 February 2018.

G. Droesse, *Membership in International Organizations*,
https://doi.org/10.1007/978-94-6265-327-6_1

sonality for it to be recognized as an international organization. The organization's autonomy is conceptualized with reference to the organization's relationship with its members and is largely seen as the corollary of the organization's international legal personality.

Membership is a core element in all traditional theories of international organization. One of the mantras of public international law is that there cannot be an international organization without members. Traditional theories of international law and international organization are also predicated on the assumption that only the unitary state can be a subject of membership and that regular membership in international organizations only comprises states and, to a limited extent, international organizations. Hence sub-state actors (e.g., technical government agencies and regulatory agencies) are not seen as eligible subjects of membership in international organizations. Dependent territories are sometimes admitted as associate members; only very few organizations admit them as full members. Private sector entities and civil society organizations, on the other hand, are generally precluded from full membership and are, if at all, only admitted to a more limited type of affiliate or sector membership.

1.2 Static and Dynamic Concepts of International Organization

One of the core problems of many theories of international organization is that they view international organizations as static structures whose legal frameworks are defined by their constituent agreements which determine their functions and powers and establish their international legal personality. This gives insufficient weight to the fact that international organizations can evolve substantially.

Judge Alvarez already remarked more than 60 years ago, that while formerly, rules of law were elaborated, and evolved, slowly:

> Today, because of the social upheaval which we have just traversed, because of the remarkable dynamism in the life of peoples, because of the new international organization and the institutions and organs which this organization has created, and finally because of the aspirations of peoples and the exigencies of modern life, the elaboration of such new rules is rapid and sometimes even sudden; this elaboration is effected by means which are different from those of former times, and in this process the factors which have just been mentioned exert their influence.[2]

Developments in the realm of international organizations have been even faster than those in the field of international law, in general. Traditional theories of international organization give insufficient weight to this fact.

---

[2] "Competence of Assembly regarding admission to the United Nations, Advisory Opinion: ICJ Reports 1950, 4". Dissenting Opinion of M. Alvarez, 13. http://www.icj-cij.org/files/case-related/9/009-19500303-ADV-01-01-EN.pdf.

As indicated by Szasz, "human institutions show many of the traits of biological systems, including a striving to grow as far as resources allow, a tendency to proliferate and a resistance to annihilation unless survival by successors is assured."[3] The "law of complexification"[4] set out by Szasz also applies to international organizations, which may change beyond recognition due to mission creep and progressive institutionalization. In certain cases, their legal structures may be transformed and their legal status may evolve. Also, constituent instruments normally only regulate the powers of organs in very general terms and only provide a general blueprint of the relations of organs. The relationship of an organization's governing bodies (e.g., those between the executive head and the organization's governing bodies) may evolve substantially based on the personalities of the actors involved and the developments of the wider political agenda. Hence, a dynamic rather than a static concept of international organization is warranted not only to achieve an accurate understanding of the special characteristics of certain international organizations, but also in relation to the interactions of the various governing bodies of international organizations.

1.3 Early Developments Tie in with Recent Trends

State-centric concepts based on the Westphalian paradigm are so entrenched in the traditional concepts of international organization and international law that they are often accepted as a given notion and not critically reviewed. In this context, it is useful and pertinent to see the concept of international organization in a wider historical perspective. Such a perspective shows that some of the early beginnings tie in with recent developments.

This relates on the one hand to the private international unions which were created in the nineteenth century. One of the underlying considerations for creating these unions with private sector frameworks, rather than as organizations with treaty foundation, was to avoid the lengthy process of establishing an international organization by way of a treaty. Similar considerations were also paramount in the mind of those who created organizations such as the Global Fund to Fight Aids, Tuberculosis and Malaria (Global Fund) and Gavi, the Vaccine Alliance (Gavi Alliance), which may be seen as a new class of dual and hybrid organizations, established under national law but with recognition of international legal personality and privileges and immunities under international law. In that sense, early beginnings tie in with recent developments. Also, some organizations established in the nineteenth century or early twentieth century which previously were classified as nongovernmental [e.g., the International Criminal Police Origination (ICPO-Interpol, hereinafter referred to as "INTERPOL") and the Inter-Parliamentary

[3] Szasz 1999, pp. 2–3.

[4] Ibid.

Union (IPU)], are now recognized as intergovernmental, respectively, international organizations. In fact, they may be seen as new paradigms of intergovernmental, respectively, international organizations.

The example of the international administrative unions (IAUs) is also instructive as these pioneered wider concepts of subject of membership by allowing dependent territories and technical government agencies admission to membership at par with states. This is relevant to the discussion on eligible subjects of membership.

In addition, it is useful to go back even further, i.e., well before 1579 when Jean Bodin wrote his book titled "*Les six livres de la République*", promoting a concept of absolute and undivided sovereignty. This relates to the concepts of sovereignty and subject of international law which were distinct and broader in the middle ages that in the time after the Peace of Westphalia.

1.4 Necessary Changes to Concepts of Membership and Subject of International Law

It is one of the main themes of this book that traditional theories regarding membership and subject of international law are no longer in line with changed realities and the evolution of international law and need to be fundamentally rethought and revised for that reason.

Contrary to conventional wisdom, international organizations do not need to have members as the parties to the constituent agreement (if there is such an agreement) do not necessarily need to become members of the new international organization that will be established; in addition, there are international organizations which do not have any formal membership structure.

Membership in international organizations also does not need to be confined to states and a few international organizations. Private sector entities and other stakeholders (including sub-state actors and regulatory agencies) potentially may be subjects of membership as well. In addition, as the relations of an international organization with its members are of an internal nature, it is not necessary for an international organization to be endowed with international legal personality for it to have members.

Far-reaching changes are required also to the legal and policy frameworks governing membership in international organizations. Membership of international organizations needs to become more diversified and should include full, partial, sector or affiliate membership of private sector entities, philanthropic and civil society organizations and other stakeholders. Moreover, international organizations should become hubs, platforms and forums for a great variety of actors, including sub-state actors.

The concept of "subject of international law" also needs to be revised. It was only with the "consolidation of nation states in the sixteenth and seventeenth century and with the pivotal role attributed henceforth to the concept of sovereignty that the characteristics of what later became known as 'subject of international law' began to be the exclusive prerogative of States." International law has no intrinsic constraint against the recognition of entities other than states or intergovernmental organizations as subjects of international law. Hence, dual and hybrid organizations incorporated under national law, but with recognized international legal personality and privileges and immunities under international law, may qualify for recognition as subjects of international law. Moreover, the concept of "subject of international law" is broader than that of "international legal personality". Hence, organizations without international legal personality which act on the international plane and organizations established as trust funds may qualify for recognition as subjects of international law.

1.5 Need for a New Definition of International Organization

Traditional concepts of international organization fail to take account of the development of international law and the emergence of new forms of international cooperation. This work proposes that some fundamental concepts of international law and the law of international organizations need to be rethought and revised.

There are various new paradigms to establish international organizations that do not follow the traditional scheme. Organizations may be established based on resolution(s) of a conference or international organization(s), the adoption of a constitution by a governing body, by parallel acts of national law, by the legal acts of one country, or merely by consensus. They may also originate from the decision of a conference or a meeting of the parties to a multilateral environmental agreement, or they may be incorporated under national law. Organizations established as subsidiary bodies or as financial mechanisms of conventions or comprising sub-state actors or national regulators as members may also qualify, in principle, for recognition as international organizations.

Rather than recognizing that new types of international organizations without treaty foundation have emerged, international lawyers often try to associate the aforementioned modes of establishing an international organization with an agreement governed by international law. These attempts are futile at best and questionable at large and completely fail in some cases. A more promising and courageous approach is to admit that in essence it does not matter how international organizations are established. Whether organizations, including cooperative undertakings of sub-state actors and entities incorporated under national law, could be recognized as international organizations does not depend on the nature of the act establishing them, or on the composition and classification of their membership, but on their powers and functions and the position which recognized subjects of international law have taken in their regard.

The constituent agreement establishing an international organization is frequently seen as a hybrid of treaty and constitution. However, an international organization does not need to be established by a treaty, nor does its constitution need to be adopted as a treaty. The constitution adopted by a plenary body of an international organization may have similar functions as a constitution adopted by a treaty, and it may also be the basis for the external action of the organization.

In the light of the foregoing, there is a need to reassess the very concepts and definitions of "intergovernmental organization" and "international organization". The term "intergovernmental organization" needs to be interpreted in a wider manner to comprise a wide range of international organizations not established by a treaty, including organizations created pursuant a decision of a conference of the parties to a multilateral convention or organizations established as trust funds. Furthermore, an "intergovernmental organization" does not necessarily need to be defined as a public international organization. Hence, also dual and hybrid organizations incorporated under national law may qualify as "intergovernmental organizations".

As regards the term "international organization", the current definition of that term by the International Law Commission was coined in the specific context of the work of the Commission on responsibility of international organizations and needs to be understood in this context. It is not suitable to be given a general application. The term "international organization" should not be understood to comprise only public international organizations. Rather, given the evolution of public international law, dual and hybrid organizations incorporated under national law may be seen as a new paradigm of international organization. However, the term "international organization" is broader than "intergovernmental organization". Therefore, also organizations which are not established by agreement between governments or which do not have predominantly or exclusively states as members may qualify for recognition as international organization.

The need for new concepts of "intergovernmental organization" and "international organization" is a corollary of new trends and developments in international law. It is related, on the one hand, to the fact that the number of participants in the international legal system is increasing. In this context, a wider definition of international organization is required to include certain actors that were previously classified as nongovernmental. Such broader definition is also necessary as the borderline between public and private is shifting. The public and private and governmental and nongovernmental dichotomies can only capture the legal nature of international organizations to a limited extent. In the past, organizations that were not established by governments, and with representation arrangements not involving government representatives, were *ipso facto* relegated to the realm of non-governmental organizations. However, such an approach is no longer appropriate. It is no longer justifiable to exclude organizations of Parliamentary cooperation and organizations involving membership of sub-state actors, or technical agencies, from the realm of international organization for the only reason that they were not established by agreement between governments.

The same also applies to cooperative frameworks of national regulators which remain below the radar of international lawyers even though these frameworks wield large power and command billions of dollars. While many traditional international organizations are in perennial crisis, the field of cooperation for regulators continues to thrive. In principle, also cooperative undertakings of national regulators may qualify for recognition as international organization, based on progressive institutionalization. Whether this is the case depends on their powers and functions and the position which recognized subjects of international law have adopted in their regard.

Hence, fundamental changes to the concepts of "intergovernmental organization" and "international organization" are necessary which will have far-reaching legal and policy implications for a great variety of matters. These changes relate to the very qualification of international organizations as members of the international community, to their membership structures, and their ability to act on the international plane. Neither establishment by international agreement, nor membership or international legal personality should be part of a definition of international organization.

While traditionally, the autonomy of international organizations was defined with reference to their relationships with their members and was seen as a corollary of the international legal personality of organizations established by a treaty, it is necessary to rethink this traditional approach. The institutional autonomy of an organization needs to be defined in wider terms, as organizations not established by a treaty and without a formal membership structure may also enjoy institutional autonomy. Moreover, international organizations can well function without being endowed with international legal personality or legal capacity under national law.

The definition of "intergovernmental organization" and "international organization" is not only of theoretical significance but has many other implications. It is of decisive importance in relation to issues such as whether an organization may obtain observer status in the United Nations, how it may protect its emblems, whether it can access administrative tribunals and the Permanent Court of Arbitration, and even what domain name it is entitled to choose.

The concept advocated by this author will substantially increase the number of recognized "intergovernmental organizations" and "international organizations", possibly to the thousands. This is a change which is long overdue and only reflects changed realities. Based on the above, a new and revised analytical framework of international organization will be developed. Moreover, it will be proposed that the power of creation of new international organizations has passed over to international organizations and entities other than states.

1.6 Outline of the Book

In line with the above, this book is organized into ten chapters. This present chapter discusses the basis of this book and identifies why there is a need for a new definition of international organization.

Chapter 2 of this book analyzes historic perspectives of membership and traces the development of the international administrative unions and private international organizations established in the nineteenth century into today's international organizations.

Chapter 3 discusses concepts, definitions and types of international organizations, and membership.

Chapter 4 of this book will review (1) the dichotomies between public and private and governmental and nongovernmental, and (2) the various implications and ramifications of organizations' constitution and constitutionalization.

Chapter 5 discusses types of membership, subjects of membership, membership procedures and termination of membership.

Chapter 6 will show *inter alia* that a wider definition of the term "subject of international law" is required and that international legal personality does not need to be conferred by the constituent agreement organization but can be provided for at a later stage based on bilateral or multilateral agreements or other arrangements.

Chapter 7 reviews paradigms of international organization not established by a treaty. It also highlights the problematic concept of "intergovernmental organization" and discusses the conceptual framework of, and the need for changes to, the concept of "international organization".

Chapter 8 will review the relationship between membership and privileges and immunities. It will discuss, in particular, ways of conferring privileges and immunities and the challenges that international organizations face in ensuring privileges and immunities in their member countries and in non-member countries.

In Chap. 9, the intrinsic link between membership and institutional frameworks and capital structures of international organizations will be highlighted and the legal implications of membership for representation in governing bodies will be reviewed. It will be shown that there may be benefits for transforming international organizations into multi-actor institutions. Also, the legal implications of membership for organizations funding structures, borrowings and operational activities will be analyzed.

In Chap. 10, based on the discussion in the chapters mentioned above, the main conclusions are summarized and a new analytical framework for international organization will be proposed. It will also be shown that the power of creation has passed over to international organizations and other actors. Finally, in this chapter, future challenges for international organizations will be highlighted.

References

Potter PB (1945) Origin of the term International Organization. Am J Int Law 39:803–806

Szasz P (1999) The complexification of the United Nations. In: Bogandy JAV, Wolfrum R (eds) Max Planck Yearbook of United Nations Law. Martinus Nijhoff, Leiden, pp 1–57. http://www.mpil.de/files/pdf2/mpunyb_szasz_3.pdf

Chapter 2
Historic Evolution of Membership Concepts

Contents

2.1 Emergence of International Organizations

The origins of international organization and the inherent constraints of state-centric concepts on which the current definition of international organization is based, may be traced to the "17th century marriage of sovereignty and statehood at Westphalia"[1] which marked the "emergence of the modern state system."[2] While

---

[1] Kelly 2005, p. 364.

[2] Mangone 1954, p. 100.

All weblinks are updated as of 28 February 2018.

G. Droesse, *Membership in International Organizations*,
https://doi.org/10.1007/978-94-6265-327-6_2

"no international organization was established by the peace of Westphalia in 1648"[3] nor during the subsequent peace of Utrecht in 1713,[4] and "there was no principle of membership which conferred an automatic right to representation or participation,"[5] the seventeenth and eighteenth century saw the development of "modern plans for [an] international organization."[6] At that time, the international community consisted of a "small group of central and western European states forming the international community of 1648, that was to become the nucleus of an ever widening system of law, which now embraces all the nations of the world."[7] The Concert of Europe was

> an exclusive club for great powers, whose members were self-appointed guardians of the European Community and executive directors of its affairs. They sometimes admitted European smaller fry to their Splendid Presence and occasionally failed to dominate the scene as completely as they wished, but they left no room for doubt that the Concert of Europe was in fact a Concert of the Great Powers.[8]

All new members entering that exclusive circle had to accept the existing rules of international law, thus giving new authority to them.[9] However, while such acceptance was a requirement for any admission to the club, it clearly was not sufficient for such an admission. "As for the states of the Near East and of the Far East, they were simply outside the circle of the European community, not recognized as being bound by the existing legal system, but merely as states with which European traders might deal at their risk, or with which European states might make such agreements as they pleased [....]."[10]

Nevertheless, there was still a long way to go from the conference mechanism of the Concert of Europe to the development of modern-day international organization. As indicated by Claude, "the setting of the stage for international organization involves the development of the *facts* of division and inter-dependence in the external world and of the *moods* of anxiety and dissatisfaction, coupled with hopeful determination and creative imagination, in the minds of men."[11] These conditions were met in the nineteenth century which brought developments at two levels: private international unions were founded, and states proceeded with public international unions to regulate technical matters with cross-border implications and the navigation of international rivers. However, the whole development of international organization proceeded "with catlike tread upon a most slippery surface,"[12]

---

[3] Mangone 1954, p. 21.

[4] Mangone 1954, p. 22.

[5] Sands and Klein 2009, p. 3.

[6] Mangone 1954, p. 23.

[7] Fenwick 1951, p. 19.

[8] Claude 1971, p. 25.

[9] Fenwick 1951, p. 20.

[10] Ibid.

[11] Claude 1971, p. 21.

[12] Mangone 1954, p. 4.

as holding "the springs of national power within the paper box of international organization requires the utmost delicacy [….]."[13]

2.2 Private International Unions

The numerous public and private congresses held during the period from 1826 to 1907 are indicative of the extent to which coordination and cooperation were seen as crucial in a wide number of sectors. Often, public congresses were the immediate consequence of private congresses, the initiative for which "has been found in individual action, prompted by considerations sometimes commercial, sometimes scientific or philosophic, sometimes altruistic."[14]

The private international unions which emerged in the nineteenth and early twentieth centuries

> had a number of interesting features. They emphasized the need for permanent, as opposed to ad hoc, association and for periodic, regular meetings. Many set up a small, permanent secretariat. Many demonstrated by their membership the artificiality of a rigid distinction between 'public and private unions' based upon function; membership sometimes comprised states, municipal authorities, national groups and societies and private individuals.[15]

The establishment of private international unions was generally prompted by the initiative of individuals.

> The relationship between the international public and private associations has usually been symbiotic. While many of the private associations clearly reflected individual interests of little concern to the state, some of them demonstrated the necessity for governmental activity and co-operation across frontiers [….]. In some cases, a private union was a forerunner of a public international union: for example, the International Association of the Legal Protection of Labour led to the establishment of the International Labour Organization in 1919.[16]

Various private unions were established in the nineteenth century that became predecessors of public administrative unions. Following the creation of the Pennsylvania Society in 1775 and other similar societies such as the Societé des Amis Noirs which denounced the slave trade[17] and the Treaty between Britain and

---

[13] Mangone 1954, p. 6.

[14] Baldwin 1907, p. 576.

[15] Sands and Klein 2009, pp. 4–5.

[16] Archer 1992, p. 14.

[17] See "1775. First American abolition society founded in Philadelphia." http://www.history.com/this-day-in-history/first-american-abolition-society-founded-in-philadelphia, and Society of the Friends of Blacks, "Address to the National Assembly in Favor of the Abolition of the Slave Trade". 5 Feb. 1790. http://chnm.gmu.edu/revolution/d/290/.

Portugal signed in 1815 to prevent slavery,[18] the World Antislavery Convention was held in London in 1840.[19] Other private unions that were established include the International Law Association (1873) and the "Institut de Droit International (1873), the International Literary and Artistic Association (1878), the International Ornithological Committee (1884), the International Dental Federation (1900), and the International Chamber of Commerce (1919)."[20] In addition to those unions, some other organizations were established, initially as non-governmental organizations, to produce public goods; some of those substantially evolved thereafter to the extent that they are now recognized as international organization.

The International Committee of the Red Cross (ICRC),[21] created in response to the moving description of the atrocities of war by Henri Dunant in his "Mémories of Solferino" (which was published in 1862),[22] is one interesting example of a non-governmental organization (NGO) which is recognized as a subject of international law due to the mandate conferred to it by the four Geneva conventions of 1949 and the fact that it enjoys recognition of "international juridical personality"[23] and privileges and immunities under its Headquarters Agreement with Switzerland and other international agreements to which the ICRC is a party. It may be seen as the predecessor of a range of organizations established under national law[24] but with privileges and immunities under international law. While organizations with similar features (e.g., the Bank of International Settlements) were rarely established in the past, since 2000, they have become a new business model for establishing international organizations, as epitomized by the Global Fund and Gavi Alliance.

The Inter-Parliamentary Union (IPU), which was originally founded at the initiative of two parliamentarians from the United Kingdom and France (William Randal Cremer and Frédéric Passy), developed from a union composed of individual parliamentarians to an "international organisation of the Parliaments of sovereign States."[25] It may be seen a new paradigm of international organization not established by agreement between governments.

---

[18] Treaty between Great Britain and Portugal, signed in Vienna on 22 January 1815. http://www.pdavis.nl/Treaty_Portugal.htm.

[19] Skidmore II, W. E. "The World Antislavery Convention of 1840." *Historians Against Slavery.* (blog) http://www.historiansagainstslavery.org/main/the-world-antislavery-convention-of-1840/.

[20] Sands and Klein 2009, p. 4.

[21] Bugnion 2004–2005, pp. 191–215.

[22] On the creation of the ICRC, see Hamburger 1942–1943, pp. 22–27.

[23] Agreement between the International Committee of the Red Cross and the Swiss Federal Council to Determine the Legal Status of the Committee in Switzerland, 1993, Article 1, https://casebook.icrc.org/case-study/agreement-between-icrc-and-switzerland.

[24] While the ICRC acquired its current name in 1875, its statutes were only drafted in 1915, and it was only registered that year as a private, non-profit organization under the Swiss Civil Code.

[25] See Article 1 of the Statutes of the Inter-Parliamentary Union (IPU Statutes), adopted in 1976 and amended on various occasions, the most recent being in Oct. 2011. http://www.ipu.org/strct-e/statutes-new.htm#1.

INTERPOL "traces its roots to an invitation by the Austrian Government (through Vienna's Chief of Police)"[26] for a conference of police officials held in Vienna in 1923. While it initially qualified as an NGO, it is now recognized as an intergovernmental organization. Hence, INTERPOL is the epitome of an intergovernmental organization not established by a treaty in which technical government agencies are represented.

2.3 International Administrative Unions

The creation of private sector unions was accompanied by the establishment of IAUs at the end of the nineteenth century and the beginning of the twentieth century. IAUs were organized to address a wide range of thematic areas which could no longer be tackled by states in their domestic sphere as these required enhanced cross-border coordination and cooperation among states.

2.3.1 Creation of IAUs

Reinsch lists "forty-five public international unions, composed of states", which were created in six areas (communication, economic interests, sanitation and prison reform, police powers, scientific purposes, special and local purposes), of which 30 were "provided with administrative bureaus or commissions."[27]

The need for cross-border coordination and cooperation for navigational and other purposes was particularly evident in the case of international water courses crossing several states, such as the rivers Rhine and Danube. Thus, it is not surprising that among the first IAUs were river commissions set up on the basis of the Final Act of the Vienna Congress, which set forth under Articles CVIII–CXVII certain principles regarding the liberty of navigation on rivers.

However, the introduction of "two of the many astounding devices of the nineteenth century, the steam engine and the electric telegraph, [that] telescoped weeks into days, days into hours, and hours into seconds,"[28] further warranted and prompted enhanced cooperation between states. Thus, the Telegraphic Union, the predecessor of the International Telecommunication Union, was set up as a comprehensive multilateral arrangement for telecommunication. The introduction of a universal regime for postal services was in response to the rise of the nation state; as when "monarchs slowly but surely succeeded in consolidating their power, a need arose for

26 Martha 2010, p. 150 (hereinafter referred to as *INTERPOL*).

27 Reinsch 1911, p. 4.

28 Mangone 1954, p. 67.

a more rapid and secure means of official communication."[29] Advances in technology also required enhanced standardization. For this reason, the International Bureau of Weights and Measures (BPIM) was established, following a preparatory conference in Paris in 1870, and the adoption of the Metre Convention of 1875[30] which as of 20 May 1875 was signed by 17 countries and entered into force on 1 January 1876.[31]

Article 1 of the Treaty relative to the Formation of the General Postal Union of 1874 states that "countries between which the present treaty is concluded shall form, under the title of *General Postal Union*, **a single postal territory** for reciprocal exchange of correspondence between their post-offices."[32] (emphasis added).

This may be seen as the epitome of an attempt to create a single administrative area comprising the territories of members. While the constituent agreements of the other IAUs do not express the same approach, the need for coordination across borders manifested itself in many other areas such as in efforts to secure the protection of intellectual property, which prompted the establishment of the International Union for the Protection of Industrial Property (1883)[33] and the International Union for the Protection of Literary and Artistic Works (1886),[34] and to guarantee minimum standards of protection of labor and social protection, which resulted in the creation of the International Labour Organization (ILO) in 1919 (see below).

Moreover, the great increase in trade and enhanced opportunities for travel between countries also facilitated the spread of infectious diseases. International cooperation in health was prompted in particular by the threat posed by cholera which "since ancient times had found its breeding ground in India and in 1830 struck Europe heavily, even crossing the Atlantic Ocean a few years later and ravaging New York State in 1854."[35] Following the fourth great cholera pandemic of 1863, a series of sanitary conferences were convened.[36] Important milestones in international cooperation were the establishment of the Pan American Sanitary Bureau in 1902 and the International Office of Public Health in 1907.[37]

---

[29] Codding 1964, p. 5.

[30] See The Metre Convention, 1875, modified in 1921. https://www.bipm.org/en/worldwide-metrology/metre-convention/.

[31] See "Convention for the Establishment of an International Bureau of Weights and Measures". 20 May 1875. Knipping et al. 1997b, pp. 93–104. See also Schmahl 2006.

[32] Treaty concerning the Formation of a General Postal Union. 9 October 1874. *The United Nations System and Its Predecessors*. Vol. II, 84–92.

[33] See Convention for the Protection of Industrial Property. 20 March 1883. *The United Nations System and Its Predecessors*. Vol. II. 105–117.

[34] See Convention concerning the Creation of an International Union for the Protection of Literary and Artistic Works. 9 September 1886. *The United Nations System and Its Predecessors*. Vol. II. 118–134.

[35] Mangone 1954, pp. 79–80.

[36] For details, refer to Strong 1921, pp. 321–322.

[37] See WHO. Archives of the Office International d'Hygiène Publique (OIHP) http://www.who.int/archives/fonds_collections/bytitle/fonds_1/en/ and Fee and Brown 2002, pp. 1888–1889. https://www.ncbi.nlm.nih.gov/pubmed/12453801.

2.3.2 *Types and Structures of IAUs*

"The qualification of an institution as international administrative union was originally meant to emphasize its non-political (in the meaning of technical/administrative nature) and that it was merely exercising co-ordinating functions on administrative matters."[38] The administrative unions established in the nineteenth century "represented at most the initiation, not the consummation, of a trend toward international control of the subjects with which they were concerned."[39] They were only "rudimentary pieces of a system of intergovernmental collaboration, dependent for their operation upon such power as could be generated in the new and drastically incomplete plant of international authority."[40] Nevertheless, the term "international administrative union" suggests a communality between the various unions, which only exists to a limited extent, as there is quite a number of important differences between the various unions as regards their establishment, powers and competencies, administrative structures, legal personality, and membership.

First, a distinction can be made between those international administrative unions which were established based on the action of public authorities from those based on private initiative. Such distinction is rather clear in some cases. Thus, the IAUs in the areas of communication and sanitation are based on public initiative, as were, in a similar way, "the unions dealing with the metric system, the suppression of the slave trade, the sugar bounties, and the publication of custom tariffs" and "the scientific union for the study of geodesy."[41] On the other hand, the unions in the fields of "literary and industrial property, labor legislation and agriculture" were "the result primarily of a determined and persistent private initiative."[42] The International Institute of Agriculture "was established as the direct result of the efforts of David Lubin, a successful merchant from California, with the active support of the King of Italy, who foresaw the advantages that would accrue to agriculture, commerce and industry from an international clearing-house for systematically collecting and disseminating official information supplied by the various governments of the world."[43] The "Convention for the Creation of the International

---

38 Wolfrum 2006, para. 2

39 Claude 1971, p. 35.

40 Claude 1971, p. 37.

41 Reinsch 1911, p. 146.

42 Reinsch 1911, p. 147.

43 See The International Institute of Agriculture. Science. 1921. New Series, Vol. 54, No. 1387, 86–87, 86. As indicated therein, the information to be collected and disseminated concerned matters such as "agricultural production, consumption, movements, surpluses, deficits, and prices of agricultural products, transportation, plant and animal diseases and insect pests, rural credits and insurance, standard of living, wages and hours of labor on farms, cooperative organizations of farmers, legislation affecting agriculture, and similar information." Ibid., 86.

Institute of Agriculture" was drafted at a series of meetings in May and June 1905.[44]

While initial proposals to establish unions such as the international freight unions were based on private initiative, there are other cases where the establishment of an IAU involved both public and private initiative. Hence, there are cases where it "is not always easy to tell with certitude whether the formation of a given union is due primarily to public or to private initiative," as "commonly an interaction of influences" is encountered.[45]

Second, there is a marked difference in the powers and competences of IAUs. Regarding the administrative powers of IAUs, Reinsch notes the "extreme reluctance which nations have hitherto felt toward endowing these international organs with positive powers."[46] When establishing the General Postal Union, states sought to prevent the union from taking unwarranted initiatives. Thus, the functions of the international office were very narrowly defined[47] and the office was under the surveillance of a designated postal administration. The International Union for the Protection of Industrial Property and the International Union for the Protection of Literary and Artistic Work had similar structures. In the case of these international administrative unions, the international bureau was also placed under the supervision of the Swiss Confederation.

Nevertheless, some IAUs—such as the Central Commission for the Navigation on the Rhine (Central Commission) and the European Commission of the Danube —had far-reaching or even supranational powers. The Central Commission, which

---

[44] See "Convention between the United States of America and Italy, Montenegro, Russia, Argentine Republic, Romania, Serbia, Belgium, Salvador, Portugal, The United Mexican States, Luxemburg, The Swiss Confederation, Persia, Japans, Ecuador, Bulgaria, Denmark, Spain, France, Sweden, The Netherlands, Greece, Uruguay, Germany, Cuba, Austria-Hungary, Norway, Egypt, Great Britain, Guatemala, Ethiopia, Nicaragua, Brazil, Costa Rica, Chile, Peru, China, Paraguay, and Turkey, Providing for the Creation of an International Institute of Agriculture". Signed at Rome, 7 June 1905. *The American Journal of International Law*. 1908. Vol. 2, Supplement: Official Documents, 358–362.

[45] Reinsch 1911, p. 144.

[46] Reinsch 1911, p. 167.

[47] Article 15 of the Treaty concerning the General Postal Union provided:

There shall be organized, under the name of the International Office of the General Postal Union, a central office, which shall be conducted under the surveillance of a Postal Administration to be chosen by the Congress, and the expenses of which shall be borne by all the Administrations of the contracting States.

This office shall be charged with the duty of collecting, publishing, and distributing information of every kind which concerns the international postal service; of giving, at the request of the parties concerned, an opinion upon questions in dispute; of making known proposals for modifying the detailed regulations; of giving notice of alterations adopted; of facilitating operations relating to international accounts, especially in the cases referred to in Article 10 foregoing; and, in general of considering and working out all questions in the interest of the Postal Union." In accordance with Article 14 of the said Convention, the "treaty does not involve any alteration in the interior postal legislation of any country, nor any restriction of the right of the contracting parties to maintain and to conclude treaties, as well as to maintain and establish more restricted unions with a view to a progressive improvement of postal relations.

is the oldest international administrative union, had both administrative and quasi-judicial powers,[48] which distinguished it from similar bodies established under other international administrative unions. Moreover,

> The European Commission was notable in that it could operate completely independent of local authorities. Its installations and works were considered neutral [….] its legislative acts, and especially its regulations on navigation and fluvial police, were directly applicable and had the force of law. Its officials were appointed autonomously and enjoyed quasi-diplomatic immunities [….]. Individual administrative and judicial acts, such as the collection of fees, the enforcement of navigational regulations and the levying of fines, were so far-reaching and its powers so vast that 19th century legal scholars struggled to adequately assess the Commission's status.[49]

For this reason, Zeilinger argues that, in hindsight, it can be attested that the European Commission "was one of the first international organizations with international legal personality, equipped with supranational powers [….] comparable to those enjoyed today by the [….] European (Economic) Community."[50]

Third, there are certain differences in the administrative structures of IAUs. It was a general feature of nearly all IAUs that they had a general conference or congress as their legislative organ and made "use of a central office or bureau as their chief administrative agency."[51] Different arrangements were made regarding the supervision of the bureaus that had been established.

Some IAUs (the General/Universal Postal Union and International Telecommunication Union [ITU] epitomize that approach) made provision for "a central office, which shall be conducted under the surveillance of a Postal Administration to be chosen by the Congress, and the expenses of which shall be borne by all the Administrations of the contracting States."[52] On the other hand, the "Convention for the Creation of an International Institute of Agriculture" provided (Article 2) that the "institute shall be composed of a general assembly and a permanent committee."[53] The general assembly exercised "supreme control over the international institute of agriculture"[54] while the executive power of the institute was vested in the permanent committee, which, under the direction and control of the general assembly, was "to carry out decisions of the latter" and was tasked to

---

48 Völderndorff 1894.

49 Zeilinger 2013, para. 5.

50 Ibid.

51 Reinsch 1911, p. 155.

52 Article 15 of the Treaty relative to the Formation of a General Postal Union. 9 October 1974. In *The United Nations System and its Predecessors*. 1997. Vol. 2, Doc. 9, 84–92. See also Article 14 of the International Telegraph Convention of St Petersburg. 10/22 July 1875. *The United Nations System and its Predecessors*. 1997. Vol. 2, Doc. 8, 78–83, 81–82, 90.

53 Convention for the Creation of an International Institute of Agriculture. 1905, Article 2. ("IIA Convention"). In *The United Nations System and its Predecessors*. 1997. Vol. 2, Doc. 13, 135–139.

54 Ibid., Article 5.

"prepare propositions to submit to" the general assembly.[55] The Convention for the Establishment of an International Bureau of Weights and Measures also provided for a governance structure comprising a general conference and an international committee.[56]

Fourth, while "the bureaux of the public international unions which are seen as the forerunners of the secretariats of later universal organizations such as the League of Nations"[57] constituted a major innovation, the public unions were "like the pebbles on a beach, thrown around by the waves of circumstance, varied in every aspect."[58] While each of them was based on a treaty, this agreement did "not always make clear whether, or how much, international legal personality the signatories intended to confer upon the institution created."[59] Nevertheless, in some instances, international public unions were able to act on the international plane. The International Committee of Weight and Measures is on record of having concluded an "agreement with France concerning the Committee's headquarters."[60] Moreover, in some cases, there are indications that some of the IAUs possessed international legal personality. Thus, Hostie qualified the Central Commission as "*une autorité internationale et non pas seulement une assemblée de représentants des Etats riverains*."[61] The international legal personality of the Central Commission may be seen as a corollary of the above. While "the Rhine River Commission was the first riparian commission whose officials and institutions were accorded special guarantees and safeguards", the

> prerogatives did not take the form of diplomatic privileges and immunities, but rather emerged as a concept of neutralization of the persons and offices enjoying the conferred status. The underlying motive, however, was the same, i.e. the protection of the agents of the international community.[62]

As shown by Michaels, the "Rhine River Commissioner and his staff, charged with responsibility of regulating the navigation of the Rhine by the Convention, were in effect the first international civil servants."[63]

---

[55] Ibid., Article 6.

[56] See Articles 7–11 of Appendix No. 1 Regulations to the Convention on the Establishment of an International Bureau of Weights and Measures of 20 May 1875, In *The United Nations System and Its Predecessors*. 1997. Vol. 2, Doc. 10, 93–104, 98–99.

[57] Archer, 13.

[58] Eagleton 1950a, p. 329.

[59] Ibid., 329.

[60] See Chiu 1966. Chiu further cites Fiore's International Law Codified, as follows: "The International Congo Association, to which international legal personality was attributed for the limited purpose for which it was formally recognized, was regarded as capable of concluding treaties, and has concluded several, including one with Italy, 19 Dec. 1884." Ibid.

[61] Hostie 1930, p. 209.

[62] Michaels 1971, p. 69.

[63] Ibid., 1.

As regards the European Commission, notwithstanding the fact that "before the Second World War, the [Permanent Court of International Justice] PCIJ perhaps only hinted that international organizations had international legal personality",[64] Amerasinghe states that by regarding in its Advisory Opinion of 8 December 1927 regarding the Jurisdiction of the European Commission of the Danube between Galatz and Braila[65] the European Commission "as being able to perform functions with international consequences, it is possible that the PCIJ had in mind that the Commission had some kind of international personality."[66] Another argument in favor of international legal personality of the European Commission is that it enjoyed, as shown by Jellinek under a treaty with Romania, complete independence and was able to enter independently in international agreements.[67]

With reference to the European Commission of the Danube, in relation to Article 53 of the Treaty signed at Berlin, Michaels states that:

> The practice in the evolution of the riparian commissions' privileges and immunities began with a concept of neutrality and by the end of the century had attained a status of 'complete independence of the territorial authorities.' However, such independence in the nineteenth century may well have constituted an equivalency to privileges and immunities.[68]

Fifth, different concepts applied to IAUs in respect of membership procedures and eligible subjects of membership. As these issues are in the context of this book of particular relevance, they will be reviewed in some detail.

2.3.3 *Membership of IAUs*

Membership in international administrative unions has several interesting aspects, first regarding admission criteria and procedures for obtaining membership, and, second, in particular, because eligibility for membership in certain IAUs extended, in addition to states, to dependent territories and technical administrations. This is of relevance for the discussion on eligible subjects of membership as it shows that the concept of "subject of membership" has been defined in wider terms in the past that this is normally done at present.

---

64 Amerasinghe 2005, p. 77.

65 "Jurisdiction of the European Commission of the Danube between Galatz and Braila", Permanent Court of International Justice, Collection of Advisory Opinions, Series B, No. 14, 8 December 1927. http://www.icj-cij.org/files/permanent-court-of-international-justice/serie_B/B_14/01_Commission_europeenne_du_Danube_Avis_consultatif.pdf.

The PCIJ stated in this Decision on p. 64: "As the European Commission is not a State, but an international institution with a special purpose, it only has the functions bestowed upon it by the Definitive Statute with a view to the fulfilment of that purpose, but it has power to exercise these functions to their full extent, in so far as the Statute does not impose restrictions upon it."

66 Amerasinghe 2005, p. 77.

67 Jellinek 1882, pp. 169–170.

68 Michaels 1971, p. 35.

2.3.3.1 Membership Criteria and Membership Procedures

Many IAUs aspired to universality, which had corresponding implications for the criteria of their admission. Once a union had been created, admission was generally granted freely so that a state could "ordinarily acquire membership by merely declaring its adherence to the conventions concluded, and by assuming the burdens imposed by them."[69] Article 6 of the Agreement respecting the Establishment of the International Office of Public Health (1907) epitomizes this approach. The said Article provides:

> Governments that have not signed the present arrangement are, on their request, admitted to adhere thereto. Their adhesion shall be notified, through the diplomatic channel, to the Royal Government of Italy, and, by the latter, to the other Contracting Governments; it will imply a pledge to contribute to the payment of the expenses of the Office in the manner referred to in Article 3.[70]

Restrictions regarding accession to conventions are epitomized by the International Convention Concerning the Carriage of Goods by Rail of 14 October 1890, to which states that had not participated could not accede by unilateral act. Rather, an admission procedure was determined by the contracting parties in 1893 when the Convention came into force. Under an additional Article adopted at that time, States, which had not acceded to the Convention of 1890, had to refer their request for admission first to the central office for examination which was charged to transmit its recommendations to the contracting states. Where agreement on admission had been reached, the state concerned and the contracting states were informed to that effect. Unanimous action of all members was necessary for any new member to be admitted.[71]

IAUs that incorporated conditions for admission to membership include the European railway freight union, the sugar convention, and the slavery convention.[72] Moreover, some unions were essentially closed in that any extension of

---

[69] Reinsch 1911, p. 149.

[70] Article 6 of the Agreement Respecting the Establishment of an International Office of Public Health of 9 December 1907. The United Nations System and Its Predecessors. Vol. II, 140–146, 141.

[71] The German version of the additional article is reproduced in Rosenthal 1894, p. 349:

> Die Staaten, welche an dem Übereinkommen vom 14. X. 1890 über den Eisenbahnfrachtverkehr nicht teilgenommen haben, können um die Aufnahme nachsuchen. Sie haben sich zu diesem Zwecke an die schweizer. Regierung zu wenden. Diese Regierung wird das Aufnahmegesuch dem Centralamt zur Prüfung übermitteln und alsdann seine Vorschläge den Vertragsstaaten zur Kenntnis bringen.
>
> Wenn ein Einverständnis erzielt ist, wird die schweizer. Regierung dem betreffenen Staate von der Aufnahme in das Übereinkommen Kenntnis geben und diese Aufnahme gleich-zeitig den übrigen VertragsStaaten mitteilen.

[72] Reinsch 1911, p. 149.

membership outside the initial pool required an amendment to their constituent agreement, such as for those unions where membership was limited to a specific group (e.g., the riparian states of a river or members of a geographical region).[73]

The Central Commission for Navigation on the Rhine (Central Commission) which was established in 1815 consistent with the Final Act of the Congress of Vienna is interesting as the composition of that commission changed as the consequence of the evolution of the treaty regime governing the river Rhine. Under the Convention of Mainz (1831) and the Mannheim Convention (1868),[74] membership in the Commission was limited to riparian states (with the exclusion of Switzerland). The Treaty of Versailles internationalized membership by admitting Switzerland and non-riparian countries, including Great Britain, Italy, and Belgium.[75] Admission of these three countries recognized their "general interest in free circulation on the rivers regarded as transit routes" and sought to enable the non-riparian members of the Commission to "act as a check on the strongest riparian State abusing her preponderating influence to the detriment of the others."[76]

The European Commission of the Danube proved to be the "more resilient"[77] of the two commissions established by the Paris Peace Treaty.[78] Its membership was

---

[73] See, with further references, Reinsch 1911, p. 149, who states,

> An exceptional method is followed in those unions in which very special burdens are imposed upon the treaty states. Thus, in the European railway freight union the request of a country to be admitted to membership must be addressed to the directing state; it is then referred to and reported on by the bureau, submitted to the member states, and acted upon by them. Unanimous action of the latter is necessary in order that a new member may be admitted. In the sugar union the request for admission must be acted on by the commission of the union, to whom it is transmitted through the Belgian government, which is, in this case, the directing state. Admission to the union for the suppression of the slave trade may be made subject to certain conditions, which are applied upon motion of the treaty states [....]. In certain unions membership is limited by natural causes or by the specific nature of the purpose for which the union has been created [....].

[74] Revised Convention respecting the Navigation of the Rhine, 17 Oct. 1968, *The United Nations System and its Predecessors*, Vol. II, 153–167, 153.

[75] The Treaty of Versailles envisaged that the Central Commission would have 19 members: 2 of the Netherlands, 2 of Switzerland, 4 of riparian German states, 2 of Great Britain and 2 of Belgium. See Article 355 of the Treaty of Peace between the Allied and Associated Powers and Germany and other Treaty Engagements, signed at Versailles, 28 June 1919. https://babel.hathitrust.org/cgi/pt?id=hvd.32044020077533;view=1up;seq=5.

[76] Cited by Borel who reproduced the reply of the Allied and Associated Powers to the observations made by the German delegates on the Peace treaty. Borel 1921–1922, p. 82.

[77] Zeilinger, para 4.

[78] The Peace Treaty of Paris, 1856 foresaw the establishment of a permanent riparian Commission and a European Commission, deemed to be temporary, established to dredge the mouths of the Danube. While the riparian commission never managed to function effectively, the European Commission was extended on various occasions. For the relevant provisions of the Paris Peace Treaty (Articles 15–19), see *The United Nations System and its Predecessors*. 1997. Vol. 2, Doc.

initially confined to Great Britain, Austria, France, Prussia, Sardinia and Turkey (being in charge of the mouths of the Danube),[79] but evolved as the political situation of the riparian states substantially changed. Its geographic scope was extended upstream to Galatz and Braila and its duration was extended on various occasions until it eventually became a permanent body.[80]

2.3.3.2 Eligible Subjects of Membership: Dependent Territories and Technical Administrations

It is important to note that historically, international organizations have admitted both technical administrations and dependent territories to membership at par with states. Hence, one important distinction between IAUs relates to those that only accept states as members and those that admit dependent territories or technical administrations to membership.

The Metre Convention (1875), which established the International Bureau of Weights and Measures, falls in the first category as it sought to encourage the adherence of as many states as possible.[81] States could adhere to the Metre Convention by unilateral declaration, subject to providing necessary contributions, but dependent territories were not eligible, either in their own right or upon presentation of their membership by the metropolitan state responsible for the conduct of their external relations. The same approach was adopted by a number of other IAUs that only allowed states,[82] respectively governments[83] to join.

17; European Commission of the Danube (Peace Treaty of Paris, 1856, Articles 15–19. A good summary of the relevant background is contained in the Summary of the "Advisory Opinion of 8 Dec. 1927 (Series B, No. 14) on the Jurisdiction of the European Commission of the Danube between Galatz and Braila prepared by the United Nations: http://legal.un.org/PCIJsummaries/documents/english/PCIJ_FinalText.pdf. For the Peace Treaty of Paris, see Sherman 1923, pp. 438–459.

[79] See the Paris Peace Treaty, Article 16.

[80] See McCaffrey 2010.

[81] Convention for the Establishment of an International Bureau of Weights and Measures. 1875. *The United Nations System and its Predecessors*. Vol. II, 93–104, 96, Article 11.

"Those governments which may take advantage of the privilege, **open to every state**, of acceding to this convention, shall be required to pay a contribution, the amount of which shall be fixed by the committee on the basis established in Article 9, and shall which be devoted to the improvement of the scientific apparatus of the bureau. (emphasis added)"

[82] For example, Article 16 of the Convention on the Protection of Industrial Property of 20 March 1883 stated: "The States that have not taken part in the present convention shall be admitted to adhere to the same upon their application. This adhesion shall be notified through the diplomatic channel [….]" See Knipping 1999, p. 109.

[83] Article 6 of the Agreement respecting the Establishment of an International Office of Public Health of Dec. 1907 read: "Governments that have not signed the present arrangements are, on their request, admitted to adhere thereto. Their adhesion shall be notified, through the diplomatic channel, to the Royal Government of Italy, and by the latter to the other contracting Government." See *The United Nations System and its Predecessors*. Vol. II, 140–146, 141.

On the other hand, the International Telegraph Union, the predecessor of the International Telecommunication Union, initially admitted dependent territories and technical administrations on a par with states.

As shown by Codding, the

> origins of this concept of membership are found in the actions of the conference at Paris, in 1865, when the delegates holding diplomatic credentials agreed to allow the 'experts' from their respective telegraph administrations to draw up the Convention and the Telegraph Regulations. The delegates with diplomatic credentials performed the formality of signing the Convention, and the experts were permitted to sign the Telegraph Regulations which were annexed to the Convention.[84]

It was further "decided at Paris that the Telegraph Regulations could be modified at any time by common agreement between the "administrations" of the contracting parties.[85]

The issues of the colonial vote and the representation of postal administrations were of paramount importance at the subsequent St. Petersburg Conference of 1875, convened to redraft the International Telegraph Convention.

While Article 18 of the St Petersburg Convention[86] only permitted States which had not taken part in the said Convention to adhere to it, the Bureau of the Union adopted the practice of referring to "the members of the Union as 'contracting administrations'", and based on that change in practice, "the telegraph administrations became accepted as members of the Union on a par with the 'sovereign' states that had drawn up and signed the Telegraph Conventions."[87]

Article 15 of the St Petersburg Convention provided that changes to the uniform rates set forth in the Convention would "be submitted to revisions at which all the States which participate in the Convention may be represented" and that to this end "Administrative Conferences will be held periodically, each Conference fixing the place and date of the next meeting." In accordance with Article 16, these "Conferences consist of delegates representing the Administrations of the Contracting States." It was further indicated in this Article:

> In the deliberations, each Administration has the right to one vote, subject to the condition, in the case of different Administrations of the same Government, that a claim for it has been made through the diplomatic channel to the Government of the Country where the Conference is to be held, before the date fixed for its opening, and that each one has a special and distinct representation.

The above underlines that the St. Petersburg Convention allowed the representation of technical administrations.

At the Berlin Radio Conference of 1906 and the London Radio Conference of 1912, the issue of the colonial vote was also of paramount importance. In the end,

---

[84] Codding 1952, p. 38.

[85] Ibid.

[86] International Telegraph Convention of St. Petersburg. 10/22 July 1875. Article 18. *United Nations System and its Predecessors*, Vol. II, 78–92, 82–83.

[87] Codding 1952, p. 41.

five colonial votes each were granted to France, Germany, Great Britain, Russia and the United States, two votes each to Italy, Netherlands and Portugal and one each to Belgium, Japan and Spain.[88]

On the subject of membership of dependent territories and technical administrations, the case of the General Postal Union of 1874 (later known in 1878 as the Universal Postal Union) is also particularly interesting.

The wording of the "Treaty relative to the formation of the General Postal Union"[89] signed in Bern on 9 October 1874 was characterized by imprecise legal drafting in various respects.[90] The fact that "such words as 'countries', 'members of the Union', 'state', 'contracting parties' and 'postal administrations' [were used interchangeably and informally, raised] doubt as to whether governments or their postal administrations were finally admitted to the Postal Union."[91] The "admission to act as parties to an international treaty, of states which did not possess an individual competence in the field of foreign relations, [was] a most significant feature of the treaty [….]."[92]

In particular, the wording of Article 17 of the Treaty of Bern regarding membership[93] was ambiguous, as this Article did not specify any conditions for admission to membership of European countries, but only set forth conditions for

---

[88] Codding 1952, p. 100.

[89] Knipping et al. 1997a, pp. 84–92.

[90] Akzin 1933, p. 652.

[91] Ibid.

[92] Akzin 1933, p. 652.

[93] The Treaty of Bern, Article 17 provides:

The entry into the Union of countries beyond sea not yet forming part of it, shall be effected on the following conditions:

> 1st. They shall make their application to the Administration charged with the management of the International Office of the Union.
>
> 2d. They shall submit to the stipulations of the treaty of the Union, subject to an ulterior understanding on the subject of the cost of sea conveyance.
>
> 3d. Their adhesion to the Union must be preceded by an understanding between the Administrations having postal conventions or direct relations with them.
>
> 4th. In order to bring about this understanding, the managing Administration shall convene, if there be occasion, a meeting of the Administrations interested, and of the Administration desiring admission.
>
> 5th. When the understanding has been arrived at, the managing Administration shall give notice of the same to all the members of the General Postal Union.
>
> 6th. If in a period of six weeks, counting from the date of that communication, no objections are presented, the adhesion shall be considered as accomplished, and notice thereof shall be given by the managing Administration to the Administration joining the Union. The definitive adhesion shall be completed by a diplomatic act between the Government of the managing Administration and the Government of the Administration admitted into the Union.

admissions of "overseas countries", without specifying whether colonies or territories were meant to be covered by this term.

The Treaty of Bern was interpreted to allow admission of dependent territories. Thus, when Great Britain applied in 1875 "for the admission of British India to the union" [, the] Swiss government called a special conference of all interested administrations to decide on the sea transit rates to be permitted between British India and the members of the union."[94] Further to this request and a similar request that had been made by the French Government, "the conference agreed on sea transport rates for British India and the French colonies [….]."[95] However, the

> significant result of this Conference was not the admission of British India and the French colonies to the Postal Union but the establishment of the unorthodox principle that non-sovereign colonial territories could be accepted as members of an international organization on an equal footing with either their mother-country or with any other sovereign and independent state [which led, in particular in 1877/78, to] an unprecedented rise of new sovereign states and colonies admitted to the union.[96]

The admission procedure was simple; the Swiss Postal Department, without making a distinction between states and colonies, simply notified

> by circular letter to the member countries of the Union that it had received a request for admission and that the terms and conditions applied to British India and the French colonies would be applicable. If no objections were raised within six weeks, admission to the Union was automatic.[97]

It is important to note that the "Swiss Postal Department considered all applications for admission equally. As no distinction was made between the admission of a state or colony, their applications were often grouped together in the same postal circular letter."[98]

As highlighted by Akzin, in accordance with para 6 of Article 17 of the Treaty of Bern,

> it is the administration, not the government, that is finally admitted to the Union. It is this provision of Article 17, coupled with the preponderant use by the treaty of the ambiguous word *country,* and with the generally informal language of the treaty, that made possible the subsequent admission of colonies and groups of colonies as members of the Union.[99]

From 1875 to 1919, the Universal Postal Union made substantial progress on the road to universality. In 1878, the admission clause was eventually revised to give all countries the right to join the Union by unilateral declaration.[100] Moreover, Article

---

[94] Codding 1964, pp. 35–36.

[95] Ibid., 36.

[96] Cotreau 1975, p. 100.

[97] Cotreau 1975, p. 101.

[98] Cotreau 1975, p. 101.

[99] Akzin 1933, p. 653.

[100] Universal Postal Union. Convention and final protocol signed at Paris, 1 June 1878, Article 18:

21 specified which dependent territories were to be considered a single country or single administration.[101] By the Congress of Rome of 1906, 17 non-independent members had joined the Union.

The creation of the International Office of Public Health was decided at a conference held in Rome in 1907. At this conference, 13 governments were represented, including that of British India,[102] but the "Agreement respecting the Establishment of an International Office of Public Health" adopted on 9 December 1907,[103] as reflected in its preamble, only covered Great Britain and Ireland but did not extend to British India. In accordance with Article 6 of the said Agreement, governments that had not signed the Agreement were, "on their request, admitted to adhere thereto." Such adhesion was to be "notified, through the diplomatic channel, to the Royal Government of Italy and by the latter, to the other Contracting Governments" and implied "a pledge to contribute to the payment of the expenses of the office [….]."[104]

Finally, the period prior to the First World War marked the beginning of an international commodity regime. The first IAU established for that purpose was the International Sugar Union. It was created in 1902 by the Brussels International Sugar Convention[105] to end "the race of subventions and surtaxes [that] threatened to ruin beet sugar production by forcing unsound world competition and stifling domestic trade."[106] A permanent commission, having headquarters at Brussels, was charged with carrying out the agreement.[107]

Countries which have not taken part in the present convention are admitted to adhere thereto upon their demand. Notice is given of this adhesion, through the diplomatic channel, to the Government of the Swiss Confederation, and by that Government to all the countries of the Union. It implies, as a right, accession to all the clauses and admission to all the advantages stipulated **by** the present Convention.

See Bevans 1968, pp. 51–62. https://www.loc.gov/law/help/us-treaties/bevans/m-ust000001-0051.pdf.

[101] Universal Postal Union, Article 21: "The following are considered as forming, for the application of Articles 16, 19, and 20 preceding, a single country, or a single Administration, as the case may be: 1st. The Empire of British India; 2d. The Dominion of Canada; 3d. The whole of the Danish Colonies; 4th. The whole of the Spanish Colonies; 5th. The whole of the French Colonies; 6th. The whole of the Netherland Colonies; 7th. The whole of the Portuguese Colonies."

[102] As indicated by Grubbs, "the following Governments were represented at the Rome meeting of 1907: Belgium, Brazil, British India, Egypt, France, Great Britain, Holland, Italy, Portugal, Romania, Russia, Spain, Switzerland and the United States." Grubbs 1909, p. 23. https://www.jstor.org/stable/pdf/4562416.pdf?refreqid=excelsior:9c867f3f6a630e65b907efb9b2cdb26f.

[103] The Agreement in reproduced in *The United Nations System and its Predecessors*, Vol. II, 140–146.

[104] Article 6 of the Agreement respecting the Establishment of an International Office of Public Health.

[105] The text of the Brussels International Sugar Convention (1902) is reproduced in *The Advocate of Peace (1894–1920)*, Vol. 64, 78–79, http://www.jstor.org/stable/25751939.

[106] Wilk 1939, p. 862.

[107] International Sugar Convention, Article 7.

Article 8 of the International Sugar Convention of 1902[108] provided that "the high contracting parties agree for themselves and their colonies and possessions" to take certain measures in respect of bounty sugars. However, such obligations were not made applicable to the "autonomous colonies of Great Britain and of the British East Indies." As provided by Article 9 of the Convention, "The states which have not taken part in this convention will be permitted to agree to it upon request, and upon agreeing to conform to the rules of the permanent commission."[109] Thus, admission to membership was conditional upon agreement to the rules of the permanent commission, but not subject to consensus of all contracting states.

These examples show that there is historic precedent for both technical administrations and dependent territories to be admitted to membership in international organizations at par with states.

2.4 League of Nations

2.4.1 The League as a New Paradigm of International Organization

The governance structure of the League of Nations drew on the experience of the concert of Europe and the IAUs. In that sense, it may be "regarded as a rationalization, focalization, and consolidation of previous organizational developments. The League was a composite of the institutional descendants of nineteenth century agencies; it pulled together the separate lines of development into a coherent system."[110]

Prior to the establishment of the League, the "body of civilized States which form the Family of Nations" had been "an unorganized community."[111] In that sense, the establishment of the League was an important new paradigm of organization of the international community based on a treaty.

The Covenant of the League of Nations (1919) did not address the question whether the League had a juridical personality. Part I of the 1926 Modus Vivendi between the Secretary-General of the League and the Swiss Government "recognized that the League of Nations, which possesses international personality and legal capacity, cannot, in principle, according to the rules of international law, be sued before the Swiss Courts without its express consent."[112] Also, authorities such as Sir Fischer Williams "argued persuasively that the League was an entity separate from its Members, which could take action of its own."[113] Notwithstanding the

[108] See also Taylor 1909, pp. 347–358.

[109] International Sugar Convention, Article 9.

[110] Claude 1971, p. 44.

[111] Oppenheim 1919, p. 29.

[112] Cited by Miller 2009, p. 11.

[113] See Eagleton 1950b, p. 334.

above, as indicated by Crawford, the status of the League of Nations remained unsettled "such that the Secretary-General of the League apparently had to sign contracts of employment in his personal capacity."[114]

While the Covenant of the League of Nations did not expressly provide for the League's treaty-making capacity, there are several provisions in the Covenant which support the conclusion that it had such capacity.[115] In fact, the League even concluded a treaty with a non-member country.[116]

2.4.2 *Membership in the League*

For an organization established to maintain international peace and security, universal membership is important. One logical approach for the League to take could have been to "start from the beginning made by the two Hague Peace conferences."[117] However, doing so met with the strong opposition from countries like France which were determined to keep Germany and other central powers out of the League, at least in the initial phase.

One intrinsic problem of the League of Nations was that even though, conceptually, it was meant to be universal, it did not accept this principle at the time of its establishment, nor did it even achieve subsequently relative universality of all key states. The founders of the League of Nations initially decided to "build the League based on homogenous universality," but its members eventually decided to renounce that policy by adopting a policy of "heterogenous universality."[118] While it substantially expanded its membership for that reason, for all practical effects, the League could never be considered as "universal." This was related to the fact that the United States declined to participate in the League despite the fact that President Woodrow Wilson was one of its major proponents, and "even though it participated for some time in various League activities."[119]

---

114 Crawford 2013, p. 152.

115 Regarding the transfer of its assets and functions, Chiu refers to Articles 8, paras 2 and 4 of the Covenant which were interpreted to authorize the League to conclude treaties in matter of disarmament" and to Article 17 of the Covenant which was construed to be the basis of an agreement between the League and a non-member. (See Chiu, 8) While recognizing that "no agreement was ever concluded under the above mentioned provisions" (Ibid., 8), Chiu shows that "the LN [League of Nations] did conclude a number of agreements with both member and non-member States." (Ibid., 8).

116 This related, as indicated by Chiu, to an "exchange of notes on registration of treaties and other international agreements of the United States with the Secretariat of the LN, 22–23 Jan. 1934." Chiu, 12 with further references.

117 Oppenheim 1919, p. 36.

118 Schwarzenberger 1936, p. 59 ss.

119 See Berdahl 1932, p. 99, with further references.

This lack of universality was also partially due to the fact that the "Peace Conference of Paris in 1919 was the worst possible environment in which the League of Nations could have been designed."[120] While the League of Nations "emerged from its birthplace as a voluntary association of sovereign and almost sovereign or prospectively sovereign entities which had not been found on the 'wrong side' of World War I,"[121] not only were the central powers who had lost the war (Germany, Austria, Hungary, Bulgaria) not allowed to join the League as original members, but a number of other States were also excluded, on rather arbitrary grounds.

Article 1 and the Annex of the Covenant of the League of Nations made a basic distinction between the "Original Members of the League of Nations, Signatories of the Treaty of Peace" and "States invited to accede the Covenant"[122] and those states, dominions and colonies who could join the League pursuant to the second paragraph of Article 1 of the Covenant which reads:

> Any fully self-governing State, Dominion or Colony not named in the Annex may become a Member of the League if its admission is agreed to by two-thirds of the Assembly, provided that it shall give effective guarantees of its sincere intention to observe its international obligations, and shall accept such regulations as may be prescribed by the League in regard to its military, naval and air forces and armaments.

While there was no difference in status between original members and other members admitted pursuant to Article 1, para 2, the fact that initial members were only admitted selectively weakened the representativeness of the League.

The Kingdom of Great Britain and Northern Ireland had a very central role among the original members of the League, as Canada,[123] Australia, South Africa, New Zealand and India were listed in the Annex to the Covenant under the rubric of the "British Empire". While the first four were considered as self-governing even before the Balfour Resolutions which recognized their independence,[124] India only became a fully independent state in 1947. Despite this, India was admitted as one of the original members of the League in view of its contribution made in the war, but only as one of the signatories of the Treaty of Versailles.

However, the same treatment was not extended to thc Philippincs as doing so appeared to be "unwise" to President Wilson.[125] Hence, the "distinction between original and admitted members allowed the drafters of the Covenant to apply the

---

[120] Smith, H. A. in the Preface to Schwarzenberger 1936, pp. xi–xiii, xi.

[121] Claude 1971, p. 86.

[122] For the membership of Argentina, which was invited by the Annex of the Covenant to accede the Covenant, see Hudson 1934, pp. 125–133.

[123] "Before 1914 Canada could only have obtained recognition of its separate international personality by successful revolt against the mother country, and no proof of its *de facto* autonomy would have entitled it to a place in the councils of the nations, although it may be noted that Canada had already secured for itself a qualified position in international affairs by reason of the separate commercial treaties [it had entered into with] other states." Fenwick 1920, pp. 484–485.

[124] Northedge 1986, p. 47.

[125] According to Schwarzenberger 1936, p. 35.

principle of heterogeneous universality in the case of India, a signatory [of the Peace Treaty], and to exclude the Philippine Islands by providing the rule of homogeneous universality for later applicants."[126]

With the admission of the four British self-governing dominions, together with India, "a new rule of international law" was introduced which permitted "a state to possess international personality while formally remaining a dependent member of a larger empire."[127] However, while this constituted an important development, it also raised the issue of whether the British Empire was "not thereby overrepresented in the assembly, and in consequence, one of the reservations adopted by a majority of the United States Senate proposed that these five votes not be counted when disputes involving Great Britain were before the assembly."[128]

Hence, "in its quality as a member of the League, the 'British Empire' [was not] to be taken to include the Dominions."[129] Thus, the "principle of identity between members of the League and subjects of the international legal community was, however, set aside in favour of a very extensive interpretation of the principle of including nations organized on a territorial basis by granting membership to dominions and colonies."[130]

In addition, a number of applicants were initially excluded from League membership even though their independence was not in doubt and statehood was not a requirement for membership. This was the case for states such as Lichtenstein,[131] where their exclusion was directly related to the concern that such countries might outvote the big powers. Other states were excluded because their governments were not recognized by some of the allied powers.

The non-acceptance of Mexico, Costa Rica, and the Dominican Republic as original members of the League of Nations "was based upon the non-recognition of the governments of these States then in office by some the Allied and Associated Powers,"[132] even though there never was any doubt that these "were recognized as States by the great majority of the nations which constitute the international community."[133] In particular, those countries adhering to the Tobar doctrine of not recognizing any government which had achieved power illegally through revolutionary means, blocked admission to membership in the League on these grounds, even though the Covenant of the League of Nations did not stipulate the recognition of government as a condition of membership.

---

126 Ibid., 36.

127 Fenwick 1920, p. 484.

128 Ibid., 485.

129 Hudson 1924, p. 441.

130 Schwarzenberger 1936, p. 26.

131 Regarding the exclusion of Lichtenstein, see Gunter 1974, pp. 496–501.

132 See Schwarzenberger 1936, p. 67.

133 Ibid.

Further, the membership of some countries was subjected to extraneous and questionable criteria of classification. "China, with a population about 10 times as great as that of France and Italy" and "Brazil with an area about 10 times as large as those of France and Italy combined" were deemed to be small member states of the League of Nations.[134] That same classification was given to a number of other member states of the League,[135] which underlined that

> smallness depends neither on population nor area. Nor does the status of a Small State stand in any relation to its place in history, to its neutrality or belligerency in the World War, to its geographical situation, to its form of government, to its possession of colonies, to its degree of civilization, to its per-capita wealth, nor to its aggressive or pacific policies. In fact the so-called Small States within the League of Nations have nothing in common which distinguishes them from others, except that they enjoy no permanent representation on the Council.[136]

2.4.3 Preservation of Peace and Relations with Non-Members

For an organization dedicated to the preservation of peace, a broad membership base is of crucial importance to ensure its ability to settle conflicts and establish a system of collective security. One important point relates to the relationship between the League and non-members and the question of whether the "Covenant vests the League with powers to impose its will on non-members if the peace of the world is in danger of being broken or is actually broken."[137] This question was considered in detail by Schwarzenberger (1936). He analyzed relevant provisions of the League Covenant,[138] the different classes of non-members, and the Briand-Kellogg Pact, and arrived at the following conclusion:

> To sum up, the Covenant assumes the competence of the League in all matters concerning the maintenance of world peace. The competence of the League is not restricted to cases in which the consent of the non-member has been obtained. The claim of the Covenant is

---

[134] Rappard 1934, p. 544.

[135] "Spain, Poland, India, Australia, Canada, [were] counted as 'small members' of the League, as [were] Sweden, Holland, Luxembourg, Albania, Belgium, Hungary, Denmark, Switzerland, Liberia and Panama." See Rappard 1934, p. 544.

[136] Ibid.

[137] Schwarzenberger 1936, p. 96.

[138] Articles 3 and 4 of the League Covenant provides that the Assembly and Council of the League, respectively, "may deal with any matter within the sphere of action of the League or affecting the peace of the world." Article 11 of the Covenant provides in pertinent part: "Any war or threat of war, whether immediately affecting any of the Members of the League or not, is hereby declared a matter of concern to the whole League, and the League shall take any action that may be deemed wise and effectual to safeguard the peace of nations…." Other relevant provisions are Articles 16, 17 and 20 of the Covenant.

> compatible with international law as it existed at the time when the Covenant came into force only with regard to non-members which were signatories of the Peace Treaties. Since the Briand-Kellogg Pact has been almost universally accepted, and has thus become a rule of international law, its signatories can resort to intervention as a means of vindicating the Pact. Those signatories which are members of the League can use the League machinery for the purposes of intervention against a member signatory as well as against a non-member signatory. Every signatory State, however, retains its sovereign right to decide for itself whether the Pact has been violated and whether it participates in its vindication.[139]

In addition to being subject to the above limitations, the security system of the Covenant, which had been "drafted under the assumption that the U.S.A. would be a member of the League,"[140] largely remained ineffective due to the fact that the League never achieved relative universality. Also, there was no agreement on a comprehensive system of settlement of disputes.

As Schwarzenberger has shown in detail, the League did not even manage to solve all disputes between its members, let alone disputes between non-members of the League.[141] Thus, the League which had been created by the Covenant "was deficient in legal authority and practical competence for making the international decisions required for the management of a collective security system."[142]

2.4.4 The League and the International Bureaux

Prior to the establishment of the League, there had barely been any coordination among the international bureaus then established. Article 24 of the League Covenant sought to change this by providing in pertinent part:

> There shall be placed under the direction of the League all international bureaux already established by general treaties if the parties to such treaties consent. All such international bureaux and all commissions for the regulation of matters of international interest hereafter constituted shall be placed under the direction of the League.

Thus, as a matter of principle, the League was given an important role of direction in respect of the "sixty odd official organizations cooperating to facilitate and improve methods of communication, to promote commerce, to carry out international police and sanitation work, to secure and disseminate scientific data, and to perform various social, economic and political matters of common interest."[143] "The Covenant stated unmistakably its supremacy over all other international legislation, and declared with equal firmness that functional organizations

---

[139] Schwarzenberger 1936, p. 118.

[140] Ibid., 150.

[141] For additional details, see Chapter VII of Schwarzenberger 1936, p. 119 ss.

[142] Claude 1971, p. 263.

[143] Eckhardt 1919, p. 437.

working in the international field should be subordinated to the League."[144] Nevertheless:

> The attempt to subordinate the international bureaus to the League had not been very successful, apart from administrative and budgetary difficulties, mainly because important members of public international unions either did not belong to the League, or were of less influence there than in the particular union whose coordination with (or rather subordination to) the League was contemplated.[145]

As has been shown by Ghebali:

> Le Conseil de la S.D.N. interpréta délibérément l'article 24 dans un sens restrictif pour démontrer aux Etats-Unis et aux Bureaux internationaux que la Société n'avait pas l'intention d'englober les Unions, qui se placeraient sous son autorité, laquelle ne serait rien d'autre qu'un magistère moral [....].[146]

Hence, it "it has been remarked that 'the League has built a large and well-equipped hotel, but the guests are slow at arriving.'"[147] For all practical purposes, Article 24 largely remained ineffective as by 1931 no "more than four organizations have been brought under the 'direction' of the League."[148] In the end, only "six agencies of minor importance became affiliated with the League of Nations."[149] Thus, the League never performed the function of direction to the extent foreseen by the drafters of its Covenant.

2.5 UN System

2.5.1 United Nations

2.5.1.1 Continuity and Innovation

The establishment of the United Nations represented a renewed effort to achieve world peace through *international organization*, as distinguished from *world government*."[150]

---

[144] Pollaczek 1946, p. 606.

[145] Ibid., 607.

[146] Ghebali, V. Y. Aux origines de l'Ecosoc—l'évolution des commissions et organisations techniques de la Société des Nations. http://www.persee.fr/doc/afdi_0066-3085_1972_num_18_1_1712.

[147] Bailey 1931, p. 418.

[148] Ibid.

[149] Klein 2006.

[150] Claude 1971, p. 69.

The "UN entered its career with four organs directly evolved by the League of Nations".[151] The General Assembly of the UN is clearly based on that of the League, as are the Secretariat and the International Court of Justice. The Permanent Court of International Justice was formally superseded by a new agency, with a revised title, but the modifications in the Statute and the technical dissociation of the two judicial bodies were not significant enough to break the effective institutional continuity of the World Court."[152] While the Council of the League of Nations had "the same powers as the Assembly", the UN Security Council was given "the exclusive task of maintaining international peace" and, in this context, "considerably widened" powers.[153]

The establishment of the UN entailed both elements of continuity and major innovations. Nevertheless, the UN "was put forward, again for psychological reasons, as a decidedly *new* organization rather than as a revived and remodeled League of Nations."[154] "The understatement of this bond of continuity with the League was a tactic designed to avoid offending the Russians, who had been alternately distrustful of, disillusioned with, and outraged by the old organization, and the Americans, who would have found it embarrassing to join an organization from which they had so long made it a cardinal point of national policy to abstain."[155]

While the UN Charter "laid down a rather simple structure" of the UN system consisting of "six principal and a number of subsidiary organs," and a "halo of specialized agencies" with which it would "maintain defined close relationships and which would be part of the 'UN System' [....], today, this simple scheme has proliferated into a veritable jungle of miscellaneous entities, including numerous quasi-autonomous bodies [....], treaty organs [....], enhanced treaty organs, two categories of specialized agencies and other related organizations [....] and a variety of other entities and arrangements in part designed to coordinate these many new actors [....]."[156]

> The United Nations system also drew upon the past in sense that it simply adopted, without fundamental alteration, significant segments of the preexisting complex of international machinery. Such special-purpose agencies as the Universal Postal Union, the International Telecommunication Union, the International Labor Organization, and the League's organ for international drug control were destined for integration in the new network.[157]

---

[151] See Mangone 1954, p. 173, and Conforti 1996, p. 2. "It was contemplated that the basic organs would be the same four organs of the League: The Assembly (consisting of all the Member States), the Council (made up of a limited number of States)."

[152] Claude 1971, p. 61.

[153] Conforti 1996, p. 3.

[154] Claude 1971, p. 66.

[155] Claude 1971, p. 66.

[156] Szasz 1999, pp. 2–3.

[157] Claude 1971, p. 61.

The UN further evolved in comparison to the League at several levels. While the Covenant of the League of Nations did not incorporate any provisions on the juridical personality or legal capacity of the League, Article 104 of the UN Charter provided that the UN organization "shall enjoy in the territory of each of its Members such legal capacity as may be necessary for the exercise of its functions and the fulfillment of its purposes." Moreover, with the Reparations of Injuries Decision,[158] the objective international juridical personality of the UN in non-member countries and the treaty-making capacity of the UN were firmly established.

2.5.1.2 Collective Security and Relations with Non-Members

Moreover, the UN Charter defined the relationship between the UN and member countries and non-member countries in a different manner than the League. In accordance with Article 1 of the UN Charter, it is the purpose of the UN to "maintain international peace and security, and to that end: to take effective collective measures for the prevention and removal of threats to the peace, and for the suppression of acts of aggression or other breaches of the peace [....]." Understood as a "halfway house between the terminal points of international anarchy and world government,"[159] the collective security system under the UN Charter was surely more satisfactory than that ineffective system of the League. This relates on the one hand to the substantial powers given to the Security Council. Gowlland-Debbas indicates:

> Those who initially framed the Charter back in San Francisco in 1945 had played sorcerer's apprentice by introducing such loaded provisions as Article 39 of the Charter, which gave the Security Council seemingly unfettered discretion to determine threats to or breaches of the peace and by entrenching a monopoly of permanent members which reflected the then power relationships of the immediate post-World War II era. To these provisions were added Article 25 of the Charter whereby Member States bound themselves to carry out in the future the unknown decisions of the Security Council in accordance with the Charter, and Article 103 under which their obligations under the Charter were to prevail over any other international agreements, well before the concept of *jus cogens* introduced different notions of non-derogability.[160]

2.5.1.3 Membership in the UN

While colonies were eligible to apply for membership to the League of Nations, the UN Charter is predicated on the assumption that colonies, even if self-governing,

[158] Reparation for injuries suffered in the service of the United Nations, Advisory Opinion: ICJ Reports 1949, 174.

[159] Claude 1971, p. 246.

[160] Gowlland-Debbas 2011, pp. 185–444, 200–201.

and other dependencies are precluded from applying for membership[161] and partake in the membership of the metropolitan state. However, these criteria were arbitrarily applied in some cases, as is underlined by the controversy on the status of the Soviet republics.

The Soviet Union had suggested "that the 16 republics which made up the U.S.S.R. be included among the initial members."[162] "[T]he issue of membership proved a cause of sharp controversy. Stalin looked at this issue in terms of voting strength and found the Soviet Union wanting as compared with the United Kingdom and its family in the British Commonwealth, or with the United States and its Pan-American family."[163] At Yalta, the decision was taken to invite the two Soviet republics of Ukraine and Byelorussia (now Belarus) to the San Francisco Conference in 1945 "to increase the weight of the Soviet Union, both in the Conference (the only other participating Communist State was Yugoslavia) and in the future organization."[164] The said republics were admitted as founding members of the UN even though these were "not sovereign until the break-up of the Soviet Union at the end of 1991[....]."[165]

Unlike the League, the UN eventually achieved universality in that at present, with a few exceptions, all independent states are members of the UN. This was a "momentous change for the Organization."[166] As UN's tortuous road to universality has been analyzed in detail in literature,[167] this process does not need to be recounted in detail in this publication. Rather, the focus of this analysis is on the great variety of concepts of membership used for the various organizations and institutions that form the "veritable jungle"[168] called the UN system.

2.5.2 Specialized Agencies and Related Agencies

In addition to the UN, specialized agencies and related agencies are part of the UN system. While they share some characteristics, they have different legal status.

161 See Simma 1994, p. 162.
162 Leonard 1951, p. 48.
163 Ibid., 74.
164 See Conforti 1996, p. 4.
165 See Simma 1994, p. 156.
166 Grant 2009, p. 1.
167 See in particular, Grant, with detailed references.
168 Szasz 1999, p. 3.

2.5.2.1 Specialized Agencies

"Functionally speaking, the United Nations was set up as a kind of loose confederation of international agencies. In contrast to the League, which had in theory, and to a lesser degree in practice, imposed central direction and control upon of the operation of agencies in nonpolitical fields, the United Nations was committed to the concept of the coexistence of a 'hub' organization and a group of autonomous 'Specialized Agencies,' looking to the United Nations proper for coordination and guidance, but enjoying essential freedom of action in their respective fields."[169]

"In structural terms the United Nations system may be described as a vast complex of international machinery, all-embracing in territorial and substantive scope, and characterized by internal decentralization and specialization."[170] Specialized agencies were conceived by Article 57 of the UN Charter as "established by intergovernmental agreement and having wide international responsibilities, as defined in their basic instruments, in economic, social, cultural, educational, health, and related fields." The term "wide international responsibilities" is understood to comprise the substantial and geographic scope of responsibilities. Thus, only organizations of global reach and universal membership qualify for recognition as a specialized agency.

UN specialized agencies are governed by the constituent agreement, a treaty or convention, which contains provisions on membership and determines the organizational, institutional, and governance structure of the organization and its decision-making procedures. Specialized agencies possess international juridical personality and are separate organizations with their own membership, budgetary and funding arrangements, and an executive head elected by the members. However, the corollary of such independence is the inclusion of the specialized agencies in the complex and involved coordination framework of the UN. Article 57 stipulates that the specialized agencies "shall be brought into relationship with the United Nations in accordance with the provisions of Article 63." This provision has a "mandatory character", as was highlighted by the Preparatory Commission in its Report to the General Assembly.[171]

In accordance with Article 63 para 1 of the UN Charter:

> The Economic and Social Council may enter into agreements with any of the agencies referred to in Article 57, defining the terms on which the agency concerned shall be brought into relationship with the United Nations. Such agreements shall be subject to approval by the General Assembly.

Moreover, Article 63 para 2 provides that the United Nations Economic and Social Council (ECOSOC) "may coordinate the activities of the specialized agencies

[169] Claude 1971, p. 68.

[170] Claude 1971, p. 69.

[171] See Repertory of the Practice of the United Nations Organs, 1945–1953, Vol. 3, Article 57, para 4. http://legal.un.org/docs/?path=../repertory/art63/english/rep_orig_vol3_art63.pdf&lang=EFS.

through consultation with and recommendations to such agencies and through recommendations to the General Assembly and to the Members of the United Nations."

The terms of the various agreements which have been concluded between ECOSOC and the specialized agencies have been analyzed in the Repertory of Practice of the United Nations Organs.[172] Special arrangements apply to the organizations of the World Bank Group and the International Monetary Fund (IMF). When tripartite negotiations with the United Nations commenced in 1947, the "representatives of the Bank and the Fund declared that, while they were anxious to co-operate with the United Nations, the safeguarding of the autonomy and independence of their institutions was vital to their very existence. In particular, the success of the Bank's operations was dependent upon the degree of confidence it could inspire among financial institutions and private investors. Any suggestion that it was in any degree open to the influence of other organizations, especially those of a political character or those in which political considerations played a part, would inevitably shake that confidence."[173] Hence, the final draft relationship agreements between the UN and International Bank for Reconstruction and Development (IBRD) and the IMF, while recognizing that they both had status of a specialized agency, stated "that the agency in question was, and was 'required to function as, an independent international organization'."[174] Despite some criticism, the draft agreements were approved by ECOSOC and the General Assembly.[175] For this reason, the IMF and the organizations of the World Bank Group enjoy substantial greater independence than other specialized agencies. This is epitomized by a comparison of their relationship agreements with those concluded by ECOSOC with the United Nations Industrial Development Organization (UNIDO) and the World Tourism Organization (UNWTO), which were the last organizations to join the specialized agencies club. They, respectively, converted to the status of a specialized agency from being a subsidiary body of the General Assembly and a non-governmental organization. Their relationship agreements with the UN set out the cooperation framework, including close budgetary cooperation between the UN and these agencies. The relationship agreement with the UN negotiated with ECOSOC mandates UNIDO "to accept the Statute of the International Civil Service Commission."[176] A similar provision is also contained in the Agreement between UNWTO and the UN.[177] While similar provisions are not set out in other

[172] Repertory of the Practice of the United Nations Organs, Article 63. http://legal.un.org/repertory/art63.shtml.

[173] Article 63, Repertory of Practice of the United Nations Organs (1945–1954), para 79. http://legal.un.org/docs/?path=../repertory/art63/english/rep_orig_vol3_art63.pdf&lang=EFS.

[174] Ibid., para 82.

[175] Ibid., para 91.

[176] See Repertory of Practice of the United Nations Organs, Article 63, Supplement 7, 1985–1988, Vol. 4, para 20.

[177] See Agreement between the United Nations and the World Tourism Organization, Article 16, para 1. In *UNWTO Basic Documents*. 2016. Vol. I, 5th ed. Madrid: UNWTO. http://cf.cdn.unwto.org/sites/all/files/docpdf/130718basicdocumentsenweb.pdf.

relationship agreements, all specialized agencies (except the IMF and organizations of the World Bank Group) follow the UN common system, either because they have accepted the statutes of the International Civil Service Commission, or, as the International Fund for Agricultural Development (IFAD) which has not, as a matter of policy.[178]

There is no uniformity between the UN and the specialized agencies either relating to their member states or regarding eligible subjects and types of membership. While states are the main subjects of membership for all specialized agencies, in a number of cases, only states are eligible to join, while other specialized agencies also allow international organizations to become members. Moreover, some specialized agencies also allow associate membership of dependent territories and affiliate or sector membership of private sector entities (see below).

Generally, specialized agencies make a distinction between original members and members admitted subsequently. This concerns only the process of admission but not the entitlements of the members. In certain cases, members of the UN are also entitled to join specialized agencies by accepting the Constitution or other constituent agreement, but generally lose membership when they cease to be a member of the UN. In some cases, the right to join a specialized agency is conditional upon the fulfillment of certain requirements (e.g., in the case of the World Meteorological Organization, only those UN members which have a metrological service are eligible to join),[179] while in other cases, the right to join by a unilateral act has been extended to non-UN member states. Moreover, other specific requirements relating to the activity of the specialized agency may apply for admission to membership.[180]

The membership of specialized agencies is not necessarily identical to membership in the UN or even to other specialized agencies. For example, Germany had been admitted as a member of some UN specialized agencies long before becoming a member of the UN. Moreover, a number of small island countries, which are not members of the UN, have been admitted to membership in certain specialized agencies.

Dependent territories are not entitled to full membership in any of the UN specialized agencies. However, some organizations such as the FAO, International Maritime Organization (IMO), UNESCO, WHO, and UNWTO, have created an

[178] The International Civil Service Commission. 2000. *A Quarter-Century Serving the United Nations Common System*. https://icsc.un.org/resources/pdfs/general/25abenglish.pdf.

[179] Article 3(b) of the Convention on the World Meteorological Organization provides the following may become members of WMO: "Any Member of the United Nations having a Meteorological Service by acceding to the present Convention in accordance with Article 33."

[180] See, for example, para 1 of Article 5 of the Convention establishing the World Intellectual Property Organization (WIPO), as amended on 28 September 1979, which provides that membership "shall be open to any State which is a member of any of the Unions as defined in Article 2 (vii)". http://www.wipo.int/wipolex/en/treaties/text.jsp?file_id=283833.

associate membership status for dependent territories.[181] Associate members may participate in the work of the organization but have no role in decision-making procedures. Thus, in the case of FAO, "Associate Members shall have the right to participate in the deliberations of the Conference but shall not hold office or have the right to vote."[182] They are not represented in the Council and may only be included without the right to vote "in the membership of commissions, committees, conferences, working parties and consultations."[183] Similar provisions are contained in the constitutions or conventions of a number of other specialized agencies.

The UNWTO constitution provides for affiliate membership for "international bodies, both intergovernmental and non-governmental, concerned with specialized interests in tourism and to commercial bodies and associations whose activities are related to the aims of the Organization or fall within its competence."[184]

ITU, on the other hand, is "an intergovernmental organization in which Member States and Sector Members, having well-defined rights and obligations, cooperate for the fulfillment of the purposes of the Union."[185] Sector Members are "entitled to participate fully in the activities of the Sector of which they are members" and "may provide chairmen and vice-chairmen of Sector assemblies" and "take part in the adoption of Questions and Recommendations and in decisions relating to the working methods and procedures of the Sector concerned."[186]

2.5.2.2 Related Agencies

In addition to specialized agencies, there are agencies such as the International Atomic Energy Agency (IAEA), the World Trade Organization (WTO) and the International Organization for Migration (IOM) which are similar, in many respects, to specialized agencies. As has been shown by Szasz, "the IAEA could not become an SA [specialized agency] principally because its relationship agreement was not negotiated with ECOSOC (as required for SAs by Articles 57 and 63 para 1) reflecting the fact that the Agency's international security related activities might require it to have access to the SC [Security Council] rather than to ECOSOC."[187] Also in the case of the WTO and IOM, their relationship agreements are with the

[181] Klein, paras 24 and 25.

[182] See the FAO Constitution, Articles II, para 11; III, para 1. *Basic Texts of the Food and Agriculture Organization of the United Nations*, 2015 ed. Vols. I and II.

[183] See the FAO Constitution, VI, para 7.

[184] UNWTO Statutes, Article 7(1). http://cf.cdn.unwto.org/sites/all/files/docpdf/unwtostatuteseng.pdf.

[185] ITU Constitution, Article 2.

[186] ITU Constitution, Article 3.

[187] Szasz 1999, p. 38.

UN rather than with ECOSOC. The General Assembly accepted the status of IOM as that of a related organization recently.[188]

Related organizations as mentioned above overall belong to the inner circle of UN agencies, but their status is different from that of the United Nations or a UN specialized agency. While the staff of related agencies can make use of the UN laissez-passer, neither the Convention on the Privileges and Immunities of the United Nations nor the Convention on the Privileges and Immunities of the Specialized Agencies are applicable in their regard (see below). Hence, in the case of related agencies their constituent agreements and any bilateral and multilateral agreements regarding privileges and immunities which are applicable in their regard are the source of their privileges and immunities.

2.5.3 Subsidiary Organs and Quasi-Autonomous Bodies

Article 7 of the UN Charter provides that "subsidiary organs as may be found necessary may be established in accordance with the present Charter." Articles 22 and 29 expressly refer to subsidiary organs that may be created by the General Assembly and Security Council and Article 63 to commissions created by ECOSOC.

Of particular interest are the "quasi-autonomous bodies" (QABs) which have been established, in most cases by a resolution of the General Assembly pursuant to Article 22 of the UN Charter. These include the United Nations University (UNU), the UN High Commissioner for Refugees (UNHCR), the United Nations Children Fund (UNICEF), the United Nations Conference on Trade and Development (UNCTAD), the United Nations Development Fund for Women (UNIFEM), the United Nations Development Programme (UNDP), the United Nations Human Settlement Programme (UN-HABITAT), the United Nations Population Fund, the United Nations Relief and Works Agency for Palestine Refugees in the Near East (UNRWA), and the World Food Programme (WFP).[189] These bodies have various organs, and in certain cases, subsidiary bodies.

The basic difference between specialized agencies and QABs is that the latter are not established by a treaty, but are generally adopted by a Resolution (of the UN General Assembly) usually formulated as a statute, while later changes "usually consist of just individual paragraphs of routine resolutions relating to or just mentioning the QAB."[190] Thus, the overall approach taken when these quasi-autonomous bodies were established was they would partake in the juridical

---

[188] See Resolution 70/296 "Agreement concerning the Relationship between the United Nations and the International Organization for Migration". http://www.un.org/en/ga/search/view_doc.asp?symbol=A/RES/70/296.

[189] The above follows the list given by Rudolf 2006.

[190] Szasz 1999, p. 6, footnote 13.

personality of the UN rather than have a separate juridical personality under international law.

In terms of membership, UNCTAD is a quasi-autonomous body with a nearly global membership. It was established as an "organ of the General Assembly"[191] and its membership was conceived as membership in the "United Nations Conference on Trade and Development", rather than as membership in a separate organization.

Its membership provisions extend membership in the Conference to "those States which are members of the United Nations or members of the specialized agencies or of the International Atomic Energy Agency."[192] On the one hand, this provision extends membership to states other than UN members that are members of the UN specialized agencies or IAEA. On the other hand, it constrains membership to those states that are members of the organizations mentioned above. Thus, States are not free to join UNCTAD as they deem fit but must first become a member of one of the international organizations mentioned above. In doing so, they become automatically members of UNCTAD.

In addition to the Conference, the General Assembly Resolution establishing UNCTAD provided for the "Trade and Development Board" as a "permanent organ of the Conference."[193] Membership in the Board is open to all members of the Conference.[194] The said Board has the same functions as the Conference.

Unlike UNCTAD, UNDP does not have a plenary body. It is governed by the Executive Board, which is "is made up of representatives from 36 countries around the world who serve on a rotating basis."[195] In the case of UNEP, General Assembly Resolution 2997 (XXVII) established a Governing Council composed of 58 members. Also, the other quasi-autonomous entities

> tend to have small governing councils made up of between 30 to 60 members, while membership is generally open to all UN member states. Some UN programmes have set limits for serving consecutive terms and conditionality that members are in good standing with the issue. Membership is also normally regionally balanced. Unlike specialised agencies, UN programmes do not have separate instruments establishing them as organisations, rather their establishment generally comes from GA resolutions and each resolution has variations in specificity of how the programme is governed. In general, the resolution establishes the mandate of the programmes, its functions, its relationship to ECOSOC or the GA along with other UN and specialised agencies, rules of procedures, funding and decision making, and the role of their secretariats.[196]

---

191 General Assembly Resolution 1995 (XIX), Section I. https://documents-dds-ny.un.org/doc/RESOLUTION/GEN/NR0/210/89/IMG/NR021089.pdf?OpenElement.

192 General Assembly Resolution 1995 (XIX), Section II, para 1.

193 General Assembly Resolution 1995 (XIX), para 4.

194 General Assembly Resolution 1995 (XIX), para 5.

195 UNDP. Executive Board. http://www.undp.org/content/undp/en/home/executive-board.html.

196 UNEP. 2010. United Nations Specialised Agencies versus United Nations Programmes. Note by the Executive Director, 10. https://www.scribd.com/document/212017488/UN-Specialised-Agencies-vs-UN-Programmes.

The case of UNIDO shows that a conversion from a QAB to a specialized agency is possible. Thus, the conversion of other QABs into a specialized agency or other type of international organization is not precluded.

General Assembly Resolution 1995 (XIX) establishing UNCTAD contemplates a review "of the effectiveness and further evolution of institutional arrangements" and, to this end, a study of "all relevant subjects, including matters relating to the establishment of a comprehensive organization based on the entire membership of the United Nations system of organizations." (para 29) While this needs to be seen in the context of the discussion of the defunct International Trade Organization, it does not preclude other types of organizational arrangements.

In particular, various options have also been considered to "upgrade"[197] UNEP and transform it into a UN Specialized Agency established by intergovernmental agreement,[198] as well as explore how to enhance its functions and legal frameworks to enhance environmental governance. Bernstein and Brunnée discuss various options of institutional reform, including, *inter alia*, whether "universal membership would increase UNEP's legitimacy and enhance its global mandate."[199] However, they note that "there is no structural reason per se that universal membership is a pre-requisite for enhanced functions."[200] Moreover, "in many ways, UNEP already is 'universal'", because as a UN programme established by UNGA, its 'members' include all UN members."[201]

The main question is whether the strings which hold QABs to the UN and the constraints resulting therefrom unduly constrain QABs in the achievement of their statutory objectives. Based on the answer to that question, a decision may be taken as to whether they should maintain their current legal status or be transformed in a UN specialized agency or other independent international organization.

---

197 The "Report of the High-Level on United Nations System-wide Coherence in the areas of development, humanitarian assistance and the environment" recommends "that the United Nations Environment Programme be upgraded and given real authority as the environmental policy pillar of the United Nations system." The aforementioned Report is an attachment to United Nations. 2006. *Follow-up to the outcome of the Millennium Summit. Note by the Secretary-General.* Doc. A/61/583, 15. http://www.un.org/en/ga/search/view_doc.asp?symbol=A/61/583.

198 See Meyer-Ohlendorf and Knigge 2007, pp. 124–141. http://www.centerforunreform.org/sites/default/files/GEG_Meyer-Ohlendorf_Knigge.pdf.

199 S Bernstein with J Brunnée. "Options for Broader Reform of the Institutional Framework for Sustainable Development (IFSD): Structural, Legal, and Financial Aspects", 9. http://www1.uneca.org/Portals/rio20/documents/cfssd7/IFSD%20FIVE%20OPTIONS%20REPORT_31Oct11.pdf.

200 Ibid.

201 Ibid.

2.6 Treaty Bodies, Conferences of Parties and Financial Mechanisms

There are a number of reasons why states opt for the establishment of treaty bodies rather than traditional international organizations. "In international environmental law, the emergence of the institutional structures in the 1970s and 1980s coincided with the dissatisfaction with traditional organizations because of their cost and bureaucracy".[202] Moreover, as shown by Ulfstein, there were a variety of reason relating to Arctic cooperation, human rights and arms control for states to opt for the creation of treaty bodies.[203] In essence, it is often a policy decision whether to pursue that option or the traditional paradigm of international organization with treaty foundation.

Szasz has indicated that the creation of treaty organs is one of the policy options which states members of an IGO often pursue "to regulate their conduct in ways not provided for in its institutional treaty."[204] As they "generally cannot do so by resolutions of any of the IGO organs but must formulate another treaty",[205] they need to "consider whether any collective action to be taken for the implementation of the treaty should be entrusted to the parent IGO itself or whether a new IGO is to be created—or to take the intermediate step of merely establishing some political and/or expert organs and having those serviced by the secretariat of the parent IGO, i.e. to establish treaty organs."[206] Often the latter option is pursued in creating "treaty organs that exist in a symbiotic relationship with their host organization."[207] They are often seen as "'IGOs manquées' lacking a secretariat of their own as well as international legal personality."[208]

Treaty bodies such as the Human Rights Committee, the Committee on Economic, Social and Cultural Rights, the Committees on the Elimination of Racial Discrimination, the Committee of Discrimination against Women, the Committee against Torture, the Committee of the Rights of the Child, and the Committee on Migrant Workers are "supervisory bodies established by conventions" which have "their legal basis in a separate treaty and their members are elected by the conference of its States Parties."[209] Their legal status is different both from that of committees of the UN General Assembly and from that of QABs. While QABs are deemed to be an extension of the legal personality of the UN and, therefore, are covered by the Convention on the Privileges and Immunities of the United Nations

[202] Ulfstein 2009, p. 49.
[203] Ibid., 49.
[204] Szasz 1999, p. 29.
[205] Ibid., 29.
[206] Ibid., 29.
[207] Ibid., 29.
[208] Ibid., 18.
[209] Rudolf 2006, para 11.

(General Convention),[210] the General Convention is generally not applicable to treaty bodies. Hence, ensuring that persons associated with treaty bodies are covered by privileges and immunities may entail major challenges.

Of particular interest are the treaty bodies of multilateral environmental conventions. These bodies, and, in particular, their "conferences of the parties" (COPs), are not merely intergovernmental conferences since they are established by treaties as permanent organs and have subsidiary bodies and a secretariat, while they also differ from traditional intergovernmental organizations (IGOs)."[211] As will be shown below, some COPs possess international legal personality and it is questioned whether "autonomous institutional arrangements"[212] may be classified as a new type of international organization. Nevertheless, such arrangements have distinctive features (e.g., no permanent seat) and other characteristics which set them apart from international organizations and it is quite doubtful for that reason whether they can be classified as international organizations, even to the extent that they are recognized as possessing international legal personality.

It is an important development that in the case of the Multilateral Fund for the Montreal Protocol and the Green Climate Fund, financial mechanisms with international legal personality have been created pursuant to a decision of the Meeting of the Parties to the Montreal Protocol and decisions of the Conference of the Parties to the United Nations Framework Convention on Climate Change, respectively. Furthermore, the Preparatory Commission of the Nuclear Test Ban Organization (CTBTO) was established by Resolution of the states signatories to a treaty and is operating on the international plane. As will be shown, organizations as mentioned above may qualify to be treated as international organizations.

2.7 International Financial Institutions

The membership and financial structures of international financial institutions have already been analyzed by this author who has shown the development of four generations of concessional windows,[213] and, in detail, the financial and institutional structures of 12 concessional windows. The major changes to the current architecture of international financial institutions took place in Asia.

The Eurasian Development Bank (EDB), which was established in 2006 by the Russian Federation and the Republic of Kazakhstan "to foster the strengthening and development of market economy" in its member states and "enhance trade and

---

[210] Convention on the Privileges and Immunities of the United Nations. Adopted by the General Assembly on 13 February 1946. http://www.un.org/en/ethics/pdf/convention.pdf.

[211] Ulfstein 2007, p. 878.

[212] Churchill and Ulfstein 2000, pp. 623–659.

[213] Droesse 2011, pp. 6–33. (Hereinafter, "Introductory Remarks"). See also Ragazzi 2014.

economic integration among them,"[214] has managed to attract new members and deliver projects. In accordance with para 1 of Article 3 of the constituent agreement of the Eurasian Development Bank, the Bank "may be joined by other states or international organisations, upon condition that they comply with the requirements and procedures set forth by the Charter of the Bank."[215] The Republics of Armenia, Tajikistan, Belarus and Kyrgyz became members of the EDB in 2009, 2010 and 2011, respectively.[216] While so far no international organization has yet been admitted to membership, international organizations are in the case of the Eurasian Development Bank eligible subjects of membership, as a matter of principle.

However, the most important development relates to the creation of an entire new infrastructure of international financial institutions in Asia comprising the Asian Infrastructure Investment Bank (AIIB), the New Development Bank and the Silk Road Fund, and the Credit Guarantee and Investment Facility (CGIF), and the ASEAN+3 Macroeconomic Research Office (AMRO).

The establishment of the Asian Infrastructure Investment Bank, the New Development Bank (previously called BRIC Bank), and the Silk Road Fund[217] reflects, as Wihtol observes, "China's and other emerging economies' frustration with the slow pace of reform of the Bretton Woods institutions, particularly the World Bank and the IMF. 'China feels it can't get anything done in the World Bank or the IMF, so it wants to set up its own World Bank that it can control itself,' one participant in the AIIB negotiations explained."[218] Also, the shareholdings of China and India in ADB are still much lower than those of Japan and the United States, with no realistic chance of China obtaining a special capital increase which would allow a similar capital share as the countries mentioned above. This further strengthened the determination of the Chinese government to sponsor a new financial infrastructure conducive to its strategic objectives. The "creation of the AIIB is an important development in global governance and reflects key shifts in the balance of world economic power. It further suggests that China has made the transition to global leadership, including building new multilateral organizations."[219]

The establishment of AIIB and the New Development Bank follows the traditional treaty-based mechanisms of establishing an intergovernmental organization. Their constituent agreements are inspired by those of other development banks. However, their membership structures are different from those of ADB.

One of the main purposes for allowing membership of non-regional countries in ADB was to mobilize additional resources for the development of ADB's region.

---

[214] Agreement Establishing the Eurasian Development Bank (EADB Charter), Article 1. https://eabr.org/upload/iblock/c91/foundation-documents.pdf.

[215] Agreement Establishing the Eurasian Development Bank, Article 3, para 1.

[216] Agreement Establishing the Eurasian Development Bank, Article 3.

[217] See Silk Road Fund, http://www.silkroadfund.com.cn/enwap/27365/index.html.

[218] Wihtol 2015, pp. 7–15.

[219] Chin 2016, p. 12.

When the ADB Charter was drafted, development assistance was, in essence, exclusively provided by developed countries. Hence, the drafters of the ADB Charter looked to non-regional developed countries as a source of funding. Therefore, while Israel "was keenly interested in the membership of the Bank" and there were indications of Saudi Arabia's interest in "securing membership of ECAFE" and Kuwait's willingness to provide funds for ADB,[220] a possible membership of these countries in ADB was not pursued by the Consultative Committee in 1965. The Preparatory Committee which finalized the draft ADB Charter adopted the same approach. Hence, under Article 3, para 1 of the ADB Charter, only "non-regional developed countries" are eligible to join ADB.

However, things have changed substantially since the ADB Charter was drafted. Developing countries are now a major source of development assistance. The establishment of the AIIB epitomizes this development, as it is predominantly funded by regional developing countries. In spite of pressure from the US that countries should not join the AIIB, there was a flood of new applications, partially received after the set deadline; thus, 57 countries have become founding members, among which countries as diverse and hostile as Israel and Iran. Some of the non-regional members will probably be able to contribute to the resources of the AIIB only to a limited extent.

In accordance with para 2, Article 3 of the AIIB Charter, in addition to the original members who ratified the AIIB Articles pursuant to Article 58, "Members of the International Bank for Reconstruction and Development or the Asian Development Bank" are eligible for membership in AIIB. Thus, while it possesses a regional character and in accordance with Article 5, para 2 of the AIIB Articles seventy-five (75) per cent of the total subscribed capital stock are reserved for regional countries, non-regional developing countries may be members of AIIB. This is a major difference in comparison to ADB. It defines the outlook and vision of AIIB as an institution which is open for participation of a wide range of regional and non-regional countries and offers opportunities and new perspectives of south-south cooperation among developing countries.

On the other hand, the five BRICS[221] countries comprise the original members of the New Development Bank. In accordance with Article 2 of the Articles of Agreement approved at Fortaleza,[222] "membership shall be open to members of the United Nations, in accordance with the provisions of the Articles of Agreement of the New Development Bank. It shall be open to borrowing and non-borrowing members." As for AIIB, the aforementioned provision allows membership of a wide range of developing countries in the New Development Bank.

Established by the ten members of the Association of Southeast Asian Nations (ASEAN) together with China, Japan, South Korea (ASEAN+3) and ADB, the CGIF was approved as an ADB trust fund to develop local bond markets and issue

[220] Krishnamurti, R., 49.

[221] Brazil, Russia, India, China, and South Africa.

[222] Agreement on the New Development Bank. http://www.ndb.int/wp-content/themes/ndb/pdf/Agr.

guarantees for local currency denominated bonds issued by investment grade companies in ASEAN+3 countries.[223] While it does not possess international legal personality or legal capacity under national law, CGIF has a quasi-equity structure involving shareholdings of contributors[224] and an elaborate governance structure involving the meeting of contributors as the highest decision-making organ. It also has a Board of Directors which is "not an executive body" but whose function is "to lead, guide and perform policy oversight of management," and a chief executive officer.[225] While ADB, the trustee, is the legal owner of CGIF assets towards third parties, most substantive decisions are taken by the governing bodies of the CGIF (i.e., the Meeting of Contributors and Board of Directors). Every decision by the Board of Directors is taken by simple majority; except as provided otherwise, the same is also the case for the Meeting of Contributors.[226] Thus, the governing bodies of the CGIF meet all the criteria for a "*volonté distincte*" traditionally seen as one of the criteria for recognition as an international organization.

One of the peculiarities of CGIF[227] is that it was established as a trust fund of ADB rather than as an entity with juridical personality under international law or as a corporation with legal capacity under municipal law. Also, the Articles of Agreement of the CGIF were not ratified by the governments involved in this initiative. As any borrowings would involve a material liability of ADB, the Articles of Agreement do not allow CGIF to leverage resources on capital markets (in fact, its Articles expressly prohibit it from borrowing, except for cash-flow purposes).[228] Also, its lack of juridical personality does not allow it to properly isolate the risk resulting from the guarantees of bonds. Thus, any lawsuits relating to such guarantees may involve a material liability of ADB.[229] Also, in order not to exceed its commitment authority, CGIF can only leverage at a very conservative rate. All these make institutional reform of the CGIF important.

AMRO, which was initially established as a company limited in Singapore (AMRO Ltd.), has already completed a process of reform and progressive institutionalization. AMRO, which is seen by some as the nucleus of a possible Asian Monetary Fund, was constituted by the "Agreement Establishing ASEAN+3

[223] http://www.adb.org/site/funds/funds/credit-guarantee-and-investment-facility.

[224] See Credit Guarantee and Investment Facility (CGIF) Articles of Agreement (as revised at the meeting of contributors of 27 November 2013 in Shanghai). http://www.cgif-abmi.org/wp-content/uploads/2016/06/CGIF-Articles-of-Agreement-as-of-May-2016_Clean.pdf (henceforth CGIF Articles of Agreement). Articles 4 and 5 contain provisions on the authorized capital of the CGIF, and the rights and obligations of contributors.

[225] See CGIF Articles of Agreement, Articles 7, 8 and 9.

[226] CGIF Articles of Agreement, Articles 7.7 and 8.6.

[227] On the CGIF, see http://www.cgif-abmi.org/.

[228] See CGIF Articles of Agreement, para 2.3. "CGIF shall not borrow from any source to finance its operations described in Article 2.2 except for the purposes of cash management."

[229] In accordance with ADB Charter, Article 50.1, ADB "shall enjoy immunity of every form of legal process except in cases arising out of or in connection with the exercise of its powers … to guarantee obligations."

Macroeconomic Research Office (AMRO)" as an international organization "with full legal personality and the legal capacity for carrying out its purpose and function."[230]

2.8 Proliferation, Privatization and Emergence of New Organizational Paradigms

In the period after World War II, there has been a substantial proliferation of international organizations. This author has shown this development in relation to four generations of concessional windows.[231] The first generation of organizations created in the wake of the Second World War until the 1950s, and the second generation covering 1960s–1970s, saw the establishment of many international financial institutions by way of a treaty; since then, however, the trend of founding new international organizations and affiliates has begun to subside.[232]

The growing disenchantment with the traditional treaty-based mechanisms was prompted, in particular, by the fact that treaties are not well suited to create funding structures that could respond quickly to new emerging needs. The third generation of international organizations (which includes institutions established in the 1980s and 1990s) saw the creation of *ad hoc* funding structures deprived of legal personality. However, in the fourth generation (which includes the period since 2000), the legal personality of international institutions once again became a matter of prime concern. As will be shown, this led to the creation of a number of dual and hybrid organizations established under municipal law but endowed with privileges and immunities under international law.

While the attention of international lawyers continues to be focused on traditional international organizations established by a treaty, it is no longer justified to limit the concept of international organization to these traditional organizations. International law and the law of international organizations need to take account of the fact that there are a number of organizations which have not been established by a treaty. Moreover, trust funds have become an important mechanism for establishing new international organizations. These can be established either with or without legal personality. A new class of international organizations with dual or hybrid character has also emerged, established under municipal law, but with privileges and immunities under international law. Moreover, it is not intrinsically impossible that in certain cases, based on progressive institutionalization, also

230 Agreement Establishing ASEAN+3 Macroeconomic Research Office (AMRO), Article 1(1).

231 Droesse 2011, pp. 6–33. [see footnote 213].

232 Droesse 2011, p. 16, citing Blokker, Blokker, Proliferation of International Organizations and Exploratory Introduction.

cooperative undertakings of regulators agencies may be qualified as international organizations.

References

Akzin B (1933) Membership in the Universal Postal Union. Am J Int Law 27:651–674

Amerasinghe CF (2005) Principles of the Institutional Law of International Organizations, 2nd edn. Cambridge University Press, Cambridge, p 77

Archer C (1992) International Organizations, 2nd edn. Routledge, London, p 14

Bailey SH (1931) Some problems of Article XXIV of the Covenant. Am Polit Sci Rev 25:406–424

Baldwin SE (1907) The International Congresses and Conferences of the last century as forces working toward the solidarity of the world. Am J Int Law 1:565–578

Berdahl CA (1932) Relations of the United States with the assembly of the League of Nations. Am Polit Sci Rev 26:99–112

Bevans CI (1968) Treaties and other International Agreements of the United States of America. 1776–1949. 1:51–62

Borel E (1921–1922) Freedom of navigation on the Rhine. Br Yearb Int Law 2:175–189

Bugnion F (2004–2005) The International Committee of the Red Cross and the Development of International Humanitarian Law. Chic J Int Law 5:191–215

Chin GT (2016) Asian Infrastructure Investment Bank: governance innovation and prospects. Glob Gov 22:11–26

Chiu H (1966) The capacity of International Organizations to conclude treaties, and the special legal aspects of the treaties so concluded. Martinus Nijhoff, The Hague

Churchill RR, Ulfstein G (2000) Autonomous institutional arrangements in multilateral environmental agreements: a little-noticed phenomenon in international law. Am J Int Law 94:623–659

Claude IL Jr (1971) Swords into plowshares: the problems and progress of international organization, 4th edn. Random House, New York

Codding GA (1952) The International Telecommunication Union. An experiment in international cooperation. Brill, Leiden, p 38

Codding GA (1964) The Universal Postal Union: coordinator of the international mails. New York University Press, New York

Conforti B (1996) The law and practice of the United Nations. Kluwer Law International, The Hague

Cotreau JD (1975) Historical development of the Universal Postal Union and the question of membership. Ph.D. diss., Boston

Crawford J (2013) Chance, order, change: the course of international law. General course on Public International Law. Collect Courses Hague Acad Int Law 365: 9–390

Droesse G (2011) Introductory remarks and overview of publication: proliferation, fragmentation, and earmarking of concessional financing. In: Droesse G (ed) Funds for development: multilateral channels of concessional financing. Asian Development Bank, Manila, pp 1–37

Eagleton C (1950a) International Organization and the law of responsibility. Collect Courses Hague Acad Int Law 76:319–426

Eagleton E (1950b) The law of responsibility. Collect Courses Hague Acad Int Law 36:319–425

Eckhardt CC (1919) The old internationalism and the New League. Sci Mon 8:437–441

Fee E, Brown TM (2002) 100 Years of the Pan American Health Organization. Am J Public Health 92:1888–1889

Fenwick CG (1920) Notes on international affairs: the outlook for international law. Am Polit Sci Rev 14:481–492

Fenwick CS (1951) The progress of International Law during the past forty years. Collect Courses Hague Acad Int Law 79:1–72
Gowlland-Debbas V (2011) The Security Council and issues of responsibility under International Law. Collect Courses Hague Acad Int Law 185–444
Grant TD (2009) Admission to the United Nations. Charter Article 4 and the rise of universal organization. Martinus Nijhoff, Leiden, p 1
Grubbs SB (1909) International Office of Public Hygiene—its inauguration at Paris, France. Public Health Reports (1896–1970) 24:23–28
Gunter MM (1974) Liechtenstein and the League of Nations: a precedent for the United Nation's ministate problem. Am J Int Law 76:496–501
Hamburger K (1942–1943) The Red Cross in the nineteenth century. Soc Forces 21:22–27
Hostie J (1930) Le Statut International du Rhin. Collect Courses Hague Acad Int Law 28:105–230
Hudson MO (1924) Membership in the League of Nations. Am J Int Law 18:436–458
Hudson MO (1934) The Argentine Republic and the League of Nations. Am J Int Law 28:125–133
Jellinek G (1882) Die Lehre von den Staatenverbindungen. In: Pauly W (ed) (1996) Die Lehre von den Staatenverbindungen (reprint of the 1882 edn. Hölder, Vienna). Keip Verlag. Goldbach,
Kelly MJ (2005) Pulling at the threads of Westphalia: 'Involuntary Sovereignty Waiver'—revolutionary international legal theory or return to rule by the great powers? UCLA J Int Law Foreign Aff 10:361–442
Klein E (2006) United Nations, specialized agencies. Max Planck Encycl Public Int Law. www.mpepil.com
Knipping F (ed) (1999) The United Nations system and its predecessors, vol II. Oxford University Press, Oxford
Knipping F, von Mangoldt H, Rittberger V (eds) (1997a) The United Nations system and its predecessors, vol I. Oxford University Press, Oxford
Knipping F, von Mangoldt H, Rittberger V (eds) (1997b) The United Nations system and its predecessors, vol II. Predecessors of the United Nations. Oxford University Press, Oxford
Leonard LL (1951) International Organization, vol 48. McGraw-Hill Book Company, Inc, New York
Mangone GJ (1954) 1975. A short history of international organization. Reprint, McGraw-Hill, New York
Martha RSJ (2010) The legal foundations of INTERPOL. Hart, Portland
McCaffrey SC (2010) European Commission of the Danube. Jurisdiction of the (Advisory Opinion), para 2. Max Planck Encycl Public Int Law. www.mpepil.com
Meyer-Ohlendorf N, Knigge M (2007) A United Nations Environment Agency. In: Swart L, Perry E (eds) Global environmental governance: perspectives on the current debate. Center for UN Reform Education, New York, pp 124–141
Michaels DB (1971) International privileges and immunities: a case for a Universal Statute. Springer, The Netherlands
Miller AJ (2009) The privileges and immunities of the United Nations. Int Organ Law Rev 6:7–115
Northedge FS (1986) The League of Nations: its life and times: 1920–1946. Leicester University Press, Leicester
Oppenheim L (1919) The League of Nations and its problems: three lectures. Longmans, Green and Co, London, p 29
Pollaczek G (1946) The United Nations and specialized agencies. Am J Int Law 40(3):592–619
Ragazzi R (2014) Financial institutions, international. Max Planck Encycl Public Int Law
Rappard WE (1934) Small States in the League of Nations. Polit Sci Q 49:544–575
Reinsch PS (1911) Public International Unions. Their work and organization: a study in International Administrative Law. Athenaeum Press, Boston, p 4
Rosenthal E (1894) Internationales Eisenbahn-Frachtrecht. Auf Grund des Internationalen Übereinkommens über den Eisenbahn-Frachtverkehr vom 14. Oktober 1890 und der Konferenzbeschlüsse vom Juni und Sept. 1893. Verlag G. Fischer, Jena

Rudolf B (2006) United Nations Committees and Subsidiary Bodies, system of. Max Planck Encycl Public Int Law. www.mpepil.com

Sands P, Klein P (2009) Bowett's Law of International Institution, 5th edn. Sweet and Maxwell (Thomson Reuters, London, p 3

Schmahl S (2006) International Bureau of Weights and Measures (BIPM). Max Planck Encycl Public Int Law

Schwarzenberger G (1936) The League of Nations and world order: a treatise on the principle of universality in the theory and practice of the League of Nations. Constable & Co, London, p 59 ss

Sherman GE (1923) The International Organization of the Danube under the peace treaties. Am J Int Law 17:438–459

Simma B (ed) (1994) The Charter of the United Nations. A Commentary. Oxford University Press, Oxford, p 162

Strong RP (1921) International Public Health Problems. North Am Rev 213:319–332

Szasz P (1999) The complexification of the United Nations. In: Bogandy JAV, Wolfrum R (eds) Max Planck Yearbook of United Nations Law. Martinus Nijhoff, Leiden, pp 1–57. www.mpil.de/shared/data/pdf/pdfmpunyb/szasz_3.pdf

Taylor B (1909) The Brussels Sugar Convention. North Am Rev 190:347–358

Ulfstein G (2007) Treaty bodies. In: Bodansky D, Brunnée J, Hey E (eds) The Oxford Handbook of International Environmental Law. Oxford University Press, Oxford, pp 877–889

Ulfstein G (2009) Institutions, structures, and competences. In: Klabbers J, Peters A, Ulfstein G (eds) The Constitutionalization of International Law. Oxford University Press, Oxford, pp 45–80

Völderndorff O (1894) Die richterliche Tàtigkeit der Centralcommission für die Rheinschiffahrt von 1832 bis 1894. Krebs-Schmitt, Frankfurt a. M

Wihtol R (2015) Beijing's Challenge to the Global Financial Architecture. Policy Forum 11:7–15

Wilk K (1939) The International Sugar Régime. Am Polit Sci Rev 33:860–878

Wolfrum R (2006) International Administrative Unions. Max Planck Encycl Public Int Law

Zeilinger AF (2013) Danube River. Max Planck Encycl Public Int Law

Chapter 3
Concepts of International Organization and Membership

Contents

3.1 Classifications of Organizations

International organizations may be classified in different ways, such as: according to (1) "the manner of their establishment (as public and private organizations)"; (2) "the division of power (as legislative, administrative, and judicial organizations);"[1] (3) "the extent of authority and power of the organization vis-à-vis states: policy-making, operative and supranational organizations;"[2] (4) the scope of their activities (as general or special organizations), or (5) in relation to their membership structures. These classifications are generally discussed with reference to traditional international organizations with treaty foundation. It is one of the themes of this book that the above approach is too narrow and that new paradigms of international organization should be recognized. Moreover, in the case of many international

[1] El-Erian 1963, p. 168.
[2] El-Erian 1963, pp. 168–169.

All weblinks are updated as of 28 February 2018.

G. Droesse, *Membership in International Organizations*,
https://doi.org/10.1007/978-94-6265-327-6_3

organizations, their functions, outlook and role in the architecture of international organizations and other entities providing public goods or fighting against public bads have dramatically changed since the time when they were established. In this context, some of the classifications listed above need to be revisited.

First, there are a number of instances where the traditional classification of an organization as either public and private or governmental and non-governmental does not adequately capture the nature of the organization.

Second, while the distinction between general and special organizations continues to be relevant, most general and special organizations operate now in an environment which is dramatically different than at the time they were founded. This entails specific challenges for special organizations, in particular, and requires that these adopt a new outlook and vision.

Third, the distinction between supranational and other international organizations concerns the core of the relationship of an organization with its members. It has multiple implications, in relation to the conditionality for admission to membership and the requirements for withdrawing from membership, but also in the context of the organizations' institutional structures and legal and policy frameworks.

Fourth, in the context of this book, the classification of organizations based on their membership (as open or closed, universal, regional or of limited membership) is particularly relevant. Also, in this regard, traditional classifications of international organizations tend to be too restrictive and require refocusing and further elaboration.

The aforementioned issues will be reviewed in further detail in the following.

3.1.1 Public and Private Organizations

Treatises on the law of international organizations and on international institutional law generally focus on the "public international organization" for which a great number of different definitions is given. Amerasinghe expresses a position which is widely adhered to as follows: "The public international organization is normally created by a treaty or convention to which states are parties and the members of the organization so created are generally states, though sometimes but rarely governments may constitute the membership."[3]

As will be shown in detail in the following chapter, the conceptual framework of "intergovernmental organization" and "international organization" can no longer be reduced to the dichotomies of public and private and governmental or non-governmental. One of the themes of this book is that the terms "intergovernmental organization" and "international organization" need to be interpreted in a wider manner than in the past, to comprise organizations not established by a treaty

[3] Amerasinghe 2005, p. 9.

and dual or hybrid organizations incorporated under national law. Moreover, the term "international organization" should not be limited to cover organizations emanating from the cooperation between governments, but may also comprise organizations of Parliamentary cooperation and, potentially, based on progressive institutionalization, cooperative undertakings of sub-state actors and national regulators.

3.1.2 General and Special Organizations

One distinction which is generally made in respect of international organizations is that between general and special organizations. As indicated by El-Erian, the "general international organization is one whose jurisdiction covers the whole fabric of international relations. It is basically interested in the political problems, but its activities extend to other fields as well, e.g., economic, social and technical."[4] Schermers and Blokker relate the characteristics of general organizations "to the vastness of the fields they may cover and the presence of diplomats or politicians in the delegations of the members. These representatives will strive to attain general political goals and are usually not experts on particular issues."[5]

General and political organizations are largely equated. The United Nations is the epitome of the general organization. However, an organization does not need to be of a universal nature to be classified as a general organization. "[A] number of organizations dealing with regional cooperation: the European Union, the Council of Europe, the Organization of American States, the African Union, and the Association of Southeast Asian Nations"[6] can also fall in the category of a general organization.

The distinction between general and special organizations has clear legal connotations as was already emphasized by the Permanent Court of International Justice[7] with regard to the European Commission of the Danube. The International Court of Justice referred to the aforementioned decision when it elaborated in its

---

[4] El-Erian 1963, p. 168.

[5] Schermers and Blokker 2011, §64.

[6] Ibid.

[7] The Permanent Court of International Justice stated: "As the European Commission is not a State, but an **international institution with a special purpose**, it only has the functions bestowed upon it by the Definitive Statute with a view to the fulfilment of that purpose, but it has power to exercise these functions to their full extent, in so far as the Statute does not impose restrictions upon it." Permanent Court of International Justice, Advisory Opinion No. 14. "Jurisdiction of the European Commission of the Danube between Galatz and Braila", In *Publications of the Permanent Court of International Justice. Series B–No. 14.* 1927. Leiden: AW Sijthoff Publishing Company. http://www.icj-cij.org/files/permanent-court-of-international-justice/serie_B/B_14/01_Commission_europeenne_du_Danube_Avis_consultatif.pdf (emphasis added).

Advisory Opinion of 8 July 1996, in response to a question by the World Health Organization,[8] on the legal implications of the "principle of specialty".[9]

Most international organizations were created to address specific problems and may therefore be comprised in the category of special organizations. As the UN may be seen as the epitome of a general organization, the UN specialized agencies may be seen as the epitome of organizations created for special purposes. In that sense, they may also be seen as representative of the deep-rooted conceptual problems that are connected with the very concept of that kind of organizations. However, the term "special organization" should not be confined to international organizations with treaty foundation. In the view of this author, also dual and hybrid organizations such as the Global Fund and organizations established as trust funds (e.g. the Global Environment Facility) may be qualified as "special organizations".

As has been shown in the first chapter, the roots of UN specialized agencies go back to the nineteenth century when organizations such as the ILO, the International Bureau for Agriculture, the Universal Postal Union, and others were created in response to the need to enhance coordination and cooperation at the international level. The intellectual basis of the creation of the specialized agencies after World

---

[8] The World Health Assembly had requested by Resolution WHA46.40 adopted on 14 May 1993 the International Court of Justice to given an Advisory Opinion on the following question: "In view of the health and environmental effects, would the use of nuclear weapons by a State in war or other armed conflict be a breach of its obligations under international law including the WHO Constitution?" "Legality of the Use by a State of Nuclear Weapons in Armed Conflict, Advisory Opinion" ICJ Reports. 1996, 66, para 1, http://www.icj-cij.org/files/case-related/93/093-19960708-ADV-01-00-EN.pdf.

[9] The International Court of Justice stated in its aforementioned Advisory Opinion of 8 July 1996:

> 25. The Court need hardly point out that international organizations are subjects of international law which do not, unlike States, possess a general competence. International organizations are governed by the 'principle of speciality', that is to say, they are invested by the States which create them with powers, the limits of which are a function of the common interests whose promotion those States entrust to them.

The Court further stated in para 25:

> In the opinion of the Court, to ascribe to the WHO the competence to address the legality of the use of nuclear weapons—even in view of their health and environmental effects—would be tantamount to disregarding the principle of speciality; for such competence could not be deemed a necessary implication of the Constitution of the Organization in the light of the purposes assigned to it by its member States.

In line with the above, while the International Court of Justice found in para 32 that it was "not able to give the advisory opinion which was requested of it under World Health Assembly resolution", it complied in a second Advisory Opinion also rendered on 8 July 1996 with the request of the General Assembly "to render its advisory opinion on the following question: 'Is the threat or use of nuclear weapons in any circumstance permitted under international law?'" "Legality of the Threat or Use of Nuclear Weapons, Advisory Opinion", ICJ Reports 1996, 226, paras 1 and 105(1). http://www.icj-cij.org/files/case-related/95/095-19960708-ADV-01-00-EN.pdf.

War II, was "the theory that a major contribution could be made to world peace by the spread of a functional rather than a political approach to international relations, i.e., nations should devote more attention to working together on solving certain practical problems of a technical character—especially problems which cut across political frontiers—and spend less time on political debate."[10]

As shown by Klabbers, "functionalism in international institutional law was already by and large in place when the 'move to institutions' took off in earnest after World War I, and was born out of an encounter with colonial administration."[11] It "has been, and is, tremendously influential"[12] and important for the development of the law of international institutions. One main proponent of the functional theory was Mitrany who stated that "[f]unctional 'neutrality' is possible, where political 'neutrality' is not" and opinioned in this context: "If Governments have the welfare of their own peoples at heart they could let such organizations get to work; and if the organizations are successful and their number grows, world government will gradually evolve through their performance."[13]

Organizations created for special purposes, in general, and the specialized agencies of the UN, in particular, face challenges at three levels. One relates to the fact that the postulations of the functional theory whereby the creation of functional agencies would allow international actors to cooperate in a non-political context have long since been revealed as a myth which contrasts with the harsh reality of increasing politicization of specialized agencies. Admission to membership in specialized agencies is one of the areas which was highly politicized in some cases, such as for the admission of Palestine and Kosovo to membership in some specialized agencies.

The second challenge faced by specialized agencies is even more fundamental, as it relates to the position of specialized agencies in the overall architecture of international organizations and other entities providing public goods or fighting public bads. While the "basic principle of separate and autonomous agencies to confront each major field of activity, on which the system was based from 1945, and even before, has remained unaltered",[14] the overall environment in which specialized agencies are operating has changed drastically since the time of their establishment.

Many of the specialized agencies of the UN are exposed to competition with other players in their field, in particular, in the non-core operational functions that they have assumed over time. Today, often UN specialized agencies are only one of many actors operating in a given sector and, at least in financial terms, not necessarily, the most important ones. At times, the budgets of philanthropic institutions, organizations established as trust funds, or dual or hybrid organizations by far

10 Williams 1987, p. 2.

11 Klabbers 2014, p. 648.

12 Ibid., 649.

13 Mitrany 1948, p. 358.

14 Luard 1977, p. 5.

exceed that of traditional specialized agencies. This is particularly evident in the health sector, which is characterized by a great number of transnational actors present in this sector. The budgets of organizations such as the Bill and Melinda Gates Foundation exceed those of many traditional international organizations. Moreover, even in its core functions, WHO is increasingly dependent on the financial support of transnational actors such as the Bill and Melinda Gates Foundation, which, together with the United States, is WHO's biggest donor. This changed environment in which specialized agencies are operating underlines the need for organizations to open themselves by allowing transnational actors, including the private sector, philanthropy and civil society, to substantially participate in their decision-making processes.

Third, drastic changes are also required in relation to the role of specialized agencies and other special organization in knowledge management. While "originally established as organizations with a mainly functional purpose to act as international clearing houses of information in their specialty"[15] they can no longer perform this task, assuming that they were ever able to do so in the past. The above concepts reflect a top-down approach to information sharing which is no longer adequate in the global information age where knowledge is dispersed through many channels and where knowledge networks have become a new "mode of governance" as "a third involution rather than an outward devolution of governance from public agencies."[16] Stone and others use the concept of "global agora" as a metaphor "to convey a fast changing, multi-level domain where new policy responsibilities are taking shape but where what is 'public' and what is 'private' becomes unclear."[17]

"As the global agora features a lower degree of institutionalization of *de jure* legal and political processes than at the national level, then the governance impact of knowledge organisations and networks may be more pervasive in terms of problem formulation, agenda-setting as well as monitoring and evaluation. The policy discourses of networks do not just describe reality but also help constitute it."[18]

International organizations need to take account of the fact that knowledge frameworks rely in the modern information age first and foremost on networking solutions and only to a lesser extent on international organizations and other institutionalized mechanisms. Hence, the specialized agencies need to open themselves to other stakeholders in their sector by becoming forums for a variety of non-state actors and entities. They should embrace and facilitate, with the support of advanced IT solutions, a wide range of networking opportunities with all relevant stakeholders in their sector, including sub-state entities, technical government agencies and regulators, and stakeholders from academia, civil society, philanthropy, and the private sector.

---

[15] Williams 1987, 14.

[16] Stone 2013, p. 183.

[17] Ibid., 185.

[18] Ibid., 183.

The UN specialized agencies and other organizations established for special purposes also often no longer have the staff, financial resources or necessary expertise to provide intellectual leadership in all areas of a given sector. This is another reason and makes it the more necessary for them to fundamentally change their focus and approach, by drawing on all available sources of expertise. Thus, rather than making the futile attempt to cover a given sector entirely with their own resources, they should open up to the outside by becoming forums which give a wide range of transnational actors a voice in their affairs and attract the best sources of knowledge and expertise.

The considerations set out above will require substantial changes to organizations' vision and outlook, and their governance and membership structures and decision-making procedures.

3.1.3 Supranational and Other International Organizations

While some use the term "supranational organizations" in a more general context,[19] overall, these organizations are a special case of international or intergovernmental organizations characterized by a high degree of coordination and integration and by the impact of their legal acts on the regulatory framework of its members. The classification of an organization as a supranational organization is intrinsically related to its relationship with its member states and concepts of national sovereignty. Some see these organizations as lying "on the outer limit of international organizations and on the border of federalism. They are hybrids which draw both on international law and municipal public law in their functioning techniques. As such, they are subject to the law of international organizations, but not in an exclusive way."[20]

According to Schermers and Blokker, the term "supranational organization" implies the following five characteristics:

> (1) The Organization should have the power to take decisions binding on the member states.
> (2) The organs taking the decisions should not be entirely dependent on the cooperation of all the member states [….].
> (3) The organization should be empowered to make rules that directly bind the inhabitants of the member states. This power enables the organization to perform governmental functions without the need or the possibility for national governments to transform the rules of the organization into domestic law.
> (4) The organization should have the power to enforce its decisions. Enforcement should be possible even without the cooperation of the governments of the states concerned [….].
> (5) The organization should have some financial autonomy [….].[21]

---

[19] Head 1994, pp. 605–666.

[20] El-Erian 1963, p. 169.

[21] Schermers and Blokker 2011, §61.

However, as Schermers and Blokker highlight, "to be completely supranational, an organization should fulfill all the above-mentioned conditions. No such supranational organization currently exists."

On the other hand, Klabbers asks whether a distinction between intergovernmental organization and supranational organizations really clarifies anything. "As things stand, there is only one organization which is usually held to be supranational in character: the EU. Hence, any description of supranational organizations will inevitably be based on the EU."[22] The United Nations "is not a supranational organization but it has supranational characteristics"[23] relating to the powers vested in the Security Council.

It has been asserted that conceptually, supranationalism involves "a re-territorialization of political power as the three key features of the modern sovereign state", i.e., "Staatsgewalt", "Staatsgebiet" and "Staatsvolk", "are re-scaled upwards and re-differentiated vertically," with mechanisms being put in place "for constitutionalizing and legitimating authority in the expanded territory."[24] However, "in the case of the upward re-scaling (or re-territorialization) of state sovereignty, the development of a multi-level government could be seen as a transitional effect of the transition."[25] The case of the EU representing a multi-level governance structure par excellence may be viewed in this manner.

While the EU is frequently seen as the epitome of a supranational organization, its classification as "supranational" touches on fundamental issues of national sovereignty and in that sense on the EU's relations with its members. This relates on the one hand to the special characteristics of EU law, which imply, as indicated by Bernhardt, that "international and national law can no longer properly be separated and states no longer have the option to adopt a dualistic path."[26] It may also be seen as a corollary of the objective of establishing "the foundations of an ever closer union among the peoples of Europe" already set out in the preamble of the Treaty of Rome.[27] However, while "since its creation in 1951, the European integration process has progressed through a mixture of closer integration in a growing number of policy domains and the expansion of the group countries participating therein,"[28] there is "an inherent tension between the two aspects of European integration, 'deepening' and 'widening'."[29] Moreover, there is an increasing resistance in some member countries against any further deepening ofthe establishment the European integration.

[22] Klabbers 2015, p. 26.

[23] Schermers and Blokker 2011, §61.

[24] Jessop 2004, p. 54.

[25] Ibid.

[26] Bernhard 1998, p. 27.

[27] Treaty establishing the European Economic Community. 25 March 1957.

[28] Blockmans and Prechal 2006, p. 1.

[29] Ibid.

This is further epitomized by the discussion on whether the EU member states have a right of withdrawal. Prior to the treaty of Lisbon, there were voices asserting that based on the European treaties and state of integration, withdrawal was only allowed in case of mutual agreement of all members. However, a different approach was notably taken, among a range of other voices, by the German *Bundesverfassungsgericht* already in the Maastricht Decision of 12 October 1993,[30] the principles thereof were further elaborated in the judgement of 30 June 2009[31] on the law to the Treaty of Lisbon.

It has always been an illusion to believe that law could prevent a member of the EU from withdrawing from the Union. This matter has been finally settled by the Treaty of Lisbon, which allows the withdrawal from EU membership. Although the members of the EU maintain this right, among other important rights, and the EU still depends, to a substantial extent, on cooperation of the members, the EU still qualifies as a supranational organization on the grounds that it possesses the following characteristics:

> (a) the possession of institutions that are independent in composition and operation; (b) the use of decision-making procedures by majority votes that nonetheless bind all Member States; (c) the implementation of EC decisions by or under the supervision of EC institutions; and (d) the creation of judicially-enforceable rights and obligations through the treaties and secondary legislation.[32]

---

[30] The Bundesverfassungsgericht stated in its judgement of 12 Oct. 1993, Entscheidungen des Bundesverfassungsgerichts (BverfGE) Vol. 89, 155 ss., under note 90: "Der Vertrag begründet einen europäischen Staatenverbund, der von den Mitgliedstaaten getragen wird und deren nationale Identität achtet; er betrifft die Mitgliedschaft Deutschlands in supranationalen Organisationen, nicht eine Zugehörigkeit zu einem europäischen Staat (II.1)." Note 95 further provides: "(b) Das Demokratieprinzip hindert mithin die Bundesrepublik Deutschland nicht an einer Mitgliedschaft in einer—supranational organisierten—zwischenstaatlichen Gemeinschaft. Voraussetzung der Mitgliedschaft ist aber, daß eine vom Volk ausgehende Legitimation und Einflußnahme auch innerhalb eines Staatenverbundes gesichert ist." Note 112 further reads: "Deutschland ist einer der 'Herren der Verträge', die ihre Gebundenheit an den 'auf unbegrenzte Zeit' geschlossenen Unions-Vertrag (Article Q EUV) mit dem Willen zur langfristigen Mitgliedschaft begründet haben, diese Zugehörigkeit aber letztlich durch einen gegenläufigen Akt auch wieder aufheben könnten. Geltung und Anwendung von Europarecht in Deutschland hängen von dem Rechtsanwendungsbefehl des Zustimmungsgesetzes ab."

[31] "Der Vertrag von Lissabon macht erstmals das bestehende Recht jedes Mitgliedstaates zum Austritt aus der Europäischen Union im Primärrecht sichtbar (Article 50 EUV-Lissabon). Dieses Austrittsrecht unterstreicht die Souveränität der Mitgliedstaaten und zeigt ebenfalls, dass mit dem derzeitigen Entwicklungsstand der Europäischen Union die Grenze zum Staat im Sinne des Völkerrechts nicht überschritten ist [....] Kann ein Mitgliedstaat aufgrund einer selbstverantworteten Entscheidungaustreten, ist der europäische Integrationsprozess nicht unumkehrbar. Die Mitgliedschaft der Bundesrepublik Deutschland hängt vielmehr von ihrem dauerhaften und fortbestehenden Willen ab, der Europäischen Union anzugehören." Urteil vom 30 Juni 2009—2 BvE 2/08, BVerfGE 123, 267–437, Note 329. https://www.bundesverfassungsgericht.de/SharedDocs/Downloads/DE/2009/06/es20090630_2bve000208.pdf?__blob=publicationFile&v=1.

[32] Cited by Goebel 2013, pp. 82–83, footnote 16.

3.1.4 Classifications Based on Membership

There is nothing that defines an organization as much as its membership. Whether an organization is open or closed, or may be classified as universal, regional or of limited membership, defines its vision and outlook, as well as the scope of the organization's activities. The discussion on this matter must not be limited to international organizations with a treaty foundation, but needs to take into account that new paradigms of international organization have emerged, without a treaty foundation and without international legal personality and legal capacity under national law. Moreover, it is necessary to take account of the fact that there may be international organizations without any membership structure.

3.1.4.1 Open and Closed Organizations

One of the basic distinctions between international organizations relates to whether, respectively to what extent, they allow the admission of new members or not. It is suggested in literature that regional organizations and other organization of limited membership should generally be classified as closed organizations "as they seek only membership from a closed group of states and no members from outside the group will be admitted."[33] In the view of this author, it is better to reserve the term "closed organization" to those international organizations, of regional or limited membership, which cannot admit any new members without amendment of their constituent instrument. The other organizations should be classified as open, subject to the different eligibility requirements which may apply.

3.1.5 Universal Organizations and Organizations of Global Reach

The idea of universality has gradually developed over time. Advances towards universality were made by some of the IAUs such as the Universal Postal Union. The League of Nations never achieved universality, and the UN went through a tortuous initial period during which many countries were barred from membership. At that time, it was discussed at length whether the principle of universality had legal connotations, and what its implications for those countries were, whose membership applications had been denied. However, the admission to UN membership transcends considerations of a merely legal nature, as is shown by the very limited effect which the judgements of the International Court of Justice regarding this matter had on influencing state behavior.

[33] Schermers and Blokker 2011, §53.

When the UN increased its membership from the 51 founding members[34] to 193, many of the specialized agencies mirrored such increase. It is necessary to emphasize the fundamental importance that this change contributed to the institutional and governance structures of the organizations concerned. The great expansion of membership of universal organizations fundamentally altered the balance of power in plenary bodies of universal organization and in certain cases, triggered the result that such bodies could no longer effectively perform the functions for which they had been created.

Universal organizations "can be said to have 'vocation' to attract all States, and this indicates that they have a field of action which makes it necessary, or at least desirable, that all States should be bound by the same obligations and invited to cooperate within the same framework."[35]

As Boisson de Chazournes had highlighted, universal organizations are defined by the criteria *ratione personae* et *ratione materiae* in the sense that (1) in principle, they are open for participation by all states (membership of all states is not a requirement) and on an exceptional basis for participation by other entities and (2) their activities are of a global or universal nature.[36]

The requirements for admission to membership are generally regulated in the constituent instrument. The fact that an international organization is universal in nature, as such, does not give any state the right to join an international organization.[37] Hence, states may only join an international organization by way of a unilateral declaration if the constituent instrument of the organization or another legal act expressly permits this. Such an "automatic procedure of admission" where admission to membership "depends solely on the will of the prospective member" concerned "was the case of the Universal Postal Union, up to 1947, and it is still the case for certain specialized agencies as regards the admission of States which are already Members of the United Nations."[38] Generally, international organizations have "regulated procedures of admission [….] which prescribe certain conditions for admission."[39] In these cases, there is an inherent tension between the aspiration of an organization to achieve universal membership and conditionality for admission to membership. The same also applies to provisions allowing international organizations to expel members and the effect is that this power often is only an "empty shell".[40]

---

[34] United Nations. UN Member States. Founding Member States. http://www.un.org/depts/dhl/unms/founders.shtml.

[35] Dominicé 2001, p. 67.

[36] Boisson de Chazournes 2010, p. 102.

[37] See, in this context, the discussion in Czerwinsky 1974, p. 48: "Die Bezugnahme auf die Völkerrechtsprinzipien macht deutlich, daβ das Prinzip der Universalität keine orignäre Spezialnorm darstellt und eine Teilnahmeberechtigung nicht zu konstituieren vermag."

[38] El-Erian 1963, pp. 159–185, para 68.

[39] Ibid., para 69.

[40] Schermers and Blokker 2011, §51.

As may be seen from the above, universal organizations, in essence, are classified as such based on their vocation and "do not have to be truly universal in membership and responsibilities."[41]

Also, an organization does not need to have a treaty foundation to be classified as universal. While the "Vienna Convention on the Representation of States in their Relations with International Organizations of a Universal Character" of 1975[42] expressly only recognizes traditional treaty-based organizations with membership structures and international legal personality as organizations of a universal character, this approach needs to be seen in the specific context of the aforementioned convention and should not be generalized or given a wider application.

There may be organizations which have universal character even though they were not established by a treaty. INTERPOL, which has 190 members, falls in this category. Moreover, lack of international legal personality or legal capacity under national law does not preclude that an entity may be classified as a universal international organization. Thus, the Global Environment Facility, which has 183 participant countries, should be recognized as a universal international organization even though its quest for being granted legal personality remained unsuccessful. Finally, also the Inter-Parliamentary Union with 173[43] members can be classified as "universal" even though it does not have a treaty foundation and does not count states as its members. As indicated by Ian Brownlie and Guy Goodwin-Gill: "The IPU is a *universal* organization, in that its membership is open to all parliaments satisfying the requirements of Article 3 of its Statutes, just as the United Nations is open to all States satisfying the requirements of Article 4 of the UN Charter."[44]

Universal organizations may have an internal regionalization. There are many examples for such internal regionalization which may be based on policy or on specific provisions of the constituent agreement.

While the UN Charter contains in Chapter VIII provisions regarding regional arrangements relating the maintenance of international peace and security, the "regional group system is not mentioned or envisaged in the United Nations Charter. However, it has become an essential part of the whole working structure of

---

[41] Ibid.

[42] Vienna Convention on the Representation of States in their Relations with International Organizations of a Universal Character, 1975, Article I, para (1) states that "'international organization' means an intergovernmental organization." Moreover, para (2) provides: "'international organization of a universal character' means the United Nations, its specialized agencies, the International Atomic Energy Agency and any similar organization whose membership and responsibilities are on a worldwide scale."

[43] The indicated numbers of members/participants of INTERPOL, GEF and IPU as of 16 September 2017....

[44] Brownlie, I. and G. S. Goodwin-Gill. 1999. "The Inter-Parliamentary Union (IPU)". Joint Opinion. Statement 2. http://www.ipu.org/finance-e/opinion.pdf.

the United Nations."[45] Currently, there are five regional commissions of the UN.[46]

Among the specialized agencies, the World Health Organization (WHO) is an example of pronounced internal regionalization. The WHO Constitution provides that the "Health Assembly shall from time to time define the geographical areas in which it is desirable to establish a regional organization" and "may, with the consent of a majority of the Members of each area so defined, establish a regional organization to meet the special needs of such area."[47] Currently, there are six regions,[48] each with a regional committee composed "of representatives of the Member States and Associate Members in the region concerned" and with "semi-autonomous regional offices".[49]

As universal organizations are defined as such based on their openness to membership by all states, a formal membership structure is a corollary of the traditional definition of universal organization. Under this aspect, organizations without a formal membership structure such as the Global Fund and Green Climate Fund would not qualify for recognition as universal organization. However, these organizations have global aspirations and worldwide activities, both with regard to representation arrangements, sources of financing, and their operational activities. Thus, the members of the Board of the Green Climate Fund represent the 196 country Parties to the UNFCCC, which number exceeds that of the UN members represented in the General Assembly. Similarly, the Global Fund is a multi-actor Fund which operates on a worldwide scale and gives, in addition to states, civil society, the private sector, philanthropy and affected communities a voice in

---

45 "Regional group system within the United Nations—Conditions for admission to a regional group—Consensus—General Assembly resolution 1192 (XII) of 12 Dec. 1957. Letter to the Acting Chief Counsel, O.I.P.C., INTERPOL. *United Nations Juridical Yearbook*, 2003, Vol. II, Chapter VI, A: Legal Opinions of the Secretariat of the United Nations, 528–529, 529: "The regional group system was established in the late fifties through the process of transformation of the system of unofficial and informal caucuses, based on loose geographical and political affinities, which had emerged following the founding of the United Nations, into a new arrangement. It was first reflected in indirect form in General Assembly resolution 1192 (XII) of 12 Dec. 1957 concerning the composition of the General Committee of the General Assembly. The concept of regional groups has subsequently been endorsed in various decisions of the General Assembly, the Security Council, the Economic and Social Council and their subsidiary bodies as the accepted mechanism for distribution of elected places according to the principle of equitable geographical distribution and as the forum for consultations and negotiations on important issue." (Ibid., 529). http://legal.un.org/docs/?path=../unjuridicalyearbook/pdfs/english/volumes/2003.pdf&lang=E.

46 United Nations. United Nations Regional Groups of Member States. http://www.un.org/depts/DGACM/RegionalGroups.shtmls.

47 Constitution of the World Health Organization, Article 44(a) and (b).

48 African Region, Region of the Americas, South-East Asia Region, European Region, Eastern Mediterranean Region, and Western Pacific Region. See http://www.who.int/healthinfo/global_burden_disease/definition_regions/en/.

49 Clift, C. 2013. "The Role of the World Health Organization in the International System". *Centre on Global Health Security Working Group Papers.* Working Group on Governance. Paper 1. London: Chatham House, The Royal Institute of International Affairs.

decision-making. Organizations such as the Green Climate Fund and the Global Fund may be seen in many ways as functional equivalents of universal organizations and might best be characterized as "global organizations."

3.1.6 Regional and Other Organizations of Limited Membership

Region is, in essence, a political and sociological rather than a geographic concept. The classification of countries as regional or non-regional may have multiple implications for eligibility for membership, organizations' capital structures, institutional frameworks, governance structures, and decision-making procedures, and for eligibility for financing, procurement and other operational matters.

3.1.6.1 Eligibility of Countries in a Region to Join a Regional Organization

As a general rule, the countries in a region may join a regional organization; however, this is not applicable in all instances. In certain cases, eligibility criteria are an amalgam of legal and policy considerations. Thus, the Charter of the Organization of African Unity, the predecessor of the African Union, contained a definition of the geographic scope of the Organization,[50] and was open for signature by "[e]ach independent sovereign African State,"[51] the purpose of which was to exclude South Africa (during Apartheid) and Rhodesia from membership.[52] Moreover, regional countries which have joined an organization may be excluded or suspended from membership.

On the other hand, non-regional countries may be admitted to membership in regional organizations. This will be discussed below, in relation to regional development banks.

3.1.6.2 Region is a Political and Not a Geographic Concept

The very definition of "region" is problematic. One basic misconception is that the term "region" is predominantly or exclusively related to geography. While some

---

[50] Charter of the Organization of African Unity, Article I, para 2.

[51] Charter of the Organization of African Unity, Article XXIV, para 1.

[52] In the case of the African Union, the Constituent Act of the African Union was open, in accordance with para. 1 or Art. 27, "for signature, ratification and accession by the Member States of the OAU [Organization of African Union]". In addition, in accordance with Art. 29 para. 1, "[a] ny African State may, at any time after the entry-in-force of this Act, notify the Chairman of the Commission of its intention to accede to this Act and to be admitted as a Member of the Union."

organizations like the BENELUX Economic Union[53] fit the definition of Cantori and Spiegel of regions as "areas of the world which contain geographically proximate states forming, in foreign affairs, mutually interrelated units,"[54] such definition cannot apply to a range of other cases, or can only be applied to a limited extent. As indicated by Boisson de Chazournes: "*Quand la géographie joue un role, la proximité ou le lien géographique peut être diffus.*"[55] She cites a number of cases where there is no direct proximity between the member countries of the organization or where the geographic scope of the organization is not clear.

Moreover, in the case of regional organizations, it is often the cultural and intellectual history, or "political affinity", rather than geographic distinctions, which are seen as decisive for the definition of region. Membership in the EU is open to "European States".[56] However, it is difficult to identify a clear geographic demarcation, particularly in South-East Europe, and the term "European" needs to be interpreted on substantive terms, to take into account not only geographic criteria but also the cultural and intellectual history of countries.[57] While this implies that countries which geographically do not belong to Europe and do not have a nexus as mentioned above are not eligible for EU membership, application of these criteria in practice involves considerations of some complexity. Hence, while the European Commission refused the application of Morocco for membership, the European Council approved the applicant status of Turkey even though there is neither a direct geographic link nor cultural or intellectual history which would allow qualification of Turkey as a European country.

As may be seen from the above, it is far from clear where the borders of Europe are.[58] Similar questions also arise in other regional organizations, as is underlined by the fact that the former Secretary-General of ASEAN, Severino, noted:

> The 1967 ASEAN Declaration states that 'the Association is open for participation to all States in the South-East Asian Region subscribing to the aforementioned aims, principles and purposes.' This raises the question: what precisely is Southeast Asia?[59]

As shown in literature, in essence, space is a "social construct that people, somehow, invent", "geography is meaningful and politically consequential principally through the ways in which it is imagined", and "the border of a region 'is not a

[53] http://www.benelux-parlement.eu/en/benelux/geschiedenis.asp.

[54] Cited according to Archer 1992, p. 46.

[55] See Boisson de Chazournes 2010, p. 107.

[56] Treaty on European Union, Article 49. See Consolidated Version of the Treaty on European Union. Official Journal of the European Union C 326/13 (26.10.2012). http://eur-lex.europa.eu/legal-content/EN/TXT/PDF/?uri=CELEX:12012M/TXT&from=EN.

[57] See Pechstein 2014, p. 835.

[58] As reported by Thomas, the Finnish Foreign Minister stated in 2006 during a press conference: "Please don't ask me where the borders of Europe are, that's something we didn't want to put on the agenda." Thomas 2017, p. 218.

[59] Thomas 2017, p. 2; citing Severino 2006.

geographic fact that has sociological consequences, but a sociological fact that takes geographic form'."[60]

It transpires, with particular clarity, from a comparison of the geographic scope and membership structures of the five UN regional economic commissions[61] established as subsidiary organs of ECOSOC that "region" is a political and sociological concept and not a geographic one. This is shown, in particular, by both the historic and current composition of the UN Economic Commission for Asia and the Far East (ECAFE), which is now known as the UN Economic and Social Commission for Asia and the Pacific (UNESCAP).

The original membership of ECAFE was considered "anomalous because the majority (six out of ten) consisted of non-Asian members."[62] This composition was due to the fact that at the time of ECAFE's birth, there was a difference of opinion among ECOSOC members as to what constituted Asia, and whether the islands of the South Pacific should be included.[63] Such difference of views persisted after the commission had been established.

Closely connected with the issue of geographic scope was the question of whether membership in ECAFE should be restricted to UN member states. A proposal to allow dependent territories to apply directly for membership was not approved, it being held that such territories were only eligible to apply for associate membership if their application was sponsored by the metropolitan state responsible for the conduct of their external relations.[64] Even some countries which were responsible for the conduct of their external relations were initially only admitted to associate membership.[65]

Moreover, even the current composition of UNESCAP defies any geographic notion generally associated with Asia. First, there is a substantial overlap between membership in UNESCAP and the European Commission for Europe (ECE) to the extent that UNESCAP membership includes countries that under any geographic classification are generally associated with Europe. On the other hand, certain Arabic countries with territories in Asia, which would have been eligible to apply for membership in UNESCAP, failed to do so for political reasons, as they preferred to be members of the UN Economic and Social Commission for Western Asia (ESCWA), whose membership is confined to Arabic countries.

Also, membership in the other economic commissions transcends any geographic definition of region. The participation of the United States in ECE and UN

---

[60] See Thomas 2017, p. 218, with further references.

[61] See http://www.un.org/regionalcommissions/about.html.

[62] Singh 1966, p. 27.

[63] See Singh, who reports that "New Zealand, presumably apprehending anti-colonialist criticism, informed ECOSOC that these territories need not come under the Commission's region, as the six powers in charge of these colonies had agreed to establish the South Pacific Commission to promote their economic and social development." Singh 1966, p. 26.

[64] On the background of the establishment of ECAFE, see Wightman 1963.

[65] The best example is Japan which was initially only admitted to associate membership in ECAFE. See Mie 2008, pp. 98–113.

Economic Commission for Latin America (ECLA) as a founding member was in fact breaking "the geographical and historical unity of these regions."[66] However, even though it had played a very crucial role in their establishment, the US acted largely "as a controller, making sure that the commissions' activities [did] not harm its own interests."[67]

At "the founding of the UN in 1945, there were only four independent African countries – the Arab Republic of Egypt, Ethiopia, Liberia and South Africa" and the colonial powers ruled the rest of Africa.[68] The colonial powers questioned the need of an economic commission for Africa and "succeeded in delaying the establishment of ECA for thirteen years."[69] Also, they sought to ensure that "the ECA would not intervene in any of their territories except at their own request."[70] Hence, dependent territories could only be admitted to associate membership upon proposal of the state responsible for their international relations.

The initial membership of ECA comprised in accordance with ECOSOC Resolution 671A (XXV) of 29 April 1958[71] various colonial powers[72] and 10 independent African states,[73] as well as several associate members. One fundamental difference between ECA and ECAFE is that in the case of ECA, the non-regional "States which shall cease to have any territorial responsibilities in Africa shall cease to be members of the Commission",[74] while they remained full members of ECAFE/UNESCAP.

ECWA's regions is marked by "broad economic inequalities between member states; great instability; and the problem raised by the question of Israel."[75] Due to the "long and painful birth of ECWA", some potential members "joined existing regional commissions: Egypt and Ethiopia joined the ECA, Afghanistan and Iran joined ECAFE, and Greece, Israel and Turkey joined the ECE."[76]

---

[66] Berthelot 2004, p. 19.

[67] Berthelot 2004, p. 19.

[68] Adedeji 2004, p. 233.

[69] Ibid., 234.

[70] Ibid., 235.

[71] United Nations Economic and Social Council. 1958. Terms of Reference of the Economic Commission for Africa (E.CN.14/1, 22 Oct.). http://repository.uneca.org/pdfpreview/bitstream/handle/10855/16002/Bib-64579.pdf?sequence=1.

[72] Resolution 671A listed Belgium, France, Italy, Portugal, Spain and the United Kingdom of Great Britain and Northern Ireland as members of the commission.

[73] In addition to the four original African UN members, Libya, Morocco, Tunisia, the Sudan, Ghana, and Guinea became members of ECA. Adedeji 2004, p. 236.

[74] See para 5 of the Terms of Reference of the Economic Commission for Africa. Resolution 671 A (XXV) adopted by the Economic and Social Council at its 1017th meeting held on 29 April 1958, as amended. http://repository.uneca.org/bitstream/handle/10855/16002/Bib-64579.pdf?sequence=1.

[75] Destremau et al. 2004, p. 307.

[76] Destremau et al. 2004, p. 310. Egypt is now a member of UNESCWA.

3.1.6.3 Different Concepts of Region in Regional Development Banks

One of the reasons why regional development banks are of particular interest is that they have adopted different practices in defining their region.

ADB is the only regional development bank which partially originated from the institutional setting of a UN regional economic commission. ECAFE (now UNESCAP) was instrumental in the process of the creation of ADB. This distinguishes the creation of ADB from that of the other regional development banks (AIIB, AfDB, EBRD and IADB) and explains why, unlike those banks, ADB's region is defined with reference to the Terms of Reference of UNESCAP.

In accordance with Article 1 of the ADB Charter, the purpose of ADB is "to foster economic growth and co-operation in the region of Asia and the Far East (hereinafter referred to as the 'region')."[77] Moreover, consistent with Article 3.1 of the ADB Charter, members and associate members included in the said territories of Asia and the Pacific are, in principle, eligible for membership as regional countries of ADB. In line with the above, the regional membership of ADB extends from countries such as Armenia, Georgia, to the islands in the Pacific.

In the AIIB, on the other hand, "the current geographical region and composition listing for Asia and Oceania by the United Nations for statistical purposes formed the basis for their consideration of 'Asia' and 'region'."[78]

ADB's sister organizations, the African Development Bank (AfDB), the Inter-American Development Bank, and the European Bank for Reconstruction and Development (EBRD), each adopted a different approach than ADB.

In the case of AfDB, the Conference of Finance Ministers on the Establishment of an African Development Bank was convened by the Executive Secretary of ECA. However, unlike ECAFE, the geographic scope of AfDB was not defined with reference to the geographic scope of ECA. Rather, para 2 of Article 3 of the Agreement establishing the African Development Bank provides that

> (1) Any African country which has the status of an independent State may become a member of the Bank [....].
> (2) The geographical area to which the membership and development activities of the Bank may extend (referred to in this Agreement as 'Africa' or 'African', as the case may be) shall comprise the continent of Africa and African islands.[79]

As in the case of the Organization of African Unity, the referenced "status of an independent State" was meant to exclude South Africa and Rhodesia, which, during Apartheid, were considered non-African states in nature even though they were located on the African continent.

---

[77] Now referred to as the region of Asia and the Pacific.

[78] Chief Negotiators for Establishing the Asian Infrastructure Investment Bank. Report on the Articles of Agreement of the Asian Infrastructure Investment Bank. 22 May 2015.

[79] Agreement establishing the African Development Bank, signed on 4 August 1963, as amended. https://www.afdb.org/fileadmin/uploads/afdb/Documents/Legal-Documents/Agreement%20Establishing%20the%20ADB%20final%202011.pdf.

The original membership of IADB was linked to that of the Organization of American States (OAS).[80] Thus, it was not necessary for the IADB Charter to define a region. However, Section 1(b) of Article II of the Agreement Establishing the Inter-American Development Bank (IADB Charter), as subsequently amended, defined additional countries eligible for membership (Canada, Bahamas and Guyana), and opened the way for the admission of non-regional countries.

The purpose of IADB is to contribute "to the acceleration of the process of economic and social development of the regional developing member countries, individually and collectively."[81]

Until recently, EBRD was the regional development bank which had given up to the farthest extent the notion of a regional scope of activities. This relates to EBRD's character as an organization based on political conditionality, which was created to "foster the transition towards open market-oriented economies and to promote private and entrepreneurial initiative in the Central and Eastern European countries committed to and applying the principles of multiparty democracy, pluralism and market economics."[82] While the geographic scope of EBRD activities was initially limited to Central and Eastern European countries, Article 1 of the EBRD Charter was amended in 2006 to clarify that its purpose "may also be carried out in Mongolia subject to the same conditions."[83] Further amendments to Article 1 of the EBRD Charter were recommended following the Arab Spring to allow EBRD to become active in the Southern and Eastern Mediterranean.[84] Thus, the focus of EBRD has moved from providing assistance to a defined region to being an instrument for facilitating the transition of countries to market-based economies in Europe, Asia and Africa. Article 2 of the EBRD Charter mandates EBRD to cooperate, "in such manner as it may deem appropriate within the terms of this Agreement", with the IMF, IBRD, IFC, MIGA, and the UN and its Specialized Agencies and other related bodies, which also includes the "Council of Europe (and in particular the Social Development Fund), the International Investment Bank, the Nordic Investment Bank and the Economic Commission for Europe."

In regional development banks, the original logic of allowing membership of non-regional countries was to mobilize additional resources for the development of

[80] IADB Charter, Article 2, Section 1(a).

[81] IADB Charter, Article 1, Section 1.

[82] EBRD Charter, Article 1.

[83] Ibid.

[84] The current wording of the second sentence of Article 1 of the EBRD Charter reads: "Subject to the same conditions, the purpose of the Bank may also be carried out in Mongolia and in member countries of the Southern and Eastern Mediterranean as determined by the Bank upon the affirmative vote of not less than two-thirds of the Governors, representing not less than three-fourths of the total voting power of the members." See Report of the Board of Directors to the Board of Governors on the Geographic Expansion of the Bank's Region of Operations to the Southern and Eastern Mediterranean. http://www.ebrd.com/downloads/board/Geographic_expansion_recommendation.pdf. On the amendment to the EBRD Charter, see the Foreword to the Basic Documents of the European Bank for Reconstruction and Development. 2013. http://www.ebrd.com/news/publications/institutional-documents/basic-documents-of-the-ebrd.html.

a given region. It is against this background that non-regional developed countries were allowed to join ADB. However, this basic logic increasingly is out of tune with the increased importance of transitional economies in the global economy. This is underlined by the fact that AfDB has members from Asia and Latin America, and IADB has members from Asia. So far, only ADB resisted this trend. While non-regional developing countries have expressed an interest in joining ADB, the latter does not have any members from Africa or Latin America to date.

The membership structure of AIIB goes substantially beyond this as, in addition to regional countries,[85] its membership is "open to members of the International Bank for Reconstruction and Development or the Asian Development Bank." Similarly, while the founding members of the New Development Bank (NDB) are the BRICS countries,[86] membership is open to all "members of the United Nations", both borrowing and non-borrowing members.[87] Thus, both AIIB and NDB are institutions which allow membership of developing countries irrespective of region.

3.1.6.4 Regional Country Designation in Regional Development Banks

Another reason why regional development banks are very interesting is that their organizational, institutional and governance structures show with particular clarity the many connotations that may result from the classification of a member as a regional country.

The importance attributed to regional membership is epitomized by the example of IADB where under Article VIII, Section 4(b),

> [n]o increase in the subscription of any member to the ordinary capital stock shall become effective, and any right to subscribe thereto is hereby waived, which would have the effect of reducing the voting power of the regional developing members below 50.005 per cent of the total voting power of the member countries [....].

The designation of a country as part of a region may have implications for a country's eligibility to receive financial assistance[88] from an international financial institution. In accordance with Article III, Section 1 of IADB Charter,

---

[85] AIIB Articles of Agreement, Article 3, para 1(a) provides: "Regional members shall be those members listed in Part A of Schedule A and other members included in the Asia region in accordance with para 2 of Article 1. All other members shall be non-regional members."

AIIB Articles of Agreement, Article 1, para 2 provides that "Wherever used in this Agreement, references to "Asia" and "region" shall include the geographical regions and composition classified as Asia and Oceania by the United Nations, except as otherwise decided by the Board of Governors."

[86] Federative Republic of Brazil, the Russian Federation, the Republic of India, the People's Republic of China and the Republic of South Africa.

[87] Agreement on the New Development Bank, Article 2.

[88] See Droesse 2011a, pp. 207–218.

> The resources and facilities of the Bank shall be used exclusively to implement the purpose and functions enumerated in Article I of this Agreement, as well as to finance the development of any of the members of the Caribbean Development Bank by providing loans and technical assistance to that institution.

The core provisions governing the categories of Board members to be elected and the procedure for their election are set forth in Article VIII, Section 3(b)(ii) of the IADB Charter. It provides for the adoption of regulations regarding these matters and any amendments thereto by "a three-fourths majority of the total voting power of the member countries, including, with respect to provisions relating exclusively to the election of directors by nonregional member countries, a two-thirds majority of the governors of the nonregional members, and, with respect to provisions relating exclusively to the number and election of directors by the remaining member countries, by a two-thirds majority of the governors of regional members."

In addition, classification as a regional country, has a direct impact on IADB's decision-making procedures.

IADB requires various double-weighted majorities involving a qualified, absolute or simple majority of all Board members and of Board members from regional countries, for the quorum of Board meetings and certain decisions of fundamental importance.

In accordance with Article VIII, Section 2(e), of the IADB Charter:

> [a] quorum for any meeting of the Board of Governors shall be an absolute majority of the total number of governors, including an absolute majority of the governors of regional members, representing not less than three fourths of the total voting power of the member countries.

Similarly, the quorum for any meeting of the Board of Executive Directors is defined in Article VIII, Section 3(f) as "an absolute majority of the total number of directors, including an absolute majority of directors of regional members, representing not less than two thirds of the total voting power of the member countries."

In addition, there are a number of actions which require decision by a qualified majority of the members of the Board of Governors, including a qualified majority of Board members from regional countries.[89]

For the election of the President, Article VIII, Section 5(a) requires "a majority of the total voting power of the member countries, including an absolute majority of the governors of regional members," and the same majority is applicable in accordance with this provision to the decision of the Board of Governors to terminate the appointment of the President.[90]

---

[89] e.g., IADB Articles of Agreement, Article II, Section 2(e).

[90] Different double-weighted voting requirements are contained in other Charter provisions. Thus, the adoption of regulations regarding the election of Executive Directors requires, "a three-fourths majority of the total voting power of the member countries, including, with respect to provisions relating exclusively to the election of directors by nonregional member countries, a two-thirds majority of the governors of the nonregional members, and, with respect to provisions relating exclusively to the number and election of directors by the remaining member countries, by a two-thirds majority of the governors of regional members." Exceptions from the principle that

In addition, there are a number of other IADB Charter provisions which require a double-weighted majority. These provisions are sometimes rather complex, such as Article IX, Section 2 which requires for any suspension of a member

> a three-fourths majority of the total voting power of the member countries, including a two-thirds majority of the total number of governors, which, in the case of suspension of a regional member country, shall include a two-thirds majority of the governors of regional members and, in the case of suspension of a nonregional member country, a two-thirds majority of the governors of nonregional members.

For the termination of IADB's operations, Section 2 of Article X of the IADB Charter requires "a decision of the Board of Governors by a three-fourths majority of the total voting power of the member countries, including a two-thirds majority of the governors of regional members."[91] The aforementioned provision, and other provisions, give the US which holds 35% of IADB shareholdings a veto right.

In addition to cases when a double-weighted majority is required, the IADB Charter for certain decisions requires a qualified majority of total voting power.[92] Such qualified majorities and the double weighted voting and quorum requirements define in IADB the equilibrium of power between members, and between regional and non-regional members.

Also in the other regional development banks (i.e. ADB, AfDB and EBRD), classification as a regional country has multiple implications. Moreover, the other regional development banks also require qualified majorities for a series of decisions. Thus, for example in the case of ADB, in addition to unanimity, the ADB Charter provides for the use of four qualified majorities for decisions of the ADB Board of Governors.[93] However, unlike IADB, double-weighted requirements including a certain percentage of voting rights of regional members are not required in the case of these institutions.

"None of the elected directors and their alternates may be of the same citizenship" are determined in the case of borrowing member countries "by the governors of the borrowing members pursuant to a three-quarters majority of their total voting power and a two-thirds majority of their total number." See the IADB Articles of Agreement, Article VIII, Section 3(c)(ii).

[91] Any amendment of the general rules regarding admission of non-regional countries requires "a two-thirds majority of the total number of governors, including two thirds of the governors of nonregional members, representing not less than three fourths of the total voting power of the member countries" [IADB Articles of Agreement, Article II, Section 1(b)]. Moreover, any increase in the authorized capital stock of IADB requires "a three-fourths majority of the total voting power of the member countries, including a three fourths majority of the total number of governors, which includes a two-thirds majority of the governors of regional members." IADB Articles of Agreement, Article II, Section 2(e).

[92] IADB Articles of Agreement, Article II, Section 2(c)(ii) and Section 4(c); Article III, Section 7 (a) and Section 12; Article IV, Section 3(f) and (g) and Section 9(b); Article V, Section 1(e); and Article VII, Section 1(iii) and Section 4(b).

[93] Droesse 2011b, pp. 341–342.

3.1.6.5 Organizations of States with Common Background and Closed Special Organizations

Regional organizations are only one type of international organizations with limited membership. Organizations which restrict eligibility to membership can either be organizations of states that share a common background or closed special organizations.[94] The Organisation for Economic Co-operation and Development (OECD) is an important example of an organization of states with a common background. While OECD is an organization with closed membership, it has opened itself towards non-members by allowing them to participate in its activities to a certain extent.

The Nordic Development Fund is another example of a closed regional institution which provides financing exclusively for the benefit of non-member countries. While the Organization of the Petroleum Exporting Countries (OPEC) is the epitome of a closed special organization, the OPEC Fund for International Development provides financing exclusively for the benefit of non-members.

3.2 Conclusions

Along with the overall concept of international organization, some of the traditional classifications of international organizations also need to be re-thought and be redefined. As discussed, a treaty foundation is not a requirement either for the definition on an organization a "universal", of "limited membership" or as "general" or "special". Moreover, the policy connotations of these definitions have changed at time dramatically, as has been shown notably in the context of special organizations which now operate in an environment that is drastically different from the time when they were established, as well as for supranational organizations, where some of the previous assumptions are being tested by Brexit. Finally, it is important to analyze the legal implications of the classifications given to international organizations. As shown, the distinction between general and special organizations is not only relevant from a policy point of view but also warranted as a matter of law. In particular, the classification as "regional" has far-reaching and multiple legal implications in relation to organizations' institutional frameworks and decision-making procedures. Moreover, regional organizations and other organizations of limited membership face particular problems in relation to recognition of their international legal personality and privileges and immunities, as set out in Chap. 5.

94 Schermers and Blokker 2011, §§53–56.

3.3 Membership, Participation, Representation and Related Concepts

There is much confusion about the definition and connotations of the terms "membership", "participation" and representation. These concepts will be clarified in the following.

3.3.1 No Consistent Definition of Membership

Joining an international organization can either be defined as "membership" or as participation. As Blokker recalls, the "English word 'member' and the French '*membre*' are both derived from the Latin word '*membrum*', which means 'part of the body' and thus indicates clearly that members are part of a whole."[95] Given that definition, membership denotes a status. "Political participation", on the other hand, "is defined as 'taking part in politics', or 'as a term to denote the actions by which individuals take part in the political process'."[96] Hence, participation relates to a process and is seen to involve "an element of 'action'",[97] that can be as minimal "as exercising the right to vote and as active as becoming a career politician."[98]

In addition to participation in decision-making, other manifestations of participation in established processes include the provision of financial support to the organization, receipt of support and financing, and the implementation of the operational activities of the organization.

In certain cases, reference is made in constituent agreements to contracting parties[99] thereby emphasizing the establishment of the organization by a treaty. In that case, the members of the organization are by implication contracting parties to the treaty establishing the organization. However, the same is not necessarily applicable in all cases, as there may be situations where the contracting parties to the constituent agreement do not become members of the organization, or where the organization does not has a membership structure.

The term "accession" implies, as set forth in Article 15 of the Vienna Convention on the Law of Treaties, "the consent of a State to be bound by a treaty." It "is the act whereby a state accepts the offer or the opportunity to become a party to a treaty already negotiated and signed by other states" (e.g. the constituent

---

[95] Blokker 2004, p. 139.

[96] Verstichel 2009, p. 28.

[97] Ibid., 28.

[98] Ibid., 29.

[99] As indicated in Chap. 7 below, in the case of the GATT, a distinction was made between "CONTRACTING PARTIES, acting jointly—designated by uppercase letters (Article XXV:1) in contrast to the sum of the individual contracting states (contracting parties), designated by lowercase letters—as a rule making organ. [....]."

agreement of an international organization) that "has the same legal effect as ratification."[100] In relation to organizations' constituent agreements, the terms "adherence" or "adhesion"[101] are used with similar connotations.

International financial institutions generally have an equity structure comprising different types of shares. In some cases, such as the Corporación Andina de Fomento (CAF), the constituent agreement refers to "shareholders", thereby emphasizing the fact that the organization's shares are owned by its members.[102] However, the World Bank and the regional development banks and various other international financial institutions use the term "member" to denote the fact that a state or entity is part of the organizational and institutional structure of the organization. In such instances, the constituent agreement defines the principles applicable to the subscription of shares by the members and the types of shares held by them, and the various other legal implications which membership may have, including, in particular, for representation on the organization's governing bodies and voting rights.

An important question is whether membership presupposes international legal personality of the organization. Generally, international financial institutions with an equity structure comprising shares are established by a treaty and have both international legal personality and legal capacity under national law. However, there are entities that may be classified as international organizations even though they do not possess either international legal personality or legal capacity (see Chap. 6). This relates, in particular, to international organizations established as trust funds.

In most cases, the terms "membership" and "participation" are used synonymously and interchangeably. This is the case, in particular, for intergovernmental organizations established by a treaty whose governing bodies are exclusively or predominantly composed of representatives of states.

To be a "membrum" of an organization, the organization should arguably exist in the first place. Following this approach, it would make perfect sense not to use the term "membership" for cases where a state or entity participates in an organization which does not possess international legal personality or legal capacity under national law, while the same constraint would not apply to the use of the term "participation", as this term relates to a process rather than a status.

---

[100] United Nations Treaty Section. Glossary of terms relating to Treaty actions. https://treaties.un.org/pages/overview.aspx?path=overview/glossary/page1_en.xml.

[101] As indicated by Oppenheim: "'Adhesion' is defined as such entrance of a third party into an existing treaty as takes place, either with regard only to a part of the stipulations, or only with regard to certain principles laid down in the treaty." However, as indicated by Oppenheim, the above distinction "is one made in theory to which the practice frequently does not correspond." See Oppenheim 1920, §533.

[102] See Chaps. II and III of the Agreement establishing the Corporación Andina de Fomento. https://www.caf.com/media/3610/ConvenioConstitutivoingles.pdf.

There are some cases where the term "participating states" rather than "member states" is used to underline that a cooperative undertaking is not endowed with international legal personality.

The use of the term "participating states" in the context of the Wassenaar Arrangement[103] needs to be seen in this context.

In the case of the UNDP, which is a quasi-autonomous body, reference to "participating states" rather than member states denotes that certain states participate in the work of the organization either as donors or as recipients[104] and underlines that UNDP was conceived to partake in the legal personality of the UN and, hence, does not have a formal membership structure.

In particular, the case of the Organization for Security and Co-operation of Europe (OSCE) adds an interesting facet to this discussion, as it is expressly stated that the reference to "'participating States' rather than 'member States'—a distinction that is more than just a matter of words,"[105] is meant to denote the fact that the OSCE is not endowed with international juridical personality. On the other hand, the case of the OSCE also clearly shows that the legal nature of an organization effectively does not depend on the semantics used to describe it, but on the organization's powers and functions and the position which recognized subjects of international law have adopted vis-à-vis the organization. As will be discussed in the following, notwithstanding the elaborate terminology used to suggest that the OSCE is not endowed with international legal personality, there are very strong arguments to the contrary which suggest that the OSCE is indeed a subject of international law and able to act on the international plane.

The issue of trust funds is particularly interesting as such funds may be established with or without juridical personality. In the case of the Global Environment Facility (GEF), whose quest for legal personality has to date been unsuccessful, it would make sense to refer to participation rather than membership, in line with the approach discussed above. While para 7 of the GEF Instrument, under the heading "Participation", provides that "Any State member of the United Nations or of any of its specialized agencies may become a Participant in the GEF by depositing with the Secretariat an instrument of participation," the aforementioned two groups of participants, i.e. countries and specialized agencies, are not equal. While both groups are represented in the GEF Assembly, the same is not true for the main governing body of the GEF, i.e. the GEF Council, which is entirely composed of (developed and developing) country representatives.[106] Moreover, the terminology used in the

---

[103] The Wassenaar Arrangement on Export Controls for Conventional Arms and Dual-Use Goods and Technologies, About us. http://www.wassenaar.org/about-us/. See the provisions of the "Scope" of the Wassenaar Arrangement and "Participation". Wassenaar Arrangement Secretariat. 2017. *Public Documents*, Vol. I, Founding Documents. Guidelines & Procedures.

[104] Berthoud 1970, p. 157.

[105] OSCE. 2010. *The Legal Framework of the OSCE*. http://www.osce.org.

[106] See para 16 of the Instrument of the Restructured Global Environment Facility (GEF Instrument). https://www.thegef.org/gef/sites/thegef.org/files/publication/GEF_Instrument-Interior-March23.2015.pdf.

GEF Instrument is not clear. While the aforementioned provision refers to participation, para 15(c) of the Governing Instrument foresees that the Assembly of the GEF shall "keep under review the **membership** of the Facility." (emphasis added)

The CGIF, on the other hand, which was established as an ADB trust fund, shows that an organization established as a trust fund without international legal personality and legal capacity under national law may have an equity-based capital structure and an organizational structure which resembles that of traditional member-owned organizations.

Hence, there is no consistent practice of limiting use of the term "membership" to entities with international legal personality and legal capacity under national law. Moreover, as will be shown in the following, membership is used with a great variety of different connotations without consistency in either approach or terminology.

In some cases, a distinction is made between *de jure* and *de facto* membership. Membership in the General Agreement on Tariffs and Trade (GATT) falls in the latter category. The involved GATT/World Trade Organization (WTO) terminology even coined the intriguing term "de facto non-member participants in the GATT" referring to the status of those post-colonial states which, prior to acquiring full autonomy in the conduct of their external commercial relations, had been under GATT jurisdiction, and, for that reason, "in contrast to the standard accession process under GATT Article XXXIII [...] were not required to negotiate new terms of trade liberalization prior to becoming contracting parties."[107]

Other organizations, such as the IMF, make a distinction between legally binding and non-binding types of membership. This is underlined, *inter alia*, by the approach adopted by the IMF in relation to the Financial Stability Board (FSB) which, before its incorporation as a non-governmental organization, was not endowed with international juridical personality or legal capacity. In this context, an IMF paper raised the question: "How can the Fund become a member of something that does not exist as a separate legal entity?" The following answer was given to this question:

> Membership in the FSB is not the same as membership in an international organization like the Fund, the latter which implies legal rights and obligations. Rather membership in the FSB would effectively involve a non-binding commitment to cooperate towards a common goal with the other members in the forum provided by the FSB.[108]

While involving "a non-binding commitment to cooperate", membership in FSB, nevertheless, was still deemed important enough to require approval by IMF Executive Board. The paper concluded that that "membership in the FSB would be the most effective mechanism for cooperation between the Fund and the FSB."[109] Based on that recommendation, the IMF's Executive Board approved the Fund's

---

[107] See with further references: Copelovitch and Ohls 2012, p. 82.

[108] IMF. 2010. "IMF Membership in the Financial Stability Board", para 16.

[109] Ibid., para 21.

acceptance of membership on the understanding that membership would "not give rise to any legal rights or obligations for the Fund" and by reserving for the IMF "the right in specific circumstances not to take part in the decision-making of the FSB where such participation would not be consistent with the Fund's legal or policy framework."[110]

Similarly, the term "membership" is also used in a conceptually different manner, i.e. not as a legal construct conferring rights and obligations, in other types of transnational frameworks, such as the International Organization of Securities Commissions (IOSCO).[111] Even though not established as a legal entity with separate international juridical personality, the IOSCO has a governance structure which resembles that of international organizations and an elaborate membership structure comprising in addition to ordinary members,[112] associate members[113] and affiliate members.[114]

Finally, the membership issue has interesting ramifications in the case of entities established under municipal law for the production of public goods. In the case of such entities, it is entirely a policy decision whether an organization is established with a dual or hybrid structure under municipal law but with privileges and immunities under international law (e.g. the Global Fund), or entirely under municipal law. Thus, entities incorporated under national law which produce global public goods or fight global public bads may potentially become dual or hybrid organizations. In either case, an entity may or may not have members.

---

[110] Ibid., para 23.

[111] "IOSCO was created in 1983, when 11 securities regulatory agencies from North and South America agreed to build their inter-American regional association into an international cooperative body. A year later, securities regulators from France, Indonesia, Korea and the United Kingdom become the first non-American agencies to join the new organization. In July 1986, IOSCO held its annual conference in Paris, the first outside the Americas and where members agreed to create a permanent General Secretariat." OICV-IOSCO. About IOSCO.

[112] Ordinary membership comprises national security commissions or similar bodies with "significant authority over securities or derivatives markets" (See IOSCO By-Laws, Section 1, Part 2, Section 6), or where there is no government regulatory body, a "self-regulatory body, such as a stock exchange." (Ibid., Section 7.1).

[113] Associate membership comprises in accordance with IOSCO By-Laws, Section 1, Part 2, 8.1 associations of "public regulatory bodies" and in accordance with Section 8.2, "(a) supranational governmental regulators; (b) subnational governmental regulators where there is a national governmental regulator; (c) intergovernmental international organizations and other international standard-setting bodies; (d) other governmental bodies with an appropriate interest in securities regulation; and (e) national governmental regulators who are not MMoU signatories and who are not ordinary members."

[114] "The following bodies are eligible for affiliate membership of the Organization. (a) self-regulatory organizations (SROs); (b) securities exchanges; (c) financial market infrastructures (including clearing and settlement agencies); (d) international bodies other than governmental organizations with an appropriate interest in securities regulation; (e) investor protection funds and compensation funds; and (f) any other body with an appropriate interest in securities regulation that the IOSCO Board may decide for the purpose of furthering the objectives of the Organization." IASCO By-Laws, Section 1, Part 2, 9.1.

The above shows that that the concepts and definitions of membership are as varied as those of "international organization". Definitions, while valuable, are no end to themselves but are only useful to the extent that they support analytical processes. In the context of this book there is little merit, if any, in defining "membership" in a manner that is not supported by the use of this term in international practice. Given the fact that there is no agreement and generally accepted definition, this book will use the term "membership" in a broad sense to denote all forms of accession, adhesion and participation of states and other entities in international organizations, including organizations which do not possess international juridical personality and legal capacity under municipal law.

3.3.2 Membership and Representation

There is a conceptual difference between the powers attributed to international organizations and the power of organs of international organizations. Such difference relates to that between membership in an organization and membership in an organ of an organization.

Membership in an international organization generally relates to the fact that a state, international organization or other entity is part of the institutional set up of an international organization, and in this context is intrinsically related to the issue of who are eligible subjects of membership in an international organization. As will be shown, in addition to states, also international organizations and other entities, including private sector entities may become members of international organizations.

States, international organizations and other entities may be assigned seats in the organs (governing bodies) of international organizations, but they generally do not become members of the organ concerned in their corporate identity. Rather, the individuals which have been elected, selected or otherwise been appointed to serve on the organ are the members.

Membership in an organ is intrinsically linked, but nevertheless separate from representation. As highlighted by Ruiter:

> Membership differs from representation in that the decisions of the members of an organ are not the decisions imputed to the organ itself. The members of an organ are only collectively, not separately, competent to take decisions on its behalf.[115]

Also, while membership in international organizations may involve representation arrangements as shown in the following, certain members of governing bodies may be appointed in a personal capacity based on their qualifications and experience, rather than as the representative of a state, international organization or other entity.

---

[115] Ruiter 2001, p. 104.

3.3.2.1 Paradigms of Representation

As indicated by Amerasinghe, "Representation of a member State in an organization concerns the question of which persons are to be recognized as entitled to represent that State in the organs of the organization. Issues of representation are not issues concerning admission to membership. Representation presupposes admission."[116]

Similar positions are taken by Duxbury[117] and by Sands and Klein who contend that representation "is concerned with the question of the persons to be recognized as being entitled to represent the member within the organs of the Organization."[118]

Schermers and Blokker contend:

> There are two different sorts of representation in public law. On the one hand, a public cooperation can only operate through a natural person, in the same way as member states of international organizations, which can only act in organs of these organizations through their representatives. On the other hand, a public corporation can be represented by another public corporation. Likewise, a member state may sometimes represent another member state in an international organ. Wherever doubts may arise, we will use the term "delegation" and "delegate" when the first form of representation is referred to, and "acting by proxy" when discussing the second.[119]

However, issues of representation cannot be reduced to a distinction between "delegation" and "acting by proxy". More promising than the approach proposed by Schermers and Blokker is that of Heywood and Verstichel who seek to identify various representation schemes, indicating that representation may involve (1) trustee arrangements involving a person or entity "vested with formal responsibility for another's property and affairs" and (2) delegation "to a person chosen to act for another on the basis of clear guidance and instructions."[120] Moreover, (3) "a representative may be a person who carries out a mandate, in the sense that such people are obliged to carry out the promises upon which they fought an election", and (4) "a representative may typify or resemble the group he or she claims to present, usually coming from the group itself."[121]

While the four paradigms of representation highlighted above are useful, they are also not fully satisfactory as they do not fully capture all types of representation in international organizations. This applies, in particular, to the arrangements set out in items (1) and (2) above.

The trustee arrangements referred to under item (1) do not represent a specific paradigm of representation arrangements but are so wide that they cover a wide range of options. While it is a common feature of trustee arrangements that the

---

[116] Amerasinghe 2005, pp. 125–126.

[117] Duxbury 2011, p. 20.

[118] Sands and Klein 2009, p. 557.

[119] Schermers and Blokker 2011, §238.

[120] Verstichel 2009, p. 29 citing Haywood 2000.

[121] Ibid., 30.

trustee is the legal owner of the assets, the powers entrusted into the trustee may vary substantially. In certain cases, the trustee has been conferred far-reaching powers, including the power to mobilize resources, signing agreements, implementing operational activities; at other times, the powers of the trustee are very narrowly circumscribed and are, in essence, limited to those of a fiscal agent competent only to deal with the administration of the organization's resources.

As regards the role which representatives of states perform toward international organizations, such roles cannot be analyzed exclusively under the aspect of delegation as suggested under item (2) above, as states play both "an internal and an external role [as] constituent parts of organs [and as] counterparts of the international organization."[122] These roles are not necessarily related to the functions performed by an organization or the type of resources it administers. As will be shown in Chap. 9, organizations have resorted to external, even extra-constitutional processes, to deal with core strategic issues. Moreover, many have resorted to external mechanisms to deal with the replenishment of their special funds which are part of their own resources, while administering trust funds which are not part of their own resources on the same terms as special fund resources. A "delegation" as defined above typically relates to the representation of states in diplomatic conferences. However, members of a governing body of an international organization (e.g. a governing body of limited membership), often do not only have an obligation towards the authorities which appointed them, but also have a fiduciary responsibility towards the organization as a member of its governing body. As will be shown in further detail below, this is discussed, in particular, with regards to the executive boards of international financial institutions.

The mandates referred under item (3) above generally relate to those of elected officials.

As regards to the paradigm of representation specified under item (4) above in respect of persons who "typify or resemble the group" which they represent, the Global Fund may be seen as the epitome of the latter case as it is a multi-actor fund. Its Board comprises representatives of developing countries as well as representatives from civil society, the private sector, and a foundation, among which one should be a "representative of an NGO who is a person living with HIV/AIDS or from a community living with tuberculosis or malaria."[123]

The four cases referred to above need be amplified by two additional paradigms of representation. First, as highlighted by Schermers and Blokker above, a member may be represented by another member, which relates to "acting by proxy". Second, a member (either a state, international organization or other member entity) can be represented by a private sector entity. This was foreseen by the INMARSAT convention which includes a provision that the

> Operating Agreement can either be signed by a State Party to the INMARSAT Convention, or by an entity, known as a 'Signatory', designated for that purpose. A 'Signatory' is

---

[122] Schermers and Blokker 2011, §66.

[123] Global Fund By Laws, Article 7.1.

> subject to the municipal legal system and the 'guidance and instructions' of the designating State. Hence, while a private legal person can be designated as a Signatory, it remains firmly under the control of the designating Party and represents nothing more than an extension of that Party.[124]

Moreover, as shown by Sands and Klein, on appeal against a ruling of an WTO Panel, the Appellate Body confirmed that "not-withstanding the intergovernmental character of the dispute settlement system, a member state was free, in accordance with customary international law and in the absence of express rules to the contrary, to nominate whoever it wished to represent its interests."[125]

3.3.2.2 Distinction Between Membership and Representation Gets Blurred

While the distinction between membership in international organizations and membership in organs of international organizations may be clear as a matter of principle, "the formal distinction between organizations and organs is far from clear-cut in practice."[126] It gets blurred in a number of cases, in particular, in the case of quasi-autonomous bodies.

For example, reference to "UNCTAD membership" is generally made without clarification that strictly speaking such membership, as originally conceived, relates to membership in the UNCTAD conference, rather than to membership in an international organization. It is enhanced in the case of UNCTAD by the fact that membership in the UNCTAD conference differs from that in the General Assembly of which UNCTAD is a subsidiary body and by the fact that subsidiary bodies like UNCTAD and UNDP do their best to mimic full-fledged international organizations, to the extent that they are sometimes considered as such by third parties.

QABs are not exempt from the transformational effect of progressive institutionalization which may entail that a subsidiary body established as an organ may evolve to an intermediate step between international organization and representation or even to a *de facto* international organization.

The characterization of quasi-autonomous bodies as organs does not take into account the large autonomy that they enjoy as well as their progressive institutionalization. They may best be conceived of as "intermediate forms between an independent organizations and organs of organizations."[127] Hence, membership in quasi-autonomous bodies such as UNCTAD may best be conceived as an intermediate form between membership in an international organization and membership in an organ.

---

[124] Majid 1996, p. 68.

[125] Sands and Klein 2009, p. 557.

[126] Schermers and Blokker 2011, §557.

[127] Schermers and Blokker 2011, §41.

References

Adedeji A (2004) The ECA: forging a future for Africa. In: Berthelot Y (ed) Unity and diversity of development ideas. Indiana University Press, Bloomington, pp 233–306

Amerasinghe CF (2005) Principles of the Institutional Law of International Organizations, 2nd edn. Cambridge University Press, Cambridge

Archer C (1992) International Organizations, 2nd edn. Routledge, London

Bernhard R (1998) Europäisches Gemeinschaftsrecht und das Recht internationaler Organisationen: Gemeinsamkeiten und Unterschiede. In: Hafner G, Loibl G, Rest A, Sucharipa-Behrmann L, Zermanek K (eds) Europäisches Gemeinschaftsrecht und das Recht internationaler Organisationen. Liber Amicorum Professor Ignaz Seidl-Hohenveldern in honour of his 80th Birthday. Kluwer International, The Hague, pp 25–35

Berthelot Y (2004) Unity and diversity of development: the regional commissions' experience. In: Berthelot Y (ed) Unity and diversity in development ideas. Perspectives from the UN Regional Commissions. Indiana University Press, Bloomington, pp 1–50

Berthoud P (1970) The United Nations Development Programme. Framework and procedures. J World Trade Law 4:155–191

Blockmans S, Prechal S (2006) The European Integration Process: a continuum of 'deepening' and 'widening'. In: Blockmans S, Prechal S (eds) Reconciling the deepening and widening of the European Union. T.M.C. Asser Press, The Hague, pp 1–12

Blokker N (2004) International Organizations and their members. International Organizations belong to all members and to none. Variations on a theme. Int Organ Law Rev 1:139–161

Boisson de Chazournes L (2010) Les relations entre organisations régionales et organisations universelles. In: Collected Courses of the Hague Academy of International Law, vol 347, pp 79–406

Copelovitch MS, Ohls D (2012) Trade, institutions, and the timing of GATT/WTO accession in post-colonial states. Rev Int Organ 7:81–107

Czerwinsky G (1974) Das Universalitätsprinzip und die Mitgliedschaft in internationalen universalen Verträgen und Organisationen. Duncker & Humblot, Berlin

Destremau B, Saywell A-S, Barroche J (2004) ESCWA: Striving for regional integration. In: Berthelot Y (ed) Unity and diversity of development ideas. Indiana University Press, Bloomington, pp 307–357

Dominicé C (2001) Co-ordination between universal and regional organizations. In: Blokker NM, Schermers H (eds) Proliferation of International Organizations: legal issues. Kluwer Law International, The Hague, pp 65–84

Droesse G (2011a) Modalities of multilateral concessional financing. In: Droesse G (ed) Funds for development: multilateral channels of concessional financing. ADB, Manila, pp 179–297

Droesse G (2011b) Concessional financing of the Asian Development Bank: The Asian Development Fund and other channels of ADB concessional financing. In: Droesse G (ed) Funds for development: multilateral channels of concessional financing. ADB, Manila, pp 299–398

Duxbury A (2011) The Participation of States in International Organization: The Role of Human Rights and Democracy. Cambridge University Press, Cambridge

El-Erian A (1963) First report on relations between states and inter-governmental organizations (A/CN.4/161 and Add.1). Yearb Int Law Commission 2:159–185

Goebel RJ (2013) Supranational? Federal? Intergovernmental? The governmental structure of the European Union after the Treaty of Lisbon. Columbia J Eur Law 20:77–142

Haywood A (2000) Key concepts of politics. MacMillan, London

Head JW (1994) Supranational Law: How the move toward multilateral solutions is changing the character of 'International' Law. Kansas Law Rev 42:605–666

Jessop B (2004) Multi-level governance and multi-level metagovernance. In: Bache I, Flinders M (eds) Multi-level governance. Oxford University Press, Oxford, pp 49–74

Klabbers J (2014) The emergence of functionalism in International Institutional Law: Colonial inspirations. Eur J Int Law 25(3):645–675

Klabbers J (2015) An introduction to International Organizations law, 3rd edn. Cambridge University Press, Cambridge

Luard E (1977) International Agencies: The emerging framework of interdependence. MacMillan Press, London

Majid AA (1996) Legal status of International Institutions: SITA, INMARSAT and Eurocontrol examined. Dartmouth Publishing, Aldershot

Mie O (2008) Japan's entry into ECAFE. In: Makoto I, Rose C, Junko T, West J (eds) Japanese diplomacy in the 1950s. From isolation to integration. Routledge, London, pp 98–113

Mitrany D (1948) The functional approach to world organization. Int Aff (Royal Institute of International Affairs) 24:350–363

Oppenheim L (1920) In: Roxburgh RF (ed) International Law. A treatise, 3rd edn, vol 1, §533 (reprint: The Lawbook Exchange, New Jersey)

Pechstein M (2014) Mitgliedschaftsordnung der EU. In: Hatje A, Müller-Graf P-C (eds) Enzyklopädie Europarecht, vol 1. Europäisches Organisations-und Verfassungsrecht. Nomos, Baden Baden, pp 833–890

Ruiter DW (2001) Legal institutions. Kluwer Academic Publishers, Dordrecht

Sands P, Klein P (2009) Bowett's Law of International Institution, 5th edn. Sweet and Maxwell (Thomson Reuters), London

Schermers HG, Blokker NM (2011) International Institutional Law: Unity within diversity, 5th edn. Martinus Nijhoff, Boston

Severino RC (2006) Southeast Asia in search of an ASEAN Community: Insights from the former ASEAN Secretary-General. ISEAS Publishing, Singapore

Singh LP (1966) The politics of economic cooperation in Asia: A study of Asian International Organizations. University of Missouri Press, Columbia

Stone D (2013) Knowledge actors and transnational governance: The private-public policy nexus in the global agora. Palgrave MacMillan

Thomas DC (2017) Beyond identity: Membership norms and regional organization. Eur J Int Relat 23:217–240

Verstichel A (2009) Participation, representation and identity, the right of persons belonging to minorities to effective participation in public affairs: Content, justification and limits. Intersentia, Antwerp

Wightman D (1963) Towards economic cooperation in Asia: The United Nations Economic Commission for Asia and the Far East. Yale University Press, New Haven

Williams D (1987) The specialized agencies and the United Nations. The system in crisis. St. Martin's Press, New York

Chapter 4
Decline or Disaggregation of the Nation State, Dichotomy of Public and Private and Constitution and Constitutionalization

Contents

4.1 Introduction

There is a variety of reasons as to why new concepts of "intergovernmental organization" and "international organization" are required. This needs to be seen in the overall context of the evolution of public international law, against the background of the decline and disaggregation of the nation state and dispersion of

All weblinks are updated as of 28 February 2018.

G. Droesse, *Membership in International Organizations*,
https://doi.org/10.1007/978-94-6265-327-6_4

authority, and the fact that the dichotomies of public and private and governmental and nongovernmental are not suitable in all cases to capture the nature of international organizations.

Also, the traditional concept of international organization established by a treaty requires amplification and revision. The constituent agreement of an international organization is widely seen as a hybrid of treaty and constitution. However, a constitution does not need to be adopted as a treaty. A constitution not adopted as treaty may largely have the same effect and may also be the basis of international action. Moreover, an international organization does not need to be established by or based on the constituent agreement as a subject of international law but may acquire that status because of progressive institutionalization.

The formal ratification requirement of the constituent agreement of an international organization is often no longer seen as a sufficient to ensure an organization's legitimacy. This merely formal criterion needs to be supplemented by substantive criteria, such as accountability, transparency, due process and the protection of human rights. This is the core of the discussion on constitutionalization that has far-reaching ramifications. This and various related issues will be discussed in this chapter.

4.2 Decline or Disaggregation of the Nation State

The centuries since 1648 have been characterized by a progressively developing "state governance framework—including international law—responding to the adaptations and adjustments made by states to fulfill their new responsibilities to people in their jurisdictions, stewardship of their territory and resources, and multilateral coordination and cooperation."[1]

The literature has analyzed in detail the development of the concept of absolute sovereignty.

As indicated by James Leslie Brierly:

> Sovereignty started in Bodin's writings as a formal juristic concept in the sixteenth century, the attribute of a personal monarch entrusted by the constitution with supreme authority over the ordinary law of the state. Sovereignty, under the momentum of the historical developments which took place in the character of European governments, then came to be regarded as power absolute and above the law. Eventually when it became impossible to fix the location of such power in any definite person or organ within the state, sovereignty became seen as the attribute of the personified state itself.[2]

What "most distinguishes the modern post-Reformation from the medieval state is the much greater strength and concentration of the powers of government in the modern state."[3] As the international community evolved into an inter-state system,

---

[1] Ku 2014, p. 38.

[2] Clapham 2012.

[3] Ibid., 2.

the public international law also developed as a separate legal discipline based on state-centric concepts. Such concepts have become in many areas the foundation of public international law doctrines, notably as regards the concepts of international legal personality, subject of international law and membership. In fact, state-centric concepts became so entrenched in concepts of international law that they were—and partially still are—often accepted as a given notion which is presumed rather than critically analyzed.

State-centric concepts of international organizations (IO) emphasize the consensual nature of the establishment of an organization by a treaty or other international agreement and the role of members of the organization as the masters of their creation. However, "[f]ounding fathers are among the most frustrated and double-crossed heroes of history; they can state the purposes of the institutions that they create, but they cannot determine those purposes or control the course of development of those institutions."[4] By creating an international organization, states give it a life of its own and face what Guzman calls the Frankenstein problem of needing "to balance the potential benefits of an IO against the risk that the IO will behave contrary to the interests of the state."[5] While states generally design strategies to keep their creation under control, they have not always managed to do so as organizations redefine their purpose or adjust their functions in response to new demands or, due to mission creep, may change beyond recognition. Moreover, organizations frequently undergo a process of progressive institutionalization and may acquire a new legal status other than what was contemplated in their respective constituent instruments. As formal international lawmaking "is increasingly superseded by 'informal international lawmaking' involving new actors, new processes, and new outputs,"[6] Pauwelyn, Wessel and Wouters conclude accordingly that "[o]n many occasions, the traditional structures of formal lawmaking have become shackles."[7]

While the nation state was "long seen as steadily amassing power, [it] is now being viewed as increasingly vulnerable, even on its way out." Oscar Schachter[8] has given a number of reasons regarding the decline of the nation-state, among which are the decreased role of the state in the global economy, the enhanced role of civil society, and the resurgence of particularisms. However, as Slaughter has shown, "[t]he state is not disappearing, but is disaggregating into its component institutions, which are increasingly interacting principally with their foreign counterparts across borders."[9] Hence, the impermeability of the nation state has been reduced.

[4] Claude 1971, p. 6.

[5] Guzman 2013, p. 1002.

[6] Pauwelyn et al. 2014, p. 733; see Pauwelyn et al. 2012.

[7] Pauwelyn et al. 2014, p. 743.

[8] Schachter 1997, pp. 7–23.

[9] Slaughter 2004, p. 31.

As indicated by Oeter:

> Fundamental for understanding the fragmented nature of global legal order is a step which has been called the 'piercing of the veil' of unitary statehood. The traditional way how international relations tried to understand the 'global order'—as product of a set of unitary actors, namely states—hinders an adequate conceptualization of the current global legal order. The state as a unitary collective actor is a fiction. States do not act with one voice in the international arena.[10]

Oeter further specifies:

> The 'unity' of international law as a legal order in itself is a mere fiction. Negotiated in specialized fora by specialized bureaucracies and agencies, international treaties form not a consistent body of rules, but a plethora of segmented legal regimes that are based on divergent assumptions and 'cognitive patterns', follow different objectives, use different tools and instruments and might end up in contradictory provisions.[11]

While the "disaggregation of the state in its component institutions" is increasingly accepted as a matter of principle, international lawyers largely have failed to draw any consequences from this finding for their analysis of organizational and institutional frameworks of international organizations, e.g. when discussing concepts such as membership or "subject of international law". Also, they have largely failed to conceptualize for their analysis of organizational and institutional frameworks that "there is also a dispersion of authority taking place,"[12] as the number of subjects of international law is increasing and authority is exercised by an increasing number of non-state actors which "compete with states for the scarce resource of politico-legal authority (i.e., the power to set authoritative standards)."[13] As the fragmentation and verticalization of international law go hand in hand,

> the system is no longer exclusively made up, as it still was in the earlier days, of independent and sovereign states who famously interact as if they are billiard balls on the green sheet of a pool table. Instead other actors have come to the fore, including international organizations, multinational corporations, international NGOs, minority groups, policy-making networks, and even (or especially) individuals, and at least some of these bring their own internal normative ('legal') orders to the table.[14]

It is indeed a "mark of international law's conservatism that it took until 1949 for the separate legal personality of an international organization like the United Nations to be recognized. The status of its predecessor, the League of Nations, for example, remained unsettled such that the Secretary-General of the League apparently had to sign contracts of employment in his personal capacity."[15] It is

---

[10] Oeter 2009, p. 14.

[11] Ibid., p. 18.

[12] Klabbers 2011, p. 11.

[13] Ibid., 12.

[14] Ibid., 14.

[15] Crawford 2013, para. 246.

equally a mark of international law's conservatism that there is a lingering resistance against taking account of new developments, the vastly increased number of international actors and the increased role for civil society.

Public goods are increasingly provided through entities not established by a treaty but by a resolution or decision of a conference, by the decision of the governing body of an organization, by the conference of the parties to a convention, or merely by consensus. Moreover, they comprise entities which are not established by governments or incorporated under national law or which do not include government representatives in their governing bodies. Taking account of the evolution of international law and the proliferation of actors at the international stage, the notions of "international organization" and "subject of international law" need to be revised to comprise entities as mentioned above.

Until recently, organizations such as IPU, which involve cooperation of Parliaments, were *ipso facto* relegated into the realm of nongovernmental organizations.[16] However, even if it is assumed that adopting this approach may have been justified in the past, it is no longer appropriate now. Any determination on whether such forms of cooperation fall within the scope of international organization must be made on a case-to-case basis, and go beyond the legal status of an entity or organization at the time of its establishment since it only represents a snapshot of the organization's status and functions at that time.

In addition, the emergence of a new hybrid or dual type of international organization and of organizations created as trust funds, means that the very concept of international organization and of who can be the subject of international law needs to be defined in a broader manner.

While the "notion that the state has to represent the symbolic identity of state subjects is a relatively new one, dating perhaps from the eighteenth or early nineteenth century"[17] and despite the partial disaggregation of the state,[18] public international law continues to look at international cooperation largely only through "the lens of the unitary states".[19] Current theories of international law and international organization are still largely based on the assumption that only the unitary state may be the subject of membership in international organizations and that international organizations are only to interact with the unitary state. Thus, forms of cooperation between sub-state actors (e.g. technical or regulatory agencies) and transnational networks, however powerful, are not included in the ambit of theories of public international law and international institutional law. As a corollary of the "partial disaggregation of the state" highlighted above, and considering the evolution of international law, this mantra is no longer adequate and needs to be revised.

[16] A similar approach is also adopted by Charnovitz who also proposes to treat the IPU "as an NGO". Charnovitz 1997, p. 187.

[17] Milliken and Krause 2002, p. 757.

[18] See Slaughter 2004, pp. 12–15.

[19] Ibid., 13.

In many cases, forms of cooperation between sub-state actors are deliberately kept informal and do not qualify for recognition as an international organization. However, whether such forms of cooperation may be considered as international organizations needs to be considered on a case-by-case basis and cannot just be ruled out because they involve cooperation among sub-state actors or technical government agencies. It is possible, as a matter of principle, that forms of cooperation between regulatory agencies or other sub-state actors may also qualify for recognition as international organization based on progressive institutionalization. Any such institutionalization is only possible with the agreement of states. However, whether an entity is to be recognized as an international organization and subject of international law is to be determined based on its functions and the position which recognized subjects of international law have adopted in its regard.

Thus, it is necessary to rethink some basic concepts of international law and the very concept of international organization, taking account of the above. This is the basic theme of this book. However, it is not only the concept of international organization which needs to change. The legal and policy frameworks of international organizations also need to substantially change to a multi-level and multi-layered setting and they need to open to the outside by enhancing their cooperation and interaction with a variety of stakeholders, including through institutionalized participation of such stakeholders through full, partial. sector or affiliate membership.

Further, to remain relevant, international organizations do need to reconsider their role and functions and relations with other actors, including the private sector, philanthropy and civil society, and open to the outside by allowing participation of a variety of stakeholders. Without the support of such stakeholders and active involvement of the private sector, it will not be possible to achieve many of the ambitious objectives which have been formulated. Climate change adaptation and mitigation is a good example. At Cancun, in 2010, developed countries committed to providing USD100 billion per year by 2020 for climate change adaptation and mitigation. There is wide-spread recognition that for achieving this objective, private sector involvement is crucial.

In certain cases, traditional funding mechanisms may be reversed to the extent that international organizations derive the bulk of their funding from the private sector (e.g. for facilitating the transition of countries to a green economy).

International organizations should transform themselves into forums and platforms that involve a great variety of stakeholders, including, *inter alia*, sub-state actors. As Abeyratne proposes in relation to the International Civil Aviation Organization (ICAO), international organizations need to ensure that they keep "abreast with the new world order in which States are increasingly being disaggregated into components which act in global networks, linking the world together in a manner that enables global trends to permeate the local environment.

In other words, ICAO should facilitate interaction between States and their components that interact in matters of civil aviation."[20] In rudimentary form,

[20] Abeyratne 2009, p. 542.

examples of interaction between government departments and international organizations are already provided for by some organizations. Thus, in case of the International Labour Organization (ILO), in accordance with Article 11 of the Constitution,

> [t]he government departments of any of the Members which deal with questions of industry and employment may communicate directly with the Director-General through the representative of their government on the Governing Body of the International Labour Office or, failing any such representative, through such other qualified official as the government may nominate for the purpose.

Moreover, Abeyratne has given some examples on the form which interactions between ICAO and sub-state actors might take.[21] Building on these examples, the scope of which might be expanded, interactions between international organizations and sub-state actors should also be considered in the case of other international organizations to the extent that these may become forums for sub-state actors.

4.3 The Public-Private and Governmental and Nongovernmental Dichotomies

Traditional theories of international law interpret the term "international organization" to comprise only "public international organizations" and exclude any organization not established by agreement between governments from the scope of international organization. In line with the evolution of international law, approaches as indicated above require amplification and revision.

4.3.1 The Public-Private Distinction

As indicated by Kotzur,[22] there is a "world of dichotomies".

> The "either/or" between constitutional unity and legal fragmentations, between a Westphalian and a post-Westphalian system, between a still national and an already post-national order pushes the search in a wrong direction. The reality all those who try to do the mapping are confronted with is a reality of 'in-betweens'. In the world of 'in-betweens' it does not help to focus only on actors, only on institutions, or only on

[21] "For example, in many member States, aviation has numerous players in different areas such as customs and immigration, medical and quarantine, tourism, police, airports, and air navigation service providers. In most instances, these players do not act in accord, thus resulting in disharmony in the ultimate delivery of an efficient air transport product. ICAO's Mission and Vision Statement exhorts ICAO to do just what is needed—to act as the global forum in the key areas of concern to international civil aviation through cooperation between its member States." Abeyratne 2009, pp. 542–543.

[22] Kotzur 2012, p. 590.

> processes. In this world, government is not the exclusive alternative to governance or vice versa. [….]

The public-private dichotomy is of utmost importance. Many have very clear ideas as to what belongs to the public and what belongs to the private sphere. This is because they are looking at this distinction through the state-centric concepts of the nation state. However, the

> public-private distinction stands out as one of the grand dichotomies of Western thought, in the sense of a binary opposition that is used to subsume a wide range of other important distinctions and that attempts (more or less successfully) to dichotomize the social universe in a comprehensive and sharply demarcated way.[23]

As stated by Horwitz, the

> distinction between public and private realms arose out of a double movement in modern political and legal thought. On the one hand, with the emergence of the nation-state and theories of sovereignty in the sixteenth and seventeenth centuries, ideas of a distinctly public realm began to crystallize. On the other hand, in reaction to the claims of monarchs and, later, parliaments to the unrestrained power to make law, there developed a countervailing effort to stake out distinctively private spheres free from the encroaching power of the state.[24]

History shows that for a long time, matters which are now considered to be public used to be considered to be part of the private sphere. It is pertinent to recall that as "late as the sixteenth century, English judges still analyzed taxation, not as an exaction by the state but as a private gift from the donor—the taxpayer."[25] Until "the nineteenth century, lawsuits involving the removal of a public official from office were analyzed more frequently than not as questions of property. The officeholder often successfully claimed a property interest in the office from which he could not be divested."[26] As "warfare and diplomacy—which we today unquestionably include in the public sphere—were marketized and internationalized well into the nineteenth century," "mercenaries were the foundation of European military power" for several centuries, and "until the early nineteenth century, diplomacy was an aristocratic pursuit; diplomats who had a sense of belonging to a single 'cosmopolitan fraternity' or 'aristocratic international' could easily change from one employer to the other."[27]

In the period since World War II, the distinction between public and private has become increasingly blurred at several levels. This relates to the fact that the borderline between public and private is moving in several respects. This is demonstrated, on the one hand, by the evolution of international investment law and the finding "that international investment law inherently brings together apparently contradictory perspectives, and that it is the amalgamation of these oppositions, of

---

[23] Weintraub 1997, p. 1.

[24] Horwitz 1981–1982, p. 1423.

[25] Ibid., 1423–1424.

[26] Ibid., 1427.

[27] Jönsson 2013, p. 1.

these 'public–private' antinomies, which lies at its foundations."[28] As shown by Mills, "many of the major issues which are matters of contention in international investment law are the products of underlying foundational uncertainties, which can be identified through analysis of the two 'public–private' antinomies explored above."[29] This also relates in particular to the discussion on the legal status of investors under international law, and whether multinational enterprises[30] or investors may be deemed to possess international legal personality. Moreover, as shown by Jönsson, there are

> four modes of global governance along the moving public-private borderline that have different consequences for international organizations. First, intergovernmental organizations may proactively open up and grant access to private actors. Second, they may become involved in informal networks around specific issues. Third, they may enter into public-private partnerships. And fourth, intergovernmental organizations may be bypassed insofar as private actors take over global regulatory functions.[31]

It needs to be added that the borderline between public and private is also moving in the realm of international organization, as shown by the emergence of a new paradigm of dual and hybrid organization.

The dichotomy and distinction between international organizations and international non-governmental organizations (INGO) also has increasingly become blurred at several levels. This relates on the one hand to the scope of their activities and the areas in which governmental or nongovernmental organizations are operating. Actions of international organizations and INGO are entwined and interconnected in many ways.

Examples of organizations which evolved from non-governmental organizations to international organizations include the World Meteorological Organization,[32] the World Tourism Organization,[33] the International Development Law Organization,

---

[28] Mills 2011, p. 477.

[29] Ibid., 502.

[30] Hansen 2010, pp. 1–129.

[31] Jönsson 2013, p. 4.

[32] The International Meteorological Organization, the predecessor of the WMO, was established in 1873 as the outcome of the Vienna Congress. It was conceived as a "governmental organization from which meteorologists in universities and private institutions were excluded", but after the First Conference of Directors of Meteorological Services held in Munich in 1891, "it became a non-governmental body in which all meteorologists could be involved, whether in government service or not. And in this body, all meteorologists were welcome to work as technical experts." See Sarukhanian and Walker.

[33] The predecessor of the World Tourism Organization, the International Union for Official Tourism Organizations (IUOTO), was an association established under Swiss private law. See Vrancken 2006.

and the now defunct Agency for International Trade Information and Co-operation.[34]

The way between international organizations and INGO is a two-way road, as some international organizations have been privatized and functions previously performed by international organizations have been absorbed by, or been delegated to, private sector entities. INMARSAT was the first of the international satellite organizations to engage in a privatization process[35] and this course was followed by other satellite agencies.

As regards the private sector, there are many reasons why international organizations should collaborate with private-sector entities.[36] Such collaboration may mobilize and leverage additional resources and enhance implementation and execution of projects and programs.

Whether an organization should be classified as public or private is, in essence, a policy decision and has nothing to do with the process of its creation or the representation arrangements in its governing bodies. This is underlined by the fact that some of the IAUs which preceded recognized international organizations were based on private initiative. On the other hand, the World Road Association, which tends to be classified as a non-governmental organization, was based on a diplomatic conference held in 1908; it "is continuing the work initiated by the first international Road Congress" held that year[37] and has a membership structure which includes national governments, regional authorities (within a national state),

---

[34] The Agency for International Trade Information and Cooperation (AITIC) was set up by the Federal Office of External Economic Affairs (OFAEE) of the Swiss Federal Administration, when within the framework of the establishment of the World Trade Organization (WTO) in Geneva, the Swiss government decided to finance a programme to strengthen the capacity of less-advantaged country missions in Geneva and neighboring capitals to lead a more effective trade diplomacy. See http://www.aitic.org.

[35] Sagar 1999, pp. 127–147. On the privatization of Intelsat, see Katkin 2005, pp. 1–66.

[36] As indicated by UNDP, "First, the private sector, the main driver of economic growth, represents the main source of employment creation in most countries and invests human capital and workforce development. Furthermore, it creates and delivers goods and services that can benefit society at all levels, develops and deploys new technologies and innovations, and has the capacity to levy scalable solutions through market-based approaches. It also represents the primary source of tax and other public revenues and directs social investment and philanthropic resources toward development. The private sector also has the ability to apply norms and standards in its operations that have impact on important UN areas such as labor rights, environment, human rights and corruption. At the same time, the private sector sometimes also contributes to a negative impact on development, including on the environment, social conditions, labor rights, corruption and conflict to name a few. UNDP should work with and influence private actors to improve their performance and reverse such negative impact." UNDP (2012) *Strategy for Working with the Private Sector*, Section 2.4. http://www.undp.org/content/dam/undp/library/corporate/Partnerships/Private%20Sector/UNDP-Private-Sector-Strategy-final-draft-2012.pdf.

[37] Statutes of the World Road Association, Article I.1, Oct. 2015. https://www.piarc.org/ressources/documents/Statutes-World-Road-Association/23758,Statutes-World-Road-Association-November-2015.pdf.

collective members, and honorary members.[38] The ILO, which is a specialized agency of the UN, has a tripartite structure comprising government, employer and worker representatives. Finally, the King Abdullah Bin Abdulaziz International Centre For Interreligious and Intercultural Dialogue (KAICIID),[39] which is an intergovernmental organization with treaty base, founded by the Kingdom of Saudi Arabia, the Republic of Austria and the Kingdom of Spain, has a Board of Directors composed of representatives of major world religions.[40] This clearly shows that it is not necessary for an entity to count in its governing bodies only representatives of governments for such entity to be classified as an "intergovernmental organization" or as an "international organization".

The Internet Corporation for Assigned Names and Numbers (ICANN)[41] serves as an example of how an organization with private sector participation may exercise public authority. While ICANN, which administers access to the internet, "has never been vested with such power by any international treaty", nevertheless, it "establishes rules which are of greater importance than most acts of international organizations and they are more widely and strictly accepted and respected than binding decisions of most international organizations."[42] ICANN "was an experiment in creating an alternative regime for global policy-making (that is, policy-making without government participation)" and "is a type of global public-policy network [....] performing alternative public policy-making."[43]

In practice, "the distinction between public and private—between the 'public sector' and the 'private sector'—usually means the distinction between 'governmental' and 'nongovernmental', with the implication that this distinction should be as clearly and sharply dichotomous as possible."[44] As the "field of the nongovernmental is conceived essentially in terms of the market,"[45] using the public-private distinction, "characteristically involved a preoccupation with questions of *jurisdiction*, and especially with demarcating the sphere of the 'public authority' of the state from the sphere of formally voluntary relations between 'private' individuals." Further, the public-private divide and the perceived dominance of the state as the main actor in international affairs are reflected in the "rather crude form of indicating dissimilarity" by distinguishing "the state and everything else",[46] i.e. making a distinction between state and non-state actors.

---

[38] See Statutes of the World Road Association, Article IV. http://www.piarc.org/ressources/documents/Statutes-World-Road-Association/23758,Statutes-World-Road-Association-November-2015.pdf.

[39] KAICIID. Who we are. About us. https://www.kaiciid.org/who-we-are.

[40] KAICIID. Who we are. Governance. https://www.kaiciid.org/governance.

[41] https://www.icann.org/en.

[42] Hartwig 2010, p. 576.

[43] Antonova, p. 3.

[44] Weintraub 1997, p. 8.

[45] Weintraub 1997, p. 2.

[46] Noortmann 2011, p. xxxviii.

One of the main problems of the current concept of international NGOs relates to their very definition as "nongovernmental", i.e. as the negation or conceptual and organizational anti-thesis of governmental forms of organization. This "semantic negation neglects the most significant part of the organizations, which is that their strength comes from 'their capacity at continuous existence and development'."[47] Furthermore, it has led to the assumption that paradigms of organizational structures not established by intergovernmental agreement, i.e. an agreement between states, or established by entities other than the government (e.g., police departments), or with members of governing bodies representing entities other than the government, should be brought in the realm of nongovernmental organization, rather than in the realm of international organization. Rather than the term "non-governmental organization" or the "term "non-state actor", this book uses the term "transnational actors" with the additional specification that it includes the private sector, philanthropy and civil society.

The basic question is whether an organization should be classified as non-governmental in nature for the only reason that it was not established by an intergovernmental agreement and has members from technical government agencies. The discussions on the legal status of the International Criminal Police Organization (INTERPOL) clearly confirm that the above concerns were of paramount importance in the minds of many government representatives. Martha has elaborately described the "arduous"[48] dealings between INTERPOL and the United Nations, in particular with the United Nations Economic and Social Council (ECOSOC), which sought to establish special arrangements with INTERPOL pursuant to Article 71 of the UN Charter, and the difficult process of recognition of the intergovernmental character of INTERPOL by the United Nations.

The traditional position on the divide between intergovernmental and non-governmental organizations is epitomized by the position that ECOSOC categorically took in 1950, stating,

> Any international organization which is not established by intergovernmental agreement shall be considered as a non-governmental organization for the purpose of these arrangements.[49]

Moreover, as shown by Martha, "[at] its 46th session, the ECOSOC, faced with the question whether INTERPOL was a non-governmental or intergovernmental organization, requested the Committee on Non-governmental Organisations to study a proposed special arrangement to be arrived at between the Council and INTERPOL.[50] He clarifies that "debates on the issue of INTERPOL's status

[47] Charnovitz 2006, p. 351, citing J. J. Lador-Lederer.

[48] Martha 2010, p. 143

[49] Resolution 288 (X), Review of Consultative Arrangements with Non-Governmental Organizations. 27 Feb. 1950, para 8. Economic and Social Council Official Records. Tenth Session. 7 Feb. to 6 March 1950, 24–33, 25. https://documents-dds-ny.un.org/doc/UNDOC/GEN/NR0/753/48/IMG/NR075348.pdf?OpenElement.

[50] Martha 2010, p. 140.

stemmed from Article 4 of the INTERPOL's statute which provides that each country may appoint as a Member of the Organization, any official police body whose functions come within the scope of the Organization's activities."[51] The aforementioned provision and INTERPOL's legal status, in general, relate to the origins of INTERPOL which was not established by treaty, but and "traces its roots to an invitation by the Austrian government (through Vienna's chief of police) to police officials around the world."[52]

Under the circumstances, whether "INTERPOL qualifies as a 'governmental' international organization or merely as a non-governmental organization thus turns partly on the question of the capacity in which those who created INTERPOL acted."[53] Martha derives from the "text of the very first International Criminal Police Commission (ICPC) charter, adopted in 1923, that the police officers' conduct implied they were acting on behalf of their governments when INTERPOL was created."[54]

The United Nations Office of Legal Affairs (OLA) took a different approach and only recognized the intergovernmental status of INTERPOL in 1982 "in view of the amended constitution of INTERPOL (dating 1956) which evidenced the international character of the organization."[55] Article 4 of the INTERPOL Constitution provides:

> Any country may delegate as a Member to the Organization any official police body whose functions come within the framework of activities of the Organization. The request for membership shall be submitted to the Secretary General by the appropriate governmental authority. Membership shall be subject to approval by a two-thirds majority of the General Assembly.

Thus, at present, INTERPOL is recognized as an "intergovernmental organization" both by the UN and by other international organizations.

The IPU is classified by Schermers and Blokker as a non-governmental organization,[56] but such classification does not properly capture the nature and legal status of IPU. It is not enough to just look at when or how an organization was initially established to determine its nature and character. Organizations can dynamically develop and often dramatically change their structures. The IPU epitomizes such development as it evolved from an association of parliamentarians to an association of Parliaments. Under its statutes initially adopted in 1976 (and extensively revised thereafter)[57] the IPU "is the international organization of the Parliaments of sovereign States."[58]

---

[51] Ibid., 140.

[52] Ibid., 150.

[53] Ibid., 150.

[54] Ibid., 153.

[55] Citing Martha 2010, p. 153.

[56] Schermers and Blokker 2011, §35.

[57] Statutes of the Inter-Parliamentarian Union (Adopted in 1976 and extensively revised in Oct. 1983, April 2003, and Oct. 2013). http://www.ipu.org/strct-e/statutes-new.htm.

[58] IPU Statutes. http://www.ipu.org/strct-e/statutes-new.htm#1.

While it may have been justified to classify the IPU as a non-governmental organization at the time it was founded, this classification is no longer appropriate. There are "still voices of doubt,"[59] yet the joint legal opinion of Ian Brownlie and Guy S. Goodwin-Gill convincingly shows that the IPU has "international legal personality and is an international organization *sui generis*, that is, it is an international parliamentary, political and representative organization."[60] They clearly state that "[t]he IPU is unique in its combination of aims and purposes with a representative character. It is distinguishable from non-governmental organizations and private voluntary organizations in its membership of parliaments, the public, legislative organs of States, rather than of private or personal interests."[61]

The principles formulated in the above legal opinion are of relevance well beyond the specific case of IPU in relation to which they were formulated. They have to be seen in the wider context highlighted by Slaughter that "[t]he state is not disappearing, but is disaggregating into its component institutions, which are increasingly interacting principally with their foreign counterparts across borders."[62] She states that "[l]ooking at the international system through the lens of unitary states leads us to focus on traditional international organizations and institutions created by and composed of formal state delegations," thinking of states as "aggregations of distinct institutions with separate roles and capacities—provides us a lens that allows us to see a new international landscape. Government networks pop up everywhere."[63]

Forms of cooperation of technical government agencies, sub-state entities, or regulatory agencies do not necessarily qualify for recognition as international organizations. However, the *ipso facto* exclusion of such forms of cooperation from the realm of international organizations for the sole reason that these were not government-initiated can no longer be justified. Instead, a better way is to consider their role and functions and the position which recognized subjects of international law have adopted in their regard, in order to determine whether they may qualify for recognition as international organizations.

Finally, the dichotomy of governmental and nongovernmental is not adequate to capture the legal nature of organizations like the Global Fund or the Gavi Alliance. While these organizations are incorporated under municipal law as NGOs or corporations, they enjoy international legal personality in accordance with their Headquarters Agreements and multilateral and bilateral agreements, and privileges and immunities in their host country and certain other countries. These organizations are best understood as a *sui generis* paradigm of organizational structure and as a new type of dual and hybrid international organization.

---

[59] See Kissling 2011. Footnote 50 with further references.

[60] I Brownlie and GS Goodwin-Gill, Statement 1, para 1.

[61] Ibid., para 11.

[62] Slaughter 2004, p. 18.

[63] Ibid., 13.

4.3.2 Implications for Organizations' Structure, Role and Functions

4.3.2.1 Forum and Service Institutions

The public and private distinction and governmental and nongovernmental dichotomy may have far-reaching implications regarding the organizations' structure, role and functions and operational activities.

One of the distinctions in literature is that between forum and service institutions.[64] The traditional function of international organizations was "to provide the representatives of members with a forum for discussion on the matters covered by their constituent Documents."[65] This continues to be one of the main functions of many international organizations and bodies, such as in the case of the World Health Organization (WTO) and United Nations Conference on Trade and Development (UNCTAD) whose main focus is on forum-related activities.

Nevertheless, there is an increasing realization that international organizations (and their governing bodies) should not only be forums for states, but should aspire to be platforms for a variety of stakeholders, including civil society and the private sector. This question is articulated with different connotations regarding boards of governors, assemblies or similar bodies which are the first tier of the traditional governance structure of international organizations, and for the boards of directors, councils of ambassadors or similar bodies which are the second tier. The third tier of the traditional governance structure of international organizations is the secretariat.

As regards boards of governors and assemblies which are the highest decision-making bodies in traditional three-tier structures, their ability to provide strategic guidance is increasingly being questioned, in particular, in the case of universal organizations. This has led in some organizations to proposals for far-reaching institutional reforms and has prompted others to move toward two-tier structures while substituting the plenary body with a forum involving a great variety of stakeholders (see Chap. 9 below).

Boards of directors or councils of ambassadors are generally bodies of limited membership, but may also be plenary bodies in which all members are represented, as will be discussed in Chap. 9 above. One core question to be addressed is whether it is still appropriate for governing bodies of international organizations (of limited membership or otherwise) to be exclusively or predominantly composed of state representatives, or whether it is advisable to transform such bodies into multi-actor institutions which give transnational actors, including the private sector, philanthropy and civil society and independent expert a voice in decision making. The latter approach is in the view of this author clearly preferable, at least for international organizations that rely on cooperation with a great variety of stakeholders.

---

64 See Majid 1996, p. 125.

65 Ibid.

4.3.2.2 International and Transnational Regulation and Standard Setting

In addition to forum-related activities, international organizations perform a range of other activities. In the specific context of this section, in particular, organizations' regulatory and standard-setting activities, as well as their service delivery and operational activities are of interest.

It is indicative of "a shift of power" from the nation state "towards international governance bodies and also to non-governmental bodies"[66] that regulation is no longer the exclusive domain of states but has become a core feature of transnational governance regimes. Cooperating "across borders in order to establish rules and standards of behavior accepted as legitimate", transnational actors "not only formulate norms, but also often have a key role in their enforcement."[67] Such transnational governance regimes "codify, monitor, and in some cases certify firms' compliance with labor, environmental, human rights, or other standards of accountability'."[68]

> They are transnational, rather than international, in the sense that their effects cross borders, but are not constituted through the cooperation of states as reflected in treaties (the latter being the principal territory of international law). They are nonstate (or private, as we prefer) in the sense that key actors in such regimes include both civil society or non-governmental organisations (NGOs) and firms (both individually and in associations).[69]

Standard setting, which is the core function of some organizations, is relegated in certain cases to a commission, or an organization specifically established for that purpose, or carried out pursuant to a convention. The Codex Alimentarius Commission, the International Office of Epizootics (OIE), International Plant Protection Convention (IPPC) that produce "international standards" regarding food safety, animal health, and plant health respectively, may serve as examples. Alternatively, standardization may be entirely performed by NGOs such as the International Organization for Standardization (ISO) which

> is not an intergovernmental organization, such as the United Nations, constituted by multilateral agreement whose members are states represented by governmental authorities. Although the ISO member from some countries is a governmental entity such as a national standardizing body, ISO is primarily a forum for coordinating standardizing efforts by private business.[70]

The thousands of standards elaborated in the context of ISO are indicative of the importance and spread of transnational private regulation. Private standards "do not simply add new rules for previously ungoverned phenomena. Rather, they add an

66 Scott et al. 2011, p. 1.

67 Jönsson 2013, pp. 12–13.

68 Scott et al. 2011, p. 3.

69 Ibid.

70 Wirth 2009, p. 81.

additional layer of rules for phenomena that are already embedded in complex political, legal, and regulatory orders."[71] The case of ISO is also interesting as it shows that the conceptual difference between legally binding standards and voluntary non-binding standards increasingly get blurred.

While ISO and other voluntary standards are not legally binding as a matter of principle, they may have legal effects if incorporated or referenced in national legislative acts or regulations or in international agreements. There is an increasing number of cases were private standards are incorporated in rules issued by public authorities. In particular, in the United States, this has become an important matter.[72] Moreover, such standards are used and referenced by international organizations and transnational regulatory networks "through a variety of mechanisms. Examples include the Financial Services Board or FSB's incorporation of international auditing standards, the Basel Committee's reference to credit rating agencies, the WTO agreements' connection with international standards established by private bodies and the EU endorsement of international accounting standards."[73]

The Director General of the WTO emphasized the "vital relationship" between WTO and ISO and the "complementary nature of the work done by the WTO and ISO" and stated in this context:

> In fact, it is the very reason that two key WTO Agreements (the Agreement on Technical Barriers to Trade[74] [TBT] and the Agreement on Sanitary and Phytosanitary Measures [SPS]),[75] explicitly urge regulators to base their measures on relevant international standards to avoid unnecessary barriers to trade. These Agreements go as far as to say that measures that are based on relevant international standards *are assumed to be in compliance with WTO rules*.[76]

The use of ISO standards is being considered in the WTO by its TBT and SPS committees with somewhat different connotations. While the WTO SPS Committee in essence refers to the Codex Alimentarius Commission, World Organization for Animal Health (OIE) and International Plant Protection Convention (IPPC) as producing international standards, the WTO TBT Committee does not link the question whether a standard is international to any specific entities or to the legal nature of the entity that has prepared a standard:

> The WTO TBT Committee has agreed on principles and procedures that should be observed when such 'international standards' are elaborated. In these principles for

[71] Bartley 2011, p. 518. http://www7.tau.ac.il/ojs/index.php/til/article/view/784/742.

[72] Strauss 2013, p. 502, ss. http://scholarship.law.wm.edu/cgi/viewcontent.cgi?article=1681&context=wmborj.

[73] Bellis 2010, p. 4.

[74] Uruguay Round Agreement. Agreement on Technical Barriers to Trade. https://www.wto.org/english/docs_e/legal_e/17-tbt_e.htm.

[75] The WTO Agreement on the Application of Sanitary and Phytosanitary Measures (SPS Agreement). https://www.wto.org/english/tratop_e/sps_e/spsagr_e.htm.

[76] "Pascal Lamy cites 'vital relationship' between WTO and ISO". ISO. 21 Sept. 2011. https://www.iso.org/news/2011/09/Ref1463.html.

> 'international standards', no distinction is made between standards developed by international governmental organizations, international non-governmental organizations or other 'private' organizations.[77]

Hence, for the WTO TBT Committee, it is the procedure adopted for preparing a standard rather than the legal nature of the agency that has prepared the standard which decides whether a standard can be classified as international. Thus, a standard may be classified as international if even if it is established by a non-governmental or private-sector entity.

4.3.3 External Cooperation with the Private Sector and Institutionalized Participation

Cooperation with the private sector and other stakeholders in the delivery of services and in the planning and implementation of the organization's operational activities may substantially strengthen the impact of the organization's activities. Traditionally, cooperation with the private sector is conducted through external mechanisms. In addition to such external mechanisms, institutionalized forms of participation involving full, associate or partial membership of transnational actors, and alliances and partnerships between public and private in dual and hybrid organizations may be ways of enhancing organizations outcomes.

Cooperation with the private sector is of particular importance in the case of international financial institutions, including the multilateral development banks (MDBs), which have created various institutional paradigms for operationalizing such cooperation. Some organizational groups, such as the World Bank Group, have created affiliated organizations with proper juridical personality under international law to conduct their private sector operations. The IFC is one such example.[78] Other organizations (e.g. ADB), administer concessional and non-concessional resources under one institutional roof and have created a private sector operations department without proper juridical personality to conduct their private sector operations. While this makes it more difficult to isolate the liabilities resulting from private sector operations, it potentially leaves a wide scope of cooperation between public and private sector operations, given the fact that private sector operations are not insulated through a separate legal personality from public sector operations. Such synergies so far have only been explored to a limited extent.

The mechanisms mentioned above involve an external relationship of the private sector and other transnational actors as partners of international organizations and recipients of their financing in financial transactions, operational activities and capacity-building measures and other activities. Transnational actors are regularly

---

[77] ISO 2010, p. 3.

[78] See the International Finance Corporation website. http://www.ifc.org/wps/wcm/connect/corp_ext_content/ifc_external_corporate_site/home.

consulted and provide advice, but they generally do not have any formal role in organizations' decision-making procedures. The problem is that such external cooperation mechanisms, while important, may at times have only limited impact, as cooperation is not continuous but sporadic and geared to specific outcomes rather than to the work of the organization in general. Against this background, institutionalized participation mechanisms involving full or partial membership of private sector institutions, philanthropy, or other stakeholders in international organizations may have a stronger impact, as they entail a long-term commitment to support a specific organization.

The Green Climate Fund (GCF) epitomizes a new approach to cooperation with the private sector. While transnational actors do not take part in any formal decision-making procedures, the private sector and civil society representatives have, as "active observers",[79] the right to speak at Board meetings on similar terms and conditions as Board members. In addition, the GCF has a "private sector facility that enables it to directly and indirectly finance private sector mitigation and adaptation activities at the national, regional and international levels."[80] Such facility seeks to "fund and mobilize institutional investors and leverage GCF's funds to encourage corporates to co-invest" and is "actively engaging with pension funds, insurance companies, corporations, local and regional financial intermediaries, and the capital markets."[81] Nevertheless, private sector investments are not limited to the private sector facility, but are supposed to be mainstreamed in all GCF operations. As GCF will provide all initial financing through accredited entities, collaboration with accredited entities offers opportunity for the Fund to scale up its financing.

Dual and hybrid organizations and multi-actor funds such as the Global Fund and alliances such as the Gavi Vaccine Alliance bring together, in addition to states, a variety of other actors and give those a voice in their governing bodies; they may be seen as the epitome of institutionalized forms of public-private partnerships and participation of transnational actors.

However, institutionalized forms of participation which involve full, associate or partial membership of transnational actors may also exist in traditional international organizations with treaty foundation and should be considered as a design option for any new international organization of that kind which is established. Full membership of private sector entities and non-state actors, including foundations, should be encouraged where they meet all requisite requirements of an acceptable donor and are able to support an organization on a continuous basis and in a sustained manner. Otherwise, special types of membership should be considered, such as in the case of ITU which "brings together more than 700 Sector Members

---

79 Governing Instrument of the Green Climate Fund, para 16.

80 Governing Instrument of the Green Climate Fund, para 41.

81 "What We Do: Private Sector Facility". Green Climate Fund. http://www.greenclimate.fund/what-we-do/private-sector-facility.

and Associates from industry, international and regional organizations, as well as academia."[82]

One advantage of institutionalized participation of transnational actors is that such participation does not need to be limited to representation in organizations' governing bodies. While such representation is important in that it transforms the organization concerned to a multi-actor institution, the full potential of institutionalized forms of cooperation can only be realized when there is interaction with the organization at all levels, including, wherever feasible and appropriate, secondment of staff of private sector entities and other transnational actors who have specific knowledge or capacities otherwise not available in the organization. Such secondment may substantially expand the knowledge base of an international organization and enhance its ability to propose new and innovative solutions.

Implementation of the above proposals requires far-reaching changes to conceptual frameworks of public international law. International law and international institutional law need to evolve to cover forms of cooperation between sub-state actors and regulatory agencies which are now often deemed to be outside the margins of international law. It is also necessary to recognize that a new type of dual and hybrid organization has emerged which is established under national law, but with recognition of international legal personality and with privileges and immunities under the law of their host country and certain other countries.

Transforming international organizations in forums and platforms involving sub-state and non-state acts requires a fundamental reorientation of organizations' visions, functions, and operational priorities.

In existing organizations, allowing for institutionalized participation of transnational actors in governing bodies will generally require amendment to the constituent agreement, which is a formidable task, given the required qualified majorities. However, as will be shown in Chap. 9, to a more limited extent, such participation can also be achieved by adopting as a matter of policy secondary governance structures under umbrella arrangements approved by the organization's governing bodies.

4.3.4 Funding Arrangements

The public-private distinction has traditionally been translated in organizations funding structures and operational frameworks. Hence, most international organizations still rely on their state members as the main source for their funding. Often, they have not even explored the full potential of funding opportunities involving civil society, the private sector, and philanthropy. At a time when the assistance provided by some philanthropic organizations by far exceeds that of many states

[82] "Sector Members, Associates and Academia". ITU. http://www.itu.int//en/membership/Pages/sector-members.aspx.

and official resources available are increasingly becoming scarce, funding from philanthropy and the private sector may substantially enhance the funding of international organizations.

However, as will be shown in Chap. 9, for attracting financing from sources as mentioned above, international organizations often have to change their outlook and *modus operandi*. While international organizations are sometimes reluctant to undertake the required fundamental review and reorientation of their policies, attracting funding from institutional investors, private-sector entities and other stakeholders has the potential to substantially enhance their impact. Moreover, in certain cases, international organizations may derive their entire operational funding from institutional investors and other private-sector entities.

4.4 Constitution and Constitutionalization

The establishment of, and membership in, international organizations are intrinsically related to concepts of constitution and constitutionalization. While there are many theories on the legal nature of the constituent agreement establishing an international organization, the most widely recognized approach appears to be predicated on the assumption that the treaty establishing an international organization has a hybrid character as a treaty and as the organization's constitution. Peters epitomizes that approach,[83] and the first part of this section will review its implications, as well as highlight the transformational potential of international agreements.

This traditional approach is predicated on the assumption that an international organization is established by way of treaty which establishes a new subject of international law. The main assumptions of the traditional theory, as formulated by Peters, is that the founding documents of an international organization may create a new political actor and a new subject of international law.[84] In the context, Peters asserts that by signing a treaty which is the constituent agreement of an international organization, states become members rather than being merely contracting parties."[85]

Consistent with the above, the term "Constitution" is widely used to denote the constituent treaty of an international organization referred to in Article 5 of the Vienna Convention on the Law of Treaties. The "Constitution" of the International

[83] See Peters 2013, pp. 1–57, with further references.

[84] "Die Besonderheit der Gründungsdokumente ist dass sie einen neuen politischen Akteur und in der Regel ein neues Völkerrechtssubjekt (also als Zurechnungsobjekt völkerrechtlicher Rechte und Pflichten) konstituieren. Gleichzeitig wird damit eine eigene und möglicherweise eigenständige Rechtsordnung erzeugt. Diese Wirkungen werden als institutionelle und konstitutionelle bezeichnet." Ibid., 6.

[85] "Die Staaten warden mit dem Vertragsabschluss, der gleichzeitig eine Gründungsakt ist, von blossen Vertragsparteien zu Mitgliedern." Ibid., 54.

Labour Organization and that of the International Telecommunication Union or the International Organization for Migration, *inter alia*, epitomize this approach. Nevertheless, while treaties are the traditional way of establishing international organizations, the treaty format is often not suitable, particularly for addressing concerns of an economic nature, or for the creation of new funding structures, nor does the constitution of an organization need to take the form of treaty. Hence, a number of organizations not established by treaty have emerged, as well as new dual or hybrid types of international organizations incorporated under national law but with privileges and immunities under international law and international organizations established as trust funds. Also, whether a new subject of international law is created is, in essence, a matter of fact.

As indicated by Gaja:

> Even if a treaty provision were intended to confer international personality on a particular organization, the acquisition of legal personality would depend on the actual establishment of the organization. It is clear that an organization merely existing on paper cannot be considered a subject of international law.[86]

Hence, it is not the constituent agreement *per se* but the effective implementation of the provisions of that agreement and the actual establishment of the organization which determine whether an organization has international legal personality and may be recognized as a new subject of international law. It is one of the themes of this book that a "subject of international law" does not necessarily need to be established by the constituent agreement of an organization. Also, there may be subjects of international law which are not endowed with international legal personality. Further, while a treaty may guarantee the autonomy of the organization, there are other ways to do so. Finally, while the parties to the constituent agreement of an organization may become members, membership is not, in fact, necessary, as shown by several examples where parties to the constituent agreement did not become members or where international organizations do not have a formal membership structure.

Constitutionalization goes substantially beyond the traditional concept of the constituent agreement as a hybrid of treaty and constitution. As highlighted by Peters, the main difference is that the

> traditional institutional-constitutional topos did not introduce a *constitutionalist* approach to the law of international organizations. The constitutionalist approach—by contrast—seeks to identify and to advocate the application of constitutionalist principles, such as the rule of law, checks and balances, human rights protection, and possibly also democracy, to the law of international organizations.[87]

There is a vast literature on constitutionalization. While this literature cannot be analyzed in any detail, it is useful to highlight the specific ramifications which

[86] G Gaja (2003). "First Report on Responsibility of International Organizations", (Doc. A/CN.4/532, 26 March), para 19. http://legal.un.org/ilc/documentation/english/a_cn4_532.pdf.

[87] Peters 2012, p. 204.

the discussion on constitutionalization has for the topic of this book. Constitutionalization is relevant in this context to a variety of matters, including the standards applied by international organizations in admitting members which may include human rights considerations or minority protection. It is intrinsically related to the "fragmentation, pluralization, verticalization (and privatization) of international law" as has been shown by Klabbers.[88] It is also related to the dispersion of authority already highlighted above and in that sense requires a wider definition of the notion of "subject of international law". It has a dimension relating to the definition of the role of the private sector and the transformation of private-sector institutions into international organizations. Finally, constitutionalization and legitimacy are directly linked. These issues will be further reviewed in the following.

4.4.1 Treaty and Constitution

Treaties traditionally have been the most important source of international law. The Vienna Convention on the Law of Treaties (VCLT) and the Vienna Convention on the Law of Treaties between States and International Organizations or between International Organizations (VCLTIO) both recognize in their preambles "the consensual nature of treaties and their ever-increasing importance as a source of international law". It is important to note that in spite of its importance, the VCLT "cannot be understood as a comprehensive source of law dealing with all aspects of the general concept on the function on treaties in the international system,"[89] as it "provides only rules on, *inter alia*, the conclusion, effect and termination of treaties, but not on their content; with the exception of Article 53 of the VCLT (jus cogens) the content of a treaty and its substantial impact on international relations can be freely determined by the contracting parties as part of their contractual autonomy."[90]

The scope of matters covered by international agreements has evolved over time. While "the period following the Westphalian Peace can be characterized as a productive time of treaty making with, however, a limited scope on political issues of a reciprocal nature," the nineteenth century marked a dramatic change "as the original age of internationalization;"[91] it also brought about the "well-known establishment of international organizations through treaties",[92] which subsequently became the standard mode of establishing international organizations.

Article 5 of the VCLT provides:

---

[88] Klabbers 2011, pp. 11–19.

[89] Tietje 1999, p. 27.

[90] Ibid., 27.

[91] Ibid., 31.

[92] Ibid., 32.

> The present Convention applies to any treaty which is the constituent instrument of an international organization and to any treaty adopted within an international organization without prejudice to any relevant rules of the organization.

While the constituent agreements of international organizations are traditionally ratified as a treaty by the legislatures of the member countries of the organization concerned, the question arises "whether, or to what extent, the constituent instrument of an international organization is to be regarded as an international treaty on a parity with any other multilateral treaty."[93]

4.4.2 *Hybrid Character of Constituent Agreements Adopted as a Treaty*

As Peters indicates, constituent agreements have two facets: She views the treaty facet as a cipher for a horizontal legal instrument with strict inter-partes effect, depending on the will of the creators, who only bind themselves thereby (temporarily). In contrast, "constitution", in her view, is a cipher for a vertical legal act with *erga omnes* effect, which to a certain extent can develop autonomously from the producers.[94]

As set out by Peters, the qualification of the constituent agreement as a hybrid of treaty and constitution has a series of implications, notably for the acceptance of reservations to the constituent agreement and for the interpretation of the constituent agreement.[95]

In this context, the International Court of Justice in its Advisory Opinion on the "Legality of the Use by a State of Nuclear Weapons in Armed Conflict"[96] stated that

> the constituent instruments of international organizations are also treaties of a particular type; their object is to create new subjects of law endowed with a certain autonomy, to which the parties entrust the task of realizing common goals. Such treaties can raise specific problems of interpretation owing to their character which is conventional and at the same time institutional; the very nature of the organization created, the objectives which have been assigned to it by its founders, the imperatives associated with the effective

93 Rosenne 1989, p. 181.

94 "Hierbei ist die Vertragsfacette eine Chiffre für eine horizontales Rechtsinstrument mit strikter Inter-partes Wirkung, in Abhängigkeit vom Willen der Erzeuger, die sich hiermit lediglich (temporär begrenzt) selbst binden. Demgegenüber ist, Verfassung' eine Chiffre für einen vertikalen Rechtsakt mit Erga-omnes Wirkung, der sich zu einem gewissen Grad autonom von den Erzeugern entwickeln kann." Peters 2013, p. 10.

95 Ibid., 13, s.s.

96 "Legality of the Use by a State of Nuclear Weapons in Armed Conflict", Advisory Opinion, ICJ. Reports 1996, 66, para 19. http://www.icj-cij.org/files/case-related/93/093-19960708-ADV-01-00-EN.pdf.

performance of its functions, as well as its own practice, are all elements which may deserve special attention when the time comes to interpret these constituent treaties.

The distinction between a constituent agreement and other multilateral treaties has implications at various levels. It is intrinsically related to the relationship between the international organization and its members, in particular, to the question of to what extent are members "Herren der Verträge", and to the ambivalent concept of international organizations as "institutionalised 'open' structures accommodating states, while at the same time they constitute independent legal entities."[97]

Admission to membership in an international organization is generally different from accession to a multilateral treaty. As stated by Rosenne, whenever

> a State exercises its right to become a party to an open or partially open treaty, the legal relationship established by the treaty will come into existence between that State and all the other States, both those which were previously parties and those which subsequently become parties to that treaty, in accordance with the treaty's terms for the entry into force of an accession or article 24, paragraph 3, of the Vienna Conventions. Reduced to its essentials, subsequent participation in an open treaty is a unilateral act undertaken in accordance with the terms of participation provisions of the treaty in question, which is to that extent a species of a treaty providing for rights for third States within the contemplation of article 36 of the Vienna Conventions.[98]

In the case of international organizations, subsequent membership is usually "only open to States meeting certain conditions, and admission consists of a dual process: (a) a unilateral application by the interested State submitted in due form, followed by (b) a determination by the competent organ or organs of the organization that the conditions are met and admitting the State to membership."[99]

However, the most important distinction relates to the "fundamental tension between the layered structure of international organisations and the one-dimensional law of treaties system. The law of treaties, given the nature of the contractual instrument, is strictly based on the principle of consensualism and by consequence is geared to equal legal partners. International organisations, however, are 'neither sovereign nor equal' [....]."[100]

4.4.3 Consensual Basis and the Transformational Potential of International Agreements

To a substantial extent, intergovernmental organizations established by a constituent agreement derive their authority from the consent of the Parties establishing

---

97 Brölmann 1999, p. 85.

98 Rosenne 1989, p. 214.

99 Rosenne 1989, pp. 214–215.

100 Brölmann 2007.

the organization. However, there is an inherent tension between that consensual basis and the transformative potential of international organizations, which are dynamic frameworks and which, over time, may change beyond recognition from the blueprint used for their establishment. In addition to the formal amendment of the constituent agreement,

> [c]onstitutional transformation can occur through the organs' exercise of their delegated powers at all levels of the system (as opposed to only the constituent level): through the enactment of important legislation, through the actions of the executive power, or through interpretation by the courts. Moreover it may occur through a variety of more subtle means, including longstanding usages, customs, and conventions of the constitution.[101]

Constitutional transformation generally connotes "two main kinds of change: the reordering of power among the organs of the organization (e.g. procedural adjustments, or the restructuring of checks and balances), or changes to the power of the organization as a whole, vis-à-vis the constituent power."[102] As highlighted by Julian Arato, the "material effect of a constitutional transformation can be just as profound as any change achieved through formal amendment."[103]

The same informal process that contributes to the autonomy of an organization can thus "undermine the consensual grounds of its authority."[104] This relates to the constitutional interpretation of constituent agreements and the provisions on their amendment. A number of organizations have changed beyond recognition since the time they were established. Such "constitutional creep"[105] is facilitated by the authentic or creative interpretation of the constituent agreement. As indicated by Arato,

> Constitutional interpretation in international organizations thus presents a familiar paradox: on the one hand, in light of the important role of these organizations in supranational governance, there is a perceived need for them to employ a flexible approach to their functions in a changing legal and political environment; on the other hand, in light of the very same importance and sensitivity of the areas regulated by these treaties, there is a countervailing pressure to stick to the bargain struck [….]. Informal change may indeed yield desirable results—any particular such development will have to be judged in its own right, case-by-case. But the specter of consent always lurks in the background: irrespective of its results, informal transformation carries in its wake the potential to produce serious problems of legitimacy and accountability.[106]

In principle, similar issues arise in the case of those organizations which allow amendment to the constituent agreement by decision of a qualified majority of the governing body of the organization without need for the consent of the parties to the constituent agreement. Nevertheless, the transformational potential of such

---

101 Arato 2013, p. 304.

102 Ibid., 305.

103 Ibid., 304–305.

104 Ibid., 291.

105 Regarding mission creep, see, *inter alia*, Hockett 2002, p. 178.

106 Arato 2013, pp. 291–292.

amendments is somewhat mitigated by the fact that amendments to constituent agreements are rare, as qualified majorities, while guaranteeing protection of minorities, are formidable obstacles for institutional reform.

As may be seen from the above, constituent agreements and other international agreements have substantial transformational potential and give substantial room for international organizations to expand their functions and respond to new needs by way of authentic interpretation of the governing instrument. Nevertheless, there are limits, as authentic interpretation is limited to matters of law; moreover, there is a fine line between matters which can be addressed by an authentic interpretation of the governing instrument and those which concern fundamental features of the governing instrument and accordingly, require amendment of the agreement.[107]

The case of the World Trade Organization (WTO) is very interesting as "[m]ultilateral instruments and procedures, some of them fairly informal, may be used to bring into WTO law new norms and interpretations, as long as the resulting rule is perceived as reflecting a common understanding of the membership."[108]

The transformational potential is particularly acute in the case of decisions taken under a framework agreement such as the United Nations Framework Agreement on Climate Change (UNFCCC).

> There are two main ways in which law making pursuant to a framework agreement might differ from the standard treaty model. First, we may be witnessing gradual shifts in the location of lawmaking decisions from the states parties to an agreement to the agreement's plenary body, its Conference (Meeting) of the Parties (COP). Second, there may be corresponding shifts in the consent basis for the norms and standards that are developed through the deliberations and decisions of COPs.[109]

As regards multilateral environmental agreements, Brunnée says that these "have become the setting for a broadening range of lawmaking methods that facilitate wide-ranging international standard setting."[110] In this context, she discusses "the attendant approaches to consent by individual states" and whether formal consent still anchors "most treaty-based environmental law making".[111]

The recourse to a framework model has connotations in three respects regarding the further development of the treaty regime:

> First, its sets an institutionalized background to the ongoing discussions and future meetings of State representatives. Second, it establishes the principles and decision-making procedures on the basis of which future agreements shall be achieved. Moreover, at least in broad terms, *ratione materiae*, it defines the boundaries of the agenda and the priorities to be addressed, and *ratione personae*, it sets eligibility criteria for the various participants.

---

[107] See Droesse 2011, pp. 139–140, with further references (hereinafter: "Organizational Structures").

[108] Vidigal 2013, p. 1030, with further detailed references.

[109] Brunnée 2005, p. 102.

[110] Ibid., 103.

[111] Ibid., 103.

> With these treaties that are 'constitutive, rather than regulatory' States establish a process for the subsequent development of substantive obligations, rather than an immediate set of specific substantive rules.[112]

As regards the law processes of multilateral environmental agreements, one of their "distinctive features" relates to the fact that they "take place under the *aegis* of the treaty's institutional core, the COP."[113] While "COPs of multilateral environmental agreements regularly engage in a number of activities, some of which follow the traditional model of international law as based on the consent of states, such as formally amending the treaty text, amending appendices or annexes, and concluding protocols," much of the discussion relates to the COP "resolutions and decisions that do not require the formal consent of states."[114] As indicated by Wiersma,

> COP decisions and resolutions are almost invariably tightly connected with the original treaty and enrich it by deepening and thickening the parties' obligations. They deepen the obligations by contributing to implementation and effectiveness. They thicken the obligations by adding to the text of the original treaty through interpretation and guidance.
>
> This tight connection to the treaty and the deepening and thickening effect makes COP activity hard to evaluate according to our traditional classifications of the sources of international legal obligation: treaties and customary international law.[115]

At times, COPs adopt resolutions or take decisions regarding matters which are not expressly contemplated in the underlying treaty, based on the mandate given to them "to promote the effective implementation of the Convention."[116] As indicated by Brunnée, "to the extent that COPs are assuming more influential law-making roles, legitimacy considerations are emerging as increasingly important topics of discussion."[117] Brunnée, in this context, raises the question whether "COPs have begun to play a global legislative role."[118]

One important issue is whether a COP may create an international organization with international legal personality or whether such personality needs to be conferred to the organization by its member states. This issue is contentious, in particular, in case of the Green Climate Fund, where the UNFCCC does not expressly provide, and was not amended to provide, for any reference to the establishment of the Green Climate Fund.

---

112 Jacur 2013, p. 24.

113 Brunnée 2002, p. 4.

114 Wiersema 2009, p. 74.

115 Ibid., 75.

116 For example, UNFCCC, Article 7, para 2, provides: "The Conference of the Parties, as the supreme body of this Convention, shall keep under regular review the implementation of the Convention and any related legal instruments that the Conference of the Parties may adopt, and shall make, within its mandate, the decisions necessary to promote the effective implementation of the Convention…."

117 Brunnée 2002, p. 5.

118 Ibid., 6.

4.4.4 *The Limited Relevance of the Treaty Format*

Laurence Boisson de Chazournes, while recalling that "treaties have traditionally been seen as among the main vehicles for the rule of law,"[119] states: "A challenging question at the beginning of this twenty-first century is whether this still is the case, and if not, what the reasons are."[120] She sets out that "the reasons for not having a treaty deal with a topic are not structural, so as to say, but of a strategic nature"[121] and indicates as one example that "international economic and financial matters in some of their aspects are not among the most suited for treaty regulation."[122]

Moreover, there are a range of other cases where the treaty-format is not chosen, e.g., because "it makes more sense to enshrine good practices and behavior modelling provisions in a non-binding document"[123] or in "other circumstances, States might show no political willingness to negotiate a treaty (often referred to in such circumstances as a hard law instrument to display its mandatory nature)."[124]

The above findings are supported by those of Pauwelyn, Wessel and Wouters, whose research confirms that "[f]ormal international law is stagnating in terms both of quantity and quality. It is increasingly superseded by 'informal international lawmaking' involving new actors, new processes, and new outputs."[125] They support this by evidence on the "slowdown" in formal international law-making.[126]

Neuhold stresses that "[t]reaties often fail to meet four requirements for an effective legal regime:

(1) speed: in a rapidly evolving international system, quick responses to new challenges are needed, also at the normative level;
(2) clarity and uniformity: the contents of legal rules ought to be clear-cut, unambiguous and identical for all parties;
(3) universality of participation: many legal regimes have to be applied by all or almost all states (and other subjects of international law) in order to achieve genuine solutions to global problems; [and]

---

[119] Boisson de Chazournes 2005, p. 463.

[120] Ibid., 463.

[121] Ibid., 464.

[122] Ibid., 464.

[123] Ibid., 465.

[124] Ibid., 466.

[125] Pauwelyn et al. 2014, p. 734.

[126] "For each decade since the 1950s, the number of new multilateral treaties deposited with the UN Secretary General was around 35. In the 10 years between 2000 and 2010, this number dropped quite dramatically to 20. In the preceding five decades it had never been below 34. Between 2005 and 2010, only nine new multilateral treaties were deposited; in 2011, 2012, and 2013 not a single one. The broader UN Treaty Series database confirms this downward trend as of the 2000s, both for bilateral treaties (12,566 concluded in the 1990s; only 9484 concluded in the 2000s) and multilateral treaties (406 entries in the 1990s; down to 262 in the 2000). Pauwelyn et al. 2014, pp. 734–735.

(4) flexibility and adaptability: rules may have to be quickly adjusted to changes in their non-legal environment."[127]

He elaborates on the "deficiencies of treaties with regard to these four requisites".[128]

This author has also shown with specific reference to concessional windows that during the third generation of such windows (which covers the 1980s and 1990s),

> the trend of establishing new international organizations and affiliates began to subside. While in the past, 'an organization was established almost automatically as soon as a new international problem and the need to cooperate were identified[,] [States instead] almost instinctively express[ed] their wish *not* to create a new organization if a new international problem and the need to cooperate present[ed] themselves.' Rather, states established 'autonomous institutional arrangements' (e.g., in the context of multilateral environmental conventions) and/or set up ad hoc financing frameworks, notably through trust funds.[129]

Other authors also note that there "is strong evidence that traditional international lawmaking is in a process of stagnation, both quantitatively (number of treaties) and qualitatively (thin state consent followed by domestic rubber-stamping by parliament)"[130] They observe:

> Whereas traditional international law is driven by thin (state) consent, new forms of cooperation are increasingly based on thick (stakeholder) consensus. No inherent or automatic benefits come with being part of international law. Yet, to conclude a treaty, in particular a multilateral one within a formal IO requires huge transaction costs, and once concluded is hard to adapt to changing circumstances. In the end, new forms of cooperation can be more (rather than less) accountable or responsive to a broader audience and better (rather than worse) adapted to the needs of modern society. To that extent, traditional international law is no longer the first-best option to which soft or informal law can only aspire.[131]

It is an important development that increasingly institutionalized forms of cooperation are agreed upon by, or based on, agreements between central banks, ministries of finance or national aid agencies.[132] The Articles of AMRO Limited and CGIF discussed below are some of many examples. Traditional unitary concepts of treaty-making do not offer an adequate conceptual framework for analyzing the nature and legal effects of such types of agreements; these raise "fundamental legal issues" as is underlined by the fact that the Office of Legal Affairs of the UN (OLA) has already stated more than 40 years ago in relation to a "draft of an Asian

---

127 Neuhold 2005, p. 40.

128 Ibid., 40–47.

129 Droesse 2011, p. 16, citing N. Blokker "Proliferation of International Organizations and Exploratory Introduction".

130 Pauwelyn et al. 2014, p. 762.

131 Ibid., 750–751.

132 See in detail, Martha 2015, pp. 22–50.

Clearing Union Agreement to be concluded between 'Central Banks and Monetary Authorities' of various countries."[133]

> The principle that an international legal person can be created by virtue of a treaty is, after all, nothing more than a rule of customary international law, and it may well be that a new customary rule of international law is emerging under which such a legal person could also be created by an agreement concluded solely by autonomous public entities, such an agreement being governed by international law pursuant to another new customary rule.[134]

Traditional concepts of treaty-making need to be amplified to reflect the development mentioned above, as well as other new paradigms of treaty making (e.g. the fact reviewed in Chap. 6 that an international organization such as the EU may have multiple legal personalities).

While this cannot be the place to attempt the development of such a new analytical framework, the question raised by the Office of Legal Affairs merits indeed further consideration. Moreover, it is necessary to take account of the fact that there may be organizations which are not established by a treaty or other agreement between governments or other state authorities.

4.4.5 Organizations Not Established by a Treaty

It is a corollary of the stagnation of formal international law-making noted above that states at times deliberately do not want to use the treaty format for creating new international organizations, either for political reasons or because of the often cumbersome and very time-consuming process of establishing an international organization by way of a treaty. This trend has accelerated during the last decades notably for the reason that the traditional paradigm of the international organization with treaty foundation is ill-suited for creating funding structures to respond quickly to emerging needs.

Hence, as will be discussed in further detail below, new paradigms of organizational structure have emerged which are widely recognized as intergovernmental or as international organizations even though they have no treaty foundation and, in certain cases, no international legal personality.

---

[133] "Fundamental legal issues raised by the draft of an Asian Clearing Union Agreement to be concluded between the "central banks and monetary authorities" of various countries—Question of the law governing such an agreement—Question whether the Clearing Union thus established would be endowed with legal personality and could claim privileges and immunities—Determination of the entities eligible to become parties to the Agreement." *United Nations Juridical Yearbook.* 1971, 215–218, 215. http://legal.un.org/docs/?path=../unjuridicalyearbook/pdfs/english/by_volume/1971/chpVI.pdf&lang=EF.

[134] Ibid., 218.

4.4.6 Legal Implications of Constitutions Not Adopted as a Treaty

Constituent agreements of international organizations generally define their legal status and organizational and institutional structure, powers and composition of organs, procedures for accession to membership, voting procedures and qualified majorities, and operational modalities, and strike an equilibrium of power between the members of the organization and the various organs of the organization. In the case of constitutions adopted as a treaty, the constituent agreement or certain parts thereof (e.g., those regarding the legal status and privileges and immunities) often have the force of law in member countries. Moreover, they may provide for the establishment of a new subject of international law. However, the constitution of an organization does not need to be adopted as a treaty. A constitution adopted by a resolution of a conference or by the decision of a governing body of an organization can establish an internal legal order of an organization and regulate its institutional and governance structure (including membership, competences of organs, voting rights and other internal matter) to the same effect as constitutions adopted as a treaty. Moreover, constitutions which are not adopted by a treaty may be the basis of international action as will be shown in detail in the following.

4.4.7 Examples of Constitutions Not Adopted as a Treaty

The Constitution adopted by the INTERPOL General Assembly at its 25th session in 1965[135] contains provisions regarding the organizational, institutional and governance structure of the organization comparable with the constitutions of traditional organizations with treaty foundation.

The situation is similar in the case of IPU. As indicated by Brownlie and Goodwin-Gill in their joint legal opinion:

> While there is no treaty foundation as such to the IPU, the IPU Statutes, as adopted and amended from time to time by the membership, play an equivalent constitutional role. That is to say, the Statutes (1) describe the character of the organization and its object and purpose; (2) provide for membership and lay down the procedure for affiliation and suspension; (3) establish and determine the structure and functions of the organs of the IPU, namely, the Inter-Parliamentary Conference, the Inter-Parliamentary Council, the Executive Committee, and the Secretariat; (4) regulate issues of representation and voting in the relevant organs; (5) prescribe authority in budgetary matters; and (6) establish the IPU's internal legal order.[136]

---

[135] Constitution of the ICPO-INTERPOL. http://www.interpol.int/About-INTERPOL/Legal-materials/The-Constitution.

[136] Brownlie and Goodwin-Gill, para 11.

As regards the GCF, the Governing Instrument which was approved by Decision 3/CP.17 by the Conference of the Parties (COP) to the United Nations Framework Convention on Climate Change may be seen as the equivalent of a constitution.

The same can also be maintained with regard to constituent instruments of certain organizations established as trust funds which may qualify for recognition as an international organization based on their functions, irrespective of whether they were established by a treaty and possess international legal personality. There is a range of theories on the legal qualification the Instrument for the Establishment of the Restructured Global Environment Facility (GEF Instrument).[137] Some view the GEF Instrument as a treaty on the grounds that following negotiations to restructure the Global Environment Facility (GEF) concluded at a GEF Participants meeting in Geneva, Switzerland, in March 1994, the GEF Instrument was accepted by representatives of 73 States, thus "transforming the GEF from an experiment into a permanent program."[138] However, such acceptance does not give the GEF Instrument the character of a treaty, nor can it be considered as being the equivalent of a treaty. While, as shown by Ragazzi,[139] there are divergent views on the classification of the GEF Instrument among the UN and World Bank, there is general agreement that the GEF does not possess legal personality. This author agrees with Freestone that the GEF Instrument is best classified as a "*sui generis* document which does not follow the format of an international treaty."[140] However, whether the GEF can be classified as an international organization does not depend on the classification of the GEF Instrument as a treaty.

There may be a difference between the legal act establishing the organization and the legal act establishing its governance structure. For instance, prior to the establishment of the ASEAN+3 Macroeconomic Research Office (AMRO) as an international organization with treaty foundation, its governance structure was set out in the "Articles of Agreement in respect of the ASEAN+3 Macroeconomic Research Office" which did not meet the traditional requirements for classification as treaty as they deliberately did not involve governments but only ministries of finance or central banks. The above agreement determined the governance of AMRO Ltd. and for that reason, may be considered as its constitution, but it did not establish the organization itself, which was actually established as a company limited by guarantee in Singapore.

Similarly, the Articles of Agreement of CGIF were not ratified by all contributing countries and do not qualify for recognition as a treaty for that reason. Nevertheless, they may be seen as the constitution of the CGIF. While the Articles of Agreement determined a quasi-equity structure and the governance structure of the CGIF, they did not establish the CGIF which was created as an ADB trust fund without legal personality.

---

[137] See Ragazzi 2011, pp. 486–488.

[138] Ibid., 486.

[139] Ibid., 486–487.

[140] Freestone 2007, p. 1081.

4.4.8 Rule of Law

As international organizations are creations of law, their normative structure needs to be consistent with the rule of law. Their constitutions are the supreme norms under a normative structure comprising various layers of legislation which need to be consistent with the constitution and other fundamental legal acts (e.g. bylaws, rules of procedure of governing bodies, etc.).

The case of the EU is special as there is both an internal hierarchy relating to the European Community Law and an external hierarchy between the European Community law and the laws of EU member countries.[141]

In principle, any bylaws, statutes, rules of procedure or similar instruments of general purport need to be interpreted in a manner consistent with the constituent instrument. Similarly, decisions of governing bodies should be consistent with both the constituent instrument, statutes, bylaws, rules of procedures, or similar instruments or general application. However, the issue cannot be merely reduced to that of a hierarchy of norms. As has been shown by Gold in his paper on the "Rule of Law" in the IMF, main issues discussed during the process leading to the establishment of the IMF were "the extent to which international norms should be accepted or discretion retained by members and the advisability of choosing between firm norms and the exercise of discretion by a new organization."[142] This relates to the extent to which mandatory and permissive norms create rights and obligations for the organization and its members, and the extent to which norms govern the organization's relations with non-members and, in general, to the manner in which decisions are taken in an international organization.[143] In particular, it is related to the manner and the extent to which international norms can be adapted to changing circumstances.[144] Thus, it is not merely the hierarchy of norms but the normative structure of an organization which defines the relation of the organization with its members and non-members.

At times, the relationship between the constituent instrument and other rules may have a horizontal and in addition to a vertical dimension. The GCF may serve as an example:

> The Governing Instrument provides in paragraph 17 that 'Additional Rules of Procedure will be developed by the Board'. The reference to 'Additional Rules of Procedure' denotes the fact that such rules are intended to supplement rather than implement the provisions contained in the Governing Instrument.[145]

---

[141] See, with further references, Wölker 2007, pp. 32–56.

[142] Gold recalls that in his proposal for a Clearing Union, Keynes expressed similar concerns. Gold 1980.

[143] See Gold 1980, pp. 7–11.

[144] Ibid., 11–26.

[145] GCF (2012) Additional Rules of Procedure of the Board (GCF/B.02–12/02, 8 Oct.), para 1. http://www.greenclimate.fund/documents/20182/24928/GCF_B.02-12_02_-_Additional_Rules_

Constitutions which do not have the hybrid status of a treaty may also create a hierarchy of laws, and policies and other rules need to be in conformity with the legal instruments. There is a hierarchy of norms in INTERPOL which is comparable to that of traditional treaty-based organizations, specifically, between its Constitution and its General Regulations which establish additional rules regarding the General Assembly and General Secretariat. Article 1 of its General Regulations[146] expressly provides that the INTERPOL Constitution shall prevail "if there are any difference between the two." Moreover, the Rules of Procedure of the INTERPOL General Assembly[147] and the Rules of Procedure of the Executive Committee[148] highlight their conformity with the Constitution and General Regulations.

There is a hierarchy of norms between the Governing Instrument of the GCF and the additional rules of procedure of its Board.[149] GCF policies also need to be in conformity with the GCF Governing Instrument.

---

of_Procedure_of_the_Board.pdf/f4243d8e-6e23-4500-95a4-a1f71e605dea. See also the discussion in para 7 of that Board paper.

146 General Regulations of the ICPO-INTERPOL. Article 1. http://www.interpol.int/Media/Files/Legal-material/Reference-Documents/General-Regulations.

147 Article 1 of the General Regulations of the International Criminal Police Organization-Interpol state: "These General Regulations and Appendices have been adopted in accordance with Article 44 of the Constitution of the Organization. Should there be any differences between the two, the Constitution shall prevail."

148 Article 66 of the Rules of Procedure of the INTERPOL General Assembly provides: "The present Rules of Procedure are adopted under the authority of, and are subject to, the Constitution and the General Regulations. In the event of a conflict between a provision of the present Rules of Procedure and a provision of the Constitution or of the General Regulations, the Constitution and General Regulations shall prevail." Similarly, Article 12 of the Rules of Procedure of the Executive Committee provides: "The present Rules of Procedure, adopted in application of Article 8(d) of the Organization's Constitution, constitute an appendix to the Organization's General Regulations. (2) Should any provision of the present Rules of Procedure diverge from a provision of the Organization's Constitution or General Regulations, the latter shall prevail." The fundamental texts of INTERPOL, including the INTERPOL Constitution, General Regulations and Rules of Procedure of the General Assembly and the Executive Committee may be accessed through INTERPOL. Fundamental Texts. https://www.interpol.int/About-INTERPOL/Legal-materials/Fundamental-texts.

149 Paragraph 50 of the Rules of Procedure of the GCF Board provides: "In the event of any conflict between any provision of these rules and any provisions of the Governing Instrument, the provisions of the Governing Instrument shall prevail." See GCF. Rules of Procedure of the Board. https://www.greenclimate.fund/documents/20182/56440/Rules_of_Procedure.pdf/9d55fae7-f4df-45fe-a3f3-754bc0d98e67. It is further indicated in para 2 of the said document:

There are a range of matters that are not expressly covered by the Governing Instrument, such as the role and functions of the two Co-Chairs, the role of the alternate member after a Board member is elected Co-Chair, actions to be taken if a vacancy occurs prior to the end of the statutory term of a Board member, membership in Board committees and a range of other procedural matters. The Governing Instrument also called on the Board in para 14 to "develop procedures for adopting decisions in the event that all efforts at reaching consensus have been exhausted" and in para 16 to "make arrangements, including developing and operating accreditation processes, to allow for effective participation by accredited observers in its meetings."

Similarly, organizations established as trust funds or dual or hybrid types of organizations may also have a hierarchy of laws.[150]

As indicated by Cogan, "constitutive elements of the international system will not appear solely in a single document labeled a treaty, convention, charter, statute, or constitution. Instead, they will manifest themselves in a variety of agreements, some formal and some informal, some written and some unwritten."[151]

> This operational constitution—the combination of formal and informal rules that together regulate how international decisions are made and applied—is especially complex in the domain of representation not only because of the variety of forms available, but also because of the multiplicity of mechanisms through which decision-making authority is allocated. Principles of representation manifest themselves in several constitutive processes: the election of states to exclusive decision-making bodies; the relative voting rights assigned to states; the election and appointment of individuals of particular nationalities to high- and mid-level offices in international organizations; and the de facto devolution of appointment authority for such offices to particular states or groups of states. Only by canvassing all these areas can one fully comprehend the intricacies of representational values and how they are implemented.[152]

The main question relates to the extent to which the operational constitution may deviate from the constituent agreement. It is recognized that some deviations from the constituent agreement are allowed for the sake for expediency. Thus, for example, the rules of procedures of MDBs generally make reference to the appointment of temporary alternate governors and temporary alternate directors even though no reference to such officials is contained in the constituent agreement. As the Rules of Procedure allowing the appointment of temporary alternate governors or directors were drafted in certain cases at the same time and by the same persons as the constituent agreement (e.g. ADB), such deviation was found to be permissible.

Nevertheless, it is problematic if the operational constitution deviates from the constituent agreement to the extent that the authority provided by the constituent agreement is ignored or redefined by unwritten practice. This author believes that Burton has well made this point:

> The extra-legal act has always played a role in the creation of a national government. Most governments owe their creation to a formally illegal act: revolution, secession, or constitutional change outside the rules of an established order. It is through such acts that a community transcends the limitations of prior contractual legality. The possibility that international institutions could evolve similarly is one that has only rarely been raised, for it is hard to envision the revolution that produces international unity. Action for unity tends to

[150] There is a hierarchy between the bylaws of the Global Fund and certain core policies such as the Board and Committee Operating Procedures (which expressly refer to the bylaws), and between the core governance and institutional documents of the Global Fund and other policies. The governance and institutional documents of the Global Fund can be found under https://www.theglobalfund.org/en/governance-policies/.

[151] Cogan 2009, p. 219.

[152] Ibid., 219.

take a less dramatic form such as the carefully thought out extension of a legitimate authority.

Evaluation of such extra-legal approaches requires immense caution, for legal restrictions are often designed precisely to guarantee justice.[153]

In international organizations, the incorporation of extra-legal and extra-constitutional acts poses major problems. Hence, the unwritten practice must not be allowed to outright redefine, beyond any limits of an acceptable interpretation of the constituent instrument, fundamental provisions of the constituent instrument, because by doing so they would change the structure of, and the balance of power enshrined in, the constituent instrument. The same concern also applies to situations where governing bodies of international organizations in essence are only given the choice to rubberstamp decisions taken in other forums, because this undermines the statutory authority of the established governing bodies and raises concerns of due process. Cases as mentioned above may give rise to serious concerns regarding organizations' legitimacy.

4.4.9 Constitutionalization

Constitutionalization has many ramifications.[154] This term is used in relation to developments of public international law, in general, and for specific areas of public international law (e.g. international environmental law) and specific international organizations (e.g. the WTO), and also with reference to non-state actors.

Constitutionalization is seen "as the process of change by which a set of social practices defined as law (rules, principles, procedures, and institutions), and generally associated with Western industrialized democracies, emerge in a relatively and unified arrangement, in relation to a particular community, and attain a level of social acceptance, defined as legitimacy."[155]

The core question is whether there are "constitutional principles which limit the powers of states."[156]

---

[153] Barton 1983–1984, p. 1530.

[154] See Kleinlein 2012, 2, ss.

[155] Cass 2005, p. 29.

[156] As indicated by Kleinlein: "Für Vertreter der Konstitutionalisierungsthese ist im Völkerrecht ein die Staateninteressen transzendierendes Gemeinschaftsinteresse der Menschheit anerkannt, setzen hirarchisch übergeordnete, Verfassungsprinzipien dem bisher bindungslos gebliebenen Willen der Staaten Grenzen, verselbständigen sich internationale Organisationen gegenüber ihren Mitgliedstaaten und verbleibt den Mitgliedstaaten nicht länger ein genuiner *domaine réserve*." Kleinlein 2012, p. 2.

The case of the European Community is of particular interest as in this case, it cannot be disputed that constitutional structures have been created.[157] While the Constitutional Treaty was not approved, the constituent treaties of the European Union are widely seen and interpreted as a constitution. As shown by Tuori: "The European Constitution possesses multiple dimensions, and in each of these dimensions discourse is conducted at both doctrinal and theoretical levels; consequently, constitutional theory is also differentiated along constitutional dimensions."[158] In particular, "the European Constitution possesses a juridical and political dimension,"[159] former of which is underlined by the fact that main constitutional principles of the EU law, "relating to supremacy and direct effect, as well as efficacy (*effet utile*) and uniformity as meta-level justificatory principles," and general principles regarding fundamental rights have been developed by way of jurisprudence.[160] The "Kadi Saga"[161] and the fact that on two occasions regulations implementing Security Council decisions were annulled underlines the incisiveness of the control exercised by the European Court of Justice.

The discussion on constitutionalization is relevant in several respects in the context of this book. This relates on the one hand "to the endorsement of constitutional rights and principles such as human rights, rule of law, democracy, and solidarity in the law of international organizations", which are, as shown by Peters, giving UN, EU, and ILO as examples, "typically not addressed at the organization itself, but exclusively or primarily at the member states."[162] Nevertheless, these principles also define an international organization as and to the extent that they are applied by international organizations as criteria for the admission of new members. Hence, there is no reason why international organizations should be allowed to dissociate themselves in their own affairs from the values which they preach tor their members.

Peters asserts that a constitutionalist perspective can explain "the current trend of the reopening of the circle of members of the international community, so as to now include international organizations, individuals, non-governmental organizations (NGOs), transnational corporations (TNCs), hybrid actors such as the public-private partnerships and quasi-governmental organizations (quangos) [….]."[163]

---

[157] Oeter, S. states: "Man kann zur gegenwärtigen Debatte um eine Verfassungsgebung für die Europäische Union, im Sinne der Setzung einer formellen Verfassungsurkunde, stehen wie man will – daß die europäische Integration Züge einer ‚Verfassungswerdung' angenommen hat, im Sinne einer allmählichen institutionellen Verdichtung, hin zu verfassungsartigen Strukturen, ist kaum zu bestreiten, ja trägt Züge eines Gemeinplatzes." Oeter 1999, p. 901.

[158] Tuori 2015, pp. 6–7.

[159] Ibid., 9.

[160] Ibid., 12–13.

[161] Lenaerts 2014, pp. 707–715. http://scholar.smu.edu/cgi/viewcontent.cgi?article=1003&context=smulr. See also, with a critical note of the decisions, Anthony 2009, pp. 293–298 and Kämmerer 2008, pp. 65–87.

[162] Peters 2012, p. 205.

[163] Ibid., 155.

While this author shares the main thrust of Peter's observations, one adjustment to her proposal is required in relation to the concept of international organization. Peters appears to adhere to the traditional concept of international organization with treaty foundation. However, in the view of this author, as part of the constitutionalization process, it is necessary to define international organizations in a wider manner than is contemplated by Peters, for such term to comprise dual or hybrid organizations incorporated under national law, as well as international organizations established as trust funds, with or without international legal personality.

Constitutionalization is immediately relevant to attempts to formalize the legal status of organizations such as the Organization for Security and Co-operation in Europe (OSCE) which are predicated on "institutional ambivalence by design."[164]

Moreover, as indicated by Klabbers:

> Constitutionalization finally also offers a riposte to privatization in two ways. First, it does so by carving out a protected public realm. If there is indeed a risk that the public sphere threatens to be overtaken by the private sphere, constitutionalization appears to put a stop to this; it appears to build a fence around the public, and protect it as well as it can. But emphasizing that few things are ever what they seem, constitutionalization also helps to discipline the public institutions that serve the global market place.[165]

In this overall context, constitutionalization is relevant to enhancing the governance structures of certain entities (such as ICANN) which, while organized as corporate entities under private law, are entrusted tasks of utmost importance and produce global public goods.

As argued by Cass in relation to WTO, "multi-level governance and flexibility should be built in any transnational constitutional theory."[166]

Kleinlein also argues that assuming that "the constitutionalist perspective classically grew as the direct opposite of a state-centric, sovereignty-oriented theory of international law", the conclusion should be that "the role and status of non-state actors in international law should lie at the heart of any international constitutionalist perspective."[167] This author shares the conclusion of Kleinlein that "an increasing role of non-state actors is both an expression of individual empowerment and a means to enhance the legitimacy of international law and to serve global welfare."[168] However, it is indeed an important "constitutional problem whether and to what extent non-state actors performing governance functions are bound by rules of public international law concerning governance, in particular human rights, and how compliance with these rules can be ensured."[169] This issue is particularly relevant with respect to forms of institutionalized participation of non-state actors in international organizations involving full, sector, or affiliate membership. In the

---

164 Klabbers 2001, pp. 403–421.

165 Klabbers 2011, pp. 18–19.

166 Cass 2005, p. 4.

167 Kleinlein 2011, p. 41.

168 Ibid., 48.

169 Ibid., 45.

view of this author there is no valid reason or justification why transnational actors associated with international organizations should be dispensed with from complying with the standards of good governance which international organizations are promoting for their member states. The obligation to comply with core principles of good governance is a corollary of, and a requirement for, institutionalized forms of participation of transnational actors in organizations' activities.

Finally, constitutionalization of international organizations is important in the context of the discussion on their legitimacy. The traditional approach to this matter is to derive the legitimacy of international organizations from the fact that the constituent agreements of organizations with treaty foundation are ratified and thus are generally approved by the legislature. However, this argument requires further elaboration, in particular, on three grounds.

First, legitimacy may derived not only from the fact that the constituent agreement of an international organization has been ratified by Parliament, but also from the fact that a Parliament has allocated budgetary resources to an entity. This is supported by the position adopted by the United States, given that the International Organizations Immunities Act defines a public international organization as one "in which the United States participates pursuant to any treaty or under the authority of any Act of Congress authorizing such participation **or making an appropriation for such participation** [….]." (emphasis added)[170] Hence, an organization without a treaty base may be recognized in the United States as a public international organization if there is a separate budget line for such organization in the federal budget. In such a case, the budgetary appropriation to an organization has the same effect as an Act of Congress authorizing the participation of the United States in the Organization. In line with the above, the case may be made also for other countries that by approving budgetary allocations to entities without a treaty base, Parliaments also confer legitimacy to them. Clearly, the German Parliament is well aware that the OSCE exists, having funded it for decades, and the fact that funding has to be provided to an entity such as the OSCE for an extended period also entails a form of legitimization.

Second, the core of the discussion on constitutionalization relates to the fact that the merely formal criterion of ratification alone is no longer deemed to be sufficient to ensure legitimacy even in traditional international organizations with treaty foundation. The fact that the constituent agreement of an organization has been ratified does not give any insight as to how an organization is coping on account of accountability, transparency, protection of fundamental rights, and effectiveness and performance delivery. Hence, this merely formal ratification criterion needs to be supplemented by substantive criteria, such as those indicated above.

Third, the discussion on the legitimizing nature of Parliamentary ratification cannot be taken to imply that entities without a treaty foundation should not exist. They do exist and increasing have become new paradigms of establishing

[170] See the definition in the International Organizations Immunities Act, 9 Dec. 1945. http://www.law.cornell.edu/uscode/text/22/288.

international organizations for the very reason that there is a need for organizations of that kind. Hence, the conclusion can only be that for entities without treaty foundation constitutionalization along the lines indicated above is even more important for international organizations with a treaty base.

The concepts of constitution and constitutionalization mentioned above will be further analyzed in the following in relation to membership and membership procedures, the concepts of intergovernmental and international organization and for the concepts of subject of international law and international legal personality.

References

Abeyratne R (2009) The role of the International Civil Aviation Organization (ICAO) in the 21st century. Ann Air Space Law XXXIV:529–544

Anthony A (2009) Kadi: Ignoring International Legal Obligations. Int Organ Law Rev 6:293–298

Antonova S (2008) Deconstructing an experiment in Global Internet Governance: the ICANN case. Int J Commun Law & Policy. pp 2–15

Arato J (2013) Treaty interpretation and constitutional transformation: informal change in International Organizations. Yale J Int Law 38:290–357

Bartley T (2011) Transnational governance as the layering of rules. Intersections of Public and Private Standards. Theor Inq Law 12:517–542

Barton JH (1983–1984) Two ideas of International Organization. Mich Law Rev 82:1520–1532

Bellis MD (2010) Public Law and Private Regulators in the Global Legal Space. In: The New Public Law in a global (dis)order. A perspective from Italy. Jean Monnet Working Paper 16/10. New York University School of Law, New York, pp 4–39

Boisson de Chazournes L (2005) Treaty-law making and non-treaty-law-making: the evolving structure of the International Legal Order. In: Developments of International Law in Treaty Making. Springer, Berlin, pp 463–479

Brölmann C (1999) The legal nature of International Organisations and the Law of Treaties. Aust Rev Int Eur Law 4:85–125

Brölmann C (2007) The Institutional Veil in Public International Law: International Organisations and the Law of Treaties. Hart Publishing, Oxford

Brunnée J (2002) COPing with consent: law-making under multilateral environmental agreements. Leiden J Int Law 15:1–52

Brunnée J (2005) Reweaving the fabric of International Law? Patterns of consent in environmental framework agreements. In: Wolfrum R, Röben V (eds) Developments of International Law in Treaty Making. Springer, Berlin, pp 101–126

Cass DZ (2005) The constitutionalization of the World Trade Organization: legitimacy, democracy, and community in the International Trading System. Oxford University Press, Oxford

Charnovitz S (1997) Two centuries of participation: NGOs and International Governance. Mich J Int Law 18:183–286

Charnovitz S (2006) Nongovernmental Organizations and International Law. Am J Int Law 100:348–372

Clapham A (ed) (2012) Brierly's Law of Nations. An introduction to the role of International Law in International Relations, 7th edn. Oxford University Press, Oxford

Claude IL Jr (1971) Swords into plowshares: the problems and progress of International Organization, 4th edn. Random House, New York

Cogan JK (2009) Representation and power in International Organization: the operational constitution and its critics. Am J Int Law 103:209–263

Crawford J (2013) Chance, order, change: the course of International Law. General course on Public International Law. Collected Courses Hague Acad Int Law 365:9–390
Droesse G (2011) Organizational structures, institutional frameworks, and decision-making procedures of multilateral concessional financing. In: Funds for development: multilateral channels of concessional financing. ADB, Manila, pp 59–177
Freestone D (2007) The establishment, role and evolution of the Global Environment Facility: operationalizing common but differentiated responsibility? In: Ndiaye TM, Wolfrum R (eds) Law of the Sea, Environmental Law and Settlement of Disputes. Liber Amicorum Judge Thomas A. Mensah. Martinus Nijhoff, Leiden, pp 1077–1107
Gold J (1980) The rule of law in the International Monetary Fund. Pamphlet Series No. 32. IMF, Washington DC
Guzman A (2013) International Organizations and the Frankenstein problem. Eur J Int Law 24:999–1025
Hansen RF (2010) The International Legal Personality of multinational enterprises: treaty, custom and the governance gap. Global Jurist 10(1):1–129
Hartwig M (2010) ICANN—government by technical necessity. The exercise of public authority by International Institutions. In: von Bogdandy A, Wolfrum R, von Bernsdorff J, Dan P, Goldmann M (eds) The exercise of public authority by International Institutions: advancing International Institutional Law. Springer, Heidelberg, pp 575–605
Hockett R (2002) From macro to micro to “mission creep”: defending the IMF’s emerging concern with the infrastructural prerequisites to global financial stability. Columbia J Transnatl Law 41:153–193
Horwitz MJ (1981–1982) The history of the public/private distinction. Univ Pa Law Rev 130:1423–1428
ISO (2010) International Standards and Private Standards. ISO, Geneva, p 3
Jacur FR (2013) The dynamics of multilateral environmental agreements: Institutional Architectures and Law-Making Processes. Editoriale Scientifica, Naples, p 24
Jönsson C (2013) The John Holmes Memorial Lecture: International Organizations at the moving public-private borderline. Glob Gov 19:1–18
Kämmerer JA (2008) Die Urteile ‘Kadi’ und ‘Yusuf’, from EuG und ihre Folgen. Europarecht:65–87
Katkin K (2005) Communication breakdown? The future of global connectivity after the privatization of Intelsat. Int J Commun Law Policy. Special Issue Global Flow of Information. Autumn, 1–66
Kissling C (2011) The legal and political status of International Parliamentary Institutions. Background Paper No. 4. Committee for a Democratic U.N., Berlin
Klabbers J (2001) Institutional ambivalence by design: soft organizations in International Law. Nordic J Int Law 70:403–421
Klabbers J (2011) 2012. Setting the scene. In: Klabbers J, Peters A, Ulfenstein G (eds) The constitutionalization of International Law. Oxford University Press, Oxford, pp 1–44
Kleinlein T (2011) Non-state actors from an International Constitutionalist perspective. Participation matters! In: d’Aspremont J (ed) Participants in the International Legal System, pp 41–53
Kleinlein T (2012) Konstitutionalisierung im Völkerrecht. Konstruktion und Elemente einer idealistischen Völkerrechtslehre. Springer, Heidelberg
Kotzur M (2012) Overcoming dichotomies: a functional approach to the constitutional paradigm in Public International Law. Goettingen J Int Law 4:585–597
Ku C (2014) The evolution of International Law. In: Weiss TG, Wilkinson R (eds) International Organization and Global Governance. Routledge, p 38
Lenaerts K (2014) The Kadi Saga and the rule of law within the EU. SMU Law Rev:707–715
Majid AA (1996) Legal status of International Institutions: SITA, INMARSAT and Eurocontrol examined. Dartmouth Publishing, Aldershot
Martha RSJ (2010) The legal foundation of INTERPOL. Hart Publishing, Portland

Martha RSJ (2015) The financial obligation in International Law. Oxford University Press, Oxford, pp 22–50
Milliken J, Krause K (2002) State failure, state collapse, and state reconstruction: concepts, lessons and strategies. Dev Change 33(5):753–774
Mills A (2011) Antinomies of public and private at the foundations of International Investment Law and Arbitration. J Int Econ Law 14(2):469–503
Neuhold H (2005) The inadequacy of law-making by international treaties: 'soft law' as an alternative? In: Wolfrum R, Röben V (eds) Development of International Law in treaty making. Springer, Berlin, pp 39–52
Noortmann M (2011) Presentation. In: d'Aspremont J (ed) Participants in the International Legal System. Multiple perspectives on non-state actors in International Law. Routledge, London, pp xxxviii–xxxvixl
Oeter S (1999) Europäische Integration als Konstitutionalisierungsprozess. Zeitschrift für ausländisches öffentliches Recht und Völkerrecht 59:901–917
Oeter S (2009) The global legal order: an international lawyers' perspective inspired by institutionalism. TranState Working Papers. No. 109, 14. https://www.econstor.eu/bitstream//29687/1/616499515.pdf
Pauwelyn J, Wessel RA, Wouters J (eds) (2012) Informal International Lawmaking. Oxford University Press, Oxford
Pauwelyn J, Wessel RA, Wouters J (2014) When structures become shackles: stagnation and dynamics in International Lawmaking. Eur J Int Law 25:733–763
Peters A (2012) Membership in the Global Constitutional Community. In: Klabbers J, Peters A, Ulfstein G (eds) The constitutionalization of International Law. Oxford University Press, Oxford, pp 153–262
Peters A (2013) Das Gründungsdokument internationaler Organisationen als Verfassungsvertrag. Zeitschrift für öffentliches Recht 68:1–57
Ragazzi M (2011) The Global Environment Facility: institutional and operational aspects. In: Droesse G (ed) Funds for development: multilateral channels of concessional financing. ADB, Manila, pp 485–500
Rosenne S (1989) Is the constituent instrument of an International Organization an international treaty? In: Developments in the Law of Treaties 1945–1986. Cambridge University Press, Cambridge, pp 181–258
Sagar D (1999) The privatization of Inmarsat—special problems. In: SP-442, 3rd ESCL Colloquium. International Organisations and Space Law. Their role and contributions. Perugia, Italy. European Space Agency Publications Division, Noordwijk, pp 127–147
Sarukhanian EI, Walker JM (1879–1950) The International Meteorological Organization (IMO). http://ane4bf-datap1.s3-eu-west-1.amazonaws.com/wmocms/s3fs-public/The_International_Meteorological_Organization_IMO_1879-1950.pdf?Td4kDN4kyR7yiUv5m1.y4vJTHhQ_STc
Schachter O (1997) The decline of the nation-state and its implications for International Law. Columbia J Transnatl Law 36:7–23
Schermers HG, Blokker NM (eds) (2011) International Institutional Law: unity within diversity, 5th edn. Martinus Nijhoff, Boston
Scott C, Cafaggi F, Senden L (2011) The conceptual and constitutional challenge of transnational private regulation. J Law Soc 38:1–19
Slaughter AM (2004) A new world order. Princeton University Press, Princeton, p 31
Strauss PL (2013) Private Standards Organizations and Public Law. William Mary Bill Rights J 22:497–561
Tietje C (1999) The changing legal structure of international treaties as an aspect of an emerging global governance architecture. German Yearb Int Law 42:26–55
Tuori K (2015) European Constitutionalism. Cambridge University Press, Cambridge
Vidigal G (2013) From bilateral to multilateral law-making: legislation, practice, evolution and the future of inter se agreements in the WTO. Eur J Int Law 24(4):1027–1053
Vrancken P (2006) World Tourism Organization (UNWTO). In: Max Planck Encyclopedia of Public International Law (www.mpepil.com)

Weintraub J (1997) The theory and politics of the public/private distinction. In: Weintraub J, Kumar K (eds) Public and private in thought and practice. Perspectives of a grand dichotomy. The University of Chicago Press, Chicago, pp 1–42
Wiersema A (2009) Conferences of the parties to multilateral environmental agreements: the new International Law-makers? Proceedings of the Annual Meeting. Am Soc Int Law 103:74–76
Wirth DA (2009) The International Organization for standardization: private voluntary standards as swords and shields. Boston Coll Environ Aff Law Rev 36:79–102
Wölker U (2007) Die Normenhirarchie im Unionsrecht in der Praxis. Europarecht:32–56

Chapter 5
Membership in International Organizations

Contents

All weblinks are updated as of 28 February 2018.

G. Droesse, *Membership in International Organizations*,
https://doi.org/10.1007/978-94-6265-327-6_5

5.1 An Organization Does Not Need to Have Members

One of the traditional mantras of international law is that an international organization established by treaty[1] needs to have members.

Blokker has expressed this under the heading "Without Members, there would be No International Organizations" as follows:

> It is of course a truism to mention that there would be no international organizations without members. An international organization does not simply spring to life, spontaneously. It must be founded.[2]

However, in the next sentence, he already concedes:

> Strictly speaking, it is not founded by its members. Those members only exist from the moment that the organization has been established. An organization is generally founded by states which draw up the founding treaty of the organization, sign it and subsequently ratify it.[3]

In the view of this author, the traditional mantra mentioned above is incorrect in three respects.

First, an international organization does not need to be established by a treaty, nor is there a need for membership structures to be established by a treaty.

Second, the parties to the treaty establishing an international organization do not need to become members of the organization.

Third, an international organization does not need to have members and in fact, there are organizations which qualify as "international" even they do not have any members.

These three points will be further elaborated in the following.

5.1.1 Membership Issues Cannot Be Reduced to the Dichotomy of Treaty and Constitution

As regards the first issue, the difference between the constituent agreement and the resulting constitution has already been discussed in detail in Chap. 4. Martha associates with such difference a distinction between the general law of treaties and international institutional law (governing membership and membership rights), which explains in his view "the differences between the legal regime for the succession to treaties as compared with that for the succession to the membership of international organizations."[4] He concludes, "Hence, [….] it is evident that the

1 Schermers and Blokker 2011, §66: "One element all organizations have in common is that they have members."

2 Blokker 2004, p. 140.

3 Blokker 2004, p. 140.

4 Martha 2010, p. 169.

question of membership in itself has no bearing on whether the constituent instruments of international organizations qualify as a treaty or not."[5]

As set out in detail in Chap. 4, the constitution of an organization does not need to take the form of a treaty, nor is there any need for membership in an international organization to be regulated by a treaty. Constitutions of organizations not established by a treaty can regulate membership on very similar terms as constitutions adopted by a treaty. Moreover, the decreasing importance of the treaty format has been highlighted. Further, organizations established as trust funds or as dual or hybrid organizations may have membership structures based on their constituent instruments. Moreover, as will be shown in detail in Chap. 7, there are effectively a number of organizations which are, or should be, classified as intergovernmental or international organization, respectively, even though they were not established by a treaty. Hence, membership issues cannot merely be reduced to the dichotomy of treaty and constitution.

5.1.2 Parties to Constituent Agreement Do Not Need to Become Members

As highlighted by Wessel:

> The situation in which there can be no confusion about the State/member State dichotomy is when the international organization does not yet exist. International organizations are based on international agreements between States (or other international organizations) and obviously States can only become a member of the new entity once that agreement has entered into force and the organization starts functioning. This implies that, during all preparatory work, States remain having the single status as 'State', irrespective of procedures that may have been agreed upon during the negotiation process. Also, in terms of responsibility, it is clear that, in this situation, States are the relevant actors.[6]

This author agrees with the statement of Wessel, however, with two qualifications. First, as has been extensively shown, international organizations may be based, but do not need to be based, on international agreements between states. Second, while it is true that states can only "become a member of the new entity once that agreement has entered into force and the organization starts functioning," there may be cases where the parties to the constituent agreement do not become members.

In certain cases, the constituent agreement expressly foresees that the contracting parties of the constituent agreement will become members. Thus:

The Agreement establishing the CAF states in Article 1:

> The High Contracting Parties hereby create the Corporación Andina de Fomento.

---

[5] Ibid.

[6] Wessel and Dekker 2015, pp. 301–302.

By implication, the High Contracting Parties specified in the preamble of the said Agreement became members, respectively shareholders, of the CAF by virtue of being contracting parties to its constituent agreement.

As regards the IMF, the IMF Articles of Agreement mandate all governments to sign the IMF Articles of Agreement and "deposit with the Government of the United States of America an instrument setting forth that it has accepted this Agreement in accordance with its law and has taken all steps necessary to enable it to carry out all of its obligations under this Agreement."[7] Thus, all IMF members need to sign and ratify the IMF Articles of Agreement.

In cases as mentioned above, members are necessarily parties to the constituent agreement of the organization. In many other international organizations, the parties to the constituent agreement are also members of the organization. However, while this is frequently the case, particularly for traditional international organizations with treaty foundation, there is no intrinsic need for the parties to the constituent agreement also to become members. This can even be derived from Blokker's statement cited above that an international organization, "[s]trictly speaking, is not founded by its members."

Martha illustrates this with several examples, including the World Customs Organization (WCO). "Article II of the Convention Establishing a Customs Co-operation Council, currently the WCO, clearly distinguishes between members and contracting parties. It stipulates that the members shall be the contracting parties as well as the government of any separate customs territory proposed by a contracting party."[8]

In addition, he refers to the Bank of International Settlements (BIS) as "one example of an organization where countries came together and created an international organization in which the central banks of the contracting countries, rather than the contracting countries themselves are members"[9] and to the IPU as "the international organization of the parliaments of sovereign states."[10] In addition, the establishing agreement of the Joint Vienna Institute "makes a distinction between the parties to the Agreement and the members," and underlines that contracting parties do not need to be members.[11]

However, the clearest example for illustrating the distinction between contracting parties and membership relates to the process of establishing the new Consultative Group for International Agricultural Research (CGIAR) Consortium. The case of the CGIAR Consortium shows that there may be international organizations with international legal personality in which none of the state parties to the constituent agreement is a member. It is different both from cases such as the BIS and IPU where the members are not governments but central banks or

7 IMF Articles of Agreement, Article XXXI, Section 2(a) and (b).

8 Martha 2010, p. 169.

9 Ibid., 169–170.

10 Ibid., 170.

11 Ibid.

Parliaments and cases such as the Joint Vienna Institute where the parties to the constituting agreement may, but do not need to become, members of the organization. In the case of the "the Agreement establishing the Consortium of International Agricultural Research Centers as an International Organization,"[12] the contracting parties do not even have the option of becoming members. The above Agreement has been merely chosen as the vehicle for establishing the CGIAR Consortium as an international organization with international legal personality and privileges and immunities. However, France, which is the depository and signed the agreement on 13 September 2011, and the other contracting parties,[13] are not become members of the CGIAR Consortium, as membership in the Consortium is reserved to the initial CGIAR member centers and any member centers admitted subsequently.

The above shows that establishing an organization by way of a treaty may nearly be a vehicle or tool for endowing it with international legal personality. The CGIAR Consortium is an important new paradigm for creating international organizations.

First, because following this scheme an international organization can be created by a small number (e.g., 3) of states which may, but do not need to, become members of the organization.

Second, because in that manner international organizations with virtually any type of membership structure may be created. Thus, it would potentially be possible to establish, following the approach adopted for the CGIAR Consortium, an international organization which has sub-state entities (e.g., federal states, municipalities or regulatory agencies of different countries) and private sector entities or other transnational actors as members. Potentially, as discussed in relation to ICANN, ISO and IATA below, an international organization so established might only have members incorporated or operating under national law.

Third, the CGIAR paradigm can also be used for creating international organizations without any formal membership structure. Furthermore, an organization with a varied membership structure as indicated above or without any formal membership structure does not need to be established necessarily by a treaty in all cases. It could also be created by the resolution of a conference or the decision of a governing body adopting its constitution, or based on a decision of the conference or meeting of the parties to a multilateral convention, or merely by consensus.

---

[12] See Agreement establishing the Consortium of International Agricultural Research Centers as an International Organization. 20 July 2012. https://cgspace.cgiar.org/bitstream/handle/10947/2592/Agreement_establishing_the_Consortium_of_International_Agricultural_Research_Centers_as_an_International_Organization.pdf?sequence=4.

[13] The following countries signed the Agreement: Republic of Hungary (13 Sept. 2011), Kingdom of Denmark (2 March 2012); Republic of Benin (April 5, 2012); Oriental Republic of Uruguay (28 Oct. 2012).

5.1.3 Whether an Organization Needs to Have Members Depends on Its Functions

5.1.3.1 Paradigms of Membership Structures

In many cases, international organizations have membership structures. Such structures are applicable to most international organization with treaty foundation. In that case, generally the constituent agreement defines the types of membership, the eligible subjects of membership and legal implications of membership for governance and decision-making.

International financial institutions have an equity structure where the members are shareholders of the organization. For such organizations, their constituent agreement also defines their capital structure and governance structure, and the rights and obligations of the members which are the shareholders of the organization. As indicated by Bradlow, IFIs have a "dual character", because as "subjects of international law, their rights and obligations arise from the applicable public international law principles" while they "engage in financial transactions, which despite their public purpose, are, by nature, similar to market-based financial transactions."[14] Consistent with their dual character, membership has multiple implications as has been shown by this author in his contributions to the book "Funds for Development". These relate to organizational, institutional and governance structures, funding modalities and financial transactions, and to operational modalities alike. Thus, membership has not only implications for internal matters which relate to the organization's relations with its members but also for its relations with external stakeholders, e.g., in the context of procurement operations or financial transactions.

In the case of the BIS, the "Bank's capital is held by central banks. Sixty central banks and monetary authorities are currently members of the BIS and have rights of voting and representation at General Meetings."[15] The case of BIS is special as it was established based on a Convention providing that Switzerland would grant a charter to the bank,[16] and based on the Bank's Charter incorporating the BIS under Swiss law[17] and the Statutes of the Organization.[18]

---

[14] Bradlow 2010, p. 1.

[15] Bank for International Settlements. BIS Member Central Banks. http://www.bis.org/about/member_cb.htm.

[16] Convention respecting the Bank for International Settlements. 1930. http://www.bis.org/about/convention-en.pdf. The said Convention contained an undertaking of Switzerland not to abrogate or amend the Charter for 15 years (see Articles 1 and 3) and provisions on dispute settlement (Article 2).

[17] Constituent Charter of the Bank for International Settlements. 1930. https://www.bis.org/about/charter-en.pdf.

[18] Statutes of the Bank of International Settlements. 1930, as amended on 7 Nov. 2016. https://www.bis.org/about/statutes-en.pdf.

The Arbitration Tribunal established pursuant to Article XV of the Agreement signed on 20 January 1930 held on 22 November 2002 that notwithstanding the internal structure of the Bank as company limited by shares, "the essential international character of the Bank is apparent from its treaty origin"[19] and that the "functions of the Bank were quintessentially public international in their character."[20] Thus, it based its finding that the BIS was a "*sui generis* creation which is an international organization"[21] both on an analysis of the mode establishment and on the functions of BIS.

As shown, the ASEAN+3 Macroeconomic Research Office (AMRO), prior to its conversion into traditional treaty-based organization, had a membership structure and was owned by the ASEAN+3 states. Its governance structure was based on an agreement among the ASEAN+3 states, which, nevertheless, did not correspond to the traditional concept of treaty, given the fact that the ASEAN+3 states were not represented by their governments but by ministries of finance or similar institutions. AMRO was established under the Companies Act, Cap. 50, of Singapore as a "Company Limited by Guarantee and not Having a Share Capital" under Articles of Association of the ASEAN+3 Macroeconomic Research Office Limited.

Similarly, CGIF was given an equity-based membership structure, even though it does not possess international legal personality and was not established by or based on a traditional treaty ratified by governments. While ADB, as the trustee, is the legal owner of CGIF assets, this "is a *sui generis* trust ownership that is enforceable against third parties",[22] but "as between the donors and the trustee it remains in the real ownership of the donors." However, from a substantive point, the contributors are the owners of CGIF resources, as set out in the Report and Recommendation of the President to the Board of Directors.

> The contributors in CGIF will be the governments of ASEAN+3 and ADB. Ownership rights will be in proportion to capital contributions, with Japan providing $200 million, the PRC $200 million, the Republic of Korea $100 million, ASEAN countries collectively $70 million, and ADB $130 million.[23]

In addition to being related to the ownership of an organization, membership is at the core of a web of duties and responsibilities which define the rights and benefits of members and their obligations based on the club principle.

---

[19] Reineccius, H. First Eagle SoGenFunds, Inc., Mathieu, Pierre and La Societé Hippique de la Châtre v. Bank for International Settlements, "Partial Award on the Lawfulness of the Recall of the Privately Held Shares on 8 Jan. 2001". Reports of International Arbitral Awards. 2002. Vol. XXIII, 183–251, paras 112 and 113. http://legal.un.org/riaa/cases/vol_XXIII/183-251.pdf.

[20] Ibid., 51.

[21] Ibid., 54.

[22] Bantekas 2009, p. 34.

[23] ADB. 2010. "Proposed Credit Guarantee and Investment Facility: Establishment of Trust Fund and Capital Contribution. Report and Recommendation of the President to the Board of Directors. Project Number: 44908-01", para 33.

As the above cases show, membership structures are often determined by a treaty and may also be incorporated in an agreement between ministries of finance or central banks. However, international organizations do not need to be created necessarily by a treaty, nor is there a need for their membership structures to be determined by a treaty or other type of international agreement. In principle, they can also be established based on other legal acts as mentioned above, such as the resolution of a conference, a constitution approved by the plenary body of the organization or based on a decision by the conference of the parties to a multilateral convention, or merely by the resolution of an international organization establishing a trust fund. Moreover, also dual or hybrid organization and international organizations established as trust funds may be owned by their members and have equity-based structures. Whether a dual or hybrid organization has a membership structure does not depend on its legal status but is entirely dependent on its functions. The same is also applicable for other international organizations without treaty foundation, including international organizations established as trust funds.

5.1.3.2 Membership and the Club Theory

The question whether an organization needs to have members is to be seen in the overall context of the discussion on the global public goods and bads, and the criticism voiced in this context against the "consensual nature of the international legal order with its strong emphasis on the sovereign equality of states," that "has been attacked for its incongruence with the realities of inequality in international politics, for its tension with ideals of democracy and human rights, and for standing in the way of more effective problem solving in the international community."[24] "The main thrust of the critique is that international law is ineffective in solving global problems as those problems become more salient."[25]

> Public goods are best understood by contrasting them with private goods. Private goods can be made excludable and exclusive in consumption. They are associated with clear property rights. And it is up to their owner to determine how to use them to consume, lease or trade them. Public goods, by contrast, are goods in the public domain: available for all to consume and so potentially affecting all people. Global public goods are public goods with benefits or costs, in the case of such 'bads' as crime and violence that extend across countries and regions, across rich and poor population groups, and even across generations.[26]

While "there is a standard definition of public goods anchored on non-rivalry and non-excludability," it is important to note that "the properties of goods do not always correspond to this standard definition" as "society can modify the (non)

[24] Krisch 2014, p. 1.

[25] Ibid., 3.

[26] Kaul et al. 2003, p. 2. https://www.g24.org/wp-content/uploads/2016/01/Why-Do-Global-Public-Goods.pdf.

rivalry and (non)excludability of a good's benefits."[27] "That is why consideration should be given to expanding the definition—to recognize that in many if not most cases, goods exist not in their original forms but as social constructs, largely determined by policies and other collective human actions."[28]

As indicated by Krisch, "International law in its classical form appears as particularly ill-suited to tackling this challenge. As a threshold matter, its consent-based structure presents a structural bias against effective action on global public goods, especially given the large number of sovereign states today."[29]

In their traditional forms, international organizations are clubs that reserve certain benefits (e.g., representation in governing bodies, access to financing and procurement, etc.) to their members, which in turn have certain obligations, in particular the obligation to contribute to the funding of the organization. The constituent agreement or other constituent documents of the organization generally define the terms, benefits and obligations of the club membership. This link between benefits and obligations of membership is particularly evident in case of those organizations such as the EU and the WTO where the terms of membership are subject to lengthy negotiations and involve a treaty of accession. Important reasons for the approach mentioned above are to provide incentives for membership in an organization and for the production of public goods and to avoid giving certain countries a free ride even though they fail to contribute to the objectives and financing of the organization.

However, the fairly simplistic correlation of benefits and obligations of membership cannot be properly applied in case of organization producing global public goods or fighting global wrongs. The traditional theory of clubs as developed by Buchanan is "in one sense, a theory of optimal exclusion, as well as one of inclusion."[30] However, as Buchanan highlights, the theory of clubs "applies in the strict sense only to the organization of membership or sharing arrangements where 'exclusion' is possible. In so far as non-exclusion is a characteristic of public goods supply, [....], the theory of clubs is of limited relevance."[31] Thus, as will be shown, exclusion would neither be possible nor appropriate in case of international organizations producing global public goods.

Moreover, a fundamental problem is that

> public goods result in the problem of underinvestment. If a particular good is a public good, then because those who invest in its production may not capture all of the benefits, a collective problem may arise and the public good may be underproduced. This is a problem of a positive externality that would be efficient to be provided, if the incentives were appropriate. On the other hand, a public bad involves adverse effects that are

[27] Kaul and Mendoza 2003, p. 80.

[28] Kaul and Mendoza 2003, pp. 80–81.

[29] Krisch 2014, p. 4.

[30] Buchanan 1965, p. 13.

[31] Buchanan 1965, p. 13.

> non-excludable and inexhaustible. Those who produce public bads may not internalize all of the detriments, and the public bad may be overproduced. This is a type of negative externality.[32]

The traditional funding mechanisms of international organizations based on the correlation of benefits and obligations resulting from membership generally do not apply in those cases (e.g. the Global Fund), where an organization does not have an established membership structure. In these cases, contributors will often be reluctant to assume a firm legal obligation to fund a certain percentage or burden-share of the organization's budget; often they will only be willing to provide voluntary contributions. However, even in those cases where an international organization has a membership structure, the ability of the organization to attract new members may be constrained and the willingness of the existing members to provide funding to the organization may be limited if there are no tangible benefits attached to membership to which only members are eligible.

Hence, it is one of the themes of this book that traditional concepts of membership based on the correlation of benefits and obligations deriving from membership are unsuitable to a substantial extent for international organizations producing global public goods or fighting global public bads.

5.1.3.3 Organizations Without Membership Structures

While effectively, most international organizations have members, a membership structure is not necessary or even suitable in some cases. In particular, for funding mechanisms and other international organizations producing global public goods or fighting global public bads, formal membership structures may often be dispensed with.

The traditional rationale for a membership structure based on the club theory cannot be properly applied in these cases. It is neither possible, nor would it be appropriate, to make assistance to countries in fighting HIV/AIDS, malaria or tuberculosis dependent on whether such countries are members of an organization or not. Similarly, it is necessary to assist countries in their adjustment to, and in their attempts to mitigate the effects of, climate change irrespective of whether they are members of a specific organization. These benefits are, therefore, not excludable and the club theory, in its various manifestations, is only relevant for that reason to a very limited extent. Finally, assistance needs to be given to countries to fight drug trafficking and human trafficking, and other heinous crimes, irrespective of their association with a specific organization. In all the cases mentioned above, resources need to be used where they are most needed and not based on formal criteria relating to the association of a country with a specific organization.

It is possible to establish an international organization without a formal membership structure following the paradigm used for the establishment of the CGIAR

[32] Trachtman 2013, pp. 28–29.

Consortium, i.e., by way of adoption of an international treaty, between two or more state parties which do not become members of the organization. Moreover, there is a range of other modes for establishing an international organization, as mentioned above.

As a matter of principle, it would have been possible to make provision to the effect that all country Parties of the UNFCCC would have become automatically members of the Green Climate Fund. The example of the CTBTO shows that automatic membership is possible. Nevertheless, there is one fundamental difference between the CTBTO and the GCF.

Article 4 of the "Text on the Establishment of a Preparatory Commission for the Comprehensive Nuclear-Test-Ban Organization" provides that the

> Commission shall be composed of all states which sign the Treaty. Each State Signatory shall have a representative in the Commission, who may be accompanied by alternates and advisors.[33]

Hence, all signatories of the Comprehensive Nuclear-Test-Ban Treaty automatically become members of the Preparatory Commission and they can participate in the decision-making of the Commission, which is covered by Article 6 of the said Text.

When the Governing Instrument of the Fund was being drafted, the Transitional Committee initially considered giving the Fund a formal membership structure. This issue was pursued up to the third meeting of the Transitional Committee for the Design of the Green Climate Fund.[34] In the end, the decision was taken not to create any formal membership structure of the Fund. It would appear that this was partially due to the fact that in the case of the Green Climate Fund there is no decision-making body in which all country Parties to UNFCCC are represented. While provision has been made in the Governing Instrument that the Fund "will be accountable to and function under the guidance of the Conference of the Parties

---

[33] Comprehensive Nuclear-Test-Ban Treaty. Resolution establishing the Preparatory Commission for the Comprehensive Nuclear-Test-Ban Treaty Organization (Adopted on 19 Nov. 1996), CTBT/MSS/RES/1; 27 Nov. 1996), Annex: "Text on the Establishment of a Preparatory Commission for the Comprehensive Nuclear-Test-Ban Treaty Organization", Article 4. https://www.ctbto.org/fileadmin/user_upload/legal/CTBT-MSS-RES-1-e_01.pdf.

[34] The following three options were considered:

Option 1: All Parties of the UNFCCC will be the members of the Fund if the Fund is provided legal personality through a decision of the COP.

Option 2: Any Party to the UNFCCC may decide to participate in the GCF if the GCF does not have a legal personality or is provided legal personality by a Party e.g. like the Global Environment Facility and Global Fund.

Option 3: Any Party to the UNFCCC may become a member of the Fund by acceding to the treaty establishing the GCF if the GCF is established through a new treaty e.g. like the MDBs. Transitional Committee. 2011. Cross-cutting issues in the design of the Green Climate Fund Background information note prepared by the Technical Support Unit the Transitional Committee under the guidance of the Co-Chairs, para 6. http://unfccc.int/files/cancun_agreements/green_climate_fund/application/pdf/tc3_inf1_rev.1.pdf.

(COP)", the center of decision-making is the Board, which is a governing body of limited membership comprising 24 members and alternates representing the two constituencies of developed and developing countries. Any automatic membership of all country Parties to the UNFCCC in essence would have been meaningless, as there was no governing body in the GCF in which all country Parties could have participated in decision-making. It appears that it was partially for that reason that the option of automatic membership of all UNFCCC country Parties was not pursued.

Hence, the case of the GCF shows that an organization without formal membership structure may also be established pursuant to a decision taken by the conference of the parties to a multilateral convention.

In addition, in principle other modes are possible for establishing an organization without a formal membership structure (e.g., a resolution adopted by a conference, etc.). Moreover, an organization of that kind can be incorporated under national law or be established as a trust fund. Whether a dual or hybrid organization needs to have a membership does not depend on the mode of its establishment but on its purpose and functions. As has been mentioned above, dual or hybrid organizations may have membership structures but they do not need to have such structures.

The declining overall importance of membership for the institutional and strategic frameworks or international institutions can be illustrated by the example of the Global Fund, which needs to focus its resources on those countries where they are most needed, irrespective of whether they are members or not. Therefore, the Global Fund does not have a formal membership structure and does not limit participation in decision-making and eligibility to receive financing to member states; it is a multi-actor fund which also involves the private sector, including philanthropy, and a representative of communities living with the disease in its decision-making procedures.[35] Moreover, it is not funded exclusively by states but actively seeks to attract funding from a variety of resources, including philanthropy and the general public. A similar approach has also been adopted by Gavi, the Vaccine Alliance (Gavi Alliance).[36]

In the cases of the Global Fund, Gavi Alliance and GCF, the legal instruments which define the governance structure of these organizations do not provide for a formal membership structure but only for representation arrangements of relevant stakeholders. This relates to the difference between membership and representation highlighted above.

Also for organizations established as trust funds with or without legal personality, the decisive criterion for whether or not they should have a membership structure is not the mode of their establishment but their purpose and functions.

In the case of organizations without any formal membership structure, the traditional logic of benefits and obligations on which funding structures of

[35] See the composition of the Global Fund Board, set forth in Article 7 of the Global Fund Bylaws. 2016. https://www.theglobalfund.org/media/6007/core_globalfund_bylaws_en.pdf.

[36] Gavi. The Vaccine Alliance. http://www.gavi.org.

international organizations are based, does not apply. As in these organizations, the incentives which are traditionally meant to encourage states to participate in the organization (e.g., procurement eligibility) do not apply, or apply only to a limited extent, states may be less inclined to contribute to the financing of the organization's expenses. For that reason, new mechanisms need to be sought to fund the expenses of international organizations without a formal membership structure and/or organizations which produce global public goods or fight global public bads. Moreover, the legal frameworks of such organizations need to be different in several respects from those of international organizations with regular membership structure in line with the club theory.

5.2 Types of Membership

Schermers and Blokker "distinguish between four sorts of members: "*full members*, which may participate with full rights in all activities of the organization; *associate* and *affiliate* members, which may participate but have no voting rights in the principal organs; and *partial* members, which only participate in some activities."[37]

Currently, in most international organizations, full members are states (or in some cases international organizations), while dependent territories may be admitted in some cases to associate membership without voting rights. The specialized agencies of the UN epitomize this traditional approach. No UN specialized agency has admitted a dependent territory to full membership; they are, if at all eligible, only considered for associate membership. Also, membership of corporate entities is only allowed in a select few cases, and then only in a limited context, e.g., in relation to the affiliate membership in the World Tourism Organization (UNWTO) or the sector membership of the International Telecommunications Union (ITU).

While full membership in the UNWTO is limited to states and associate membership is open to dependent territories, the UNWTO Statutes provide for an affiliate membership which is open "to international bodies, both intergovernmental and non-governmental, concerned with specialized interests in tourism and to commercial bodies and associations whose activities are related to the aims of the Organization or fall within its competence."[38]

While, as shown, the International Telegraph Union, the predecessor of the ITU, admitted dependent territories and technical administrations at par with states, ITU only provides for full membership of states. However, one of the distinguishing features of the ITU Constitution is that it makes provision for the sector

[37] Schermers and Blokker 2011, §69.

[38] UNWTO Statutes, Article 7, para 1. For full and associate membership, see UNWTO Statutes, Articles 5 and 6. See *UNWTO Basic Documents*. 2016. http://cf.cdn.unwto.org/sites/all/files/docpdf/unwtostatuteseng.pdf.

membership from industry, international and regional organizations, as well as academia.[39]

Hinricher calls the ITU the "Sleeping Beauty among international organisations" because "it has not been disturbed in its slumber by many academic writers" and "rarely steps out into the limelight of public attention."[40] Nevertheless, ITU may be seen as an example for other organizations as it allows sector members to "participate in all activities of the Sector concerned, with the exception of formal votes and some treaty-making conferences."[41] Moreover, the assembly or conference of a sector may decide to admit entities or organizations to participate as associates in the work of a given study group or subgroups thereof.[42] The inputs of private sector entities to ITU have made important contributions to global standards and best practices, and "have played a vital role in the work of the Union, helping Member States address emerging issues and rapid changes in the telecommunication/ICT sector."[43]

Generally, the distinction between original members and other members does not relate to the membership status of countries and other entities concerned but only to the procedure of their admission. Other distinctions can also be made (e.g., between regional and non-regional members, borrowing and non-borrowing members, and developed and developing countries). While these may have multiple legal implications (e.g. for the geographic scope of activities funded by the organization, the organization's capital structure, and the appointment of the executive head of the organization), generally these distinctions do not relate to a special institutional status of member countries in terms of voting rights and decision-making procedures.

Nevertheless, it is not intrinsically impossible that distinctions as mentioned above may also have institutional implications. For example, OPEC makes a distinction between the founder members and other full members; for any admission of full or associate members "the concurrent vote of all Founder Members" is

---

[39] See ITU Constitution, Article 3 (http://www.jus.uio.no/english/services/library/treaties/07/7-06/itu_const.xml#treaty-header1-1) and ITU. "Sector Members, Associates and Academia". https://www.itu.int/en/membership/Pages/sector-members.aspx.

[40] Hinricher 2004, p. 489.

[41] See Resolution 14 (Rev. Antalya). 2006. "Recognition of the Rights and Obligations of all Sector Members of the Union". *Collection of the Basic Texts of the International Telecommunication Union adopted by the Plenipotentiary Conference*, Edition 2015. (cited as "ITU Collection"), pp. 251–252. https://www.itu.int/pub/S-CONF-PLEN-2015. See also Resolution 170 (Rev. Busan). 2014. ITU Collection, pp. 689–690, and Resolution 187. 2014. "Review of the Current Methodologies and Development of a Future Vision for the Participation of Sector Members, Associates and Academia in the Activities of ITU". ITU Collection, pp. 768–771.

[42] ITU Collection No. 241A, 125.

[43] "ITU's Evolving Membership", ITU, 2. https://www.itu.int/en/plenipotentiary/2014/newsroom/Documents/backgrounders/pp14-backgrounder-evolving-membership.pdf.

required.[44] The Charter of the AIIB also confers a special status to the founding members, who are allocated "six hundred (600) Founding Member votes."[45]

The Central American Bank for Economic Integration (BCIE), on the other hand, has created a special category of beneficiary country (beneficiary countries do not need to be members).[46]

This underlines that there is nothing cast in stone regarding different types of membership. The determination of types of membership needs to be driven by the functions and the specific circumstances of each organization and can be tailored to the needs of each organization.

De lege ferenda, for the establishment of new international organizations, consideration should be given on whether to incorporate in their constituent instruments an express provision that full membership does not need to be limited to states and international organizations, but may include transnational actors, including the private sector, philanthropy and civil society. Also, there is no need or intrinsic justification for excluding associate, affiliate or sector members from participation in any formal decision making. It is possible, as a matter of principle, to create special types of associate, affiliate, or sector membership which afford to transnational actors additional opportunities to participate in formal decision-making and voting (e.g., for certain types of decisions). Allowing this would give transnational actors a more enhanced role and transform their role in governance of international organizations. In the case of existing organizations, such transformation of their governance structure is possible, as a matter of principle, but would generally require amendment of their constituent instrument, which is a formidable task, given the applicable qualified majorities. However, short of such amendment, it is possible as a matter of policy to create secondary governance structures under umbrella operational arrangements approved by organizations' statutory governing bodies, which give defined decision-making powers to a variety of stakeholders. This will be discussed in further detail in Chap. 9.

5.3 Subjects of Membership

The topic of "eligible subjects of membership in international organizations" is colored by state-centric concepts. The concept that international organizations, in addition to states, can be a subject of membership in international organizations took a long time to be accepted. The discussion on this matter is largely informed by the membership of the European Union in international organizations, even

---

[44] OPEC Statute. 2012. Article 7, C and D. http://www.opec.org/opec_web/static_files_project/media/downloads/publications/OPEC_Statute.pdf.

[45] AIIB Articles of Agreement, Article 28.1(iii).

[46] Currently, Belize is the only country in this category. http://www.bcie.org/index.php?id=81&L=1.

though there are some other cases where international organizations are also members of other international organizations.

It is firmly established by historic precedent and current legal frameworks of international organizations that in addition to states and international organizations, dependent territories may also be eligible subjects of membership. Unlike the Covenant of the League of Nations, the Charter of the United Nations does not allow membership of dependent territories. However, there are some other international organizations which permit dependent territories to accede to full membership and various others which allow dependent territories to become associate members. Thus, it is firmly accepted that dependent territories can be subjects of membership.

Some of the IAUs established in the nineteenth century allowed technical government agencies and administrations to join the organization on the same terms as states. As regards sub-state actors and national regulators, it is for each state to decide whether and to what extent technical government agencies, national regulators, and other sub-state entities may participate in international cooperation. However, there is no reason to exclude the aforementioned agencies, regulators or entities from eligibility for membership in international organizations, as a matter of principle.

The question of whether transnational actors (including civil society, philanthropic institutions and private sector entities) may be considered as eligible objects of membership, is generally not raised, let alone answered. As will be shown in the following, the concept of "subject of membership" needs to be defined in a much wider term than it has been in the past. As a matter of principle, it may also comprise institutionalized forms of participation of transnational actors involving full or limited types of membership.

5.3.1 States, Countries, Nations and Governments

In international organizations, states were, and to a large extent still are, the main subject of membership. The constituent agreements of a number of organizations expressly provide that only states may join, while "partially due to the absence of agreement on the definition of a state, the constituent instruments of the IMF, the World Bank, and several development banks adopted a different approach, defining 'countries' rather than 'states' as subjects of membership. In some international organizations, the term "country" includes dependent territories of members."[47] In certain cases, such as the Caribbean Development Bank (CDB) and the International Coffee Organization, provision has been made for several countries to be considered one member. Under Article II of the Constitution of the Food and Agriculture Organization (FAO) of the United Nations, nations are referred to as

---

[47] For a more detailed discussion, see Droesse, "Organizational Structures", 91.

subjects of membership.[48] As the term "country", "nation" is related to, but not necessarily identical, with the term "state". Finally, as highlighted by Amerasinghe, "sometimes but rarely governments may constitute the membership."[49]

This is not the place to review the vast literature on concepts and criteria for statehood or recount the story of the many changes in membership of the United Nations and the specialized agencies due to secession, succession, unification, annexation and change of status which have been analyzed in detail in literature.[50]

Articles 3 and 4 of the UN Charter do not contain a definition of the term "states". "In practice, the decision-makers seem to have followed a number of criteria and have given a wide variety of meanings to the term."[51]

Also, as highlighted by Crawford,

> the question of admission to the United Nations raises somewhat different issues from those simply of statehood. Thus, the obligations of a State towards a fellow Member are greater than those towards a non-Member State: there would seem to be grounds for refusing United Nations membership to any State the territory of which was subject to a serious and genuine unresolved claim of another Member.[52]

However, membership issues tend to transcend considerations of a merely legal nature. Moreover, the case of Palestine, in particular, shows that the discussion on statehood may also transcend any schematic application of the criteria set out in Article 1 of the Montevideo Convention of 1933 (i.e., "(a) a permanent population; (b) a defined territory; (c) government; and (d) capacity to enter into relations with other States."

Overall, at present, it is fairly well established which states are eligible to be a member of the United Nations, given a few exceptions, such as the cases of Kosovo, Palestine, and a few small island countries.

Following the advisory opinion rendered by the International Court of Justice (ICJ) at the request of the General Assembly on the unilateral declaration of independence of Kosovo,[53] Kosovo was admitted to membership by the IMF and World Bank; however, so far, it has not become a member of the UN, as a direct result of the different membership procedures followed by these organizations, which, as in the case of Palestine, proved to be more important than substantive admission criteria.

---

48 See FAO 2015.

49 Amerasinghe 2005, p. 9.

50 On the concepts and criteria for membership, see as representative of many others and with detailed references the studies of Crawford 1977, pp. 93–182 and Crawford 2006. On issues of succession in relation to membership in international organizations, see with detailed references, Bühler 2001; and with regard to the IMF, Gold 1974.

51 Chen 2001, p. 25.

52 Crawford 2006, p. 49.

53 "Accordance with International Law of the Unilateral Declaration of Independence in Respect of Kosovo, Advisory Opinion", ICJ Reports, 2010, 403. http://www.icj-cij.org/files/case-related/141/141-20100722-ADV-01-00-EN.pdf.

Finally, there is some difference between international organizations in their appreciation of the legal status of some small islands like the Cook Islands, the case of which is particularly interesting, as it sheds light on the different concepts and criteria applied by international organizations for admission to membership.

Even though the Cook Islands is responsible for the conduct of their external relations, the UN does not consider them as an independent country. In a legal opinion, the UN Office of Legal Affairs said:

> 3. [....] The question is whether the Cook Islands in their present status, can be considered as an independent country for the purposes of the above-mentioned decision of the Governing Council. The term 'independent country' (or 'independence') has not been defined by the Governing Council, but the legislative history indicates that the decision was intended to apply to fully sovereign independent States within the meaning of that term in international law and the practice of the United Nations [....].
>
> xxx xxx xxx
>
> 4. An independent State under the generally accepted definition in international law must have inter alia one central political authority—the government which represents the State internally and externally. In that sense, independence means that a state may conduct its internal and international affairs unrestricted legally except through the operation of international law. Thus, a self-governing territory which does not possess the full capacity to enter into foreign relations cannot be regarded as a sovereign independent state. In other words, every independent country is by definition also a self-governing territory but a self-governing territory is not necessarily an independent country.
>
> xxx xxx xxx
>
> 6. In view of the essential characteristics of independent States as described above, it follows that the status of the Cook Islands is not sovereign independence in the juridical sense.[54]

While the Cook Islands were not deemed to be eligible for membership in the UN, and were admitted by UNESCAP as only an associate member, several UN specialized agencies have admitted the Cook Islands to full membership.[55] Hence, there is no common approach that has been adopted within the UN family in relation to membership of the Cook Islands.

Moreover, Cook Islands is also a member of various other international organizations outside the UN system. ADB does not consider Cook Islands to be a dependent territory and has admitted it to full membership as one of its member

[54] Question whether the Cook Islands are Eligible to Receive a United Nations Development Programme Indicative Planning Figure (IPF) Independence Bonus—Distinction between Self-Governing Territories and Independent States under International Law. Memorandum addressed to the Chief of Division One, Regional Bureau for Asia and the Pacific of the United Nations Development Programme. *United Nations Juridical Yearbook 1979*, pp. 172–174. http://legal.un.org/unjuridicalyearbook/pdfs/english/volumes/1979.pdf.

[55] A good overview of the legal and constitutional situation of the Cook Islands is contained in ILO. 2015. "Cook Islands' Application for Membership". *Background Paper for the International Labour Conference*. Provisional Record 3–1. 104th Session, Geneva, June. http://www.ilo.org/wcmsp5/groups/public/%2D%2D-ed_norm/%2D%2D-relconf/documents/meetingdocument/wcms_372015.pdf.

countries. The decisive criterion for ADB on whether an applicant for membership can join pursuant to Article 3.1 or Article 3.3 of the ADB Charter is not independence but whether the applicant is responsible for the conduct of its international relations.

These two criteria, while closely related, are not identical. On the one hand, while the ability to conduct its external relations is generally seen as one of the attributes of an independent state, the exercise of sovereign rights of states may be restricted for a variety of reasons, e.g. as a result of a treaty obligation or due to military and other concessions.[56] "Actual independence is relative, or in Rousseau's terms 'quantitative': it is a matter of degree.[57] On the other hand, the fact that a territory is responsible for the conduct of its external relations does not necessarily imply that the territory has attained independence. The capacity of the applicant to conduct its external relations is "a conflation of the requirements of government and independence" as it "depends partially on the powers of the internal government of a territory without which international obligations may not be carried into effect, and partly on the entity concerned being separate for the purpose of international relations so that no other entity both carries out and accepts responsibility for them."[58] As shown by the example of Cook Island, there are associated states responsible for the conduct of their external relations that are admitted to full membership by some international organizations, while they are considered ineligible for membership by others as they are deemed falling short of the requirement of independence.

5.3.2 International Organizations as Subjects of Membership

It is now firmly established that an international organization may become a party to a convention. This is epitomized by the accession of the European Union (EU) to the "Convention for the Protection of Human Rights and Fundamental Freedoms", widely known as the "European Convention on Human Rights" which was permitted by Article 59, para 2 of this Convention and was expressly mandated for the EU by Article 6, para 2 of the Treaty on European Union (TEU). Moreover, it is equally firmly established that as a matter of principle, international organizations may also become members of international organizations.

Organizations frequently interact with other international organizations and follow their work as observers. Cases where international organizations become full members of other international organizations are not very common. Nevertheless, such membership is expressly permitted in the constituent agreements of some of

---

[56] See Crawford 2006, pp. 67–71.

[57] Ibid., 72.

[58] Ibid., 62.

the newer international organizations, particularly for the European Union, which is a member of more than 30 international organizations.

As shown by Odendahl,[59] with regard to EU membership in international organizations, there is a distinction between sole membership (*Alleinige Mitgliedschaft*), additional membership (*Zusätzliche Mitgliedschaft*), and complimentary membership (*Komplementäre Mitgliedschaft*), also referred to as parallel, mixed, or partial membership of the EU, depending on whether the EU has exclusive competence in certain matters, a competence which is independent from that of the EU member states, or a shared competence.

In certain cases, international organizations are able to participate in the creation of new international organizations to ensure recognition of their membership status in the constituent agreement. The most important example was related to the EU's eligibility, in accordance with Articles XI and XIV of the Marrakesh Agreement, to become an original member of the WTO together with 12 EU members who were also members of the General Agreement on Tariffs and Trade (GATT) in 1947.

However, in a number of cases, international organizations have had to amend their constituent agreement to accommodate the membership of other international organizations. One example is the amendment of the Constitution of the Food and Agriculture Organization (FAO) by Resolution 7/91, which empowered the FAO Conference to admit by a two-thirds majority, any regional economic integration organization (REIO) meeting the following criteria: "constituted by sovereign States, a majority of which are Member Nations of the Organization, and to which its Member States have transferred competence over a range of matters within the purview of the Organization, including the authority to make decisions binding on its Member States in respect of those matters."[60] While the EU is, at present, the only organization that meets these criteria (incorporated in Article II, para 4 of the FAO Constitution), the wording of this Article is not specifically geared to the EU; hence, any regional integration organization that meets the required criteria is eligible for admission to membership.[61]

Another international organization which counts other international organizations as its members is the European Bank for Reconstruction and Development (EBRD), whose members include the EU as well as the European Investment Bank.

---

[59] Odendahl 2014, pp. 273–319, §5.

[60] See section on "Membership of regional economic integration organizations in FAO" in the Report of the Conference of FAO. 26th session. 9–27 November 1991. http://www.fao.org/docrep/x5587E/x5587e0b.htm#membership.

[61] FAO Constitution, Article II, para 3 provides:

The Conference may by a two-thirds majority of the votes cast, provided that a majority of the Member Nations of the Organization is present, decide to admit as a Member of the Organization any regional economic integration organization meeting the criteria set out in paragraph 4 of this Article, which has submitted an application for membership and a declaration made in a formal instrument that it will accept the obligations of the Constitution as in force at the time of admission [….].

5.3.3 Technical Government Agencies, Sub-State Actors and Regulatory Agencies as Subjects of Membership

A core question is whether technical government agencies, sub-state actors or cooperative undertakings of regulatory agencies may be eligible subjects of membership.

As previously discussed in the preceding chapters, in their early stages, the Universal Postal Union (UPU) and the ITU allowed the participation of technical administrations on a par with governments. These are important precedents as they underline that technical agencies have been recognized in the past as subjects of membership.

In the case of INTERPOL, the origins of which can be traced to a conference held in 1923 at the invitation of Vienna's chief of police, the intergovernmental character of the organization was affirmed based on a rule of attribution of the conduct of police authorities to governments, both in relation to the creation of INTERPOL and the representation of police authorities in its governing bodies.

However, an organization does not need to possess the characteristics of an intergovernmental organization to be qualified as an international organization. Hence, the members of an international organization do not need to be states and the conduct of the members of the organization's governing bodies does not need to be attributed to a government.

It is now widely accepted that the IPU may be considered an international organization even though its members are not governments but Parliaments. Applying the same rationale, other types of international organizations which do not have governments as members are also conceivable. Hence, as a matter of principle, an international organization may have as members federal states of various countries (e.g. belonging to a specific geographic area), or associations of municipalities, or national regulators.

As regards cooperative undertakings of national regulators, some of these (e.g., IOSCO and Financial Stability Board) already underwent progressive institutionalization and increasingly resemble traditional organizations.

Whether an organization composed of sub-state actors and national regulators may qualify for recognition as an international organization does not depend on its legal status or the manner of its establishment but on its functions and the position which recognized subjects of international law have adopted in its regard.

5.3.4 Dependent Territories as Subjects of Membership

The term "dependent territory" already appeared "to nineteenth-century writers strange and anachronistic."[62] In addition to being questionable *per se* from a

[62] See Crawford 2006, p. 283.

conceptual point of view, it suggests a communality of the legal status of such territories which effectively does not exist. The term "dependent territory" lacks clear definition as it refers to various territories with fundamentally different status. While, "the etymological origins of the term 'dependent territories' are unclear",[63] it appears that this term was increasingly used in the United Kingdom since the early 1900s to refer to "four categories: Colonies, Protectorates, Protected States and Trust Territories",[64] so as to avoid the "derogatory connotations"[65] of the term "colonies" which previously had been employed in a wider sense to refer to all four categories. It merely denoted the fact that the responsibility for the external relations of such territories was vested in the United Kingdom[66] but did not take account of the fact that such territories had a substantial different history and legal status.

Traditionally, dependent territories partake in the international relations of the metropolitan state responsible for the conduct of their external relations. The reason why the British dominions were able to apply for membership in the League of Nations before having attained full independence was not for the benefit of these territories, let alone their inhabitants, but to increase the voting rights and power of the United Kingdom, which had a core role in the League.

In case of the UN, the traditional state-centric approach prevailed as only states, not dependent territories, are eligible for membership. The fact that the established criteria were not properly applied in case of some of the original members of the UN may be seen as a derogation of the rule rather than an opening towards the membership of dependent territories.

Nevertheless, while Article 23(b) of the Covenant of the League of Nations only mandated the members of the League to "secure just treatment of the native inhabitants or territories under their control," Articles 73–74 of the UN Charter established important principles with regard to "non-self-governing territories" (as the dependencies of colonial and other powers were euphemistically addressed). While the League of Nations did not rule out colonial rule and domination by foreign powers, subsequently, the UN strongly advocated the independence of non-self-governing territories.

---

63 Drower 1992, p. xvii.

64 Ibid., xviii. The differences between the cited four categories have been elaborated by Fawcett:

Colonies are British possessions which were acquired by settlement and are administered by the Crown in accordance with the provisions of the British Settlements Act, 1887, or were conquered by or ceded to the Crown and are administered by the Crown under its prerogative powers or under a specific Act of Parliament. A British protectorate is not part of His Majesty's dominions and is therefore not a British possession, but foreign territory, over which the Crown exercises jurisdiction under the Foreign Jurisdiction Act, 1890. A British-protected state is a foreign territory, having a local ruler who has by treaty transferred responsibility for its external relations to the Crown. Trust territories of the United Kingdom are territories which have been placed by the Crown under the trusteeship system of the United Nations, in accordance with Chapter XII of the United Nations Charter, and of which His Majesty's Government in the United Kingdom is the administering authority. Fawcett 1949, p. 88.

65 Drower 1992, p. xvii.

66 Ibid., xviii.

The IMF and the World Bank adopted a similar state-centric approach as the UN. Thus, Section 2(g) of Article XXXI of the IMF Articles of Agreement provides:

> By their signature of this Agreement, all governments accept it both on their own behalf and in respect of all their colonies, overseas territories, all territories under their protection, suzerainty, or authority, and all territories in respect of which they exercise a mandate.

Moreover, an equivalent provision is contained in Section 2(g) of Article XI of the IBRD Articles of Agreement.

There are other cases where organizations discontinued the ability of dependent territories to apply for membership. As has been shown above, the representation of dependent territories was an important issue from the time the ITU was established. However, under Article 2 of ITU Constitution of 1975, membership is now limited to states. Thus, dependent territories are no longer eligible subjects of membership. The UPU founders wanted to admit as members not only sovereign States but also certain territorial and political entities that were not totally independent (in particular protectorates or colonies) [….]. That is why they chose [in Chapter 1, Article 1] the term 'country' in order to embrace all the entities admitted as member countries of the UPU."[67] In accordance with Chapter 1, Article 2 of the UPU Constitution, "member countries of the Union shall be:

a. countries which have membership status at the date on which the Constitution comes into force;
b. countries admitted to membership in accordance with article 11."

Hence, those "non-self-governing territories" which had membership status when the Constitution came into force continued to be members. However, "non-self-governing territories" cannot be admitted as new members pursuant to Chapter 1, Article 11 of the UPU Constitution as in accordance with paras 1 and 2 of this Article admission to membership is only available to "[a]ny member of the United Nations" and "[a]ny sovereign country which is not a member of the United Nations."

The World Meteorological Organization (WMO) did not adopt a similar approach as the ITU or the UPU. Thus, under Article 3(d) of the Convention of the World Meteorological Organization, "[a]ny territory or group of territories maintaining its own Meteorological Service and listed in Annex II [of the Convention]" may become a member of WMO upon application of the metropolitan state (see Annex I of the Convention) "responsible for its international relations."

Moreover, membership in the WTO is open to states as well as to any "separate customs territory possessing full autonomy in the conduct of its external commercial relations and of the other matters provided for" in the Marrakesh Agreement and the multilateral trade agreements.[68]

---

[67] See commentary to Article 1 of the UPU Constitution. UPU. 2014. *Organic Acts of the UPU*. Berne. (cited as UPU Commentary). http://www.upu.int/uploads/tx_sbdownloader/actInFourVolumesConstitutionManualEn.pdf.

[68] See Agreement Establishing the World Trade Organization, Article XII, para 1.

The ADB and the CDB are of particular interest as they allow full membership of dependent territories.

The fact that five of the six "dependent territories" which joined ADB pursuant to Article 3.3 of the Charter subsequently became responsible for the conduct of their external relations also clearly underlines that the term "dependent territory" merely reflects a snapshot of their development status at the time when they applied for ADB membership.[69]

It was not intrinsically necessary for ADB to admit dependent territories to membership to be able to extend financing to such territories.[70] Nevertheless, ADB

---

[69] In fact, some effectively achieved independence within a few months after joining ADB. As for Hong Kong, China, however, it subsequently became an integral part of the territory of the People's Republic of China (PRC), and its legal status can also no longer properly characterized as that of a dependency, but it remains a member of ADB independent of PRC's membership.

[70] This was already clearly set out by Otto Schachter, the Director of the UN General Legal Division, after the Executive Secretary of ECAFE, U Nyun, requested him on 10 Sept. 1965 to provide advice on the legal aspects of making the facilities of the proposed ADB available to assist ECAFE members such as Brunei and Hong Kong and dependent territories in the Asian region such as Fiji and Papua and New Guinea. This shows that the drafters of the ADB Charter were well aware that membership of dependent territories in ADB was not per se necessary to enable ADB to provide assistance to such dependent territories. In his legal opinion of 7 October 1965, Schachter said:

> There are three possible ways in which the facilities of the Bank could be made available to Territories not responsible for the conduct of their own foreign relations (referred to in this note as Territories), namely:
>
> 1. Through the exercise by such a Territory of the membership rights of the Metropolitan Power;
> 2. By a grant to such a Territory of membership in its own right under a provision to the be inserted in the Agreement establishing this Bank; and
> 3. By means of a special provision in the Agreement permitting loans to co-operations in Territories even where neither the Territories nor the Metropolitan Powers concerned are members of the Bank.

While indicating that all three alternatives would require consent on the part of the Metropolitan Power and the assumption by it of international responsibility for the fulfillment of any obligations which could devolve upon the territory, Schachter observed that the first alternative would require no special provision in the ADB Charter and could be based on the broadly worded authorization granted the Bank to provide or facilitate financing to any member, or agency, instrumentality or political subdivision thereof. The second option, on the other hand, involved issues of share capital and voting rights while the third option would only require a simple enabling clause expressly permitting the bank to provide or facilitate financing to Territories in the region not responsible for the conduct of their own foreign relations, with the consent of the Metropolitan State and under such conditions as the Board of Governors may determine.

He further elaborated on this in a second legal opinion of 15 October 1965:

In my letter of 7 October I also briefly touched on the question of granting a territory membership in its own right under a provision to be inserted in the draft charter. As I have I think made clear, such a provision is not necessary for the purpose of providing for the eligibility of such territories for assistance. There is, however, no legal obstacle to including a provision on these lines provided that the State internationally responsible grants its consent. Such membership or

deliberately took a different approach than the UN, IMF and World Bank, which include dependent territories in the membership of the metropolitan state. Considering that the General Assembly of the United Nations had passed its "Declaration on the granting of independence to colonial countries and peoples" in 1960,[71] and given ADB's character as a regional institution founded to "foster economic growth and co-operation" in its region and "to contribute to the acceleration of the process of economic development of the developing member countries in the region, collectively and individually,"[72] it would not have been appropriate for ADB to extend financing to dependent territories within its region as a dependency of a developed country outside the region. Thus, unlike the case of the IMF and IBRD, the non-regional countries responsible for the conduct of the international relations of certain territories were not called upon to accept the ADB Charter on behalf of such territories.

ADB followed the IMF and World Bank in determining that countries rather than states were subjects of ADB membership. This was to avoid the many issues surrounding the definition of "state", which term does not have a defined meaning and is even seen to have "metaphysical attributes."[73] The eligibility of "countries" to apply for membership in ADB as a regional country is linked to their membership or associate membership in UNESCAP/ECAFE, or membership in the UN or a specialized agency. This implies that

> membership and eligibility issues are to some extent 'pre-digested' by the relevant United Nations agencies before they reach the Bank. According to a former UNESCAP senior official, the reason for this was probably to quarantine a development body such as the Bank from some of the politically charged membership eligibility issues that have plagued the early United Nations. By making UNESCAP or UN agency membership a prerequisite for ADB membership, the founders were probably ensuring that the possibly acrimonious membership issues were fought out in the UN, rather than in the ADB.[74]

There are three special aspects to the employment of the term "country" in ADB.

First, in the case of countries with dependent territories, the term "country" only comprises the metropolitan territory of ADB's member country and does not include any dependent territories or territories held in trust. Thus, the Government of the United Kingdom of Great Britain and Northern Ireland (United Kingdom) ratified the ADB Charter on 19 September 1966 only on behalf of the United

---

associate membership would give rise to problems of determining voting rights and possibly share capital for such territories and would require new provisions. Such membership arrangement entails a more complicated norm for providing for the extension of facilities to such territories and is not necessary for that purpose.

[71] Declaration on the Granting of Independence to Colonial Countries and Peoples. Adopted by General Assembly Resolution 1514 (XV) of 14 Dec. 1960. http://www.un.org/en/decolonization/declaration.shtml.

[72] Agreement establishing the Asian Development Bank, Article 1. https://www.adb.org/sites/default/files/institutional-document/32120/charter.pdf.

[73] See Chen 2001, citing Reisman.

[74] Wesley 2003, p. 100.

Kingdom and its membership did not extend to Hong Kong, Fiji, the British Solomon Islands Protectorate, and the Gilbert and Ellice Islands,[75] which were subsequently admitted to ADB membership as dependent territories pursuant to Article 3.3. Similarly, the membership of France only extends to the "Republic of France" classified as a "non-regional developed country",[76] which implies that none of the French overseas territories or dependencies are included in France's membership. The same also applies to regional countries such as Australia and New Zealand. The Commonwealth of Australia ratified the Charter for "Australia"[77] and the Government of New Zealand did so for "New Zealand", the implication being that their membership did not extend to Papua New Guinea and Cook Islands, respectively. Finally, even though Macau is deemed to be an "inalienable part"[78] of the People's Republic of China (PRC), based on the Basic Law of the Macau Special Administrative Region of the People's Republic of China (Basic Law), ADB's Charter does not extend to Macau. Similarly, Hong Kong, China, in spite of the transfer of power to the PRC, is not comprised in the membership of the PRC and continues to be an ADB member in its own right.[79]

Second, consistent with the above, one of the particularities of the ADB Charter is that it defines a country to "include a territory which is an associate member of the United Nations Economic Commission for Asia and the Far East [now known as the United Nations Economic and Social Commission for Asia and the Pacific or UNESCAP]."[80] ADB is one of the few organizations that admit dependent territories to full membership. Thus, the term "country" is used both for an original and a derived subject of international law.

Third, currently not all associate members of UNESCAP are dependent territories. Some of the associate members of UNESCAP were admitted to ADB membership pursuant to Article 3.1 of the Charter after they had become responsible for the conduct of their external relations while others joined ADB pursuant to Article 3.3 of the Charter as dependent territories, but subsequently became

---

75 Now the separate countries of Kiribati and Tuvalu.

76 ADB. 1970. Admission of the Republic of France to Membership in the Asian Development Bank (Resolution No. 31, adopted by ADB's Board of Governors on 24 March) See also ADB. 1970. Membership of the Republic of France (Sec.M9-70, 17 Feb.).

77 Commonwealth of Australia. 1966. Instrument of Ratification of the Agreement Establishing the Asian Development Bank (signed by John Grey Corton, Acting Minister of State for External Affairs for the Commonwealth of Australia on 15 September).

78 See Article 1 of the Basic Law of Macau. http://www.umac.mo/basiclaw/english/ch1.html.

79 See: Agreement Establishing the Asian Development Bank. Status of Ratifications. End Note 1. https://treaties.un.org/pages/ViewDetails.aspx?src=TREATY&mtdsg_no=X-4&chapter=10&clang=_en which refers, in addition to Hong Kong, to five other previously "non-autonomous territories" that became members of ADB.

80 ADB Charter, Article 3.3.

responsible for the conduct of their external relations while remaining an associate member of UNESCAP. In each case, ADB had to assess their current development status. In doing so, ADB applied its own criteria and did not necessarily rely on the classification by UNESCAP or any other international organization.

Thus, as a matter of practice and even though not expressly recognized by the Charter, the term "country" in Article 3 of the ADB Charter may extend, in addition to dependent territories, to associate members of UNESCAP which are responsible for the conduct of their international relations.

This use of the term "country" in three different and distinct connotations underlines that this term is subject to substantial complexity. Such complexity is further compounded by the fact that the term "dependent territories" used in Article 3.3 of the ADB Charter is unclear, misleading and questionable from a conceptual point of view.

A similar approach, even though following a somewhat different procedure, has been adopted by the CDB which also admits dependent territories as full members of the Bank.[81]

The EU has yet again adopted a different approach in respect of the overseas territories of EU member countries. These territories were neither admitted to membership in the European Union, nor are they deemed to be part of the metropolitan territory of EU member states. Rather, these are associated with the EU pursuant to Articles 198–204 of the TFEU (Association of the Overseas Countries and Territories).

"Although OCTs are not third countries and their nationals are in principle EU citizens, they do not form part of the single market and must comply with third country obligations regarding trade, notably rules of origin, (plant) health, and safeguard measures" and "hence EU law applies to them only insofar as necessary to implement the association agreements."[82]

---

[81] See CDB Charter, Article 62(2). As indicated by Droesse, "Organizational Structures", 97:

> While both the ADB and CDB charters allow membership of dependent territories, there are certain differences regarding their procedures for admitting dependent territories to membership. Both organizations require the presentation of an application for membership by the member responsible for the international relations of the applicant. While ADB requires that member to assume responsibility for all obligations of the applicant until such time that the applicant itself assumes such responsibility, CDB requires confirmation from said member that the dependent territory has authority to enter into a membership agreement with CDB and to assume the rights and obligations of the agreement. Thus, the state responsible for conducting the international relations of the dependent territory generally does not assume a legal obligation to CDB for the borrowings and other financial obligations of the dependent territory.

[82] Baetens 2012, note 3. www.mpepil.com. See also, in great detail: Murray 2012.

5.3.5 *Corporations or Other Transnational Actors as Members of International Organizations*

5.3.5.1 Membership of Private-Sector Entities in International Organizations

The question whether corporations and other transnational actors may be full members of international organizations is generally not even raised, let alone answered. As set out under hereunder, there is no reason why such a form of institutionalized participation should be excluded. It is also conceivable, as shown under Sect. 5.3.7.1 below that there may be international organizations with a membership structure consisting entirely of corporations and other non-state actors. Moreover, affiliate or sector membership of private sector entities and other transnational actors which so far have only been given marginal application and other types of partial membership should be encouraged.

5.3.6 *Examples of Participation of Private-Sector Entities*

The East African Development Bank (EADB) and the West African Development Bank (WADB), both of which have a treaty foundation, are two examples of international financial institutions which have corporations (e.g., banks, export credit agencies, or national development corporations incorporated under national law) as members.

Article 2 of the EADB Treaty expressly provides for the membership of "bodies corporate, enterprises or institutions."[83] Consistent with the above, in addition to four regional members,[84] a number of corporate entities are institutional

[83] Article 2 of the Treaty and Charter of the East African Development Bank, on "Membership in the Bank", provides:

1. The original members of the Bank shall be the United Republic of Tanzania, the Republic of Uganda and the Republic of Kenya and **such bodies corporate, enterprises or institutions** who remain members of the Bank on the date of entry into force of the amendments to this Charter adopted by the Member States in the Treaty of 23.7.1980 amending and re-enacting this Charter. (emphasis added)
2. Upon an affirmative decision of the Governing Council, any state in the region, **body corporate enterprise or institution**, which has not become a member under para 1 of this Article, may be admitted to membership of the Bank under such terms and conditions consistent with this Charter, as the Bank may determine. [….] (emphasis added)

See Treaty and Charter of the East Africa Development Bank, Treaty Amending and Re-Enacting the Charter of the East African Development Bank. http://eadb.org/?wpdmdl=1540.

[84] Tanzania, Uganda, and Kenya, the three original members specified in Article 2 of the EADB Treaty and Charter, and the Republic of Rwanda.

shareholders of EADB classified as B members; these include the Netherlands Development Company; German Investment and Development Company; SBIC Africa Holdings, Commercial Bank of Africa, Standard Chartered Bank and Barclays Bank Plc., which joined EADB.[85]

In addition to eight West African countries and the Central Bank of the West African States that hold A shares, the WADB also counts countries and agencies from outside the West African subregion among its shareholders and members. Its B membership comprises countries (France, Belgium and Morocco), international organizations (African Development Bank [AfDB] and European Investment Bank [EIB], acting on behalf of the European Union), and other entities such as the Kreditanstalt für Wiederaufbau of Germany, Exim Bank of India, acting for the Republic of India, and the People's Bank of China, acting on behalf of the People's Republic of China.[86]

The CAF distinguishes between its A, B and C series of capital shares. While the A series shares are available "for subscription by the Government of each Member Country or by public, semipublic or private institutions as the former may designate," capital B shares are reserved for subscription "by governments or public, semipublic or private entities of Member Countries", and capital C shares are available for "subscription by legal entities or natural persons from outside the Member Countries."[87]

Finally, the Regulations of the Islamic Solidarity Fund for Development (ISFD) contain provisions which are relevant in this context. While the ISFD does not possess international legal personality, arrangements for participation in the ISFD are set forth in the said Regulations, which are separate from those applicable to the Islamic Development Bank (ISDB). Article 6.02 of the said Regulations provides:

> Any member country of the Bank, or **any institution of a member country of the Bank**, other than those named in Annex A hereto, may participate in the Fund upon such terms as may be decided by a vote of the majority of the total number of Governors representing a majority of the votes of the Governors. (emphasis added)

Article 10 of the said Regulations further stipulates: "Those Participant institutions whose paid contribution is US$ 20,000,000 (US Dollars Twenty Million) or more, individually or collectively, may participate in decision-making in the Board of Governors." Other participants merely participate as observers.[88]

---

85 For the detailed list of B shareholders of EADB, see http://eadb.org/about-us/shareholding/.

86 BOAD. "Who we are?" https://www.boad.org/en/who-we-are/.

In accordance with Article 6, para 2 of the Articles of Association of the West African Development Bank k (BOAD), category B shareholders include,

- Non-member countries of the Union or their designated financial institutions,
- The international financial institutions, desirous of lending their support to the development of the Union and approved by the Council of Ministers of the Union.

87 See Agreement Establishing the Corporation Andina di Fomento, Article 5, paras 1(A), (B), and (C). https://www.caf.com/media/1412720/agreement-establishment-caf-march-2012.pdf.

88 Regulations of the Islamic Solidarity Fund for Development as of 2007. Author's copy.

While currently, the ISDB is the only institution participating in the ISFD, in principle, other institutions are also entitled to participate in the ISFD if the Board of Governors of the ISFD agrees. The wording of the ISFD Regulations allows institutions incorporated under national law or foundations to participate in the ISFD. The example of the ISFD is particularly interesting as the right of any Participant institution to decision-making in the Board of Governors is linked to the amount of its contribution. This could be an approach that might be adopted for institutions participating in international organizations, in general. To be able to be considered for participation in the work and decision-making of international organizations, reputable institutions which meet all requirements may be requested to make a long-term commitment to supporting the organization, including through financial contributions.

5.3.7 *Private-Sector Entities Can Be Full Members of International Organizations*

There is no intrinsic reason why private sector corporations, agencies incorporated under national law, or other state actors should not be full members of international organizations. First, in a number of cases, countries provide financial support and assistance to beneficiary countries through entities which are organized as private corporations, even though they are fully state owned and operating under the supervision and authority of the central government. Unlike the Danish[89] and Swedish[90] development corporations DANIDA and SIDA, which form part of their respective countries' Ministry of Foreign Affairs, the German Gesellschaft für Internationale Zusammenarbeit (GIZ), is organized as a corporation under private law (Gesellschaft mit beschränkter Haftung [GMBH]).[91] Moreover, the German Kreditanstalt für Wiederaufbau Banking Group (KFW)[92] is also governed by corporate law. As both GIZ and KfW are fully owned and are operating under the supervision and authority of the German federal government, it is irrelevant whether the Federal Republic of Germany or GIZ or KfW as corporate entities are members of an international organization. In either case, they represent the German government. In addition to GIZ and KfW, there are a range of other organizations which are incorporated under national law and pursue matters of public policy. In the case of WADB, Exim Bank is expressly acting as a shareholder on behalf the Republic of India, while the People's Bank of China is acting similarly on behalf of the People's Republic of China.

89 See Ministry of Foreign Affairs of Denmark. Danida. http://um.dk/en/danida-en/.

90 See Sida. http://www.sida.se/English/.

91 See Deutsche Gesellschaft für Technische Zusammenarbeit (GIZ) GmbH. www.giz.de/en/html/our_services.html.

92 See KfW. KfW Group. https://www.kfw.de/KfW-Group/.

However, full membership of private sector entities in international organizations does not need to be limited to national developing agencies incorporated under national law, such as GIZ and KfW. It might be extended to reputable private sector entities that meet all the requirements of a reputable donor and commit to providing substantial and sustained financial or other equivalent support to an organization on a long-term basis which will enhance the effectiveness and performance of the organization concerned.

Full membership of reputable transnational actors which meet all the requirements of an acceptable donor might be linked to a contribution in a defined minimal amount (e.g., USD 20 million as in the case of the ISFD mentioned above). Hence, the institutionalized participation of transnational actors including the private sector, philanthropy and civil society may become a major source of financial support. However, it would be a mistake to focus only on the financial support which transnational actors may provide. Their support to international organizations may come in different forms. For example, some countries may face constraints in providing financial inputs to international financial institutions, but may be able to facilitate the provision of risk mitigation instruments through their export credit agencies or through re-insurance companies. In the case of international financial institutions, such support would substantially enhance the risk-bearing capacity of the organization and its ability to leverage resources. If a reputable export credit agency or re-insurance company would be willing to provide to an international financial institution substantial support on untied terms and on a long-term basis, an institutionalized participation of that entity in the work of the organization through full membership might be considered. Moreover, full membership in international organizations might also be extended to other transnational actors (e.g., philanthropic organizations).

Institutionalized participation of private sector entities in the work of international organization may not only enhance the financial support to an international organization but may also substantially expand its knowledge base. In a number of areas, the main knowledge base is outside international organizations. This is markedly the case for risk assessment and risk mitigation mechanisms, including re-insurance and export insurance. The limited financial and staffing resources which international financial institutions can muster on these matters are tiny if compared with the financial and staffing resources available to re-insurance companies and export credit agencies. Thus, to engage with such companies and agencies and get them involved in the work of international organizations would boost the knowledge base of such organizations and their ability to provide innovative finance mechanisms and to leverage additional resources.

However, for full effect, the institutionalized participation of private sector entities in the work of international organizations should not be limited to such entities providing advisory services to an organization. The full potential of such institutionalized forms of participation can only be maximized if it is enhanced by additional measures, such as staff secondment, and interaction at all levels between the private sector entity and the international organization concerned. While advisory services may facilitate the engagement of an organization in new types of activities, staff secondment may greatly enhance the knowledge base of an organization and contribute to the effective implementation of its activities and the design of innovative solutions.

There are a number of other areas where main sources of knowledge are outside international organizations. One of these areas relates to global value chain (GVC) issues which are central to any discussion on trade policy and investment policy. As indicated by Pascal Lamy, any discussion on such matters "that fails to acknowledge the centrality of GVCs would be considered outmoded and of questionable relevance."[93] International organizations, which generally have very limited expertise, if any, in GVC matters, might substantially benefit from outside inputs on GVC issues in optimizing their policy agenda and operational activities.

Any membership (either full, associate or affiliate, partial or sector membership) would only be available to reputable foundations, private sector institutions, and other entities willing to support such organizations on a long-term basis and to make a substantial contribution to the work of these organizations. While full membership of transnational actors in international organization will only be possible in a limited number of cases, transnational actors, including the private sector and civil society, may be involved in the work of international organizations on a regular basis through a more limited type of membership, i.e., an associate, affiliate or sector membership.

Thus, *de lege ferenda*, institutionalized forms of participation of transnational actors, which may entail full membership or a more limited forms of membership (associate, affiliate, or sector), should be considered as design options for all new international organizations that are established.

Consistent with the mandate of the organization, action may be taken to transform international organizations from state-governed institutions into multi-actor institutions wherever such transformation may enhance their effectiveness and performance. There is nothing in international law which forbids providing for such membership. On the contrary, this book has identified a few examples which show that such form of participation is indeed possible.

For newly established international organization, institutionalized participation of transnational actors may expressly be incorporated in their constituent agreement. In the case of existing organizations, allowing the involvement of transnational actors may require amendment of their constituent agreements. As has been shown by this author,[94] any such undertaking is very difficult as qualified majorities may be required for the amendment of constituent instruments, which may offer a small group of countries, or, possibly one country alone, a veto right. Thus, generally, institutional reform is a formidable task. However, organizations that face such constraints can open themselves toward transnational actors as a matter of policy. Moreover, as will be shown in Chap. 9, secondary governance structures that involve the private sector under an overall strategic framework approved by the

93 Lamy 2013, p. xv. https://www.wto.org/english/res_e/booksp_e/aid4tradeglobalvalue13_e.pdf.

94 Droesse, "Organizational Structures", 59–177.

organization's governing bodies can be created as a matter of policy and do not necessarily involve an amendment to the constituent agreement.

Hence, it is necessary to rethink not only the forms of interaction between international organizations and the private sector but also the current paradigms of organizational structure, particularly for organizations which have been established to finance global public goods. The proposed changes to current membership concepts highlighted above are in line with the increased importance of the private sector, philanthropy and non-state actor in global governance and may enhance the effectiveness and impact of international organizations.

5.3.7.1 Membership Structures Comprising Only Transnational Actors

It is not impossible to fathom an international organization whose membership is entirely composed of private sector entities. Organizations such as the Internet Corporation for Assigned Names and Numbers (ICANN), which was incorporated as a nonprofit public benefit corporation, organized under California law,[95] the International Standard Organization (ISO), and the International Air Transport Association (IATA) might be possible candidates for conversion into an international organization of that type.

As highlighted, "one of the main revelations of the research on global governance is that institutions based on private law or hybrid institutions which lack any relevant delegation of authority may carry out activities which are just as much of public interest as those based on delegations of authority."[96] A typical instance of such functional equivalence is "any governance activity which directly affects public goods, by which global infrastructures are managed, or which unfolds in a situation where the collision of fundamental interests of different social groups has to be dealt with."[97] In the case of ICANN, the roles of the private sector entities and government are reversed, as the "principal participants in settling the standards and organizing the Internet are private corporations," while national governments, although involved, "are formally reduced to an advisory role vis-à-vis the organization."[98] While ICANN is incorporated under national law, it produces global public goods and its functions are of great importance.

The discussion on ICANN on the privatization and restructuring of ICANN[99] has gained momentum since the U.S. Commerce Department's National

---

[95] See Articles of Incorporation of ICANN as revised on 21 Nov. 1998. https://www.icann.org/resources/pages/governance/articles-en.

[96] von Bogdandy et al. 2010, p. 14.

[97] von Bogdandy et al. 2010, p. 14.

[98] Hartwig 2010, p. 576.

[99] Report on the Transition of the Stewardship of the Internet Assigned Numbers Authority (IANA) Functions. https://www.ntia.doc.gov/files/ntia/publications/iana_report_013015.pdf; see also the letter conveying NTIA's assessment to the Congress of the United States: http://www.ntia.

Telecommunications and Information Administration (NTIA) announced on 14 March 2014 its intent to release its limited control over ICANN and transition the stewardship of key internet functions to the global multi-stakeholder community. The proposal which was made to that effect in March 2016[100] met with a positive response from NTIA.[101] The expiry on 1 October 2016 of the contract between ICANN and NTIA, under which NTIA performed the Internet Assigned Numbers Authority (IANA) functions, was a "historic moment" which "marks the transition of the coordination and management of the Internet's unique identifiers to the private-sector."[102]

The purpose of the ISO is "to promote the development of standardization and related activities in the world with a view to facilitating international exchange of goods and services and to developing cooperation in the spheres of intellectual, scientific, technological and economic activity."[103] ISO, which is generally classified as a non-governmental organization, "brings together experts to share knowledge and develop voluntary, consensus-based, market relevant International Standards that support innovation and provide solutions to global challenges."[104]

The ISO Statutes provide for association of national standards bodies as subscriber, correspondent and as full member, which categories "give increasing access to, and influence in, the ISO system."[105] Regular membership is reserved for "national standards bodies most broadly representative of standardization in their respective countries" (one member body per country).[106]

IATA is a member organization representing over 280 of the world leading airlines and cargo operators.[107] Most of the functions of IATA could also have been performed by an international organization, as is underlined by the fact that Great Britain proposed during the Chicago conference of 1944 "an international organization which would have at least equal, if not more, power than the United States

---

doc.gov/files/ntia/publications/ntia_letter_to_congress_transmitting_ntias_assessment_of_iana_-transition_proposal_06.09.16.pdf.

100 Proposal to Transition the Stewardship of the Internet Assigned Numbers Authority (IANA) Functions from the U.S. Commerce Department's National Telecommunications and Information Administration (NTIA) to the Global Multi-stakeholder Community IANA Stewardship Transition Coordination Group (ICG). March 2016. https://www.icann.org/en/system/files/files/iana-stewardship-transition-proposal-10mar16-en.pdf.

101 National Telecommunications and Information Administration. "NTIA Finds IANA Stewardship Transition Proposal Meets Criteria to Complete Privatization". Press Release. https://www.ntia.doc.gov/press-release/2016/iana-stewardship-transition-proposal-meets-criteria-complete-privatization.

102 Stewardship of IANA Functions Transitions to Global Internet Community as Contract with U.S. Government Ends. https://www.icann.org/news/announcement-2016-10-01-en.

103 ISO Statutes, Article 2.1. http://www.iso.org/iso/statutes.pdf.

104 About ISO. http://www.iso.org/iso/home/about.htm.

105 ISO membership manual. http://www.iso.org/iso/iso_membership_manual.pdf, 6.

106 ISO Statutes, Article 3.1.1. http://www.iso.org/iso/statutes.pdf.

107 See IATA. "Current Airline Members". http://www.iata.org/about/members/Pages/airline-list.aspx?All=true.

Civil Aeronautics Board. According to her proposed plan, the 'International Air Authority' would be empowered to determine and distribute frequencies and capacity, and to fix rates, while routes were to be agreed upon bilaterally or multilaterally between nations."[108]

For different reasons, traditional concepts of international organization are not suitable for each of the three organizations mentioned above. Neither ICANN, ISO, nor IATA can limit their functions to public institutions or standard setting bodies, because this would exclude many institutions and bodies which are privately organized or have a mixed composition. The inclusiveness of their procedures is core to their ability to perform their functions. In the case of ICANN, this relates to the perceived need of guaranteeing the openness of the internet and maintaining a multi-stakeholder model; for ISO, this relates to the fact that "ISO standards are developed in over 3,000 technical bodies by around 100,000 experts from industry and commerce, government, consumers, labour organizations, academic and research bodies, standards bodies and non-governmental organizations in over 160 countries."[109] Finally, it is deemed essential to involve airline carriers in IATA's operations, including both privately-owned and government-owned carriers as well as mixed types of corporations.

Organizations such as ICANN, ISO or IATA involve matters of public interest. Hence, it is necessary to give a role in such institutions to governments and other stakeholders if they are structured in such manner that their membership comprises entities incorporated or operating under national law.

While this cannot be the place to discuss in detail options for converting the entities as mentioned above into international organizations, it is to be highlighted that there are a great variety of different design options both regarding the potential membership structure of such an international organization and its accountability mechanisms, which may involve states in a supervisory or advisory capacity.

Membership structures may include, depending on the role and functions of the organization to be established, equity-based arrangements which may involve states and other entities in addition to their role as members in the quality of shareholders. Such arrangements are appropriate, in particular, in those cases where the participating entities own the organization.

The involvement of states may be tailored to the organization's role and functions. A variety of different guidance mechanisms may be conceived. Following the example of the Green Climate Fund, provision might be made for the organization to be "accountable to and operate under the guidance of" the parties to a convention. Alternatively, consideration might be given, to creating one or more advisory bodies. Depending on the functions and purpose of the organization, such advisory bodies might be composed of states or comprise, in addition to states, other stakeholders.

An organizational structure as indicated above would imply the reversal of the governance structures of international organizations to the extent that private sector

[108] Chuang 1972, p. 22.

[109] ISO Membership Manual, 6.

entities would be members while states would have an advisory role. Recognizing that an international organization can be established in that manner would imply a constitutionalization of entities such as ICANN, ISO, and IATA which so far operate in a grey zone of uncertain legal and supervisory arrangements which give rise to many concerns regarding accountability and transparency; it would imply clarifying their legal status and rationalizing their governance structure.

Organizations such as ICANN, ISO and IATA could be converted into international organizations based on an international agreement between three or more states that would not become members of the organization. Rather, the agreement would merely be a vehicle for conferring international personality to the organization and the parties to the agreement would not become members of the international organization established in that manner. As has been shown above, this method was used for the establishment of the CGIAR Consortium.

Thus, it is necessary for international organizations to adjust to changed realities by giving up the concept that only states and international organizations can be subjects of membership. Allowing the participation of transnational actors, including the private sector, philanthropy and civil society, may substantially enhance the organization's access to resources, as well as its knowledge base and ability to produce innovative solutions.

5.3.7.2 Affiliate, Sector and Partial Membership of Transnational Actors

The cases where private sector entities and other transnational actors become full members of international organizations will necessarily remain limited. First and foremost, all transnational actors considered for admission to membership must meet all the requirements of reputability, accountability and transparency. Moreover, generally any full membership of transnational actors requires (i) a sustained and long-term commitment to support the organization and (ii) a substantial financial or equivalent contribution. These requirements cannot easily be met.

In those cases where full membership of private sector entities is not possible, other forms of participation of private sector entities should be promoted. As shown above, such forms of participation exist at present in a rudimentary form in relation to the affiliate membership of the UNWTO and the sector membership of the ITU. Building on these examples, similar forms of institutionalized participation should be implemented by most international organizations. This should be considered as a design option for any new international organizations to be established. For existing international organizations, the qualified majorities required for amendments of constituent instruments are a formidable constraint for taking such action. However, as has been shown by this author, in such a case it is possible to involve transnational actors as a matter of policy by creating secondary governance structures under the overall purview of the statutory governing bodies of international organizations (see Chap. 9).

5.4 Membership Procedures

Generally, the constituent agreement or instrument reflects the consensus among the members of an organization as to which subjects may be admitted to membership and on conditions for admission to membership. It often also contains core provisions on the applicable membership procedure which may be further defined and elaborated in the organization's bylaws or other basic instruments, or by decisions of the organization's governing bodies.

At times, membership procedures are as important, or even more important, than substantive eligibility requirements. This is applicable, in particular, in those cases where certain states have the opportunity to veto applications for membership.

There is a range of distinctions that can be made as regards membership procedures. Such differences relate, on the one hand, to the fact that the constitutions of some organizations require ratification, while the constitutions of other entities were adopted by the resolution or a decision of a governing body of the entity concerned and, hence, were not subject to ratification. This distinction is a corollary of that between international organizations established by a treaty and those not created in that manner.

Another fundamental distinction relates to open organizations (who allow the admission of new members) and closed organization. There is a wide spectrum of different eligibility requirements and conditionalities for admission to membership.

On one end of the spectrum are universal organizations that aspire to have a membership as comprehensive as possible, including membership of technical administrations and dependent territories, and require virtually no conditions for countries and other entities to be admitted to membership. A paradigm for such organization may be seen in the General/Universal Postal Union prior to its transformation into a specialized agency when states could join the organization through unilateral action and technical administration and dependent territories, alike, were admitted to membership. Organizations of that kind may be seen as the epitome of an open organization. On the other end of the spectrum are closed organizations such as the Nordic Development Fund (NDF) where an amendment to the constituent agreement is required to admit new members. Organizations whose constituent instruments contain restrictions regarding the eligibility requirements of new members are often also seen as closed organizations. In between, there is a range of varying eligibility requirements and conditionalities which apply to the admission of new members.

At times, procedural criteria are as important, or even more important, than substantive eligibility criteria. One important distinction between membership procedures relates to the requirement of ratification of the governing instrument. Moreover, membership procedures may be classified based on their complexity, based on the criteria which are applied in the membership process, and in relation to the procedures which are applied to different subjects of membership. These issues will be reviewed in *seriatim*.

5.4.1 Procedure May Prevail Over Substance

The UN membership procedures are an epitome of the fact that procedural requirements (embodied in the need for the Security Council to recommend admission to membership to the UN and the right of permanent Security Council members to veto such recommendation) may prevail over the five substantive eligibility criteria set forth in para 1 of Article 4 of the UN Charter. The International Court emphasized in the second admissions case that

> the admission of a State to membership in the United Nations, pursuant to paragraph 2 of Article 4 of the Charter, cannot be effected by a decision of the General Assembly when the Security Council has made no recommendation for admission, by reason of the candidate failing to obtain the requisite majority or of the negative vote of a permanent Member upon a resolution so to recommend.[110]

Hence, in the case of a negative vote by one of the five permanent Security Council members, a candidate state cannot be admitted to membership even if there is otherwise overwhelming support for admission among the members of the Security Council and the members of the General Assembly.

It is true that the number of instances where permanent Security Council members have used or threatened to use their veto right has greatly reduced since the package deal of 1955 when the Security Council, "without substantive comment, recommended sixteen States for admission as member States of the UN."[111] The above package entailed the "eclipse of substantive admission criteria"[112] and was an important milestone on the way towards universality of the United Nations. It also meant in essence that the Security Council ceased to review whether a candidate country is "peace-loving" and "able and willing to carry out" its obligations under the UN Charter. This did not mean, however, that the permanent members of the Security Council had surrendered their right to veto applications for membership on political grounds. The two cases of Palestine and Kosovo demonstrate that there are still cases where permanent members use their veto right in spite of the fact that there is widespread support for an application.

The utmost importance of procedural issues is highlighted by the intricate web of unity and diversity that characterizes the relation between membership in the UN and membership in the specialized agencies. Such relation is particularly strong in the case of those specialized agencies such as UNESCO and ICAO where membership in the UN automatically carries the right to membership in these organizations. Their relationship agreements with the UN included a provision that they

---

110 Competence of Assembly regarding Admission to the United Nations, Advisory Opinion. ICJ Reports 1950, 4–57, 10. http://www.icj-cij.org/docket/files/9/1883.pdf.

111 Grant 2009, p. 87.

112 See Grant 2009, Chapter 4, on "Admission to the United Nations".

had to accept a recommendation of ECOSOC[113] and the General Assembly,[114] respectively, to reject the application for membership of non-UN members. When this requirement was removed for UNESCO,[115] the door for the admission of Palestine in a highly-politicized decision was opened, which clearly contradicts the assumptions of the functional theory that specialized agencies can isolate themselves from general political issues and that admission to specialized agencies is governed only by the specific functions of the organization.

The issue of Palestinian membership, which had already been the subject of intensive discussion in relation to the regional commissions of the UN,[116] again became the subject of debate after Yasser Arafat applied in a letter to the Director General of UNESCO dated 27 April 1989 "for the admission of the 'State of

[113] "The agreement with UNESCO provides, in article II, that applications for membership by States not Members of the United Nations shall be immediately transmitted to the Economic and Social Council which 'may recommend the rejection of such applications'. Any such rejection 'shall be accepted' by UNESCO. If no recommendation for rejection is made by the Council within six months, the application is governed by the normal procedure under the Constitution of UNESCO, that is to say, it becomes subject to a two-thirds majority vote of the General Conference of the agency, upon recommendation of its Executive Board." See *Repertory of Practice of United Nations. (1945–1954)*, Vol. 3 Extracts Relating to the Charter of the United Nations, Article 63, para 118, http://legal.un.org/repertory/art63/english/rep_orig_vol3-art63_e.pdf.

[114] Similar provisions were also contained in the relationship agreement between ICAO, and the United Nations. This relationship agreement provided in Article II, that applications for membership from States other than those provided for in Articles 91 and 92(a) of the Convention on International Civil Aviation, namely States signatory to the Convention, States Members of the United Nations and States associated with them, and States which remained neutral during the Second World War, shall at once be referred to the General Assembly of the United Nations, which may, within one year, recommend rejection.

Failing such a recommendation, the application is governed by the normal procedure set Civil Aviation, that is to say, it is open to approval by a four-fifths majority of the Assembly of ICAO, subject to such conditions as the Assembly may prescribe, and provided that in each case the assent of any State invaded or attacked during the Second World War by the State seeking admission shall be a necessary prerequisite for admission to membership.

It appears that the aforementioned provision of the relationship agreement with the UN did not create any problems for ICAO. While there were cases where non-members of the UN were admitted to ICAO, the General Assembly did not reject such applications. As regards UNESCO, the relationship agreement with the UN was amended to dispense with the requirement of ECOSOC approval of membership applications of States who are not members of the UN.

[115] "At its thirty-third session the Council [ECOSOC] approved the suggestion of UNESCO of an amendment calling for the deletion of article II of the Agreement between the United Nations and UNESCO, the adoption of which would eliminate the need for UNESCO to consult with the Council on applications of States not Members of the United Nations for membership in that Organization." *Repertory of Practice of United Nations. Supplement No. 3 (1959–1966)*, Vol. 2. http://legal.un.org/repertory/art63/english/rep_supp3_vol2-art63_e.pdf.

[116] See Meron 1979, pp. 52–64.

Palestine as a member of" UNESCO.[117] The Israeli ambassador expressed serious reservations on behalf of Israel regarding qualification of Palestine as a state.[118] Following the aforementioned application and a decision taken by the General Conference in 1989 "to provide for the closest possible participation of Palestine in the action of UNESCO"[119] and a study on possible options, the General Conference decided at its thirty-sixth session in 2011 "to admit Palestine as a Member of UNESCO."[120]

In the United Nations, the Palestine issue has been on the UN agenda "in one form or another since the Organization's earliest days" and "has been the subject of countless hours of debate, discussion and negotiation. Yet, despite all the intensive and extensive efforts, the Palestine issue remains unresolved, and continues to require the urgent attention of the international community."[121]

To date, Palestine is not a member of the UN. While an "Application of the State of Palestine for admission to membership in the United Nations"[122] was submitted in 2011, "deep divisions within the Council have led to a stalemate; no vote has been taken on the matter. To circumvent this, Palestine then pursued non-member-State status through the UN [General Assembly], which voted by 138 to 9 (with 41 abstentions) in favor of its request on 26 November 2012."[123]

Consequently, for UN purposes, Palestine may now be referred to as state or country and its government as the Government of Palestine.

Kosovo is another case where its application for membership in the UN was blocked by a permanent member of the Security Council. The Russian envoy made it clear that "Moscow will not allow Kosovo to join the organization and that UN Resolution 1244, which confirms Serbia's territorial integrity, will not be

[117] United Nations Educational Scientific and Cultural Organization (UNESCO). Executive Board. Hundred and thirty-first Session (131 EX/45, 18 May 1989). Item 9.4 of the provisional agenda. Application for the admission of Palestine as a Member State of UNESCO. https://unispal.un.org/DPA/DPR/unispal.nsf/28ead5e67368b9ea852579180070e4d6/a49be78bcaadcc71852579220070828f?OpenDocument.

[118] The Ambassador, Permanent Delegate of Israel to UNESCO, forwarded on 18 May 1989 a letter regarding this matter to the Director-General of UNESCO, which was transmitted the following day by the Director-General to the Chairman of the Executive Board. UNESCO. Executive Board. 131st Session. Item 9.4 of the agenda (131 EX/INF. 7, 26 May 1989). http://unesdoc.unesco.org/images/0008/000827/082713EO.pdf.

[119] UNESCO. Records of the General Conference. 25th Session, Paris 1989, Vol. 1 Resolutions, 9–10, 9. http://unesdoc.unesco.org/images/0008/000846/084696E.pdf.

[120] See UNESCO. Records of the General Conference. 36th Session, Paris, 25 Oct.–10 Nov. 2011, 79. http://unesdoc.unesco.org/images/0021/002150/215084e.pdf.

[121] United Nations. 2008. "The Question of Palestine and the United Nations". New York, iii. https://unispal.un.org/pdfs/DPI2499.pdf.

[122] United Nations. "Application of Palestine for admission to membership in the United Nations". Note by the Secretary-General (Document A/66/371–S/2011/592; 23 Sept. 2011). https://unispal.un.org/DPA/DPR/unispal.nsf/0/F6CF1ED25A5D8FE9852579170050C37F.

[123] See Burgis-Kasthala 2014, p. 678, with further references.

amended."[124] However, Kosovo was admitted to membership in the IMF and World Bank, which was the direct result of the fact that OECD countries still can muster a majority of voting power in these organizations, in spite of some limited constitutional reforms aimed at increasing the voting power of developing countries.

Article XII, Section 5(c) of the IMF Articles of Agreement provides:

> Except as otherwise specifically provided, all decisions of the Fund shall be made by a majority of the votes cast.

There may be doubts whether weighted voting is an appropriate means to solve institutional issues, e.g., related to admission of new members, as in expressing an opinion on the legal status of an applicant country, states act in their capacity as subject of international law rather than in their capacity as a member, or, to put it differently, in their identity as a state rather than as a member state.[125] This issue was raised during the deliberation on Kosovo's membership in the IMF. In this context, the General Counsel explained that

> the decision by the Executive Board to recommend to the Board of Governors a resolution on membership would be based on a majority of votes cast. A decision by the Board of Governors to actually approve membership, which was to offer the terms of membership to Kosovo, was also based on a majority of votes cast. However, there was a need for a quorum, which required a majority of the governors having not less than two thirds of the total voting power at the meeting for purposes of approving the request.[126]

Whether the decision on admission to membership is taken by the majority of the votes cast or by the majority of the governors who have voted is likely to determine in many instances the fate of applications for membership. Evidently, results may be very different depending on whether the one-country-one-vote rule, or weighted voting rules, are used for admission to membership. Hence, this is not a merely technical issue but a legal and policy matter of utmost importance, which underlines that the weight which needs to be attributed to considerations of a procedural nature may at times well exceed that which needs to be given to substantive eligibility requirements.

5.4.2 Ratification Requirement of Constituent Instruments

As the term "international organization" needs to be interpreted to comprise entities not established by a treaty, including entities incorporated under national law, an important difference between membership procedures of international organizations

[124] Russia Today. 2010. "UN membership door closed for Kosovo–Moscow". 4 August. http://rt.com/politics/churkin-kosovo-un-resolution/.

[125] See Wessel and Dekker 2015, pp. 293–318.

[126] IMF. 2009. "Minutes of Executive Board Meeting 09/10-1, 2 Feb. (19 May)", 8.

relates to whether the constituent agreement of an organization requires ratification or not. Ratification or approval of an international agreement need to comply with a number of formal requirements.[127] Moreover, it has far-reaching implications for the relation of an international organization to its members and the legal status of the organization in its member countries.

As regards membership obligations, the wording of constituent agreements often reflects a dualist concept of the relation of municipal law and public international law. This is underlined by the fact that in certain cases, the constituent agreement expressly mandates members to make certain provisions of the constituent agreement (e.g., those providing for privileges and immunities) effective in their territory.[128] However, in the case of countries like the Republic of Korea which adhere to monistic concept, the treaty itself has the "the same effect as the domestic laws."[129]

While the ratification requirement does not apply to an international organization not established by a treaty, the constituent instrument of such an international organization can regulate the membership procedure to the same effect as a constituent agreement which has been ratified by the organization's member countries, given that the relations of an organization with its members are not of an external nature. Against this background, it is indicative to analyze the membership procedures of organizations such as INTERPOL, the IPU, and the OSCE, which are now widely recognized as international organizations in spite of the fact that they do not have a treaty foundation.

Article 45 of the INTERPOL Constitution of 1956,[130] which was not ratified or submitted to government approval, provides for an "opting-out technique"[131] for the countries listed in Annex 1 of the Constitution to become members of INTERPOL. While this technique also called "non-objection technique"[132] is used in international organizations, it is generally not applied in traditional international

---

[127] See United Nations. 2012. *Treaty Handbook*, Rev. Ed., 9–10. https://treaties.un.org/doc/source/publications/THB/English.pdf.

[128] For example, Article 57 of the Agreement Establishing the Asian Development Bank provides: "Each member, in accordance with its juridical system, shall promptly take such action as is necessary to make effective in its own territory the provisions set forth in the Chapter and shall inform the Bank of the action which it has taken on the matter."

[129] Paragraph 1 of Article 6 of the Constitution of the Republic of Korea provides: "Treaties duly concluded and promulgated in accordance with the Constitution and the generally recognized rules of international law shall have the same effect as the domestic laws of the Republic of Korea."

[130] Article 45 of the INTERPOL Constitution of 1956 provides: "All bodies representing the countries mentioned in Appendix I shall be deemed to be Members of the Organization unless they declare through the appropriate governmental authority that they cannot accept this Constitution. Such a declaration should be made within six months of the date of the coming into force of the present Constitution." INTERPOL. Constitution of the ICPO-INTERPOL (adopted by the ICPO-INTERPOL General Assembly at its 25th session, Vienna, 1956). https://www.interpol.int/About-INTERPOL/Legal-materials/The-Constitution.

[131] Martha 2010, p. 160.

[132] Ibid.

organizations with treaty foundation for admitting members to join the organization. In the case of countries other than those listed in the said Annex 1 of the INTERPOL Constitution, any "request for membership shall be submitted to the Secretary General by the appropriate governmental authority. Membership shall be subject to approval by a two-thirds majority of the General Assembly."[133]

In the case of IPU which is the "international organization of the Parliaments of sovereign States,"[134] parliaments, either "constituted in conformity with the laws of a sovereign State" or "in conformity with the basic law of a territorial entity whose aspirations and entitlement to statehood are recognized by the United Nations, and which enjoys the status of Permanent Observer to the United Nations with substantial additional rights and privileges"[135] may become full members, while "[i]nternational parliamentary assemblies established under international law by States which are represented in the IPU" may be admitted to associate membership.[136] The IPU Governing Council, which normally holds two sessions a year and which is composed of three representatives of each IPU member,[137] takes decisions "on the admission and re-admission" of IPU members.[138]

The term "participating countries" is related to OSCE being viewed as not possessing international legal personality.

> Despite this anomalous terminology, procedures exist for the admission of new states in the organisation. The procedure, established by practice consists in a letter of request of admission by the candidate state to the OSCE. The Permanent Council decides by unanimity on the admission.[139]

In essence, the increase in membership of OSCE was related to the disintegration of the former Soviet Union and Yugoslavia and the emergence of new states which arose from that disintegration. These states had to apply for new membership. Thus, in case of the former Republic of Yugoslavia, the issue was resolved by application for membership of the new political entities (Croatia, Slovenia, Bosnia and Herzegovina, Former Yugoslavia Republic of Macedonia), and a new application by the Former Republic of Yugoslavia (Serbia and Montenegro).[140] The case of Mongolia was special as it was admitted as a participating state of OSCE despite the fact that it was not included in the zone of application for CSBMs as defined in

---

[133] INTERPOL Constitution of 1956, Article 4. http://www.interpol.int/About-INTERPOL/Legal-materials/The-Constitution.

[134] IPU Statutes, Article 1.

[135] IPU Statutes, Article 3.

[136] See IPU Statutes, Article 3, paras 1, 2, and 5. http://www.interpol.int/About-INTERPOL/Legal-materials/The-Constitution.

[137] See IPU Statutes, Article 17, para 1, and Article 18, para 1.

[138] IPU Statutes, Article 21(a).

[139] See Odello 2006, p. 387.

[140] Ibid., 387–388.

Annex 1 of the Vienna Document 2011 on Confidence- and Security-Building Measures.[141] Therefore, the problems which arose were quite complex. The decision on Mongolia's admission was taken in 2012 by the Ministerial Council of OSCE[142] following "receipt of the letter from the Minister for Foreign Affairs of Mongolia [….] in which Mongolia expressed its willingness to join the OSCE as a participating State and its acceptance of all commitments and responsibilities contained in OSCE documents [….]."

Finally, organizations established as trust funds, with or without international legal personality, may also have membership structures. Whether an organization established as a trust fund is given a membership structure does not depend on the legal status of that organization or whether it possesses international legal personality, but is entirely dependent on the functions of the organization. Also, the organization's functions determine whether its membership structures are open or closed, and equity-based or not. In this context, the Global Environment Facility (GEF) and the Credit Guarantee and Investment Facility (CGIF) may be seen as different paradigms of international organizations established as trust funds.

During the pilot phase from 1991 to 1994, when the resources of the GEF were held in the Global Environment Trust (GET) established by the World Bank, a minimum contribution of US$4 million was required also for developing countries that wished to participate in the Fund. Under the restructured GEF, such minimum contribution was dispensed with. Hence, all members of the United Nations and its specialized agencies may join the GEF by way of an unilateral act.[143]

> To become a GEF participant, a state must provide the Secretariat with an instrument of participation, substantially in the form set out in Annex A of the GEF Instrument. For a state contributing to the GEF Trust Fund, an instrument of commitment (in the form of Attachment 2 in Annex C of the GEF Instrument) serves as its instrument of participation. In practice, after receiving an instrument of participation or commitment, the GEF Secretariat verifies that the country in question is a member of the UN or a specialized agency. Generally, no legal opinion confirms that the instrument was signed by a duly authorized representative. Instead, the GEF Secretariat relies on the implicit representation that the signatory of the instrument (usually the minister for the environment) has the required authority to represent the country in question. Participation takes effect on the date the notification is deposited with the GEF CEO.[144]

The CGIF, on the other hand, even though not endowed with international legal personality or legal capacity under national law, is a closed organization with an equity-based structure. The CGIF Articles specify the capital shares held by the

[141] For details, see OSCE. "Vienna Document 2011 on Confidence- and Security-Building Measures". https://www.osce.org/fsc/86597?download=true.

[142] OSCE. 2012. Decision No. 2/12 "Accession of Mongolia to the OSCE". MC.DEC/2/12. 21 Nov. http://www.osce.org/mc/97736?download=true.

[143] GEF Instrument, para 7 provides: "Any State member of the United Nations or of any of its specialized agencies may become a Participant in the GEF by depositing with the Secretariat an instrument of participation substantially in the form set out in Annex A. I…."

[144] Ragazzi 2011, p. 495.

contributors which may be seen as members of the CGIF. As no provision is made in the Articles for other contributors to subscribe to the shares of the CGIF, any such enlargement of the group of contributors would require an amendment to the CGIF Articles.

5.4.3 Classification of Membership Procedures Based on Complexity

There is benefit to classifying membership procedures based on their complexity. Magliveras suggests classifying them into three categories:

> The first category covers procedures which could be described as straightforward in the sense that either they involve only one organ (primarily the plenary organ encompassing representatives of all members) reaching the relevant decision (e.g., International Organization for Migration, World Tourism Organization, Organization of Black Sea Economic Cooperation) or the decision is reached by the existing members directly (e.g., African Union, World Hydrographic Organization). The second category includes those procedures that are more complex and involve two or more organs, where at least one organ plays a recommendatory role (e.g., United Nations, United Nations Industrial Development Organization) and may additionally require the members to be admitted to accede to the constitutive instrument (e.g. Council of Europe, Organization of American States, Organisation of Economic Co-operation and Development). Finally, the third category covers even more complicated procedures that entail not only the consent of one or more organs but also require that the future member/s conclude a treaty of accession (e.g., European Union, International Monetary Fund, World Trade Organization, European Free Trade Association, European Space Agency).[145]

The above classification according to the complexity of membership procedures is useful, but requires some further elaboration and refocusing.

5.4.3.1 First Category

For this first category, Magliveras cites the IOM, the WTO, and the Organization of Black Sea Economic Cooperation as organizations where the acceptance only involves one organ.[146]

---

[145] Magliveras 2011, p. 90.

[146] E.g. Article 2 of the IOM Constitution provides:

> The Members of the Organization shall be: (a) the States being Members of the Organization which have accepted this Constitution according to Article 29, or to which the terms of Article 30 apply; (b) other States with a demonstrated interest in the principle of free movement of persons which undertake to make a financial contribution at least to the administrative requirements of the Organization, the rate of which will be agreed to by the Council and by the State concerned, subject to a two-thirds majority vote of the Council and

While the above classification is useful, the fact that only one organ decides does neither imply that admission to membership is easy nor that the admission procedure is simple. Even if the acceptance to membership only involves one organ of the organization concerned, applicants for membership are often required to ratify the constituent agreement of the organization or accept its provisions.

One example is the ADB where countries other than the original members may

> be admitted, under such terms and conditions as the Bank may determine, to membership in the Bank upon the affirmative vote of two-thirds of the total number of Governors, representing not less than three-fourths of the total voting power of the members.[147]

In accordance with Article 28.2(i) of the ADB Charter, the decision on admission to membership is vested in the Board of Governors and cannot be delegated. In accordance with Article 57 of the ADB Charter,[148] parliamentary approval of the Charter is required in many of the ADB member countries. Submission of an instrument of ratification or acceptance of the ADB Charter is generally one of the conditions precedent which must be met for the membership to take effect.

The African Union and International Hydrographic Organization referred to byMagliveras in the first category are interesting examples where the members have

---

upon acceptance by the State of this Constitution in accordance with its constitutional processes. https://www.iom.int/constitution#ch2.

In the case of UNWTO, for "sovereign states" that are eligible for full membership (UNWTO Statutes, Article 5), different procedures apply depending on whether states were full members of the International Union of Official Travel Organizations (IUOTO). Those who were full members, "shall have the right to become Full Members of the Organization, without requirement of vote, on formally declaring that they adopt the Statutes of the Organization and accept the obligations of membership. of IUOTO," (UNWTO Statutes, Article 5, para 2).

Article 5, para 3 of the UNWTO Statutes provides: "Other States may become Full Members of the Organization if their candidatures are approved by the General Assembly by a majority of two-thirds of the Full Members present and voting provided that said majority is a majority of the Full Members of the Organization." Statutes of the World Tourism Organization, UNWTO. 2016. UNWTO Basic Documents, Vol. I. http://cf.cdn.unwto.org/sites/all/files/docpdf/130718basicdocumentsenweb.pdf.

As regards the Organization of Black Sea Economic Cooperation, the "BSEC is open to any State which desires to become a Member and is deemed to be able and willing to fulfill the principles and objectives of the BSEC as set forth in the present Charter. Applications for new membership shall be submitted to the Council of Ministers of Foreign Affairs, hereinafter referred to as the Council, for consideration and approval according to the Rules of Procedure."

[147] ADB Charter, Article 3.

[148] ADB Charter, Article 57. "Each member, in accordance with its juridical system, shall promptly take such action as is necessary to make effective in its own territory the provisions set forth in the Charter."

not delegated the decision on acceptance of a new member to the governing body of the organization, but take the decision themselves.[149]

5.4.3.2 Second Category

According to Magliveras, the "second category includes those procedures that are more complex and involve two or more organs, where at least one organ plays a recommendatory role (e.g. United Nations, United Nations Industrial Development Organization) and may additionally require the members to be admitted to accede to the constitutive instrument (e.g. Council of Europe, Organization of American States, Organization for Economic Co-operation and Development)."[150]

As already discussed above, applicants for membership may be required to ratify the constituent agreement of an organization even if only one organ is involved in the review of membership applications. Hence, whether applicants have to accede to constituent agreement is conceptually distinct from whether one or two organs are involved in the membership process.

While there are several organizations where applications for membership involve two organs, membership procedures in the second category are best epitomized by the example of the UN where, for states not included in the original membership, Article 4 of the UN Charter provides:

> 1. Membership in the United Nations is open to all other peace-loving states which accept the obligations contained in the present Charter and, in the judgment of the Organization, are able and willing to carry out these obligations.
> 2. The admission of any such state to membership in the United Nations will be effected by a decision of the General Assembly upon the recommendation of the Security Council.

The requisite conditions in Article 4, para 2

> are five in number: to be admitted to membership in the United Nations, an applicant must (1) be a State; (2) be peace-loving; (3) accept the obligations of the Charter; (4) be able to carry out these obligations; and (5) be willing to do so.

---

[149] Article XX of the Convention on the IHO provides:

After it has entered into force this Convention shall be open for accession by the Government of any maritime state which applies to the Government of the Principality of Monaco specifying the tonnage of its fleets, and whose admission is approved by two-thirds of the Member Governments. Such approval shall be notified by the Government of the Principality of Monaco to the Government concerned. The Convention shall enter into force for that Government on the date on which it has deposited its instrument of accession with the Government of the Principality of Monaco which shall inform the Member Governments and the President of the Directing Committee. https://www.iho.int/mtg_docs/com_wg/ISPWG/Documents/R11_iho_convention.pdf.

[150] Magliveras 2011, p. 90.

> All these conditions are subject to the judgment of the Organization. The judgment of the Organization means the judgment of the two organs mentioned in paragraph 2 of Article 4, and, in the last analysis, that of its Members.[151]

As is well known and widely documented, the International Court of Justice (ICJ) held in its Advisory Opinion of 1948 that that text of para 1 of Article 4 "by the enumeration which it contains and the choice of its terms, clearly demonstrates the intention of its authors to establish a legal rule" and that the conditions set forth therein "constitute an exhaustive enumeration and are not merely stated by way of guidance or example. The provision would lose its significance and weight, if other conditions, unconnected with those laid down, could be demanded. The conditions stated in paragraph 1 of Article 4 must therefore be regarded not merely as the necessary conditions, but also as the conditions which suffice."[152]

> Moreover, the spirit as well as the terms of the paragraph preclude the idea that considerations extraneous to these principles and obligations can prevent the admission of a State which complies with them.[153]

The Court concluded

> that, in particular, a Member of the Organization cannot, while it recognizes the conditions set forth in that provision to be fulfilled by the State concerned, subject its affirmative vote to the additional condition that other States be admitted to membership in the United Nations together with that State.[154]

While in the 1948 Advisory Opinion of the ICJ,

> the majority's opinion may be rationally impeccable, it poses in near-textbook fashion the question of the limits of adjudication in what is essentially a politico-diplomatic dispute. Since no member is required to state the reason for its vote in either the General Assembly or the Security Council, the effect of juridically precluding a specific motive for voting is likely to be that the member's true motive will thereafter not be revealed, but the vote will remain unaffected.[155]

The ICJ further emphasized in its Advisory Opinion of 1950 that "the General Assembly can decide to admit only on the basis of a recommendation of the Security Council" as admission by the General Assembly in the absence of such

---

[151] Admission of a State to the United Nations (Charter, Article 4), Advisory Opinion. ICJ Reports 1948, 57, 62. http://www.icj-cij.org/files/case-related/3/003-19480528-ADV-01-00-EN.pdf.

[152] Ibid.

[153] Ibid., 63.

[154] Ibid., 65.

[155] Franck, T. M. "Admission of a State to Membership in the United Nations (Advisory Opinions)", para 7. www.mpepil.com.

recommendation "would be to deprive the Security Council of an important power which has been entrusted to it by the Charter."[156]

Hence, notwithstanding the said Advisory Opinion, "between 1951 and 1954, no States were admitted, despite the fact that there were some 25 applicants."[157] This only changed after the "package deal" of 1955 already mentioned above.

The above decisions and the tortuous way of the UN to universality have been analyzed in detail in literature and do not need to be reviewed in this book.[158] However, it is important to note that the well-documented problems which arose in the admission process highlight the great importance of procedural issues which at times carry greater weight even than substantive considerations.

5.4.3.3 Third Category

The third category referred to by Magliveras covers "even more complicated procedures that entail not only the consent of one or more organs but also require that the future member/s conclude a treaty of accession."[159] In addition to the European Union and the World Trade Organization and European Free Trade Association, he also includes in this category the IMF and European Space Agency. However, in the view of this author, classification of the IMF in the third category is misplaced as it does not involve conclusion of a treaty between a new member and existing members.

Both the Organization for Economic Co-operation and Development (OECD) and the Council of Europe employ a rigorous accession procedure.[160] However, the European Union and World Trade Organization reflect indeed the utmost in complexification of membership negotiations. In both cases, negotiations can take years. The membership negotiations relating to these organizations will be reviewed in some detail below.

In the case of the WTO:

> Becoming a Member of the WTO is a lengthy process. All candidate Members have observer status in the WTO before joining the organization. Candidates have to submit to the Director-General of the WTO a formal written request for accession. The first step of the

[156] International Court of Justice, Advisory Opinion of 3 March 1959, 9. http://www.icj-cij.org/docket/files/9/1883.pdf.

[157] Franck, T. M. "Admission of a State to Membership in the United Nations (Advisory Opinions)", para 4.

[158] See in particular Grant, who refers to the Committee on Admissions used in the early years for reviewing applications for membership in the UN, and the subsequent disuse of that Committee (52–62), and describes in Chapters 4, 5, and 6 the evolution of the admission criteria on the road to universality of the United Nations.

[159] Magliveras 2011, p. 90.

[160] For OECD, see OECD. "The Accession Process". https://www.oecd.org/legal/accession-process.htm and OECD. "OECD and Enlargement". http://www.oecd.org/about/membersandpartners/enlargement.htm.

> accession process is the establishment of a working party by the General Council. The working party is open to all interested WTO Members. This working party will examine the applicant's trade regime. To this end, the candidate has to submit a memorandum describing among others its trade rules, tariffs and policies. The proposed memorandum contains seven main headings [….].
>
> The working party's focus is especially on the consistency of this regime with the WTO Rules. If measures are found inconsistent, they have to be adjusted or removed. Next, parallel bilateral talks start. Candidate Members will negotiate with each existing Member commitments and concessions to ensure market access. Members can take this opportunity, but are obliged to negotiate with the candidate. Much depends on the trade interests of members.[161]

As regards the European Union, its enlargement policy is portrayed by the EU "to be a powerful tool for societal transformation," and through that policy, the EU sought to extend "its zone of peace, stability, democracy, and prosperity."[162] Nevertheless, while the deepening and widening of the EU are not necessarily in conflict, there is an inherent tension between these two objectives which are often seen as complementary. As indicated by Schäfer, it needs to be examined whether there is a trade-off between enlargement and deepening.[163]

While considered as one of the EU's successes, there has been less enthusiasm in case of the most recent applications for enlargement that this was applicable previously, to the extent that some are talking of an "Enlargement fatigue".[164] Moreover, given the success of the British referendum on leaving the EU, the enlargement process, for the first time, is being reversed to the effect that a member will be leaving the EU.

"Through the so-called 'pre-accession strategy', the Union has forged an 'EU Member-State making policy' which has articulated in sizeable detail the putative attributes of membership."[165] For that purpose, the EU has systematically used a variety of agreements (e.g., association agreements and stability and association agreements) to manage and support the association process during the pre-accession phase. Thus, for example, the Stabilisation and Association Process of the western Balkans, the ultimate purpose of which was membership in the EU, involved a

---

161 Wouters and de Meester 2007, pp. 154–155.

162 European Commission. "Communication from the Commission to the European Parliament and the Council. Enlargement Strategy and Main Challenges 2011–2012", 2. https://ec.europa.eu/neighbourhood-enlargement/sites/near/files/pdf/key_documents/2011/package/strategy_paper_2011_en.pdf.

163 "Zu prüfen ist, ob Erweiterung und Vertiefung der EU nicht vielmehr in einem eher substitutionalen Verhältnis stehen, daß also mit jeder Erweiterungsrunde grundsätzlich ein Schritt zu weniger Vertiefungspotential gegangen wird. In diesem Sinne stehen Erweiterung und Vertiefung also in einer trade-off-Beziehung." Schäfer 2007, p. 51.

164 "EU Accession Procedure". Library of the European Parliament, 1. http://www.europarl.europa.eu/RegData/bibliotheque/briefing/2013/130437/LDM_BRI(2013)130437_REV3_EN.pdf.

165 Ibid.

"progressive partnership with a view of stabilising the region and establishing a free-trade area."[166]

As the Commission seeks to dissuade "applications of those deemed not sufficiently ready," generally, "a unilateral declaration of intent" precedes the formal membership application.[167] The EU provides support to candidate countries during the pre-accession stage, *inter alia* through the Community assisting partner countries in institution building [TAIEX (Technical Assistance and Information Exchange)][168] and monitors the candidate country's efforts to implement the *acquis*.

The complexity of pre-accession arrangements is underlined by the fact that in the case of Bosnia-Herzegovina, in "2000, an EU 'Road Map' identified eighteen initial 'Steps to be taken by Bosnia and Herzegovina to prepare for a Feasibility Study on opening Negotiations on a Stabilisation and Association Agreement'."[169] Following completion of these steps, a "Feasibility Study on opening Negotiations on a Stabilisation and Association Agreement" was prepared by the Commission in 2003[170] which assessed in detail the progress made by Bosnia-Herzegovina against political and economic criteria and its ability to assume obligations resulting from a Stabilization and Association Agreement. This study showed that Bosnia and Herzegovina had "made considerable progress in stabilisation since the conflicts of the 1990's",[171] but identified a series of challenges and priorities which Bosnia and Herzegovina had to address and where further progress was required. It took until 2016 for Bosnia Herzegovina to be able to submit a formal membership application.[172]

---

[166] See with further references: European Commission. Enlargement. http://ec.europa.eu/enlargement/policy/glossary/terms/sap_en.htm.

[167] "EU Accession Procedure", 2.

[168] http://eur-lex.europa.eu/summary/glossary/taiex.html.

[169] Commission of the European Communities. 2013. Report from the Commission to the Council on the preparedness of Bosnia and Herzegovina to Negotiate a Stabilisation and Association Agreement with the European Union. 18 Nov. http://eur-lex.europa.eu/legal-content/EN/TXT/PDF/?uri=CELEX:52003DC0692&from=EN.

[170] This study is contained in the aforementioned 18 November 2013 Report from the Commission to the Council on the preparedness of Bosnia and Herzegovina to Negotiate a Stabilisation and Association Agreement with the European Union.

[171] Ibid., 39.

[172] For details, see EU. Bosnia and Herzegovina, Membership status. http://ec.europa.eu/enlargement/countries/detailed-country-information/bosnia-herzegovina/index_en.htm; European Commission. 2015. Commission Staff Working Document. Bosnia and Herzegovina 2015 Report. https://ec.europa.eu/neighbourhood-enlargement/sites/near/files/pdf/key_documents/2015/20151110_report_bosnia_and_herzegovina.pdf.

The formal procedure for joining the EU is set forth in Article 49 of the TEU and involves an initiation phase, a negotiation phase and an end phase.[173]

Following notification of the application for membership to the European Council (Article 49, para 1, TEU), the Commission draws up, as instructed by the Council, "a preliminary opinion on the application assessing the general feasibility and problems of accession by the country concerned."[174] Such opinion considers in great detail the circumstances of candidate countries, as may be seen *inter alia* from the opinions prepared by the Commission in relation to the applications of Serbia[175] and Croatia.[176] Candidate status is extended to a country following the favorable opinion of the Commission and consent of the European Parliament. However, formal negotiations "cannot start until all EU governments agree, in the form of a **unanimous decision by the EU Council**, on a framework or mandate for negotiations with the candidate country."[177] (emphasis added)

As indicated by Balász, the "extremely detailed and sophisticated negotiation process on EU membership assures, in principle, the compliance with the *acquis communitaire* on behalf of the new member."[178] As the "sophisticated set of the EU *acquis* is the fruit of Western European legal and institutional development of well-established market economies and parliamentary democracies", those "candidates whose traditions are enrooted in that political and legal culture can swiftly adapt", while other candidates may have problems in doing so.

Negotiations with candidate countries are conducted in intergovernmental conferences. "The body of EU law (acquis) is divided into policy areas each to be

[173] Article 49 of the TEU states: "Any European State which respects the values referred to in Article 2 and is committed to promoting them may apply to become a member of the Union. The European Parliament and national Parliaments shall be notified of this application. The applicant State shall address its application to the Council, which shall act unanimously after consulting the Commission and after receiving the consent of the European Parliament, which shall act by a majority of its component members. The conditions of eligibility agreed upon by the European Council shall be taken into account.

The conditions of admission and the adjustments to the Treaties on which the Union is founded, which such admission entails, shall be the subject of an agreement between the Member States and the applicant State. This agreement shall be submitted for ratification by all the contracting States in accordance with their respective constitutional requirements."

[174] Pechstein and Kubicki 2001, pp. 197–240.

[175] European Commission. 2011. Communication from the Commission to the European Parliament and the Council. Commission Opinion on Serbia's application for membership of the European Union. COM (2011) 688 final. http://ec.europa.eu/enlargement/pdf/key_documents/2011/package/sr_rapport_2011_en.pdf.

[176] Commission of the European Communities. 2004. Communication from the Commission. Opinion on Croatia's Application for Membership of the European Union. http://eur-lex.europa.eu/legal-content/EN/TXT/PDF/?uri=CELEX:52004DC0257&from=EN.

[177] European Commission. European Neighbourhood Policy and Enlargement Negotiations. "Steps towards Joining". https://ec.europa.eu/neighbourhood-enlargement/policy/steps-towards-joining_en.

[178] Balász 2014, p. 525.

negotiated separately. (There are currently 35 policy areas or 'chapters').[179] These are based under each chapter on the following elements:

> **Screening** – the Commission carries out a detailed examination, together with the candidate country, of each policy field (chapter), to determine how well the country is prepared. The findings by chapter are presented by the Commission to the Member States in the form of a screening report. The conclusion of this report is a recommendation of the Commission to either open negotiations directly or to require that certain conditions – **opening benchmarks** - should first be met.
>
> **Negotiating positions** – before negotiations can start, the candidate country must submit its position and the EU must adopt a common position. For most chapters the EU will set closing benchmarks in this position which need to be met by the Candidate Country before negotiations in the policy field concerned can be closed. [...]
>
> The pace of the negotiations then depends on the speed of reform and alignment with EU laws in each country. The duration of negotiations can vary – starting at the same time as another country is no guarantee of finishing at the same time.[180]

Each EU member must be satisfied that the candidate has made sufficient progress in any chapter for that chapter to be closed. All chapters must be closed for negotiations to be completed.[181]

Accession to the European Community takes the form of a treaty. This treaty "contains the detailed terms and conditions of membership, all transitional arrangements and deadlines, as well as details of financial arrangements and any safeguard clauses.

It is not final and binding until it:

- wins the support of the EU Council, the Commission, and the European Parliament
- is signed by the candidate country and representatives of all existing EU countries
- is ratified by the candidate country and every individual EU country, according to their constitutional rules (parliamentary vote, referendum, etc.).[182] (emphasis added)

Pechstein lists 17 steps for the membership negotiations pertaining to the initial phase, negotiating phase, and final phase of these negotiations.[183]

---

[179] See European Commission. European Neighbourhood Policy and Enlargement Negotiations. "Chapters of the Acquis". http://ec.europa.eu/enlargement/policy/conditions-membership/chapters-of-the-acquis/index_en.htm.

[180] See European Commission. "Steps Towards Joining".

[181] Ibid.

[182] See European Commission. "Steps towards Joining". https://ec.europa.eu/neighbourhood-enlargement/policy/steps-towards-joining_en. The Treaty regarding the "Accession of Croatia to the European Union" is reproduced in the Official Journal of the EU: http://eur-lex.europa.eu/legal-content/EN/TXT/PDF/?uri=OJ:L:2012:112:FULL&from=EN.

[183] Pechstein 2014, p. 839.

5.4.4 *Classification of Membership Procedures Based on Criteria for Admission to Membership*

Membership procedures may also be classified according to the criteria they use for admitting states or dependent territories to membership. This has already been touched upon in the discussion of open and closed organizations and universal and regional organizations above. However, the issue cannot be reduced merely to a question of whether a state can join an international organization by unilateral decision or if an application for membership would require acceptance by the governing bodies of the organization (and if so with what qualified majority, and eligibility criteria and conditionality).

First, while the criteria for admission to membership should ideally be related to the organization's functions, the Palestine and Kosovo issues discussed above clearly show the potential of politicization even for technical organizations. Second, the criteria for admission to membership need to be seen in the further context of the constitutionalization of international organizations. In this context, the question arises to what extent admission to an international organization should be subject to compliance with certain standards, e.g., regarding human rights, democracy and protection of minorities.

The constitutions of a number of organizations enshrine the principle of non-interference into internal affairs. This principle is formulated in a particularly strong manner in Article 3 of the INTERPOL Constitution, which provides:

> It is strictly forbidden for the Organization to undertake any intervention or activities of a political, military, religious or racial character.

Consistent with the above, Article 4 of the INTERPOL Constitution does not prescribe any substantive criteria for admission to membership.

In the case of international financial institutions such the IMF and multilateral development banks such as the World Bank, ADB, AfDB and IADB, their charters provide that these can only be guided by economic considerations and must not interfere into the political affairs of any member.[184] Nevertheless, it is convincingly argued that they "are not only free to take sustainable development concerns into account but have an international legal obligation to do so."[185] So far, they have only done so to a very limited extent.[186] In particular, decisions regarding admission to membership have not been based on the human rights record or democratic record of a country.

---

[184] Article 36.2 of the ADB Charter provides: "The Bank, its President, Vice-President(s), officers and staff shall not interfere in the political affairs of any member, nor shall they be influenced in their decisions by the political character of the member concerned. Only economic considerations shall be relevant to their decisions. Such considerations shall be weighed impartially in order to achieve and carry out the purpose and functions of the Bank."

[185] Handl 2001, p. 35.

[186] See Droesse, "Modalities of Multilateral Concessional Financing", 196.

However, the EBRD has adopted a different approach. As set out in the preamble of its Articles of Agreement, EBRD is "committed to the fundamental principles of multiparty democracy, the rule of law, respect for human rights and market economics." Article 1 provides that:

> the purpose of the Bank shall be to foster the transition towards open market-oriented economies and to promote private and entrepreneurial initiative in the Central and Eastern European countries committed to and applying the principles of multiparty democracy, pluralism and market economics [....].

Hence, political aspects[187] are part of EBRD's relations with its member countries and with the countries where the EBRD is operating.

In the case of the Council of Europe, the human rights record of any applicant country is a matter of utmost concern, as epitomized by Article 3 of the Statute of the Council of Europe, which states:

> Every member of the Council of Europe must accept the principles of the rule of law and of the enjoyment by all persons within its jurisdiction of human rights and fundamental freedoms, and collaborate sincerely and effectively in the realisation of the aim of the Council as specified in Chapter I.[188]

In addition to the Council of Europe, also EU and North Atlantic Treaty Organization epitomize the importance which is given to human-rights considerations in the membership process, as has been shown, *inter alia*, by Duxbury.[189]

Moreover, the Organisation for Economic Co-operation and Development (OECD) is also

> 4. [....] committed to fundamental values, which candidate countries are expected to share. These fundamental values serve as the foundation of the likemindedness of OECD Members and have been expressed in various OECD Ministerial Communiqués. Accepting these values, along with the established body of OECD instruments, standards and benchmarks, is a requirement for membership.
> 5. These fundamental values include a commitment to pluralist democracy based on the rule of law and the respect of human rights, adherence to open and transparent market economy principles and a shared goal of sustainable development.[190]

---

[187] See Political Aspects of the Mandate of the European Bank for Reconstruction and Development, http://www.ebrd.com/news/publications/instituational-documents/political-aspects-of-the-mandate-of-the-ebrd.html.

[188] Article 3 of the Statute of the Council of Europe provides: "Every member of the Council of Europe must accept the principles of the rule of law and of the enjoyment by all persons within its jurisdiction of human rights and fundamental freedoms, and collaborate sincerely and effectively in the realisation of the aim of the Council as specified in Chapter I." http://www.coe.int/en/web/conventions/full-list/-/conventions/rms/0900001680306052.

[189] See Duxbury, 126–137, on "Human rights, democracy and participation in Europe".

[190] See OECD. 2007. "Roadmap for the Accession of Chile to the OECD Convention". Doc. C(2007)100/FINAL C(2007)100/FINAL of 3 Dec. 2007 with further references. https://www.oecd.org/legal/41463062.pdf.

Such values are monitored under the accession road map established for potential new members which is a "tailor-made process of accession in respect of each candidate."[191]

As regards the European Union, the core of the accession modality are the so-called Copenhagen criteria adopted during the Copenhagen European Council of 21–22 June 1993 which concluded that

> Membership requires that the candidate country has achieved stability of institutions guaranteeing democracy, the rule of law, human rights and respect for and protection of minorities, the existence of a functioning market economy as well as the capacity to cope with competitive pressure and market forces within the Union. Membership presupposes the candidate's ability to take on the obligations of membership including adherence to the aims of political, economic and monetary union.[192]

In the case of the EU, the Charter of Fundamental Rights of the European Union of 7 December 2000[193] referenced in Article 6, para 1 of the TEU incorporated fundamental human rights principles.

Article 6 of the TEU provides:

> The Union is founded on the principles of liberty, democracy, respect for human rights and fundamental freedoms, and the rule of law, principles which are common to the Member States.

These are fundamental principles which all states wishing to join the EU must comply with. This may be seen from Article 49 of the TEU, which states:

> The conditions of admission and the adjustments to the Treaties on which the Union is founded, which such admission entails, shall be the subject of an agreement between the Member States and the applicant State. This agreement shall be submitted for ratification by all the contracting States in accordance with their respective constitutional requirements.

Pechstein observes that Article 49 of the TEU requires active state conduct for the realization of these values ("aktives Verhalten des Staates zur Verwirklichung dieser Werte)."[194]

---

[191] OECD. 2007. "A General Procedure for Future Accessions". (adopted by the Council at its 1155th session of 10–13 May 2007). C(2007)31/FINAL, 16 May 2007. http://www.oecd.org/officialdocuments/publicdisplaydocumentpdf/?doclanguage=en&cote=C(2007)31/Final.

[192] European Parliament. "Official positions of the other Institutions and Organs - European Council". Copenhagen European Council. 21–22 June 1993. http://www.europarl.europa.eu/enlargement/ec/cop_en.htm.

[193] Charter of Fundamental Rights of the European Union. http://eur-lex.europa.eu/legal-content/EN/TXT/HTML/?uri=CELEX:12012P/TXT&from=EN.

[194] Pechstein 2014, note 8, p. 836. He further states in this context (Ibid.): "Die Achtung und Förderung der Werte des Article 2 EUV ist eine Voraussetzung bereits für die Zulässigkeit des Beitrittsantrags und nicht lediglich eine zwingende Voraussetzung für den Beitritt selbst. Art. 2 EUV stellte eine materiellrechtliche Fundamentalnorm der Europäischen Union dar. Es kann keine hinreichende Grundlage für die Beitrittsverhandlungen sein, dass der antragstellende Staat Werte wie Freiheitlichkeit, Demokratie, Menschenrechte sowie Rechtstaatlichkeit lediglich in Zukunft achten und fördern will."

Consistent with the above, there is a very extensive pre-application conditionality and monitoring which was shown above regarding the case of Bosnia Herzegovina. The fact that human rights record of countries, rule of law, and protection of minorities are extensively reviewed before a formal membership application is even accepted is indicative of the extent of the constitutionalization of the EU membership process.

Nevertheless, it is a core problem of the EU that the standards which are applied in the pre-accession process and accession process are not equally applied to the current members of the EU. Hillion states that the "*décalage* between accession conditions and membership obligations has been a curse for the EU, not only because it undermines the credibility of its message, but more fundamentally because the Union's confined ability to react to domestic fundamental right problems might hamper its very functioning."[195]

Moreover, in addition to the political criteria mentioned above, a number of other issues are considered. The wide range of conditionality which is applicable in the membership process of the EU is, in particular, shown by the opinion rendered by the Commission in relation to new applications. Thus, for example in the European Commission's opinions on the application of Croatia to membership in the EU, in addition to the political criteria already mentioned above (i.e., democracy and the rule of law and human rights and the protection of minorities), a number of other criteria are being reviewed and are subject to conditionality. This relates, in particular, to a detailed economic assessment of the candidate country and its ability to assume obligations to each chapter of the acquis, as well as special conditions relating to the candidate country, in particular.

5.4.5 Membership Procedures for Different Subjects of Membership

Different membership procedures apply to different subjects of international law.

5.4.5.1 Admission of International Organizations to Membership

While it is now widely accepted that international organizations can be subjects of international law, it is still quite rare for international organizations to join an organization at the time it is established, as the EU did in the case of the WTO,[196] and there may be a need to amend the constituent agreement of the organization to allow for membership of international organizations.

---

[195] Hillion 2014, p. 558.

[196] In accordance with Article XI, para 1 of the Marrakesh Agreement Establishing the World Trade Organization, the EU is one of the original members of the WTO.

The history of the relations between the European Economic Union (EEC) and the FAO before and after the accession of the EEC, and the rationale for the amendment of the FAO Constitution allowing EEC membership, have been set out in detail by Frid.[197] What is important to highlight in this context is that Article II, para 3 of the FAO Constitution, as amended, applies to any regional integration organization. However, while in principle, also other regional integration organizations would be eligible for membership, so far, the EU is the only such organization which has met the requisite criteria. The relations between the EU and other international organization have been analyzed in detail in Vol 10 of the "Enzyklopädie Europarecht" by Arnaud.[198]

As regards EBRD, Article 3, para 1(II) of the Agreement establishing the European Bank for Reconstruction and Development Bank expressly stated that membership was open to the EU (European Economic Union) and the European Investment Bank.

5.4.5.2 Procedures for Admission of Sector Members and Affiliate Members

Special procedures apply to the admission of sector members, associates and academia in the International Telecommunication Union (ITU) and to the admission of affiliate members in UNWTO. These generally involve approval or support requirements of appropriate national authorities.

ITU is special as in addition to 193 states, well over 800 sector members, associates and academia members have joined the organization.[199] Hence, "ITU membership represents a cross-section of the global ICT sector, from the world's largest manufacturers and carriers to small, innovative players working with new and emerging technologies, along with leading R&D institutions and academia."[200]

Applications from companies, organizations and Academia must be approved by the relevant national telecommunication administration in the Member State where the organization is located.[201]

---

[197] Frid 1995.

[198] Arnaud 2014.

[199] ITU. List of Sector Members + Associates + Academia. https://www.itu.int/online/mm/scripts/gensel11?_memb=SAU.

[200] ITU. ITU's Evolving Membership. ITU Backgrounders. https://www.itu.int/en/plenipotentiary/2014/newsroom/Documents/backgrounders/pp14-backgrounder-evolving-membership.pdf. See also: ITU. Private Sector Involvement in ITU. http://itunews.itu.int/en/5897-Private-Sector-Involvement-in-ITU.note.aspx.

[201] See ITU. Frequently Asked Questions. https://www.itu.int/en/join/Pages/OLD_faqs.aspx.

The rights and obligations of sector members and the types of entities and organizations which are eligible to become ITU sector members are set forth, respectively, in Article 3 and Article 19 of the ITU Convention.[202]

Affiliate membership to the UNWTO is, in accordance with Article 7 of the Statutes of the World Tourism Organization, "open to international bodies, both intergovernmental and non-governmental, concerned with specialised interests in tourism and to commercial bodies and associations whose activities are related to the aims of the Organisation or fall within its competence."

Generally, applications for affiliate membership have to be addressed to Secretary General and are referred, following receipt of a "letter of support from the national tourism administration of the government of the state of residence of the applicant", to the UNWTO Executive Council for approval and, subsequently, to the UNWTO General Assembly for ratification.[203]

5.4.5.3 Different Membership Procedures for Independent Countries and Dependent Territories

As shown, often, dependent territories are only admitted to associate membership, which carries only limited rights and obligations. However, some organizations, such as ADB and the CDB admit dependent territories to full membership. The case of ADB is interesting as the procedure for admitting dependent territories differs from that applicable to independent countries and involves fundamental issues regarding the status of the territories so admitted. Therefore, the case of ADB will be analyzed in some detail. Moreover, the difference in procedure followed by CDB will be highlighted.

---

[202] Each of the three sectors of ITU (Radiocommunications, Telecommunication Standardization and Telecommunication Development) "has a number of Study Groups related to the Sectors' specific field. Organizations/entities can join any or all Sectors of ITU. Full Sector Members are entitled to participate in all of the Study Groups, while organizations/entities that have a specific focus can choose to participate in a single Study Group as an Associate. Academia, universities and their associated research establishments benefit from preferential rates, as do Sector Members from some developing countries." ITU. ITU'S Evolving Membership.

[203] See UNWTO Statutes, Article 3, paras 2 and 3. The detailed admission procedure for affiliate members is set out in World Tourism Organization. UNWTO Affiliate Members. "How to join?" http://affiliatemembers.unwto.org/content/how-join.

5.4.6 *Asian Development Bank*

5.4.6.1 Countries Responsible for the Conduct of Their External Relations

The power to admit new members and determine the conditions of their admission is listed in Article 28.2(i) of the ADB Charter in the first place among those which cannot be delegated by the Board of Governors. This underlines that admission to ADB membership is considered a very important decision which concerns the membership at large and is for that reason exclusively vested in the Board of Governors. Admission as a new member requires in accordance with Article 3.2 of the Charter "the affirmative vote of the total number of Governors, representing not less than three-fourths of the total voting power of the members." Thus, no country can join ADB if the two largest shareholders (i.e. Japan and the United States of America) or a group of shareholders carrying more than 25% of the votes do not agree. Consistent with the above, regularly the procedure has been followed that an application is only submitted to the Board of Governors "when an informal general consensus is established in favor of admitting an applicant."[204]

In ADB, the "formal membership process is generally preceded by informal inquiries and discussions among existing ADB members"[205] and efforts of the potential new member to gain support of existing members of their application. Often, potential members liaise informally (e.g., at Annual Meetings which they may attend as observers) or through their embassies or other channels with other ADB's current members to seek their support for membership. ADB is generally not involved in such consultations; except that a potential candidate may keep ADB management informed on the outcome of its bilateral discussions with other members and may seek clarification from ADB management on membership procedures. "Upon receiving a firm written expression of interest in membership in ADB addressed to the President, which is signed by a person of ministerial rank and above, the President seeks, as appropriate, the views of existing members through the Board of Directors regarding the applicant's interest."[206] Whether there is an informal consensus (i.e., broad support by most members) for an application is determined based on a sufficiently comprehensive set of responses from members. Where such informal consensus has been ascertained, "the Office of the Secretary requests the applicant to provide basic legal and economic information to enable ADB to assess, inter alia, the number of shares in the capital stock of ADB to which the applicant is eligible to subscribe and, where, appropriate, the applicant's contribution to the ADF."[207]

[204] ADB 2005, p. 2.
[205] Ibid., para 4.
[206] Ibid., para 6.
[207] Ibid., para 7.

Section 16 of the ADB By-Laws[208] foresees a two-step process for the formal membership applications submitted to the Board of Governors by countries that are responsible for the conduct of their external relations. It is for the Board of Directors to recommend "the number of shares of capital stock to be subscribed and such other conditions, as, in the opinion of the Board of Directors, the Board of Governors may wish to prescribe." Thus, the Board of Governors takes a decision based on the recommendation of the Board of Directors, which, in turn, is generally predicated on a staff study recommending, based on various economic factors, the amount of shares to be offered to a candidate country (see below), and consultations with the candidate country concerned.

> 8. ADB prepares, on the basis of the best available country economic data, a preliminary assessment regarding the applicant's terms and conditions of membership (shareholding, subscriptions, etc.).
> 9. The Office of The Secretary subsequently requests that a delegation visit ADB (or that ADB visit the applicant) to explain the formal process of membership and to discuss terms and conditions of membership related to capital subscriptions, ADF contributions (if applicable), mode and method of payment, and related issues [....].[209]

Section 16 of the ADB By-Laws has consistently been interpreted to imply that it governs the formal procedure to be followed for submitting applications for membership to the Board of Governors for approval, but does not give a right to an applicant country to demand that an expression of interest for ADB membership is immediately brought to the Board of Governors for decision.

In the case of countries that are responsible for the conduct of their external relations, the formal membership process is generally triggered by the letter of application of the candidate country which contains an offer to subscribe the agreed number of shares of ADB's capital stock and other undertaking of the candidate country (e.g. a contribution to the Asian Development Fund). This letter is generally signed by the head of state, head of government, minister of foreign affairs or minister of finance.[210]

In practice, the proposed number of shares to be offered to a candidate country is agreed with the candidate country which offers in its letter of application to subscribe to the agreed number of shares. The Board of Directors takes its decision on the President's recommendation with the required quorum (a majority of the directors representing not less than two thirds of the total voting power)[211] by "a majority of the voting power represented at the meeting" (see Article 33.3 of the

[208] ADB By-Laws. Section 16. "Application for Membership in the Bank. When submitting an application to the Board of Governors, the Board of Directors, after consultation with the applicant country, shall recommend to the Board of Governors the number of shares of capital stock to be subscribed and such other conditions as, in the opinion of the Board of Directors, the Board of Governors may wish to prescribe."

[209] ADB 2005, p. 2, paras 8 and 9.

[210] ADB 2005, para 4, footnote 2.

[211] See ADB Charter, Article 32.2.

Charter). After the Board of Directors has approved transmission of its report and the resolution to the Board of Governors, the applicant is informed accordingly.

Admission to membership does not fall in the category of decisions which can only be taken at an annual or special meeting of the Board of Governors. Therefore, generally, the Board of Directors invokes, on the recommendation of the President, Section 3 of the By-Laws to seek approval of the Board of Governors of its report and the proposed resolution admitting the applicant country to membership, which a request for a vote (generally, within 30–40 days).

To ensure consistency in the treatment of applicant countries, the resolutions of the Board of Governors admitting the applicant to membership are mostly very similar; they generally specify:

(a) the number of shares to be subscribed by the applicant country (including the number of paid-in shares and callable shares);
(b) the date by which the first installment payment for the paid-in portion of the applicant's capital subscription needs to be made;
(c) the currenc(y)(ies) for the paid-in portion of the capital subscription;
(d) arrangements pending a decision on the valuation of ADB's capital stock; and
(e) the following conditions precedent to membership;

i. the applicant country shall have deposited with ADB an instrument that it accepts, in accordance with its laws, the Articles of Agreement set forth in the resolution and that all necessary steps have been taken to enable the applicant country to carry out its obligations under the Articles of Agreement and the resolution;
ii. the applicant country shall have furnished ADB evidence satisfactory to ADB that the instrument referred to in (i) above has been executed and deposited in accordance with all relevant authorities; and
iii. the applicant country shall have paid the first installment of its subscription in accordance with the Resolution.[212]

The Resolutions consistently specify that the applicant country shall not become a member until on or before a specified date "or such later date as the Board of Directors may determine,"[213] such conditions precedent to membership have been met.

5.4.6.2 Dependent Territories

While dependent territories may become full members of ADB, their situation differs in several respects from that of countries responsible for the conduct of their foreign relations.

First, in case of dependent territories, problems may arise in defining the subject of membership. The issue of the legal personality of dependent territories has been extensively discussed in literature, in particular with reference to Chapter XI of the UN Charter and the General Assembly Declaration on Friendly Relations and

---

[212] See the outline of a Resolution provided in ADB. Rules and Procedures for Membership in ADB. Appendix 9.

[213] Ibid.

Co-Operation among States.[214] In relation to the above declaration, Crawford asserts that the "people of a Charter XI territory enjoy a separate legal status and with it a measure of legal personality."[215] Nevertheless, the fact that a dependency enjoys a certain degree of autonomy does not imply in all cases that it has international standing and can be the subject of membership in an international organization. The situation may arise that a territory, while endowed with autonomy, does not have an identifiable international juridical personality. In such cases, application for membership may be made on behalf of the government of the dependent territory rather on behalf of the territory itself.[216]

Second, the membership procedure applicable to dependent territories differs from that applicable to countries which are responsible for the conduct of their international relations. Such countries, including countries which are still associate members of UNESCAP but have become responsible for the conduct of their international relations, may directly apply for membership in ADB pursuant to Article 3.1 of the Charter, while in accordance with Article 3.3 of the Charter the application of dependent territories for membership has to be presented by "the member of the Bank responsible for the international relations of the applicant." While, subject to such presentation, dependent territories may apply for membership and, as a matter of principle, may be involved in membership negotiations, under national constitutions, they may not have the power to engage in international relations. In such cases, membership negotiations may entirely be driven by the metropolitan state responsible for the conduct of the international relations of the territory.

Third, in relation to the above, the further question arises whether the same derogations and reservations of the ADB Charter apply to dependent territories as to countries which join ADB pursuant to Article 3.1 of the ADB Charter. While the ADB Charter does not expressly specify whether dependent territories may retain for them the right under Article 56.1 of the ADB Charter to tax the salaries and emoluments of their citizens and nationals and may avail of derogations to the ADB Charter as those contained in Article 24.2, it would appear that they should be given these rights.

---

[214] This declaration provides: "The territory of a colony or other Non-Self-Governing Territory has, under the Charter, a status separate and distinct from the territory of the State administering it; and such separate and distinct status under the Charter shall exist until the people of the colony or Non-Self-Governing Territory have exercised their right of self-determination in accordance with the Charter, and particularly its purposes and principles." General Assembly Resolution 2625 (XXV). Declaration on Principles of International Law concerning Friendly Relations and Co-operation among States in accordance with the Charter of the United Nations (A/8082) of 24 Oct. 1970. See http://daccess-dds-ny.un.org/doc/RESOLUTION/GEN/NR0/348/90/IMG/NR034890.pdf?OpenElement.

[215] Crawford 2006, p. 618.

[216] This issue was discussed, in particular, in relation to Hong Kong. Being a possession of the British Crown, Hong Kong could "be best described as an entity with virtually no formal or *de jure* autonomy." Olivier 1992–1993, pp. 61–88. The UK presented for that reason application for membership of Hong Kong in ADB on behalf of the government of Hong Kong, rather than on behalf of the crown colony of Hong Kong.

Fourth, the question arises regarding the extent of the liability of the metropolitan state responsible for the external relations of the dependent territory. In accordance with Article 3.3 of the Charter, the presentation of application for membership of dependent territories shall be accompanied "by an undertaking by such member that, until the applicant itself assumes such responsibility, the member shall be responsible for all obligations that may be incurred by the applicant by reason of admission to membership in the Bank and enjoyment of the benefits of such membership."

Both presentation of membership by the metropolitan state and the undertaking of responsibility of the metropolitan are compulsory requirements which cannot be dispensed with. As dependent territories are full members of ADB, the metropolitan state responsible for the conduct of the external relations of the territory is generally not required to guarantee its loans.[217] The undertaking under Article 3.3 of the Charter, even though similar to a guarantee, is distinguishable from it in several respects. One the one hand, it is limited *in tempore* until the date when the dependent territory assumes itself responsibility for its external relations and in that sense more restricted than a guarantee. On the other hand, the undertaking under Article 3.3 of the ADB Charter may also extend to non-financial obligations of the dependent territory. As a matter of principle, the obligation under Article 3.3 is unqualified and does not require any additional undertaking on the part of the metropolitan state.

5.4.7 Caribbean Development Bank

The Caribbean Development Bank (CDB) follows somewhat different procedures in admitting dependent territories:

> While both the ADB and CDB charters allow membership of dependent territories, there are certain differences regarding their procedures for admitting dependent territories to membership. Both organizations require the presentation of an application for membership by the member responsible for the international relations of the applicant. While ADB requires that member to assume responsibility for all obligations of the applicant until such time that the applicant itself assumes such responsibility, CDB requires confirmation from said member that the dependent territory has authority to enter into a membership agreement with CDB and to assume the rights and obligations of the agreement. Thus, the state responsible for conducting the international relations of the dependent territory generally does not assume a legal obligation to CDB for the borrowings and other financial obligations of the dependent territory.[218]

[217] See the wording of Article 15.2 of the ADB Charter: "**Where the recipient of loans or guarantees of loans is not itself a member**, the Bank may, when it deems it advisable, require that the member in whose territory the project concerned is to be carried out, or a public agency or any instrumentality of that member acceptable to the Bank, guarantee the repayment of the principal and the payment of interest and other charges on the loan in accordance with the terms thereof." (emphasis added)

[218] See Droesse, "Organizational Structures", 97, with further references.

5.5 Withdrawal, Suspension and Termination of Membership

Sands and Klein state that "apart from the case of dissolution of the organization, termination of membership is likely to arise in three different ways: by withdrawal, as the voluntary act of the member; by expulsion, as a measure taken by the organization against a member; and by loss of membership consequent upon a member's refusal to accept an amendment to the constitution of an organization."[219]

Schermers and Blokker add the fourth obvious case that "membership ends if the member ceases to exist."[220] Neither that case, which may relate to the disappearance of a member or the fact that a "member ceases to fulfil the requirements of statehood as an essential condition of membership,"[221] or the dissolution of an organization, will be discussed in any detail. As regards the other criteria listed by Sands and Klein, they require some elaboration. A fifth case which needs to be added relates to the fact that the suspension of a member may automatically entail the termination of membership if it is not lifted within a certain period.

Withdrawal, suspension and expulsion (termination of membership) have been analyzed in detail in literature, and by this author, in relation to international financial institutions.[222] It may suffice for that reason to give a succinct overview of relevant issues without entering in a discussion of individual cases which are extensively covered by the cited publications.

5.5.1 *Withdrawal*

As regards withdrawal from an organization, such right is often expressly recognized in an organization's constitutions, often with specification of a shorter or longer time period after which the withdrawal shall take effect. However, there is wide agreement that even without a specific provision in the constitution of the organization, states have the right of withdrawal. Hence, "on a number of occasions states have withdrawn from international organizations, the constitutions of which do not contain provisions on withdrawal."[223]

The case of the EU is special, as in that case it was argued in the past that states would not have the right of unilateral withdrawal based on the state of European integration and the powers conferred to the European Community. Given the above,

[219] Sands and Klein 2009, p. 550.

[220] Schermers and Blokker 2011, §118.

[221] Amerasinghe 2005, p. 124.

[222] See amongst many others: Magliveras 1999; and Singh 1958, pp. 99–103.

[223] See regarding the above Schermers and Blokker 2011, §125.

it is somewhat paradoxical that Article 50 of the TEU, which expressly permits EU members to leave the EU, is, as highlighted by Pechstein, a corollary of the further deepening of European integration which the Treaty of Lisbon entailed.[224] However, this is not the only paradox which surrounds the aforementioned provision. It may also be seen as a paradox that the Commission which is heavily involved in dealing with applications for EU membership, in so to a lesser degree in the process of a member to leave the EU. The exit of the United Kingdom (UK) following the referendum of June 2016 invoked by Prime Minister Theresa May on 29 March 2017[225] has put Article 50 of the TEU to a test. As indicated by Douglas-Scott, it involves complex issues involving EU and UK law related to the concepts of Parliamentary sovereignty, popular sovereignty, and the external sovereignty of the UK.[226]

5.5.2 Suspension and Expulsion/Termination of Membership

As regards suspension and expulsion/termination of membership by an organization, these are measure of last resort which are only used rarely and sparingly.

There are a number of cases where the suspension automatically leads to termination of membership if it is not lifted within a certain period. This has been shown by this author in relation to international financial institutions.

> If a member fails to fulfill any of its obligations, the [International Development Association] (IDA) Articles provides for suspension of membership by a majority of the governors exercising a majority of the total voting power. The suspended member automatically ceases membership 1 year from the date of its suspension unless the same majority decides to restore the member in good standing. The constituent instruments of ADB, IADB, and IFAD contain provisions regarding suspension and consequent termination if the member is not restored to good standing; such provisions are modeled on those of IBRD and IDA. The NDF Agreement does not include a provision regarding suspension or termination of membership. The IMF Articles, on the other hand, gives the board of

---

[224] "Die Schaffung eines förmlichen Austrittsrechts durch den Vertrag von Lissabon lässt sich – auf den ersten Blick mag dies paradox wirken—verstehen als Konsequenz einer zumindest intendierten deutlichen Vertiefung der Integration durch diesen Vertrag. Verstanden als Realisierung der wichtigsten Ziele des gescheiterten Verfassungsvertrags mit anderen Mittlen, erhebt der Vertrag von Lissabon, mit dem die Eurpäische Union ja auch erstmal Rechtspersönlichkeit erhielt, den Anspruch einen entscheidenden Schritte nach vorne getan zu haben. Vor diesem Hintergrund ist es plausibel, den Mitgliedern die Möglichkeit einzuräumen, die schicksalhafte Einordnung in den weiterhin integrationsprogessiven Verbund regelkonform rückgängig machen zu können, bevor es dafür endgültig zu spät ist." Pechstein 2014, p. 834.

[225] Asthana, A, H. Stewart, and P. Walker. "May Triggers Article 50 with Warning of Consequence for UK", The Guardian, 29 March 2017. https://www.theguardian.com/politics/2017/mar/29/theresa-may-triggers-article-50-with-warning-of-consequences-for-uk.

[226] Douglas-Scott 2016, pp. 1019–1020. See also: Armstrong 2017.

governors the power to require a member to withdraw from membership if such member persists, after having been declared ineligible to use the general resources of the IMF, in fulfilling its obligations under the IMF Articles.[227]

It is indicative of the constitutionalization of some organizations that suspension and expulsion may be based on the failure of a member to respect certain fundamental freedoms. The Council of Europe (CoE) epitomizes this development, as in accordance with Article 8 of Chapter 2 of the CoE Statutes[228] "[a]ny member of the Council of Europe which has seriously violated Article 3 [which sets out the values of the CoE] may be suspended from its rights of representation and requested by the Committee of Ministers to withdraw under Article 7. If such member does not comply with this request, the Committee may decide that it has ceased to be a member of the Council as from such date as the Committee may determine."

In the case of the European Union, Article 7 of the TEU provides for a multi-level procedure for the suspension of members involving a determination by the European Council of "the existence of a serious and persistent breach by a Member State of the values referred to in Article 2" (Article 7, para 2, TEU) and a decision on sanctions taken by the European Council (Article 7, para 3, TEU), both involving a qualified majority. The decision on sanctions may be varied or revoked only by qualified majority.[229]

An important question is whether expulsion of a member is possible in the absence of an express constitutional provision. In a number of cases, the constituent instrument of an organization does not expressly provide for termination of membership. While in these cases organizations generally do not have the right to expel members, it has been "accepted in doctrine that *in exceptional* cases these organizations may expel a member."[230] As regards the EU, the maximum sanction which may be imposed under Article 7 of the TEU is a suspension. Nevertheless, as indicated by Pechstein, if a state continuously disregards the values set forth in Article 2 TEU, termination of membership must be possible to preserve the identity of the European Union.[231]

[227] Droesse, "Organizational Structures", 100, with further references.

[228] http://assembly.coe.int/nw/xml/RoP/Statut_CE_2015-EN.pdf.

[229] For details regarding the procedure set out in Article 7 of the TEU, please see Pechstein 2014, pp. 844–848.

[230] Schermers and Blokker 2011, §148.

[231] "Sofern die auf Grundlage von Art. 7 EUV ergriffenen Sanktionen erfolglos geblieben sind und der betreffende Staat die Werte des Art. 2 EUV weiterhin dauerhaft missachtet (bspw durch Errichtung eines diktatorischen Regimes), muss auch in einem solchen Fall die Beendigung seiner Mitgliedschaft nach dem allgemeinen Völkerrecht möglich sein, um die Identität der Union zu wahren." Pechstein 2014.

5.6 Opening of International Organizations to Non-members

The fact that an international organization has a limited membership clearly does not imply that its interests are limited to its members. This is shown not only by organizations such as the Nordic Development Fund and the OPEC Fund for International Development, which conduct their operations entirely in non-member countries.[232] Other international organizations, which focus mainly on interaction with their member countries and conduct their activities and/or operations exclusively or predominantly in member countries, also often have interests which transcend the limited scope of their membership. In many cases, given progressive globalization, problems can no longer be addressed exclusively by the member states of an organization, or at a regional or national level, but require collaboration among many states and other actors. Thus, opening international organizations to non-members is required.

The example of the OECD shows the benefits which an organization of limited membership may derive from collaborating actively with non-member countries and other stakeholders. While the membership of OECD is restricted, it "has been used as an incubator of new ideas or as a forum in which new, and/or higher, standards could be developed, for over fifty years. Its innovative approaches to new or unaddressed difficulties faced by governments have led non-members to express interest in participating in some OECD legal instruments [....]. Some OECD standards were later accepted as the universal standard or incorporated into other legal frameworks (e.g. the Arrangement on Export Credits)."[233] OECD is remarkable as it gives non-member countries a voice in its deliberations.

> One of the features of the OECD is that while a non-member country cannot become an observer to the OECD, it can join selected bodies, on the basis of 'mutual benefit.' A second important feature is that, in this context of selective participation, the non-member can even decide to participate with equal rights and obligations as OECD members, with the status of 'full participant'. This is more proof of the flexibility and the pragmatism of the OECD.[234]

The open approach of OECD to collaboration with non-member countries may be seen as an example for other organizations. In particular, it is important for regional organizations and other organizations of limited membership to improve their cooperation with non-member countries to address global issues which transcend the limited geographic scope of their membership and enhance their innovativeness, performance and development outcomes.

So far, both membership in international organizations and representation in the governing bodies of such organizations are generally limited to states and

---

[232] Droesse, "Organizational Structures", 14 and 191, with further references.

[233] Bonucci 2011, pp. 248–249.

[234] Bonucci 2011, p. 252.

international organizations. While international organizations cooperate and engage with transnational actors, generally, they do not allow their institutionalized participation (such as full or partial membership), and only permit such transnational actors very limited roles in the organization's decision-making procedures and operational mechanisms.

However, it is necessary and important to take the relationship between international organizations and transnational actors to the next stage where civil society and the private sector are not only engaged as interlocutors of international organizations, and as partners in their activities and operational modalities, but are also an integral part of organizational, institutional and governance structures. This may imply that transnational actors, including the private sector, philanthropy and civil society, are admitted to full or partial membership in international organization and that representatives of such actors may be admitted to membership in governing bodies of international organizations. It would mean introducing institutionalized forms of cooperation (including membership) between international organizations and transnational actors, thus transforming international organizations into multi-actor institutions.

Making this shift to more inclusive organizational and governance structures requires substantial changes to organizations' legal and policy frameworks. In certain cases, the constituent agreements of organizations may have constraints for such transformation, as this may concern the legal status of subjects of membership (which in a number of cases is limited to states), and the legal qualification of members of governing bodies (which may be limited to representatives of the member). Given the qualified majorities applicable to amendment of constituent agreements, these are formidable obstacles for institutional change.

5.7 Conclusions

Hence, current concepts of membership need to be fundamentally revised. The main issues where a fundamental reorientation is required is that (i) international organizations may have, but do not need to have members; (ii) their membership structures may, but do not need to involve states and international organizations; and (iii) private sector entities and other transnational actors are also eligible subjects of membership.

References

ADB (2005) Rules and procedures for membership in ADB. ADB, Manila.

Amerasinghe CF (2005) Principles of the Institutional Law of International Organizations, 2nd edn. Cambridge University Press, Cambridge

Armstrong KA (2017) Brexit time. Leaving the EU – why, how and when? Cambridge University Press, Cambridge
Arnaud AV (ed) (2014) Europäische Außenbeziehungen. In: Hatje A, Müller-Graff P-C (eds) Enzyklopädie Europarecht, vol 10. Nomos Verlagsgesellschaft, Baden-Baden
Baetens F (2012) European Community and Union, Association of Overseas Countries and Territories. Max Planck Encyclopedia of Public International Law
Bantekas I (2009) Trust funds under International Law: trustee obligations of the United Nations and International Development Banks. T.M.C. Asser Press, The Hague
Balász P (2014) Enlargement conditionality of the European Union and future prospects. In: Govaere I, Lennon E, Esluwege PV, Adam S (eds) The European Union in the world. Essays in honour of Marc Maresceau. Martinus Nijhoff, Leiden, pp 523-540
Blokker N (2004) International Organizations and their members. International Organizations belong to all members and to none—variations on a theme. Int Organ Law Rev 1:139–161
Bonucci N (2011) The OECD at fifty: some observations on the evolving nature of an International Organization. George Wash Int Law Rev 43:239–254
Bradlow DD (2010) International Law and the operations of International Financial Institutions. In: Bradlow DD, Hunter DB (eds) International Financial Institutions. Kluwer Law International, The Netherlands, pp 1–30
Buchanan JM (1965) An economic theory of clubs. Economica 32, 1–14
Bühler KG (2001) State succession and membership in International Organizations: Legal Theories versus Political Pragmatism. Kluwer Law International, The Hague
Burgis-Kasthala ML (2014) Over-stating Palestine's UN membership bid? An ethnographic study on the narratives of statehood. Eur J Int Law 25(3):677–701
Chen FT (2001) The meaning of 'states' in the membership provisions of the United Nations Charter. Indiana Int Comp Law Rev 12:25–51
Chuang RY (1972) The International Air Transport Association: a case study of a quasi-governmental organization. A.W. Sijthoff, Leiden, p 22
Crawford J (1977) The criteria for statehood in International Law. Br Yearb Int Law 48:93–182
Crawford J (2006) The creation of states in International Law, 2nd edn. Clarendon Press, Oxford
Douglas-Scott S (2016) Brexit. Article 50 and the contested British constitution. Mod Law Rev 79:1019–1089
Drower G (1992) Britain's dependent territories: a fistful of islands. Dartmouth Pub. Co., Aldershot, p xvii
FAO (2015) Basic texts of the Food and Agriculture Organization of the United Nations, vols I and II
Fawcett JES (1949) Treaty relations of British Overseas Territories. Br Yearb Int Law 26:86–107
Frid R (1995) The relations between the EC and International Organizations: Legal Theory and Practice. Kluwer Law International, The Hague
Gold J (1974) Membership and nonmembership in the International Monetary Fund: a study in International Law and Organization. IMF, Washington DC
Grant TD (2009) Admission to the United Nations. Charter Article 4 and the rise of universal organization. Martinus Nijhoff, Leiden
Handl G (2001) Multilateral Development Banking: environmental principles and concepts reflecting General International Law and Public Policy. Kluwer Law International, The Hague.
Hartwig M (2010) ICANN–governance by technical necessity. In: The exercise of public authority by International Institutions, pp 575–605
Hillion C (2014) Enlarging the European Union and its fundamental rights protection. In: Govaere I, Lannon E, Elsuwege PV, Adams S (eds) The European Union in the world. Essays in honour of Marc Maresceau. Nijhoff, Leiden, pp 557–573
Hinricher J (2004) The law-making of the International Telecommunication Union (ITU): providing a new source of international law? Zeitschrift für ausländisches öffentliches Recht und Völkerrecht 64:489–501
Kaul I, Mendoza R (2003) Advancing the concept of public goods. In: Providing global public goods: managing globalization, pp 78–111

Kaul I, Conceição P, Le Goulven K, Mendoza R (2003) Why do global public goods matter today? In: Kaul I, Conceição P, Le Goulven K, Mendoza R (eds) Providing global public goods: managing globalization. Oxford University Press, Oxford, pp 3–20

Krisch N (2014) The decay of consent: International Law in an age of global public goods. Am J Int Law 108:1–40

Lamy P (2013) Foreword. In: Elms DK, Low P (eds) Global value chains in a changing world. Fung Global Institute and World Trade Organization, Geneva, pp xv–xviii

Magliveras KD (1999) Exclusion from participation in International Organizations. The law and practice behind Member States' expulsion and suspension of membership. Kluwer Law International, The Hague

Magliveras K (2011) Membership in International Organizations. In: Klabbers J (ed) Research handbook on the Law of International Organizations. Edward Elgar, Cheltenham, pp 84–107

Martha RSJ (2010) The legal foundation of INTERPOL. Hart Publishing, Portland

Meron T (1979) The composition of the UN Regional Commissions and the PLO. Int Comp Law Q 28:52–64

Murray F (2012) The European Union and Member State territories: a new legal framework under the EU treaties. T.M.C. Asser, The Hague

Odello M (2006) The developing legal status of the organisation for security and co-operation in Europe. Anuario Español de Derecho Internacional 22:351–393

Odendahl K (2014) Beziehungen zu Drittstaaten und internationalen Organisationen. In: Hatje A, Müller-Graff P-C (eds) Enzyklopedie Europarecht, vol 10. Nomos, Baden-Baden, pp 273–319

Olivier M (1992–1993) Hong Kong: an exercise in autonomy. S Afr Yearb Int Law 18:61–88

Pechstein M (2014) Mitgliedschaftsordnung der EU. In: Hatje A, Müller-Graf P-C (eds) Enzyklopädie Europarecht, vol 1. Europäisches Organisations-und Verfassungsrecht. Nomos, Baden, pp 833–890

Pechstein M, Kubicki P (2001) The legal framework of accession to the European Union. Polish Yearb Int Law XXV:197–240

Ragazzi M (2011) The Global Environment Facility: institutional and operational aspects. In: Droesse G (ed) Funds for development: multilateral channels of Concessional Financing. ADB, Manila, pp 485–500

Sands P, Klein P (2009) Bowett's Law of International Institution, 5th edn. Sweet and Maxwell (Thomson Reuters, London

Schäfer W (2007) Europäische Union: Erweiterung cum Vertiefung? Erweiterung versus Vertiefung! Jahrbuch für die Ordnung von Wirtschaft und Gesellschaft (ORDO) 58:51–65

Schermers HG, Blokker NM (eds) (2011) International Institutional Law: unity within diversity, 5th edn. Martinus Nijhoff, Boston

Singh N (1958) Termination of membership of International Organizations. Stevens & Sons, London.

Trachtman JP (2013) The future of International Law: Global Government. Cambridge University Press, Cambridge.

von Bogdandy A, Dann P, Goldmann M (2010) Developing the publicness of Public International Law: towards a legal framework for global governance activities. In: von Bogdandy A, Wolfrum R, von Bernstorff J, Dann P, Goldmann M (eds) The exercise of public authority by International Institutions: advancing International Institutional Law. Springer, Heidelberg, pp 3–32

Wesley M (2003) Membership expansion and change. In: Wesley M (ed) The regional organizations of the Asia-Pacific: exploring institutional change. Palgrave Macmillan, pp 97–115

Wessel RA, Dekker IF (2015) Identities of states in International Organizations. Int Organ Law Rev 12:293–318

Wouters J, de Meester J (2007) The World Trade Organization: a legal and institutional analysis. Intersentia, Antwerp, pp 154–155

Chapter 6
Subjects of International Law and International Legal Personality

Contents

All weblinks are updated as of 28 February 2018.

G. Droesse, *Membership in International Organizations*,
https://doi.org/10.1007/978-94-6265-327-6_6

6.1 Subjects of International Law

6.1.1 The Need for a Wider Concept of Subject of International Law

State-centric concepts are so entrenched in current theories of the subject of international law that this term is widely conceived and interpreted in a very restrictive manner. Therefore, it is useful to see the discussion on the "subject of international law" in a historic context, because such a historic reflection shows that in the Middle Ages a much wider concept of "subject of international law" was prevalent. Given the evolution of international law and law of international organizations, it is necessary to redefine "subject of international law" to comprise a wide range of actors present on the international plane. In this regard, many of the current assumptions regarding subject of international law and international juridical personality need to be revised.

The discussion on the concept of "subject of international law" is intrinsically entwined with that on "international legal personality". Current theories on the subject of international law are largely predicated on the assumption that the constituent agreement of an organization establishes its legal personality, which is distinct from that of the members, and that such legal personality is a precondition for organizations to be qualified as subjects of international law. While the above legal construct may overall adequately describe the situation of traditional international organizations established by a treaty, it requires amplification and revision as it is no longer in line with changed realities of an international system characterized by the proliferation of international actors.

There is no denying that despite such proliferation, states remain the main (even though not the only) gatekeepers[1] of access to the international system. However, two things have changed in the last decades, in particularly in the last decades.

First, the range of entities that are allowed to pass through the "gate" to join the global community is much wider than in the past. These are no longer limited to traditional public international organizations established by a treaty but include, among others, entities not established by a treaty, and dual and hybrid forms of organizations incorporated under national law, but endowed with privileges and immunities under international law, as well as other forms of international cooperation. It is necessary to recognize these as new paradigms of organizations acting

[1] Parlett provides the following background for the emergence of the concept of "gatekeeper": "in the middle of the 19th century, recognition of belligerency was detached from recognition of independence. Thus belligerent (international law) rights were recognized for groups and individuals who did not necessarily have a valid claim to statehood. This occurred through a process of recognition by states: in this way, states remained gatekeepers of the international legal system; the ability of individuals to acquire international law rights was dependent on a specific intentional act by a state adopted as a matter of policy." Parlett 2012, p. 65.

on the international plane and amplify the definitions of "international organization" and "subject of international law" to this end.

Second, the decision of admission to the international legal system is no longer necessarily linked to the establishment of an organization. While it may be taken when the organization is established, it can also be taken subsequently, based on progressive institutionalization, recognition of international legal personality or assignment of duties and responsibilities under international law.

Sometimes, questions of "subject of international law" and "international legal personality" are discussed with nearly metaphysical connotations, i.e., in relation to whether international organizations have the power of creation. The argument generally given is that international organizations can only create subsidiary bodies but not new international organizations. There is no denying that there may be constraints to the ability of an international organization to create a new international organization with international legal personality. This discussion is particularly relevant in relation to the EU, which is one of the areas of greatest proliferation of new agencies, as well as for quasi-autonomous bodies that, in theory, constitute an extension of the legal personality of the United Nations but have developed their own identity. Nevertheless, even regarding such agencies and QABs, there are indications of progressive institutionalization that may give rise to a discussion on their legal status.

Overall, it is a matter of fact whether an entity may be recognized as possessing international legal personality and hence as a subject of international law. Also, there are clear indications that the power of creation of international organizations has passed over to international organizations and COPs.

Finally, the relationship of the two notions of "subject of international law" and "international legal personality" need to be reevaluated. This author agrees with Klabbers that "a plea for personality, and the consequent acceptance thereof, has more to do with political recognition of relations between actors and those relations' relevancies, than with anything else."[2] As will be shown, the notion of subject of international law is broader than that of international juridical personality. Hence, organizations such as the OSCE and organizations established as trust funds with or without juridical personality may qualify for recognition as subjects of international law. The same is also true for dual and hybrid organizations, incorporated under municipal law but with recognition of international legal personality and privileges and immunities under international law. In addition, subsidiary bodies may also qualify for recognition. Thus, it is not how they were established which is relevant but their functions and whether they are acting on the international plane.

---

[2] Klabbers 2005, p. 38.

6.1.2 Historical Connotations of Subjects of International Law

Current concepts of subject of law and international juridical personality are largely the result of the state-centric concepts that evolved during the eighteenth and nineteenth centuries, in contrast with the concepts of sovereignty and subject of international law that prevailed in the Middle Ages.

Steinberger has shown that "Political organizations and institutions in medieval Europe did not correspond to the notion of the State as used since the 17th century, nor did their mutual legal relationships correspond to an international legal order of a plurality of interdependent States."[3]

Moreover, as indicated by Oeter, the idea of a "summa potestas", in the sense of an unlimited power of the ruler over a certain territory and people, the Middle Ages did not know, and could not know it.[4]

Under Roman law and in the Middle Ages, there was a much wider concept of subject of international law than at present.

As Vinogradoff has clarified, the *jus gentium* appeared as "the common law of intercourse between free individuals"[5] and formed "the main stock of private international law in societies constructed on the principle of free individual association."[6] This also ties in with the point made by Michoud:

> Les jurisconsultes romains n'ont jamais employé le nom de personne pour désigner l'Etat en tant que sujet de droits de souveraineté. Pour eux, être une personne, c'etait seulement être capable de droits privés, tels que le droit patrimoniaux et les droits de famille. L'Etat était en dehors et au-dessus des personnes: et si à une époque plus ou moins tardive on l'a considéré comme une personne *en tant que fisc, on ne l'a considéré que comme une personne de droit privé.*[7]

---

[3] Steinberger 2000, p. 501.

[4] "Die Vorstellung einer *summa potestas*, als konzentrierte und gedanklich unbeschränkte Gewalt über ein bestimmtes Gebiet und Volk zu Händen eines Herrschers, kannte das Mittelalter gerade nicht, konnte es nicht kennen." Oeter 2002, p. 262.

[5] Vinogradoff 1939, p. 99.

[6] Vinogradoff clarifies that the "introduction of this new body of laws—the *jus gentium* was not brought about by legislative acts. The *leges and senatus consulta* applied directly to civil law and touched the intercourse between nations only in an indirect and subsidiary way. The edicts of the praetors and of the governors who wielded the administrative *imperium* in the province referred frequently to rules based on natural reasonableness and assisted materially in establishing them. But these edicts themselves were in no way the product of the magistrates' personal opinion: normally, they presented the juridical results of ideas elaborated by business practice and by professional analysis. And it is in the domain of *jus gentium* that these sources of law conceived as authoritative opinions of jurists (*responsa prudentium*) found their widest application [….]." Vinogradoff 1939, p. 93.

[7] Michoud 1906, pp. 21–22. https://archive.org/stream/lathoriedelaper00michgoog#page/n6/mode/2up.

In the Middle Ages, the concepts of personality remained inspired by the Roman law concept of *jus gentium* and were firmly anchored in private law:

> Pour qualifier la nature des groupes, le canonistes parlent de *nomen intellectuale* ou de *persona repraesentata.* Mais le moyen âge ne formula la personnalité ni de l'Eglise ni de l'Etat, malgré la doctrine des corporations ou la *persona ficta* de la jurisprudence.[8]

For representatives of the Spanish Theological School such as Francisco de Vitoria, "the law of nations regulated an international community encompassing also individuals '*Respublica est pars totius orbis*'"[9] and based "on the view of Thomas Aquinas it was held that any governance was not affected by the status of mortal sin but was linked to human personhood. Thus, it could later be allowed that individuals as part of this *societas humana* had a certain standing in the context of international law."[10] Blackston also did not distinguish between States and individuals."[11]

In the same vein, Pauwelyn, Wessel and Wouters state:

> Over the centuries, the subjects and lawmaking process and outputs in the international legal order have dramatically evolved. In the Middle Ages, for example, the main actors were not states, but the spiritual and temporal regime of the two universal powers, the Holy Roman Emperor and the Pope, with, under them, kings and princes, the clergy, and independent cities, tied up in complex feudal relationships. In the 17th century, states emerged but also the semi-state, semi-private trading companies operating on the basis of concessions and privileges granted to them by states including trade monopolies and sovereign rights.[12]

This author joins Pauwelyn, Wessel and Wouters in recalling that "as the ICJ (*sic*) opined in the *Reparations case*, 'throughout its history, the development of international law has been influenced by the requirements of international life'"[13] and shares their view that this "had led to new 'instances of action upon the international plane by certain entities which are not States' and may, in turn, lead to 'new subjects of international law' that are 'not necessarily … States or possess the rights and obligations of statehood'."[14]

It is pertinent to recall these historical developments because they underline that the notion of subject of international law may be thought about in a much wider context that its current application. It was substantially only towards the end of the eighteenth century, under the influence of authors such as Vattel and Hobbes, that "States were personalized and were regarded as the only addressees of international

[8] Carroz and Probst 1953, p. 10.

[9] Hafner 2013, p. 289.

[10] Hafner 2013, pp. 289 and 290.

[11] Hafner 2013, p. 291, with further references.

[12] Pauwelyn et al. 2014, p. 744.

[13] Ibid., 744.

[14] Ibid., 744–745.

law."[15] Hence, states were considered to be the only subjects of international law.[16] This process reached its culmination at the beginning of the last century. As recent as 1904, "international law was canonically seen as a system designed exclusively by States exclusively for states—as a system with 73 participants, 74 including the Pope."[17]

The theory that states are the only subjects of international law has been superseded by events, as have been the mystical concepts of the State which emerged in the seventeenth and eighteenth centuries.

It is indeed a "mark of international law's conservatism that it took until 1949 for the separate legal personality of an international organization like the United Nations to be recognized,"[18] to the extent "that the Secretary-General of the League apparently had to sign contracts of employment in his personal capacity", due to the unsettled status of the League of Nations.[19]

It is equally a mark of international law's conservatism that there remains a lingering resistance against taking account of new developments and the increased role for civil society in international relations which Oscar Schachter sees as one of the reasons for the decline of the nation-state.[20]

Traditional state-centric concepts, while they greatly contributed to the development of public international law and continue to be relevant to traditional organizations established by treaties, have become sterile as they fail to consider new developments, such as, in particular, the increased role of transnational actors, including the private sector, philanthropy and civil society. The failure to take account of such developments has become a burden for the further development of public international law.

Higgins has stated,

> it is not particularly helpful, either intellectually or operationally, to rely on the object-subject dichotomy that runs through so much of the writings. It is more helpful, and closer to perceived reality, to return to the view of international law as a particular decision-making process. Within that process (which is a dynamic and not a static one), there are a variety of participants, making claims across state lines, with the object of maximizing various values. [....]
>
> xxx xxx xxx
>
> Now, in this model, there are no 'subjects' and 'objects, but only *participants*. Individuals *are* participants along with states, international organizations (such as the United Nations), or the International Monetary Fund (IMF) or the ILO, multinational corporations, and indeed private non-governmental groups.[21]

---

[15] Hafner 2013, p. 291.

[16] Carroz and Probst 1953, p. 13.

[17] Crawford 2013, p. 146.

[18] Ibid., 152.

[19] Ibid., 152.

[20] Schachter 1997, pp. 12–15.

[21] Higgins 1991, p. 81.

This author fully shares Higgins's view that it is necessary to recognize a wider group of participants in the international legal system. However, two qualifications need to be made. First, the term "international organization" must not be limited to traditional organizations with treaty foundation such as the United Nations, the IMF or the UN specialized agencies, but must be interpreted in a wider manner to comprise international organizations not established by a treaty, including dual or hybrid organizations such as the Global Fund and international organizations established as trust funds. Second, this author attributes less importance to questions of terminology than Higgins who deliberately avoids not only using the term "subject of international law" but also "international legal personality". The term "participant" used by Higgins refers to a process, while the terms "subject of international law" and "international legal personality" both denote a status. As long as the term "subject of international law" is not understood in the sense formerly proposed to imply that only states can be subjects of international law and is deemed to comprise any entity which is acting on the international plane and may be the subject of duties and responsibilities under international law, such term can be used interchangeably with that of participant. The notion of "subject of international law" is broader than international legal personality, as also entities without international legal personality may be qualified as subjects of international law. Hence, both terms have different connotations and should be used accordingly.

6.1.3 Dual and Hybrid Organizations

The question of whether an organization established under municipal law may enjoy international juridical personality and privileges and immunities under international law has long since been a point of discussion. This is underlined by the fact that at the beginning of last century this issue already surfaced at the Union of International Associations, established in 1910, following a resolution of the First World Congress of International Associations.

> This forum was the first to propose that a '*supra-national status be established through diplomatic convention*, for the use of international associations without lucrative object, which, by reason of their nature or aim, cannot or do not wish to be subject to a fixed society legislation'. In that same year, the International Law Association (ILA) adopted a similar resolution, calling 'to establish by *diplomatic convention, an extra-national or supranational* statute or governing law' which may be adopted by international associations formed for non-profit. Most significantly, however, the matter was discussed for the first time by the Institute of International Law (Institute). These discussions led to the formulation of the first *Draft Convention on the Legal Status of International Associations* presented by the Institute member, von Baar, in 1912.[22]

[22] Ben-Ari 2013, p. 5.

While the convention presented by von Baar in 1912 focused on the recognition of the juridical personality of international associations under domestic law,[23] it also contained in para 6 a reference to the recognition of the international juridical personality of international associations ("reconnaissance comme personne juridique internationale"). The draft prepared by Nicolas Politis in 1923 set out in the Preamble that it was necessary to determine for international associations "an international status of which they can avail themselves on the territories of the Contracting Powers to an extent which is compatible in each of the same with the requirement of public order."[24] Politis "understood that a universal status required the specification of certain secured rights" and envisioned a "more balanced universal system of control", suggesting for that reason "an improved international bureau, supervised by a diplomatic (that is, a state-controlled commission)."[25]

In accordance with Article 5 of the said draft, international Association had to lodge their original articles of association and any amendments thereto with a "Permanent Commission" set up under Article 4. While the Contracting Powers maintained, according to Politis's draft, the right to refuse recognition of an international association, Article 7 of the draft provided in pertinent part:

> The refusal so motivated shall be notified by the permanent Commission to the association concerned which, within four months following such notification, may contest the same on the grounds of action *ultra vires* before the permanent International Court of Justice.

The convention proposed by Politis sought to regulate the legal capacities of international associations, as well as their ability to receive gifts, fiscal advantages, use of their name, mark and emblem, access to jurisdiction and specified to what extent these associations were subject to national jurisdiction. While Politis's proposal went way beyond what was considered acceptable at the time and was not approved, the above discussion shows that even at the beginning of the last century an international status of non-governmental organizations was not deemed to be intrinsically impossible. Thus, the discussion on the international legal personality of transnational actors goes back for some 100 years.[26]

---

[23] "Les gouvernements signataires de la présente convention s'engagent (sauf la faculté, pour chacun d'eux, d'apprécier suivant ses propres lois, dans chaque cas particulier, s'il y a lieu d'autoriser l'acceptation des donations ou legs faits par ses ressortissants à des associations internationales, ou ayant pour objet des biens situés sur son territoire), à reconnaître comme personnes juridiques ayant le droit de faire des contrats, d'acquérir par donation ou testament ainsi que la faculté d'ester en justice, les sociétés internationales d'utilité publique …" See Draft Convention on the Legal Status of International Associations. von Bar, L. 2012. Reproduced in Appendix 4.1 of the International Associations Statutes Series, Vol 1. Union of International Associations (UIA) eds (1988) http://www.uia.org/archive/legal-status-4-1.

[24] Draft Convention on International Associations. Politis, N. 1923. Appendix 4.5 of the International Associations Statutes Series. Vol. 1, UIA eds (1988) http://www.uia.org/archive/legal-status-4-5.

[25] Ben-Ari 2013, p. 8.

[26] See also Charnovitz 1997, p. 189.

The case of the International Committee of the Red Cross (ICRC) also shows that "[p]ersonality may be acquired by a combination of treaty provisions and recognition or acquiescence by other international persons."[27] It has long-since been recognized that the ICRC is a subject of international law. However, along with the order of Malta and the Holy See, it has been placed in the category of special or "atypical subjects[28]" of international law. It is time to remove it from that niche and recognize the ICRC as the predecessor of a new class of international organizations with dual or hybrid character, established under national law but with privileges and immunities under international law and operating on the international plane.

The ICRC is not the only international organization established under municipal law which operates at the international level and has been afforded privileges and immunities. The Bank of International Settlements (BIS), which was founded on 20 January 1930 to implement Germany's reparations payments as determined under the Treaty of Versailles, is another example of an institution incorporated under national law but endowed with international legal personality and enjoying privileges and immunities under international law.

The establishment of the BIS is remarkable in various ways, first because consistent the Convention respecting the Bank of International Settlements of 20 January 1930 (Hague Convention of 1930),[29] under the constituent charter of 1930 granted by the Swiss Government, it was not created by governments; rather, the central banks of Belgium, France, Germany, Great Britain, Italy and Japan and a banking group of the United States "have undertaken to found the said Bank and have guaranteed or arranged for the guarantee of the subscription of its authorised capital."[30] The BIS was given a dual status as it enjoys privileges and immunities similar to those accorded to other international organizations in Switzerland. Its Charter provided for the exemption and immunity of the Bank from all taxation. Additional privileges and immunities were extended to the BIS under the Protocol regarding the immunities of the Bank for International Settlements of 30 July 1936.[31]

BIS was created as a commercial bank and adopted the legal structure of a Swiss limited company with publicly held shares. "The bank's immunity from Swiss government interference and taxes in both peace and war was guaranteed by the Hague Convention of 1930, which established BIS as an international organization governed by international law with the privileges and immunities necessary for the performance of its role."[32]

[27] Shaw 2003, p. 243.

[28] Walter 2007, para 7. http://opil.ouplaw.com/home/EPIL.

[29] Convention respecting the Bank of International Settlements of 20 Jan. 1930. https://www.bis.org/about/convention-en.pdf.

[30] Constituent Charter of the Bank for International Settlements of 20 Jan. 1930. https://www.bis.org/about/charter-en.pdf.

[31] Protocol regarding the immunities of the Bank for International Settlements of 30 July 1936. https://www.bis.org/about/protocol-en.pdf.

[32] Felsenfeld and Bilali 2004, p. 955, with further references.

> The international legal personality of BIS and the privileges and immunities which it has enjoyed in Switzerland since its founding were also 'reconfirmed' in other documents such as the Brussels Protocol of July 30, 1936 and the Headquarters Agreement entered between BIS and the Swiss government on February 10, 1987.[33]

The case of the BIS shows that incorporation of an organization under national law does not necessarily imply that it is also subject to national law. The background of the establishment of the BIS is analyzed in detail in the partial award of the Permanent Court of Arbitration of 2002.[34] As shown therein, the reason for the "the rather complicated manner in which the Bank was established must be seen in light of the stage of development of international law in 1930. Apparently, at that time some of the parties to the treaty had doubts as to whether a treaty could establish under public international law a company limited by shares and whether such a company could be generally recognized."[35]

> For these reasons the parties to the treaty chose to adopt a model whereby pursuant to the treaty obligation Switzerland undertook to grant the Constituent Charter of the Bank and thereby create the company. At the same time, however, the parties made clear that, even though the Charter, as an Annex to the treaty, was also issued under Swiss law, the company would not be subjected to Swiss law. This complicated system does not exclude the applicability of Swiss law for formalities, for instances as to the procedure for general meetings of the Bank, where this is not in conflict with the relevant instruments of international law."[36]

Hence, while "the internal structure of the Bank was, according to Article 1 of the Statutes, 'a Company limited by Shares,' and the Board of the Bank was comprised, on a permanent basis, of the governors of the central banks of the seven founding States and their nominees, the essential international character of the Bank is apparent from its treaty origin."[37]

The example of the BIS shows that it is possible, in principle, to exempt a dual or hybrid organization from the applicability of national law.

Such exemption from the application of national law can be based on a treaty, as in the case of the BIS. However, it may also be predicated on national legislation if this is permissible in accordance with the constitution and laws of the country concerned. The International Rice Research Institute (IRRI) offers an interesting example. As shown in Chapter 7, after having been incorporated initially in 1960

---

[33] Ibid., 956.

[34] "Partial Award on the Lawfulness of the Recall of the Privately Held Shares on 8 Jan. 2001". Dr. Reineccius, Horst, First Eagle SoGen Funds, Inc., Mathieu, Pierre and La Societé de Concours Hippique de la Châtre v. Bank for International Settlements, Reports of International Arbitral Awards. 2002. Vol. XXIII, 183–251. http://legal.un.org/riaa/cases/vol_XXIII/183-251.pdf

[35] Ibid., para 105.

[36] Ibid., para 106.

[37] Ibid., para 112.

under the laws of the Philippines by the Securities and Exchange Commission[38] "as an autonomous, non-stock, philanthropic, nonprofit corporation".[39] IRRI was recognized in 1979 by Presidential Decree No. 1620[40] "as an international organization" (Article 1) and was granted "all the immunities and privileges normally accorded to international organizations of a universal character." (Article 2) The said Presidential Decree provided in Article 3 for "Immunity of Legal Process" and for other privileges and immunities generally enjoyed by international organizations (for communications, taxation and customs, free disposal of funds, freedom from entry and sojourn and privileges and immunities for the Institute's Board of Trustees, officials and other persons associated with IRRI (Articles 4–8).

To the extent that an entity providing public goods incorporated under national law is not exempted from the application of national law either as consequence of a treaty obligation or on the basis of a legal act adopted by the appropriate national authority, national law applies subsidiarily to the entity concerned. This fact does not preclude that the entity concerned may be qualified as a dual or hybrid organization if the country concerned recognizes its international legal personality and extends to it privileges and immunities under a headquarters agreement or through other arrangements. Nevertheless, the establishment of dual and hybrid organizations of that type is not feasible in all countries.

As Muller highlights, "in the relationship between international organizations and their host states, the notions of *functional necessity* and *state sovereignty* or *sovereign powers* are essential. The functional needs of the organization provide both the source and the limitations of an organization's special status in the host country."[41] As they restrain sovereign powers, headquarters agreements are generally concluded as treaties. However, in some countries, it is not possible to conclude an international agreement such as a Headquarters Agreement with an entity incorporated under national law. This is case for example for the Republic of Korea, the Constitution of which is based on a monistic conception of the relationship between international and domestic law. While there is no explicit provision of the Korean Constitution which would prevent concluding an international agreement with an entity incorporated under national law, this is not deemed possible under Article 6 of the Constitution of the Republic of Korea (South Korea), which provides: "Treaties duly concluded and promulgated under the Constitution and the generally recognized rules of international law shall have the same effect as

[38] Certificate of Incorporation for the International Rice Research Institute signed at Manila on 8 March 1960 by the Philippines Securities and Exchange Commission. http://library.cgiar.org/bitstream/handle/10947/233/irri002.pdf?sequence=1.

[39] Article 1, para 1 of the By-Laws of the International Rice Research Institute, Inc. (IRRI), as amended on 17 Sept. 2017.

[40] Presidential Decree 1620 of 19 April 1979. http://www.lawphil.net/statutes/presdecs/pd1979/pd_1620_1979.html http://library.cgiar.org/bitstream/handle/10947/944/irri004.pdf?sequence=1.

[41] Muller 1995, p. 281.

the domestic laws of the Republic of Korea."[42] As a treaty has the same effect as domestic laws, it is not considered possible to grant privileges and immunities by way of treaty to an entity which is incorporated under and subject to the authority of national law.[43]

Where dual or hybrid organizations have not been exempted from the application of national law, the law of the country where they are incorporated may impose some constraints. As has been previously analyzed by this author, the appointment of Board members to the Global Fund or the Gavi Alliance may require a formal sanction by the supervisory authority of the country concerned, and there may be requirements regarding the composition and number of Board members; approval of said supervisory authority may also be required for certain fundamental decisions such as amendment of the organization's statute or the dissolution of the organization and the disposal of its assets.[44] Due to the above, the dual or hybrid organizational model can only flourish in countries that are willing to guarantee the autonomy of the organization and exercise the right of supervisory authorities selectively and restrictively.

The emergence of hybrid or dual organizations as a new paradigm of organizational structure needs to be seen in the context of wider developments in international law. As has been shown above, the borderline between public international law and private international law is moving for a variety of reasons. It increasingly gets blurred in the context of the internationalization of the investment law. Such internationalization is epitomized by the "shift from the traditional hegemony of national jurisdiction in international investment law to the internationalization of international contracts,"[45] the discussion on the legal status of investors which some characterize as "partial international personality", and, in this context, in particular, by the "the fundamental question of whether the investor's rights are of a direct, a derivative or a contingent nature."[46]

As indicated by Shaw:

> Another possible method of acquiring international personality is by subjecting an agreement between a recognized international person and a private party directly to the rules of international law. This would have the effect of rendering the latter an international person in the context of the arrangement in question so as to enable it to invoke in the field of international law the rights it derives from that arrangement.[47]

---

[42] Constitution of the Republic of Korea of 17 July 1948, as subsequently modified. http://english.ccourt.go.kr/cckhome/images/eng/main/Constitution_of_the_Republic_of_Korea.pdf.

[43] It transpired from a discussion of this author with Korean lawyers that, if all, privileges and immunities could only be extended to an entity incorporated under national law unilaterally by the Republic of Korea in statute adopted for that purposed. However, any such statute would be subject to the legislative discretion of the Korean Parliament and could be repealed or amended as the Parliament deems it fit.

[44] Regarding the dissolution, See Droesse, "Organizational Structures", p. 103.

[45] Cantegreil 2011, p. 442.

[46] See with further references: Braun 2014, p. 73.

[47] Shaw 2003, p. 243.

Moreover, there is a variety of participants in the international legal system which are recognized having partial legal personality. As a result of the "emancipation of the individual from the State,"[48] the individual has been recognized as possessing partial international legal personality, respectively as a participant in the international legal system.

In the view of this author there is no convincing reason why, given these circumstances, a dual or hybrid organization which is recognized as having international legal personality and enjoys privileges and immunities in its host country and certain other countries, should not be qualified as a subject of international law?

In the Barcelona Traction Case, the ICJ recognized that

> 37. [….] From its origins closely linked with international commerce, diplomatic protection has sustained a particular impact from the growth of international economic relations, and at the same time from the profound transformations which have taken place in the economic life of nations. **These latter changes have given birth to municipal institutions, which have transcended frontiers and have begun to exercise considerable influence on international relations. One of these phenomena which has a particular bearing on the present case is the corporate entity.**
> 38. **In this field international law is called upon to recognize institutions of municipal law that have an important and extensive role in the international field.** This does not necessarily imply drawing any analogy between its own institutions and those of municipal law, nor does it amount to making rules of international law dependent upon categories of municipal law. All it means is that international law has had to recognize the corporate entity as an institution created by States in a domain essentially within their domestic jurisdiction. This in turn requires that, whenever legal issues arise concerning the rights of States with regard to the treatment of companies and shareholders, as to which rights international law has not established its own rules, it has to refer to the relevant rules of municipal law. Consequently, in view of the relevance to the present case of the rights of the corporate entity and its shareholders under municipal law, the Court must devote attention to the nature and interrelation of those rights.[49] (emphasis added).

The Court further stated: "If the Court were to decide the case in disregard of the relevant institutions of municipal law it would, without justification, invite serious legal difficulties. It would lose touch with reality, for there are no corresponding institutions of international law to which the Court could resort. Thus the Court has, as indicated, not only to take cognizance of municipal law but also to refer to it."[50]

Higgins contends that the latter statement "seems to come close to an abdication of its international judicial function."[51] Moreover, some members of the International Court of Justice have criticized the approach adopted by the majority

[48] See Hafner.

[49] "Barcelona Traction, Light and Power Company, Limited, Judgment", *ICJ Reports 1970,* 3, paras 37 and 38. http://www.icj-cij.org/docket/files/50/5387.pd http://www.icj-cij.org/files/case-related/50/050-19700205-JUD-01-00-EN.pdf.

[50] Ibid., para 50.

[51] Higgins 1970–1971, p. 333.

of the Court, such as the dissenting opinion of Judge Riphagen who states categorically:

> This complete separation between. the rules of customary international law concerning responsibility for the treatment of aliens, and the rules and principles of municipal law, is much more than a mere legal construct permitting of the substitution of legal relations between States for the legal relations between the government and the private citizen or between private citizens inter se.
>
> It reflects a reality of international life: it determines the very content of the rights and obligations of States on the international plane.
>
> xxx xxx xxx
>
> The considerations which determine the choice of a particular system of municipal private law with respect to what the Court has called 'the nature and interrelation' of 'the rights of the corporate entity and its shareholders' are completely foreign to the problems which are the concern of the rules of public international law relating to responsibility for the treatment of aliens.[52]

Also Judge Fitzmaurice has stressed in his separate opinion that it is necessary

> to insist on the principle that when private law concepts are utilized, or private law institutions are dealt with in the international legal field, they should not there be distorted or handled in a manner not in conformity with their true character, as it exists under the system or systems of their creation. But, although this is so, it is scarcely less important to bear in mind that conditions in the international field are sometimes very different from what they are in the domestic, and that rules which these latter conditions fully justify may be less capable of vindication if strictly applied when transposed onto the international level.[53]

This author does not share the criticism of the aforementioned decision. Rather, the deliberations of the majority of the Court in the Barcelona Traction Case cited above are relevant and important well beyond the specific context in which they were made. This reflects the basic issue that the traditional dichotomies of public and private and governmental and non-governmental no longer capture properly the evolution of international law. International law needs to take account of institutions of national law, not only in the field of diplomatic protection, but also in the field of international organization where a series of new paradigms of organizational structure have emerged, among which a new class of dual and hybrid organizations incorporated under national law but with recognition of international legal personality and privileges and immunities under international law. In line with the principles set out by the International Court of Justice, "international law is called upon to recognize [these] institutions of municipal law that have an important and extensive role in the international field". Doing so does not mean to make international law dependent on national law nor does it entail any obstacle to the

[52] Dissenting Opinion of Judge Riphagen, W. para 4. http://www.icj-cij.org/files/case-related/50/050-19700205-JUD-01-11-EN.pdf.

[53] Separate Opinion of Judge Fitzmaurice, Sir G., para 5. http://www.icj-cij.org/files/case-related/50/050-19700205-JUD-01-04-EN.pdf.

development of international law. It only means taking account of the evolution of international law that already took place.

Also, there is nothing in international law which would prevent recognized subjects of international law from concluding agreements with an entity incorporated under national law that recognizes the international legal personality of that entity for the purposes of the agreement. Nor are there any constraints under international law for states to assign duties and responsibilities under international law to an entity incorporated under national law.

As a corollary of its sovereignty, each state can decide on which matters to conclude agreements governed by international law and with which entities to conclude such agreements. This is also reflected in Article 6 of the Vienna Convention on the Law of Treaties, which is widely seen to have codified a general principle of customary law. As stated in the commentary by Dörr and Schmalenbach, the purpose of this provision is to "safeguard the treaty capacity of States against any attempts to limit its scope." In contrast, Article 6 does not deal with the competence of States to conclude certain treaties.[54]

It is further indicated in the same commentary that the "wording of Article 6 implicates the **legal irrelevance** of any agreed or imposed limitation on the treaty-making capacity while remaining a sovereign State" and that, accordingly, the "treaty-making capacity of any state is unassailable under the Convention."[55]

It is prerogative of each state to decide whether to enter into a bilateral agreement covered by international law with an entity that has been incorporated under national law or to become a party to a multilateral agreement which assigns duties and responsibilities under international law to such an entity or provides for recognition of its legal personality and privileges and immunities.

It is pertinent to recall in this context that, as shown above, the internationalization of the status of transnational actors including civil society has been discussed for more than 100 years. Also, there are various cases where states have expressly recognized the international status of organizations incorporated under national law. As will be shown below in further detail, both the headquarters agreements of the Global Fund and Gavi Alliance with the Swiss Federation expressly provide for international legal personality of these organizations. While these agreements are similar to the headquarters agreements concluded between states and traditional international organizations with treaty foundation, they differ from those as they transform the status of the aforementioned organizations by converting them from nongovernmental organizations to dual and hybrid organizations.

The international status of the Global Fund can also be derived from the fact that it is recognized in the United States as a public international organization. Moreover, the Global Fund was the first entity of its kind to propose to the countries where it is operating to become party to a multilateral agreement which recognizes the legal personality of the Global Fund and attributes to it privileges and

[54] See Schmalenbach 2012, p. 105.

[55] Ibid.

immunities. Thus, the Global Fund has become the epitome of a new dual or hybrid organization established under national law but with recognition of its international legal personality by its home country and other countries. It is a subject of international law and participant in the international legal system.

6.1.4 Relationship of Subjects of International Law and International Legal Personality

There are a number of theories on "subjects of international law". "The idea of 'subjects' of international law is a confusing idea, and the confusion stems in part from being conflated with the notion of international legal personality."[56] The traditional approach, which is still widely reflected in literature, is that the constituent instrument of an international organization (generally in the form of a treaty) establishes the (international) juridical personality of an organization and that being a subject of international law is the consequence of an organization possessing international juridical personality.

Broches[57] is among those who most categorically "use the term 'international personality', that is the quality of being an international person, as synonymous with the quality of being a subject of international law."[58]

Indeed, the constituent agreements of traditional international organizations frequently contain provisions on the legal capacity of the organization in member countries and, in some cases, on the international juridical personality of the organization. Hence, the first test applied by the Court of Justice in the *Reparations for Injuries Case* to ascertain whether the United Nations has international legal personality was to look into whether the UN Charter had "given the Organization such a position that it possesses, in regard to its Members, rights which it is entitled to ask them to respect. In other words, does the Organization possess international personality".[59]

Also, there can be no doubt about the usefulness of the concept of personality:

> Without personality, an organization would not be able to appear in its own right in legal proceedings, whether at the international level or non-international level. There would also not be a single international person as such having the capacity in its own right to have rights, obligations and powers, whether implied or expressed, both at the international level or non-international level.[60]

---

[56] Klabbers 2015, p. 42

[57] Broches 1959, p. 316.

[58] Ibid.

[59] Reparation for Injuries Suffered in the Service of the United Nations. Advisory Opinion: ICJ Reports, 1949, 174, 178. http://www.icj-cij.org/files/case-related/4/004-19490411-ADV-01-00-EN.pdf.

[60] Amerasinghe 2010, pp. 97–105.

Nevertheless, the traditional position that the international legal personality is established by the constituent agreement and the equation of the terms "subject of international law" and "international legal personality" need to be rethought in three respects:

First, the decision whether an entity should be endowed with international legal personality may be, but is not necessarily taken, at the time when the organization is established. The constituent agreement of an organization may, and often does, but does not need to, provide for international legal personality. Whether an organization can be recognized as a subject of international law is first and foremost based on the organization's functions and the position which recognized subjects of international law have adopted in its regard. Thus, organizations such as IPU and INTERPOL may qualify for recognition, and are effectively recognized, as subjects of international law, even though they are not established by a treaty. Even if an entity is established under local law, it may subsequently acquire international legal personality based on progressive institutionalization of its activities, by the fact that its international legal personality is recognized in bilateral or multilateral agreements or in other arrangements, or because duties and responsibilities under international law are conferred to the entity.

Second, over "the last few decades, international cooperation has increasingly been organized through mechanisms that were deliberately kept at the fringes of international law, or even outside it altogether"[61] and this should induce international lawyers to reflect on whether current concepts of international law and international organization are still adequate. While, as shown above, the disaggregation of the state in its component institutions is increasingly accepted, so far international lawyers have not drawn any conclusions from such disaggregation for their analysis of institutional frameworks of international organizations. Hence, currently, forms of cooperation among national regulators and other forms of cooperation between sub-state actors generally are not deemed to qualify for recognition as international organization or as subject of international law. However, it is conceivable, as a matter of principle, that such forms of cooperation may be provided with a structure and endowed with powers for them to be classified as international organization and as subject of international law. As will be shown, the FSB manifests tendencies in this direction. Whether forms of cooperation between sub-state actors are to be recognized as international organization and as subjects of international law does not depend on the mode of their establishment or on whether their membership involves sub-state actors or national regulators, but on their functions and powers. Similar considerations also apply to those cases where states seek to artificially withhold international legal personality from their creation.

In the view of this author, a much wider definition of "subject of international law" is required to include entities not established by a treaty and dual or hybrid organizations incorporated under national law. Moreover, forms of cooperation

---

[61] Klabbers 2001, p. 405.

between technical government agencies, entities at the sub-state level, and regulatory agencies should not be excluded from recognition as international organizations" merely for the reason that they were not established by an agreement of governments. In that case, the question of whether an entity may qualify as a subject of international law and whether it meets all the requirements of an international organization should be determined on a case-to-case basis, taking account of their functions and the position adopted by recognized subjects of international law in their regard.

Third, as stressed by Amerasinghe,

> a question that arises 'in *limine*' is whether it is necessary to have a concept of personality for international organizations or whether such organizations can function without having legal personality at all. The question has sometimes been raised but hardly ever been discussed in any detail.[62]

Consistent with the statements made by the International Court of Justice in its Advisory Opinion of 1949,[63] the fact that an organization is an "international person" can be taken to mean that "it is a subject of international law and capable of possessing international rights and duties, and that it has capacity to maintain its rights by bringing international claims."[64] However, the opposite is not true: An organization may qualify as a subject of international law without possessing international legal personality. Runavot mentions "the Belgo–Luxemburg Economic Union (BLEU) and the Benelux Union that illustrate the paradox of 'intergovernmental organizations' in their composition and functioning, but devoid of international personality."[65] In addition to organizations such as OSCE incorporating "institutional ambivalence by design", international organizations established as trust funds may be other examples of international organizations which operate on the international plane without possessing international legal personality and may qualify as subjects of international law. Hence, international legal personality should neither be a requirement for an institution to qualify as a "subject of international law" nor should it be an integral part of the definition of international organization. This author agrees with Frid:

> Being a subject of international law is a precondition for having a legal personality but being a subject of international law does not necessarily indicate the possession of legal personality. Thus, the concept of subject of international law is broader than the concept of international persons because it encompasses also subjects who do not have legal personality.[66]

---

[62] Amerasinghe 2005, pp. 68–69.

[63] Reparation for injuries suffered in the service of the United Nations, Advisory Opinion: ICJ Reports 1949, 174, 179. http://www.icj-cij.org/files/case-related/4/004-19490411-ADV-01-00-EN.pdf.

[64] Ibid.

[65] Runavot 2015, p. 38.

[66] Frid 1995, p. 10.

The term “international organization”, on the other hand, is even wider than that of “subject of international law”.

Hence, an entity may be classified as a subject of international law even if it is deprived of international legal personality. This will be further reviewed below in relation to international organizations characterized by “institutional ambivalence by design” and international organizations established as trust funds. However, possession of international legal personality and classification as a subject of international law do not necessarily imply that an entity may be considered as an international organization.

6.1.5 Organizations with Institutional Ambivalence by Design as Subjects of International Law

International lawyers who have espoused state-centric concepts have problems coming to grips with the analysis of OSCE which appears like a marshmallow: “it may look enticing, but it is difficult to give it a good bite. For what can a lawyer do with an organisation which is not treaty-based and therefore has no international personality [....]?”[67]

Traditional concepts of international law refer to the intention of the participating states to determine whether an entity is endowed with international legal personality. In the case of the OSCE, its historic and factual background is quite clear. Its predecessor was the Conference for Security and Co-operation in Europe (CSCE) and during “the Cold War, the CSCE was a ‘process’ among its participating states and was never endowed with the formal and organizational attributes of an international institution.”

“This lack of structure was well suited to its role in this period: it captured whatever little common ground existed between East and West and allowed the exploration of ways to bridge the divide between them.”[68] When the CSCE changed its name to OSCE in 1994, the participating states did not mean to confer international juridical personality to the OSCE. Thus, inasmuch as the intention of the participating states is concerned, there cannot be any doubt that these “did not intend to change the legal status of the entity or its institutions, much less to conclude an agreement to create an international legal personality.”[69]

In the view of the above, and based on the origins of the OSCE and taking account of the fact that powerful states such as the United States are of the opinion that the OSCE “has no status in international law”, the OSCE itself was for many years in search of its own identity, as may be seen from the OSCE Handbook of 2007 which states:

---

67 See Odello, citing Kooijmans 1996, p. 33.

68 Flynn and Farrell 1999, p. 514.

69 Sapiro 1995, p. 631.

> The short answer to the question 'What is the OSCE?' is that it is the continuation of the Conference on Security and Co-operation in Europe that began in Helsinki more than 30 years ago.[70]

It was further indicated in this context:

> With all these institutional developments, the CSCE had, de facto, evolved from a conference process into a full-fledged organization. At the Budapest Summit on 5 and 6 December 1994, participating States adopted a U.S. proposal to rename it the Organization for Security and Co-operation in Europe. This decision took effect on 1 January 1995. As part of the same decision, the CSCE Council was renamed the Ministerial Council, the Committee of Senior Officials became the Senior Council and the Permanent Committee the Permanent Council. **The changes in name, however, altered neither the character of CSCE commitments nor the status of the CSCE and its institutions, as the decision explicitly noted.** A proposal by the Russian Federation at the Rome Council meeting the previous year to transform the CSCE into an international organization with legal status had not been accepted.[71] (emphasis added)

In line with the above, Epping und Brunner merely conceive the OSCE as a common forum of the participating states.[72]

As the international legal personality of the OSCE was not recognized by participating states, it had previously a fragmented legal status which different arrangements applicable to different countries and OSCE missions. It was only on 14 June 2017 that OSCE eventually managed to sign a headquarters agreement with Austria regulating the presence of OSCE in Austria.[73] Also, on 28 June 2017 OSCE and Poland signed a headquarters agreement.[74] Unlike previous fragmented

[70] OSCE Handbook 2007, p. 1.

[71] Ibid., 8.

[72] "Es liegt daher nahe, die OSZE in toto noch als gemeinsames Forum der Teilnehmerstaaten zu begreifen. Zwar zeigt sich gerade an der der OSZE eingeräumten Möglichkeit, unabhängig von den Teilnehmerstaaten Erkundungs—und Berichterstattermissionen zu entsenden sowie friedenserhaltende Maßnahmen durchzuführen, bereits ein der OSZE zur eigenständigen Wahrnehmung übertragener Aufgabenbereich. Gleichwohl muss man angesichts der angeführten Umstände Fastenrath zustimmen, der die Umbenennung der KSZE und die Einführung einiger neuer Bezeichnungen für im Übrigen unverändert gebliebene Organe zutreffen als 'Augenwischerei' titulierte." Epping and Brunner 2014, p. 1313.

[73] As regards the conclusion of a headquarters agreement with Austria, Tichy and Köhler state that "in 2007 a proposal that OSCE should simply conclude a headquarters agreement with Austria, which would implicitly grant it international legal personality, surprised the participants in the long discussions on the legal status of the OSCE. Austria quickly made it clear that it was 'able to take a flexible position in this regard and would be ready to conclude a headquarters agreement under international law with the OSCE along the lines of existing headquarters agreements between Austria and International Organizations, if the OSCE is in a position to do so'. However, not surprisingly there was no consensus within the OSCE to such an implicit approach." Tichy and Köhler 2008, p. 470. Hence, it took until 2017 for host country agreements to be signed with Austria and Poland. See OSCE Press Release. 14 June 2017. Austrian Deputy Foreign Minister Linhart and OSCE Secretary General Zannier sign Headquarters Agreement regulating presence of OSCE in Austria. http://www.osce.org/chairmanship/322916.

[74] OSCE Press Release. Warsaw, 28 June 2017. OSCE/ODIHR and Polish Foreign Ministry sign host country agreement. http://www.osce.org/odihr/326711.

arrangements, such agreements do not only cover OSCE's missions to certain countries but the relations between OSCE and Austria and Poland, respectively. This constitutes an important new development.

As shown above, it is clear that states neither wanted to provide for firm legal obligations either in the context of the Final Act of Helsinki, the creation of the CSCE, or in the context of the conversion of the CSCE into OSCE in 1994. However, the real question is whether the founders of an organization can decide that an organization should be outside the realm of international law and whether they can artificially withhold international legal personality from the organization even though it meets all the objective criteria for international legal personality and effectively conducts itself in a manner suggesting that it does possess international legal personality. These questions, along with the question of whether an international organization must possess international legal personality to qualify as a subject of international law, will be addressed in the following discussion.

One way to establish whether an entity is a subject of international law is to examine whether it is endowed with international legal personality. This question has been discussed prior to the adoption of the Treaty of Lisbon, mostly with reference to, and against the background of, the "will theory"[75] in relation to the European Union on the grounds that no express provision for the international legal personality of the EU had been made. This author agrees with Klabbers that the EU met all the criteria for international legal personality even before the Treaty of Lisbon recognized that the EU possesses such personality.[76] Highlighting inherent problems relating to the traditional "will theory" and Seyersted's objective theory,[77] Klabbers tries to capture this under the term "presumptive personality" arguing that "the activities of the union can only be understood on the presumption that the Union possesses international legal personality."[78] Others, such as Pachinger, already concluded before the Treaty of Lisbon that the EU possessed a "de facto" international legal personality.[79]

Similarly, as in the case of the EU, it might be argued that the OSCE possesses, based on objective assessment of its powers and functions, international legal personality despite the intention of the participating states to withhold such personality from OSCE.

In the view of this author, it has been convincingly shown that

> it is not up to the drafters to decide on legal personality: that is rather something to be decided by the legal system concerned. All the drafters can do this, so to speak, apply for a

[75] Klabbers 1998, pp. 238–239.

[76] Ibid., 231–253.

[77] See Seyersted 1964, pp. 1–74 (hereinafter, Seyersted, "International Personality") and Seyersted, *Common Law of International Organizations*.

[78] Ibid., 233.

[79] Pachinger 2003, p. 135. For the evolution of the international legal personality of the EU, see, with further references, Tührer and Marro 2012.

> certain status, but the legal system decides. And no matter what the precise intentions of the drafters are, if the legal system decides otherwise, then so be it.[80]

Hence, while the legal personality of OSCE is not recognized by some participating states, it is indeed possible to maintain that based on objective criteria, the OSCE possesses *de facto* international legal personality. A number of the states participating in the OSCE effectively have adopted a position to that effect while others either deny that the OSCE possesses international legal personality or have not taken a clear position on this matter.[81]

Seyersted, while highlighting that OSCE "possesses the essential criteria to enable it to be categorized as an intergovernmental organization"[82] states in this context:

> Yet, the OSCE seems to aim for the advantages of not being an intergovernmental organization proper (the perceived freedom of exercising coordinated actions under the 'veil' of an international institution without being accountable for the result of such performances) while at the same time making sure that there is no difference between acts of OSCE and those of other, formal intergovernmental organizations. There is no reason to treat the OSCE any differently than other IGOs [....].[83]

Furthermore, the arguments that the OSCE indeed possesses international legal personality have gained recently strength and merit due to the fact that both Austria and Poland have agreed to enter into headquarter agreements with the OSCE, which are applicable to the OSCE, in general, and not only to the OSCE field operations. The willingness of these two countries to enter into headquarters agreements with the OSCE governed by international law may be seen as an implicit recognition of the international legal personality of OSCE.

If it is found that the OSCE possesses, contrary to the express intentions of its founders, *de facto* international legal personality, this necessarily implies that it can be classified as a subject of international law. However, the question arises whether the *detour* over affirmation of international legal personality is indeed required and whether it is necessary to show that an entity possesses (possibly contrary to the express intentions of its founders) international legal personality to assert that it is a subject of international law. In the view of this author, this is not necessary as the question whether an organization is the subject of duties and responsibilities under international law is separate from whether it possesses international legal personality. Thus, even if the participating states deliberately and artificially decided to withhold international legal personality from an organization, or if an entity is deprived of international legal personality, the entity concerned may still qualify as a subject of international law, provided that there is evidence that it is has duties and responsibilities under international law.

---

80 See, with further references, Klabbers 2001, pp. 403–421.

81 See Stribis 2013, pp. 113–114.

82 Seyersted 2008, p. 51.

83 Ibid., 51–52.

In the case of the OSCE, even before the signature of the recent headquarters agreements between the OSCE and Poland and Austria, respectively, there could hardly be any doubt that it was acting on the international plane. This derives from (i) an analysis of the OSCE commitments, (ii) the fact that the OSCE performs actions under international mandates and (iii) the recognition of its status in participating countries.

6.1.5.1 OSCE Commitments

The OSCE functions in a very similar manner as traditional international organizations. Klabbers argues that:

> Whether the organization takes legally binding decisions or non-legally binding decisions is deemed to be of little relevance, a finding supported by research and theorization.
>
> Also in the types of discourse to which commitments are subjected, there is no apparent difference, dixit the OSCE. Despite being 'political', OSCE commitments are nonetheless drafted as legal instruments and analyzed by means of the standard techniques of international law.[84]

In the same vein, Stribis contends:

> The character of a decision as 'politically binding' does not authorize states which have consented to it, to disregard it. The distinction between legally binding and politically binding force concerns exclusively the consequences attached to its violation, not the binding character of its commitment; the disrespect of legally binding commitments entails international legal responsibility; the non-observance of politically-binding commitments does not give rise to a claim under international law.[85]

As Christian Berger highlights:

> The Final Act of Helsinki and other CSCE/OSCE agreements and decisions are not legally binding, and accordingly are not eligible for registration under Article 102 of the Charter of the United Nations. However, they contain numerous clauses which stem from international law and refer to international law, or can be traced to international agreements by which a great number of all the OSCE states are legally bound. OSCE commitments and the relations of participating states with each other are generally based on the principles of public international law, while the norms of international humanitarian law and the law of war are given special attention in various documents and decisions of OSCE bodies.[86]

Finally, also Odello states:

> An interesting possibility would be the classification of the Helsinki Declaration within the category of non-conventional concerted acts *(actes concertés non conventionnels)*. These acts do not create legal obligations, but they are established to govern mutual relationships and the conduct of states. The relationship between 'political', 'moral' and 'legal' obligations has been addressed as well, and political obligations have been considered

[84] Klabbers 2001, p. 410.

[85] Stribis 2013, p. 115

[86] Berger 1996, p. 38.

> particularly useful to define commitments among states. Even if they 'do not create legal obligations nevertheless formulate community or shared expectations of state behaviour'. Therefore, there is a possibility that political obligations when receive a strong level of compliance can be seen as legal obligations.[87]

The underlying thought of all the theories mentioned above is that the OSCE participating states are not entitled to ignore politically binding commitments to which they have consented.

6.1.5.2 OSCE Actions Under International Mandates

As regards (ii) above, that the OSCE is a subject of international law may be derived from the fact that it is the subject of duties, responsibilities and privileges and immunities under international law under UN Security Council resolutions. For example, the OSCE mission to Kosovo was governed by UN Security Council resolutions as a distinct component of the United Nations Interim Administration Mission in Kosovo (UNMIK). Further to UN Security Council Resolution 1244 (1999),[88] UNMIK Regulations No. 2000/47 defined in Section 1 "UNMIK" as the "international civil presence established pursuant to Security Council resolution 1244 (1999)" and integrated the OSCE for institution-building.[89] It can be derived from Section 9 of these Regulations[90] governing the applicability of the General Convention, that this convention applies to UNMIK personnel to a limited extent. Hence, the functional immunity from legal process and immunity from any form of arrest or detention which UNMIK personnel enjoy under UNMIK Regulations also extends to UNMIK personnel from OSCE.

6.1.5.3 Recognition of Status

Finally, in relation to (iii), even before Austria and Poland expressed their willingness to enter into headquarters agreements with OSCE, OSCE has entered into a

---

[87] Odello 2006, p. 370.

[88] See para 5 of UN Security Council Resolution 1244. Adopted on 10 June 1999. http://peacemaker.un.org/sites/peacemaker.un.org/files/990610_SCR1244%281999%29.pdf. The Security Council decided in this para "on the deployment in Kosovo, under United Nations auspices, of international civil and security presences, with appropriate equipment and personnel as required, and welcomes the agreement of the Federal Republic of Yugoslavia to such presences."

[89] UNMIK Regulation No. 2000/47 of 18 Aug. 2000 ("on the Status, Privileges and Immunities of KFOR and UNMIK and their Personnel in Kosovo"). http://www.unmikonline.org/regulations/2000/reg47-00.htm.

[90] Section 9 of UNMIK Regulation No. 2000/47 provides: "Applicability of the Convention on the Privileges and Immunities of the United Nations. The provisions of the present regulation are without prejudice to the privileges and immunities enjoyed by UNMIK under the Convention on the Privileges and Immunities of the United Nations."

number of Memoranda of Understanding (MOUs) and arrangements with the host states of its field operations. While OSCE has a fragmented legal nature in the countries where its field missions operate and some maintain that these are "legally not binding,"[91] this author believes that a different conclusion is warranted, given the content of these MOUs and the fact that some of them are ratified by Parliament. For example, the MOU between OSCE and the Government of Ukraine on the Deployment of an OSCE Special Monitoring Mission (2014),[92] contains provisions on inviolability of premises and cars (Article 4), privileges and immunities of the mission and its staff (Article 5), tax exemption (Article 6), communications (Article 7), visas and diplomatic cards and plates (Article 8) and settlement of disputes (Article 9) which would not make any sense if it was assumed that the MOU was non-binding. Also, the fact that the MOU was ratified by the Ukraine Parliament[93] clearly suggests that both OSCE and the Government of Ukraine consider it as legally binding.

Proponents of traditional treaty-based concepts of international organization such as Sands and Klein now recognize that

> one may take the view that the OSCE now qualifies as a full-fledged international organization. It has been endowed with legal capacity in the various states hosting CSCE/OSCE institutions and has been vested—together with its officials—with some privileges and immunities; it also has permanent organs and its obviously able to undertake legal international commitments in its own name at the international plane.[94]

Also Stribis convincingly contends:

> In fact, there are several elements, recognized under international law disproving the allegation that the OSCE is not an international organization. To name a few: the institutionalization of the OSCE, the permanence and autonomous decision-making of its structures, its wide-spread operational activities, its participation in international relations in general and, in particular in international agreements and related instruments, its institutionalized cooperation with other international actors, the fact that it bears rights and obligations under international law and even its name and self-qualification as an organization and regional arrangement under Chapter VIII of the UN Charter.[95]

Thus, even before thc recent developments regarding the headquarters agreements between the OSCE and Austria and Poland respectively which may be seen as the implicit recognition of OSCE's international legal personality by the states concerned, the OSCE could be classified in the view of this author both as a subject of international law and as an international organization. While it may be argued

[91] Tichy and Köhler 2008, p. 463.

[92] The text of the MoU in Ukrainian is available at http://zakon1.rada.gov.ua/laws/show/975_026/paran2#n2; and a summary of the MoU is available at http://zakon1.rada.gov.ua/laws/anot/1282-18 http://zakon1.rada.gov.ua/laws/anot/1282-18.

[93] The law of ratification is available on the website of the Parliament http://www.zakon1.rada.gov.ua/laws/show/1282-18 and the chronology of law under http://www.w1.c1.rada.gov.ua/pls/zweb2/webproc4_1?pf3511=50947, both in the Ukrainian language.

[94] Sands and Klein 2009, p. 203.

[95] Stribis 2013, pp. 115–116.

that the OSCE possesses *de facto* international legal personality despite the original intention of participating states not to confer to it such personality, it is not necessary to prove that the OSCE possesses international legal personality to conclude that it can be classified as a subject of international law. As the latter term is wider than that of international legal personality, it only needs to be determined whether the OSCE is operating on the international plane and has duties and responsibilities under international law. In the view of this author, this is amply documented.

6.1.6 Trust Funds as Subjects of International Law

6.1.6.1 International Organizations Do Not Need to Possess International Legal Personality

Another area involving the fundamental question of the relationship between notions of subject of international law and international legal personality relates to organizations established as trust funds. Current theories of public international law do not recognize that international organizations may be created as trust funds, either with or without international legal personality. To be clear, the term "trust funds" in this context does not refer to the many thousands of trust funds that are administered by UN organizations, MDBs or other organizations to supplement their regular activities, sometimes without any detailed legal framework. Rather, it refers to trust funds with a proper institutional and governance structure which enjoy substantial autonomy and have become a new paradigm of international organization. This author has given a detailed overview of such funds in the 2011 publication, "Funds for Development: Multilateral Channels of Concessional Financing". The World Bank generally refers to them as "financial intermediary funds", but this term does not fully reflect their characteristics, and some qualify for recognition as international organization and should be referred to as such.

Amerasinghe has made it clear that international organizations do not necessarily need to possess international legal personality:

> The practical convenience of personality is what makes it theoretically justified. The choice is not between recognizing personality and chaos. Organizations can well function in the same way as unincorporated associations or partnerships in national law where the group has no legal personality as such. What is useful or even necessary is that states have the *option* of creating an organization which has personality and can function as a legal person rather than as an 'unincorporated' group because primarily it facilitates action and is deemed to be necessary for the functioning of the organization.[96]

There are other voices which affirm that international legal personality is not an essential requirement for international organizations. Martha states, "No rule prevents the creation of an entity under international law that lacks international legal

---

[96] Amerasinghe 2005, pp. 68–69.

personality, i.e., the capacity to perform legal acts governed by international law."[97]

Schermers and Blokker noted that when "an international organization is created, it is usually created as a legal person," and that "in exceptional cases have international organizations been created without such capacity."[98] The Global Partnership Network and the Global Water Partnership Organization[99] are in their view such examples.

There is no rule that prevents the creation of an entity under public international law that lacks international legal personality. Hence, there is nothing to preclude an organization established as trust fund without international legal personality from operating at the international level and qualify as a subject of international law. An organization established as trust fund can operate at the international level even though deprived of international legal personality. If it meets all other requirements further discussed below, its lack of international legal personality neither precludes its classification as a subject of international law, nor is at variance with its recognition as an international organization.

6.1.6.2 Traditional Theories of International Law Are Ill-Suited for Trust Funds

In traditional international organizations with treaty foundation there is generally a clear correlation between their international legal personality and classification as subject of international law and their capacity to be the bearer rights and subject of responsibilities under international law. The problem is that traditional theories of international law are often ill-suited to grasp the special characteristics of international organizations established as trust funds without international legal personality.

Sui generis Ownership of Trustee

The above relates on the one hand to thc deep-felt need to identify "the bearer of the rights and duties." Kelsen has observed in this context:

> The concept of a legal person is another general concept used in the presentation of positive law and closely related to the concepts of legal duty and legal right. The concept of the legal person—who by definition, is the subject of legal duties and legal rights—answers the need of imagining a bearer of the rights and duties. Juristic thinking is not satisfied with the insight that a certain human action or omission forms the contents of a duty or a right. There must be something that "has" the duty or the right. In this idea, a general trend of human thought is manifested. Empirically observable qualities, too, are interpreted as qualities of an object or a substance, and grammatically they are represented as predicates of a subject.

---

97 Martha 2010, p. 145.

98 Schermers and Blokker 2011, §44.

99 Ibid.

> This substance is not an additional entity. The grammatical subject denoting it is only a symbol of the fact that the qualities form a unity.[100]

While there is need to know which entity is the "bearer of the rights and duties", to refer to Kelsen's words cited above, law would be directed to the wrong addressee if it were to refer to the trustee for the purpose mentioned above. As shown by Gold using the example of the IMF, the following six principles apply in relation to trust funds:

(i) "The rights of ownership of property subject to a trust are divided between the trustee and the beneficiary or beneficiaries."[101]
(ii) "A trustee must keep trust property separate from his own property and from the property of other trusts, and must earmark trust property as such, unless relieved of this obligation by law or the terms of the trust."[102]
(iii) "A trust is not a legal entity in the sense that is the bearer of rights and subject of duties."[103]
(iv) "A trustee may not engage in 'self-dealing' in administering the trust."[104]
(v) "A trustee must administer the trust solely in the interest of the beneficiary."[105]
(iv) "In administering a trust the trustee must use reasonable care and skill and must avoid unreasonable risk."[106]

Hence, while the trustee is the formal owner of a fund's assets towards third parties, such ownership is merely a "*sui generis* trust ownership that is enforceable towards third parties" and which entails that "*vis-à-vis* third parties (i.e., not the donors) the assets of the fund are deemed for all legal purposes as assets of the trustee and are thus covered by the privileges and immunities of the trustee, assuming in all cases that particular trustees, such as international financial institutions, possess these privileges."[107] However, the trustee is not the owner of the assets from a substantive point of view. Rather, substantive ownership depends on the trustee arrangements.

Also, the difference between trust funds endowed with international legal personality and those deprived of such personality is less important than would appear. International organizations established as trust funds without international legal personality cannot be a party to any formal contribution or financing agreements governed by international law. However, there is nothing to prevent the trustee from delegating the signature of such agreements to the chief executive officer or chief operations officer of the international organization established as a trust fund. This

[100] Kelsen 2007, p. 93.
[101] Gold 1978, p. 863.
[102] Ibid., 863.
[103] Ibid., 864.
[104] Ibid., 864.
[105] Ibid., 864.
[106] Ibid., 865.
[107] Bantekas 2009, p. 34.

was discussed in the case of GEF[108] and a delegation is in place for the CGIF.[109] Moreover, irrespective of the above, there is nothing to preclude the governing bodies of the trust fund from entering into a direct relationship with other parties (e.g. such as the COP for GEF) in the form of an MOU or other cooperative arrangement. Finally, irrespective of whether a trust fund possesses international legal personality, the rights of the trustee are merely formal and the assets of trust fund need to be held and administered separately from the trustee's own assets.

Trust Funds and the Institutional Veil

Another fundamental issue relates to the concept that international legal personality provides the "institutional veil" which protects the members from being held liable for the organization liabilities.[110]

> Doctrine proceeds on the assumption that international organizations can be responsible for breaches of obligation in their own right, consistent with the idea that they can be the 'bearers' of a right or obligation. In addition, the default rule appears to be that such responsibility is not coupled with *concurrent* responsibility on the part of the member states, unless this is provided for in the organization's constitution. In other words, the organization appears primarily as a closed legal entity, in the same way as when it independently assumes primary obligations under the law of treaties.[111]

As Brölmann further highlights, the "difference with the law of treaties context is that member states may assume a part in the responsibility of the organization at a later stage through the mechanism of 'secondary responsibility', which is triggered once the organization itself cannot meet its obligations."[112]

Hence, as may be seen from the above, the "institutional veil" which the international legal personality provides is not absolute as there may "be a concurrent liability" (if expressly provided for) or secondary liability of the members of international organizations. However, while there is much discussion on the

[108] "The GEF's structure has given rise to significant conflict between the Secretariat and the World Bank as the GEF has grown in size and stature. The desire of the GEF Secretariat for more independence than allowed by the GEF's structure (under which the GEF lacks independent legal personality or capacity, and the World Bank, as Trustee, is the only entity with legal capacity to act in respect of the GEF Trust Fund assets, surfaced as a key issue in the third replenishment. The issue was resolved at that time by a number of band-aid arrangements. Subsequent developments in the early stages of the fifth replenishment suggest that the shelf life of those band-aids has now expired" (Smyth 2011, p. 524).

[109] Article 10.3.2 of the CGIF Articles of Agreement (as amended on 27 November 2013 and 31 May 2016), provides for a delegation of all powers of the trustee, except those "expressly reserved by Article 10.1," "to the Meeting of Contributors which, in turn, may delegate such powers to the Board of Directors." http://www.cgif-abmi.org/wp-content/uploads/2016/06/CGIF-Articles-of-Agreement-as-of-May-2016_Clean.pdf.

[110] On "Institutional Veil and International Responsibility", see Brölmann 2007, pp. 262–267.

[111] Ibid., 262–263.

[112] Ibid., 263.

circumstances and conditions for piercing the institutional veil, there appears to be widespread acceptance that in circumstances where a body or entity is not endowed with legal personality the members of the body or entity may directly be liable. Amerasinghe states:

> It is easy to see that, if an organization has no international personality its actions are no more than actions of all its member states, whoever acts ostensibly in the name of the organization being only an agent of some or all of the member states.[113]

Based on this logic, the International Court of Justice admitted in its 1992 judgment in the case "Certain Phosphate Lands in Nauru (Nauru v. Australia)" the claim against Australia as a member of the authority administering Nauru, noting

> that the three Governments mentioned in the Trusteeship Agreement constituted, in the very terms of that Agreement, 'the Administering Authority' for Nauru; that this Authority did not have an international legal personality distinct from those of the States thus designated; and that, of those States, Australia played a very special role established by the Trusteeship Agreement of 1947, by the Agreements of 1919, 1923 and 1965, and by practice.[114]

Consistent with the above, the International Court of Justice did not consider

> that any reason has been shown why a claim brought against only one of the three States should be declared inadmissible *in limine litis* merely because that claim raises questions of the administration of the Territory, which was shared with two other States. It cannot be denied that Australia had obligations under the Trusteeship Agreement, in its capacity as one of the three States forming the Administering Authority, and there is nothing in the character of that Agreement which debars the Court from considering a claim of a breach of those obligations by Australia.[115]

However, the principle that the members of an organization are liable if an international organization does not possess international legal personality does not apply to international organizations established as trust funds without international legal personality. The trustee is generally an entity with international legal personality and endowed with privileges and immunities which provides its services for a fixed financial compensation. While the trustee, as the legal owner of the assets, is the respondent of any legal action, trustee arrangements make it painstakingly clear beyond any doubt that any liability which is incurred by the trustee is a material liability of the trust fund.[116] Thus, the responsibilities of the

---

[113] Amerasinghe 2005, p. 412.

[114] "Certain Phosphate Lands in Nauru (Nauru v. Australia), Preliminary Objections, Judgment", *ICJ Reports*, 1992, 240, para 47. http://www.icj-cij.org/files/case-related/80/080-19920626-JUD-01-00-EN.pdf.

[115] Ibid., para 48.

[116] See as one of many examples the "Amended and Restated Agreement on the Terms and Conditions for the Administration of the Green Climate Fund Trust Fund between Green Climate Fund and International Bank for Reconstruction and Development, serving as the Interim Trustee of the Green Climate Fund Trust Fund". Paragraph 2.2 of that Agreement provides: "The Fund agrees that the Trustee shall be fully indemnified, out of the assets of the Fund, including the Trust Fund resources, for any liabilities, claims, losses, costs and expenses, including attorneys' fees and

trustee in respect of the assets held in trust are merely formal. Moreover, the participating countries do not incur any liability for obligations incurred by or on behalf of the trust fund even if the organization concerned does not possess international legal personality.

Hence, while in case of cooperative arrangements between states that are not endowed with legal personality, the participating states are generally liable for any obligations in the context of that cooperation, the same is not applicable in case of international organizations established as trust funds that do not possess international legal personality. In that case, the legal personality of the trustee shields the contributors or participants from any liability.

6.1.6.3 Varying Responsibilities of Trustee

The responsibilities of the trustee may vary. In all instances, one of its core responsibilities relates to the administration of the organization's financial resources. In some organizations, the functions of the trustee are confined to this core role and, in essence, are equivalent to those of a fiscal agent. The arrangements between the Global Fund and the World Bank fall into this category. In other cases, such as the GEF, the trustee may have a role in resource mobilization and may perform additional functions as implementing and administering agency. In either case, and irrespective of whether a trust fund is endowed with international legal personality, the governing bodies of the organization established as a trust fund may take the substantive decisions regarding the use of the assets of the fund and may meet all the requirements of autonomous and independent decision-making which is generally conceptionalized under the heading of *volonté distincte*.

6.1.6.4 Establishment of International Organizations as Trust Funds

The legal basis for the establishment of an international organization as a trust fund without international legal personality may be a treaty. The treaty may either directly provide for the establishment of the trust fund, either with or without international legal personality, or it may set out the constitution for the organization which is then established by a resolution or decision of one or more organizations or through another process. Hence, the legal act incorporating the constitution of an organization and the act providing for the establishment of the trust fund can be different. Also, the constitution of an international organization established as a trust fund does not need to be adopted by a treaty in all cases. It can be based on an

expenses, incurred by the Trustee in connection with or in any way arising out of its activities as Trustee under this Agreement. Such indemnity shall not include any liabilities, claims, losses, costs or expenses incurred by the Trustee as a direct result of its own gross negligence or willful misconduct." http://www.greenclimate.fund/documents/20182/24868/Trust_Fund_Agreement_between_GCF_and_IBRD__Amended_.pdf/7ca07ac8-7a83-4f18-847e-e260b32b3e9a.

agreement between state authorities (e.g., ministries of finance or central banks) which does not meet the traditional requirements of a treaty (as applicable to AMRO, Inc. and CGIF). It may also be based on the resolution of a conference or the resolution or decision of a governing body of an international organization, or merely on consensus. Moreover, in principle, it not impossible for the governance and membership structure of an international organization established as a trust fund to be merely contained in the resolution or decision of the organization or other authority establishing the trust fund.

There are a number of cases where fairly complex governance structures have been created by the resolution or decision of an organization establishing a trust fund, which is the case for the Heavily Indebted Poor Countries (HIPC) Initiative[117] and the Prototype Carbon Fund.[118] While the HIPC Initiative did not result in the creation of an international organization and the contributors to the HIPC Initiative were not members of an organization, it is not intrinsically impossible that membership structures can be created by the decision or resolution of an international organization establishing a trust fund. Whether an organization established in that manner can be recognized as international organization and subject of international law, respectively, does not depend on the mode of its establishment but on its functions and on the attitude of other recognized subjects of international law.

In the following, the Global Environment Facility (GEF) and the Credit Guarantee and Investment Facility (CGIF) will be reviewed in some further detail. The GEF is widely recognized as an international organization even though it does not possess international legal personality. In the view of this author, the same is also applicable for the CGIF, which may even be seen as a new paradigm for establishing an international organization.

6.1.6.5 Global Environment Facility

During the discussions on the restructuring of the GEF,

> a range of options was considered: (1) to establish a new international organization as an affiliate of the World Bank for at least the financial administration of global environmental programs; (2) to amend the Articles of Agreement of the World Bank to undertake the new function; (3) to establish separate funds in the context of each global environmental activity that would finance implementation by the World Bank with the UNDP and the UNEP, as was done for the Montreal Protocol; or (4) to proceed as finally agreed to by having trust funds in the World Bank with a rather heavy superstructure of governance and institutional arrangements.[119]

[117] Droesse, "Modalities of Multilateral Concessional Financing", 259, ss.

[118] Smyth 2005, pp. 28–34 and 80–81, ss.

[119] Silard 1995, p. 622.

Thus, a treaty-based mechanism for establishing the GEF was reviewed during the restructuring process but was not pursued. In the end, the trust fund option was adopted because it assured maximum flexibility. Hence,

> the restructured GEF was implemented neither by virtue of an interstate treaty nor as result of an agreement between international organizations destined to create a new institution. Instead, the seventy-three states attending the meeting that reached final agreement about the restructured GEF merely 'accepted' the new structure of the mechanism. They reached agreement on the Instrument of the Restructured Global Environment Facility, which lays down the main rules and the governance of the Facility. The governments did not sign the Instrument but it was 'adopted' by the three Implementing Agencies. In spite of that, the approval of the countries to the restructured GEF was a preliminary condition by international law and concluded between states or international organizations) to the decisions of the Implementing Agencies.[120]

The GEF Instrument is "unique", precisely "because it is not an international treaty (i.e., an international agreement governed by international law and concluded between states or international organizations)."[121]

While there are different interpretations given of the GEF Instrument,[122] it is firmly established that the GEF does not possess international legal personality. This is plain given that "the GEF participants decided not to provide the GEF with legal personality, as their intention was not to create a new institution"[123] and the fact that the quest of the GEF for legal personality during the third and fifth replenishment of GEF resources remained unsuccessful.[124] However, this lack of legal personality does not preclude GEF's classification as a subject of international law.

That it is able to act on the international plane may be derived *inter alia* from Article 27 of the GEF Instrument, which provides:

> The Council shall consider and approve cooperative arrangements or agreements with the Conferences of the Parties to the conventions referred to in paragraph 6, including reciprocal arrangements for representation in meetings. Such arrangements or agreements shall be in conformity with the relevant provisions of the convention concerned regarding its financial mechanism and shall include procedures for determining jointly the aggregate GEF funding requirements for the purpose of the convention [….].

Pursuant to the aforementioned provision, GEF entered into cooperative arrangements with the Conference of the Parties (COP) of each of the three environmental conventions for which the GEF serves as a financial mechanism: i.e. the United Nations Framework Convention on Climate Change [UNFCCC], the Convention on Biological Diversity [CBD], and the Stockholm Convention on Persistent Organic Pollutants. It did so by way of memoranda of understanding

---

[120] Streck 2000.

[121] Ragazzi 2011, p. 487.

[122] See Ragazzi 2011, pp. 486–487.

[123] Ibid., 486.

[124] Smyth 2011, pp. 525, 547–548.

which were approved by the GEF Council and the COP of the respective conventions."[125] The GEF clearly acted on the international plane when entering into such memoranda which are not governed by any national law and contain provisions on the guidance provided by the COP in operating the financial mechanism under the respective convention, reporting, monitoring and evaluation, determination of funding requirements, reciprocal representation and a variety of other matters.[126]

In case of the financial agreements with contributors, the GEF is not a party to these agreements which are entered into by the World Bank in its capacity as trustee of the GEF.[127] Similarly, the GEF is not a party to the financial procedures agreements[128] with executing and implementing agencies or to other agreements with international organizations, bilateral agencies or other entities. Nevertheless, the World Bank acts in these cases as trustee on behalf of the GEF. The fact that an entity does not possess treaty-making capacity does not imply that it cannot be the subject of duties and responsibilities. The GEF is the material source of all commitments and obligations.

In case of the GEF, the World Bank has a powerful position as trustee, implementing entity and provider of administrative support. This contrasts with its much more limited role in the case of the Global Fund where the World Bank, in essence, only fulfills the role of a fiscal agent responsible for the administration of financial assets, and its role in the case of the Green Climate Fund which can be a party to bilateral[129] or tripartite agreements.[130]

---

[125] Ragazzi 2011, pp. 493–495.

[126] See Decision 12/CP.2 Memorandum of Understanding between the Conference of the Parties and the Council of the Global Environment Facility, http://www.unfccc.int/resource/docs/cop2/15a01.pdf#page=55 and Decision 12/CP.3 Annex to the Memorandum of Understanding on the determination of funding necessary and available for the implementation of the Convention, http://unfccc.int/resource/docs/cop3/07a01.pdf#page=43. Council of the Global Environment Facility. Memorandum of Understanding between the Conference of the Parties to the Convention on Biological Diversity and the Council of the Global Environment Facility. http://www.iisd.ca/biodiv/cop3/cop30008.htm.

[127] See Annex C to the GEF Instrument, paras 1(a) and (b). Contributors deposit their instrument of contribution with the World Bank as trustee in accordance with para 2(a) of the said Annex.

[128] Financial procedures agreements are executed between the agency concerned and the IBRD, acting as the trustee of the GEF. See as one of many examples the Financial Procedures Agreement between the Asian Development Bank and the International Bank for Reconstruction and Development as Trustee of the Global Environment Facility Trust Fund of 23 October 2008: https://www.thegef.org/sites/default/files/documents/ADB_FPA_-_Oct_2008_-_Fully_Executed_Original_0.pdf.

[129] The "Accreditation Master Agreements" are bilateral agreements between the Green Climate Fund and the accredited entity. See "Accreditation Master Agreements" Library. https://www.greenclimate.fund/library/-/docs/list/383065.

[130] Contribution Agreement are concluded as tripartite agreement involving the Green Climate Fund, the IBRD (as interim trustee) and the donor country concerned. See "Contribution Agreements" Library. https://www.greenclimate.fund/library/-/docs/list/574026.

Nevertheless, the difference between the three situations mentioned above is effectively less than it would appear at first sight. While as a matter of law, the situation of the GEF is different from that of the Global Fund and that of the GCF, in that the GEF does not possess international legal personality and, hence, cannot be a party to any international agreement, as a matter of practice very similar results might also be achieved by way of a mere delegation of authority. There is nothing to prevent the World Bank from delegating its power to sign agreements to the Chief Executive Officer of the GEF. A limited delegation of authority was discussed on various occasions for the GEF,[131] but was not approved as the World Bank refused to release its firm hold on the GEF.

The GEF Instrument specifies a number of specific competences to be performed by the GEF Council, its main decision-making body, and by the Assembly and Secretariat. Hence, the GEF meets all the requirements of *a volonté distincte*.

Under the circumstances, the GEF needs to be qualified both as subject of international law and as an international organization in spite of the fact that it was not established by a treaty and does not possess international legal personality.

6.1.6.6 Credit Guarantee and Investment Facility (CGIF)

The CGIF "was established in November 2010 to promote financial stability and to boost long-term investment in the ASEAN+3 region."[132] To this end, "CGIF aims to address the challenges of currency and maturity mismatches faced by corporations. It does so by providing credit guarantees to enable them to raise long-term funding to meet their financing needs."[133]

While ASEAN+3 countries approved the Articles of Agreement of CGIF,[134] the countries opted not to establish a traditional international organization with a treaty foundation. Rather, the CGIF was established as a trust fund of the ADB, based on a decision of the ADB Board of Directors.[135] Hence, CGIF is an example of an organization whose constitution is based on an agreement between states but whose legal status is that of a trust fund.

While the CGIF does not possess international legal personality, nevertheless, it was given an independent governance and equity-based structure, and is owned by contributors in proportion to the amount of their capital contributions. As a trust

[131] See Smyth 2011, pp. 527–528.

[132] http://www.cgif-abmi.org/about.

[133] ADB. 2010. Report and Recommendation of the President to the Board of Directors. Proposed Credit Guarantee and Investment Facility: Establishment of Trust Fund and Capital Contribution. http://www.adb.org/projects/documents/proposed-credit-guarantee-and-investment-facility-rrp.

[134] http://www.cgif-abmi.org/datas/pdf/CGIF%20Articles%20of%20Agreement%20(as%20of%20December%202013).pdf.

[135] ADB. 2010. Report and Recommendation of the President to the Board of Directors. Proposed Credit Guarantee and Investment Facility: Establishment of Trust Fund and Capital Contribution. http://www.adb.org/projects/documents/proposed-credit-guarantee-and-investment-facility-rrp.

fund of ADB, CGIF is required "to follow applicable ADB operational policies and to present an annual activity report including audited financial statements for the information of the ADB Board of Directors. Operating as a trust fund of ADB, CGIF [enjoys] ADB's privileges and immunities."[136] ADB holds "in trust all CGIF funds and other property"[137] and, accordingly, is the legal owner of the assets of the CGIF. Nevertheless, while ADB exercises influence as a contributor, its role as trustee is narrowly circumscribed, as with the exception of the certain powers relating mostly to financial fund management, all other powers as trustee under the CGIF Articles of Agreement are delegated to the "Meeting of Contributors, which, in turn, may delegate such powers to the [CGIF] Board of Directors [....]."[138]

Hence, ADB, in its capacity as trustee, has no substantive role in the governance of the CGIF. Most relevant decisions are taken by the governing bodies of the CGIF in accordance with the CGIF Articles of Agreement. Also, even though it was established as an ADB trust fund, CGIF operations are "financed solely from funds that are contributed from time to time in accordance with the provisions of these Articles of Agreement, and any other CGIF property."[139]

It is important to note that the establishment of CGIF did not involve any delegation of functions normally performed by ADB. Hence, constraints based on principles of "*compétence d'attribution*" and the "principle of specialty" discussed in further detail below above in relation to the European Agencies and the QABs do not apply to ADB's assistance in the creation of the CGIF. Rather, ADB support is consistent with its purpose and functions set forth in Articles 1 and 2 of its Charter and in line with its strategy for a regional initiative. As set out in the document submitted to the ADB Board of Directors for approval, "CGIF will provide a useful model for further regional initiatives."[140] In fact, the support which ADB provided for the establishment of CGIF may be seen as indicative for the support which international organizations may provide for the establishment of new international organizations. It may be considered a new institutional paradigm for establishing new organizations.

Hence, some of the traditional concepts of international law regarding subjects of international law need to be revised, taking account of the proliferation of actors at the international stage and the development of international law.

---

[136] ADB. 2010. Report and Recommendation of the President to the Board of Directors. Proposed Credit Guarantee and Investment Facility, para 34.

[137] CGIF Articles of Agreement, Article 3.1.2(a).

[138] CGIF Articles of Agreement, Article 10.3.2.

[139] CGIF Articles of Agreement, Article 3.1.1.

[140] ADB. 2010. Report and Recommendation of the President to the Board of Directors. Proposed Credit Guarantee and Investment Facility.

6.2 International Legal Personality and Its Legal Implications

The discussion on international legal personality and international organization has a multitude of facets. This relates to the scope of personality, its implications for the relations of an organization with its members, the participation of actors in the international system, the recognition of juridical personality in member and non-member countries of the organization, and the organization's responsibilities and any residual responsibilities of its members.

As for the subjects of international law that are not identical, also the scope of organizations' juridical personality may differ. There are various shades of legal personality. On the one side of the spectrum are institutions with limited international status. The Human Rights Committee (HRC), which, as shown by Tomuschat, "under Article 28 of the International Covenant on Civil and Political Rights enjoys a definite international status in that it has been mandated to carry out the functions mandated in the Covenant,"[141] belongs into this category. Institutions such as the HRC are generally classified as treaty bodies which "act under a mandate which is nearly exclusively spelled out in the relevant treaties and which, generally, does not permit of any extension."[142] They have the power to interact with judicial institutions and states to a very limited extent, but are generally established on a permanent or *ad hoc* basis, and their international legal personality is circumscribed by their functions.

On the other side of the spectrum are organizations such as the UN and its specialized agencies which are parties to many international agreements and whose ability to act at the international scale is firmly established. In between, there is a range of international organization with a varying scope of international legal personality.

There are a multitude of problems involving international organizations' international legal personality and legal capacity under national law. The relevant doctrines are well known and have been discussed at length in literature, int. al. recently by Portman who distinguishes five theories which have been developed, and are succinctly characterized by him as follows:

(1) "**States-only**: The first position reserves international personality exclusively to states. There are no conditions for international personality other than having acquired statehood. The corollaries of personality are synonymous with those of being a state [....]."
(2) "**Recognition**: The second position conceives of states as the original or primary persons of international law. However, other entities can also acquire international personality, often called derivative or secondary international persons. The mechanism through which this is possible is explicit or implicit recognition by states. [....]."

---

141 Tomuschat 1999, p. 142.
142 Ibid., 142.

(3) "**Individualistic**: The third position states a presumption for the individual as an international person in the field of so-called fundamental norms of international law. In addition, states and various other entities can be international persons if there are international norms addressing them [….]." Individuals become internationally responsible for violations of fundamental international norms irrespective of whether they act in a public or private function.
(4) "**Formal**: The fourth position declares international law an open system. There is no presumption as to who is a legal person. International personality becomes an a posteriori concept: Every entity is an international person that according to general principles of interpretation is the addressee of the norms of international law [….]."
(5) **Actor**: The fifth position, rejecting the concept of international personality as traditionally understood, stipulates a presumption that all effective actors of international relations are relevant for the international legal system. The specific rights and duties held by particular actors are determined in an international decision-making process in which the actors themselves participate depending on their effective power.[143]

As the regards the first category identified by Portland, this author believes that it does not require any detailed discussion as it has clearly been superseded by events.

This author shares the view of Dewey that "the entire discussion on personality [….] is needlessly encumbered with a mass of traditional doctrines and remnants of old issues."[144] As regards remaining overall positions described by Portman as above, the differences between these positions are to some extent less profound that it would appear at first sight inasmuch as their application to international organizations is concerned. No organization will be able to function properly unless it is recognized by a number of states. These states do not necessarily have to be members of the organization, but their recognition of the organization generally implies that they recognize the international legal personality and/or legal capacity of the organization under municipal law, and may imply that they confer privileges and immunities to the organization concerned. Thus, the issue of international legal personality of international organizations relates, in particular, to the question whether international organizations have objective juridical personality in all countries, as proposed by Seyersted,[145] or relative juridical personality in only those countries which have recognized them.

Gaja argues from a conceptual point of view, that

> [a]lthough the view has been expressed that an organization's personality exists with regard to non-member States only if they have recognized it, this assumption cannot be regarded as a logical necessity. Should a State conclude a headquarters agreement with an organization of which it is not a member, it is hard to imagine that by so doing the State bestows on the organization a legal personality that would not otherwise exist. The very conclusion of the headquarters agreement shows that the organization is already a subject of international law. It should be noted that the organization's legal personality does not necessarily imply that the organization is entitled to enjoy immunities from non-member States under general international law. Nor can it be assumed that member States' responsibility

---

[143] Portmann 2010, p. 242.

[144] Cited according to Eagleton 1950, p. 326.

[145] Seyersted 1964, and Seyersted 2008.

for the conduct of an organization of which they are members is identical towards other members and towards non-members.[146]

Nevertheless, while there is a strong point in affirming that international organizations with universal membership have objective juridical personality in all countries, and not only in those countries which have recognized them, there is very little evidence of a general recognition of such objective juridical personality in the case of regional organizations or other international organizations with limited membership. In particular, in countries that follow the dualist tradition, the question of the recognition of the legal existence of an organization may be subject to specific legislative action, as underlined, inter alia, by the approach adopted by the House of Lords towards the International Tin Council.[147] As indicated by Shaw,

> [I]n the UK, the approach has been rather different. The International Organizations Act 1968 grants the legal capacity of a body corporate to any organization declared by Order in Council to be an organization of which the UK and one or more foreign states are members. The view of the House of Lords in the Tin cases was that the legal effect of the Order in Council of 1972 concerning the International Tin Council (ITC) was to create the ITC as a legal person separate and distinct from its members, **since 'as an international legal persona [it] had no status under the laws of the United Kingdom.' In other words, without such legislative action, an international organization would have no legal existence in the UK.**[148] (emphasis added)

While the legal personality of regional international organizations and organizations of limited membership is often recognized in non-member countries, either on the basis of international law or private international law,[149] this is in essence a matter which is determined by each country in accordance with its constitution and law. No regional organization or organization of limited membership will be able to rely on recognition of its legal personality in a non-member country, the authorities of which may not have even heard of the organization, let alone be aware that it enjoys international legal personality and privileges and immunities. Thus, for practical reasons, any regional organization or organizations with limited membership or geographic scope will need to address this in their dealings with non-member countries.

With regard to the fifth position, to a large extent, this author shares the view of the proponents of the New Haven school, although he does not concur with the proposal that any reference to international legal personality should be avoided. In

---

146 G. Gaja, *First Report on Responsibility of International Organizations* (Document A/CN.4/532, 26 March 2003), 105–116, 111. http://legal.un.org/ilc/documentation/english/a_cn4_532.pdf.

147 Sandurska and Chinkin 1989–1990, pp. 845–890; Warbrick and Cheyne 1987, pp. 931–935; Lowe et al. 1990, pp. 945–952. https://doi.org/10.1093/iclqaj/39.4.945; Seidl-Hohenveldern 1994, pp. 255–274.

148 Shaw 2003, pp. 1190–1191.

149 See the approach adopted in "House of Lords Judgment of 21.2.91: Arab Monetary Fund (Appellants) Hashim, V. and others (Respondents)". http://www.unife.it/giurisprudenza/giurisprudenza/studiare/international-institutional-law/allegati-pubblici/6ArabLQ90.pdf/at_download/file.

this regard, this author instead agrees with d'Aspremont that there is still some benefit in the use of the term "international legal personality".

> It should again be made clear, however, that the participation-based outlook of this volume is not at loggerheads with scholarly inquiries about legal personality, law and non-law or bindingness. Although there is some benefit at looking at law-making from the angle of participation, law primarily remains a set of norms, which like other social norms need to be ascertained at some point in the process between their creation and their enforcement. The ascertainment of international legal rules and the determination of their effects simultaneously require formal categories.[150]

It is not possible in the context of this book to discuss the aforementioned theories in any detail. Rather, this author wishes to focus only on the following three issues only: First, it will be shown that international legal personality is not a requirement for membership. Thus, international organizations without international legal personality may also have membership structures. Second, international legal personality does not need to be conferred to an organization at the time of its establishment, in the constituent agreement or otherwise. Hence, organizations may acquire international legal personality subsequently, based on bilateral or multilateral agreements which recognize their international legal personality or legal capacity, or through a variety of other means. Effectively, international legal personality may also be conferred to dual and hybrid organizations incorporated under national law and organizations characterized by "institutional ambivalence by design", as described above, by multilateral or bilateral agreements or through other means. Third, entities established as a subsidiary body or as a financial mechanism of an international convention may possess international legal personality. Whether this is the case, is not to be determined with reference to the mode of their establishment but based on their functions and the position which recognized subjects of international law have adopted in their regard. These three issues will be reviewed in the following *seriatim.*

6.2.1 International Legal Personality Not a Requirement for Membership

This book focuses on the relationship between organizations and their members. In this context, it is to be noted first of all that the legal personality of an organization, under international and domestic law, it not a requirement for membership and/or participation in international organizations, the reason being that "[r]elations established by an international organization with its Member States are only external to the extent to which they do not pertain exclusively to their status under the internal law of the organization."[151]

150 d'Aspremont 2011, p. 3.

151 Rensmann 2009.

Arangio-Ruiz has analyzed the implications of international legal personality for the functioning of an international organization as follows:

> Of course, international personality allows the organisation to participate in legal relationships which are essential for its actual existence and operation (*siège*, privileges and immunities, communications, active and passive legation, protection of staff, claims for damages, agreements). In turn, this will affect the organisation's functioning indirectly. **In so far, however, as the functioning *per se* is concerned, the organisation does not operate as a person in legal authority more than the arbitral tribunal and the arbitrating State do so. Although endowed with international personality for the purposes of its primary activities, the United Nations has no such international personality under the Charter as an inter-State compact. That compact creates rights and obligations for the contracting States, not for the organisation. The international personality of the United Nations is thus not really functional in the sense in which the personality of municipal corporations is such.**[152] (emphasis added)

Thus, participation or membership in an organization is only related to the organization's international legal personality as and to the extent that the relations with the member can be qualified as external. This relates to cases where the organization enters into an agreement with the member as a subject of international law or to those cases where a change in status is concerned (e.g. expulsion or termination of membership which the corresponding obligation to conduct a financial settlement). Upon termination of membership by either withdrawal or expulsion, the relations between the organization and its former member are henceforth of an external nature. This does not imply, however, that the obligations resulting from membership are extinguished on the date of effective termination of membership. This is particularly clear from the constituent agreements of MDBs and other international financial institutions.[153]

6.2.2 Consensual Basis of International Legal Personality and Transformation of International Organizations

International legal personality is related to the consensual basis of the establishment of international organizations inasmuch as it is conferred by their constituent agreements. There are cases where the constituent agreement expressly refers to the international legal personality of the organization. However, often the constituent agreement only contains a provision on the legal capacity of the organization in member countries. This is the case for the United Nations, as Article 104 of the UN Charter "is concerned with domestic law. It therefore did not confer international legal personality on the Organization: but it obligated members as a matter of international law to ensure that their domestic law recognizes the legal personality

152 Arangio Ruiz 1972, pp. 679–680.

153 See for example, Article 43 of the ADB Charter regarding settlement of accounts.

of the UN so that it is able to carry out in States in which it operates."[154] A number of other organizations have similar provisions in their constituent agreements. As has been made plain by the International Court of Justice in the Reparations for Injuries Decision,[155] the fact that no express reference to an international juridical personality is contained in the constituent agreement does not prevent the conclusion that the organization concerned is nevertheless endowed with international juridical personality. On the other hand, where the constituent agreement contains an express provision that the organization possesses international juridical personality, this is generally deemed to imply that the organization also has legal capacities under the law of its member or host country or countries.

The discussion below identifies cases where the organization's legal status and privileges and immunities are specified in a protocol to a treaty or in a multilateral agreement or in bilateral agreements on the organization's legal status and privileges and immunities. In those instances where the constituent agreement or similar instrument already provides for international legal personality or mandates recognition of the organization's legal capacity under national law, such agreement or protocol merely confirms, or elaborates on, the legal status of the organization provided under the constituent instrument. However, in cases of organizations without treaty foundation (e.g. dual and hybrid organizations incorporated under national law), multilateral or bilateral agreements and other arrangements which recognize their international legal personality may transform the status of the organization.

6.2.3 Non-Ratified Constitution Can Be the Basis for International Action

An international organization does not need to be established by a treaty to have international legal personality. As has been shown in Chapter 4 above, constituent instruments of organizations which were not submitted for ratification may regulate the organization's governance structure, the powers of its organs, decision-making procedures and voting rights, budgetary and financial procedures and other internal matters which concern the organization relation with its members on very similar terms as constitutions submitted for ratification. Moreover, while the constitution of an organization which was not submitted for ratification may not have legal effects under national law, it may, nevertheless, be the basis for the organization's international action, if this is agreed by the members. Hence, international legal personality does not necessarily need to be specified in the constituent instrument, but it may be extended to an organization subsequently, on the basis of the

[154] Miller 2007, p. 13.

[155] Reparation for injuries suffered in the service of the United Nations, Advisory Opinion: International Court of Justice Reports 1949, pp. 174–220.

organization's progressive institutionalization and the organization's evolving status. In such cases, the adoption of a multilateral agreement or of bilateral agreements or arrangements regarding privileges and immunities may convert the legal status of entities classified as non-governmental, including entities characterized by "institutional ambivalence by design" and entities incorporated under national law, to recognized intergovernmental or international organizations.

INTERPOL is one example of an organization without treaty foundation but with international legal personality. As indicated by Martha, various "European Union legal documents have recognized INTERPOL's status as an international organization."[156] While "no rule prevents the creation of an entity under international law that lacks international legal personality" and "as international organizations are generally presumed to have international legal personality, it would follow that unless the contrary is intended, the recognition of the status of an international organization includes the recognition of its international legal personality."[157] Moreover, Martha has shown that "INTERPOL has entered into numerous international agreements with States and international organizations" based on four articles in the INTERPOL constitution that "lay the foundations for the recognition of INTERPOL's international legal personality."[158]

The Green Climate Fund is another example of a new type of international organization which possesses international legal personality even though it was not established by a treaty. While financial mechanisms of the UNFCCC do not necessarily enjoy international legal personality,[159] there is ample evidence to support that the Green Climate Fund has such personality.

Paragraph 7 of the Governing Instrument of the Green Climate Fund incorporates[160] some deliberate ambiguity to alleviate the concerns of countries who wanted to avoid the use of the term "international legal personality." Nevertheless, and irrespective of the diverging views on whether the GCF possesses international legal personality based on the COP decision or such personality had to be conferred by country Parties, it is now firmly established that the GCF has international legal personality. Both the Board of the Fund and country Parties to the UN recognized that the Fund can be a party to agreements governed by international law. For example, the Headquarters Agreement between the GCF and the Republic of Korea

---

156 Martha 2010, p. 144.

157 Ibid., 145.

158 Ibid., 146.

159 The Adaptation Fund is an example where the first approach was followed, as in that case legal capacity under German law was conferred to the Adaptation Fund Board. Similarly, the Secretariat of the UNFCCC only has legal capacity under German law under the agreement between the United Nations, the Government of the Federal Republic of Germany and the secretariat of the United Nations Framework Convention on Climate Change. See Droesse 2011, pp. 21–22.

160 Paragraph 7 of the Governing Instrument provides, "In order to operate effectively internationally, the Fund will possess juridical personality and will have such legal capacity as is necessary for the exercise of its functions and the protection of its interests."

is a treaty under Article 6 of the Korean Constitution. In addition, consistent with a COP Decision[161] and reference provisions approved by the GCF Board,[162] the Secretariat, as authorized by the Board, "had sent draft agreements on the privileges and immunities of the GCF to a cumulative total of 121 countries", and "13 bilateral privileges and immunities agreements have been signed" and are in force.[163]

6.2.4 International Legal Personality of Organizations Incorporated Under National Law

In the case of organizations incorporated under national law, the conclusion is that a headquarters agreement which recognizes their international legal capacity and the conclusion of other bilateral or multilateral agreements regarding their legal status and privileges and immunities may transform their status to that of a "dual or hybrid" organization. Organizations such as the Global Fund and Gavi Alliance, which were incorporated under Swiss law, fall in this category. Their international legal status derives from the recognition of their international legal personality by the country where they are located and incorporated, i.e. Switzerland, and recognition in a number of other countries.

As shown, there is nothing in international law which would preclude assigning an entity incorporated under national law duties and responsibilities under international law or which would prevent a state from concluding a bilateral agreement, or becoming party to a multilateral agreement, which recognizes the international legal personality of an entity incorporated under national law.[164]

---

161 Paragraph 21 of Decision 7/CP.20. http://www.ciesin.columbia.edu/repository/entri/docs/cop/FCCC_COP20_dec07.pdf.

162 Decisions of the Board—Tenth Meeting of the Board. 6–9 July 2015 (GCF/B.10/17, 21 July 2015). Annex XXV: Draft provisions for privileges and immunities, 125–127. http://www.greenclimate.fund/boardroom/on-record?p_p_id=122_INSTANCE_8e72dTqCP5qa&p_p_lifecycle=0&p_p_state=normal&p_p_mode=view&p_p_col_id=_118_INSTANCE_jUGwSITWV8c5__column-2&p_p_col_pos=1&p_p_col_count=2&p_r_p_564233524_resetCur=true&p_r_p_564233524_categoryId=23988#nav-category.

163 GCF. 2017. Report on the activities of the Secretariat (GCF/B.18/Inf.04, 21 September), para 102 http://www.greenclimate.fund/documents/20182/820027/GCF_B.18_Inf.04_-_Report_on_the_activities_of_the_Secretariat.pdf/09454489-7819-4d80-ac92-8c788b588040.

164 Article 1 of the Headquarters Agreements between the Global Fund and the Swiss Federal Council contains the following provision:

> Article 1: Personality and capacity
>
> The Swiss Federal Council recognizes for the purposes of this Agreement the international juridical personality and legal capacity in Switzerland of the Global Fund to Fight AIDS, Tuberculosis and Malaria (hereinafter referred to as the Global Fund)." https://www.theglobalfund.org/media/3375/bm07_07gpcreportannex92_annex_en.pdf.

Article 1 of the "Headquarters Agreement between the Global Fund and the Swiss Federal Council, recognizes the international legal personality of the Global Fund.[165] A similar provision is contained in Article 1 of the "Headquarters Agreement between the Gavi Alliance (Global Alliance for Vaccines and Immunization) and the Swiss Federal Council to determine the legal status of the Gavi Alliance in Switzerland."[166]

In addition to the recognition of the international juridical personality of the Global Fund contained in the Headquarters Agreement between the Global Fund and the Swiss Federation, the Global Fund proposed to the countries where it is operating that they become parties to the "Agreement on Privileges and Immunities of the Global Fund to Fight AIDS, Tuberculosis and Malaria". Article 1 of said agreement provides:

> The Global Fund shall be accorded by each of the State Parties to this Agreement juridical personality, and it shall have the capacity (i) a to contract, (ii) acquire and dispose of immovable and movable property, and (iii) to institute legal proceedings.[167]

This agreement avoids express reference to international legal personality and only provides for an obligation by the countries to recognize the legal capacity of the Global Fund under their domestic law. Nevertheless, considering that the agreement requires ratification and is not subject to any national law, it must be presumed that it is meant to be governed by international law. It can be seen as a new paradigm for conferring international legal status to an organization incorporated under national law.

6.2.5 Transformation of International Organization Acquiring International Legal Personality

There have been various instances where states sought to create forms of international cooperation outside the realm of international law. The OSCE, as one of these cases, is particularly interesting as a series of mechanisms were considered for conferring to it international legal personality. While such enhancement of its legal status had been blocked in the past, for different reasons, mainly by the United States and Russia, the discussion on the conversion of its legal status shows that a series of techniques can be used for converting the status of an organization

[165] Agreement between the Swiss Federal Council and the Global Fund to Fight AIDS, Tuberculosis and Malaria in view of determining the legal status of the Global Fund in Switzerland.

[166] Headquarters Agreement between the Gavi Alliance (Global Alliance for Vaccines and Immunization) and the Swiss Federal Council to determine the legal status of the Gavi Alliance in Switzerland done in Berne on 23 June 2009, in the French language.

[167] See https://www.theglobalfund.org/media/4138/bm32_19-pandis_report_en.pdf.

incorporating "institutional ambivalence by design" (see above) into an organization with recognized international legal personality.

The issue of the OSCE's legal status has been on the agenda for a long time since the 1993 decision of the Rome Ministerial Council,[168] which was not implemented by a large number of participating states, as noted in 2000 in the Istanbul Summit Declaration. The heads of state of the participating States of the OSCE noted that "a large number of participating States have not been able to implement the 1993 Rome Ministerial Council decision on legal capacity of the OSCE institutions and on privileges and immunities."[169] The matter gained momentum after a working group was set up in 2000[170] and the 2005 report of the eminent persons group which recommended that "Participating States agree on a convention recognising the OSCE's legal capacity and granting privileges and immunities to the OSCE."[171] However, no agreement could be reached by the working group, on the recommendation of the Eminent Persons Group, or on the "Draft Convention on the International Legal Personality, Legal Capacity, and Privileges and Immunities at the OSCE."[172] Hence, while the change in status met with the support of the majority of OSCE participating countries, this matter was not resolved.

---

[168] "11. The Ministers have taken note with appreciation of the report of the ad hoc Group of Legal and Other Experts. The Ministers adopted a decision on legal capacity and privileges and immunities that recommends implementation of the following three basic elements (CSCE/4-C/Dec.2):

- The CSCE participating States will, subject to their constitutional, legislative and related requirements, confer legal capacity on CSCE institutions in accordance with the provisions adopted by the Ministers;
- The CSCE participating States will, subject to their constitutional, legislative and related requirements, confer privileges and immunities on CSCE institutions, permanent missions of the participating States, representatives of participating States, CSCE officials and members of CSCE missions in accordance with the provisions adopted by the Ministers;
- The CSCE may issue CSCE Identity Cards in accordance with the form adopted by the Ministers."

See OSCE. 1993. Fourth Meeting of the Council. CSCE and the New Europe. Our Security in indivisible. Decisions of the Rome Council Meeting. VII. CSCE Structures and Operations, 16–17, para 11. http://www.osce.org/mc/40401?download=true.

[169] Cited according to OSCE. 2000. Decision No. 383. Report on OSCE Legal Capacity and on Privileges and Immunities to the Ministerial Council. (PC.DEC/383, 26 Nov.), para 1. http://www.osce.org/pc/24379?download=true.

[170] Decision No. 383. 2000. Report on OSCE Legal Capacity and on Privileges and Immunities to the Ministerial Council. (PC. DEC/383, 26 November), 1, para 1 http://www.osce.org/pc/24379?download=true.

[171] Common Purpose. Towards a More Effective OSCE. Final Report and Recommendations of the Panel of Eminent Persons on Strengthening the Effectiveness of the OSCE. 27 June 2005. 19–20. http://www.osce.org/cio/15805?download=true.

[172] A copy of the draft Convention is reproduced in OSCE. 2007. Fifteenth Meeting of the Ministerial Council 29–30 Nov. 2007, 65, ss. http://www.osce.org/mc/33180?download=true.

Tichy and Köhler[173] have given a detailed account on the tortuous quest of OSCE for international legal personality. Their analysis is particularly interesting as they have given a detailed account of the options, and their implications, considered by the "open-ended working group which met in 2000 and 2001 following the Istanbul Summit Declaration and in the group of experts tasked with reviewing the implications of the lack of international legal status and uniform privileges and immunities of the OSCE which met in 2006.[174] As shown, the "chairman of this group gave the following overview over the various options in a document of 5 July 2006":

> Convention on the International Legal Personality, Legal Capacity and Privileges and Immunities of the OSCE: to be adopted by the appropriate body of the OSCE, then open for signature, subject to ratification, acceptance or approval, binding for all States parties in this convention (this option is not favoured by all Participating states);
>
> Statute of OSCE: convention addressing not only the international legal personality, legal capacity and privileges and immunities of the OSCE, but also its functions and institutional structure, to be adopted by the appropriate body of the OSCE, then open for signature, subject to ratification, acceptance or approval, binding for all States parties to this convention (this option is not favoured by a majority of the Participating states);
>
> Convention on Privileges and Immunities of the OSCE: to be adopted by the appropriate body of the OSCE, then open for signature, subject to ratification, acceptance or approval, binding for all States parties to this convention (under this variant, the issue of international legal personality would have to be addressed separately, e.g. through a separate convention or through an OSCE decision; not all Participating States would be able to follow that approach;"
>
> OSCE Decision on International Legal Personality of the OSCE: decision of the appropriate body of the OSCE that the OSCE is to be regarded as an international organization and that, therefore, it can conclude agreements binding under international law (under this variant, the issue of privileges and immunities would have to be addressed separately, e.g. through a convention on Privileges and Immunities of the OSCE; not all Participant would be able to follow this approach;
>
> (declaratory) OSCE decision on International Legal Personality of the OSCE: declaratory decision of the appropriate body of the OSCE that the OSCE, in view of its development, has already acquired the status of an international organization and that, therefore, it can conclude agreements binding under international law (under this variant, the issue of privileges and immunities would have to be addressed separately, e.g. through a Convention on Privileges and Immunities of the OSCE; not all Participating States would be able to follow this approach);
>
> (new) OSCE decision on the International Juridical Personality, Legal Capacity and Privileges and Immunities of the OSCE: to be adopted by the appropriate body of the OSCE, politically binding for all Participating States of the OSCE, to be implemented through legislation of the Participating States (which some Participating States say is not possible to them);
>
> Model law on the International Legal Personality, Legal Capacity and Privileges and Immunities of the OSCE: to be adopted by the appropriate body of the OSCE, political

173 Tichy and Köhler 2008, pp. 455–478.

174 Tichy and Köhler 2008, p. 466.

obligation for all Participating States of the OSCE to adopt such a law at the national level (which some Participating States say is not possible for them);

Model bilateral agreement between the OSCE and mission receiving countries: to be adopted by the appropriate body of the OSCE, model text for agreements (with unclear status) with certain countries; this option – already in practice to a certain extent – does not solve the issue of lack of international legal personality nor does it provide a uniform system of privileges and immunities.[175]

The above options listed by Tichy and Köhler show that many participating countries preferred mechanisms, other than treaty-based ones, to confer international legal personality to the OSCE. Some of the proposed solutions resemble those chosen, as described above, for the establishment of international organizations without treaty foundation. Hence, the case of the OSCE is very instructive as it shows that it was possible, in the view of many participating countries of the OSCE, to confer international legal personality to the OSCE without resorting to treaty-based mechanisms for doing so.

Nevertheless, OSCE is currently not covered by any multilateral agreement providing for privileges and immunities. However, the fact that both Austria and Poland have agreed, in principle, to enter into headquarters agreements with the OSCE gives further weight to those who argue that the OSCE must be deemed to possess international legal personality.

6.2.6 European Agencies

The question of whether international organizations may create an organization with international legal personality and hence a new subject under international law has been controversial for a long time. This issue has multiple ramifications. The point of departure for approaching this issue is for many the principle of "*compétence d'attribution*," according to which international organizations may not generate their own powers or determine their own competence[176] and the corresponding "principle of speciality" formulated by the International Court of Justice in its Advisory Opinion of 1996." (see above) Consistent with these principles, constraints may apply to the powers that may be delegated by an organization to an agency or organization established by it.

From an institutional perspective, a corollary of a discussion on the limits of delegation is the question whether, and under which circumstances, organizations may have multiple legal personalities, and, potentially, but not necessarily, different membership structures. This, in turn, has implications for the legal effects of international agreements concluded by an organization and its subsidiary bodies, an issue which the ILC opted not to address, stating that it

[175] Tichy and Köhler 2008, pp. 466–467.

[176] See Schermers and Blokker 2011, §209, with further references.

> would be useful to make it clear that, unless there is a properly established indication to the contrary, when an international organization binds itself by treaty, it also binds all these other bodies. Conversely, a treaty concluded on behalf of a subsidiary organ should bind the entire organization as well. However, as pointed out elsewhere, this is an area in which notions, vocabulary and the practice of international organizations are not settled, and it seemed wisest to leave aside a subject which it is too early to codify.[177]

The issue of constraints on the ability of an organization to create a new subject of international law under its constitution and laws is relevant in the case of the European Union which has become one of the areas of greatest proliferation of new technical agencies. Such proliferation of EU agencies has many interesting ramifications and involves several fundamental questions, such as the institutional balance in the European Union which gives the Council the power to represent the EU in external relations, the procedure for such representation, new paradigms of mixed administration, legal issues relating to the limits of delegation, and the scope of the legal personality of the EU agencies. These issues will be addressed in the following discussion in relation to the agencies of the European Union.

6.2.6.1 Types of EU Agencies

As of 31 January 2016, there are 40 EU agencies in five groups:

(i) decentralized agencies, carrying out "technical, scientific or managerial tasks that help the EU institutions make and implement policies";[178]
(ii) agencies under a common security and defense policy carrying "out very specific technical, scientific and management tasks" within the framework of that policy;[179]
(iii) executive agencies "set up for a limited period of time by the European Commission to manage specific tasks related to EU programmes";[180]
(iv) EURATOM agencies "created to support the aims of the European Atomic Energy Community Treaty (EURATOM), which are to: coordinate national nuclear research programmes, for peaceful purposes provide knowledge,

[177] See Draft articles on the law of treaties between States and international organizations or between international organizations with commentaries. Commentary (3) to Article 29 "Territorial Scope of Treaties", Yearbook of the International Law Commission. 1982. Vol. II, Part Two, 17–77, 40. http://legal.un.org/ilc/texts/instruments/english/commentaries/1_2_1982.pdf.

[178] European Union. Decentralized Agencies. https://europa.eu/european-union/about-eu/agencies/decentralised-agencies_en.

[179] European Union. External Action. CSDP structure, instruments, and agencies. https://eeas.europa.eu/headquarters/headquarters-homepage/5392/csdp-structure-instruments-and-agencies_en.

[180] European Union. About the EU. Agencies and other EU bodies. https://europa.eu/european-union/about-eu/agencies#type_of_agencies.

infrastructure and funding for nuclear energy ensure sufficient and secure supplies of nuclear energy";[181] and

(v) Other organizations (set up as part of EU programs or as public-private partnerships.[182]

The decentralized agencies are of particular interest as—unlike executive agencies—they are not limited to a fixed period and have more far-reaching authority. As there "is no single legal framework governing the establishment of agencies and no set criteria for choosing the agency option", agencies are "being created on an *ad hoc* basis."[183]

6.2.6.2 External Action of EU

There are different approval requirements for EU Agencies to engage in international action. While in some cases, an act of international cooperation requires approval of the EU Council or Commission, in other cases, agencies need to ask for the opinion of the Commission or are not expressly subject to the supervision of the Council or Commission. Based on that distinction, such agencies may be classified as Category 1, 2 or 3.[184] The EU Agencies have a threefold international dimension:

> First, agencies have themselves acquired a larger breadth than being 'pure EU' bodies, as third countries may participate in agencies' internal structure [….].
>
> Second, they increasingly give support to the EU institutions in global fora [….].
>
> Third, they increasingly cooperate with third states' authorities, international programmes and organisations. Here agencies at times conclude various forms of arrangements such as memoranda of understanding and working arrangements as independent actors.[185]
>
> In addition, they also play an important role in the enlargement process.[186]

6.2.6.3 Limits of Delegation of Powers to European Agencies

As the EU agencies are to assist the EU Council and European Commission in their responsibilities regarding the external relations of the EU, the legal status of the EU Agencies has been discussed under the aspect of limits of delegation of discretionary powers and with reference to the legal status of the European Agencies,

---

[181] Ibid.

[182] Ibid. See, with further references: http://europa.eu/about-eu/agencies/index_en.htm.

[183] European Union. Analytical Fiche Nr° 2. Creation of agencies. https://europa.eu/european-union/sites/europaeu/files/docs/body/fiche_2_sent_to_ep_cons_2010-12-15_en.pdf.

[184] Ott et al. 2013, pp. 20–34. http://www.asser.nl/media/1642/cleer_13-7_web.pdf.

[185] Ott et al. 2013, p. 8.

[186] Coman-Kund 2012, pp. 335–367.

notably relating to the question whether they only possess legal capacity under the law of EU member countries or may be considered as subjects of international law possessing international legal personality.

As regards the discretionary powers which may be delegated to European Agencies, principles for such delegation were defined in the Meroni Decision of 1958[187] which has been the guiding principle for the last 50 years.[188] This decision authorized the establishment of agencies, and defined criteria for such delegation. While the ECJ in the case of *Romana and Institut National D'assurance*

---

[187] Meroni v High Authority. Judgement of 13.6. 1958—Case 9/56. http://eur-lex.europa.eu/legal-content/EN/TXT/PDF/?uri=CELEX:61956CJ0009&from=EN.

[188] In the aforementioned Decision, the Court reviewed the limits of delegation to agencies involved in a scrap metal equalization scheme. Core parts of the decision read as follows:

> [….] Decision No 14/55 brings about a true delegation of powers, and the question whether such delegation accords with the requirements of the Treaty must be examined. (p. 149)
>
> xxx xxx xxx
>
> The consequences resulting from a delegation of powers are very different depending on whether it involves clearly defined executive powers the exercise of which can, therefore, be subject to strict review in the light of objective criteria determined by the delegating authority, or whether it involves a discretionary power, implying a wide margin of discretion which may, according to the use which is made of it, make possible the execution of actual economic policy. A delegation of the first kind cannot appreciably alter the consequences involved in the exercise of the powers concerned, whereas a delegation of the second kind, since it replaces the choices of the delegator by the choices of the delegate, brings about an actual transfer of responsibility. (p. 152)
>
> xxx xxx xxx
>
> The objectives set out in Article 3 are binding not only on the High Authority, but on the 'institutions of the Community [….] within the limits of their respective powers, in the common interest'. From that provision there can be seen in the balance of powers which is characteristic of the institutional structure of the Community a fundamental guarantee granted by the Treaty in particular to the undertakings and associations of undertakings to which it applies. To delegate a discretionary power, by entrusting it to bodies other than those which the Treaty has established to effect and supervise the exercise of such power each within the limits of its own authority, would render that guarantee ineffective. (p. 152)
>
> xxx xxx xxx
>
> In reserving to itself the power to refuse its approval, the High Authority has not retained sufficient powers for the delegation resulting from Decision No 14/55 to be contained within the limits defined above.
>
> In the paragraph of the statement of defence set out above the High Authority has made it clear that it 'adopts the data furnished by the Brussels agencies without being able to add anything thereto'. In those circumstances the delegation of powers granted to the Brussels agencies by Decision No 14/55 gives those agencies a degree of latitude which implies a wide margin of discretion and cannot be considered as compatible with the requirements of the Treaty. (p. 154)

Maladie-Invalidité[189] did not expressly refer to the Meroni principles, it emphasized the limits of delegation to administrative commissions.[190]

The question as to the limits of delegation resurfaced very recently in the case C-270/12, *United Kingdom v European Parliament and Council of the European Union,*[191] which concerned the power vested in the European Securities and Markets Authority (ESMA) to intervene in the financial markets, notably by prohibiting or imposing conditions into a short sale or other financial instrument that confers a financial advantage in the event of a decrease in the price or value of another financial instrument. The United Kingdom did not impugn the establishment of ESMA by Regulation of the European Parliament and the Council but sought the annulment of Article 28 of Regulation (EU) No 236/2012 "adopted on the basis of Article 114 TFEU, which confers power on the European Parliament and the Council of the European Union to adopt measures for the approximation of the provisions laid down by law, regulation or administrative action in the Member States which have as their object the establishment and functioning of the internal market."[192] The United Kingdom alleged that this Regulation entailed "'a very large measure of discretion" as well as "a wide range of choices as to which measure or measures to impose" and "highly subjective factors." While rejecting the plea of the United Kingdom, the Court reaffirmed the principles formulated in *Meroni* and *Romana* while adjusting them to a certain extent and putting them into

[189] Judgement of 14 May 1981—Case 98/80, Romana, Guiseppe and Institut National D'Assurance Maladie-Invalidité. http://www.eur-lex.europa.eu/legal-content/EN/TXT/PDF/?uri=CELEX:61980CJ0098&from=EN.

[190] Paragraph 20 of the said Judgment states:

> As regards that question, as framed by the Tribunal du Travail, it follows both from Article 155 of the Treaty and the judicial system created by the Treaty, and in particular by Articles 173 and 177 thereof, that a body such as the Administrative Commission may not be empowered by the Council to adopt acts having the force of law. Whilst a decision of the Administrative Commission may provide an aid to social security institutions responsible for applying Community law in this field, it is not of such a nature as to require those institutions to use certain methods or adopt certain interpretations when they come to apply the Community rules. Decision No. 101 of the Administrative Commission does not therefore bind the Tribunal du Travail.

[191] European Court of Justice, Judgment of 22 Jan. 2014, Case C-270/12, United Kingdom of Britain and Northern Ireland v European Parliament and Council of the European Union, Judgment of 22 Jan. 2014. http://curia.europa.eu/juris/document/document.jsf?text=&docid=146621&pageIndex=0&doclang=EN&mode=lst&dir=&occ=first&part=1&cid=1824444.

[192] See para 8 of Judgment of 22 Jan. 2014, Case C-270/12. http://curia.europa.eu/juris/document/document.jsf?text=&docid=146621&pageIndex=0&doclang=EN&mode=lst&dir=&occ=first&part=1&cid=1824444.

the context of the Treaty of Lisbon.[193] Thus, it would appear that in the view of the ECJ, limits to the scope of discretionary powers that may be delegated to European Agencies continue to apply.

6.2.6.4 International Legal Personality of European Agencies

The legal acts establishing the EU agencies only provide for their legal capacity under the law of EU member countries and do not address their international legal personality. While this would not necessarily preclude them from enjoying international legal personality, this discussion needs to be seen in the overall context of the discussion of the multiple international legal personalities of the European Union.

There has been a progressive institutionalization of the status of European agencies. While EU Agencies do not have any general treaty-making capacity, a clear indication in this regard is that

> host countries of independent community bodies have recognized a restricted international legal personality that is limited to the power to conclude treaties on the seat of the bodies. The form of the agreements resembles that of public international treaties. They contain, *inter alia*, preambles and entry-into-force provisions as in other international treaties [….].[194]

---

[193] The Court "observed that the bodies in question in Meroni v High Authority were entities governed by private law, whereas ESMA is a European Union entity, created by the EU legislature." (para 43). It noted that "unlike the case of the powers delegated to the bodies concerned in Meroni v High Authority, the exercise of the powers under Article 28 of Regulation No 236/2012 is circumscribed by various conditions and criteria which limit ESMA's discretion." (para 45) and that "the powers available to ESMA under Article 28 of Regulation No. 236/2012 are precisely delineated and amenable to judicial review in the light of the objectives established by the delegating authority. Accordingly, those powers comply with the requirements laid down in Meroni v High Authority." (para 53) In addition, the Court held:

> It is clear from Article 28 of Regulation No 236/2012 that ESMA is required, in strictly circumscribed circumstances, to adopt measures of general application under that provision. Such measures may also include rules affecting any natural or legal person who has a specific financial instrument or specific class of financial instruments or who enter into certain financial transactions. (para 64)
>
> However, that does not mean that Article 28 of Regulation No 236/2012 is at odds with the principle established in Romano. It should be recalled that the institutional framework established by the FEU Treaty, in particular the first paragraph of Article 263 TFEU and Article 277 TFEU, expressly permits Union bodies, offices and agencies to adopt acts of general application. (para 65)
>
> Accordingly, it cannot be inferred from Romano that the delegation of powers to a body such as ESMA is governed by conditions other than those set out in Meroni v High Authority, as referred to at paras 41 to 42 above. (para 66)
>
> In addition, the other pleas of the United Kingdom were rejected.

[194] Schusterschitz 2004, p. 175.

The possession of international legal personality was so far mainly discussed in relation to the ECB and the EIB. The ECB is included in the list of community institutions set forth in Article 13 of TEU and is regulated by Section 6 (Articles 282 to 284) and other provisions of the Treaty on the Functioning of the European Union (TFEU). Paragraph 3 of Article 282 TFEU provides:

> The European Central Bank shall have legal personality. It alone may authorize the issue of the euro. It shall be independent in the exercise of its powers and in the management of its finances. Union institutions, bodies, offices and agencies and the governments of the Member States shall respect that independence.

The ECB is the "main decision-making institution of the common monetary policy, and only the implementation of the monetary policy is decentralized between the ECB and national central bank of the Euro zone. For these purposes, the ECB enjoys both legal personality under national law and international legal personality."[195]

The European Investment Bank is regulated in Chapter 4 (Articles 308[196] and 309), and other provisions of the TFEU and is also recognized as having international legal personality in addition to legal capacity under national law.

In relation to the ECB, the judgment of the European Court of Justice in Case C-11/00 *Commission of the European Communities v. the European Central Bank* (2003) has brought some clarity, as the Court stated, while recognizing the legal personality of the ECB, "that the ECB, pursuant to the EC Treaty, falls squarely within the Community framework."[197] The ECJ opted "clearly in favor of a limited notion of independence, confined by the functions, tasks, and powers specifically conferred upon the ECB" and upheld a concept of 'independence within the Community structure' (not independence from the Community) that is reminiscent of the notion of "independence within government."[198]

Also as regards the EIB, there are some uncertainties regarding its legal personality. As indicated in a report of the research service of the European Parliament:

> In order to be able to carry out its necessary financial functions, the European Investment Bank, by virtue of Article 266 EC Treaty, has been awarded autonomous legal personality. It is free to conclude agreements and function as a bank as long as it stays within the limits of the rights conferred to it by the EC Treaty and its own Statute. However, the extent of its freedom of activity is unclear, as it is possible that the EIB may be bound by directions/instructions from other Community institutions. Interestingly, the breadth of the legal

[195] Puccio 2013, p. 226.

[196] The first paragraph of Article 308 of TFEU states: "The European Investment Bank shall have legal personality."

[197] European Court of Justice. Judgment of 10. 7. 2003—CASE C-11/00, para 92. See http://curia.europa.eu/juris/showPdf.jsf?text=&docid=48494&pageIndex=0&doclang=en&mode=lst&dir=&occ=first&part=1&cid=161058.

[198] Lastra 2012, p. 1278.

personality awarded to the European Central Bank (ECB) by Article 107 (2) of the EC Treaty, appears to be greater than that awarded to the EIB [....].[199]

Moreover, as indicated in the aforementioned report, it adds to the uncertainties regarding the status of EIB that has a "dual character, on the one hand an autonomous financial body, and on the other an EU body."[200]

As for the EU agencies that have been mushrooming, in accordance with a common approach to decentralized agencies recommended in 2012.[201] jointly by the European Commission, European Council and European Parliament, "Guidelines with standard provisions for headquarters agreements of EU decentralised agencies" were developed.[202] According to the "Common Approach on EU decentralised agencies, 'all agencies should have headquarters agreements, which should be concluded before the agency starts its operational phase'"[203] Agencies still lacking a headquarters agreement and the host country in question should reach an agreement in accordance with the legal order of the relevant Member State. However, effectively, this did not prove possible in all cases. For those agencies which have not entered into a headquarters agreement with their host country, the Protocol on the Privileges and Immunities of the European Union remains applicable.[204]

The prevailing opinion appears to be that European Agencies do not possess international legal personality and, hence, may not be qualified as subjects of international law. Nevertheless, there are some dissenting opinions.[205]

Schusterschitz discusses whether "host states of independent community bodies have recognized a restricted international legal personality that is limited to the power to conclude treaties on the seat of the bodies".[206] While the form of such agreements "resembles that of public international treaties" as they "contain, *inter*

---

[199] European Parliament. Directorate for Research. Institutional Status of the European Investment Bank. *Economic Affairs Series*. ECON 132 EN, 16. http://www.europarl.europa.eu/RegData/etudes/etudes/join/2003/332624/DG-4-ECON_ET(2003)332624_EN.pdf.

[200] Ibid.

[201] See detailed references to background documents, European Union. Decentralized Agencies: 2012 Overhaul. https://europa.eu/european-union/about-eu/agencies/overhaul_en. See also EU Agencies Network. Agencies activities in 2013 relating to the Common Approach. http://www.europarl.europa.eu/document/activities/cont/201401/20140116ATT77602/20140116ATT77602EN.pdf.

[202] "Guidelines with standard provisions for headquarters agreements of EU decentralised agencies. https://europa.eu/european-union/sites/europaeu/files/docs/body/2013-12-10_guidelines_hq_agreements_en.pdf.

[203] Ibid., 2.

[204] See with further details on the seat agreements of European Agencies, "European Union. Agencies Seat and the role of the host country". https://europa.eu/european-union/sites/europaeu/files/docs/body/fiche_3_sent_to_ep_cons_2010-12-15_en.pdf.

[205] Constantinecso 1977, §374.

[206] See Schusterschitz 2004, p. 175, with further references.

alia, preambles and entry-into-force provisions as in other international treaties",[207] the form itself may, as Schusterschitz highlights, "not prove the international legal personality of the independent community bodies."[208] Moreover, even assuming that when concluding a headquarters agreement, one individual member state of the Community sought to recognize the international legal personality of an European agency, this may not be sufficient to establish that such agency is a subject of international law. Nevertheless, the fact that member countries of the EU enter into headquarters agreements with EU agencies is an important precedent. Thus, there is room for further institutionalization which may lead to the recognition of EU Agencies as subjects of international law with international legal personality. There can hardly be any doubt that it would possible to attribute a limited international legal personality to EU Agencies similar that enjoyed by EIB and the European Central Bank, if this meets with the agreement of all members of the EU, e.g. if all EU members were to recognize through bilateral or multilateral agreements, that EU agencies are acting on the international plane and are entitled to international legal personality.

The discussion on subjects of international law and international legal personality frequently focuses on their normative implications. However, as shown by Ruiter,

> Generally spoken, a valid legal person is a legal institution playing the role of a subject in order to enable a social group to act as a single agent. [...]. In order to make it possible for legal persons of a certain category to play the role of subjects, the content rules and consequential rules of the institutional legal concept designating the category in question, as well as the legal regimes of valid legal persons falling within that category, must have the purport of effectuating social practices that can be interpreted as resting on a common belief that the legal persons are capable of responsible behaviour.[209]

Referring to the "institutional theory of law", as developed in the works of MacCormick and Weinberger, Ruiter, Wróblewski and others,[210] Wessel highlights:

> 'Legal persons' are institutional legal facts since they exist by virtue of a constitutive legal rule that makes their creation possible. However, the legal person may only exercise its rights, duties and competences (and thus become a 'successful' legal person) when a relation is established between the institutional fact (being a legal person) and the rights, powers and responsibilities attached to the existence of that institutional fact (the 'legal capacities'). The institutional fact as such is something of which the existence cannot be denied (being a fact) once a constitutive rule decides on its existence. This also underlines the view that partial legal personality is impossible: it either exists or it does not. The institutional legal fact of being a legal person is not something that can be counted and measured; its reality consists in its being used and accepted. On the other hand, the legal capacities attached to the institutional legal fact are not fixed and may indeed vary according to the amount of rights, duties and competences conferred on the legal person.[211]

[207] Ibid., 175.

[208] Ibid., 175.

[209] Ruiter 2001, p. 102.

[210] Wessel 2000, p. 512, footnote 19 with detailed references.

[211] Ibid., 514.

The constitutive legal rule referred to above may be but does not need to be a treaty. It can also relate to a resolution or decision of the governing bodies of an organization or the conference of a party of a party to a multilateral convention. Thus, the attitude which recognized subjects of international law take towards that rule is of great importance.

Hence, it is not the manner how the European agencies were established but their attribution and powers and the attitudes of recognized subjects of international law which determines whether they can be classified as subjects of international law. While this is currently not the case, there is a potential for further development.

6.2.7 Quasi-Autonomous Bodies

Similar considerations also apply regarding the question whether certain subsidiary bodies of the United Nations may be endowed with international legal personality and hence may be qualified as subjects of international law.

In relation to quasi-autonomous bodies (QAB), Szasz highlights that "the substantive interchangeability of some of these complex organs with specialized agencies [….] can be illustrated by the fact that one short-lived specialized agency, the International Refugee Organization (IRO), was, on its dissolution, replaced by a complex subsidiary body, the UN High Commissioner for Refugees."[212]

Indeed, in "several cases it was only a matter of chance that a new institution was established as an organization based on a treaty, rather than as an organ based on a resolution by another organization."[213] This is clearly shown by the case of UNIDO, as

> the constitutional form of the new organization that emerged from the deliberations of the General Assembly was a compromise arrangement. Although the organization was given comprehensive terms of reference (a) as regards promotion of industrialization in the developing countries and (b) co-ordination of the industrialization activities within the United Nations family, it was set up as an autonomous organization within the framework of the United Nations. It was a 'compromise arrangement'.[214]

Hence, the General Assembly decided in 1966 to establish UNIDO "as an organ of the General Assembly".[215]

In principle, the status of subsidiary bodies is subject to a number of legal constraints, notably under Articles 7 of the UN Charter, which provides the general basis for establishing subsidiary bodies in accordance with the UN Charter; and Articles 22 and 29, which expressly give the General Assembly and Security

---

[212] Szasz 1999, pp. 3, 5.

[213] Schermers and Blokker 2011, §40.

[214] Plasil-Wenger 1971, p. 190.

[215] Repertory of Practice of United Nations Organs, Article 59, Supplement No. 6 (1979–1984), Vol. 4, para 3. http://legal.un.org/repertory/art59/english/rep_supp6_vol4-art59_e.pdf.

Council, respectively, the power to establish subsidiary bodies. Most of the subsidiary bodies are established by the General Assembly. Thus, the General Assembly, in principle, has the authority to modify the terms of reference of the bodies that it has established. The same also applies in relation to the subsidiary bodies established by the Security Council. Subsidiary bodies are tied to the United Nations through various administrative and financial strings; they are subject to constraints regarding their budgetary independence and have reporting obligations, among others.

As regards UNIDO, although it was "given comprehensive terms of reference (a) as regards promotion of industrialization in the developing countries and (b) co-ordination of the industrialization activities within the United Nations family,"[216] it initially functioned as an autonomous organization within the United Nations [....]."[217]

It was only following General Assembly Resolution of 1975 and on the recommendation of the Second General Conference of UNIDO and upon the endorsement of that recommendation by the General Assembly[218] that the demand of the developing countries for conversion of UNIDO into a specialized agency was eventually pursued, and only after complicated negotiations was the Constitution of UNIDO adopted on 8 April 1979.[219] It took until 1985 for the requirements for its effectiveness to be completed and until 1986 for a special agreement between UNIDO and the United Nations to be concluded upon which UNIDO eventually became the 16th specialized agency of the UN.[220]

UNIDO is indicative in three respects: First, it shows that often it is entirely a matter of policy whether the entity that is established is a specialized agency of the UN or a quasi-autonomous body. Second, it shows that conversion from a quasi-autonomous body to specialized agency is possible. Third, it underlines the difficult and lengthy process of converting a QAB into a specialized agency by way of a treaty.

---

216 Plasil-Wenger 1971, p. 190.

217 UN General Assembly Resolution 2152 (XXI). https://documents-dds-ny.un.org/doc/RESOLUTION/GEN/NR0/004/55/IMG/NR000455.pdf?OpenElement.

218 General Assembly Resolution 3362 (S-VII). Development and international economic co-operation, IV, para 9: "The General Assembly endorses the recommendation of the Second General Conference of the United Nations Industrial Development Organization to convert that organization into a specialized agency and decides to establish a Committee on the Drafting of a Constitution for the United Nations Industrial Development Organization, which shall be an intergovernmental committee of the whole, including States which participated in the Second General Conference, to meet in Vienna to draw up a constitution for the United Nations Industrial Development Organization as a specialized agency, to be submitted to a conference of plenipotentiaries to be convened by the Secretary-General in the last quarter of 1976."

219 Repertory of Practice of United Nations Organs. Extracts relating to Article 59 of the Charter of the United Nations: Supplement No. 6 (1979–1984), Vol. 4. para 3. http://legal.un.org/repertory/art59/english/rep_supp6_vol4-art59_e.pdf http://legal.un.org/docs/?path=../repertory/art59/english/rep_supp6_vol4_art59.pdf&lang=EF.

220 See Rau-Mentzen and Koppenfels 1995, p. 1329, with further references.

The fact that UN bodies such as UNCTAD, UNDP, UNEP, UNHCR were established as subsidiary bodies does not fully capture their legal status, and the fact that they enjoy a large scale of autonomy. While Schermers and Blokker refer to them as the "'minors' in the UN family: institutions that operate more or less autonomously but without international legal personality,"[221] this author believes with Szasz that they are better referred to as QABs.[222] The basic principle that subsidiary bodies do not enjoy separate international legal personality but partake of the legal personality of the United Nations also applies in respect of these quasi-autonomous bodies. The Office of Legal Affairs of the UN has rendered a number of legal opinions which highlight the limited scope of authority of subsidiary bodies of the United Nations.[223] In particular, when UNDP signed an agreement with a member state of the United Nations to establish the "Centre for Environment and Development Programme for the Arab Region and Europe (CEDARE)" as an international organization, OLA sought to convey to UNDP in no uncertain terms its limited authority, reiterating categorically the traditional mantra that:

> The capacity to establish international intergovernmental organizations having separate legal personality is, under international law, conferred upon States through the conclusion of agreements. International intergovernmental organizations which are the creation of States cannot in and of themselves create new international organizations, endowed with the same international legal personality, unless; they are specifically mandated to do so by States.[224]

---

[221] Schermers and Blokker 2011, §1695.

[222] Szasz 1999, p. 7. Szasz lists a number of UN Bodies in addition to those referred to above which may qualify as QABs.

[223] E.g. Question whether the United Nations Development Programme could become a founding member of a corporate body under the national law of a Member State—Character of United Nations activities in the territories of Member States—Submission of. UNDP to the national law of the corporate body could be construed to constitute a waiver of the privileges and immunities to which UNDP is entitled. Memorandum to the Director, Policy Division, Bureau for Programme Policy and Evaluation, United Nations Development Programme. United Nations Juridical Yearbook 1990, Part Two, 259–260. http://legal.un.org/docs/?path=../unjuridicalyearbook/pdfs/english/volumes/1990.pdf&lang=E.

[224] Legal Capacity of International Intergovernmental Organizations to Establish Other International Organizations—Legal Capacity of the United Nations Development Programme to Participate in the Establishment of Other International Organizations or to Establish Its Own Subsidiary Organs. United Nations Juridical Yearbook 1991, 296–301, 297. The Office of Legal Affairs recalled in para 6 of the cited decision: "The United Nations Development Programme was created by the General Assembly in its resolution 2029 (XX) of 22 November 1965, as a combined organ of the Expanded Programme of Technical Assistance and the Special Fund, to be administered under the authority of the Economic and Social Council and the General Assembly. It is a subsidiary organ of the United Nations, and as such it has only those powers which are vested in it in its founding resolution, and in General Assembly resolution 2688 (XXV) of 11 Dec. 1970 ('the Consensus Resolution')." http://legal.un.org/docs/?path=../unjuridicalyearbook/pdfs/english/by_chapter/chpVI/1991/chpVI.pdf&lang=E.

OLA concluded in para 17 of the said opinion:

> that UNDP does not possess the legal capacity to establish a new international organization alone or with only one other State; nor does it have the capacity to establish a United Nations subsidiary organ absent a legislative authority of the General Assembly or of the UNDP Governing Council.[225]

This legal opinion reflects the attempt of OLA to affirm the overall authority and hold of the United Nations over its quasi-autonomous bodies. However, this attempt is countered by quasi-autonomous bodies seeking to evade the firm grip of the United Nations by conducting themselves as international organizations.

There has been substantial institutionalization of the status of QABs, in particular, in relation to their capacity to enter into agreements governed by international law. This has led some authors to attribute international legal personality to those quasi-autonomous bodies. Thus, Berthoud observes that UNDP "has a number of constitutional features which give it a personality separate from that of the United Nations, in a legal situation which is not devoid of all ambiguity."[226] He notes that, "The UNDP, for instance, may enter into agreements with subjects of international law; it has the capacity to demand recognition of its rights and reparation of their violation; and it has the power to acquire, hold and transfer property."[227]

However, the fact that UNDP has authority to enter into international agreements does not necessarily imply that it has an international legal personality separate from that of the UN. For an organization to be qualified as a legal person which maintains external relations, "the legal person's internal practice has to be related to the surrounding societal practice."[228] As indicated by Ruiters:

> In order to gear the legal person's internal and external practices to one another, at least the following points must be attended to: First, the potential of legal persons to be bearers of rights and owers (sic) of duties (capacity for rights), as well as their capacity of performing legal acts (legal capacity) must be established. Secondly, it must be determined which organs can conduct transactions with others on behalf of the legal persons (agency). Thirdly, the responsibility of legal persons for violations of the law imputable to its organs has to be defined (legal liability).[229]

In the case of quasi-autonomous bodies, their internal practices are sometimes unrelated "to the surrounding societal practice."[230] Often, quasi-autonomous bodies conduct themselves like independent international organizations. Thus, UNDP, to give an example, indicates in the international agreements that it enters into, that these are concluded by UNDP, rather than referring to the UN as a party to the agreement, and without making reference to the status of UNDP. However, the UN Secretariat registers the agreement as having been concluded between the country

---

[225] Ibid., 300.

[226] Berthoud 1970, p. 155.

[227] Ibid.

[228] Ruiter 2001, p. 106.

[229] Ibid.

[230] Ibid., 106.

concerned (e.g. Brazil)[231] and the United Nations (United Nations Development Programme) and thus makes it clear that the United Nations rather than UNDP is the party to that agreement.

The main issue relates to the question of who would be the respondent in arbitration proceedings or other legal proceedings which may be initiated in relation to an agreement or contract concluded by UNDP. The UN Administrative Tribunal has been quite clear on this matter in ruling that any legal action against a decision or action taken by UNDP needs to be directed against the Secretary-General of the United Nations.[232] However, the review of national jurisdiction conducted by August Reinisch "has revealed some difficulties for national courts facing subsidiary organs, notably on the legal personality of these subsidiary organs."[233]

It would appear to this author that the quality of "subject of international law" in respect of quasi-autonomous bodies is not yet firmly established. On the other hand, the mere characterization of these bodies as subsidiary bodies of the United Nations is not particularly helpful either, as it does not capture the large degree of autonomy enjoyed by these bodies. Thus, they are best conceived as "intermediate forms between independent organizations and organs of organizations.[234] As indicated by Schermers and Blokker, the existence of such intermediate forms "is not objectionable. On the contrary, it reflects practical needs. No sharp theoretical distinction should present obstacles to the effective organization of governmental functions at the international level."[235]

In the cases of the European Agencies and the quasi-autonomous bodies analyzed above, it is not the fact that they were established by the European Community as agencies, or, by the General Assembly, as subsidiary bodies of the UN that precludes their recognition as subjects of international law, but the fact that they are currently still subject to a number of constraints based on their specific legal status and that their ability to act on the international plane and be the subject of duties and responsibilities under international law is not yet firmly established.

In many instances, the gap which separates quasi-autonomous bodies from full-fledged international organizations is very narrow. While the establishment of a specialized agency of the UN requires, in accordance with para 1 of Article 57, an "intergovernmental agreement", it is conceivable that there may be ways for converting a quasi-autonomous body into an independent international organization other than concluding a constituent agreement in the form of a treaty. In some cases, it might be sufficient for the UN and participants in the international legal system to recognize a quasi-autonomous body as an independent international organization and to cut the remaining ties which link it to the UN by giving it full powers and

[231] See representative for many: UN Treaty Series. 2007. Vol. 2474, No. 44415, 83–86.

[232] UN Administrative Tribunal Judgment No. 380, Case No. 400: ALAM http://repository.un.org/bitstream/handle/11176/188272/AT_DEC_380-EN.pdf?sequence=1&isAllowed=y.

[233] Reinisch 2010, p. 81.

[234] Schermers and Blokker 2011, §41.

[235] Ibid.

competence to decide on its budget and policies, and to elect the head of the secretariat. This could be followed by a multilateral agreement, or by bilateral agreements between the organization and the countries where it operates or which are represented in its governing bodies, which recognize the organization's international legal personality and extend to it privileges and immunities.

6.2.8 Financial Mechanisms of Multilateral Environmental Conventions as Subjects of International Law

As regards the UNFCCC, it is recognized that the COP of this convention enjoys international legal personality and thus may be classified as a subject of international law. The Office of Legal Affairs stated in relation to the UNFCCC:

> Once this convention enters into force it will establish an international entity/organisation with its own separate legal personality, statement of principles, organs and a supportive structure in the form of a Secretariat.[236]

The said opinion concluded that

> in accordance with the relevant provisions of the Convention, the COP has the legal capacity, within the limits of its mandate, to enter into agreements and other arrangements with entities, such as states, intergovernmental and non-governmental organizations and bodies, which also have the authority to do so.[237]

While there is wide agreement on the legal personality of the UNFCCC COP, the question whether the COP or the meeting of the Parties to the Kyoto Protocol can establish an international organization with international legal personality is less clear. The example of the Adaptation Fund shows that a financial mechanism established by the Meeting of the Parties to a Convention does not necessarily need to be endowed with international legal personality. In case of the Adaptation Fund, only the Board of the Fund has legal personality under German law, the reason being that the Adaptation Fund is administered by the World Bank and all persons assigned to it have the status of staff members of the World Bank.[238] Moreover, the GEF which is also a financial mechanism of the UNFCCC neither possesses international legal personality nor legal capacity under national law. As discussed, this does not preclude that the GEF is classified as a subject of international law, nor that it can be considered an international organization.

---

[236] Memorandum from The Legal Counsel of the UN Carl-August Fleischhauer to Mr. Michael Zammit Cutajar, Executive secretary, Intergovernmental Negotiating Committee for a Framework Convention on Climate Change of 4 Nov. 1993 titled: "Arrangements for the implementation of the provisions of Article 11 of the UN Framework Convention on Climate Change concerning the financial mechanism. United Nations Juridical Yearbook 1993, 427–433, 428, para 4. http://legal.un.org/docs/?path=../unjuridicalyearbook/pdfs/english/volumes/1993.pdf&lang=E.

[237] Ibid., 429, para 7.

[238] See Droesse, "Introductory Remarks", 21, with further references.

Organizations such as the Multilateral Fund for the Implementation of the Montreal Protocol (Multilateral Fund) and the Green Climate Fund (GCF) show that an entity established by a meeting or the conference of the parties to a multilateral environmental convention can indeed enjoy international legal personality and hence be a subject of international law (see below).

As regards the Multilateral Fund, the Montreal Protocol was amended in 1990 to provide that the financial mechanism to be established under para 1 of Article 10 "shall include a Multilateral Fund."[239]

Further to this "London Amendment of the Montreal Protocol, the Sixth Meeting of the Parties to the Montreal Protocol held in Nairobi from 6 to 7 October 1994 decided (Decision VI/16):

> to clarify the nature and legal status of the Fund as a body under international law as follows:
>
> (a) *Juridical personality:* The Multilateral Fund shall enjoy such legal capacity as is necessary for the exercise of its functions and the protection of its interests, in particular the capacity to enter into contracts, to acquire and dispose of movable and immovable property and to institute legal proceedings in defence of its interests.
> (b) *Privileges and immunities:*
>
> (i) The Fund shall, in accordance with arrangements to be determined with the Government of Canada, enjoy in the territory of the host country, such privileges and immunities as are necessary for the fulfilment of its purposes;
> (ii) The officials of the Fund Secretariat shall similarly enjoy such privileges and immunities as are necessary for the independent exercise of their functions in connection with the Multilateral Fund.[240]

It is discussed whether this decision may be construed as a transfer of legal personality at the international level or merely at the domestic level. While the wording of Decision VI/16 only addresses the legal capacity of the Multilateral Fund under national law, this does not preclude that the Multilateral Fund may have international legal personality. Whether this is the case does not depend on the wording of the aforementioned Decision VI/16, but on the functions of the Multilateral Fund and the position which recognized subjects of international law have adopted in its regard.

Jacur contends that decision VI/16 "seems to refer to the recognition of an internal, domestic capacity rather than to legal personality at the international level",[241] but does not appear to have given adequate consideration to all relevant facts in coming to that conclusion.

The Agreement between the United Nations and the Government of Canada relating to the Multilateral Fund only covers the UNEP staff assigned to the Ozone

[239] Ozone Secretariat. The London Amendment (1990): The Amendment to the Montreal Protocol Agreed by the Second Meeting of the Parties (London, 27–29 June 1990) http://ozone.unep.org/en/handbook-montreal-protocol-substances-deplete-ozone-layer/27609.

[240] "Decision VI/16: Juridical personality, privileges and immunities of the Multilateral Fund". In Ozone Secretariat, UNEP 2016, p. 436.

[241] See Jacur 2013, p. 171.

Secretariat. Hence, it does not concern the Multilateral Fund but only the UN officials servicing the Fund.[242] The Fund was deemed competent both by its Executive Committee[243] and by the Government of Canada to be a party to a bilateral agreement with Canada[244] which provides for the Fund's "juridical personality and capacity" (Article 2), as well as for inviolability of the Multilateral Fund's premises (Article 3) and for privileges and immunities, exemptions and facilities for the Multilateral Fund and the persons associated with it (Articles 4–6 and 8–10). Moreover, in accordance with Article 14 of the said Agreement, the Multilateral Fund is the respondent in case of any dispute with the Government of Canada.

It can be derived from the above that the Multilateral Fund's international legal personality was recognized by the Government of Canada at least for the purposes of the said Agreement with the Multilateral Fund.

Moreover, there are a number of cases where the Multilateral Fund has entered into agreements with international organizations.[245] This clearly suggests that the Fund is able to act on the international plane. Against this background, the Multilateral Fund was proposed to the Interim Committee which prepared the Governing Instrument of the Green Climate Fund as the example of an organization with "international legal personality."[246]

As regards the Green Climate Fund (GCF), as part of the Cancun Agreement, the COP decided[247]

> to **establish** a Green Climate Fund, to be designated as an operating entity of the financial mechanism of the Convention under Article 11, with arrangements to be concluded between the Conference of the Parties and the Green Climate Fund to ensure that it is accountable to and functions under the guidance of the Conference of the Parties, to support

[242] See Agreement between the Government of Canada and the United Nations Concerning the Privileges, Immunities and other Facilities of United Nations Officials Servicing the Secretariat of the Multilateral Fund for the Implementation of the 1987 Montreal Protocol on Substances that Deplete the Ozone Layer. http://treaty-accord.gc.ca/text-texte.aspx?id=103122.

[243] The Agreement was signed by Marco A. Gonzalez-Salazar on behalf of the Executive Committee of the Multilateral Fund.

[244] Agreement between the Government of Canada and the Multilateral Fund for the Implementation of the 1987 Montreal Protocol on Substances that Deplete the Ozone Layer, Regulating Matters Resulting from the Establishment in Canada of the Multilateral Fund and its Organs. The Agreement was signed in Cairo on 23 Nov 1998. See http://www.treaty-accord.gc.ca/text-texte.aspx?id=103123. http://www.treaty-accord.gc.ca/text-texte.aspx?id=103123.

[245] See also UNEP. Multilateral Fund for the Implementation of the Montreal Protocol. Policies, Procedures, Guidelines and Criteria (as of Nov. 2010), 515–565.

[246] Transitional Committee. Workstream II: Governance and Institutional Arrangements. 2011. Background note: Review of the legal status of select international funds and financial institutions. Second meeting. TC-2/WSII/2, 29 June 2011, 9.

https://unfccc.int/files/cancun_agreements/green_climate_fund/application/pdf/tc2_ws2_2_290611.pdf, 9.

[247] Decision 1/CP. 16, The Cancun Agreements: Outcome of the work of the Ad Hoc Working Group on Long-term Cooperative Action under the Convention, para 102.

projects, programmes, policies and other activities in developing country Parties using thematic funding windows. (emphasis added)

The competences of the UNFCCC COP are set forth in Article 7 UNFCCC. Moreover, the provisions regarding the financial mechanism are set forth in Article 11 UNFCCC.

There is no agreement on whether the COP was in a position to "establish" the GCF with international legal personality, with the consequence that the country Parties to the UNFCCC only have to recognize such personality, or whether personality has to be conferred by each country Party to the UNFCCC. Decision 3/CP. 17, in essence leaves it to each country Party to adopt an approach regarding this matter.[248] Similarly, para 7 of the Fund's Governing Instrument incorporates some ambiguity. It provides that in "order to operate effectively internationally, the Fund will possess juridical personality and will have such legal capacity as is necessary for the exercise of its functions and the protection of its interests." While the aforementioned provision does not expressly refer to the international legal personality of the Green Climate Fund, it clearly envisages that the Fund will work on the international plane.

This discussion on whether a COP is entitled to establish an organization, such as the Green Climate Fund, with international legal personality has multiple ramifications. It needs to be seen in the wider context of the discussion on the legal nature and legal effects of multilateral framework agreements and on COP decisions and resolutions.[249] Also, COP decision-making does not fit well the traditional classification of sources of international law and any notion that an international organization can be created by COP decision is at variance with all traditional mantras of public international law.

The many facets of the discussion on the issues mentioned above would deserve a detailed study of its own. As fascinating as such a study would be, it is neither possible, nor is it necessary to engage in such a discussion in this section. The reason is that irrespective of whether one believes that the COP was able to establish the GCF or whether legal personality needed to be conferred to the Fund, there cannot be any reasonable doubt that the GCF is currently acting on the international plane and can be the subject of duties and responsibilities under international law. As has been shown below, the Headquarters Agreement between the Green Climate Fund and the Republic of Korea is a treaty under Article 6 of the

---

[248] While Decision 3/CP.17 decided in para 11 "that the Green Climate Fund be **conferred** juridical personality and legal capacity", para 12 (a) of the said Decision invited the countries offering to host the Fund to submit expressions of interest for the evaluation of expressions of interest of countries offering to host the Fund to submit expressions of interest based, inter alia, on the following criterion: "The ability **to confer and/or recognize** juridical personality and legal capacity to the Fund for the protection of its interests and the exercise of its functions, to give effect to paragraphs 7 and 8 of the governing instrument, including but not limited to the ability to contract, acquire and dispose of immovable and movable property, and institute legal proceedings."

[249] Wiersema 2009, pp. 231–287.

Constitution of the Republic of Korea that has "the same effect as the domestic laws of the Republic of Korea". Moreover, the GCF is party to a number to other agreements governed by international law which recognize the legal personality of the GCF and confer to it privileges and immunities.

Under the circumstances, it is well established that the GCF possesses international legal personality and, hence, qualifies for recognition as a subject of international law. This is important as it underlines that whether an entity is to be recognized as a subject of international law does not depend on the mode of its establishment but on its functions and the position taken by recognized subjects of international law in respect of that entity.

6.2.9 Preparatory Commission of the Nuclear Test Ban Organization (CTBTO)

Finally, the Preparatory Commission of the Nuclear Test Ban Organization (CTBTO) is yet another interesting example which needs to be considered in this context. Established by Resolution of the states signatories to the Comprehensive Nuclear Treaty adopted on 19 November 1996,[250] para 7 of the Annex to that Resolution ("Text on the Establishment of a Preparatory Commission for the Comprehensive Nuclear Test Ban Treaty") expressly states that the "Commission shall have standing as an international organization, authority to negotiate and enter into agreements, and such other legal capacity as necessary for the exercise of its functions and the fulfilment of its purposes." Consistent with the aforementioned provision, CTBTO has concluded a Headquarters Agreement with the Republic of Austria and a number of agreements with states and international organizations.[251] Hence, the international legal personality of the CTBT is firmly established.

6.3 Conclusions

While in traditional organizations with treaty foundation, the constituent agreement generally provides for the legal capacity of the organization under national law or its international legal personality, there is no intrinsic need or justification as to why an international organization should only be able to acquire international legal personality and/or legal capacity under national law up its establishment.

[250] Resolution establishing the Preparatory Commission of the Nuclear Test Ban Organization. Adopted on 19 Nov. 1996 (CTBT/MSS/RES/1, 27 Nov. 1997. https://www.ctbto.org/fileadmin/user_upload/legal/CTBT-MSS-RES-1-e_01.pdf.

[251] See detailed references: CTBT Legal Resources. https://www.ctbto.org/member-states/legal-resources/.

International legal personality may be acquired subsequently based on its progressive institutionalization and taking account of the position which other recognized subjects of international law have adopted in its regard.

The most tangible expression of such position may be seen in bilateral and multilateral agreements which expressly recognize the international legal personality and/or legal capacity of the organization. In those cases where an organization does not possess legal personality or is incorporated as nongovernmental organization or corporation under national law, the recognition of its international legal personality in a headquarters agreement and in other bilateral agreements or a multilateral agreement may transform its legal status. Moreover, in the case of organizations such as the Green Climate Fund where it is contested whether an organization possesses international legal personality based on its constituent instrument (i.e. the Governing Instrument), a subsequent agreement can clarify its status and give effect to the provisions set forth in the constituent agreement.

However, as the various solutions discussed in the case of the OSCE show, there are other ways of conferring international personality to an organization (e.g. adoption of parallel national laws, based on a model law approved by the governing body of the organization concerned).

References

Amerasinghe CF (2005) Principles of the Institutional Law of International Organizations, 2nd edn. Cambridge University Press, Cambridge

Amerasinghe CF (2010) A Twentieth Century contribution to International Personality: the International Organization. In: Vukas B, Šošić TM (eds) International law: new actors, new concepts, continuing Dilemmas. Martinus Nijhoff, Leiden, pp 97–105

Arangio Ruiz G (1972) The normative role of the general assembly of the United Nations and the declaration of principles of friendly relations (with an appendix on the concept of International Law and the theory of International Organization). Collect Courses Hague Acad Int Law 137:419–742

Bantekas I (2009) Trust funds under International Law: trustee obligations of the United Nations and International Development Banks. T.M.C. Asser Press, The Hague

Ben-Ari RH (2013) The legal status of International Non-governmental Organizations: analysis of past and present initiatives (1912–2012). Martinus Nijhoff, Leiden

Berger C (1996) OSCE and International Law. Int J Legal Inf 24:36–47

Berthoud P (1970) The United Nations Development Programme. Framework and procedures. J World Trade Law 4:155–191

Braun TR (2014) Globalization-Driven Innovation: the investor as a partial subject in Public International Law. An inquiry into the nature and limits of investor rights. J World Invest Trade 15:73–166

Broches A (1959) International Legal Aspects of the Operations of the World Bank. Collect Courses Hague Acad Int Law 98:301–408

Brölmann C (2007) The Institutional Veil in Public International Law: International Organisations and the Law of Treaties. Hart, Oxford

Cantegreil J (2011) The Audacity of the Texaco/Calasiatic Award: René-Jean Dupuy and the Internationalization of Foreign Investment Law. Eur J Int Law 22(2):441–458

Carroz J, Probst Y (1953) Personnalité Juridique Internationale et Capacité de conclure des Traités de l' O.N.U. et des Institutions Specialisées. Foulon, R., Paris
Charnovitz S (1997) Two centuries of participation: NGOs and International Governance. Mich J Int Law 18:183–286
Coman-Kund F (2012) Assessing the role of EU agencies in the enlargement process: the case of the European Aviation Safety Agency. Croat Yearb Eur Law Policy 8:335–367
Constantinecso LJ (1977) Das Recht der Europäischen Gemeinschaften. Das Institutionelle Recht, vol 1. Nomos Verlagsgesellschaft, Baden Baden
Crawford J (2013) Chance, order, change: the course of International Law. General course on Public International Law. Collect Courses Hague Acad Int Law 365: 9–390
d'Aspremont J (2011) Introduction. Non-state actors in International Law: oscillating between concepts and dynamics. In: d'Aspremont J (ed) Participants in the International Legal System. Routledge, London, pp 1–21
Droesse G (2011) Introductory remarks and overview of publication: proliferation, fragmentation, and earmarking of concessional financing. In: Droesse G (ed) Funds for development: multilateral channels of concessional financing. Manila, Asian Development Bank, pp 1–37
Eagleton C (1950) International Organization and the law of responsibility. Collect Courses Hague Acad Int Law 76:319–425
Epping V, Brunner M (2014) Organisation für Sicherheit und Zusammenarbeit in Europa (OSZE). In: Hatje A, P-C-Müller-Graff (eds) Enzyklopädie Europarecht, vol 1. Nomos, Baden-Baden, pp 1301–1339
Felsenfeld C, Bilali G (2004) The role of the bank for international settlements in shaping the World Financial System. Univ Pa J Int Law 25:945–1045
Flynn G, Farrell H (1999) Piecing together the democratic peace: the CSCE, norms, and the 'Construction' of security in post-Cold War Europe. Int Organ 53(3):505–535
Frid R (1995) The relations between the EC and International Organizations: legal theory and practice. Kluwer Law International, The Hague
Gold J (1978) Trust funds in International Law: the contribution of the International Monetary Fund to a code of principles. Am J Int Law 72:856–866
Hafner G (2013) The emancipation of the individual from the state under International Law. Collect Courses Hague Acad Int Law 358:263–454
Higgins R (1970–1971) Aspects of the Case concerning the Barcelona Traction, Light and Power Company, Ltd. Virginia J Int Law 11:327–343
Higgins R (1991) International law and the avoidance. Containment and resolution of disputes. General course on Public International Law. Collect Courses Hague Acad Int Law 230:9–342
Jacur FR (2013) The dynamics of multilateral environmental agreements: institutional architectures and law-making processes. Editoriale Scientifica, Naples
Kelsen H (2007) General theory of law and state. The Lawbook Exchange Ltd., Clark, p 93
Klabbers J (1998) Presumptive personality: the European Union in International Law. In: Koskenniemi M (ed) International Law aspects of the European Union. Kluwer Law International, The Hague, pp 231–253
Klabbers J (2001) Institutional ambivalence by design: soft organizations in International Law. Nordic J Int Law 70:403–421
Klabbers J (2005) The concept of juridical personality. Ius Gentium 11:35–66
Klabbers J (2015) An introduction to International Organizations law, 3rd edn. Cambridge University Press, Cambridge
Kooijmans P (1996) The Code and International Law. In: De Nooy G (ed) Cooperative security, the OSCE, and its code of conduct. Kluwer Law International, Hague, p 33
Lastra RM (2012) The evolution of the European Central Bank. Fordham Int Law J 35:1260–1281
Lowe AV, Warbrick C, Cheyne I III (1990) International Tin Council (3). Int Comp Law Q 39 (4):945–952
Martha RSJ (2010) The legal foundation of INTERPOL. Hart, Portland
Michoud L (1906) La Théorie de la Personnalité Morale et son Application au Droit Français. Première Partie. Librairie Genérale de Droit & de Jurisprudence, Paris, pp 21–22

Miller AJ (2007) Privileges and Immunities of United Nations officials. Int Organ Law Rev 4 (2):169–257

Muller AS (1995) International Organizations and their host states: aspects of their legal relationship. Kluwer Law International, The Hague

Odello M (2006) The developing legal status of the organisation for security and co-operation in Europe. Anuario Español de Derecho Internacional 22:351–393

Oeter S (2002) Souveränität—ein überholtes Konzept? In Tradition und Weltoffenheit des Rechts. Festschrift für Helmut Steinberger. In: Cremer H-J, Giegerich T, Richter D, Zimmermann A (eds) Springer, Berlin, pp 259–290

OSCE Handbook (2007) The organization for security and co-operation in Europe. OSCE, Vienna.

Ott A Vos E, Coman-Kund F (2013) EU agencies and their international Mandate: a new category of global actors? Cleer Working Papers 2013/7. Centre for the Law of EE External Relations, T.M.C. Asser Instituut Inter-university Research Centre, pp 20–34

Ozone Secretariat, UNEP (2016) Handbook for the Montreal Protocol on Substances that Delete the Ozone Layer, 9th edn. Nairobi, p 436

Pachinger MM (2003) Die Völkerrechtspersönlichkeit der Europäischen Union. Peter Lang, Frankfurt.

Parlett K (2012) The individual and structural change in the International Legal System. Camb J Int Comp Law 1(3):60–80

Pauwelyn J, Wessel RA, Wouters J (2014) When structures become shackles: stagnation and dynamics in International Lawmaking. Eur J Int Law 25:733–763

Plasil-Wenger F (1971) UNIDO: The United Nations Industrial Development Organization. J World Trade Law 5:188–207

Portmann R (2010) Legal personality in International Law. Cambridge University Press, Cambridge. p. 242

Puccio L (2013) The EU and the IMF: the financial crisis as a catalyst for a stronger Union representation? In: de Waele H, Kuipers J-J (eds) The European Union's emerging international identity: views from the global Arena. Nijhoff, Leiden, pp 211–238

Ragazzi M (2011) The global environment facility: institutional and operational aspects. In: Droesse G (ed) Funds for development: multilateral channels of concessional financing. ADB, Manila, pp 485–500

Rau-Mentzen BL, Koppenfels GV (1995) UNIDO: United Nations Industrial Development Organization. In: United Nations: law, policies and practice. Verlag C.H. Beck, Munich and Martinus Nijhoff, Dordrecht, Vol. 2, 1329–1334

Reinisch A (2010) Challenging acts of International Organizations before national courts. Oxford University Press, Oxford,

Rensmann T (2009) International Organizations or Institutions, external relations and co-operation. Max Planck Encyclopedia of Public International Law. www.mpepil.com

Ruiter DW (2001) Legal institutions. Kluwer Academic Publishers, Dordrecht

Runavot M-C (2015) The Intergovernmental Organization and the Institutionalization of International Relation: the modelling of International Organization at Stake. In: Virzio R, Ingravallo I (eds) Evolutions in the Law of International Organizations. Brill. Nijhoff, Leiden, pp 17–43

Sands P, Klein P (2009) Bowett's Law of International Institution, 5th edn. Sweet and Maxwell (Thomson Reuters), London

Sandurska R, Chinkin CM (1989–1990) The collapse of the international Tin Council: a case of state responsibility? Virginia J Int Law 30:845–890

Sapiro M (1995) Changing the CSCE into the OSCE: legal aspects of a political transformation. Am J Int Law 89:631–637

Schachter O (1997) The decline of the Nation-State and its implications for International Law. Columbia J Transntl Law 36:7–23

Schermers HG, Blokker NM (eds) (2011) International Institutional Law: unity within diversity, 5th edn. Martinus Nijhoff, Boston

Schmalenbach K (2012) Article 6. Capacity of states to conclude treaties. In: Dörr O, Schmalenbach K (eds) Vienna Convention on the Law of Treaties. A commentary. Springer, Berlin, pp 105–117
Schusterschitz G (2004) European agencies as subjects of International Law. Int Organ Law Rev 1:163–188
Seidl-Hohenveldern I (1994) Failure of controls in the Sixth International Tin Agreement. In: Blokker N, Muller S (eds) Towards more effective supervision by International Organizations. Essays in Honour of H. G. Schermers, vol 1. Nijhoff, Dordrecht, pp 255–274
Seyersted F (1964) International Personality of Intergovernmental Organizations. Do their capacities really depend upon their constitutions? Indian J Int Law IV:1–74
Seyersted F (2008) Common Law of International Organizations. Martinus Nijhoff, Leiden
Shaw MN (2003) International Law, 5th edn. Cambridge University Press, Cambridge. p. 243
Silard SA (1995) The Global Environment Facility: a new development in International Law and Organization. George Wash J Int Law Econ 28:607–654
Smyth S (2005) The prototype carbon fund: a new departure in international trusts and securities law. Sustain Dev Law Policy 5:28–34 and 80–81
Smyth S (2011) A practical guide to creating a collective financing effort to save the world: the Global Environment Facility experience. In: Droesse G (ed) Funds for development: multilateral channels of concessional financing. Asian Development Bank, Manila, pp 501–548
Steinberger H (2000) Sovereignty. In: Bernhardt R (ed) Encyclopedia of Public International Law, vol 4. Elsevier, Amsterdam, pp 500–521
Streck C (2000) The network structure of the Global Environment Facility. UN Vision Project on Global Public Policy Networks, 26. http://citeseerx.ist.psu.edu/viewdoc/download?doi=10.1.1.549.2573&rep=rep1&type=pdf
Stribis I (2013) Organization for security and co-operation in Europe and European Union: a matter of status. In: Gianniou M (ed) Greek Foreign Policy: global trends and challenges, Vol I. Hellenic Centre for European Studies, Athens, pp 112–117
Szasz P (1999) The complexification of the United Nations. In: Bogandy JAV, Wolfrum R (eds) Max Planck Yearbook of United Nations law. Martinus Nijhoff, Leiden, pp 1–57. www.mpil.de/shared/data/pdf/pdfmpunyb/szasz_3.pdf
Tichy H, Köhler U (2008) Legal personality or not – the recent attempts to improve the status of the OSCE. In: Buffard I, Crawford J, Pellet A, Wittich S (eds) International Law between universalism and fragmentation. Festschrift in Honour of Gerhard Hafner. Brill | Nijhoff, pp 455–478
Tomuschat C (1999) International Law: ensuring the survival of Mankind on the Eve of the Century. General course on Public International Law. Recueil des Cours 281:9–438
Tührer D, Marro P-Y (2012) The Union's legal personality: ideas and questions lying behind the concept. In: Blanke H-J, Mangiameli S (eds) The European Union after Lisbon: constitutional basis, economic order and external action. Springer, Berlin
Vinogradoff P (1939) On the history of International Law and International Organization. Collected papers of Sir Paul Vinogradoff. In: Butler WE (ed) Law Book Exchange Edition, 2009, Clark, p 99
Walter C (2007) Subjects of International Law. In: Max Planck Encyclopedia of Public International Law
Warbrick C, Cheyne I (1987) The international Tin Council. Int Comp Law Q 36:931–935
Wessel RA (2000) Revisiting the international legal status of the EU. Eur Foreign Aff Rev 5:507–537
Wiersema A (2009) The new International Law-makers? Conferences of the parties to multilateral environmental agreements. Mich J Int Law 31(1):231–287

Chapter 7
Changing Concepts of Intergovernmental Organization and International Organization

Contents

All weblinks are updated as of 28 February 2018.

G. Droesse, *Membership in International Organizations*,
https://doi.org/10.1007/978-94-6265-327-6_7

7.1 Emergence of New Organizational Paradigms

International lawyers who have espoused the traditional concept of international organization (i.e., established by treaty, with international legal personality and members which are exclusively or predominantly states) have problems in coming to terms with emerging new paradigms of organizational structure. While a treaty remains an important, and perhaps still the most important, way of establishing new international organizations, new forms of international cooperation without treaty foundation and, in certain cases, without international legal personality, have been created. The reaction of many international lawyers to the emergence of these new paradigms of organizational structure has been to attempt associating the legal instrument establishing them, however remotely related, with a treaty, or to describe them as exceptions to the traditional concept of international organization with treaty foundation. Such attempts are questionable at best and futile for most part and completely fails in some cases. Rather than pursuing the aforementioned approach, it is necessary to recognize that new types of organizational structures have emerged which are not adequately captured by the traditional concept of international organization.

The following chapter reviews several such new organizational paradigms, and will propose revised concepts of "intergovernmental organization" and "international organization" without treaty foundation and membership requirements that are not limited to international public organizations, taking account of the development of international law.

7.1.1 Progressive Institutionalization

7.1.1.1 General Agreement on Tariffs and Trade (GATT)

The GATT is one of many examples which confirms the potential of progressive institutionalization which may imply a substantial transformation and change of legal status of an entity after the time of its establishment.

The GATT 1947 was to become part of the Havana Charter of the proposed International Trade Organization (ITO) that was negotiated during the United Nations Conference on Trade and Employment held in Cuba from 21 November 1947 to 24 March 1948. The links between the GATT and the proposed ITO have been elaborated in literature[1] and were particularly evident at the third negotiation

[1] Dam 1970, pp. 10–12.

meeting held in Geneva in 1947.[2] Unlike the Havana Charter, the GATT did not provide for a detailed institutional framework as it was designed to be applicable only until the Havana Charter entered into force. This Charter did not materialize, however, as US President Harry S. Truman declined to submit the Charter to the Senate for ratification. Neither did the plan for an Organization of Trade Cooperation "designed to pick up the ITO institutional pieces"[3] succeed. Hence, the GATT 1947 continued to be applied on the basis of the Protocol of Provisional Application.

> As the GATT was not conceived as an international organization, the Agreement foresaw only the assembly of the contracting parties, acting jointly—designated by uppercase letters (Article XXV:1) in contrast to the sum of the individual contracting states (contracting parties), designated by lowercase letters—as a rule making organ. The other institutions of the GATT 1947 [including the Council of Representatives] owe their existence and scope of competences to an act of delegation by the contracting parties.[4]

One very interesting aspect concerns the relations between the GATT and the UN. To provide the necessary support to the GATT, the contracting parties decided at their second session that the secretariat of the Interim Commission for the International Trade Organization (ICITO) "would be employed on a reimbursable basis to serve as secretariat to the Contracting Parties."[5] Thus, the Executive Secretary of ICITO served as the Executive Secretary (Director General as of 1965) of the Contracting Parties. This arrangement was confirmed in an exchange of letters between the then Executive Secretary of GATT and the then UN Secretary-General in August 1952. While the GATT Secretariat initially was "minuscule", it subsequently was characterized by "dramatic growth".[6]

Despite "the lack of an institutional framework, despite lack of financial support except of the most meager sort, and despite powerful forces for trade protection which killed the [ITO] and tried to kill GATT, GATT survived"[7] and developed into a successful organization on the basis of the work of its Secretariat and institutional amendments. The extent to which the GATT transformed itself from its humble beginning to an organizational setting with an institutional framework and hundreds of staff members shows that a cooperative effort among nations cannot be properly defined just by the legal act instituting that effort. In view of this progressive institutionalization of the GATT, the Repertory of Practice of the United

---

[2] As indicated by Jackson: "This conference had a dual function. On the one hand, the Committee continued its drafting of an ITO Charter, preparing for the Havana Conference. On the other hand, twenty-two nations undertook negotiations with a view to reducing tariffs and embodied the results of these negotiations in the General Agreement on Tariffs and Trade." Jackson 1967, pp. 135–136.

[3] Dam 1970, p. 337.

[4] von Bogdandy 2001, p. 626.

[5] GATT. 1976. Ad Hoc Committee on Restructuring of the Economic and Social Sectors of the United Nations System. Addendum (L/4306/Add.1, 14 April 1976), 3.

[6] Dam 1970, pp. 340–341.

[7] Jackson 1967, p. 132.

Nations Organs characterizes it as "a United Nations Specialized Agency on a *de facto* basis."[8]

There is no reference to membership in the GATT, even though this term was regularly used on an informal basis. Nevertheless, the question of accession to the GATT was a core policy issue due to the fact that "an entrant to the GATT automatically becomes the beneficiary of a large number of tariff concessions through the operation of Article II:1. In order to assure that the new contracting party gives something of value for these benefits, the institution of 'entrance fee' negotiations has arisen,"[9] which may however, be dispensed with in certain cases.

Jackson has summarized the relevant provisions as follows:

> There are basically four ways to become a 'contracting party' (loosely referred to as a 'member') of GATT. Three involve accession by a government: by the Protocol of Provisional Application, subsequent protocol and agreement under Article XXXIII[10] of GATT, and by directly accepting the GATT itself under Article XXVI:2[11] (only one nation has accepted the GATT in this manner and then only after acceding to GATT through a protocol). These methods of accession are preceded by tariff negotiations, the 'ticket of admission' and often these negotiations extend for several years, during which time, by special Declaration (protocol) the applicant government is given 'provisional accession to GATT,' or relations with GATT are established by other special arrangements.[12]

The "fourth 'route'" referred to by Jackson[13] relates to Article XXVI:5 of the GATT which provides as follows:

> If any of the customs territories, in respect of which a contracting party has accepted this Agreement, possesses or acquires full autonomy in the conduct of its external commercial relations and of the other matters provided for in this Agreement, such territory shall, upon sponsorship through a declaration by the responsible contracting party establishing the above-mentioned fact, be deemed to be a contracting party.[14]

---

[8] Repertory of Practice of UN Organs. Extracts relating to Article 57 of the Charter of the United Nations. Supplement No. 8 (1989–1994), para 10, http://legal.un.org/docs/?path=../repertory/art57/english/rep_supp8_vol4_art57.pdf&lang=E.

[9] Dam 1970, p. 345.

[10] Article XXXIII of the GATT provides: "A government not party to this Agreement, or a government acting on behalf of a separate customs territory possessing full autonomy in the conduct of its external commercial relations and of the other matters provided for in this Agreement, may accede to this Agreement, on its own behalf or on behalf of that territory, on terms to be agreed between such government and the Contracting Parties. Decisions of the Contracting Parties under this paragraph shall be taken by a two thirds majority."

[11] Article XXVI, para 2 of the GATT provides: "This Agreement shall be open for acceptance by any contracting party which, on 1 March 1955, was a contracting party or was negotiating with a view to accession to this Agreement."

[12] Jackson 1967, pp. 143–144.

[13] Jackson 1967, pp. 143–144.

[14] See in this context, the explanations given by Dam, who clarifies that contracting party status is not automatic and that "a system of de facto application" of the GATT has been established. Dam 1970, p. 348.

7.1.1.2 Other Examples of Progressive Institutionalization

Other examples of the potential of progressive institutionalization which may change the legal status of an organization are the INTERPOL and IPU which are now widely recognized as an intergovernmental and international organization, respectively, as well as the OSCE and the International Rice Research Institute (IRRI) (see below).

An interesting indication of the potential of progressive institutionalization may also be seen in recent developments regarding cooperative undertakings of national regulators. The economic importance of international regulatory schemes such as the Basel Commission on Banking Supervision (BCBS),[15] the International Organization of Securities Commissions (IOSCO), the International Association of Insurance Supervisors (IAIS), and other similar cooperative undertakings, which involve multi-billion dollar amounts and some of the most powerful national institutions (such as central banks), is reversely proportionate to the attention which international lawyers have given to those schemes.

The potential of progressive institutionalization and legal transformation of such forms of cooperation is highlighted, in particular, by the evolution of the Financial Stability Board (FSB), which previously did not have legal personality, but has been converted into an association incorporated under Swiss law, with the potential of further transformation.[16]

The very creation of the Financial Stability Forum (FSF), the predecessor the FSB, "with representatives from all of the Basel-based regulatory groupings, IOSCO, the IMF and the World Bank, along with 21 representatives of the G7, could be seen in part, then, as the logical outcome of this process of institutionalization of the regime for international financial regulation."[17] The FSF "was called into life in 1999 after the collapse of an American hedge fund, Long Term Capital Management (LTCM), which threatened to unleash a chain reaction of financial collapses in the United States and then Europe."[18] The G7 Finance Ministers and Central Bank Governors founded the FSF in same year as the G20, on the recommendation of the President of the German Bundesbank, to bring together national authorities responsible for financial stability, sector-specific

---

[15] In the case of the Basel Commission, the concern of members to avoid any formal status and legally binding force of decisions is paramount, as may be seen from Section 3 of the Charter of the BCBS, which provides:

"The BCBS does not possess any formal supranational authority. Its decisions do not have legal force." Basel Committee Charter. https://www.bis.org/bcbs/charter.htm. Nevertheless, despite its insistence on informality, the Basel Committee has designed methods intended to compel its members to apply the regulations it promulgates to their banks upon their return from committee meetings.

Zaring 1998, p. 290.

[16] See Financial Stability Board. "About the FSB. Our History". http://www.financialstabilityboard.org/about/history/. On the Financial Stability Forum, see also Porter 2000; Liberi 2014, pp. 549–575; and Donnelly 2012, pp. 261–275. https://ris.utwente.nl/ws/portalfiles/portal/5583898.

[17] See Porter.

[18] Donnelly 2012, p. 262.

international groupings of regulators and supervisors engaged in developing standards and codes of good practice as well as international financial institutions and committees of central bank experts. "The strong and overt political guidance exercised by the G7 over the FSF was a marked change from the earlier heavily technical governance of the regime."[19]

At Pittsburgh, the Heads of State and Government decided to establish the FSB "to include major emerging economies and welcome its efforts to coordinate and monitor progress in strengthening financial regulation."[20] The FSB was conceived as a "stronger institution than its predecessor [….] with the capacity not just to compile international standards but actively to promote higher quality and effectiveness for financial market activity as a whole."[21] Such expanded mandate given to the FSB was notably reflected in Article 2 of the FSB Charter (2009). As highlighted by Donnelly, there were a number of other differences as to how the FSF and FSB were structured, involving "membership, both in terms of countries and the type of representatives they send, as well as differences in their internal structures, the means by which they interact with national authorities, and the way they interact with a variety of international bodies, including the G20, international standard-setting bodies (ISSBs), and international financial institutions: the IMF and the World Bank."[22] Moreover, the FSB "Board is more institutionally developed than its predecessor" and the institutional changes that were made in establishing the FSB "reflect and support a higher degree of political commitment within the G20."[23]

Under its Charter of 2009, the FSB had a well-established institutional framework similar to that of a traditional international organization comprising a Plenary, a Steering Committee, a Chairperson and the Secretariat (Articles 6–15). The Plenary, the "decision-making body of the FSB,"[24] was mandated by Article 7(2) of the original 2009 Charter to take "decisions by consensus." In this context, the practices were adopted by the FSB under which:

> the Chair makes clear on what issue a decision is being sought, and then asks for the views of members. If there is no immediate convergence of views, the different points of view are discussed and attempts are made to reconcile competing or conflicting views. In practice, a consensus, in the sense of general agreement, is reached when there is no sustained opposition to the Chair's proposal for decision.[25]

Annex A of the 2009 original Charter listed the IMF as a member together with the Bank for International Settlements (BIS), OECD and World Bank with the

---

[19] See Porter.

[20] See G20 Information Centre. The G20 Pittsburgh Summit Commitments. http://www.g20.utoronto.ca/analysis/commitments-09-pittsburgh.html.

[21] Donnelly 2012, p. 261.

[22] Ibid.

[23] Ibid.

[24] FSB Charter, Article 7(1).

[25] IMF. 2013. "IMF Membership in the Financial Stability Board", 5. https://www.imf.org/external/np/pp/eng/2013/022213.pdf.

proviso that "The acceptance of membership by the international financial institutions in the FSB is subject to the approval of their respective governing bodies."[26] Nevertheless, Article 16 of the Charter provided: "This Charter is not intended to create any legal rights or obligations." Thus, the IMF paper regarding "IMF Membership in the Financial Stability Board" stressed that

> the FSB itself is not a legal entity, has no capacity to enter into agreements, and has no privileges or immunities. Moreover, the Charter is a political rather than a legal document, and is explicit in its non-binding legal effect.[27]

However, the same document stressed that the "regulatory impact of 'soft law' should not be underestimated" as by "means of its adoption into the domestic framework, 'soft law' becomes 'hard law' and acquires the same effect as traditional instruments of regulation."[28]

The G20 summit in Cannes in 2011 agreed "to strengthen FSB's capacity, resources and governance," "through the establishment of the FSB on an enduring organizational footing", by giving the FSB "institutional standing, with legal personality and greater financial autonomy, while preserving the existing and well-functioning strong links with the BIS."[29]

---

[26] Financial Stability Board Charter. 2009. Annex A, Footnote 1. http://www.fsb.org/wp-content/uploads/r_090925d.pdf?page_moved=1.

[27] IMF. 2010. "IMF Membership in the Financial Stability Board", para 4. https://www.imf.org/external/np/pp/eng/2010/081010.pdf.

[28] Ibid., para 15.

[29] The Cannes Summit Final Declaration—Building Our Common Future: Renewed Collective Action for the Benefit of All (http://www.g20.utoronto.ca/2011/2011-cannes-declaration-111104-en.html), contained in paras 37–39 under the heading "Strengthening the FSB capacity resources and governance" the following statements:

"37. The FSB has played a key role in promoting development and implementation of regulation of the financial sector.

38. To keep pace with this growing role, we agreed to strengthen FSB's capacity, resources and governance, building on its Chair's proposals. These include:

- the establishment of the FSB on an enduring organizational footing: we have given the FSB a strong political mandate and need to give it a corresponding institutional standing, with legal personality and greater financial autonomy, while preserving the existing and well-functioning strong links with the BIS;
- the reconstitution of the steering committee: as we move into a phase of policy development and implementation that in many cases will require significant legislative changes, we agree that the upcoming changes to the FSB steering committee should include the executive branch of governments of the G20 Chair and the larger financial systems as well as the geographic regions and financial centers not currently represented, in a balanced manner consistent with the FSB Charter;
- the strengthening of its coordination role vis-à-vis other standard setting bodies (SSB) on policy development and implementation monitoring, avoiding any functional overlaps and recognizing the independence of the SSBs.

39. We call for first steps to be implemented by the end of this year and will review the implementation of the reform at our next Summit."

On the proposal of a High-Level Working Group on FSB Capacity, Resources, and Governance, the following recommendation were adopted by the FSB and subsequently endorsed by the G20 leaders at the Los Cabos Summit in June 2012:

> Sound Permanent Institutional Footing
>
> 11. The FSB considers a treaty-based inter-governmental organisation not to be an appropriate legal form at this juncture.
> 12. For vesting the FSB with a legal personality, creating an association under Swiss law would be an appropriate option. Appropriate Articles of Association should be formulated for this purpose, the draft of which is under review that will recognise that policy making activities will continue to be governed by the Charter.
>
> Options for Conferring Immunities and Privileges on the Legal-Form FSB
>
> 13. The FSB should adopt a gradual approach towards its institutionalisation and, at this stage obtain the needed immunities by operating as an association under the BIS Headquarters Agreement. However, the FSB should evaluate towards the end of a period of five years, in light of experience and needs at that time, whether to vest the FSB with specific immunities and privileges by negotiating a separate HQA with Swiss authorities or go beyond this.[30]

Under Article 1 of its Articles of Association of 28 January 2013,[31] the FSB was established pursuant to Article 60 of the Swiss Civil Code. "Accordingly, FSB activities will be governed by two separate documents that will co-exist: (i) the FSB Articles that are subject to Swiss law, and (ii) the FSB Charter that remains a non-legally binding document."[32] While the IMF until then had never been become a member of a "domestically-incorporated legal entity", it sought approval of its Executive Board for becoming a member of the restructured FSB, as the "activities in which the Fund engages as a member of the FSB are consistent with the Fund's purposes, and support all of the Fund's functions [….]."[33]

The Articles of Association adopted at the FSB Plenary Meeting held on 28 January 2013 in Zurich specify in Article 3 that the "following are eligible to be a Member of the Association:

> a. authorities from jurisdictions that are responsible for maintaining financial stability, such as ministries of finance, central banks, supervisory and regulatory authorities;
> b. international financial institutions; and
> c. international standard setting, regulatory, supervisory and central bank bodies."

---

30 Financial Stability Board. 2012. "Report to the G20 Los Cabos Summit on Strengthening FSB Capacity, Resources and Governance". http://www.fsb.org/wp-content/uploads/r_120619c.pdf.

31 Articles of Association of the Financial Stability Board (FSB). 28 Jan. 2013. http://www.fsb.org/wp-content/uploads/FSB-Articles-of-Association.pdf.

32 IMF. 2013. "IMF Membership in the Financial Stability Board", para 17. https://www.imf.org/external/np/pp/eng/2013/022213.pdf.

33 Ibid., para 21.

The history of the FSB recounted above shows that it is not possible or appropriate to exclude organizations from the realm of international organization for the sole reason that they count among their members sub-state actors and national regulators. It will only be a question of time until the FSB will gain a status similar to that currently applicable to the Global Fund and Gavi Alliance, if it will not convert to an organization with treaty foundation.

While the FSB may be seen as a forerunner of progressive institutionalization of cooperative undertaking of national regulators, there are other cooperative frameworks of national regulators that follow suit.

The International Organization of Securities Commissions (IOSCO), which is "now the pre-eminent international organization for securities commissions and one of the most important forums for international cooperation among capital market regulators,"[34] increasingly resembles a traditional international organization. It "was incorporated by a private bill of the Quebec National Assembly"[35] and has an elaborate membership structure.

Membership in IOSCO in regulated in detail in the By-Laws of IOSCO, which were revised in 1996 by a decision of the President's Committee.[36] It consists of ordinary members (which may comprise a national securities commission or a similar governmental body with significant authority over securities or derivatives markets, or if there is no such national authority, provincial authorities with authority over securities or derivatives markets),[37] associate members (supranational governmental regulators, subnational governmental regulators, intergovernmental international organizations and other international standard-setting bodies, and other governmental bodies and national regulators)[38] and affiliate members (self-regulatory organizations, securities exchanges, financial market infrastructures, international bodies other than governmental organizations with an appropriate interest in securities regulation, investor protection funds and compensation funds, any other body with an appropriate interest in securities regulation).[39] Membership is a prerequisite for representation in the governing bodies of IOSCO, i.e., the President's Committee in which all ordinary members are represented, and the IOSCO Board and Board committees.[40]

[34] IOSCO. Reformed By-Laws. Explanatory Memorandum. https://www.iosco.org/library/by_laws/pdf/IOSCO-By-Laws-Section-2-English.pdf.

[35] Zaring 1998, p. 292 and Footnote 77, with further references.

[36] IOSCO. Reformed By-Laws. Explanatory Memorandum, 1. https://www.iosco.org/library/by_laws/pdf/IOSCO-By-Laws-Section-2-English.pdf.

[37] IOSCO By-Laws, Part 2, Sections 6 and 7.1, https://www.iosco.org/library/by_laws/pdf/IOSCO-By-Laws-Section-1-English.pdf.

[38] IOSCO By-Laws, Part 2, Sections 8.1 and 8.2.

[39] IOSCO By-Laws, Part 2.

[40] See IOSCO By-Laws, Parts 4 and 5.

The International Association of Insurance Supervisors (IAIS) was established pursuant to Article 60[41] of the Swiss Civil Code as a Swiss non-profit organization; it possesses legal personality and legal capacity in Switzerland. Article 6 of the By-Laws specifies the entities eligible for membership.

These two regulatory schemes so far do not have the same status as the Global Fund or the Gavi Alliance, both of which have concluded headquarters agreements with Switzerland. Also, neither IOSCO nor IAIS were given a similar status to the International Air Transport Association (IATA), which enjoys limited fiscal privileges in Switzerland. However, there is a potential that with further institutionalization they may become full-fledged dual and hybrid organizations, established under national law but with privileges and immunities in their host country and other countries.

7.1.2 Established by Resolution of a Conference

The Pan American Institute for Geography and History (PAIGH) and the Organization of the Petroleum Exporting Countries (OPEC) are examples of international organizations that were not established by treaty.

PAIGH was established on 7 February 1928 by the Sixth American Conference held in Havana, Cuba that resolved to create the Institute.[42] The Organic Statutes of the PAIGH were approved in 1969, and subsequently amended, by the General Assembly of the PAIGH, which is the "supreme organ of the PAIGH".[43]

Similarly, OPEC was not established by a treaty, but was "created as a permanent intergovernmental organization in conformity with the Resolutions of the Conference of the Representatives of the Governments of Iran, Iraq, Kuwait, Saudi Arabia and Venezuela, held in Baghdad from September 10 to 14, 1960."[44] The Statute of OPEC recalls in Article 1 such creation.[45] The OPEC Statutes contain provisions on the objectives of the Organization, (full and associate) membership, organs, governance structures and voting rights, financial provisions and stipulations on other related matters; their substance is comparable with the content of constitutions of traditional treaty-based organizations.

[41] See Article 3 of the IAIS By-Laws. http://www.iaisweb.org/page/about-the-iais/by-laws#.

[42] "The Resolution by means of which the PAIGH is Created" "Organic Statutes. Rules of Procedure and Agreements 2009–2013", 129–136. For the historic background of PAIGH, see Ibid., 119–127. See also OAS. Our History. http://www.oas.org/en/about/our_history.asp.

[43] Ibid., 14.

[44] See OPEC. Brief History. http://www.opec.org/opec_web/en/about_us/24.htm.

[45] OPEC Statute. 2012. http://www.opec.org/opec_web/static_files_project/media/downloads/publications/OPEC_Statute.pdf.

Other organizations that fall under this category include, per Schermers and Blokker, the Asian-African Consultative Committee, the Inter-American Defense Board, and the International Wool Study Group.[46]

7.1.3 Adoption of Constitution by a Plenary Body

An entity may be established, or be transformed into an international organization based on the adoption of a constitution by a governing body (generally, a plenary body).

The INTERPOL and IPU are important examples of organizations without treaty foundation that are recognized as an intergovernmental organization and an international organization, respectively. As discussed in detail above, their constitutions were adopted by their plenary bodies. Moreover, as highlighted by Kissling, IPU was not the only organization of Parliamentary cooperation which was established in this manner. While there are some organizations established by a treaty:

> Mostly, however, the institution is established by a simple decision of parliaments or an international parliamentary treaty. Examples for this are the Euro-Latin American Parliamentary Assembly (EuroLat), the Forum of the Presidents of the Legislative Powers of Central America (FOPREL), and the South Caucasus Parliamentary Initiative (SCPI).[47]

7.1.4 Established Based on National Law

The Nordic Council was established "by parallel but originally not identical decisions of the Parliaments of the member states—without any common document and without approval in all countries by the Head of State or government who is the organ competent to conclude international agreements—and the fact that these decisions (i.e. the original Statute of the Nordic Council) specifically avoided provisions which would involve an obligation to participate in the Council."[48] Hence, the Statutes of the Nordic Council providing the details on its functioning were drawn up in the different languages of its members with "nothing to guarantee that the different texts of the Charter will have exactly identical contents." Effectively, the original texts were characterized "by slight departures from each other."[49] Notwithstanding the above, Schermers and Blokker state that in cases like

---

[46] Schermers and Blokker 2011, §34.

[47] Kissling 2011, p. 17.

[48] Seyersted 2008, pp. 46–47.

[49] Petrén 1959, p. 347.

the Nordic Council "there is also an agreement between states", but they concede that "it may be more difficult to prove its existence" and that the "borderline may be vague."[50] In fact, there is very little evidence, if any, to support the above conclusion.

IRRI represents another very interesting case of progressive institutionalization. It was initially established as a non-governmental organization and subsequently transformed in an international organization possessing international juridical personality,[51] not only in its host country but also in other countries.

The Rockefeller and Ford Foundations were instrumental for the establishment of IRRI for which they provided the main initial funding.[52] When approving the "proposal to establish an international rice research institute in the Philippines with the cooperation of the Ford and Rockefeller Foundations," the Philippine "Cabinet also authorized the granting of a free import franchise" enabling "the Institute when chartered, to import into the Philippines, on an automatic tax and duty-free basis, all equipment and supplies required for the establishment and operation of the Institute's program[….]" and "exemption from taxation of the salaries and stipends paid to Institute employees in dollars."[53]

As agreed upon in the MOU, IRRI was incorporated in 1960 under the laws of the Philippines by the Securities and Exchange Commission[54] "as an autonomous, nonstock, philanthropic, nonprofit corporation."[55] Article 2 of the Articles of Incorporation provides that:

> The organization shall be established and its purposes and objectives implemented principally through the support of the Ford and Rockefeller Foundations of the United States of America in cooperation with the Government of the Philippines [….].[56]

---

50 Schermers and Blokker 2011, §35.

51 See Chandler 1992; "International Rice Research Institute. Legal Status of the International Rice Research Institute". (undated) https://cgspace.cgiar.org/bitstream/handle/10947/205/irri013.pdf?sequence=1&isAllowed=y; Hargrove and Coffman 2006; and IRRI. About us. Our history. http://irri.org/about-us/our-history.

52 The Memorandum of Understanding between the Rockefeller and Ford Foundations regarding the establishment of IRRI (hereinafter, "IRRI MOU") is reproduced in Chandler, Annex 2, 196–199.

53 IRRI MOU. The tax exemption of IRRI was implemented by Republic Act No. 2707, "An Act to Exempt the International Rice Research Institute or its Successors from the Payment of Gift, Franchise, Specific, Percentage, Real Property, Exchange, Import, Export, and All Other Taxes, and the Members of Its Scientific and Technical Staff from the Payment of Income Tax". The said Act is reproduced in Chandler, Appendix 5, 206.

54 Certificate of Incorporation for the International Rice Research Institute, 8 March 1960. https://cgspace.cgiar.org/bitstream/handle/10947/233/irri002.pdf?sequence=1&isAllowed=y.

55 IRRI Articles of Incorporation, Article 1, para 1. Reproduced in Chandler, Annex 4, 200–202.

56 IRRI Articles of Incorporation, Article 2.

There was subsequent progressive institutionalization of IRRI, based on the Presidential Decree No. 1620[57] (1979) which granted IRRI the Status, Prerogatives, Privileges and Immunities of an International Organization.

The preamble of the Presidential Decree provided:

> WHEREAS, the International Rice Research Institute, by virtue of the objectives and incidental powers assigned and granted to it as set forth above, was clearly intended to be an international organization, **yet its ability to operate as such in the Philippines is greatly hampered by the fact that it was organized and registered with the Securities and Exchange Commission as a private corporation and, therefore, is subject to all laws and regulations covering private corporations, which is in conflict with its international status, and which is not conducive to the free operation of the Institute's routine activities and its efforts towards the attainment of its objectives.** (emphasis added)

Article 1 of the said decree recognized IRRI "as an international organization" and accorded "it such status in the Philippines." The following articles conferred to IRRI privileges and immunities, including immunity from legal process and other privileges and immunities (regarding archives, communications, exemption from taxation and customs, free disposal of funds and freedom of entry and sojourn) equivalent to those enjoyed by other international organizations.

Presidential Decree 1620 is important as it converted IRRI from a private corporation subject "to all the laws and regulations covering private corporations" to an international organization" and exempted IRRI from the application of the laws of the Philippines. It shows that an international organization can, as a matter of principle, be established based on a legal act of a single country that recognizes its (international) legal personality and confers to it privileges and immunities.

The Agreement Recognizing the International Legal Personality of the International Rice Research Institute signed in 1995 by the government of 12 countries[58] marked a further step of the institutionalization of IRRI. Paragraph 1 of Article I of the Agreement recognized the "status of the Institute as an international organization" and its "juridical personality" and para 2 stipulated that "the Institute may cooperate and/or conclude agreements or arrangements with governments and/or organizations."[59]

[57] See Presidential Decree No. 1620 of 19 April 1979 granting to IRRI the Status, Prerogatives, Privileges and Immunities of an International Organization. http://www.lawphil.net/statutes/presdecs/pd1979/pd_1620_1979.html.

[58] Agreement Recognizing the International Legal Personality of the International Rice Research Institute (IRRI), 19 May 1995. https://cgspace.cgiar.org/bitstream/handle/10947/147/irri_legalpersonality.pdf?sequence=1&isAllowed=y.

[59] As highlighted in the IRRI Agreement, Article III, para 1, while the Agreement was meant to bestow "international status upon the Institute" it was not meant to "bind any Party to automatically grant to the Institute privileges and immunities", nor did it entail, as stated in para 2 of the said Article, any obligation "to provide any form of financial contribution or support."

7.1.5 Establishment by Conference or Meeting of the Parties to a Convention

It is an important new development that an organization with international legal personality can be established by a resolution or decision taken by the Parties or the Conference of the Parties to a multilateral Convention. The Multilateral Fund for the Implementation of the Montreal Protocol (Multilateral Fund), the Preparatory Commission for the Comprehensive Nuclear-Test-Ban Treaty Organization (CTBTO) and the Green Climate Fund (GCF) epitomize such development.

7.1.5.1 Multilateral Fund for the Implementation of the Montreal Protocol

The Multilateral Fund shows that an entity established by a meeting or the conference of the parties to a multilateral environmental convention can indeed enjoy international legal personality.

The Multilateral Fund, being provided for by Article 10 of the Montreal Protocol,[60] advanced the discussion on this matter. While the said Article 10 did not provide for the legal nature of the financial mechanism to be established which was to include a Multilateral Fund, such legal status was clarified by Decision VI/16[61]

---

[60] Reference to the Multilateral Fund was included in the London Amendment to the Montreal Protocol of 1990. The new Article 10 introduced by that amendment reads:

1. The Parties shall establish a mechanism for the purposes of providing financial and technical co-operation [….].
2. **The mechanism established under paragraph 1 shall include a Multilateral Fund.** It may also include other means of multilateral, regional and bilateral co-operation [….]. https://treaties.un.org/doc/Treaties/1992/08/19920810%2003-51%20AM/Ch_XXVII_02_bp.pdf.

[61] "The Sixth Meeting of the Parties decided in Dec. VI/16, recalling decision IV/18 of the Fourth Meeting of the Parties, which established the Financial Mechanism, including the Multilateral Fund for the Implementation of the Montreal Protocol, provided for in Article 10 of the Montreal Protocol, as amended in London on 29 June 1990, to clarify the nature and legal status of the Fund as a body under international law as follows:

a. Juridical personality: The Multilateral Fund shall enjoy such legal capacity as is necessary for the exercise of its functions and the protection of its interests, in particular the capacity to enter into contracts, to acquire and dispose of movable and immovable property and to institute legal proceedings in defence of its interests;
b. Privileges and immunities:

   i. The Fund shall, in accordance with arrangements to be determined with the Government of Canada, enjoy in the territory of the host country, such privileges and immunities as are necessary for the fulfilment of its purposes;

titled "Juridical Personality, Privileges and Immunities of the Multilateral Fund" which set out in "detail the legal nature of that Fund." Moreover, Canada concluded a Headquarters Agreement with the Multilateral Fund which expressly recognized its juridical personality[62] prior to concluding an agreement with the United Nations on November 1998 regarding the privileges and immunities of the Multilateral Fund.[63] Hence, it is possible to maintain that the Multilateral Fund was endowed with international legal personality.

7.1.5.2 Preparatory Commission of the Nuclear Test-Ban Treaty Organization

Article II of the Comprehensive Nuclear-Test-Ban Treaty (CTBT)[64] provides for the establishment of a Comprehensive Nuclear-Test-Ban Treaty Organization "to achieve the object and purpose of this Treaty, to ensure the implementation of its provisions, including those for international verification of compliance with it, and to provide a forum for consultation and cooperation among States." Even though the Treaty has been signed by 183 and has been ratified by 164 states, it is still not effective as the signature and ratification of several specific nuclear technology holder countries are missing. Therefore, and to ensure the rapid and effective establishment of the future Comprehensive Nuclear-Test-Ban Treaty, the Preparatory Commission for CTBTO has been created, which is an international organization in its own right. The CTBTO Preparatory Commission was created on by a resolution adopted on 19 November 1996 by the states signatories to the CTBT.[65] Paragraph 7 of that Resolution provides:

---

ii. The officials of the Fund Secretariat shall similarly enjoy such privileges and immunities as are necessary for the independent exercise of their functions in connection with the Multilateral Fund (UNEP 2018)."

UNEP, 2018. Handbook for the Montreal Protocol on Substances that Deplete the Ozone Layer, 12th edition, 555. http://ozone.unep.org/sites/default/files/MP_handbook-english-2018.pdf.

[62] Agreement between the Government of Canada and the Multilateral Fund for the Implementation of the 1987 Montreal Protocol regulating matters resulting from the establishment in Canada of the Multilateral Fund and its Organs. 23 Nov. 1988. http://www.multilateralfund.org/Our%20Work/webhelp/index.html#!anneIAgreBetwTheGoveOfCanaAndThe.

[63] Agreement between the United Nations and the Government of Canada concerning the Privileges, Immunities and Other Facilities of United Nations Officials servicing the Secretariat of the Multilateral Fund for the Implementation of the 1987 Montreal Protocol on Substances that Deplete the Ozone Layer. Cairo, 23 Nov. 1998. In the *United Nations Treaty Series*, Vol. 2042, Vol. 3, 3–11. https://treaties.un.org/doc/Publication/UNTS/Volume%202042/v2042.pdf.

[64] Comprehensive Nuclear-Test-Ban Treaty. https://www.ctbto.org/fileadmin/content/treaty/treaty_text.pdf.

[65] Resolution establishing the Preparatory Commission for the Comprehensive Nuclear-Test-Ban Treaty Organization, adopted on 19 Nov. 1996 (CTBT/MSS/RES. 1), https://www.ctbto.org/fileadmin/user_upload/legal/CTBT-MSS-RES-1-e_01.pdf.

> The Commission shall have the standing of an international organization, authority to enter into agreements, and such other legal capacity as necessary for the exercise of its functions and the fulfillment of its purposes.

The Preparatory Commission has entered into a headquarters agreement with Austria[66] and in various other agreements with states and international organizations. Hence, its ability to act the international plane is clearly established.

7.1.5.3 Green Climate Fund

When the UNFCCC was negotiated, the issues regarding the financial mechanism were among the most controversial ones.

> The basic question was whether the FCCC should establish a new institution, a—so-called, 'climate' or 'green fund'—or channel financial assistance through the GEF, which was established in 1991 by the World Bank, United Nations Development Programme and the United Nations Environment Programme (UNEP). [….]
>
> In the end, developed and developing countries agreed on a compromise solution that neither established a new institution nor exclusively designated the GEF as the convention's financial mechanism. Instead, the convention simply defines governance (Article 11), and then entrusts the operation of the financial mechanism on an interim basis to the GEF. This compromise left open the possibility of creating a new institution, which the parties finally did almost twenty years later at the COP16 in Cancun, when they established the GCF as a separate operating entity of the FCCC's financial mechanism.[67]

However, unlike the case of the Montreal Protocol, no amendment to the UNFCCC was approved by the parties to the Convention to expressly allow for the establishment of the GCF. The Fund is governed by COP Decisions 1/CP.16[68] and 3/CP.17,[69] by the Governing Instrument attached to and approved by Decision 3/CP.17 and by the policies, rules and procedures approved by the Board of the Fund. The aforementioned COP Decisions were taken by consensus pursuant to the powers entrusted to the COP under Article 7 UNFCCC, in particular, those set forth in para 2 of the said Article.

Defining the relationship between the COP and GCF was a crucial topic when the Governing Instrument for the Green Climate Fund was developed.

---

[66] Agreement Between the Preparatory Commission For The Comprehensive Nuclear-Test-Ban Treaty Organization and the Republic of Austria Regarding the Seat of the Commission. https://www.org/fileadmin/content/reference/legal_resources/host_country_agreement_e.pdf.

[67] Bodansky et al. 2017, pp. 145–146.

[68] Decision 1/CP.17. The Cancun Agreements: Outcome of the work of the AdHoc Working Group on Long-term Cooperative Action under the Convention. Paragraphs 100–111. https://unfccc.int/resource/docs/2010/cop16/eng/07a01.pdf.

[69] Green Climate Fund. Decision 3/CP.17. Launching the Green Climate Fund. http://intlmgt.cipa.cornell.edu/sessions/climate/Governing%20Instrument%20of%20the%20Green%20Climate%20Fund.pdf.

> It was discussed at Cancún 'whether the Fund should be accountable to and under the guidance or whether it should also be under the authority of the COP.' This distinction is important as it relates to the question of whether the COP has the power to select the members of the executive board and approve general rules and guidelines. The majority of developed countries argued at Cancún that the relationship between the future executive board of the Fund and the COP should be modeled on the COP's relationship with the Global Environment Facility (GEF), which is one in which the GEF is 'accountable to and under the guidance of the COP.[70]

Thus, provision was made in Decision 3/CP.17 and the Governing Instrument of the Fund to the effect that the Fund "will be designated as an operating entity of the financial mechanism under Article 11 of the Convention and will be accountable to and function under the guidance of the Conference of the Parties (COP)."

While there is an inherent tension between that provision and Article 5 of the Governing Instrument which provides that the "Fund will be governed and supervised by a Board that will have full responsibility for funding decisions," the GCF enjoys autonomy and institutional independence and the ability to act on the international plane and can be classified for that reason as an international organization.

7.1.6 Dual and Hybrid Organizations Incorporated Under National Law

The establishment of dual or hybrid organizations has now become a well-established feature of the international organization architecture and they deserve to be recognized as a special category of international organizations. They are not just a transitional phase of the progressive institutionalization of an entity eventually leading to the establishment of a traditional treaty-based organization. While this may be the case in certain instances, such as ASEAN+3 Macroeconomic Research Office (AMRO) which was created as a corporation before its conversion into a traditional treaty-based organization, the dual or hybrid organization model has its own rationale and merits.

First, said model is increasingly being used for the very reason that traditional treaty-based paradigms for the establishment of international organizations do not allow for a quick response to emerging new needs.

Second, dual and hybrid organizations can adapt more easily to changing circumstances than traditional treaty-based organizations where qualified majorities combined with ratification requirements for amendment to the constituent agreement, constitute formidable obstacles to institutional reform.

Third, they have greater flexibility in involving stakeholders other than states in their governing structures.

---

70 See Droesse 2011, pp. 31–32.

Fourth, they frequently involve partnerships between the public and private sectors.

As indicated by Hatje, the public-private partnership (PPP) is not a legal concept but a heuristic category that aims to bundle a relatively diffuse variety of technical phenomena.[71]

Generally, PPPs are predicated on a contractual relationship between a government, international organization or other entity and a private-sector entity and involve mechanisms of external cooperation and collaboration. What makes organizations such as the Global Fund so interesting is that they are institutionalized forms of public-private sector cooperation with a multi-actor governance structure giving a voice not only to governments, but also to the private sector, civil society and a variety of other stakeholders. It is one of the themes of this book and is extensively argued that a new class of dual and hybrid international organizations has emerged, incorporated as a non-governmental organization or corporation under municipal law but with privileges and immunities under international law.

The governance structure of a dual or hybrid organization may be predicated on a treaty (as in the case of the BIS) or an agreement between central banks, or ministries of finance (as in the case of AMRO, prior to its conversion in an international organization with treaty foundation), but it can also be entirely based on the articles of association or a similar document concerning incorporation under national law or on the basic documents adopted by the organization's governing bodies. Nor does the international status of hybrid or dual organizations need to be recognized at the time of the establishment of the organization; such recognition may occur subsequently, based on bilateral or multilateral agreements between the organization and states and other subjects of international law.

Whether or not a hybrid or dual organization has members does not depend on the mode of its establishment but depends on its functions. There may be cases where dual organizations established under municipal law but with privileges and immunities under international law may have full-fledged membership structures. Such structure is particularly appropriate if the members have a financial interest in the organization and "own" the organization, as in the case of SITA, which is an example of "a membership-owned organization with over 400 active members from across the air transport community."[72] There are two types of SITA membership: Tier I and Tier II.[73]

However, as the case of the Global Fund and that of the Gavi Alliance show, a dual or hybrid organization does not need to have a membership structure,

---

71 "Allerdings ist PPP [public-private partnership] kein Rechtsbegriff sondern eine heuristische Kategorie, die eine relativ diffuse Vielfalt technischer Phänomen bündeln soll." Hatje 2003, p. 117.

72 SITA. About SITA. SITA membership. http://www.sita.aero/about-us/sita-membership.

73 "Tier I membership is open to any company whose primary business is air transport related. Tier II membership is only available to an air transport company that does less than USD 100,000 per annum of business with SITA or an organization meeting the criteria of an eligible institution." SITA. Together we transform Air Travel. Introduction to SITA Membership. https://www.sita.aero/globalassets/docs/brochures/sita-membership-brochure.pdf.

particularly, if its purpose is related to producing global public goods or fighting global bads. Both organizations have been recognized as possessing international legal personality for the purpose of their headquarters agreements with the Swiss Federation. In Switzerland, where both are based, they enjoy a full range of privileges and immunities equivalent to those applicable to UN organizations also based there. The Global Fund also enjoys privileges and immunities in the United States and it has proposed to the countries where it is operating to become party to an international agreement recognizing the status and privileges and immunities of the Global Fund (see above).

There is also a range of other organizations which enjoy more limited privileges and immunities. The International Air Transport Association (IATA), which was incorporated on 18 December 1945 under the Statutes of Canada by a special act approved by the Canadian Parliament[74] and counts among its 281 members[75] the world's leading cargo and passenger airlines, may be associated with the category of dual or hybrid organizations to a certain extent. While it does not possess the full range of privileges and immunities extended to dual or hybrid organizations such as the Global Fund, for fiscal purposes (i.e., tax exemption), the Swiss authorities recognized IATA in an agreement with that organization as an international organization under the General Law of Public Taxes, and such classification was upheld in the case of *Jenni and others v. Conseil d'Etat of the Canton of Geneva* where IATA was classified as "a quasi-governmental organization."[76]

As shown by Martha:

> One can notice that the Tribunal's decision was neither based on the constituent instrument of IATA, nor its membership, since IATA was not constituted by an intergovernmental agreement and is composed of commercial airlines; but rather on IATA's function, which was deemed to be of a predominantly intergovernmental character.[77]

Similarly, prior to its conversion into an international organization with a treaty foundation, the AMRO had only rather limited privileges and immunities which were essentially limited to those of a fiscal nature.

The governance structure of AMRO was determined by the "Articles of Agreement in respect of the ASEAN+3 Macroeconomic Research Office ('AMRO')" of 9 November 2010 (AMRO Articles of Agreement 2010). The AMRO Articles of Agreement 2010 cannot be classified as an international agreement in the traditional sense, as the parties were not the governments of the ASEAN+3 countries but ministries of finance, central banks and similar institutions; nevertheless, these Articles of Agreement are important as they determine the purposes (Article 2) and functions (Article 3) of AMRO, the location and status of AMRO (Article 4), the obligations of Parties and the "Organization and

---

[74] Act of Incorporation. An Act to Incorporate International Air Transport Association. https://www.iata.org/about/Documents/chapter-1-english-%20aoI.pdf.

[75] As at 11 Nov. 2011.

[76] Martha 2010, p. 186.

[77] Ibid.

Management" structure (Article 6) and other relevant matters (confidentiality, relations with other organizations, undertakings in good faith, budget and finance etc.). As specified in para 1 of Article 6 of the AMRO Articles of Agreement 2010, the governance structure of AMRO was then comprised of the "Executive Committee, an Advisory Panel, a director and staff." The Executive Committee was composed of the "Finance Deputy and the Central Bank Deputy of each member of the ASEAN+3 Countries" (para 6.2 of Article 6), and provision was made that these "shall exercise the voting power held by their country in a unified manner and shall, prior to casting the votes allotted to their country [….] agree on whether the unified vote will be cast for or against the particular proposition to be decided." (para 6.14 of Article 6).

The AMRO Articles 2010 may be seen as the constitution of AMRO and the parties to these articles as members of the organization, in the wider definition proposed above.

On 20 April 2011, AMRO was incorporated, consistent with para 4.2 of Article 4 of the AMRO Article of Agreement 2010, as a "Company limited by Guarantee and not having a Share Capital" (AMRO Limited) under the Companies Act, Cap. 50 of the Republic of Singapore.[78] The AMRO Articles of Association[79] were drawn up for that purpose.

In accordance with the AMRO Articles of Agreement and the AMRO Articles of Association, the Executive Committee appointed the members of AMRO Limited and had "the absolute discretion to remove any Member who, in the reasonable opinion of the Executive Committee, is guilty of conduct derogatory to the dignity or injurious to the reputation or interest of the Company, or is, in the reasonable opinion of the Executive Committee, deemed unsuitable or undesirable to continue to be a Member of the Company."[80]

The "Societé Internationale de Telecommunications Aeronautiques" (SITA) was entirely conceived and is owned and governed by membership airlines. The origins of SITA go back to 23 February 1949 when it was "constituted as a 'Cooperative Society'" by a deed received that day, which "was subsequently amended to meet changing circumstances with 'Proces-Verbaux.'"[81] SITA enjoys a certain fiscal immunity in Switzerland under the terms of an agreement of 1992[82] and has been recognized in 1992 by Switzerland as a "quasi-intergovernmental organization"[83]

---

78 A copy of the AMRO Articles of Association is possession of the author.

79 The Companies Act, Cap. 50, Company Limited by Guarantee and not Having a Share Capital, Articles of Association of ASEAN+3 Macroeconomic Research Office Limited.

80 Paragraph 9 of the Articles of Association of ASEAN+3 Macroeconomic Research Office Limited.

81 Majid 1996, p. 23.

82 "Accord entre le Conseil fédéral Suisse et la Société internationale de télécommunications aéronautiques (SITA) pour régler le statut fiscal de la SITA et de son personnel en Suisse" of 4 June 1992 (which entered into force on 4 June 1992). https://www.admin.ch/opc/fr/classified-compilation/19920135/index.html.

83 SITA. SITA in Switzerland. https://www.sita.aero/about-us/who-we-are/sita-in-switzerland.

While at present SITA does not meet the requirements of a dual or hybrid organization, there can hardly be any doubt that it has the potential to become one. There is nothing that prevents the Swiss Federation from concluding a headquarters agreement with SITA, or precludes the Swiss Federation or other countries from extending additional privileges and immunities to it. Whether this is done is entirely a policy decision.

7.1.7 Institutional Ambivalence by Design

Increasingly, entities are, to use Klabbers' words, created which incorporate "institutional ambivalence by design,"[84] where states seek to establish forms of cooperation based only on politically binding obligations, outside the realm of public international law, and deliberately opt not to endow such forms of cooperation with international legal personality. The Arctic Council, the Wassenaar Agreement, and the Organization for Security and Co-operation in Europe (OSCE) epitomize that approach, as do the international regulatory agencies which, despite their great importance and political clout exceeding that of many traditional international organizations, continue to be disregarded and neglected by most international lawyers. As has been extensively discussed, some of these forms of cooperation such as the OSCE may qualify for recognition as international organization even though states expressly decided to withhold international legal personality from their creation.

7.1.8 Trust Funds

There are a number of international organizations established as trust funds. In the view of this author, both the Global Environment Facility (GEF) and CGIF fall into this category despite of the fact that both do not have a traditional treaty foundation and even though they do not possess international legal personality or legal capacity under national law. As already extensively argued above, the Instrument of the Restructured Global Environment Facility cannot be considered as the equivalent of a treaty. Also the Articles of Agreement of the CGIF do not fit the traditional concept of a treaty as they were not ratified by all ASEAN+3 countries.

As the organization's relations with its members are of an internal nature, i.e., not part of the organization's external relations, an organization is not required to have legal personality to have a membership structure. Thus, organizations established as trust funds without international legal personality may have membership structures. The number of participants in the GEF has dramatically increased to 183

[84] Klabbers 2001, pp. 403–421.

since the establishment of the restructured Global Environment Facility in 1994. While both states and specialized agencies of the UN are entitled to be participants in the GEF, these two categories of participants do not have equal status as only states can be represented in the GEF Council.[85] Both GEF and CGIF enjoy substantial political and institutional autonomy and can therefore be classified as international organizations and subjects of international law.

7.1.9 *Conclusions*

This short *tour d'horizon* shows that there is a range of new paradigms of organizational structure which cannot simply be pressed in the traditional schemes of intergovernmental organization and international organization. Rather than portraying these new forms of organizational structure as exceptions to the traditional concepts of intergovernmental organization and international organization with treaty foundation and members, or making the futile attempt to associate any act establishing an organization with a treaty, it is necessary to take account of the development of international law by recognizing that the very definitions and concepts of intergovernmental organization and international organization must change.

7.2 The Problematic Concept of Intergovernmental Organization Established by Intergovernmental Agreement

7.2.1 *Traditional Concepts Require Adjustment*

As indicated by Runavot:

> In the late 19th and early 20th centuries, international representation of the State still was the Members of national governments' monopoly. The institutionalization of international relations was then reduced to an alternative: whether or not there was a personification of the common inter-state action. Thus the inter-governmental organization (IGO) was distinguished from the non-governmental organization (NGO), while IGO and IO tended to become synonymous.[86]

The traditional concept of an intergovernmental organization is reflected in the definition given by Alvarez who states that intergovernmental organizations, as

[85] GEF Instrument, para 16. https://www.thegef.org/gef/sites/thegef.org/files/publication/GEF_Instrument-Interior-March23.2015.pdf.

[86] Runavot 2015, p. 20.

opposed to transnational or multinational corporations and nongovernmental organizations,

> are typically **collections of sovereign states that have banded together as states to create, under a constitutive international agreement governed by international law** usually known as a 'charter' or a 'constitution,' an apparatus, more or less permanent, charged with the pursuit of certain defined common ends.[87] (emphasis added)

The terms "international organization" and "intergovernmental organization" are often used interchangeably. The definition of "international organization" in the "Vienna Convention on the Law of Treaties", the "Vienna Convention on the Law of Treaties between States and International Organizations or between International Organizations" and other conventions epitomize such approach.[88]

In its commentary to the Vienna Convention on the Law of Treaties, the International Law Commission (ILC) clarified that the term "international organization" had been defined as "an *intergovernmental* organization in order to make it clear that the rules of non-governmental organizations are excluded."[89]

Some countries have even enshrined the concept of international organization with treaty foundation in their law. The position adopted by the United States is a good example of this approach; it has defined an international organization as

> a public international organization in which the United States participates **pursuant to any treaty** or under the authority of any Act of Congress authorizing such participation or making an appropriation for such participation, and which shall have been designated by the President through appropriate Executive order as being entitled to enjoy the privileges, exemptions, and immunities herein provided.[90]

Thus, in the United States, by law, only organizations established by treaty are *ipso facto* considered to be "public international organizations." For any other

---

[87] Alvarez 2005, p. 1.

[88] Article 2, para 1(i) of the Vienna Convention on the Law of Treaties (23 May 1969) provides: "'international organization' means an intergovernmental organization." https://treaties.un.org/doc/publication/unts/volume%201155/volume-1155-i-18232-english.pdf. An equivalent provision is contained in Article 2, para 1(i) of the Vienna Convention on the Law of Treaties between States and International Organizations or between International Organizations (21 March 1986). http://legal.un.org/ilc/texts/instruments/english/conventions/1_2_1986.pdf. Also, see Article 2, para 1(n) of the Vienna Convention on Succession of States in respect of Treaties (23 Aug. 1978) and Article 1, para 1(1) of the Vienna Convention on the Representation of States in their Relations with International Organizations of a Universal Character (14 March 1975). See http://legal.un.org/ilc/texts/instruments/english/conventions/3_2_1978.pdf and http://legal.un.org/ilc/texts/instruments/english/conventions/5_1_1975.pdf. The intergovernmental character of specialized agencies is reflected in the definition of "specialized agency" in Article 57 of the UN Charter, which requires an organization to be "established by intergovernmental agreement" for it to be recognized as a UN specialized agency.

[89] Draft Articles on the Law of Treaties with Commentaries. *Yearbook of the International Law Commission*, 1966, Vol. II., 187–274, 190.

[90] See the definition in the International Organizations Immunities Act, 9 Dec. 1945. http://www.law.cornell.edu/uscode/text/22/288.

organization to be considered as such requires an Act of Congress "authorizing such participation or making an appropriation for such participation."[91]

As highlighted by Schermers, the "word 'government' has different meanings" and is used both "in a wide sense, covering all organs that participate in governing the nation" (including legislative and judicial branches) and "in the narrow sense indicating only the executive."[92] In the context of the terms "intergovernmental agreement" and "intergovernmental organization", the notion of "government" was traditionally used in the narrow sense to refer to organizations established by governments, with the additional implication that such organization were established by international agreement and with governing bodies exclusively or predominantly composed of government representatives.

However, the traditional concept of intergovernmental organization described above is being questioned. This relates to the premise that an intergovernmental organization needs to have a treaty foundation but also, in a wider context, to the very purpose of that term which is to eliminate any organization not established by governments or with representation arrangements involving governments.

As indicated by Archer:

> This state- and government-oriented view of the word 'international' has been increasingly challenged over the past three decades. The belief has grown that the term should not be used synonymously with 'intergovernmental' to mean 'interstate' or relations between the official representatives of sovereign states. Instead, the term has come to include activities between individuals and groups in one state and individuals and groups in another state, as well as intergovernmental relations.[93]

Hence, as will be shown in the following, the term "intergovernmental organization" is intrinsically problematic. It should only be used as and to the extent that this is warranted by law or that some legal qualifications or policy implications are attached to the qualification of an organization as "intergovernmental".

7.2.1.1 Intergovernmental Organizations Do Not Need to Have a Treaty Foundation

It is widely accepted now that there may be intergovernmental organizations without formal treaty foundation.

This is underlined by the fact that the Office of Legal Affairs of the United Nations already recognized as early as 1982 that an "intergovernmental organization" does not need to be established by a treaty:

> There is thus far, however, no authoritative definition in international law of the term 'intergovernmental organization'. Indeed, the definition proposed by the Rapporteur of the

---

[91] As will be shown below, the US followed this process for classifying the Global Fund as an international organization.

[92] Schermers and Blokker 2011, §58.

[93] Archer 1992, p. 1.

> International Law Commission during the elaboration of the Vienna Convention on the Law of Treaties, which included, among others, the requirement of a constituting treaty, was not retained because this criterion was not always met in practice. It had gradually been recognized that the substance of the constitution or statute of an organization may be more relevant to the determination of the intergovernmental character of the organization than the form in which it is cast. Even if its constitution does not qualify as a formal international treaty, an international organization may well be called intergovernmental as a result of the role which that constitution ascribes to Governments with regard to such matters as membership, representation, financing, etc. A non-governmental organization may thus change its status to intergovernmental without a change to the non-treaty form of its statute, but as a result of appropriate amendments to the relevant provisions of the statute. This possibility of conversion to intergovernmental status has been pointed out and elaborated upon by the Secretary-General of the United Nations in a report on the constitutional, organizational and financial implications of the establishment of an intergovernmental tourism organization, submitted to the Economic and Social Council in 1969. The acceptance of this possibility also seems to be implied in a letter, dated 8 August 1955, through which the Secretariat of the United Nations informed the Secretary-General of the International Criminal Police Commission (as INTERPOL was named before 1956) that "if participation in the Commission [INTERPOL] becomes exclusively governmental, as envisaged in article 3 of the draft statute, it will obviously no longer be possible for the new organization to be included in the list of non-governmental organizations recognized by the Economic and Social Council." In the light of this possibility of an international organization acquiring intergovernmental status through changes to its existing constitution (which, incidentally, may be considered an international agreement in simplified form), it may be considered that the present constitutional provisions of INTERPOL fully justify the decisions of the Economic and Social Council to consider INTERPOL as an intergovernmental, rather than a non-governmental, organization.[94]

The above legal opinion is important as it stipulates that there is "no authoritative definition in international law of the term 'intergovernmental organization'" and because it recognizes that an organization may transform itself based on progressive institutionalization from a non-governmental organization to an intergovernmental organization.

7.2.1.2 Evolution of the Position of the International Law Commission

The International Law Commission, whose concept of "intergovernmental organization" was initially colored by the traditional interpretation of that term reflected by the VCLT and the other conventions cited above, has also recognized the intrinsic ambiguity of the term "intergovernmental organization". While the Special Rapporteur of the ILC, Leonardo Diaz Gonzalez, proposed in 1985 in his "Second report on relations between States and international organizations" that the ILC should maintain the position that "an 'international organization' means an

[94] Status of the International Criminal Police Organization (INTERPOL) with the United Nations. Letter to the Secretary-General of the International Criminal Police Organization (INTERPOL). Annex: Status of INTERPOL with the United Nations, in the *United Nations Juridical Yearbook 1982*, Part Two, 179–180, 180.

intergovernmental or inter-State organization,"[95] the ILC subsequently changed its position. As indicated by Gaja in 2003, while the "definition of international organizations as 'intergovernmental' appears to give decisive importance to the fact that membership of the organizations is composed of States" and "[i]ntergovernmental organizations are generally established by treaty", there are some organizations that "do not fall clearly into one or the other category."[96] Gaja highlighted that "there are also examples of organizations which were established by States only under an instrument governed by one or more municipal laws."[97] The ILC's changed position is well summarized in the Report of the ILC of 2009. As highlighted by the ILC in this report, "the adoption of a different definition is preferable for several reasons.

> First, it is questionable whether by defining an international organization as an intergovernmental organization one provides much information: it is not even clear -whether the term 'intergovernmental organization' refers to the constituent instrument or to actual membership. Second, the term 'intergovernmental' is in any case inappropriate to a certain extent, because several important international organizations have been established by State organs other than governments or by those organs together with governments, nor are States always represented by governments within the organizations. Third, an increasing number of international organizations include among their members entities other than States as well as States; the term 'intergovernmental organization' might be thought to exclude these organizations, although with regard to international responsibility it is difficult to see why one should reach solutions that differ from those applying to organizations of which only States are members.[98]

Thus, in line with the above, an examination as to whether an entity has the characteristics of an intergovernmental organization is called for as and to the extent that specific legal consequences are linked to such qualification. In such cases, and to the extent that a convention does not define "intergovernmental organization" expressly for the purpose of that convention as an organization established by intergovernmental agreement, the term "intergovernmental organization" should be interpreted taking account of the evolution of international law, to reflect the functions of the organization, rather than the mode of its establishment or the composition of its membership.

---

[95] Díaz-González, L. 1985. "Second report on relations between States and international organizations (second part of the topic) (Doc. A/CN.4/391 and Add.1 and Corr.1)", para 26. http://legal.un.org/docs/?path=../ilc/documentation/english/a_cn4_391.pdf&lang=EFS.

[96] See, in detail, Gaja, "First report on responsibility of international organizations", para 14.

[97] Ibid.

[98] Report of the International Law Commission. 61st session (4 May–5 June and 6 July–7 Aug. 2009). General Assembly. Official Records. Sixty-fourth Session, Supplement No. 10. NY: United Nations, 44. http://legal.un.org/docs/?path=../ilc/reports/2009/english/chp4.pdf&lang=EFSRAC.

7.2.2 *Need for a New Concept of Intergovernmental Organization*

The question which the ILC so far has not yet addressed is whether intergovernmental organizations are by definition public international organizations, or whether dual or hybrid organizations, such as the Global Fund, may also qualify for recognition as intergovernmental. Given the evolution of international law, in the view of this author, it is necessary and appropriate to adopt a wider definition of the term "intergovernmental organization".

Martha argues, "that when government representatives establish an international organization to pursue an objective that could be qualified as act '*jure imperii*', this leads to the unavoidable conclusion that such organization is of an intergovernmental nature."[99] While this is convincing, it does not imply, however, that only public international organizations or organizations performing *acta jure imperii* can be qualified as intergovernmental. Given the evolving concepts of public international law, the term "intergovernmental organization can no longer be deemed to exclude organizations with dual or hybrid character such as the Global Fund. Thus, this author fully agrees with Michael Reisman who has affirmed in a legal opinion that the Global Fund is intergovernmental in character:

> 46. The Global Fund is an international organization. While there is no authoritative definition for intergovernmental organizations, one can extract criteria such as significant participation of governments, governmental sources of funds, and recognition by other states of the status of international organization in order to make a case-by-case judgment. Tested by all of these criteria, the Global Fund may clearly be considered an international intergovernmental organization.
> 47. By contrast to some international organizations which have been granted observer status by the General Assembly, the Global Fund is effectively intergovernmental. Most of its directorate is composed of governments and governments provide 95 percent of its budget and are the preponderant recipients of its assistance. Thus, granting observer status to the Global Fund would not run counter to the General Assembly's concern about allowing routine non-governmental organizations to achieve observer status.
> 48. The fact that the Global Fund was organized under national law does not belie its international and intergovernmental character, any more than the fact that the Bank for International Settlements is organized under Swiss law has negated its manifest international and intergovernmental character. Indeed, the Swiss government has already accorded the Global Fund the privileges and immunities of an international organization similar to those with headquarters in Switzerland; the United States has 'also recognized it as such.
> 49. Such state practice confirms the well-founded view that the Global Fund is an international organization with an intergovernmental character.[100]

[99] Martha 2010, pp. 22–23.

[100] Reisman, M. 2009. "Opinion with Respect to the Qualifications of the Global Fund for Observer Status at the United Nations", paras 46–49 (unpublished paper).

The Global Fund is currently listed as one of the "intergovernmental organizations having received a standing invitation to participate as observers in the sessions and the work of the General Assembly and not maintaining permanent offices at Headquarters [….]."[101]

Hence, the term "intergovernmental organization" does not necessarily refer to public international organizations, but also comprises organizations such as the Global Fund which are incorporated under national law.

Moreover, it would be appropriate for a similar interpretation to be adopted in relation to other provisions which refer to "intergovernmental organizations" without expressly requiring their establishment by an intergovernmental agreement, e.g., for the purpose of the Permanent Court of Arbitration. Arbitration Rules 2012 which "are for use in arbitrating disputes involving at least one State, State-controlled entity, or **intergovernmental organization**"[102] or for Article 6*ter* of the Paris Convention for the Protection of Industrial Property" adopted in 1883[103] which extends, based on the amendments of the Paris Convention of 1958, to "international intergovernmental organizations" protection of armorial bearings, flags, other emblems, abbreviations, and names, on similar terms as afforded to the countries of the Paris Union. However, while the Permanent Court of Arbitration has not adopted any interpretation to the contrary, World Intellectual Property Organization's (WIPO's) position is still colored by the traditional paradigms of an intergovernmental organization with treaty foundation and members.[104]

As may be seen from the above, there are specific cases where a determination is expressly required by applicable law whether an organization has an intergovernmental character.

Notwithstanding the above, it is the very definition of an international organization as "intergovernmental" organization which is problematic for the very reason that the main purpose of defining an international organization as an "intergovernmental organization" is to exclude, based on the dichotomy of governmental and nongovernmental, organizations not established by governments from the realm of international organization. Hence, this term should be used only in those cases where its use is expressly mandated by a convention or other legal act or as a matter

---

101 United Nations: Permanent Observers. Intergovernmental organizations. http://www.un.org/en/sections/member-states/intergovernmental-organizations/index.html.

102 Permanent Court of Arbitration. Arbitration Rules 2012. https://pca-cpa.org/wp-content/uploads/sites/175/2015/11/PCA-Arbitration-Rules-2012.pdf.

103 WIPO. Paris Convention, Article 6ter. http://www.wipo.int/article6ter/en/legal_texts/article_6ter.html.

104 See WIPO's procedure which requires, inter alia, to submit "a copy in English or French of the Statutes or Constituting Charter of the organization submitting the request and a list of the member states of that organization, except in the case of an organization belonging to the United Nations system or an organization that has already communicated such information to WIPO." WIPO. Procedure for IGOs. http://www.wipo.int/article6ter/en/igos.html.

of policy; it should generally be interpreted, in that case, in a wider manner as suggested above to include intergovernmental organizations without a treaty base and dual and hybrid organizations.

7.3 The Concept of "International Organization"

7.3.1 Definitions of International Organization in Literature

There are a number of authors who emphasize the treaty base of any international organization. Representative of this view in particular is Bindschedler who observes:

> The term international organizations denotes an association of States[105] established by and based upon a treaty, which pursues common aims and which has its own special organs to fulfill particular functions within the organization.
>
> Since international organizations are necessarily based upon multilateral treaties, the law of treaties forms part of the law of international organizations.[106]

Regarding membership, Bindschedler further adds:

> Membership is restricted to States, including dependent States with limited legal capacity and can be either with full or with limited rights.[107]

A range of other definitions is proposed in literature. In many cases, such definitions postulate both the establishment by a treaty and membership as elements of an international organization. Thus, Sands and Klein observe

> that for an entity to qualify as an international organization, it must have the following characteristics:
>
> - its membership must be composed of states and/or other international organisations;
> - it must be established by treaty or other instrument governed by international law, such as a resolution adopted in an international conference;
> - it must have an autonomous will distinct from that of its members and be vested with legal personality;
> - It must be capable of adopting norms (in the broadest sense) addressed to its members.[108]

[105] See also Virally 1981, p. 51. He defines an organization "as an association of States, established by agreement among its members and possessing a permanent system or set of organs, whose task it is to pursue objectives of common interest by means of co-operation among its members."

[106] Bindschedler 1983, p. 120.

[107] Bindschedler 1983, p. 121.

[108] Sands and Klein 2009, pp. 15–16.

Sands and Klein clarify that their definition, while excluding non-governmental organizations and inter-state enterprises, includes treaty-based organizations established within the framework of agreement establishing institutional arrangements.[109]

Amerasinghe indicates that a "public international organization is normally created by a treaty or convention to which States are parties and the members of the organization so created are generally States, though sometimes but rarely governments may constitute the membership."[110]

> International organizations range from the inter-State body created by multilateral treaty or convention with potential and openings for universal membership and a very broad range of interests, such as the United Nations, to the specialized agencies of the UN with potential for openings for universal membership but with a narrow focus (e.g., the FAO, the IBRD, and the UNESCO), to organizations with select or closed membership but relatively wide interests (e.g., the Council of Europe, the OAS and OAU), to agencies which are restricted both as to membership and as to subject matter (e.g. the international river commissions) to organizations which are composed entirely of non-governmental entities (NGOs).[111]

According to Clive Archer, an international organization is defined "as a formal, continuous structure established by agreement between members, whether governmental representatives or not, from at least two sovereign states with the aim of pursuing the common interest of the membership."[112]

Schermers and Blokker define an international organization "as a form of cooperation

1. founded on an international agreement;
2. having at least one organ with a will of its own; and
3. established under international law."[113]

The above definitions are all predicated on the concept of a public international organization established by treaty, with members which are generally states, and partially assume that an international organization is also defined by its international legal personality. While still applicable to traditional international organizations with treaty foundation, the above concept is in the view of this author no longer in line with the development of international law and the proliferation of actors at international plane.

[109] Ibid., 16.

[110] Amerasinghe 2005, p. 9.

[111] Ibid., 9–10.

[112] Archer 1992, p. 38.

[113] Schermers and Blokker 2011, §33.

7.3.2 *The Definition of an International Organization as Proposed by the International Law Commission*

Traditional concepts of international organization are epitomized by the definition given by Fitzmaurice in his report on the Law of Treaties,[114] as

> a collectivity of States established by treaty, with a constitution and common organs, having a personality distinct from that of its member-States, and being a subject of international law with treaty-making capacity.

The articles on the responsibility of international organizations prepared by the ILC, of which the General Assembly of the United Nations General Assembly took note by resolution 66/100, contain in Article 2(a) the following definition of international organization:

> 'International organization' means an organization established by a treaty or other instrument governed by international law and possessing its own international legal personality. International organizations may include as members, in addition to States, other entities;

The ILC observed in this context that

> Most international organizations are established by treaties. Thus, a reference in the definition to treaties as constituent instruments reflects prevailing practice. However, forms of international cooperation are sometimes established without a treaty. In certain cases, for instance with regard to the Nordic Council, a treaty was subsequently concluded. In other cases, although an implicit agreement may be held to exist, member States insisted that there was no treaty concluded to that effect, as for example in respect of the Organization for Security and Co-operation in Europe (OSCE). In order to cover organizations established by States on the international plane without a treaty, article 2 refers, as an alternative to treaties, to any 'other instrument governed by international law.' This wording is intended to include instruments, such as resolutions adopted by an international organization or by a conference of States. Examples of international organizations that have been so established include the Pan American Institute of Geography and History (PAIGH), the Organization of the Petroleum Exporting Countries (OPEC), and OSCE.
>
> The reference to "a treaty or other instrument governed by international law" is not intended to exclude entities other than States from being regarded as members of an international organization. This is unproblematic with regard to international organizations which, so long as they have a treaty-making capacity, may well be a party to a constituent treaty. The situation is likely to be different with regard to entities other than States and international organizations. However, even if the entity other than a State does not possess treaty-making capacity or cannot take part in the adoption of the constituent instrument, it may be accepted as a member of the organization so established.[115]

---

[114] "Law of Treaties (Doc. A/CN.4/101, 14 March 1956)", Report by Fitzmaurice, G. G. In *Yearbook of the International Law Commission*, Vol. II, 104–128, 108. http://legal.un.org/ilc/publications/yearbooks/english/ilc_1956_v2.pdf.

[115] Report of the International Law Commission, 63rd session (26 April–3 June and 4 July–12 Aug. 2011), Supplement No. 10 (A/66/10), Chapter V, Responsibility of international organizations, 52–170, 72–73. http://legal.un.org/docs/?symbol=A/66/10.

The approach adopted by the ILC is intrinsically related to the work of the ILC on responsibility of international organizations. The rationale of adopting a rather narrow definition of international organization is discussed by Gaja in his First Report on the Responsibility of International Organizations:

20. [….] It is clearly preferable only to address questions relating to a relatively homogeneous category of international organizations. If the present study is intended to be a sequel to the draft articles on responsibility of States for internationally wrongful acts, it is appropriate to limit the scope of this study to questions relating to organizations that exercise certain functions, that are similar, and possibly identical, to those exercised by States. These functions, whether legislative, executive or judicial, may be called governmental.
21. This choice would imply first of all that the study should not encompass questions of responsibility of NGOs, because they do not generally exercise governmental functions and moreover would not raise the key question of the responsibility of member States for the conduct of the organization. This delimitation of the scope of application of the future draft articles corresponds to the views expressed by a large number of delegations in the Sixth Committee in response to an invitation to comment addressed by the Commission [….].[116]

It is under this specific angle that the ILC decided to restrict the scope of its study. This is a choice which the ILC was called upon to make and entitled to make. While this author shares the view of Mendelson that the definition proposed by the ILC is "unsatisfactory in several respects,"[117] this publication will not discuss the appropriateness of the ILC's definition of international organization in the specific context in which it has been coined; rather, the emphasis will be showing that the ILC's definition is not suitable in nearly all respects to be used as the basis for a general definition of the term "international organization". This relates not only to the proposed definition of international organization as an "organization established by a treaty or other instrument governed by international law," but also to the proposal that international organization should be defined by its membership and that it should be a requirement for recognition as international organization for an institution to "possess international legal personality". On all these points, a different approach needs to be adopted in the view of this author. While "experience has shown that many (though not all) codifications by the ILC exercise a sort of gravitational pull on decision-makers and writers,"[118] such pull would be in the wrong direction if indeed the definition of "international organization" would be based in general terms on that adopted by the ILC.

---

[116] First Report on Responsibility of International Organizations, by Gaja, G. Doc. A/CN.4/53, para 20, http://legal.un.org/ilc/documentation/english/a_cn4_532.pdfp. 111.

[117] Mendelson 2005, p. 373.

[118] Ibid., 373.

7.3.3 *Treaty or Instrument Governed by International Law Is Not an Element of Definition*

As has been extensively argued, the importance of treaty-based mechanisms has been decreasing over the last decades. Moreover, while in the first and second generations of international organizations which comprised the period from the wake of War II to the end of the 1970s, generally organizations with treaty foundation were created, this trend subsided during the third generation and fourth generations which cover the period from the 1980s until now.[119] "Whereas once an organization was established almost automatically as soon as a new international problem and the need to cooperate were identified, the opposite is often true today. At present, States almost instinctively express their wish *not* to create a new organization if a new international problem and the need to cooperate present themselves."[120]

As shown, there are a number of organizations not established by a treaty but by the resolution of a conference or organization, by parallel provisions of national or even by one country only, or merely by consensus. Thus, it can be questioned whether it is still the "prevailing practice" that international organizations are established by a treaty. However, even assuming that most organizations are still predominantly established by a treaty, this would not be a sufficient reason to make such treaty or agreement a constitutive element of the definition of international organization.

The ILC has clarified in its comments on Article 2(a) of the articles on the responsibility of international organizations cited above, that reference to "other instrument covered by international law" has been incorporated in the ILC article, as this "wording is intended to include instruments, such as resolutions adopted by an international organization or by a conference of States." However, this does not appear to be a convincing reason, as in cases as mentioned above, it is generally the acceptance of the instrument, rather than the instrument itself, which may have legal effects. This has been pointedly underlined by Seyersted:

> It is true that most IGOs have been established by a convention concluded between the member states. **However, this is not, as generally assumed, a necessary requirement, neither to establish an IGO, nor to establish it as a subject of international law.** Quite a number of IGOs have been established pursuant to a mere resolution adopted by an international conference or to some other form of understanding between the member States. It may of course be maintained that the member States, by taking part in the organs and the work of the Organization, **have tacitly accepted** the resolution, or any other text, which may embody certain basic organizational provisions, in such a manner that it may be said to constitute and (sic) international agreement. **However, it is not a crucial element**

[119] On the concept of four generations of international organizations, see Droesse 2011, pp. 6–33.

[120] Blokker 2001, p. 10.

> **that members have legally bound themselves to participate in the work of the organization. Indeed, such obligation does not really exist even if there is a convention, if this allows for withdrawal from membership at any time without previous notice.**[121] (emphasis added)

It is a positive development that the ILC has recognized that "forms of international cooperation are sometimes established without a treaty." However, it is regrettable that the ILC maintains notwithstanding the above that "a treaty or other instrument governed by international law" should be regarded as a core element of the definition of international organization. The more appropriate and courageous conclusion would have been to dispense with the aforementioned requirement altogether and to conclude that, in essence it does not matter how an international organization is established. What matters are the functions which the organization performs and whether it acts on the international plane.

In the view of this author, a "treaty or other instrument governed by international law" is not, and should not be taken as, a constituent element of any definition of international organization, for three main reasons. First, as recognized by the ILC, there are ways of establishing an international organization other than by treaty, which should be equally considered in the context of a definition of "international organization" and cannot simply be associated with the traditional treaty-based paradigm. Second, the approach of requiring a treaty foundation of international organizations does not consider the evolution of international law. Thus, as for the term "intergovernmental organization," the definition of an "international organization" should not be limited to public international organizations but should incorporate dual or hybrid organization and organizations established as trust funds with or without legal personality. Third, an international organization is defined by its functions not by the act that establishes it. The status of an organization at the time of its establishment reflects only a snapshot of its powers and functions at that time. Organizations are not only capable of expanding their powers but may also substantially transform themselves by changing their status, e.g., from a non-governmental organization to an international organization.

Hence the very concept of "international organization" needs to change and be defined in a wider manner. Adopting such a wider interpretation of international organization has far-reaching ramifications. The concept of international organization is core to many concepts of the law of international organizations and international institutions. It is immediately related to concepts of membership and representation and the ability or organizations to act on the international plane. Moreover, as shown, it has many more concrete applications as it defines the ability of an organization for matters such as its ability to resort to arbitration, protect its emblems or have access to an administrative tribunal.

[121] Seyersted 2008, p. 46.

7.3.4 *"International Organizations" are Defined by Their Functions*

It is this author's view that the determination whether an entity is an international organization should be based on the organization's functions and the recognition of its status by the international community rather than the legal character of the instrument establishing the organization.

Gaja has stated this with admirable clarity:

> What seems to be significant for the purposes of the present report is not so much the legal nature of the instrument that was adopted for establishing the organization, as the functions that the organization exercises. A reference to the governmental functions that the organization exercises is directly relevant, while the nature of the constituent instrument has only a descriptive value. **Even if it is true that in most cases an agreement was concluded under international law for establishing the organization, it is not necessary to mention the existence of such an agreement in the definition.** Should two States intend to cooperate between themselves by creating an organization for constructing and running an industrial plant, they may do so through a contract that is concluded under one of the municipal laws. They could also achieve the same purpose by concluding an agreement under international law. It is less likely that they would establish by contract an organization that is endowed with certain governmental functions, but there is no necessary link between the constituent instrument of an organization and its functions. (emphasis added)[122]

As indicated by Gaja, "there is no necessary link between the constituent instrument of an organization and its functions"[123] or, in general, between the way an organization is established and its qualification as an "international" organization. The fact that international organizations traditionally have been, and still are, established by international agreement does not mean that such agreement needs to be part of the definition of international organization.

As stressed by Brownlie and Goodwin-Gill in their joint legal opinion on IPU:

> However, not all 'international organizations', that is, entities having the capacity to bear rights and duties and to act on the international plane, are necessarily 'inter-governmental' in the strict sense. **What counts is the degree of recognition and acceptance of such entities manifested by States in their dealings with them, which also goes to the measure of personality, the amount of which in turn depends upon a functional analysis of aims and purposes. [....].**[124] (emphasis added)

Hence, whether an international organization exists depends first and foremost on the organization's functions and the degree of its institutional independence, not on the terms of its establishment.

---

[122] Responsibility of International Organizations. Doc. A/CN.4/532. First report on responsibility of international organizations, by Gaja, G. Special Rapporteur. *Yearbook of the International Law Commission,* 2003, Vol. II, Part One. Documents of the 55th Session. NY: United Nations. 105–116, paras 20, 113.

[123] Ibid., para 25.

[124] Brownlie and Goodwin-Gill, para 60.

7.3.5 *The Dynamic Character of Intergovernmental and International Organizations*

There is ample evidence that progressive institutionalization can fundamentally change the character of an international organization. Therefore, it somewhat escapes this author why text books on the law of international organizations and international institutions, starting with that of Schermers and Blokker, still invariably refer to the act establishing an organization as a constitutive element of the definition of international organization. To base the definition of an international organization on the existence of an establishing agreement disregards the dynamic nature of development. The functions that an organization has in accordance with its constituent agreement at the time of its establishment are only a snapshot of the state of its development at that time. "International *organization* is a process; international *organizations* are representative aspects of the phase of that process which has been reached at a given time."[125] Thus, there may be entities (e.g., INTERPOL) that did not qualify for recognition at the time they were established but were subsequently recognized as such.

A non-governmental organization may thus change its status to intergovernmental as a result of appropriate amendments to the relevant provisions of its statute without, however, changing the non-treaty character of the same. In addition to the IPU analyzed above, the Commonwealth Secretariat is another example of an entity that evolved to an international organization "after adoption of the Declaration of Commonwealth Principles at the 1971 Singapore Meeting."[126]

Moreover, a treaty foundation of an international organization is neither a *conditio sine qua non* for its international legal personality nor for its autonomy and own will. As will be shown in the following, international legal personality may be acquired subsequent to the establishment of an organization. Moreover, while the existence of an international agreement may facilitate the conclusion that an organization has a separate will or *volonté distincte*, there are international organizations without treaty foundation that are endowed with institutional independence and proper autonomy.

7.3.6 *Evolution of International Law*

It is somewhat paradoxical that the definition of "international organization" which in the past generally was either perceived to be identical or wider than that of "intergovernmental organization", now tends to be more restrictive than that of an intergovernmental organization.

---

[125] Claude 1971, p. 4.

[126] Brownlie and Goodwin-Gill, para 64.

In certain respects, the definition of "international organization" needs to be aligned with the new concept of intergovernmental organization advocated above. This relates to the need to dispense with the requirement of a treaty foundation and to recognize that international organization does not necessarily mean a public international organization.

In the case of the International Committee of the Red Cross (ICRC), it has long-since been recognized that the ICRC is a subject of international law and able to act on the international plane.

Crawford states with regard to the ICRC:

> It has now developed a dual character. From an organizational point of view it remains a Swiss entity, yet it is increasingly recognized as performing public international functions and it is clear that the ICRC is as a separate international legal person in respect of the exercise of those functions—a status recognized by the Red Cross Conventions of 1949, by the Security Council and (in the context of non-disclosure of information) by the ICTY.[127]

The ICRC and BIS have become predecessors of a new class of international organizations with a dual or hybrid character that has emerged since 2000—organizations incorporated under municipal law as a non-governmental organization or a corporation, but with international juridical personality and privileges and immunities under international law. Organizations such as the Global Fund and the Gavi Alliance have become new business models for establishing international organizations. In the view of this author, dual and hybrid organizations need to be recognized as a new paradigm of international organization.

Nevertheless, it is important to stress that the term "international organization" is wider than the term "intergovernmental organization" as it also covers organizations which are not established by governments, such an organization of Parliamentary cooperation such as IPU or, potentially, cooperative undertakings of technical government agencies or regulatory agencies.

As indicated by Brownlie and Goodwin-Gill in their Joint Opinion regarding IPU:

> The IPU possesses international legal personality and is an international organization *sui generis*, that is, it is an international parliamentary, political and representative organization.[128]

However, international legal personality is not a requirement for recognition as subject of international law or as international organization. Moreover, as shown in detail above, an international organization does not need to have members.

It is necessary to rethink current concepts of international organization and revise them taking account of the above.

---

[127] Crawford 2013, p. 154.

[128] Brownlie and Goodwin-Gill, The Inter-Parliamentary Union. Joint Opinion. Statement 1.

References

Alvarez JE (2005) International Organizations as Law-makers. Oxford University Press, Oxford.

Amerasinghe CF (2005) Principles of the Institutional Law of International Organizations, 2nd edn. Cambridge University Press, Cambridge

Archer C (1992) International Organizations, 2nd edn. Routledge, London

Bindschedler RL (1983) International Organizations, general aspects. In: Bernhard R (ed) Encyclopedia of Public International Law 5:119–140

Bodansky D, Brunnée J, Rajamani, L (2017) International Climate Change Law. Oxford. Oxford University Press

Blokker NM (2001) Proliferation of International Organizations. In: Blokker NM, Schermers HG (eds) Proliferation of International Organizations: legal issues. Kluwer, The Hague, pp 1–49

Chandler Jr RF (1992) An adventure in applied science: a history of the International Rice Research Institute. IRRI: Manila. http://books.irri.org/9711040638_content.pdf

Claude IL Jr (1971) Swords into plowshares: the problems and progress of International Organization, 4th edn. Random House, New York

Crawford J (2013) Chance, order, change: the course of International Law. General course on Public International Law. Collect Courses Hague Acad Int Law 365:152

Dam KW (1970) The GATT: Law and International Economic Organization. The University of Chicago Press, Chicago, pp 10–12

Donnelly S (2012) Institutional change at the top: from the Financial Stability Forum to the Financial Stability Board. In: Mayntz R (ed) Crisis and control: institutional change in Financial Market Regulation. M. Campus and University of Chicago Press, Frankfurt, pp 261–275. https://ris.utwente.nl/ws/portalfiles/portal/5583898

Droesse G (2011) Introductory remarks and overview of publication: proliferation, fragmentation, and earmarking of Concessional Financing. In: Droesse G (ed) Funds for development: Multilateral Channels of Concessional Financing. Asian Development Bank, Manila, pp 1–37

Hargrove T, Coffman WR (2006) Breeding History. Rice Today. Oct–Dec. http://www.goldenrice.org/PDFs/Breeding_History_Sept_2006.pdf

Hatje A (2003) Public Private Partnership und europäisches Wettbewerbsrecht. In: Studiengesellschaft *für Wirtschaft und Recht (ed), Public Private Partnership. Wien, pp. 115–133.*

Jackson JH (1967) The Puzzle of the GATT. J World Trade Law 1:131–161

Kissling C (2011) The legal and political status of International Parliamentary Institutions. Background Paper No. 4. Committee for a Democratic U.N., Berlin

Klabbers J (2001) Institutional ambivalence by design: Soft Organizations in International Law. Nordic J Int Law 70:403–421

Liberi J (2014) The Financial Stability Forum: a step in the right direction…not far enough. J Int Law 24(2):549–575

Majid AA (1996) Legal status of International Institutions: SITA, INMARSAT and Eurocontrol examined. Dartmouth Publishing, Aldershot

Martha RSJ (2010) The legal foundation of INTERPOL. Hart, Portland

Mendelson M (2005) The definition of "International Organization". In: Ragazzi M (ed) International responsibility today. Essays in memory of Oscar Schachter. Martinus Nijhoff, Leiden, pp 371–389

Petrén G (1959) The Nordic Council: a unique factor in International Law. Nordisk Tidsskrift International Ret 29:346–362

Porter T (2000) The G-7, the Financial Stability Forum, the G-20, and the politics of International Financial Regulation. Paper prepared for the International Studies Association Annual Meeting. Los Angeles, California, 15 March 2000. www.g8.utoronto.ca/g20/biblio/porter-isa-2000.pdf

Runavot M-C (2015) The Intergovernmental Organization and the Institutionalization of International Relation: the modelling of International Organization at stake. In: Virzio R,

Ingravallo I (eds) Evolutions in the Law of International Organizations, vol 20. Brill. Nijhoff, Leiden, pp 17–43
Sands P, Klein P (2009) Bowett's Law of International Institution, 5th edn. Sweet and Maxwell (Thomson Reuters, London
Schermers HG, Blokker NM (eds) (2011) International Institutional Law: unity within diversity, 5th edn. Martinus Nijhoff, Boston
Seyersted F (2008) Common Law of International Organizations. Martinus Nijhoff, Leiden, pp 46–47
UNEP (2018) Handbook for the Montreal Protocol on Substances that Deplete the Ozone Layer, 12th edition. http://ozone.unep.org/sites/default/files/MP_handbook-english-2018.pdf
Virally M (1981) Definition and classification of International Organizations: a legal approach. In: Abi-Saab G (ed) The concept of International Organization. UNESCO, Paris, pp 50–66
von Bogdandy A (2001) Law and politics in the WTO—strategies to cope with a deficient relationship. Max Planck Yearb U N Law 5:609–674
Zaring D (1998) International Law by other means: the twilight existence of International Financial Regulatory Organizations. Tex Int Law J 33:281–330

Chapter 8
Membership and Privileges and Immunities

Contents

The law of immunities is an "extremely fascinating topic where fundamental questions on the basic structure of international law are at stake" as it "functions like a mirror that allows us to espouse a different perspective on our beliefs of what international law is and should be, where it comes from and where it is going in its further development."[1] As for the other topics discussed in this book, also in relation to privileges and immunities, a basic question is whether states still are

> the central actors in this system, and non-state actors a marginal phenomenon that should not detract us from the centrality of inter-state relations? Or do states play only an auxiliary role in a global legal order that finally must serve the causes of mankind, with the well-being of the individuals as the ultimate point of orientation, and yardstick? Depending on the answers one gives to these fundamental questions one's position on role and functions of sovereign immunities, and its relations to human rights (and international criminal law) will differ.[2]

What matters most in the context of this book is that the role and functions of privileges and immunities are directly relevant for the very concept of international

All weblinks are updated as of 28 February 2018.

[1] Oeter 2015, p. 355.
[2] Ibid.

G. Droesse, *Membership in International Organizations*,
https://doi.org/10.1007/978-94-6265-327-6_8

organization and have many implications for organizations' legal and policy frameworks.

No international organization will be able to function properly if it is subject to all the laws of the countries where the organization is operating. Hence, immunity of legal process and the other privileges and immunities normally extended to international organizations are a corollary of their independence and essential for the ability of international organizations to perform their functions effectively.

As regards organizations' officials, the conceptual basis of their privileges and immunities has been set out in the "Reparations for Injuries Decision" of 1949:

> In order that the agent may perform his duties satisfactorily, he must feel that this protection is assured to him by the Organization, and that he may count on it. To ensure the independence of the agent, and, consequently, the independent action of the Organization itself, it is essential that in performing his duties he need not have to rely on any other protection than that of the Organization [....]. In particular, he should not have to rely on the protection of his own state.[3]

Moreover, important principles have been set out in the Advisory Opinions of the International Court of Justice of 29 April 1999[4] and 15 December 1989.[5]

Privileges and immunities are intrinsically related to membership concepts. In their member countries, privileges and immunities are generally extended to international organizations under their constituent agreements, and under multilateral agreements and/or headquarters agreements and other bilateral agreements. Moreover, there are instances where countries have extended privileges and immunities by way of a unilateral decision or through other arrangements. In certain cases, privileges and immunities may transform the status of an organization.

Privileges and immunities are increasingly viewed critically and there is wide-spread recognition that they do not afford untrammeled freedom for international organizations to conduct themselves as they deem fit. Both international courts and the national courts of organizations' member countries scrutinize whether international organizations have complied with requirements of due process. In some cases, courts have made such compliance a condition for the grant of privileges and immunities, and it is being discussed whether adopting such an approach is advisable in contractual matters but also in the case of claims based on tort.

A serious problem, in particular, for regional organizations and organizations of limited membership, is how to ensure the protection of the organization in non-member countries. In this regard, it will be shown that at times it may be

---

[3] "Reparation for injuries suffered in the service of the United Nations". Advisory Opinion: ICJ Reports 1949, 174, 183. http://www.icj-cij.org/files/case-related/4/004-19490411-ADV-01-00-EN.pdf.

[4] "Difference Relating to Immunity from Legal Process of a Special Rapporteur of the Commission on Human Rights, Advisory Opinion". ICJ Reports 1999, 62. http://www.icj-cij.org/files/case-related/100/100-19990429-ADV-01-00-EN.pdf.

[5] "Applicability of Article VI, Section 22, of the Convention on the Privileges and Immunities of the United Nations", Advisory Opinion, *ICJ Reports*, 1989, 177. http://www.icj-cij.org/files/case-related/81/081-19891215-ADV-01-00-EN.pdf.

advisable for international organizations to renounce to privileges and immunities limited to the enforcement of international arbitration awards, in those areas where they enjoy absolute immunity of jurisdiction. In doing so, they gain certainty of the law, as they have a better chance of enforcing arbitration awards.

Finally, legal regimes applicable to privileges and immunities are fragmented and there is a *lacuna* in the regulatory framework of privileges and immunities, as there is a widening group of persons who, while contributing in an official capacity to the production of global public goods or the fight against global wrongs, are not covered by any privileges and immunities. New solutions are needed for the protection to this class of persons. The problems mentioned above will be discussed in the following.

8.1 Paradigms for Extending Privileges and Immunities

8.1.1 Constituent Agreements and Multilateral Conventions

In traditional organizations with treaty foundation, the constituent agreement provides for privileges and immunities which may be further elaborated in a convention or other multilateral agreement and in bilateral agreements or arrangements. This will be illustrated with reference to the UN system.

Privileges and immunities are intrinsically related to membership in those cases where the consensual basis of the international organization as set forth in the constituent agreement includes provisions governing privileges and immunities. While not all constitutions contain such provisions,[6] most constitutions do. However, their content may vary substantially, as some constitutions only contain provisions of a general nature, while others list specific privileges and immunities.

In addition to the United Nations, there are other international organizations which enjoy privileges and immunities under a convention, protocol, or multilateral agreement. However, not all international organizations are covered by a multilateral agreement. In such cases, the provisions of the constituent agreement are often supplemented by a headquarters agreement and other bilateral agreements with states. Such agreements may also be concluded with entities incorporated under national law and organizations characterized by "institutional ambivalence by design" (see Chap. 6).

[6] The Constitution of UPU contains no provisions "establishing the legal status of the Union on the territory of member countries"; however, the "Agreement on privileges and immunities of the United Nations" dated 1 July 1946 concluded by the Swiss Federal Council and the Secretary-General of the United Nations is applied by analogy to UPU. See Constitution. General Regulations. Rules of procedure. Legal status of the UPU, by the UPU International Bureau, Commentary, commentaries on D.11. UPU: Berne, 2014. http://www.upu.int/uploads/tx_sbdownloader/actInFourVolumesConstitutionManualEn.pdf.

8.1.1.1 United Nations

Article 105 of the UN Charter only has a very generic content. It provides:

1. The Organization shall enjoy in the territory of each of its Members such privileges and immunities as are necessary for the fulfilment of its purposes.
2. Representatives of the Members of the United Nations and officials of the Organization shall similarly enjoy such privileges and immunities as are necessary for the independent exercise of their functions in connection with the Organization.

The Rapporteur of the Preparatory Committee that drafted the said provision, explained:

> It is to be noted that this provision is [....] confined to a statement of the obligation incumbent upon each Member State to act in such a way that the Organization enjoys in its territory a juridical status permitting it to exercise its functions. The Organization should be capable, in effect, as regards internal law, of performing the juridical acts required to put its capacities into operation. The Organization must be able, in its own name, to contract, to hold movable and immovable property, to appear in court. These are only examples. The Committee has preferred to express no opinion on the procedures of internal law necessary to assure this result. These procedures may differ according to the legislation of each Member State [....].
>
> As regards the question of international juridical personality, the Committee has considered it superfluous to make this the subject of a text. In effect, it will be determined implicitly from the provisions of the Charter as a whole.[7]

The approach adopted in the UN Charter is based on a functional approach to privileges and immunities that was already reflected in the Constitution of the International Labour Organization which preceded the UN Charter.[8] Detailed provisions on the organization's legal and privileges and immunities are contained in the General Convention on the Privileges and Immunities of the United Nations (General Convention) which the General Assembly approved by Resolution No. 22.[9] Although the General Convention was submitted to all members of the

---

[7] Cited by Miller 2009, p. 13.

[8] Article 40 of the ILO Constitution provides:
Privileges and immunities:

1. The International Labour Organization shall enjoy in the territory of each of its Members such privileges and immunities as are necessary for the fulfilment of its purposes.
2. Delegates to the Conference, members of the Governing Body and the Director-General and officials of the Office shall likewise enjoy such privileges and immunities as are necessary for the independent exercise of their functions in connection with the Organization.
3. Such privileges and immunities shall be defined in a separate agreement to be prepared by the Organization with a view to its acceptance by the States Members.

[9] For the drafting history of the General Convention, see Miller 2007b, pp. 17–19; Miller 2007a, pp. 180–183; Miller 2009, pp. 16–19.

United Nations for accession,[10] only 160[11] out of the 193 UN members[12] acceded to it. Thus, not all UN members are parties to the General Convention.

The General Convention is applicable to the United Nations, including any subsidiary bodies and autonomous bodies which have been established as an extension of the legal personality of the United Nations, and under the terms of an institutional linkage, to the secretariats of the United Nations Framework Convention on Climate Change (UNFCCC)[13] and the United Nations Convention to Combat Desertification (UNCCD).[14] The institutional linkage that exists between the UN and the two secretariats allows UNFCCC and UNCCD a certain degree of autonomy, while their staff may benefit from the applicability of the General Convention. An interesting case also relates to the applicability of the General Convention to OSCE as an integral part of UNMIK, which has been discussed above.

The question as to the permitted degree of deviation from UN rules arose when the Green Climate Fund (GCF) sought an institutional linkage with the UN on similar terms as the UNFCCC and UNCCD Secretariats, but with an increased degree of autonomy, given the fact that the GCF does not adhere to the UN common system. The proposal of the Board of the Green Climate Fund for the Conference of Parties (COP) to recommend an institutional linkage to the General Assembly has not yet been acted upon.[15] Thus, the General Convention does not apply to the GCF at present.

---

[10] See Final Article, Section 31 of the General Convention.

[11] As of 5 Oct. 2017, 162 Parties have acceded to the General Convention. See https://treaties.un.org/Pages/ViewDetails.aspx?src=IND&mtdsg_no=III-1&chapter=3&lang=en.

[12] For the status of ratification of the UN Charter as at 5 Oct. 2017, please see https://treaties.un.org/pages/viewdetails.aspx?src=ind&mtdsg_no=i-1&chapter=1&lang=en.

[13] The institutional linkage of the UNFCCC secretariat to the United Nations was initially approved by UNFCCC COP decision 14/CP.1, "Institutional linkage of the Convention secretariat to the United Nations" (7 April 1995) and endorsed by United Nations General Assembly resolution 50/115, "Protection of global climate for present and future generations of mankind" (20 Dec. 1995). It was subsequently extended on various occasions. Regarding the terms of the institutional linkage, see UNFCCC. 2005. Continuation of the institutional linkage of the secretariat to the United Nations. Note by the Executive Secretary (FCCC/SBI/2005/15, 30 Aug.). http://unfccc.int/resource/docs/2005/sbi/eng/15.pdf.

[14] The institutional linkage of the UNCCD secretariat to the United Nations was initially approved by General Assembly resolution 52/198 (http://www.un.org/ga/documents/gares52/res52198.htm) and UNCCD COP decision 4/COP.1, and was subsequently extended.

[15] The background is summarized in GCF. 2014. Options for an Institutional Linkage between the United Nations and the Fund. (GCF/B.08/39, 8 Oct. 2014) The UNFCCC COP did not make, as requested by the Board of the Green Climate Fund a recommendation to the UN General Assembly but, taking "note of Green Climate Fund Board decision B.08/24 on the institutional linkage between the United Nations and the Green Climate Fund, [requested] the Board of the Green Climate Fund to continue further deliberations on privileges and immunities, and to report on this matter to the Conference of the Parties at its twenty-first session (Nov.–Dec. 2015)"; Decision 7/CP. 20, "Report of the Green Climate Fund to the Conference of the Parties and guidance to the Green Climate Fund", para 20. http://unfccc.int/resource/docs/2014/cop20/eng/10a02.pdf#page=14.

In the case of the UN specialized agencies, the legal basis of their privileges and immunities "is to be found in their constitutional instruments, their agreements with the United Nations and the Convention on the Privileges and Immunities of the Specialized Agencies [CPISA] [….]." Besides, national legislation and the headquarters agreements between the specialized agency and the host state are other valuable sources."[16]

While the Articles of Agreement of the IMF spell out in detail the applicable privileges and immunities,[17] the constitution of the Food and Agriculture Organization of the United Nations (FAO), in the tradition of the League of Nations, associates the legal status of the organization with that of a diplomatic mission, that of the Director General and senior staff with diplomatic staff, and that of other personnel with non-diplomatic staff of diplomatic missions.[18]

While considering the advantages of a unification of the privileges of the UN and those of the specialized agencies, the UN "recognized that not all agencies would need all of the privileges and immunities accorded to the UN because of their specialized functions and that others may need privileges and immunities not needed by the UN itself."[19] For this reason, the standard clauses of CPISA are subject to modifications[20] in the Annexes to the CPISA which take account of the features of the specialized agencies and may be revised on a regular basis to reflect any necessary adjustments. The framework set forth in Article X of the CPISA is of substantial complexity. For those specialized agencies mentioned in Article 1 CIPSA, the relevant Annexes are included in the CPISA. In case of new members

---

[16] Ahluwalia 1964, p. 51.

[17] See Article IX of the IMF Articles of Agreement. https://www.imf.org/external/pubs/ft/aa/.

[18] Article XVI, para 2 of the FAO Constitution provides:

> 2. Each Member Nation and Associate Member undertakes, insofar as it may be possible under its constitutional procedure, to accord to the Organization all the immunities and facilities which it accords to diplomatic missions, including inviolability of premises and archives, immunity from suit and exemptions from taxation.

In addition, Article VIII, para 4 of the FAO Constitution provides:

> 4. Each Member Nation and Associate Member undertakes, insofar as it may be possible under its constitutional procedure, to accord to the Director-General and senior staff diplomatic privileges and immunities and to accord to other members of the staff all facilities and immunities accorded to non-diplomatic personnel attached to diplomatic missions or, alternatively, to accord to such other members of the staff the immunities and facilities which may hereafter be accorded to equivalent members of the staffs of other public international organizations.

See Basic Texts of the Food and Agriculture Organization of the United Nations. 2017. Vols. I and II. http://www.fao.org/3/a-mp046e.pdf.

[19] Miller 2007b, p. 14.

[20] CPISA, Article X, Section 33. https://treaties.un.org/doc/Publication/UNTS/Volume%2033/v33.pdf.

of the specialized agency club not mentioned in Article 1, draft annexes recommended by ECOSOC are transmitted to the agencies concerned by the Secretary-General (Section 35) and are approved by each agency "in accordance with its constitutional procedure" (Section 36); upon transmission of the final relevant annex and acceptance of the modified standard clauses and other relevant provisions of the Convention, the CPISA becomes applicable to the agency concerned. The Secretary-General communicates to all members of the UN and the specialized agencies certified copies of all annexes (Section 37); any revisions to annexes approved by an agency in accordance with its constitutional procedure are transmitted to the Secretary-General pursuant to Section 38.[21]

While the potential scope of the CPISA exceeds that of the General Convention (in addition to all UN members, members of specialized agencies which are not UN members are also entitled to accede to the Convention),[22] the actual number of Parties that have ratified the Specialized Agencies Convention is substantially lower than the number of Parties which have acceded to the General Convention.[23] Furthermore, not all Parties to the CPISA have recognized that Convention to the full extent for all specialized agencies and not all Parties to the CPISA have recognized all amendments to the Annexes. As shown by Burci and Ganziera, Annex VII of the CPISA which is applicable to WHO has been revised on three occasions and not all such amendments have been accepted by all parties to the CPISA; hence, "the overall picture of the scope of the obligations accepted by WHO's member states under the Specialized Agencies Convention is somehow fragmented."[24]

The General Convention and the CPISA define standards for privileges and immunities that are widely recognized and replicated.

There are several organizations which are part of the wider UN family but are not covered by either the General Convention or the CPISA. These include related agencies such as the IAEA, WTO and IOM, and other autonomous independent organizations with a working relationship with the UN, such as the International Criminal Court (ICC), the Organization for the Prohibition of Chemical Weapons

---

[21] CPISA, Article X, Sections 35–38.

[22] See CPISA, Article XI, Section 41; In addition, CPISA, Article XI, Section 42 provides:

> Each specialized agency concerned shall communicate the text of this Convention together with the relevant annexes to those of its members which are not Members of the United Nations and shall invite them to accede thereto in respect of that agency by depositing an instrument of accession to this Convention in respect thereof either with the Secretary-General of the United Nations or with the executive head of the specialized agency.

[23] As of 25 Nov. 2017, 128 countries have ratified the Specialized Agencies Convention. See https://treaties.un.org/pages/ViewDetails.aspx?src=TREATY&mtdsg_no=III-2&chapter=3&lang=en.

[24] Burci and Granziera 2015, p. 93.

(OPCW), the Preparatory Commission for the Comprehensive Nuclear-Test-Ban Treaty Organization, and the International Seabed Authority, all of which have concluded relationship agreements with the United Nations.

The first of these relationship agreements, which was concluded between the United Nations and the IAEA in 1959, recognized the IAEA as "as the agency, under the aegis of the United Nations [....] responsible for international activities concerned with the peaceful uses of atomic energy in accordance with its Statute, without prejudice to the rights and responsibilities of the United Nations in this field under the Charter"[25] and further recognized that "the Agency, by virtue of its inter-governmental character and international responsibilities, will function under its Statute as an autonomous international organization in the working relationship with the United Nations established by this Agreement."[26]

The relationship agreement between IAEA and the United Nations does not imply that the General Convention or the CPISA are made applicable to the IAEA, as IAEA is neither part of the United Nations, nor a specialized agency as defined in Article 1(j) of the CPISA. While IAEA tried to have such an extension approved, as Szasz recounts, none of the six approaches which were considered in this context proved to be feasible.[27] Thus, coverage under the CPISA could not be extended to

---

[25] Agreement Governing the Relationship Between the United Nations and the International Atomic Energy Agency. Article I, para 1. Reproduced in IAEA. 1959. Information Circular. The Texts of the Agency's Agreements with the United Nations (INFCIRC/11, 30 Oct. 1959). https://www.iaea.org/sites/default/files/publications/documents/infcircs/1959/infcirc11.pdf.

[26] Ibid., Article I, para 2. The Agreement which contains a variety of provisions on cooperation and collaboration with the UN and the respective responsibilities of the UN and IAEA, among which in Article XIX, para under the heading "Administrative rights and facilities" the following:

> 1. Members of the staff of the Agency shall be entitled, in accordance with such administrative arrangements as may be concluded between the Secretary-General of the United Nations and the Director General of the Agency, to use the United Nations laissez-passer as a valid travel document where such use is recognized by States parties to the Convention on the Privileges and Immunities of the United Nations.

[27] As indicated by Szasz, the following six approaches were investigated:

(a) To apply the Specialized Agencies Convention to the Agency by amending that instrument;
(b) To apply the Specialized Agencies Convention to the Agency by means of a resolution of the UN General Assembly (which had originally formulated that instrument), by which the Agency would be defined to be a specialized agency for the purpose of the Convention (as had been done with respect to UNJSPF);
(c) To apply the Specialized Agencies Convention to the Agency by means of a special multilateral "protocol" to be presented by the Board to the Members of the Agency;
(d) To apply the Specialized Agencies Convention to the Agency by means of bilateral agreements between the Agency and each Member State;
(e) To present to the Member States a new agreement formulated by the Board but based as far as possible on the Specialized Agencies Convention;
(f) To conclude separate bilateral agreements with each Member State. The Secretariat of the Agency originally preferred solution (b), to which it saw no substantial legal obstacle.

the IAEA through the mechanism in Article X discussed above, i.e. involving the transmission of a draft annex to the CPISA recommended by ECOSOC (Section 35), the approval of the final annex "by the specialized agency in question in accordance with its constitutional procedure" and the transmission of the approved annex to the Secretary-General (Section 36). Instead, Article XV.C of the IAEA Statute provides that "the legal capacity, privileges and immunities referred to in this Article shall be defined in a separate agreement or agreements between the Agency, represented for this purpose by the Director General acting under the instructions of the Board of Governors, and the members";[28] such agreement was enacted on 1 July 1959 and took effect on 29 July 1960.[29]

The other relationship agreements concluded by the United Nations with the agencies mentioned above generally follow the same outline of the IAEA relationship agreement. In the case of the International Criminal Court (ICC) which was established as an international organization with juridical personality separate from the UN rather than a judicial organ of the UN, Article 12 of its relationship agreement authorizes the persons concerned (judges, the prosecutor, deputy-prosecutor and the staff/officials of the Office of the Prosecutor and the registry) "to use the *laissez-passer* of the United Nations as a valid travel document where such use is recognized by States in agreements defining the privileges and immunities of the Court."[30] However, the relationship agreement only provides for the use of the *laissez-passer* as a travel document. Its substantive privileges and immunities derive from Article 48 of the Rome Statute of the Court, the Agreement on the Privileges and Immunities of the International Criminal Court[31] and the Headquarters Agreement of the ICC with the government of the Netherlands.[32] In the case of the International Seabed Authority, the use of the laissez-passer is authorized in its relationship agreement with the UN[33] while its substantive privileges and immunities derive from the Protocol on the Privileges and Immunities of

---

However, the UN Legal Counsel concluded that the General Assembly had no power at that stage to change the scope of the Convention by an interpretative definition.

Szasz 1970, p. 971.

[28] IAEA Statute. https://www.iaea.org/about/statute#a1-15.

[29] Agreement on the Privileges and Immunities of the International Atomic Energy Agency, http://www.jus.uio.no/english/services/library/treaties/14/14-04/immunities-atomic-agency.xml.

[30] Negotiated Relationship Agreement between the International Criminal Court and the United Nations. http://legal.un.org/ola/media/UN-ICC_Cooperation/UN-ICC%20Relationship%20Agreement.pdf.

[31] See Agreement on the Privileges and Immunities of the International Criminal Court. ICC-ASP/1/3, Adopted by the Assembly of States Parties, First session, New York, 3–10 Sept. 2002. http://www.icc-cpi.int/NR/rdonlyres/23F24FDC-E9C2-4C43-BE19-A19F5DDE8882/140090/Agreement_on_Priv_and_Imm_120704EN.pdf.

[32] See Nilsson 2004, p. 562.

[33] Agreement concerning the relationship between the United Nations and the International Seabed Authority. 14 March 1997. United Nations Treaty Series. No. 1165, Vol. 256, 255–264. https://www.isa.org.jm/sites/default/files/documents/EN/Regs/UN-ISA-Agrmnt.pdf.

the International Seabed Authority[34] and its Headquarters Agreement[35] and the Supplementary Agreement thereto.[36]

The situation of the OPCW and the Preparatory Commission for the Comprehensive Nuclear-Test-Ban Treaty Organization is similar in that both relationship agreements[37] allow the use of the *laissez-passer*, but do not entail applicability of the General Convention or the CPISA; however, somewhat different arrangements have been made to extend to these organizations privileges and immunities.[38]

---

[34] Protocol on the Privileges and Immunities of the International Seabed Authority. http://www.isa.org.jm/files/documents/EN/Regs/Protocol-Priv-Imms.pdf.

[35] Agreement between the International Seabed Authority and the Government of Jamaica regarding the Headquarters of the International Seabed Authority. http://www.isa.org.jm/sites/default/files/documents/EN/Regs/HQ-Agrmt.pdf.

[36] Supplementary Agreement between the International Seabed Authority and the Government of Jamaica Regarding the Headquarters of the International Seabed Authority and the Use of the Jamaica Conference Centre Complex. https://www.isa.org.jm/sites/default/files/documents/EN/Regs/ISA-Ja-SuppAg.pdf.

[37] Pursuant to Article VIII, para 34(a) of the Convention on the Prohibition of the Development, Production, Stockpiling and Use of Chemical Weapons and on Their Destruction (Chemical Weapons Convention), https://www.opcw.org/fileadmin/OPCW/CWC/CWC_en.pdf, the United Nations and Organization for the Prohibition concluded a relationship agreement that was approved by the OPCW Conference of the States Parties on 17 May 2001 and by the United Nations General Assembly in resolution A/RES/55/283 dated 24 Sept. 2001. https://www.opcw.org/fileadmin/OPCW/LAO/a55r283.pdf. Article IX refers to the right of OPCW officials to "to use the laissez-passer of the United Nations as a valid travel document where such use is recognized by States Parties in the applicable instruments defining the privileges and immunities of OPCW and its officials." (UN. 2001. Agreement concerning the Relationship between the United Nations and the Organization for the Prohibition of Chemical Weapons. Note by the Secretary-General [18 June, A/55/988], http://www.un.org/documents/ga/docs/55/a55988.pdf). However, the legal basis for the privileges and immunities of OPWC is set out in Article VIII (E) of the Chemical Weapons Convention.

An overview of the legal framework and privileges and immunities of the Preparatory Commission for the Comprehensive Nuclear-Test-Ban Treaty Organization is provided In CTBTO preparatory commission for the comprehensive nuclear-test-ban treaty organization. 2012. National Implementation Measures: Legislation, Privileges and Immunities and Facility Agreements. Note by the Executive Secretary (CTBT/PTS/INF. 1204, 21 Sept. 2012). https://www.ctbto.org/fileadmin/user_upload/pdf/Legal_documents/2015/CTBT-PTS-INF1204.pdf.

[38] The legal basis for the privileges and immunities of OPWC is set out in Article VIII (E) of the Chemical Weapons Convention. https://www.opcw.org/chemical-weapons-convention/articles/article-viii-the-organization/#c11980. For details, See Organization for the Prohibition of Chemical Weapon. Privileges and Immunities of the OPCW. https://www.opcw.org/about-opcw/technical-secretariat/privileges-immunities/.

The cooperation arrangements between the UN and WTO of 1995[39] succeeded the "de facto working arrangements" already applicable between the UN and the General Agreement on Tariffs and Trade (GATT) under which GATT officials were entitled to use the UN laissez-passer.[40] The IMF and WTO, are, as shown by Siegel,[41] "asymmetrical organizations despite complementary objectives". As the functions of the WTO, IMF, and the International Bank for Reconstruction and Development (IBRD) are partially complementary, Article 3 para 5 of the Marrakesh Agreement contains for that reason an express provision to the effect that "With a view to achieving greater coherence in global economic policy-making, the WTO shall cooperate, as appropriate, with the [IMF] and with the [IBRD] and its affiliated agencies."[42] However, there is no equivalent provision on the relations between the WTO and the UN. Nevertheless, after "the adoption on 31 January 1995 of the Report of the Preparatory Committee which saw no grounds for formal institutional links between the WTO and the United Nations although the need for the establishment of cooperative ties between the two organizations was underscored,"[43] at the request of the WTO General Council, a global arrangement was agreed by the UN and WTO secretariats, based on a letter exchange between the Director-General of the WTO and the Secretary-General of the UN dated 29

[39] WTO. 1995. "General Council. Arrangements for Effective Cooperation with other Intergovernmental Organizations". Relations between the WTO and the United Nations. Communication from the Director-General (WT/GC/W/10, 8 Nov. 1995). See also the paper submitted on 12 Feb. 1976 to the Ad Hoc Committee on Restructuring of the Economic and Social Sectors of the United Nations System, titled: "Relations of GATT with the United Nations" (L/4306/Add.1, 14 April) (GATT. 1976. "Relations of GATT with the United Nations", *Ad Hoc Committee on Restructuring of the Economic and Social Sectors of the United Nations System*, 5. https://www.wto.org/gatt_docs/English/SULPDF/90920196.pdf.

[40] See GATT. 1976. *Ad Hoc Committee on Restructuring of the Economic and Social Sectors of the United Nations System.* Addendum. Relations of GATT with United Nations (L/4306/Add. 1, 14 April 1976) which indicates on page 5 under the heading Personnel Arrangements the following: "Under present arrangements members of the GATT staff may use the United Nations laissez-passer as a travel document." https://www.wto.org/gatt_docs/English/SULPDF/90920196.pdf.

[41] Siegel 2002, p. 563.

[42] Detailed references regarding the agreements between WTO and IMF and IBRD and related documents are contained on the IMF website under "Work with Other International Organizations. The WTO and the International Monetary Fund". https://www.wto.org/english/thewto_e/coher_e/wto_imf_e.htm.

[43] WTO. 1995. General Council. Arrangements for Effective Cooperation with other Intergovernmental Organizations. Relations between the WTO and the United Nations. Communication from the Director-General (WT/GC/W/10, 8 Nov. 1995).

September 1995.[44] One that basis, WTO staff continue to avail of the UN *laissez-passer*, but also in case of the WTO the CPISA is not applicable inasmuch as the privileges and immunities of WTO staff are concerned. This is notwithstanding Article VIII, para 4 of the Marrakesh Agreement, which provides:

> The privileges and immunities to be accorded by a Member to the WTO, its officials, and the representatives of its Members shall be similar to the privileges and immunities stipulated in the Convention on the Privileges and Immunities of the Specialized Agencies, approved by the General Assembly of the United Nations on 21 November 1947.[45]

While the CPISA is referenced in the aforementioned provision, the legal basis for the grant of privileges and immunities is the Marrakesh Agreement, not the CPISA. As a consequence, any reservations made to the CPISA are not applicable under the Marrakesh Agreement in the case of the WTO.

The "Agreement concerning the Relationship between the United Nations and the International Organization for Migration" is the last one that was approved by General Assembly Resolution 70/296 of 25 July 2016.[46] It also allows IOM staff to "use the *laissez-passer* of the United Nations as a valid travel document where such use is recognized by States in agreements defining the privileges and immunities of the International Organization for Migration."

---

[44] The 29 Sept. 1995 letter from the Director-General of WTO to the UN Secretary General reads:

> The conclusion which we have reached, as a result of these consultations and taking into account the experience in the relations between the United Nations and the GATT, is that a flexible framework for cooperation, liable to further review and adaptation in the light of developments and emerging requirements, is the most desirable course of action.
>
> We agreed, in that light, that the arrangements and practices described in the attached United Nations General Assembly document of 9 March 1976 (A/AC.179/5) in respect of the United Nations/GATT relationship provide a suitable basis to continue to guide relations between the United Nations and the World Trade Organization.

The letter exchange is contained in the Annex of WTO. 1995. "General Council. Arrangements for Effective Cooperation with other Intergovernmental Organizations". Relations between the WTO and the United Nations. Communication from the Director-General (WT/GC/W/10, 8 Nov. 1995). https://docs.wto.org/dol2fe/Pages/FE_Search/FE_S_S009-DP.aspx?language=E&CatalogueIdList=6887,13692,26254,21280,3316,32374,14512,28305,37959,24645&CurrentCatalogueIdIndex=9&FullTextHash=&HasEnglishRecord=True&HasFrenchRecord=True&HasSpanishRecord=True.

[45] Agreement Establishing the World Trade Organization. https://www.wto.org/english/docs_e/legal_e/04-wto.pdf.

[46] Resolution 70/296 "Agreement concerning the Relationship between the United Nations and the International Organization for Migration" adopted by the General Assembly on 25 July 2019. http://www.un.org/en/ga/search/view_doc.asp?symbol=A/RES/70/296.

8.1.1.2 Other Organizations with Multilateral Conventions on Privileges and Immunities

There are a number of other organizations not covered by the General Convention or CPISA which enjoy privileges and immunities under a multilateral agreement without having a relationship agreement with the United Nations.

ASEAN belongs to this category. Initially, only the ASEAN Secretariat enjoyed legal capacity and privileges and immunities under an agreement with Indonesia of 1979.[47] Subsequently, the Agreement on the Privileges and Immunities of ASEAN of 2009 entered into force, which confers to ASEAN international legal personality and privileges and immunities.

The Statute of the International Renewable Energy Agency (IRENA) provides for a decision of the members "upon a separate agreement on privileges and immunities".[48] Consistent with that provision, the IRENA council recommended the "Agreement on Privileges and Immunities for the International Renewable Energy Agency"[49] to members for further action under their respective internal procedures.[50]

Inasmuch as the founding members of the OECD are concerned, the privileges and immunities of the organization and the persons associated with the organization are set out in two protocols to the Convention for European Economic Co-operation,[51] while "separate Privileges and Immunities Agreements have been concluded with all new Members and with a number of non-Members."[52]

The Global Fund is the first case where an organization incorporated under national law sought approval of the countries where it operates to become party to a multilateral agreement extending to it privileges and immunities. This can be seen as a new paradigm for extending privileges and immunities to an organization incorporated under national law.[53]

---

[47] Agreement Between the Government of the Republic of Indonesia and the ASEAN Relating to the Privileges and Immunities of the ASEAN Secretariat of 20 Jan. 1979. http://agreement.asean.org/media/download/20140416011141.pdf.

[48] Statute of the International Renewable Energy Agency, Article XIII(B). http://www.irena.org/documents/uploadDocuments/Statute/IRENA_FC_Statute_signed_in_Bonn_26_01_2009_incl_declaration_on_further_authentic_versions.pdf.

[49] IRENA. 2012. Draft Agreement on Privileges and Immunities for the International Renewable Energy Agency. http://www.irena.org/documents/uploadDocuments/4thCouncil/C_4_13_Agreement%20P%20and%20Is.pdf.

[50] IRENA 2013. Decision on an Agreement on Privileges and Immunities for the International Renewable Energy Agency. https://www.irena.org/DocumentDownloads/2013/Assembly/A_3_DC_5_Decision_Privileges%20and%20Immunities.pdf.

[51] OECD. Convention on the Organisation for Economic Co-operation and Development. http://www.oecd.org/general/conventionontheorganisationforeconomicco-operationanddevelop-ment.htm.

[52] http://www.oecd.org/legal/privileges-immunities-agreements.htm.

[53] Global Fund. 2014. Thirty-Second Board Meeting. Privileges and Immunities of the Global Fund. https://www.theglobalfund.org/media/4138/bm32_19-pandis_report_en.pdf.

Similarly, the proposed "Draft Convention on the International Legal Personality, Legal Capacity, and Privileges and Immunities of the OSCE",[54] which expressly recognized in Article 3 the "international legal personality" of the OSCE, and provided in Articles 4 for the legal capacity of, and in Articles 5 ss. for privileges and immunities for, OSCE, had the potential of transforming the legal status of OSCE. However, it did not meet with the approval of all participating states.

In the case of the Green Climate Fund, the Secretariat noted in its "Report on the activities of the Secretariat" of 21 June 2017 that it "intends to propose offering to Parties to the UNFCCC the alternative option of entering into a multilateral agreement that will in substance follow" the template for bilateral agreements that has been developed by the Secretariat.[55] However, this matter is still subject to consideration and no multilateral agreement has yet been offered to country parties to the UNFCCC.

It is possible, as a matter of principle, that a multilateral agreement regarding privileges and immunities can be made immediately applicable following its signature based on a protocol of provisional application. However, in most cases such agreements only take effect upon ratification by a determined number of parties. This may delay for many years the effectiveness of the agreement in question.

8.1.1.3 Headquarters and Host Country Agreements

In many ways, the most important relations of an organization are those with its host country. As there are specific aspects to such relationship "that may not easily be resolved by reference to general principles of international law or even the provisions of general conventions on privileges and immunities,"[56] in many cases, headquarters agreements contain detailed provisions on the organization's premises, their protection and public services, their legal status, privileges and immunities, access and visas, facilities, and other related matters. Such agreements also normally contain provisions on the inviolability of the headquarters district or premises which are generally not contained in the organization's constituent agreements. The provisions on privileges and immunities in headquarters agreements may replicate those of the constituent agreement, or may substantially expand and further elaborate them. In addition to the functional immunity often provided to officials by the constituent agreement, headquarters agreements often extend to the executive head of the organization and other senior staff (e.g. staff at UN level P-5 and above) full

[54] "Draft Convention on the International Legal Personality, Legal Capacity, and Privileges and Immunities of the OSCE". In OSCE. 2007. *Fifteenth Meeting of the Ministerial Council, 29 and 30 Nov. 2007*, Madrid. 65 ss. http://www.osce.org/mc/33180?download=true.

[55] GCF. 2017. Report on the activities of the Secretariat (Doc. GCF/B.17/Inf.01, 21 June 2017), para 54. https://www.greenclimate.fund/documents/20182/751020/GCF_B.17_Inf.01_-_Report_on_the_activities_of_the_Secretariat.pdf/08db0fe2-e40c-44cd-baba-f3d749001ecb.

[56] Mensah 2012, p. 1463.

diplomatic privileges and immunities. This is not only a standard feature of many headquarters agreements of UN agencies,[57] but also applicable in other cases. Hence, also the headquarters agreement of the Green Climate Fund provides for the

> Executive Director and senior Staff of the Secretariat having a professional level equivalent to level P-5 and above of the United Nations position classification [....] the same privileges and immunities, exemptions and facilities as the Government accords to members of comparable rank of the diplomatic staff of missions accredited to the Government.[58]

Another area where the headquarters agreement often goes beyond what is provided for by constituent agreements relates to taxation, in particular to the exemption from indirect taxes, and to the exemption from customs duties.

As headquarters agreements are meant to have legal effects under national law, they are normally adopted by way of a treaty. The wording of organizations' constituent agreement is often geared to countries that follow the dualist tradition. Against this background, for example the Charter of the Asian Development Bank contains in Article 57 expressly provides:

> Each member, in accordance with its juridical system, shall promptly take such action as is necessary to make effective in its own territory the provisions set forth in the Chapter [Chapter VIII. Status, Immunities, Exemptions and Privileges] and shall inform the Bank of the action which it has taken on the matter.

However, in the countries that follow the monist tradition, the headquarters agreement has, as under Article 6 of the Constitution of the Republic of Korea, "the same effect as the domestic laws". This is also the case for the headquarters agreement of the Green Climate Fund, which is a treaty under the said Article 6.

One point that this author wishes to stress is that it is not a requirement for an organization to be established by a treaty for it to be able to conclude an agreement governed by international law with the country where it has its headquarters. Hence, similar agreements can be concluded not only with traditional international organizations with treaty foundation but also with entities incorporated under national law, and with subsidiary bodies and organizations established based on a decision of the Conference of the Parties to a multilateral convention.

The agreement concluded between the Swiss Federation and the Global Fund expressly recognizes "for the purposes of this Agreement the international juridical

[57] See Article 16 of the "Agreement between the Swiss Federal Council and the International Labour Organization concerning the legal status of the International Labour Organization in Switzerland": "The Director of the International Labour Office and officials of the categories designated by him and agreed to by the Swiss Federal Council shall enjoy the privileges, immunities, exemptions and facilities granted to diplomatic agents in accordance with international law and custom." http://www.ilo.org/global/about-the-ilo/how-the-ilo-works/departments-and-offices/jur/legal-instruments/WCMS_441510/lang%2D%2Den/index.htm.

[58] Headquarters Agreement, Article 13, para 2(b). https://www.greenclimate.fund/documents/20182/56440/Headquarters_Agreement.pdf/13df1525-af90-456b-8d76-5b83be9b39d4.

personality and legal capacity in Switzerland of the Global Fund [….].”[59] A similar provision is contained in the corresponding Agreement between the Gavi Alliance and the Swiss Federation.[60] There is one major difference between these two agreements and headquarters agreements with international organizations with treaty foundation. For such traditional international organizations, any provisions in their headquarters agreements regarding their international legal personality and legal capacity are generally only declaratory in nature in that they confirm those already contained in the constituent agreement. Agreements between states and organizations incorporated under national law that recognize the international legal personality of the latter, on the other hand, determine the legal status of the organization concerned in its host country. Such agreements have the potential of transforming the legal status of the organization. By recognizing the international legal personality of an organization incorporated under national law, states promote the creation of a new institutional paradigm of international organization, i.e. that of the dual and hybrid organization incorporated under national law, but with recognition of international legal personality and privileges and immunities in their host country (and certain other countries).

As due “to the ongoing dispute over the international legal personality of the OSCE, no headquarters agreement had previously been concluded between Austria and the OSCE”, action was taken by Austria to regulate the status of OSCE and its officials “by the statutory act of 1993 (the ‘OSCE Act’).”[61] The fact that Austria and Poland recently agreed to enter into headquarters agreements with OSCE (see above) constitutes an important new development that supports the position of those who claim that the OSCE possesses international legal personality.

8.1.1.4 Bilateral Agreements Supplementing Multilateral Agreements

In addition to headquarters agreements, there are a range of other bilateral agreements which have been concluded by international organizations (e.g. with countries where they maintain offices) which supplement multilateral agreements on privileges and immunities. Such bilateral agreements often provide for additional specificity and privileges and immunities. Thus, while under Article V, Section 19 of the General Convention, only the Secretary-General and all Assistant Secretaries-General are accorded in respect of themselves and their families “privileges and immunities, exemptions and facilities accorded to diplomatic

[59] Article 1 of the “Agreement between the Swiss Federal Council and the Global Fund to Fight AIDS, Tuberculosis and Malaria in view of determining the legal status of the Global Fund in Switzerland”. https://www.theglobalfund.org/media/3393/bm08_07annex4aagreement_annex_en.pdf.

[60] Article 1 of the “Agreement between the Gavi Alliance (Global Alliance for Vaccines and Immunization) and the Swiss Federal Council in order to determine the legal status of the Gavi Alliance in Switzerland” signed in July 2009.

[61] Schmalenbach 2013, p. 453 with further details.

envoys, in accordance with international law", under the terms of the bilateral host country agreements negotiated by the UN with those countries where they maintain offices or representations, diplomatic immunity is often extended to professional staff at level P-5 and above.

Similarly, bilateral agreements have been negotiated by specialized agencies with those countries where they have offices.

Moreover, there is a wide range of other bilateral agreements and arrangements concluded between the United Nations and UN specialized agencies and countries, regarding technical assistance, conferences and workshops and a variety of other matters.

8.1.1.5 Organizations Not Covered by Multilateral Agreements on Privileges and Immunities

In organizations not covered by multilateral agreements, the bilateral agreements are of particular importance to ensure that the organization is covered by privileges and immunities.

There are a number of organizations that are not covered by any multilateral agreement on privileges and immunities. This is the case for most regional organizations. As the term "wide international responsibilities" referenced in para 1 of Article 57 of the United Nations is understood both in a substantive and geographic sense, only universal organizations with a wide scope of activities qualify for recognition as a specialized agency of the United Nations. Thus, regional institutions do not qualify for recognition as a specialized agency of the United Nations. While some regional organizations (e.g. ASEAN)[62] are covered by multilateral agreements other than the General Convention and CPISA, there are various organizations which are not covered by any multilateral agreement. Such organizations generally only enjoy privileges and immunities on the basis of their constituent agreement and specific agreements and arrangements which they conclude with those countries where conduct their operations or maintain offices.

The case of the Asian Development Bank (ADB) epitomizes that approach. Chapter VII of the ADB Charter contains only certain core provisions which members are required to give force of law in their countries. However, said Chapter does not contain any provisions relating to ADB premises (inviolability, protection, public services.) as these are covered by its Headquarters Agreement with the Philippines.[63] Moreover, the ADB Headquarters Agreement provides for additional privileges and immunities for senior ADB officials (Article XII, Section 44) and

[62] See the "Agreement on the Privileges and Immunities of the Southeast Asian Nations". http://www.asean.org/storage/images/archive/15thsummit/Agreement-on-Privileges-and-Immu-nities.pdf.

[63] Agreement Between the Asian Development Bank and the Government of the Republic of the Philippines regarding the Headquarters of the Asian Development Bank. http://www.adb.org/sites/default/files/institutional-document/32422/files/adb-phil-agreement.pdf.

contains additional provisions regarding inter alia ADB's "Communications" (Article VIII), "Property of the Bank and Taxation" (Article IX), and "Access and Residence" (Article XI).

To ensure that ADB's resident missions and representative offices are covered by an appropriate legal framework consistent with that set forth in the headquarters agreement with the Philippines, ADB has concluded host country agreements with those countries where it maintains missions or offices. Also, in addition to the general provisions set forth in the ADB Charter, additional specific assurances are required for ADB to be able to provide effective technical assistance and commence private sector operations. ADB has concluded with its member countries a series of other agreements relating to its technical-assistance and private-sector operations.[64] Hence, ADB is an organization that has entered into a net of bilateral agreements which confer privileges and immunities to it. Such agreements address not only the status, privileges and immunities and exemptions and facilities applicable to resident missions and other representative offices of the ADB, but bear relevance to a variety of other matters, such as, in particular, ADB's technical assistance and private sector operations.[65]

The Governing Instrument of the GCF was adopted by the UNFCCC COP by Decision 3/CP.17.[66] Hence, the Governing Instrument which contains in paras 7 and 8[67] provisions regarding the juridical personality and the privileges and immunities of the GCF was not ratified by the country Parties to the UNFCCC, but, nevertheless, has been the basis of external action by the GCF Secretariat. "As at 8 September 2017, the Secretariat had sent draft agreements on the privileges and immunities of the GCF to a cumulative total of 121 countries. By that date, 13 bilateral privileges and immunities agreements had been signed."[68] This is one of

[64] ADB regularly concludes a "Technical Assistance Framework Agreement" and "Private Sector Framework Agreement" with those countries where it conducts technical assistance and private-sector operations. Templates of a "Technical Assistance Framework Agreement" and "Private Sector Framework Agreement" are reproduced in ADB 2005, pp. 33–45.

[65] See the templates of ADB's Technical Assistance Framework Agreement and Private Sector Framework Agreements In ADB 2005, Appendices 10 and 11.

[66] Decision 3/CP.17. Launching the Green Climate Fund. http://unfccc.int/resource/docs/2011/cop17/eng/09a01.pdf#page=55.

[67] 7. In order to operate effectively internationally, the Fund will possess juridical personality and will have such legal capacity as is necessary for the exercise of its functions and the protection of its interests.

> 8. The Fund will enjoy such privileges and immunities as are necessary for the fulfilment of its purposes. The officials of the Fund will similarly enjoy such privileges and immunities as are necessary for the independent exercise of their official functions in connection with the Fund.

[68] GCF. 2017. "Report on the activities of the Secretariat". (GCF/B.18/Inf.04., 21 September), para 102. https://www.greenclimate.fund/documents/20182/820027/GCF_B.18_Inf.04_-_Report_on_the_activities_of_the_Secretariat.pdf/09454489-7819-4d80-ac92-8c788b588040.

the most extensive attempts which any organization has undertaken to ensure the respect of privileges and immunities through bilateral agreements.

Unlike for the BIS, the establishment of dual and hybrid organizations is generally not based on a treaty. In that case, the constitution of the organization does not have the force of law in the countries where the organization has its seat or where it operates. Thus, bilateral (and multilateral) agreements are generally the main basis conferring privileges and immunities to such organizations. These agreements have the potential of transforming the legal status of a corporation or nongovernmental organization incorporated under national law to that of a dual and hybrid organization.

There is no reason why the countries where an organization operates or has an office should not be invited to conclude a bilateral agreement in addition, or as an alternative, of becoming party to a multilateral agreement on privileges and immunities. Adopting this approach has certain disadvantages. As bilateral agreements generally need to be adjusted to the specific circumstances of countries, there is the risk of a fragmented legal framework regarding privileges and immunities. Also, the process of having to negotiate bilateral agreements with each country is very time consuming and tedious, in particular, in the case of international organizations of global reach, such as the Green Climate Fund.

On the other hand, opting for the conclusion of bilateral agreements to supplement a multilateral agreement or as an alternative to such an agreement, has certain advantages. While the provisional application of treaties is expressly permitted by Article 25 VCLT, cases of provisional application of multilateral agreements are quite rare. Hence, in most cases, these only become effective upon ratification by a defined number of parties. On the other hand, the provisional application of bilateral agreement is more common. Hence, these agreements often become effective upon the signature by the parties thereto in those cases where they may be concluded as executive agreements. Also, where the agreement requires ratification, it is often possible that the provisions of the agreement may be applied provisionally pending ratification. Thus, there are clear benefits in pursing the route of bilateral agreements in addition to or as an alternative to that of a multilateral agreement.

To ensure consistency of the bilateral agreements negotiated by an organization, model agreements may be adopted by the governing bodies of the organization. This approach was considered in the case of the OSCE[69] and has been adopted in the case of the OPCW.[70] In the case of the Green Climate Fund, the Board did not

---

[69] As shown by Tichy and Köhler 2008, p. 467, one option discussed for transforming the legal status of the OSCE was a: "Model bilateral agreement between the OSCE and mission receiving countries: to be adopted by the appropriate body of the OSCE".

[70] See "Draft Agreement between the Organization for the Prohibition of Chemical Weapons and [State Party] on the Privileges and Immunities of the OPCW". https://www.opcw.org/fileadmin/OPCW/LAO/privileges_immunities_agreem/Model_privileges_and_immunities_agreement_en.pdf.

adopt the template of model agreement that had been proposed by the Secretariat,[71] but only core reference provisions to be incorporated in the bilateral agreements with country parties to the UNFCCC.[72] This leaves the Secretariat flexibility in adjusting the bilateral agreement to the constitutional requirements of country parties to the UNFCCC.

8.1.1.6 Other Mechanisms for Conferring Privileges and Immunities

Privileges and immunities may be extended to an organization by the unilateral decision of a government, either, as in the case of the US, by including an organization in the list of organizations covered by the International Organizations Immunities Act (IOIA), or by way of a unilateral commitment made by a state, e.g. in the form of a letter to an organization signed by the Minister of Foreign Affairs. Other ways for conferring privileges and immunities to an organization comprise mechanisms, as reported by Tichy and Köhler in relation to the OSCE, including adoption of a Statute and various types of decisions (either of a declaratory or merely politically-binding nature) adopted by the appropriate governing bodies of the organization.[73]

8.2 Scrutiny of Privileges and Immunities by National and International Courts

8.2.1 Immunity from Legal Process

While the United Nations and a number of other international organizations enjoy unqualified immunity from legal process provided for by their governing instrument, other organizations face express exceptions to their immunity from legal process. This is the case for international financial institutions which would not be able to have access to capital markets if they were to invoke absolute immunity from legal process in relation to their borrowings, securities and guarantees. One example is the ADB, as Article 50.1 of its Charter provides that

---

[71] GCF. 2015. Template for the Bilateral Agreement on Privileges and Immunities (GCF/B.09/19, 17 Feb.). https://www.greenclimate.fund/documents/20182/24949/GCF_B.09_19_-_Template_for_the_Bilateral_Agreement_on_Privileges_and_Immunities.pdf/f569da2d-1b35-4958-8a0b-d5d38374825e.

[72] Green Climate Fund. Board Decision B/10.12, Decisions of the Board – Tenth Meeting of the Board, 6–9 July 2015 (GCF/B.10/17, 21 July), 13. https://www.greenclimate.fund/documents/20182/24952/GCF_B.10_17_-_Decisions_of_the_Board_-_Tenth_Meeting_of_the_Board__6–9_July_2015.pdf/1238c5ad-8686-4cf9-a401-aa4893818215.

[73] Tichy and Köhler 2008, pp. 466–467.

> The Bank shall enjoy immunity from every form of legal process, except in cases arising out of or in connection with the exercise of its powers to borrow money, to guarantee obligations, or to buy and sell or underwrite the sale of securities, in which cases actions may be brought against the Bank in a court of competent jurisdiction in the territory of a country in which the Bank has its principal or a branch office, or has appointed an agent for the purpose of accepting service or notice of process, or has issued or guaranteed securities.

ADB's Charter is much clearer in this regard than the "clumsy and inartfully drafted language of Article VII Section 3"[74] of the Articles of Agreement of the IBRD,[75] for which the scope of the IBRD's immunity essentially had to be developed by jurisprudence.

As and to the extent that there are no express exceptions to the organization's immunity from legal process, such immunity may be seen as being absolute. Nevertheless, there is no general agreement on this matter as even in absence of any specific exception, challenges to the absolute immunity of international organizations are occasionally made (i) in relation to commercial transactions of international organizations or, (ii) on functional grounds, in relation to acts which are perceived not to have been taken in pursuance of the organization's statutory purpose and functions.

8.2.2 Restrictions to Immunity for Commercial Transactions

One approach taken by jurisprudence and proposed in literature is to transpose the distinction between *acta jure imperii* and *acta jure gestionis* made in state immunity to international organizations. However, in the view of this author, this is the wrong approach as it ignores the substantial difference which exists between state immunity and immunity of international organizations.

This is not to deny that a few courts have indeed espoused the above concept. One of the most famous cases relates to the decision of the Corte di Cassazione which caused friction between the FAO and Italy for some 10 years until it was

[74] Mendaro, Susana v. The World Bank, a/k/a International Bank For Reconstruction And Development, No. 82-2247, United States Court of Appeals for the District of Columbia Circuit. 1983. http://www.leagle.com/decision/19831327717F2d610_11226/MENDARO%20v.%20WORLD%20BANK.

[75] Article VII, Section 3 of the Articles of Agreement of the IBRD reads: "Actions may be brought against the Bank only in a court of competent jurisdiction in the territories of a member in which the Bank has an office, has appointed an agent for the purpose of accepting service or notice of process, or has issued or guaranteed securities. No actions shall, however, be brought by members or persons acting for or deriving claims from members. The property and assets of the Bank shall, wheresoever located and by whomsoever held, be immune from all forms of seizure, attachment or execution before the delivery of final judgment against the Bank." http://siteresources.worldbank.org/EXTABOUTUS/Resources/ibrd-articlesofagreement.pdf.

finally revoked.[76] Moreover, there have been a few more recent cases where courts sought to transpose the aforementioned distinction to international organizations. However, more often, courts have refused to take such action. As Ryngaert has shown with reference to the jurisprudence of Austrian, Swiss and Danish courts, once "the immunity of the international organization is enshrined in a treaty, courts are generally unwilling to recognize exceptions to that immunity, e.g., for acta jure gestionis, under customary international law."[77]

This is not to say that organizations enjoy untrammeled freedom to conduct them in their fiscal activities as they deem fit. First, it indeed begs the question whether an organization that wishes to participate in economic affairs on a par with private sector partners should not do so on equal terms. At times, privileges and immunities unnecessarily constrain an organization from engaging in commercial activities. Thus, if international financial institutions create corporations, funds, or other vehicles for equity investments or engage in other exclusively commercial transactions, it may be advisable for them to operate in these matters on commercial terms.

In the case of the International Telecommunications Satellite Organization (INTELSAT), criticism was voiced over the fact that the organization was exempt from paying taxes and entitled to immunity from jurisdiction and other immunities (relating to archives and assets).[78] Its eventual privatization was eventually triggered by that criticism and the perception that it was given an unfair advantage over private sector competitors. The privatization of the International Maritime Satellite Organization (INMARSAT) was prompted by similar concerns.

Hence, an organization should sustain litigation if it conducts exclusively commercial activities, rather than showing, as a colleague of the author once put it delicately in a discussion with this author, its "soft belly" by invoking privileges and immunities whenever claims out of its commercial transactions are made against it. Thus, while the Gavi Alliance and its staff enjoy privileges and immunities in Switzerland in line with those of the UN organizations that have their seat there, the members of the board of the International Finance Facility for Immunisation (IFFIm), Gavi's funding vehicle incorporated under the laws of England and Wales, do not enjoy any.

The same considerations do not apply, however, to international financial institutions such as the MDBs. While these institutions may also conduct equity investments and other financial transactions, they have an important role in global governance and public policy, and perform many functions other than purely commercial ones. Thus, to the extent that international financial institutions enjoy absolute immunity of legal process, such immunity must also apply, in principle, to their private sector operations except to the extent that such operations are expressly

[76] See for that jurisprudence and the jurisprudence of Italian courts, in general: Bonfatè 2015, pp. 246–278.

[77] Ryngaert 2010, p. 125.

[78] See Katkin 2005, p. 12.

exempted from the scope of immunity of legal process (as are under Article 50.1 of the ADB Charter which provides as exceptions, "cases arising out of or in connection with the exercise of its powers to borrow money, to guarantee obligations, or to buy and sell or underwrite the sale of securities.")

Nevertheless, to be able to invoke absolute immunity from legal process, international organizations need to proceed judiciously. This implies that they need to avoid situations where their obligations, and those of their staff, toward third parties may entail a potential conflict of interest. This situation may potentially occur, for example, if staff members of an organization in active service are appointed as directors of a corporation fully or partially owned by an international financial institution. In that case, it may well be argued that the fiduciary obligations that the appointed directors have toward the corporation prevail over their status as staff members of an international financial institution and that for this reason the privileges and immunities of the institution cannot be invoked.

International organizations are also required to deal judiciously with issues of privileges and immunities in other areas, such as referral of allegations of corruption to national jurisdiction in relation to deeds which may constitute criminal offenses in the country where they have been committed.

Special problems arise in those cases where the referral concerns the misconduct of the organization's officials. The referral may require in such cases that the organization waives the immunity of an official (e.g. in cases where an official enjoys full diplomatic immunity) and there are both arguments supporting the need for, as well as cautioning against, referrals.[79] Moreover, if the organization has made a referral to national jurisdiction, the further question arises as to what extent the organization can refuse to participate in discovery ordered by a national court on a matter that had been referred to it. Organizations may limit the discovery by expressly indicating in the act of referral on what matters the staff of the organization may or may not make statements or provide information. To the extent that no such statement is made, the question arises whether the referral may be construed as a waiver of privileges and immunities. While this can only be assumed in special circumstances, a refusal of an organization to cooperate with national authorities on a matter which had been referred to such authorities by the organization, may be seen as *venire contra factum proprium,* as such refusal may make it impossible for the national authorities to prosecute a case referred to them.

8.2.3 Other Attempts to Restrict Immunity on Functional Grounds

International organizations may be alleged to have infringed upon the personal property rights of private persons, and they "might be accused of libel and slander,

[79] See Münch 2006, pp. 71–88. http://www.mpil.de/files/pdf3/mpunyb_03_muenchneuii1.pdf.

even of false imprisonment, of infringing other property rights, of causing harm by violating competition (anti-trust rules), or domestic employment legislation".[80]

There have been attempts to restrict the scope of absolute immunity of the United Nations and other organizations on functional grounds. The line of argument advanced in support of such a claim is that it is not part of the functions of an international organization to commit tortious acts as indicated by above and that for this reason any such acts cannot be covered by privileges and immunities. This approach is epitomized by the stern position of the Supreme Court of the Philippines which denied in the Jerry Liang case[81] the applicant's plea of immunity and held upon a motion of reconsideration that:

> After a careful deliberation of the arguments raised in petitioner's and intervenor's Motions for Reconsideration, we find no reason to disturb our Decision of January 28, 2000. As we have stated therein, the slander of a person, by any stretch, cannot be considered as falling within the purview of the immunity granted to ADB officers and personnel. Petitioner argues that the Decision had the effect of prejudging the criminal case for oral defamation against him. We wish to stress that it did not. What we merely stated therein is that slander, in general, cannot be considered as an act performed in an official capacity. The issue of whether or not petitioner's utterances constituted oral defamation is still for the trial court to determine.[82]

The above decision must be seen as intrinsically related to the specifics of the case[83] which prompted the Supreme Court to reverse its long-standing jurisprudence that a Protocol of the Department of Foreign Affairs affirming an official's immunity and, thus, regarding the "political question of immunity,"[84] was binding on the courts. The problem of the approach mentioned above is that applicants can take an organization to court by merely making allegations of slander or tortious acts. As the procedural question relevant for the grant of privileges and immunities and the substantive question to be addressed by the courts, i.e., whether there has been a tortious act, are, in essence, identical, an organization would be forced to sustain litigation for the competent court to conduct at least a *prima facie* review of whether there has been a tortious conduct. This would fundamentally undermine and weaken the privileges and immunities of international organizations.

The Advisory Opinion of the International Court of Justice of 1999 underlines the problematic nature of such charges in relation to statements made by officials in their official functions. A restrictive approach is warranted and appropriate, in particular, as there are substantial differences between the defamation laws of

---

[80] Reinisch 2000, p. 28.

[81] "Liang, Jeffrey (Huefeng) versus People of the Philippines". 28 Jan. 2000. GR No. 125865. http://sc.judiciary.gov.ph/jurisprudence/2000/jan2000/125865.html.

[82] "Jeffrey Liang (Huefeng) versus People of the Philippines". 26 March 2001. GR No. 125865. http://sc.judiciary.gov.ph/jurisprudence/2001/mar2001/125865.htm.

[83] See Lacson 2002, pp. 882–928.

[84] See with further references, Department of Foreign Affairs versus National Labor Relations Commission. G.R. No. 113191. 18 Sept. 1996, http://sc.judiciary.gov.ph/jurisprudence/1996/sept1996/113191.htm.

countries and in how countries strike a balance between the competing objectives of protecting liberty of expression and reputation of individuals. Such differences concern the standards which are being applied and the extent to which countries resort to criminal proceedings to prosecute defamation cases. While such criminal action is quite rare in some countries such as Australia, it is very common in certain other countries. The ICJ has emphasized in the aforementioned Advisory Opinion (the Cumaraswamy case) that

> the Secretary-General, as the chief administrative officer of the Organization, has the primary responsibility to safeguard the interests of the Organization; to that end, it is up to him to assess whether its agents acted within the scope of their functions and, where he so concludes, to protect these agents, including experts on mission, by asserting their immunity.[85]

It further held that when

> national courts are seized of a case in which the immunity of a United Nations agent is in issue, they should immediately be notified of any finding by the Secretary-General concerning that immunity. That finding, and its documentary expression, creates a presumption which can only be set aside for the most compelling reasons and is thus to be given the greatest weight by national courts.[86]

Based on the above, the court concluded that by necessary implication, questions of immunity are "preliminary issues which must be expeditiously decided in *limine litis*". It held that the above is "a generally recognized principle of procedural law" which Malaysia was under an obligation to respect, but failed to do so.[87] This principle must apply in relation to charges of slander made against officials of international organizations.

In spite of the approach proposed by the Special Rapporteur of the International Law Commission in her "Fifth report on immunity of State officials from foreign criminal jurisdiction"[88] to define corruption as a "limitation or exception to the immunity of State officials from foreign criminal jurisdiction",[89] the same considerations must also apply inasmuch as allegations of corruption are made against international organizations and their officials. While this author has considerable

---

[85] "Difference Relating to Immunity from Legal Process of a Special Rapporteur of the Commission on Human Rights, Advisory Opinion", ICJ Reports 1999, 62–91, 87. http://www.icj-cij.org/files/case-related/100/100-19990429-ADV-01-00-EN.pdf.

[86] Ibid.

[87] Ibid.

[88] In her "Fifth report on immunity of State officials from foreign criminal jurisdiction", the Special Rapporteur, Concepción Escobar Hernández, states that cases of corruption (involving "embezzlement, diversion and misappropriation of public funds, money-laundering and other manifestations of corruption" cannot be deemed to "involve acts that can be considered as having been carried out in an official capacity. In principle, therefore, there appears to be no need at present to analyse them from the perspective of limitations or exceptions." Hernández, C. E. 2016. Fifth report on immunity of State officials from foreign criminal jurisdiction, UN General Assembly (Doc. CN.4/701, 14 June), paras 231 and 234.

[89] Ibid., para 234.

concerns regarding the approach proposed by the Special Rapporteur, this issue will here not be discussed in the specific context in which it has been coined, i.e. in relation to State officials. Rather, it needs to be stressed that a similar approach would not be suitable for being applied to the immunity from legal process of international organizations or their officials, as otherwise a mere allegation of corruption might be sufficient for courts to disregard the immunity of legal process of international organizations and their officials. This would be contrary to the principle set out by the International Court of Justice in the cited Cumaraswamy Decision that questions of immunity are "preliminary issues which must be expeditiously decided in *limine litis*".

This is not to minimize the need for international organization to take decisive action against all forms of corruption. Effectively, many international organizations have adopted anticorruption policies for that purpose. Moreover, headquarters and host country agreements generally emphasize that privileges and immunities "are not designed for the personal benefit of [....] officials but are designed solely to ensure the free functioning of the" organization concerned.[90] They oblige the executive head to "waive the immunity of any official in any case in which he considers that immunity would impede the course of justice and can be waived without prejudice to the interests" of the organization;[91] finally, they mandate international organizations to "facilitate the proper administration of justice, secure the observance of police regulations and prevent any abuse in connection with the privileges, immunities and facilities".[92]

Hence, international organization must be expected to investigate all allegations of corruption and take appropriate action, by imposing appropriate disciplinary measures and, where appropriate, waiving privileges and immunities and referring matters to national jurisdiction. Nevertheless, it is first and foremost for the executive head of an international organization and established bodies (e.g. a Disciplinary, Oversight or Sanctions Committee) to decide, based on appropriate investigation, whether there is a basis to an allegation of corruption. In cases where this cannot be ascertained, and the executive head of the organization certifies that an official enjoys immunity, in line with the Cumaraswamy Decision, this finding needs to be given "greatest weight by national courts" and can only be "set aside for the most compelling reasons".

Attempts to restrict international organizations' immunity from legal process on functional grounds must not be allowed to succeed. Ryngaert has shown the problematic nature of any such approach in relation to a Dutch court decision

---

[90] See as representative for many, Article 21, para 1 of the Agreement between the Swiss Federal Council and the International Labour Organization concerning the legal status of the International Labour Organization in Switzerland. http://www.ilo.org/global/about-the-ilo/how-the-ilo-works/departments-and-offices/jur/legal-instruments/WCMS_441510/lang%2D%2Den/index.htm.

[91] Agreement between the Swiss Federal Council and the International Labour Organization, Article 21, para 2.

[92] Agreement between the Swiss Federal Council and the International Labour Organization, Article 22.

rejecting Euratom's plea of immunity, "after observing that the frequent and significant violations of the regulations committed by the international organization could not possibly be considered as being part of the supposed mission of the organization, and that criminal liability would not hinder the fulfilment of its mission."[93] He stressed in this context:

> The criterion used by the appeals court was a broad one. Simply put, the court argued that organizations are expected to be 'good' actors, and that they forfeit their immunity if they commit 'bad acts'. In so doing, the court in fact makes a mockery of the immunity clause in the Euratom Treaty, since it subjects Euratom to the full force of the law, just like domestic establishments in a similar position.[94]

This squarely underlines the questionable nature of approaches seeking to restrict absolute immunity of international organizations on functional grounds.

8.2.4 Immunity of Jurisdiction and Due Process

8.2.4.1 Contractual Matters

It is now widely recognized that international organizations need to ensure due process to be able to invoke privileges and immunities in certain countries. The jurisprudence of the European Court of Human Rights (ECHR), starting with the case Waite and Kennedy, has anchored this principle in Article 6 of the European Convention of Human Rights.[95] Moreover, similar principles as set forth in Article 6 of the European Convention of Human Rights are set forth "in Articles 8 and 10 of the Universal Declaration of Human Rights; Articles 2(3) and 14 of the International Covenant on Civil and Political Rights; Articles 8 and 25 of the American Convention on Human Rights; Articles 6 and 13 of the European Convention on Human Rights; Article 7 of the African Charter on Human and Peoples' Rights; and Article 9 of the Arab Charter on Human Rights",[96] and in national constitutional law. The application of these principles to the grant of immunity from legal process may be seen as an indication of the constitutionalization of international organizations which has prompted discussion on the applicability of human rights law to international organizations.

The jurisprudence of the ECHR and the jurisprudence of national courts are extensively documented in literature[97] and do not need to be described in detail in this book. National courts have taken divergent positions on the jurisprudence of

---

[93] Ryngaert 2010, p. 130.

[94] Ibid.

[95] de Cooker and Süss 2009, pp. 541–570.

[96] See Barros 2015, p. 349.

[97] See with detailed references, *inter alia*, Reinisch and Bachmayer 2016, pp. 72–79; Ryngaert 2010, pp. 132–144.

the European Court of Human Rights. While some made the guarantee of due process a condition for the grant of privileges and immunities, others rejected such a proposal.

While there have been divergent interpretations of the requirements incumbent upon international organizations, it would appear to this author that is incumbent on international organizations to accept that they need to afford due process and give a fair opportunity to their staff and third parties to have their case heard. In their own interest, international organizations should embrace this principle rather than oppose it. First, given the jurisprudence of several national courts, at least there is a risk in certain countries that the grant of privileges and immunities may be made conditional on the organization complying with the requirements of due process. International organizations may minimize such risk by guaranteeing due process. In doing so, they increase their chance of defending their absolute immunity in cases where such immunity is challenged. Second, and even more important, international organizations enjoy immunity from legal process to safeguard their independence and ability to operate effectively, but are not given a license to avoid the settlement of just claims. By invoking immunity from jurisdiction on merely formal grounds while refusing to offer equitable dispute settlement procedures, international organization weaken the overall acceptance of their privileges and immunities in the countries where they are operating. Effectively, there is no good reason as to why international organizations such as the multilateral development banks, whose activities are meant to promote and enhance good governance, should be dispensed with from following in their own affairs the principles of good governance which they promote for their member countries.

The above has important implications at various levels. First, it may require international organizations to strengthen the independence of their administrative tribunals to address challenges to their immunity from legal process based on the grounds that their administrative tribunals lack independence and fail to guarantee due process. Moreover, it requires international organizations, in general, to guarantee due process in all contractual matters.

To this end, it is not sufficient that the contractual arrangements of international organizations contain an arbitration clause. Rather, international organizations need to offer not only to their staff, but also to contractors and consultants and other persons and entities associated with them, an effective dispute settlement mechanisms. This would not be the case, for example, if an international organization were to offer an individual contractor with a low remuneration package dispute settlement involving the International Chamber of Commerce, to be conducted by a panel of three arbitrators. In view of the substantial amount incurred by similar types of arbitration, it would be tantamount to denial of justice including a similar clause in contractual arrangements with low-paid contractors and consultants. For these categories, simplified arbitration proceedings should be implemented.

Given the "Kadi" decisions already cited above and other international decision highlighted by Reinisch,[98] there cannot be any reasonable doubt about the great importance which has to be attributed to the due process requirement of which even decisions of the UN Security Council are not exempt. A related obligation is to guarantee the equality of parties in legal proceedings, as Judge Cançado Trindade, in particular, has highlighted in his separate opinion to the Advisory Opinion of 1 February 2012.[99] Moreover, international organizations are required to consider in their affairs a range of other non-economic issues.

As has been convincingly shown by Handl, this also is the case for MDBs, notwithstanding the fact that these are called upon by their charters not "to interfere in the political affairs of any member":[100]

> It should be evident, then, that the Banks have not only an inherently economic and political incentive, but also a clear international legal obligation to avoid causing environmental harm in developing member countries, and indeed to incorporate environmental protection and social development activities into all of their activities in DMCs. In this sense, international public law and policy merely underline the status of MDBs as critical agents of change towards sustainable development.[101]

Handl concludes that there is no need to amend MDBs' constituent agreement for the purpose mentioned above, as "these are not only free to take sustainable development concerns into account but have an international legal obligation to do so—not despite their constituent instruments, but rather, it has been submitted, because of them."[102]

Hence, also MDBs and other international financial institutions should be required to take sustainable development concerns into account and abide with the core principles of the international human rights law, as set out inter alia in the Universal Declaration of Human Rights.

8.2.4.2 Claims Based on Tort and Class Actions

While the requirement for international organizations to guarantee due process in relation to an organization's contractual and employment matters is now widely recognized, the question of whether and to what extent an international organization needs to offer appropriate settlement procedures in case of claims based on tort is still in a grey area and largely unsettled.

---

98 Reinisch 2009, pp. 257–291.

99 See Judgment No. 2867 of the Administrative Tribunal of the International Labour Organiza-tion upon a Complaint Filed against the International Fund for Agricultural Development, Advisory Opinion, I.C.J. Reports 2012, p. 10. Separate Opinion of Judge Cançado Trindade. http://www.icj-cij.org/files/case-related/146/146-20120201-ADV-01-01-BI.pdf.

100 See as one example para 36.2 of the ADB Charter.

101 Handl 2001, p. 34.

102 Ibid., 35.

Special problems have arisen regarding mass tortious claims that have been made in relation to the UN peace keeping operations, e.g., by "over 5,000 plaintiffs, filed under the [Status of Forces Agreement for Peacekeeping Operations] SOFA between the United Nations and Haiti, alleging that the United Nations negligently introduced a cholera epidemic in Haiti"[103] and by "864 members of the Roma, Ashkali, and Egyptian community in Kosovo, who alleged that they suffered lead poising as a result of lead contamination in the Internally Displaced Persons camps in north Mitrovica".[104]

"In similar fashion to the Haiti cholera claims, they were informed that compensation was provided only with respect to 'claims of a private law character,' whereas the complainants' claims concerned 'alleged widespread health and environmental risks arising in the context of the precarious security situation in Kosovo."[105] In both cases, the approach adopted by the United Nations did not meet even basic standards of equitable treatment and due process.

In particular, the staunch refusal of the UN to accept any responsibility for the cholera outbreak which was claimed to be connected with the presence of UN peacekeepers in Haiti and cost more than 9000 lives, shows that it entails high reputational risks for an organization to refuse in a case as mentioned above any dispute settlement by merely invoking its immunity from legal process. While the legal challenges which the victims filed in the United States proved not to be successful,[106] the UN's actions were severely criticized as "morally unconscionable, legally indefensible and politically self-defeating", as well as "entirely unnecessary" and as upholding "a double standard according to which the U.N. insists that member states respect human rights, while rejecting any such responsibility for itself."[107]

The latter is the core problem. If organizations dissociate themselves from the values which they propagate by refusing in tort cases any dispute settlement to alleged victims of their actions, they may raise serious concerns as to the justification of their privileges and immunities and thereby weaken the basis on which their privileges and immunities are predicated. While the Secretary General of the United Nations finally agreed on 20 September 2016 to a compensation package for

[103] See Lewis 2014, p. 269, with further references. http://scholarship.law.unc.edu/cgi/viewcontent.cgi?article=2014&context=ncilj.

[104] Ibid., 270.

[105] Ibid., 270.

[106] See U.S. Court of Appeals for the Second Circuit in Georges and others v. United Nations, Case 15–455, Doc. 257-2, Decision of 18 Aug. 2016. http://www.ijdh.org/wp-content/uploads/2011/11/2d-Circuit-Decision.pdf.

[107] See remarks of Alston, P. reported in the New York Times article of 17 Aug. 2016 by Katz, J. M. "U.N. Admits Role in Cholera Epidemic in Haiti". http://www.nytimes.com/2016/08/18/world/americas/united-nations-haiti-cholera.html.

the Haitian victims of the cholera outbreak,[108] this could not undo the fact that the reputation of the United Nations had seriously been tainted by its failure to take timely and appropriate action.

The question of whether the principles developed by the ECHR based on Article 6 of the European Convention on Human Rights may also apply to claims against international organizations based on tort has been reviewed in *Stichting Mothers of Srebrenica v Netherlands*. Faith[109] has given a detailed account of this case which was filed on 4 June 2007 by a Dutch non-profit foundation representing the relatives of the victims of the Srebrenica Massacre of 1995 in the District Court of the Hague on the grounds that the Netherlands State and the United Nations failed to protect the victims of the massacre, and on the decisions of the Court of Appeal and the Supreme Court of the Netherlands which were subsequently seized with this matter. While all three courts upheld the immunity of the United Nations from legal process, they adopted somewhat diverging positions on this matter.

It is significant that the Supreme Court concluded that the Court of Appeal had "erred by examining whether the right of access to the courts guaranteed to the Association by Article 6 of the European Convention on Human Rights and Article 14 of the International Covenant on Civil and Political Rights prevailed over immunity on the basis of the criteria of legitimacy and proportionality."[110]

As shown by Schrijver, the "possible unlawfulness of United Nations behavior, the virtual lack of alternative procedures, and the human right of access to the courts have thus far, however, not yet undermined the immunity of the United Nations."[111] Hence not only the Supreme Court of the Netherlands but also the European Court of Justice upheld in the case mentioned above the absolute immunity of the United Nations. It appears that the ECHR[112] was swayed by the involvement of the Security Council, as may be derived from the following passage of the said decision:

> The Court finds that since operations established by United Nations Security Council resolutions under Chapter VII of the United Nations Charter are fundamental to the mission of the United Nations to secure international peace and security, the Convention cannot be interpreted in a manner which would subject the acts and omissions of the Security Council to domestic jurisdiction without the accord of the United Nations. To bring such operations

[108] See article of E.A. Health of 30 Sept. 2016 titled, "UN Secretary General Ban Ki-moon Indicates Compensation Package for Haitian Victims of Cholera Outbreak is Forthcoming", https://www.asil.org/blogs/un-secretary-general-ban-ki-moon-indicates-compensation-package-haitian-victims-cholera.

[109] Faith 2014, pp. 359–375.

[110] See the case summary: "Mothers of Srebrenica et al v. State of The Netherlands and the United Nations". http://www.internationalcrimesdatabase.org/case/769/mothers-of-srebrenica-v-the-netherlands-and-the-un/.

[111] Schrijver 2015, pp. 329–341.

[112] Ibid., para 129.

within the scope of domestic jurisdiction would be to allow individual States, through their courts, to interfere with the fulfilment of the key mission of the United Nations in this field, including with the effective conduct of its operations [....].[113]

While under this aspect, the decision of the ECHR is understandable, it cannot be seen as satisfactory, given that—as highlighted by the Court—the Secretary-General of the United Nations "had recognised that errors of judgement and fundamental mistakes had been made"[114] and had indicated "that the survivors of the Srebrenica massacre were 'absolutely right' to demand justice for 'the most heinous crimes committed on European soil since World War II;'"[115] furthermore, the claims commission to be set up in accordance with Article 48 of "the Agreement on the status of the United Nations Protection Force in Bosnia and Herzegovina of 15 May 1993" was never established.[116] The Court could have well concluded on that basis that immunity from legal process should be denied to the United Nations, but failed to reach that conclusion, probably taking account of the special circumstances highlighted above, contending that it "does not follow, however, that in the absence of an alternative remedy the recognition of immunity is *ipso facto* constitutive of a violation of the right of access to a court."[117]

While, so far, the bulwark of absolute immunity has been upheld, international organizations would be mistaken to derive from the aforementioned decision that the matter is finally settled. Rather, "the decision has given international organizations some respite" and it "is likely that the question whether international organizations are entitled to refuse claims based on tort without considering their substance by invoking immunity will again come to the agenda in the future."[118]

8.2.4.3 Private Law Matters

Article VIII, Section 29 of the General Convention sets out the basic principle that provision for appropriate mechanisms for the settlement of disputes, including disputes relating to claims based on tort and disputes of persons full diplomatic immunity, has to be made by the UN. The said provision states:

The United Nations shall make provisions for appropriate modes of settlement of:

(a) disputes arising out of contracts or other disputes of a private law character to which the United Nations is a party;
(b) disputes involving any official of the United Nations who by reason of his official position enjoys immunity, if immunity has not been waived by the Secretary-General.

---

[113] Cited according to European Court of Human Rights. Application no. 65542/12. "Stichting Mothers of Srebrenica and Others v. The Netherlands", para 154. http://hudoc.echr.coe.int/eng?i=001-122255.

[114] Ibid., para 127.

[115] Ibid., para 129.

[116] Ibid., para 162.

[117] Ibid., para 164.

[118] Droesse 2017, p. 55.

As indicated by the Secretary-General of the United Nations, claims of a private nature primarily include "claims for compensation submitted by third parties for personal injury or death and/or property loss or damage incurred as a result of acts committed by members of a United Nations peace-keeping operation within the 'mission area' concerned."[119]

Hence, the term "disputes of a private law character" in essence includes claims based on tort. Immunity from legal process afforded to international organizations does not give international organizations the right to reject claims based on tort merely on formal grounds by invoking immunity from legal process. In the view of this author, a human-rights based approach needs to be followed with regards to these claims. As a matter of principle, international organizations should also be required in tort cases to comply with the requirements of due process by offering aggrieved persons and entities an appropriate dispute settlement procedure.

There is no reason or justification to exempt claims based on tort in general from the requirement that international organizations need to offer equitable dispute settlement procedures to third parties.

In the most common tort cases (i.e. traffic accidents), there is an increasing trend to exempt civil liability proceedings from the immunity regime. While this trend is reflected in some recent headquarters agreements,[120] there is not sufficient evidence of an *opinio juris* to assume that the above reflects a new rule of common international law. Nevertheless, the examples cited above are important evidence of new trends in the development of international law. Effectively, there is no reason or justification to exempt an international organization from the obligation to adequately insure its vehicles and offer adequate compensation to third parties in case of traffic accidents. There are many examples which show how strongly the public reacts to cases where diplomats involved in traffic incidents fail to settle claims relating to such accidents by invoking their immunity of legal process. If international organizations would resort to such action, they would open themselves to criticism and to fundamental questions as to the justification of privileges and immunities granted to international organizations.

---

[119] Cited according to Lewis 2014, pp. 269–270.

[120] Article 20 of the "Agreement between the Swiss Federal Council and the Global Fund to Fight AIDS, Tuberculosis and Malaria in view of determining the legal status of the Global Fund in Switzerland" (https://www.theglobalfund.org/media/3375/bm07_07gpcreportannex92_annex_en.pdf?u=636486806830000000) provides that the individuals covered by the provisions of that agreement "shall not enjoy immunity from legal process in the event of civil liability proceedings initiated against them for damages caused in Switzerland by any vehicle belonging to or driven by them, or in the event of offences punishable by fines under federal road traffic regulations."

Similarly, the "Agreement between the Republic of Korea and the Green Climate Fund concerning the Headquarters of the Green Climate Fund" (https://www.greenclimate.fund/documents/20182/574763/Headquarters_Agreement.pdf/13df1525-af90-456b-8d76-5b83be9b39d4) also provides in Article 13, para 5 that the "persons referred to in this Article shall not enjoy immunity from legal process and execution of judgement in the case of civil liability proceedings initiated against any such person for damages caused in the Republic of Korea by any vehicle belonging to such a person or operated on his/her behalf."

There are many other cases conceivable where international organizations would be ill-advised to invoke privileges and immunities on merely formal grounds while refusing to offer equitable dispute settlement procedures to third parties in cases of claims based on tort. This is evident, for example, in the straightforward case that a person suffered bodily harm due to the failure of an organization to properly secure the safety of its premises. International organizations are required to make appropriate insurance arrangements to cover any such eventuality. While generally international organizations will not invoke privileges and immunities in cases as mentioned above, they also have a legal obligations to secure due process in more complex cases. In principle, this also applies in cases like the one which occurred in Haiti described above. In such cases, international organizations cannot be dispensed with from properly reviewing the claims. Provision for appropriate dispute settlement mechanisms, at least on an *ad hoc* basis, should be made in such cases to guarantee due process.

8.2.4.4 Tortious Claims of Staff

As regards claims of staff members against an organization based on tort, decision No. 5 of the ADB Administrative Tribunal *Cynthia M. Bares, Lauren Bares, Christopher Bares, and the Estate of Robert E. Bares v. Asian Development Bank*[121] shows the difficulties which an organization faces in dealing with claims of tort. This case was filed by the widow and children of an ADB staff member who had been stabbed by an ADB security guard; they pursued a case with the ADB Administrative Tribunal, invoking ADB's liability for his death.

The ADB Administrative Tribunal stressed in this regard:

> The Applicants presented their claim as one founded on the law of tort. That, no doubt, might have been a reasonable way to frame the cause of action had the proceedings been commenced in a national court. However, the Bank, as an international organization, is immune from suit in national courts and, short of a waiver of immunity by the Bank (which the Applicants do not appear to have requested), the Applicants would not have been able to get such a proceeding off the ground.[122]

The Tribunal stressed that it "is not akin to one of general jurisdiction within the national sphere"[123] and that "proceedings in this forum are limited to claims in contract."[124] It discussed, nevertheless, the "theoretical possibility that the parties might have agreed to resort to this Tribunal not as the Administrative Tribunal of the Bank subject to its Statute but as a group of individuals who, though happening to be the Members of the Tribunal, have agreed, at the request and with the consent

121 Bares v. Asian Development Bank, ADB Administrative Tribunal Decision No. 5, 31 May 1995. http://www.adb.org/sites/default/files/institutional-document/31489/adbt0005.pdf.

122 Ibid, para. 10.

123 Ibid., para 11.

124 Ibid., para 12.

of the parties and, for the purposes of the particular proceedings, to act as a special tribunal or arbitral body outside the scope of the Tribunal's Statute",[125] but noted that.

The Tribunal concluded "that it has not been established that the death of Mr. Bares was proximately caused by any failure on the part of the Bank to take due care" and dismissed the claims for that reason. However, it noted in this context:

> 46. The liability of the Bank has had to be assessed exclusively in terms of the contractual relationship between Mr. Bares and the Bank. If the jurisdiction of the Tribunal had extended to obligations in tort then consideration would obviously have been given to the question of vicarious liability.[126]

Given the special circumstances of the case, the Tribunal recommended in a Rider that ADB consider making an *ex gratia* payment to the family of Mr. Bares. This clearly shows the unease of the Tribunal in dealing with the case.

8.2.5 Possible Solutions

Currently, international organizations are largely in a state of denial. Generally, they do not consider in their rules and regulations to any extent that there might be claims based on tort, nor have they made appropriate provision to ensure that any such claims are reviewed in accordance with the requirements of due process.

Schrijver outlines five alternative procedures for settling claims against the United Nations.

- Alternative 1: Restrict the Immunity of the United Nations and Hold the Organization responsible.
- Alternative 2: Hold the Member States Responsible.
- Alternative 3: Towards an Independent Claims Commission within the United Nations System.
- Alternative 4: An Ombudsperson for Complaints against the United Nations.
- Alternative 5: Expansion of the United Nations Administrative Tribunal or Comparable Tribunals[127]

In the view of this author it is necessary to admit that due process requirements are applicable also to claims based on tort. In this context, some of the options proposed by Schrijver should be given further consideration.

For their staff, international organizations should consider extending the competence of their administrative tribunal to tortious actions or establish *ad hoc* a special tribunal for such cases, if the circumstances so warrant. In other cases, special claim commissions or other mechanisms to review tortious claim should be

[125] Ibid., para 14.
[126] Ibid., para 46.
[127] Schrijver 2015, pp. 334–338.

created, wherever feasible, and where provision for such commissions has been made, such provisions need to be applied and implemented. In creating special claims commissions, it is necessary to ensure compliance with the requirement of guaranteeing due process.

Hence, it is incumbent on international organizations to guarantee due process not only in the case of contractual claims but also with regard to claims of tort made against international organizations.

8.3 Privileges and Immunities in Non-Member Countries

Specific problems concern the relation of international organizations with non-member countries. In this context, there is some support in literature[128] for the position that international organizations may also enjoy privileges and immunities in non-member countries. However, as indicated by Gaja with detailed references,

> [c]urrent views on the existence of rules of general international law covering immunities of international organizations are divided. While some studies still deny the existence of any such rule, the prevailing trend in recent works is more favourable to admitting that some form of immunity – sometimes, even absolute immunity – is part of international law. Immunity of jurisdiction from execution is more widely admitted.[129]

Wood disagrees with the proposition that international organizations enjoy immunities in non-member countries and concludes, based on an analysis of relevant national court decisions and writings of leading authors, "Notwithstanding certain pronouncements of domestic courts, generally *obiter,* to the effect that organizations do enjoy immunity under customary international law [....] it would be difficult to conclude that any such rule exists."[130]

It would appear to this author that in this regard a distinction between universal organizations and regional and other organizations of limited membership should be made. It is necessary to recall the ruling of the International Court of Justice in the Reparation for Injuries Case:

> On this point, the Court's opinion is that fifty States, representing the vast majority of the members of the international community, had the power, in conformity with international law, to bring into being an entity possessing objective international personality, and not merely personality recognized by them alone, together with capacity to bring international claims.[131]

---

[128] See discussion in Wood 2015, pp. 29–60.

[129] See Gaja 2006, p. 202. http://legal.un.org/ilc/publications/yearbooks/english/ilc_2006_v2_p2.pdf. Gaja gives on pages 203–205 detailed bibliographic indications.

[130] Wood 2015, p. 59.

[131] Reparation for injuries suffered in the service of the United Nations, Advisory Opinion: ICJ Reports 1949, 174, 185. http://www.icj-cij.org/files/case-related/4/004-19490411-ADV-01-00-EN.pdf.

Hence, the court based its opinion that the UN had objective international personality and the capacity to bring international claims on the fact that the members of the UN represented the "vast majority of the members of the international community". Thus, it matters whether an international organization has universal membership or not.

As indicated by Gaja, that an international organizations enjoys legal personality in non-member countries "does not necessarily imply that the organization is entitled to enjoy immunities from non-member States under general international law."[132] Nevertheless, this author believes that it may well be argued that universal organizations enjoy privileges and immunities in non-member countries. However, at least for regional organizations or organizations of limited membership, there is no evidence of any principle of international law according to which they would enjoy immunity in non-member countries. To the extent that such immunity has been recognized, this generally was the case based on provisions of national law, rather than in recognition of a principle of international law. Hence, it is not axiomatic, and regional organizations and organization cannot place any reliance on a proposition that privileges and immunities would be granted to them in non-member countries.

However, while the geographic scope of privileges and immunities of organizations is limited, their exposure to legal claims is not limited to their member countries. There are many reason why such action might be taken in a non-member country.

Such claims may relate to tort in cases where actions of an organizations impact individuals or entities in non-member countries. While claims based on tort in non-member countries are quite rate, there may be a variety of instances where claims based on contract are made against an international organization in a non-member country. This is not limited to the case that an international organization enters into a contractual arrangement with any entity incorporated in a non-member country. It is conceivable that an entity may attempt to sell its claims against an international organization to an organization incorporated in a non-member country. For multi-national corporations, it is also conceivable that that such a corporation may attempt to take legal action against an international organization in a non-member country where it owns a subsidiary or maintains an office. While the options for international organizations to address legal claims based on tort are limited, they may ensure through the wording of their arbitration provisions that any arbitration proceedings based on contractual claims are required to take place in a country, the courts of which recognize the organization's privileges and immunities.

[132] First report on responsibility of international organizations, by Gaja, G. Doc. A/CN.4/532, 26 March 2003, 105–116, 111. Available at http://legal.un.org/ilc/documentation/english/a_cn4_532.pdf.

Special challenges arise in case of sanctions imposed by international organizations on corrupt entities. As has been shown by this author in relation to ADB:

> In the United States, a 'single publication rule' was adopted, which protects defendants from multiple law suits. This rule combines the right to a cause of action in each jurisdiction where the defendant disseminated the defamatory material into a single cause of action in any one jurisdiction where the dissemination occurred (generally, in the jurisdiction where the publisher is located or where the information is uploaded to the server). However, this has not been given general recognition in literature or in the jurisprudence of the House of Lords, the Australian High Court or the European Court of Justice. Thus, there is clearly a risk that dissemination of information through the internet may give rise to legal action for defamation in a wide range of countries. Potentially, this may be the case wherever the disseminated information is downloaded [....].[133]

As may be seen from the above, a corporation sanctioned for corruption on the website of an international organization may seek to pursue claims against an international organization in a jurisdiction of a non-member country where the organization does not enjoy any privileges and immunities under its constituent agreement or any bilateral or multilateral agreement or any other applicable arrangement.

Organizations that operate in non-member countries often conclude with such countries agreements on privileges and immunities. The Nordic Development Fund, which provides "concessional financing exclusively to nonmember countries",[134] epitomizes this approach, as they are concluding agreements with all the countries where they are operating.

To the extent that an organization has not concluded an agreement with a non-member country on privileges and immunities and that such a country does not extend privileges and immunities to international organizations in accordance with its laws and practices, regional organizations and other international organizations of limited membership face special challenges in asserting privileges and immunities in non-member countries.

International organizations may enhance their legal protection in nonmember countries by renouncing in the arbitration clauses of their contracts to a limited extent to their privileges and immunities. This approach may be a good strategy for effective dispute settlement, in particular, for regional organizations and other organizations of limited membership. These organizations may derive substantial benefits from waiving for their contractual arrangements their privileges and immunities even in those areas where they enjoy absolute immunity, limited, however, to the enforcement of international arbitration awards. By doing so, organizations may bring their contractual relations under the realm of the "Convention on the Recognition and Enforcement of Foreign Arbitral Awards" of

133 Droesse 2009, pp. 411–412.

134 Droesse 2011, p. 191.

1958[135] (also known as the New York Convention) ratified by 157 states,[136] which are required in accordance with Article III "to recognize arbitral awards as binding and enforce them in accordance with the rules of procedure of the territory where the award is relied upon [....]." While this requires that the organizations "sacrifice" their privileges and immunities to a limited extent, such sacrifice is not very significant, considering that international organizations are required, in any event, to provide due process and adequate mechanisms for settlement of claims. However, by adopting the approach proposed above, the organizations may enhance certainty of law, as they can rely on the recognition of arbitration awards in 157 countries. This shows that a bit less in terms of protection by privileges and immunities may result in the substantial improvement of the organization's position in terms of certainty of the law.

8.4 Lacuna in the Provision of Privileges and Immunities

The proliferation of international organizations and institutions has led to a *lacuna* in the grant of privileges and immunities at various levels, which may adversely affect international organizations and institutions in the performance of their functions. Even universal organizations such as the United Nations and its specialized agencies are not totally immune from this phenomenon, as they often only enjoy limited privileges and immunities under their constituent agreements; moreover, not all members of the United Nations and the specialized agencies are parties to the General Convention and CPISA.

Regional organizations face greater challenges than universal organizations as they normally only enjoy limited privileges and immunities, if any, under their constituent agreements and are generally not covered by privileges and immunities in non-member countries, either based on international agreements or in accordance with general principles of international law. However, they may address this problem by concluding bilateral agreements with member and nonmember countries that provide for privileges and immunities. Moreover, as shown above, they may bring their contractual relations under the realm of the "Convention on the Recognition and Enforcement of Foreign Arbitral Awards" by sacrificing some of their privileges and immunities in exchange for enhanced security of the law.

While international organizations generally enjoy privileges and immunities based on their constituent agreement or headquarters agreements, or other bilateral or multilateral agreements or under national law, it is a matter of serious concern that there are groups of persons serving international institutions producing global

[135] Convention on the Recognition and Enforcement of Foreign Arbitral Awards (New York, 1958) http://www.uncitral.org/pdf/english/texts/arbitration/NY-conv/New-York-Convention-E.pdf.

[136] Convention on the Recognition and Enforcement of Foreign Arbitral Awards. Status as at 15 February 2018. https://treaties.un.org/pages/ViewDetails.aspx?src=TREATY&mtdsg_no=XXII-1&chapter=22&lang=en.

public goods or fighting global public badswhich are not covered by any bilateral or multilateral agreement granting privileges and immunities. This relates, in particular, to the persons serving on governing bodies of international organizations established as trust funds and in relation to constituted bodies under international conventions where this *lacuna* manifests itself. Moreover, special problems apply to dual and hybrid organizations incorporated under national law and international organizations established as trust funds.

In the case of organizations such as the Global Fund, their headquarters agreements generally provide for international legal personality and privileges and immunities. In other countries, they need to find ways to ensure the grant of privileges and immunities.

They may do so by giving their staff the legal status of staff members of an international organization which is covered by the General Convention or the CPISA. However, the downside of such arrangements is that these are not in line with clear accountability as they impose on staff a double loyalty towards the organization for which they serve and the organization which appointed them as staff members. This has the potential of creating frictions. The Global Fund terminated for this reason the "May 2004 service agreement between the Global Fund and the World Health Organization (WHO)—under which WHO provided administrative services to the Global Fund and the staff of the Global Fund enjoyed the privileges and immunities of WHO staff (e.g., under the CPISA)."[137] Following the termination of its agreement with the WHO, the Global Fund sought to pursue, as shown above, the grant of privileges and immunities for the Fund and the persons associated with it by proposing to the countries where it is operating to become parties to a multilateral agreement regarding privileges and immunities, or alternatively, to extend privileges and immunities under national law.

As regards international organizations such as the GEF established as trust funds, the trustee is the legal owner of the assets held in trust and may, therefore, invoke in respect of such assets privileges and immunities under its constituent agreement and any bilateral or multilateral agreements to which it is a party. Moreover, the GEF staff have the status of staff members of the trustee and are for that reason covered by the legal regime applicable to the staff of the trustee. (i.e. the World Bank).

While "the CEO's bid for full legal independence for the GEF fell short, the power of the Secretariat to interact with the COPs, and of the CEO to manage Secretariat staff, were expanded by the compromises forged in response to that bid."[138] Nevertheless, the overall relationship between the GEF and the World Bank did not fundamentally change. Hence, the staff of the GEF still have the status of World Bank staff and are, therefore, covered by the Articles of Agreement of the World Bank, the CPISA and any supplementary agreements which may been

137 Droesse 2011, p. 183.

138 Smyth 2011, p. 529.

entered into by the World Bank with countries where they have offices or conduct operations.

However, the same does not apply to the participants of the GEF Assembly. Therefore, special arrangements have to put in place regularly to extend privileges and immunities to the participants of meetings of the GEF Assembly.

> In addition to any privileges and immunities they may have by virtue of their office, irrespective of the GEF, all those participating in the Assembly in an official capacity enjoy the privileges and immunities ensured by a memorandum of understanding (MoU) that is signed before each Assembly by and among the government of the host country, the Secretariat, and the World Bank as trustee. The MoU also spells out the rights and obligations regarding meeting services and facilities.[139]

Special problems apply to persons serving on constituted bodies under international conventions.

This was raised in 2005 in relation to the constituted bodies under the Kyoto Protocol. The "Executive Board of the Clean Development Mechanism (CDM), in its report to the Conference of the Parties serving as the meeting of the Parties to the Kyoto Protocol (COP/MOP), at its first session, has expressed concern about the absence of privileges and immunities for its members and the impact this may have on the functioning of the CDM."[140] The problem arises as "The Convention and the Kyoto Protocol do not contain any provisions conferring privileges and immunities on their organs or on officials and representatives serving on these organs"[141] and also the "privileges and immunities in the Headquarters Agreement [between UNFCCC and Germany that encompass the activities of the COP and its subsidiary and constituted bodies are limited to Germany."[142]

Further, the institutional linkage between the UNFCCC Secretariat and the United Nations only extends to the staff of the UNFCCC Secretariat.

> Accordingly, the secretariat enters into conference agreements with other States that host meetings of the COP or other bodies. These agreements are based on the model United Nations conference agreement and ensure that the detailed regime of privileges and immunities in the General Convention is applicable to all who attend meetings under the auspices of the Convention and the Kyoto Protocol. The agreements also extend the regime of the General Convention to observers, to others invited to attend meetings and to personnel provided by Governments for meeting services. Moreover, these conference

---

[139] Ragazzi 2011, p. 489.

[140] Conference of the Parties Serving as the Meeting of the Parties to the Kyoto Protocol. 2005. *Privileges and Immunities for Individuals serving on Constituted Bodies established under the Kyoto Protocol. Note by the Secretariat.* (FCCC/KP/CMP/2005/6, 16 Sept. 2005). http://unfccc.int/resource/docs/2005/cmp1/eng/06.pdf.

[141] Ibid., para 9.

[142] Ibid., para 11.

> agreements deal with matters not covered in the General Convention. They provide for unimpeded access to and departure from the meeting venue, ensure that the host government is responsible for third-party claims that may arise out of services provided by it, and provide mechanisms for the effective settlement of disputes.[143]

Such arrangements, while mitigating the risk, do not preclude, however, that action against members of constituted bodies might be taken. While no claims can be filed against constituted bodies as they do not have juridical personality, this, "however, is not the case for the individual members of the constituted bodies who serve in their personal capacities, thereby increasing their risk of enduring lawsuits."[144] The UNFCCC Secretariat concluded for that reason:

> It is our opinion that, due to the considerable success and financial impact of the different mechanisms under the Kyoto Protocol, it will only be a matter of time before legal proceedings are brought against individual members of the constituted bodies. Furthermore, claims made against these individuals could amount to millions of euros.[145]

How real is the risk that action may be taken against a constituted body was underlined by the fact that during "the period October 2006–August 2007, the Executive Secretary received 12 letters addressed to the Executive Board from private legal entities expressing concern or raising issues regarding project activities under the CDM."[146]

The problem is not limited to the Executive Board of the CDM, but also extends to other constituted bodies under the Kyoto Protocol, such as the Joint Implementation Supervisory Committee, the Compliance Committee and the expert review teams established under Article 8 of the Kyoto Protocol.[147] Hence, there are hundreds of persons who might potentially be affected.[148]

The issue of privileges and immunities for constituted bodies under the Kyoto Protocol was subsequently reviewed by the Subsidiary Body of Implementation (SBI) which concluded its consideration of this matter in 2012, forwarding a draft to

---

143 Ibid.

144 UNFCCC. 2008. Privileges and immunities for individuals serving on constituted bodies under the Kyoto Protocol: report on the feasibility study on possible insurance for individuals serving on constituted bodies. Technical Paper. FCCC/TP/2008/1 30 May 2008, para 4. http://unfccc.int/resource/docs/2008/tp/01.pdf.

145 Ibid., para 5. See also UNFCCC. 2007. "Privileges and Immunities (for Individuals Serving on Bodies Established by these Organizations: Review of the Legal Regime and Practice of Organizations in the United Nations System". *Technical Paper*. (FCCC/TP/2007/2, 30 July). http://unfccc.int/resource/docs/2007/tp/02.pdf.

146 Privileges and immunities for individuals serving on constituted bodies under the Kyoto Protocol: Implementation of decision 9/CMP.2. Note by the secretariat. FCCC/KP/CMP/2007/2, 13 Nov. 2007, 5. https://unfccc.int/resource/docs/2007/cmp3/eng/02.pdf.

147 Ibid., footnote 1.

148 Doc. FCCC/TP/2008/1, paras 9–11.

the CMP.[149] However, The CMP did not approve the draft submitted, nor did SBI make any progress regarding this matter in 2014.[150]

In May 2016, the Subsidiary Body of Implementation recommended conclusion of the discussions regarding privileges and immunities for constituted bodies under the Kyoto Protocol[151] and for individuals serving on constituted bodies serving under the Convention.[152] A decision to that effect was taken accordingly.[153]

8.4.1 Possible Solutions

The question arises as to the solutions which can be adopted to address the situation that many organizations and bodies are not covered, or only partially covered by privileges and immunities. As had been shown, the current situation is a patchwork of conventions and protocols, multilateral agreements and bilateral agreements, memoranda of understanding, letter exchanges and other *ad hoc* arrangements.

Michaels has made a proposal for a general statute on privileges and immunities.[154] As Blokker highlights, the CPISA "has demonstrated that it is feasible in practice to draft immunity rules that apply to more than one single organization and its staff."[155] While the CPISA shows that is possible to differentiate to a certain extent between different organizations covered by a convention on privileges and immunities, it must not be forgotten that all organizations covered by the CPISA are traditional intergovernmental organizations established by a treaty. Even for these organizations, a "one-size-fit-all" approach was not considered possible, as shown by the fact that the regime on privileges and immunities under the CPISA is subject to substantial fragmentation.

While a fairly rudimentary and basic general statute on privileges and immunities indeed would be desirable, the scope of application of such statute is the main contentious issue. It is pertinent to recall in this context that there is a substantial

---

149 UNFCCC. 2012. Subsidiary Body for Implementation. Report of the Subsidiary Body for Implementation on its 36th session, held in Bonn from 14 to 25 May 2012. Addendum (FCCC/SBI/2012/15/Add.2, 6 July 2012) and UNFCCC. 2012. Subsidiary Body for Implementation. 36th session. Bonn, 14–25 May 2012. Privileges and immunities for individuals serving on constituted bodies established under the Kyoto Protocol, Draft conclusions proposed by the Chair. FCCC/SBI/2012/L.9, 23 May 2012.

150 Privileges and immunities for individuals serving on constituted bodies established under the Kyoto Protocol. Draft conclusions proposed by the Chair. Draft conclusions proposed by the Chair. Subsidiary Body for Implementation Fortieth session Bonn, 4–15 June 2014, FCCC/SBI/2014/L.6, 10 June 2014.

151 http://unfccc.int/resource/docs/2016/sbi/eng/l03.pdf.

152 http://unfccc.int/resource/docs/2016/sbi/eng/l04.pdf.

153 https://unfccc.int/meetings/marrakech_nov_2016/items/9980txt.php.

154 See Michaels 1971.

155 Blokker 2013, p. 275.

number of traditional intergovernmental organizations which are not covered under any multilateral agreement. Alone, covering all these organizations under a general statute would be a very difficult task. However, doing so would only solve problems to a very limited extent. The challenge that organizations are facing at present is to find a solution for organizations which are established as trust funds, as dual and hybrid structures established under municipal law, or as mechanisms under international conventions. It is no longer justifiable to deprive a big group of persons associated with such organizations and mechanisms that produce global public goods or fight global wrongs of any privileges and immunities, thereby exposing them potentially of high claims of damages or even arrest.

The likelihood of ever achieving a general statute for international organizations, including non-traditional institutions without a treaty base, appears to be very remote, at best. This is underlined by the excruciating discussions on the privileges and immunities of constituted bodies under the Kyoto protocol and for individuals serving on constituted bodies established under the Convention [UNFCCC] i.e. a narrowly defined group, which did not produce any tangible outcome after having been conducted for well over 10 years. Thus, while such a general statute might be appealing on intellectual grounds, any such approach faces formidable challenges, in particular inasmuch as it purports to cover, in addition to regional organizations and organizations of limited membership, also international organizations established as trust funds, or as dual and hybrid organizations, or mechanisms under international conventions.

It is very unlikely that it will possible, within a foreseeable time-frame, to get agreement on covering all the organizations and mechanisms under one global statute. Thus, from a medium-term perspective, the only realistic option would appear to propose to states to accede to a convention which allows them to extend to international organizations of their choice, including organizations of limited membership and organizations established as trust funds, as dual and hybrid organizations, or as financial mechanisms of, or constituted bodies under, multilateral conventions, privileges and immunities, based on executive action. In accordance with a convention of that kind, each Government would have the right to notify the names of the organizations to which the provisions of the Convention shall apply. Moreover, the scope of the privileges and immunities which are applicable may be varied for organizations, on similar terms as are currently applicable to the CPISA. While this would not automatically extend privileges and immunities to non-traditional forms of cooperation as indicated above, it would facilitate it for states to have them covered. In a sense, this would be a mechanism similar to that applicable under the International Organizations Immunities Act of the US, albeit at the international level and without the restriction to traditional treaty-based organizations which is applicable in case of the IOIA.[156] As each country could determine the entities and mechanisms to which the proposed

[156] See Young 2012, pp. 311–364. https://www.law.georgetown.edu/academics/law-journals/gjil/recent/upload/zsx00113000311.PDF.

convention would apply, a similar framework is likely to have greater chances of implementation than any proposal for a general statute on privileges and immunities.[157]

References

ADB (2005) Rules and procedures for membership in ADB. ADB, Manila
Ahluwalia K (1964) The legal status, privileges and immunities of the specialized agencies of the United Nations and certain other international organizations. Martinus Nijhoff, The Hague
Barros AS (2015) Member States and the International Legal (Dis)order. Accounting for the notion of responsible governance. Int Organ Law Rev 12:333–357
Blokker N (2013) International Organizations: the untouchables? Int Organ Law Rev 10:259–275
Bonfafè BI (2015) Italian courts and the immunity of International Organizations. In: Blokker N, Schrijver N (eds) Immunity of International Organizations. Brill Nijhoff, Leiden, pp 246–278
Burci GL, Granziera E (2015) Privileges and immunities of the World Health Organization: practice and challenges. In: Blokker N, Schrijver N (eds) Immunity of International Organizations. Brill Nijhoff, Leiden, pp 91–114
de Cooker C, Süss G (2009) Immunity of International Organisations from national jurisdiction in staff matters. In: de Cooker C (ed) Law and Management Practices in International Organisation. Martinus Nijhoff, Leiden, pp 541–570
Droesse G (2009) Accountability, investigation and due process: the example of the Asian Development Bank. In: de Cooker C (ed) International Administration: Law and Management Practices in International Organisations. Martinus Nijhoff, Leiden, pp 381–460
Droesse G (2011) Modalities of Multilateral Concessional Financing. In: Droesse G (ed) Funds for development: Multilateral Channels of concessional Financing. ADB, Manila, pp 179–297
Droesse G (2017) Green climate fund and its role in promoting and funding sustainable investment. In: Dispute resolution and climate change. The Paris Agreement and beyond. International Chamber of Commerce, Paris, pp 52–55
Faith K (2014) Stichting Mothers of Srebrenica v. The Netherlands: does U.N. immunity trump the right of access to a court? Tulane J Int J Int Comp Law 22:359–375
Gaja G (2006) Jurisdictional immunity of International Organizations. Yearb Int Law Comm 2 (Part II, Annex II):201–205
Handl G (2001) Multilateral Development Banking: environmental principles and concepts reflecting General International Law and Public Policy. Kluwer Law International, The Hague
Katkin K (2005) Communication breakdown? The future of global connectivity after the privatization of INTELSAT. Int J Commun Law Policy. Special Issue Global Flow of Information:1–66
Lacson JCO (2002) Jeffrey Liang (Huefeng) v. People of the Philippines: rethinking the immunities of international organizations. Ateneo Law J 46:882–928
Lewis PJ (2014) Who pays for the United Nations' torts? Immunity, attribution, and 'appropriate modes of settlement'. N C J Int Law Commer Regul XXXIX:259–332
Mensah TA (2012) Headquarters agreements and the Law of International Organizations. In: Hestermeyer HP, König D et al (eds) Coexistence, cooperation and solidarity, vol II. Martinus Nijhoff, Leiden, pp 1463–1495
Michaels DB (1971) International privileges and immunities: a case for a universal statute. Springer, The Netherlands

[157] See Michaels 1971.

Miller AJ (2007a) Privileges and immunities of United Nations officials. Int Organ Law Rev 4 (2):169–257

Miller AJ (2007b) United Nations experts on mission and their privileges and immunities. Int Organ Law Rev 4:11–56

Miller AJ (2009) The privileges and immunities of the United Nations. Int Organ Law Rev 6:7–115

Münch W (2006) Wrongdoing of International Civil Servants – referral of cases to national authorities for criminal prosecution. Max Planck Yearb U N Law 10:71–88

Nilsson C (2004) Contextualizing the agreement on the privileges and immunities of the International Criminal Court. Leiden J Int Law 17(03):559–578

Oeter S (2015) The law of immunities as a focal point of the evolution of International Law. In: Peters A, Lagrange E, Oeter S, Tomuschat C (eds) Immunities in the age of Global Constitutionalism. Brill, Leiden, pp 355–366

Ragazzi M (2011) The Global Environment Facility: institutional and operational aspects. In: Droesse G (ed) Funds for development: Multilateral Channels of Concessional Financing. ADB, Manila

Reinisch A (2000) International organizations before national courts. Cambridge University Press, Cambridge, p 28

Reinisch A (2009) Should judges second-guess the UN Security Council? Int Organ Law Rev 6:257–291

Reinisch A, Bachmayer P (eds) (2016) The conventions on the privileges and immunities of the United Nations and specialized agencies: a commentary. Oxford University Press, Oxford, pp 72–79

Ryngaert C (2010) The immunity of International Organizations before domestic courts: recent trends. Int Organ Law Rev 7:121–148

Schmalenbach K (2013) Austrian Courts and the Immunity of International Organizations. Int Organ Law Rev 10:446–463

Schrijver N (2015) Beyond Srebrenica and Haiti. Exploring alternative remedies against the UN. In: Blokker N, Schrijver N (eds) Immunity of International Organizations. Brill Nijhoff, Leiden, pp 329–341

Siegel DE (2002) Legal aspects of the IMF/WTO relationship: the fund's articles of agreement and the WTO agreements. Am J Int Law 96(3):561–599

Smyth S (2011) A practical guide to creating a collective financing effort to save the world: the Global Environment Facility experience. In: Droesse G (ed) Funds for development: Multilateral Channels of Concessional Financing. Asian Development Bank, Manila

Szasz PC (1970) The law and practices of the International Atomic Energy Agency. IAEA, Vienna, p 971

Tichy H, Köhler U (2008) Legal personality or not – the recent attempts to improve the status of the OSCE. In: Buffard I, Crawford J, Pellet A, Wittich S (eds) International Law between universalism and fragmentation. Festschrift in honour of Gerhard Hafner. Brill, Nijhoff, pp 455–478

Wood M (2015) Do international organizations enjoy immunity under Customary International Law? In: Blokker N, Schrijver N (eds) Immunity of International Organizations. Brill Nijhoff, Leiden, pp 29–60

Young AI (2012) Deconstructing International Organization Immunity. Georgetown J Int Law 44:311–364

Chapter 9
Legal Implications of Membership

Contents

All weblinks are updated as of 28 February 2018.

G. Droesse, *Membership in International Organizations*,
https://doi.org/10.1007/978-94-6265-327-6_9

9.1 Introduction

Based on the club principle discussed in the previous chapter, membership has multiple legal implications and ramifications.

One of the major benefits of membership in international organizations is that members have the right to participate in organizations' decision-making procedures and be represented in the organizations' governing bodies. However, traditional state-centric representation mechanisms based on a three-tier governance structure involving governing bodies composed exclusively or predominantly of state-appointed representatives increasingly have become questionable with regard to their functionality, inclusiveness and legitimacy. Substantial benefits may be gained from transforming organizations into multi-actor structures which do not give only states but also other stakeholders a voice in decision making. Moreover, there are new trends relating to organizations' decision-making procedures which may be considered being given a wider application in international organizations.

Fundamental changes are also required in relation to organizations' funding mechanisms. So far, organizations look to their state members as their main or only source of funding. However, as public funds are increasingly become scarce, traditional funding mechanisms are not sufficient and organizations have to look for new sources of funding. This relates, in particular, to the funding of organizations producing global public goods or fighting global public bads for which traditional funding mechanisms are particularly ineffective.

In the case of international financial institutions, there is a direct correlation between membership and organizations' capital structures and the legal structures of concessional funding windows. Moreover, membership has implications for organizations' borrowings on capital markets and for their operational legal and policy frameworks.

This chapter will discuss the issues related above. Moreover, it will also succinctly review the nexus between membership and organizations' operational frameworks and procurement arrangements.

9.2 Membership and Representation

Many organizations have a three-tier governing structure involving a plenary body, a board or council of ambassadors or similar body and a secretariat. This system may be supplemented by parliamentary and judicial organs.

The following discussion will not give an overview of the classification and different types of organs (governing bodies) of international organizations, as this topic has already been amply discussed by scholars of international institutions, like Schermers and Blokker.[1] Rather, the focus will be to elaborate on the challenges

[1] Schermers and Blokker 2011, §§383–702.

faced by international organizations regarding their legitimacy, the functionality of their traditional three-tier system, and their decision-making procedures. It will be shown that in many instances there is a strong case and benefit for transforming international organizations into multi-actor institutions which give a voice to transnational actors and allow representation of transnational actors and individuals in their governing bodies.

9.2.1 *Legitimacy*

9.2.1.1 Democratic Deficit and Lack of Inclusiveness and Representativeness

The fact that traditionally only governments are represented in organizations' governing bodies, has resulted in challenges to their democratic deficit and contentions that national Parliaments are the "losers of internationalization; they are often sidelined in international negotiations, limited to rubber-stamping international deals struck by national governments, and constrained in their national legislation by international agreements."[2]

> The real or anticipated decline of parliament has triggered several kinds of responses. First, national parliaments have reasserted their oversight capacities and rights regarding international decision-making [….]. Second, alternative forms of citizen representation have been theorized and in some sort put in practice. [….] Third, there has been movement towards the parliamentarization of international organizations, i.e. the establishment of parliamentary bodies and the growth of parliamentary competencies and activities within international organizations.[3]

The European Parliament, in particular, epitomizes the rise of a parliamentary institution and the expansion of its powers. While various other organizations (e.g. the Council of Europe followed suit, most international organizations still do not have any parliamentary organ. In the case of such organizations, it is the more important to adopt participatory approaches that involve transnational actors in their institutional frameworks and decision-making procedures.

There are challenges to organizations' legitimacy on account of lack of representativeness. In relation to international financial institutions which have adopted weighted decision-making procedures, this charge is made on the grounds that that their capital structures no longer reflect the weight of countries in the world economy. In UN organizations and other organization which follow the one-country-one-vote principle, lack of representativeness may be seen in the fact that a county like Niue with just over 1500 inhabitants may have the same voting rights as countries with hundreds of millions of inhabitants. While this may be

---

[2] Rocabert et al. 2014, p. 1.

[3] Ibid.

consistent with the principle of sovereign equality of members, it poses major governance problems for the organization.

As discussed above, it increasingly is argued that international organizations should not be only forums for states but also for transnational actors, including the private sector, philanthropy and civil society. As will be shown by this author,[4] there are many challenges to the legitimacy of international organizations which relate to their lack of inclusiveness and failure to give a voice to transnational actors in decision-making. This has resulted in attempts to diversify the composition of their governing bodies by transforming them into multi-actor institutions. Finally, challenges to organizations' legitimacy are made due to lack of transparency and accountability and their failure to guarantee due process and other fundamental rights, and to espouse the human rights agenda.

9.2.1.2 Internal and External Roles of Members

As indicated by Wessels, there is an inherent "tension States may experience between being a State and a member State at the same time. This tension is particularly visible in the European Union—where member States' obligations under EU law increasingly collide with general obligations those States may have under international law—but also become apparent in other international 'integration' organizations as well."[5]

The "internal and external role" which states play as "constituent parts of organs" and as "counterparts of the international organization"[6] are a corollary of the different roles which they play as states and as member states.

"The internal role or capacity can easily be recognized in the composition and functioning on non-plenary, executive organs of international organizations. Members of these organs are often expected to act on behalf of all members of the organization."[7] In particular, in their internal role, members of governing bodies may have fiduciary responsibilities towards the organization, as set out in the Zedillo Report in relation to the World Bank's executive directors:

> Under current governance arrangements, Executive Directors at the World Bank Group have an ambiguous status. They are not 'ambassadors' or 'permanent representatives' of governments, as are their counterparts at OECD, WTO, or most United Nations agencies, but neither are they Bank staff accountable only to the institution. Because of their hybrid status, Directors have two sets of duties—their representational duties to their governments and their fiduciary duties to the membership as a whole.[8]

---

4 Droesse 2020.

5 Wessel and Dekker 2015, p. 294.

6 Schermers and Blokker 2011, §66.

7 Ibid.

8 "Repowering the World Bank for the 21st Century: Report of the High-Level Commission on Modernization of World Bank Group Governance (hereinafter "Zedillo Report")", p. 31. http://siteresources.worldbank.org/NEWS/Resources/WBGovernanceCOMMISSIONREPORT.pdf.

In their external role, states are “the counterparts of the organization”[9] that may enter into agreements with international organizations, e.g. as the recipient of financing or technical assistance or, as the host country of an organization or the office of an organization, in the context of headquarters agreements or host country agreements.[10] As regards the governance of international organizations, the external role of members in the governance of international organization is largely associated with the participation of delegations of member countries in conferences organized by international organizations, however, it is not limited to such representation mechanisms.

Countries may adopt external roles also while dealing with core strategic matters and the organization’s financial resources. At times, the distinction between internal and external roles may relate to a distinction between constitutional and extra-constitutional processes of international organizations. Moreover, the distinction between internal and external roles is not necessarily related to the type of resources administered by international organizations. Countries may adopt external roles in relation to the replenishment of organizations ordinary or special funds resources and internal roles in relation to trust funds which are not part of organizations’ special funds resources.[11]

So far, transnational actors are generally only consulted by international organizations, but cannot participate in decision-making. The inclusiveness of organizations decision-making procedures may contribute to their legitimacy. Hence, it may strengthen the legitimacy of international organizations if they give a voice to transnational actors in their decision-making procedures. However, this requires that also the transnational actors concerned meet in their composition, policies and procedures basic requirements of good governance and legitimacy. As has already been stressed above, this requirement is a corollary of any enhanced role given to transnational actors in the governance of international organizations.

9.2.1.3 Extra-Constitutional Processes

While international organizations have demonstrated limited ability and inclination to include transnational actors in their decision-making processes, their ability to incorporate external and even extra-constitutional processes has proved quite remarkable, as shown by the example of the international financial institutions. The core pillars of the international financial system and, in this context, the core strategic functions of each international financial institution, have been coined by decisions of the G-7/8 (G10) and G-20 or other external processes. Moreover, replenishment negotiations of concessional windows of international financial institutions are often conducted outside organizations’ institutional frameworks.

---

[9] Schermers and Blokker 2011, §66.

[10] Ibid., §§1688–1689.

[11] See Droesse 2011c, p. 91.

Both gives rise to serious concerns regarding the legitimacy of these processes, and their transparency and accountability.

The power which G-7/8/10 countries wield on international financial institutions is amply documented in literature. Foch has well explained the "G-7 and G-10's influence on World Bank decisions,"[12] which some have associated with "institutionalized hegemony".[13] It is intrinsically problematic, that core strategic decisions of international financial institutions are taken through extra-constitutional processes. This does not only apply to the G-7, G-8 and G-10, but also to the G20, which has been instrumental in determining the core principles governing the international financial system. As shown by Warren, a total of "120 IFI reform commitments" have been made by the G20.[14] At the London summit of 2009, when an "an all-time high of 29 IFI reform commitments" was made, the G20 left no doubt that the IFI reform would be driven by the G20.[15]

While international financial institutions such as the IMF are not formally bound by G-7, G-8, G-10, or G-20 decisions, they are not given the option to ignore them, as the participants in the aforementioned forums are the main shareholders and contributors of all international financial institutions. This is particularly evident for G20 decisions, as G-20 members can muster in international financial institutions that have espoused weighted voting any qualified majority short of unanimity. While this ensures effective implementation of G20 decisions, it does not justify the fact that many countries, including most developing countries, are not involved in the process because they do not belong to these privileged clubs. Legitimacy not only relates to the majority by which decisions are adopted but also to the process which is followed in adopting decisions. While it is recognized that there is a need to coordinate the work of international financial institutions, other alternative coordination mechanisms that also give a voice to developing countries could have been considered. This could have been done, for example, by strengthening the two committees which advise the Board of Governors of the IMF (i.e. the International Monetary and Financial Committee and the Development Committee) and converting them into decision-making bodies.

The fact that in implementation of G-7/G8 and G-20 decisions extra-constitutional processes are used to determine core strategic objectives of

---

[12] Foch 2013.

[13] Bailin 2001.

[14] Warren 2017.

[15] G20 Communiqué: London Summit – Leaders' Statement, 2 April 2009, para 20: "In order for our financial institutions to help manage the crisis and prevent future crises we must strengthen their longer term relevance, effectiveness and legitimacy. So, alongside the significant increase in resources agreed today we are determined to reform and modernise the international financial institutions to ensure they can assist members and shareholders effectively in the new challenges they face. **We will reform their mandates, scope and governance to reflect changes in the world economy and the new challenges of globalisation, and that emerging and developing economies, including the poorest, must have greater voice and representation.**" (emphasis added) https://www.imf.org/external/np/sec/pr/2009/pdf/g20_040209.pdf.

international financial institutions as such is a matter of serious concern. It is further aggravated by the lack of representativeness and accountability of decisions taken in the aforementioned forums. The lack of representativeness is particularly evident in the case of the G-7, which only comprises industrialized countries with democratic governance structures, but it equally applies to the G20. As Sverdrup and Nahem have indicated,

> the G20 is premised on several structural weaknesses. First, the G20 is a self-appointed club. It is in principle not mandated to act on behalf of anybody apart from its member states. Hence, there is always a risk that it will secure 'club goods' rather than global public goods. Secondly, the G20 is not representative. Although the G20 countries represent around 85 per cent of world GDP, 80 per cent of world trade, and around two thirds of the world's population, its (sic) does not represent the 193 UN[16] member states.[17]

Among those excluded from G-20 participation are the Nordic countries, which led the former Foreign Minister of Norway to the following remark:

> We have to be careful that we don't lift all the substance out [of the UN]. If you do that, you have to be sure that what you lift it into has a minimum legitimacy that is respected.[18]

He warned the G20 "against trying to impose 'pre-cooked' decisions on the UN and the Bretton Woods institutions",[19] called for a "debate over the legitimacy and representation of the G20" and proposed "members of the Nordic Council—Norway, Sweden, Denmark, Finland and Iceland—could share a rotating seat together with the Baltic states and possibly Poland.[20]

Also as regards developing countries, the interests of those countries who are not members of the G-20 are not necessarily identic to those of the G-20 members. Thus, as highlighted by Homi Kharas, at the London G20 summit "no one in the G-20 spoke up for the fact that average incomes in the United States are now 44 times the average income in sub-Saharan Africa (compared to only 17 times in 1980)."[21] Also the President of the African Development Bank, Kaberuka observed with reference to the Pittsburgh G20 summit of 2009, that given the way the G20 is structured "the low-income countries' priorities are still an appendix, a footnote."[22] The situation has not changed substantially ever since. Thus, while the "G20 Compact with Africa (CWA) Initiative" discussed at the G20 meeting in Hamburg in 2017, aims to increase investment in Africa, in particular in infrastructure, by improving the

---

[16] Ibid.

[17] Sverdrup and Nahem 2017.

[18] Cited according to A. Ward. Norway seeks representation at the G20. Financial Times, 9 Nov. 2009. https://www.ft.com/content/1f2e17fa-cc44-11de-8e30-00144feabdc0?mhq5j=e1.

[19] Cited according to Financial Times of 9 Nov. 2009.

[20] Ibid.

[21] Kharas 2009.

[22] Kharas 2009.

macroeconomic, political, and financial environment",[23] overall there was very little in this initiative which was of interest for the poorer African countries.

The above shortcomings in representation and accountability mechanisms of the G20 are not mitigated by the fact that certain countries are invited as guests to G20 meetings and that key international institutions attend G20 meetings.[24] They fundamentally undermine the legitimacy of G20 determinations regarding international financial institutions.

9.2.2 Functionality and Inclusiveness of the Three-Tier System

Most international organizations have a three-tier system comprising a board of governors, conference or similar plenary body in which all members are represented, a board (of directors), council of ambassadors or similar body, and a secretariat. Generally, the powers of the organization are vested in the Board of Governors or other similar plenary body. There are only a few international organizations (e.g., IADB) where the members of the plenary body contribute to policy formulation in between annual meetings.[25] In most organizations, plenary bodies do not have any such role; they generally only convene once a year to take decisions on certain matters of crucial importance for which decision cannot be delegated. Thus, there is an intrinsic need for institutional decisions to be made in the interval between annual meetings of plenary bodies. Generally, the boards of directors or similar bodies that have been created for that purpose are governing bodies of limited membership; they "particularly strengthen the autonomy international organizations may enjoy from their member States."

While governing bodies of limited membership are not necessarily subordinated to plenary bodies (e.g. the Security Council in not subordinate to the General Assembly of the United Nations), often there is a hierarchy between those bodies. This is the case for all those organizations where all the powers of the organization are vested in the plenary body, often with the *proviso* that such powers can be delegated—with certain exceptions—to a board of directors of similar body.[26] In these situations, there is a hierarchy of laws between the legal acts adopted by the

---

[23] "Compact with Africa Recommendations". https://www.b20germany.org/priorities/compact-with-africa/compact-with-africa-recommendations/.

[24] See Participants of the G20 Summit in Hamburg in 2017. https://www.g20.org/Webs/G20/EN/G20/Participants/participants_node.html.

[25] See Droesse 2011c, p. 127.

[26] For example, Article 28.1 of the ADB Charter provides: "All the powers of the Bank shall be vested in the Board of Governors." Section 8 of ADB's By-Laws contains a general delegation of powers to the Board of Directors, as follows: "The Board of Directors is authorized by the Board of Governors to exercise all the powers of the Bank with the exception of those expressly reserved to the Board of Governors by para 2 of Article 28 and other provisions of the Agreement."

plenary body and those adopted by the body of limited membership, which may sometimes be difficult to ascertain.

Boards of Directors or similar bodies are often designed as non-plenary bodies. The existence of such bodies particularly strengthens

> the autonomy international organizations may enjoy from their member States. Precisely because of their non-plenary nature, these Boards rely less on difficult compromises among a large number of member States, and are better able to focus on the institutional objectives rather than on individual national political preferences.[27]

It is not intrinsically impossible, however, for all members of the organization to be represented in the board of directors or similar body. This will be only possible, however, in those cases where the size of the membership is rather limited.

As regards boards and similar bodies, Martinez-Diaz makes a distinction between three governance models, one of which is the "Delegate-and-Control Model" of the IMF, MDBs and other international financial institutions, which is characterized by: "(1) a compact board of directors (relative to the total membership size) whose members are elected or appointed by member countries, and which meets very frequently; (2) a system in which most members are represented indirectly through multi-country constituencies and share a single director; (3) a CEO who is also chair of the board, and (4) a decision-making system nominally based on 'consensus' but underpinned by weighted voting."[28]

The above system contrasts, as shown by Martinez-Diaz with the "Direct-Representation Model"[29] to which the EIB, the Organization for Economic Cooperation and Development, and to a lesser extent, the BIS adhere; "despite their differences, all three organizations share the basic elements of this governance model: (1) a 'plenary' board of directors in which all members are directly represented; (2) a board or equivalent that meets only a few times per year, typically monthly or bi-monthly; and (3) voting systems that either rely completely on the principle of one-nation-one-vote or combine it with some form of double majority voting."[30] The "Direct Representation Model" is different from the "Delegate-and Control Model" as the board of the aforementioned three institutions "are relatively distant from the operations of the institution and leave more of the day-to-day business to the management."[31]

Finally, the third system referred to by Diaz-Martinez is the "Constituency-Based Oversight Model" that is common among UN agencies.

> As in the delegate-and-control model, member states delegate power to a non-plenary board, and members are represented through constituencies. However, these organizations have several distinguishing features: they have (1) boards of directors that are large in absolute terms but small relative to the size of the membership; (2) non-resident boards that

[27] Wessel and Dekker 2015, p. 304.

[28] Martinez-Diaz 2009, p. 395.

[29] Ibid., 387–401.

[30] Ibid., 399.

[31] Ibid., 399.

meet only two or three times per year; (3) board directors who represent constituencies with rotation schemes; (4) one-nation-one-vote or double-majority voting systems; and (5) separate CEOs and board chairs.[32]

The distinctions made by Martinez-Diaz between the three systems mentioned above are useful and appropriate, in particular, also as they facilitate assessing the strength and weaknesses of the three systems mentioned above. As indicated and further elaborated by Martinez-Diaz: "The delegate-and-control model is the strongest when it comes to the board's role as political counterweight, with the direct representation model in second place. As democratic forums, the direct representation and constituency-based oversight models have the most to offer, though they were conceived for two different membership sizes. In terms of strategic thinking, the direct representation model is the least inadequate."[33]

9.2.2.1 Proposals for Adjustment of the Three-Tier System: The Examples of the IMF and World Bank

The need for institutional reform and adjustment to the current three-tier system was articulated, in particular, in the case of the IMF and World Bank, which adhere to the "Delegate-and-Control Model" described above, as the current institutional set-up of these two institutions does not support a strategic focus of their governing bodies.

A potentially problematic point attached to the expansion of membership in international organizations is that, particularly in organizations with universal membership, plenary bodies are not well suited to perform strategic guidance and control in view of the very size of their membership. This has been highlighted with particular clarity in the report of the Report of the High-Level Commission on Modernization of the World Bank Group, called the Zedillo Report, after its chair, the former President of Mexico, Ernesto Zedillo.

The Zedillo Report identified fundamental deficits of the process of strategy formulation of the World Bank Group. It concluded that both the "Development Committee and the Executive Board, as currently structured, lack the capacity to play this role effectively",[34] as the "Development Committee's role in strategy formulation is constrained by its advisory nature, its limited tools [….] and the *pro forma* nature of its meetings" and that of the Executive Board, "is limited by the fact that neither the Board nor individual directors are formally held responsible for the World Bank Group's overall strategic direction. Also, given the Board's many other responsibilities, the body has insufficient time to devote to strategic matters."[35]

The Report proposed (i) reconstituting the World Bank's (resident) Executive Board as a (non-resident) body with ministerial composition, thereby, in essence,

---

[32] Ibid., 401.

[33] Ibid., 403–404.

[34] Zedillo Report. Summary of Findings, x.

[35] Ibid.

converting the Development Committee which currently only has advisory functions into a decision-making body. Other main recommendations contained in the Report were (ii) a far-reaching delegation of all financing operations to Management and (iii) the creation of a resident Advisory Council of Representatives supporting the reconstituted Board.[36]

Similar recommendations were contained in the Report of the "Committee on IMF Governance Reform" of 2009 (Manuel Report), which proposed the (i) activation of a Council of Ministers and Governors as a forum for coordination and strategy formulation, (ii) giving most authority for member-specific surveillance to Fund management, and (iii) elevation of the IMF Executive Board from day-to-day operational decisions to giving advice on strategic issues and delivering a critical supervisory function.[37]

The recommendations of the Zedillo Report were too far-reaching to be easily digested and were eventually doomed for failure by the very fact that they would have required amendments to the IBRD's Articles of Agreement, which, in view of the required qualified majorities which give one country or a group of countries the power to block any amendment, are formidable obstacles for institutional reform.

The example of the IMF shows that important changes to an organization's governance structure are not easy to implement even if they do not require an amendment to Articles of Agreement. In accordance Article XII, Section 1 of the IMF Articles of Agreement, "an eighty-five percent majority of the total voting power" is required for any decision to apply the provisions on the Council in Schedule D of the IMF Articles of Agreement. As the activation of the "Council" was not supported by such a qualified majority, the recommendations of "Committee on IMF Governance Reform" to activate the IMF Council have not been acted upon.

9.2.2.2 Plenary Body or Partnership Forum

In traditional international organizations with treaty foundation, the plenary body is the highest decision-making organ. Resolutions and decisions of the Board of Directors, council of ambassadors or similar bodies therefore need to conform with the decisions of the board of governors.

Also, traditionally, governing bodies of international organizations are an amalgam of the combined executive power of states. This is particularly evident in relation to plenary bodies of international organizations which are the pillar of consensual decision making, as they are traditionally composed of state representatives, with international organizations joining the club only fairly recently and generally only to a very limited extent.

---

[36] Ibid., xv–xvi.

[37] Committee on IMF Governance Reform. Final Report. 24 March 2009. https://www.imf.org/external/np/omd/2009/govref/032409.pdf.

Schermers and Blokker state categorically: "Each organization has at least one plenary organ: an organ which is composed of the representatives of all member states."[38] In the view of this author, this is another mantra which needs to be rethought and revised.

As has been shown above in relation to the IMF and World Bank, the functionality of the three-tier system is currently being questioned. Moreover, the system is under attack in relation to its lack of inclusiveness.

Some of the newer organizations also do no longer fully correspond to the traditional blueprint of the three-tier system. The institutional structures of the Global Environment Facility, the Global Fund, and Green Climate Fund, which each have some special features, are of interest in this context.

In the GEF, the Assembly has a role and functions which are different from those of traditional plenary bodies. This is underlined by the fact that the Assembly, unlike once every 3 years as provided in para 13 of the Instrument for the Restructured Environment Facility, effectively only meets every 4 years.[39] Moreover, the only function where "approval by consensus" by the Assembly is required relates to amendments to the present Instrument on the basis of recommendations by the Council."[40] The other functions that the Assembly has are to "review the general policies of the facility", "review and evaluate the operation of the Facility", and "keep under review the membership of the Facility" (Article 14, (a), (b) and (c) of the GEF Instrument).

De facto, the GEF assemblies have become forums for a great variety of stakeholders. Thus, inter alia, in connection with the fifth GEF Assembly in Cancun, a civil society forum was held which brought together "over 200 representatives of civil society organizations and indigenous peoples groups from more than 80 countries around the world."[41] Nevertheless, in the governance structure of the GEF, the Council is the center of decision-making;[42] transnational actors have no role in the formal decision-making by GEF Assembly and GEF Council.

In the case of the Green Climate Fund, the Board is at the core of the Fund's decision-making. While provision has been made that the Fund "will be accountable to and function under the guidance of the Conference of the Parties (COP),"[43] it was also clarified that the "Fund will be governed and supervised by a Board that

---

[38] Schermers and Blokker 2011, §237.

[39] Ragazzi 2011, p. 488.

[40] Paragraph 14(d) of the GEF Instrument. https://www.thegef.org/sites/default/files/documents/GEF_Instrument-Interior-March23.2015.pdf.

[41] GEF-CSO Network. CSO Forum during the 5th GEF Assembly. http://www.gefngo.org/index.cfm?&menuid=260&parentid=140.

[42] See paras 15–20 of GEF Instrument.

[43] Paragraph 4 of the Governing Instrument of the Green Climate Fund. https://www.greenclimate.fund/documents/20182/574763/Governing_Instrument.pdf/caa6ce45-cd54-4ab0-9e37-fb637a9c6235.

will have full responsibility for funding decisions."[44] The role and functions of the Board are detailed in para 18 of the Governing Instrument.

The COP is not authorized to overrule Board decisions. It also neither functions as, nor can it be construed to be the equivalent of, a traditional plenary body even though any decision on a potential termination of the Fund would be vested in the COP. Rather, the Governing Instrument has established a complex accountability and guidance framework for the Green Climate Fund which involves reporting obligations not only for the Fund but also for the evaluation and accountability mechanisms.[45]

It is a particular feature of the GCF Governing Instrument that "two civil society representatives, one each from developing and developed countries, and two private sector representatives, one each from developing and developed countries" are invited to participate in all Board meetings as "active observers".[46] These have the right to speak at these meetings on similar terms at the Board members. However, as for the GEF, also in the case of the GCF, transnational actors have not formal role in decision-making.

In the case of organizations that rely heavily on interaction with civil society and other stakeholders, in particular, it may indeed be questioned whether a plenary body that is exclusively composed of state representatives is still an appropriate institutional paradigm.

Creating a platform for the participation of a wide range of stakeholders instead of a traditional plenary body shows that institutions are committed to seriously considering suggestions and proposals from civil society organizations, the private sector, and philanthropy and are ready to interact with these transnational actors. Even if no express provision for such a forum is made in the constituent instrument of the organization, such forum can be introduced as a matter of policy based on decisions of the governing body of the organization concerned.

The Global Fund reflects the move to two-tier structures and may be seen as the epitome of a governance structure which also gives civil society, philanthropy and the private sector a voice in decision making.

The Global Fund opted with its "Partnership Forum" for an "innovative approach to consultation with a broad range of stakeholders, moving beyond the usual participants to reach those who are not normally involved in Global Fund processes."[47] The Partnership Forum is open to those "stakeholders that actively support the Global Fund's objectives, including representatives of donors, multilateral development cooperation agencies, developed and developing countries, civil society, NGO and community based organizations, technical and research

44 Paragraph 5 of the Governing Instrument of the Green Climate Fund.

45 See Droesse. 2017, pp 52–53.

46 Governing Instrument, para 16.

47 Global Fund. "Partnership Forum". Overview. https://www.theglobalfund.org/en/partnership-forum/.

agencies, and the private sector."[48] The Partnership Forum is to provide "input into the development and implementation of the Global Fund strategic plan"[49] and is to provide "an important and visible platform for debate, advocacy, continued fundraising, and inclusion of new partners [….]."[50] Introduction of a similar forum might also be considered for other international organizations.

9.2.3 Strategic Focus, Resident Boards and Secondary Governing Structures

The question whether governing bodies of limited membership should be resident, or non-resident is intrinsically related to manner how such bodies conduct their business. Moreover, if governing bodies of restricted membership focus on strategic frameworks regarding certain sectors or countries rather than on specific projects, this may facilitate the approval of secondary governance structures under umbrella operational arrangements approved by the governing bodies concerned.

There is increasing recognition that governing bodies of international organizations need to sharpen their strategic focus. This concerns in particular IFIs, which, in addition to being involved in issues of public policy, conduct extensive project and program financing activities.

Thus, the High-Level Panel convened by the African Development Bank opinioned as follows:

> In line with best practice in both the public and private sectors, the board must focus on providing strategic direction, fiduciary oversight, and monitoring performance while giving management its proper space for day-to-day implementation. It should resist the urge to become involved in micromanaging the Bank, say, by allowing smaller projects to be approved by management. It should collaborate more with management with a sense of collective responsibility for achieving the Bank's goals.[51]

Very similar considerations have also been articulated in the Zedillo and Manuel Reports already mentioned above which have highlighted the strategic deficit

---

[48] The Global Fund. 2016. Bylaws of the Global Fund to Fight Aids, Tuberculosis and Malaria (Global Fund Bylaws). Article 6.1.

[49] "A number of Partnership Forum consultations were held in 2015 to support the development of the Global Fund Strategy 2017–2022. The consultations included three regional Partnership Forums with over 300 participants from 128 countries, a 12-week online consultation with over 1,200 participants from 143 countries, and dozens of focused meetings and consultations on specific aspects of the strategy." Global Fund. Partnership Forum. Overview.

[50] Global Fund Bylaws, Article 6.2.

[51] High Level Panel for the African Development Bank. 2007. *Investing in Africa's Future*: *The ADB in the 21st Century. Report of the High Level Panel.* 37. http://www.afdb.org/fileadmin/uploads/afdb/Documents/Publications/27842402-EN-HLP-REPORT-INVESTING-IN-AFRICAS-FUTURE.PDF.

regarding the IMF and World Bank Executive Boards and have proposed far-reaching institutional reforms.

Hence, the question arises whether resident governing bodies of limited membership are still warranted or may be abolished. A strategic focus of organizations governing bodies is required for organizations to "contribute effectively to the long 'production chain" of global public goods."[52] An organization whose governing bodies have such strategic focus may be better served by a non-resident board at a ministerial level than by a resident board of a more technocratic nature.

Sharpening the strategic focus of boards also allows them to focus on sectors or countries, rather than on specific projects, with the consequence that approval of programs and projects which are covered by the strategic framework approved the governing body may be delegated to the executive head of the organization concerned. Adopting such a strategic approach may pave the way for adopting secondary governance structures which may be composed in a different manner that the primary ones. As this author has shown in relation to organizations' concessional windows:

> Under umbrella operational arrangements approved by organizations governing bodies, supplementary governance structures (e.g. annual donor meetings, steering committees and other bodies) could be created which are composed in a different manner than organizations' regular governing bodies and are applicable to all types of resources administered by organizations.[53]

As shown:

> While a complete delegation of financing decisions to the executive head of an organization is often not possible under MFDIs constituent agreements, organizations' governing bodies (e.g., board of governors or board of directors) generally have the power to establish under umbrella operational arrangements for countries or sectors approved by them supplementary governance structures (e.g., a council, steering committee, annual donors' meeting or other similar body) which are applicable to all resources administered by them, including trust funds (financial intermediary funds) and other types of co-financing arrangements comprising nongovernmental organizations and other stakeholders) than organizations' regular governing bodies and different decision-making procedures might apply. Adopting this approach, organizations could be transformed in multi-donor (and possibly) multi-actor platforms which are structured in a similar manner. Such transformation could be achieved as a matter of policy and would not necessarily require, even though it could be combined with, amendments to organizations' constituent agreements. The bodies so established may be composed in a different manner (e.g. comprising nongovernmental organizations and other stakeholders) than organizations' regular governing bodies and different decision-making procedures might apply. Adopting this approach, organizations could be transformed in multi-donor (and possibly) multi-actor platforms which are structured in a similar manner. Such transformation could be achieved as a matter of policy and would not necessarily require, even though it could be combined with, amendments to organizations' constituent agreements.[54]

---

[52] Zedillo Report, 13.

[53] Droesse 2011d, p. 297.

[54] Droesse 2011c, pp. 164–165.

9.2.4 *From State-Centric to Multi-Actor Governance Structures*

One core question is whether the three-tier structure is still an appropriate paradigm of institutional structure. A separate but related question is whether governing bodies of international organizations may, and should, include representative arrangements involving technical government agencies and transnational actors, including the private sector, philanthropy and civil society, as well as individual experts appointed in a personal capacity.

Currently, in most traditional international organizations, representation in governing bodies is limited to states and a few international organizations.

There are various examples where expressly representation of technical government agencies in the governing bodies of an international organization is required. In the case of the World Meteorological Organization (WMO), provision to that effect has been made both in relation to the World Meteorological Congress which is the plenary body of the organization and for the Executive Council which is a governing body of limited membership. For the World Meteorological Congress, each member "shall designate one of its delegates, who should be the Director of its Meteorological or Hydrometeorological Service, as its principal delegate at Congress."[55] The Executive Council consists of, in addition to the President and Vice-Presidents of the Association and the presidents of regional associations, of 27 "Directors of Meteorological or Hydrometeorological Services of Members of the Organization, who can be replaced at sessions by alternates."[56] The governing bodies of INTERPOL are predominantly composed of police officials, considering that in accordance with Article 4 of the Constitution of 1956 "Any country may delegate as a Member to the Organization any official police body whose functions come within the framework of activities of the Organization."

The two organizations mentioned above are classified as intergovernmental as the actions of representatives of the technical agencies concerned are attributed to government. However, it is not a requirement for the classification of an organization as "intergovernmental" that all members of its governing bodies are exclusively government representatives. Hence, the International Labour Organization (ILO), which is the epitome of tripartism involving representatives from governments, employers, and workers in the ILO Conference and Governing Body, is an intergovernmental organization.[57] As indicated by Vogel-Polsky: "la composition tripartite de la delegation nationale des États-Membres fait apparaître que les

---

[55] WMO Constitution, Article 7(b).

[56] WMO Constitution, Article 13(c).

[57] ILO Constitution, Article 3, para 1 provides: "The meetings of the General Conference of representatives of the Members shall be held from time to time as occasion may require, and at least once in every year. It shall be composed of four representatives of each of the Members, of whom two shall be Government delegates **and the two others shall be delegates representing respectively the employers and the workpeople of each of the Members**." (emphasis added).

governments nationaux ne sont plus the seuls à jouer le rôle des gouvernants dans les relations internationales."[58] Also, the Global Fund qualifies, as discussed above, for recognition as an "intergovernmental organization".

The "King Abdullah Bin Abdulaziz International Centre for Interreligious and Intercultural Dialogue" is a very interesting example of an intergovernmental organization with treaty foundation[59] whose Board of Directors is entirely composed of religious leaders. In that specific case, the states that have founded KAICIID may be seen as members of the organization; they are represented in the "Council of Parties", which is an organ of KAICIID, the functions of which are defined by Article V of the KAICIID Agreement.

As has been extensively argued in the preceding chapters, the term "international organization" is wider than "intergovernmental organization". Hence, also organizations which were not established by an agreement between governments and whose members are not states or other public entities, may qualify for recognition as international organization, including organizations of parliamentary cooperation and cooperative undertakings of sub-state actors and national regulators. Potentially, also organizations like ICANN, ISO and IATA whose members are entirely or predominantly private-sector entities or entities incorporated and operating under national law might be transformed in international organizations. The composition of governing bodies of organizations of that kind would reflect the composition of their membership (which consists of entities incorporated or operating under national law) and, therefore, would be very different from that of traditional international organizations. As in the case of ICANN the normal governance structure of international organizations is reversed, private sector entities would take the decisions in the organization's governing bodies, while states could be involved in an advisory capacity. Similar structures might also be contemplated for ISO and IATA.

Finally, an important question is to what extent individual experts should be included in a personal capacity in governing bodies of international organizations.

To a limited extent, participation of external experts is currently allowed in committees (such as the EBRD Enforcement Committee[60]) where it is seen as important to strengthen the independence of the process. External experts and

ILO Constitution, Article 7, para 1 provides: "The Governing Body shall consist of fifty-six persons, twenty-eight representing governments, fourteen representing the employers, and fourteen representing the workers." http://www.ilo.org/public/english/bureau/leg/download/constitution.pdf.

[58] Vogel-Polsky 1966, p. 71.

[59] Paragraph 1 of the "Agreement for the Establishment of the King Abdullah Bin Abdulaziz International Centre for Interreligious and Intercultural Dialogue" (KAICIID Agreement) expressly establishes "the Centre as an international organization". Moreover, para 2 of that Article provides: "The Centre shall possess international legal personality." https://www.kaiciid.org/node/2001.

[60] http://www.ebrd.com/cs/Satellite?c=Content&cid=1395248598994&d=&pagename=EBRD%2FContent%2FDownloadDocument.

stakeholders may also be included in panels, working groups or commissions which provide advisory services on certain matters. However, so far there are very few cases where a board (of directors) or similar body has transnational actors as members.

The Global Fund is one such case and it may be seen as the epitome of a multi-actor institution involving a variety of stakeholders. Its Board, which is prime decision-making body of the Global Fund, incorporates representation of transnational actors. The voting members of the Board consist, in addition to seven representatives from developing countries and 8 representatives from donor countries, of

> five representatives from civil society and the private sector (one representative of a non-governmental organization ("NGO") from a developing country, one representative of an NGO from a developed country, one representative of the private sector, one representative of a private foundation, and one representative of an NGO who is a person living with HIV/AIDS or from a community living with tuberculosis or malaria).[61]

The Gavi Alliance has a similar governance structure. The Gavi Alliance Statutes provide that

> Two-thirds of the voting members of the Board shall be representatives from key Gavi Alliance partner institutions and stakeholders (each such representative a "Representative Board Member") and one-third of its voting members shall be unaffiliated individuals who are appointed in their personal capacity on the basis of their skills and networks (each such member an "Unaffiliated Board Member"), all as defined and described herein and in the By-laws.[62]

While a similar multi-actor structure may not be suitable for all international organizations, it offers decisive advantages in a number of cases, in particular, for organizations producing or funding global public goods and relying on country ownership and close interaction with stakeholders at various levels.

As may be seen from the above, representation in organizations' governing bodies does not need to be limited to governments but may include a variety of transnational actors and individual experts or representatives of communities. The state-centric representation arrangements which characterize traditional plenary bodies are increasingly seen as a constraint to their effectiveness, in particular, in organizations which rely on country-driven activities and on interaction with transnational actors in the design and implementation of projects.

Thus, giving a voice to transnational actors in organizations governing bodies may enhance an organization's impact. It may also help mobilizing additional resources, as many contributors require a say in the strategy and on operational decisions if they contribute high amounts to an international organization. Representation of transnational actors may be linked to their commitment to

---

61 Global Fund Bylaws, Article 7.1. https://www.theglobalfund.org/media/6007/core_globalfund_bylaws_en.pdf.

62 Gavi Alliance Statutes, Article 9. http://www.gavi.org/library/gavi-documents/legal/gavi-alliance-statutes/.

support the organization. There is no reason why a foundation such as the Bill and Melinda Gates Foundation contributing amounts well in excess of those provided by most states should not be represented on the governing bodies of international organizations. Effectively, this foundation is represented on the Board of the Global Fund.[63]

However, financial contributions are not the only, nor even the most decisive criterion for allowing representation of transnational actors in the governing bodies of international organizations. Even more important is the experience which transnational actors may contribute to an organization. To allow international organizations to benefit as much as possible from the experience of transnational actors, it is essential that their representatives are selected based on merit and have the necessary background and experience. Merit-based appointment is of paramount importance in the case of persons appointed to be a member of a governing body in their personal capacity, but should not be limited to those cases. Also, representatives of civil society organizations, private sector entities and philanthropy should be selected for their participation in governing bodies first and foremost based on the contribution which they can make to the work of the organization, rather than based on other considerations. It is possible and legitimate for international organizations to require that persons representing transnational actors in governing bodies, committees or working groups need to meet minimum standards of relevant experience.

From a design perspective, there are good arguments for creating new international organizations as multi-actor institutions giving a voice to a variety of stakeholders.

Making changes to the composition of governing bodies of existing organizations often requires amendment to the constituent agreement which is a formidable obstacle for institutional changes, given the applicable qualified majorities and quorum requirements which may give one country, or a small group of countries, the opportunity to block any such amendment. However, these constitutional constraints can be addressed by creating secondary and supplementary governance structures with delegated authority to take decision regarding certain matters.

9.2.5 The Alternative of a Two-Tier System with an Accountability and Guidance Mechanism

A two-tier organizational structure which comprises a guidance or accountability mechanism involving the conference or meeting of the parties to a convention may be the functional equivalent of creating a traditional three-tier structure comprising a plenary body, a board or council of ambassadors and a secretariat. In such a

63 For the composition of the Global Fund Board, see Global Fund. Board. Members. https://www.theglobalfund.org/en/board/members/.

two-tier structure, the powers which the conference or meeting of the parties is empowered to exercise may vary substantially.

The Adaptation Fund, the Green Climate Fund and the GEF represent three paradigms on how relations with a conference, respectively a meeting of the Parties to a multilateral convention can be structured.

The Adaptation Fund stands for the case where a funding mechanism operates under the authority and guidance of the parties to a convention. The Conference of the Parties serving as the meeting of the Parties to the Kyoto Protocol (CMP) decided by Decision No.1/CMP.3[64]

> that the Adaptation Fund Board shall be established to supervise and manage the Adaptation Fund, **under the authority and guidance** of the Conference of the Parties serving as the meeting of the Parties to the Kyoto Protocol, and **shall be fully accountable to the Conference of the Parties serving as the meeting of the Parties to the Kyoto Protocol, which shall decide on its overall policies in line with relevant decisions**. (emphasis added)

The Adaptation Fund Board comprises 16 members "representing Parties to the Kyoto Protocol."[65]

> Upon invitation of the parties, the GEF provides secretariat services and the World Bank performs the functions of trustee. In Copenhagen, in December 2009, the parties accepted an offer of Germany to confer legal capacity to the Adaptation Fund Board, which was implemented a year later on the sidelines of the climate change conference in Cancun by the signature of an MOU between Germany and the Adaptation Fund Board.[66]

As a corollary of the fact that in accordance with the cited Decision the Adaptation Fund Board operates under the "authority and guidance" of the "Conference of the Parties serving as the meeting of the Parties to the Kyoto Protocol" (CMP), the CMP decides the "overall policies" of the Adaptation Fund (para 4) and elects the members and alternate members of the Adaptation Fund Board (para 6). The Board, on the other hand, has executive functions and even managerial functions, as may be seen from the long list of competences in para 5 of the said Decision and the fact that the secretariat, in accordance with para 18, is meant "to render secretariat services to the Adaptation Fund Board in a functionally independent and effective manner." Hence, the Secretariat of the Adaptation Fund is the secretariat to the Board rather than a secretariat of the Fund.

Finally, as is shown above, given that the World Bank is the trustee of the Adaptation Fund and the staff of the Adaptation Fund secretariat are World Bank staff, the decision was taken to endow the Adaptation Fund Board with legal capacity under German law. Thus, the Board is able to enter into contracts with

[64] Decision 1/CMP.3 Adaptation Fund. FCCC/KP/CMP/2007/9/Add.1, 14 March 2008. http://unfccc.int/resource/docs/2007/cmp3/eng/09a01.pdf#page=3.

[65] See para 6, Decision 1/CMP.3, which determines the composition of the Adaptation Fund Board.

[66] See Droesse 2011a, p. 21, with further references.

recipients and perform duties under German law. However, neither the Board, nor the Adaptation Fund itself possess international legal personality.

The relationship with the UNFCCC COP is different in the case of the GEF and or the Green Climate Fund. As shown by this author, during the 16th session of the UNFCCC COP in 2010:

> It was discussed at Cancún 'whether the Fund should be accountable to and under the guidance or whether it should also be under the authority of the COP.' This distinction is important as it relates to the question of whether the COP has the power to select the members of the executive board and approve general rules and guidelines. The majority of developed countries argued at Cancún that the relationship between the future executive board of the Fund and the COP should be modeled on the COP's relationship with the Global Environment Facility (GEF), which is one in which the GEF is 'accountable to and under the guidance of the COP.' The COP resolved that the Green Climate Fund be designated as an operating entity of the financial mechanism of the UNFCC under Article 11, with arrangements to be concluded between the Conference of the Parties and the Green Climate Fund to ensure that it is accountable to and functions under the guidance of the Conference of the Parties, to support projects, programmes, policies and other activities in developing country Parties using thematic funding windows.[67]

The COP is performing certain functions which normally would be vested in the plenary body of an international organization (e.g. in taking a decision on termination of the Fund on recommendation of the Board),[68] but its relations to the Fund's board cannot be compared with those of a plenary body of an international organization and a body of limited membership.

The GCF is linked to the COP at various levels. While provision is made in accordance with para 5 of the Governing Instrument that the "Fund will be governed and supervised by a Board that will have full responsibility for funding decisions", para 6 stipulates that:

> Arrangements will be concluded between the COP and the Fund, consistent with Article 11 of the Convention, to ensure that the Fund is accountable to and functions under the guidance of the COP. In order to ensure accountability to the COP, pursuant to Article 11, paragraph 3, the Board will
>
> a. Receive guidance from the COP, including on matters related to policies, programme priorities and eligibility criteria, and matters related thereto;
> b. Take appropriate action in response to the guidance received;
> c. Submit annual reports to the COP for its consideration and receive further guidance.

While there is an inherent tension between those two provisions, it is clear from the above and other provisions of the Governing Instrument that the UNFCCC COP is neither competent to appoint the members and alternate members of the GCF Board, nor to adopt the policies of the GCF. While the COP cannot overrule decisions by the GCF Board, the Board is, nevertheless, mandated to "take appropriate action in response to the [UNFCCC] guidance received." Moreover, there is a direct link between the COP and the independent evaluation unit, the

[67] Droesse 2011a, pp. 31–32.

[68] GCF Governing Instrument, para 72.

reports of which "will be provided to the COP for purposes of periodic reviews of the financial mechanism of the Convention[69]" and with the independent redress mechanism.[70] Under the circumstances, the relationship between the COP and the Fund's Board may best be understood as an intricate system of checks and balances, rather than as a vertical relationship.

The interim Secretariat of the GCF set up after the 17th session of the UNFCCC COP in 2011 "as an autonomous unit within the UNFCCC secretariat premises" was given the task to "provide technical, administrative and logistical support to the Board until the independent secretariat of the Green Climate Fund is established."[71] Similar, to the Adaptation Fund secretariat, it functioned as a secretariat to the GCF Board with narrowly circumscribed circumstances. The independent GCF Secretariat established by the GCF Board in October 2013,[72] on the other hand, was set up as the secretariat of the Fund, "responsible for the day-to-day operations of the Fund, providing administrative, legal and financial expertise" with a much wider set of competencies, as specified in para 23 of the Governing Instrument. Hence, its responsibilities are distinguishable from those of the Adaptation Fund Secretariat. The independent secretariat is headed by the Executive Director.[73]

As explained, notwithstanding the ambiguity of para 7 of the Governing Instrument, the GCF must be deemed to possess international legal personality. The status of the GCF is different for this reason from that of the Adaptation Fund, but also distinguishable from that of the GEF.

---

[69] GCF Governing Instrument, para 61.

[70] The independent redress mechanism is covered by para 69 of the GCF Governing Instrument. "An interesting new approach has been adopted in case of the independent redress mechanism of the Green Climate Fund, which is being added to the existing mechanisms. In line with the functions of other accountability mechanisms, it is to address "the grievances and complaints by communities and people who have been directly affected by the adverse impacts through the failure of the project or programme funded by the Fund to implement the Fund's operational policies and procedures, including environmental and social safeguards." However, in addition to that function, the independent redress mechanism is to the address "the reconsideration of funding decisions in accordance with paras 6–10 of the Arrangements between the Fund and the Conference of the Parties." Thus, in case of the Green Climate Fund, the accountability mechanism will have a two-pronged function relating to the review of grievance of aggrieved communities and the review of funding proposals." Droesse 2020. See: GCF. 2017. *Decision on the Updated Terms of Reference of the Independent Redress Mechanism (Revised).* (B.BM-2017/10. 25 September 2017), 3. https://www.greenclimate.fund/documents/20182/620292/B.BM-2017_10_-_Decision_of_the_Board_on_updated_Terms_of_Reference_of_the_Independent_Redress_Mechanism__Revised_.pdf/dc4fef96-fd30-4aae-bcf6-dd9088d7123b.

[71] Decisions 3/CP.17, para 18.

[72] Decision B.05/10. GCF. 2013. Decisions of the Board—Fifth Meeting of the Board, 8–10 Oct. 2013 (GCF/B.05/23, 8 Nov.), 7–8. https://www.greenclimate.fund/documents/20182/24937/GCF_B.05_23_-_Decisions_of_the_Board_-_Fifth_Meeting_of_the_Board__8-10_October_2013.pdf/ea60c39e-444d-4505-86b7-e87eecd94fb3.

[73] See GCF Governing Instrument, paras 20 and 21.

As regards the GEF, provision has been made in para 6(a)–(d) of the GEF Instrument, that the GEF operates as a financial mechanism for four conventions and "shall function under the guidance of, and shall be accountable to" the conferences of the parties of these conventions (UNFCCC, Convention on Biological Diversity, Stockholm Convention on Persistent Organic Pollutants and UNCCD). In accordance with para 27 of the GEF Instrument, the GEF Council has approved cooperative arrangements with the COPs of the aforementioned convention "which, in practice, have taken the form of MoUs approved in parallel by the COPs and the Council (the Council having given its approval only after the COPs adopted the MoU, except in the case of the MoU for the Climate Change Convention, for which the reverse order of approval was followed)."[74] While the GEF is not endowed with either international legal personality or legal capacity under national law, it is, nevertheless, a subject of international law, as extensively argued above.

9.2.6 Weighted and Non-weighted Voting Systems

A structural problem relates to the fact that the number of members of international organizations has vastly increased since their establishment. This increase has entailed great challenges both for organizations with weighted voting rights which are tied to country quotas, respectively capital shares, and those which espoused the traditional one-country-one vote system.

The IMF and World Bank had to struggle with the fact that their capital structures and corresponding voting rights were not adjusted to recognize the increased weight of transitional economies such as India and China in the world economy and that the basic votes allocated to all members on equal terms were eroded in the context of the IBRD's capital increases. Also, the reforms in which both institutions eventually engaged brought too little, came too late, and took too long, with the result that that there is still a large gap between quotas/shareholdings in these institutions and the weight of countries in the global economy.[75]

However, organizations like the UN which still follow the one-country-one-vote system also did not remain immune from the effects of the expansion of their membership, as this entailed that a number of mini-states[76] with very few inhabitants have the same voting rights as countries with hundreds of millions of inhabitants such as the US, China, India or Russia. While this is consistent with the sovereign equality of states, it entailed serious governance problems resulting from the fact that the voting rights of countries are unrelated to their size, population, economic power and financial contributions to the work of the organization.

74 Ragazzi 2011, p. 493. For further details, see Ragazzi 2011, pp. 493–495.

75 See "IMF Governance – Summary of Issues and Reform Options". 1 July 2009. http://www.imf.org/external/np/pp/eng/2009/070109.pdf.

76 Conforti and Focarelli 2016, pp. 34–36.

A similar structure is not suitable to mobilize additional financial resources. It also has contributed to the proliferation of new organizations as states opted to create new organizations where they could impose governance structures and voting rights conducive to their interests, rather than navigating the difficult process of institutional reform, for which the required qualified majorities are a formidable obstacle.

The question of the organization's governance structure is intrinsically related to the Organization's voting rights and decision-making procedures. As indicated by Guzman, for states the "most obvious strategy" for avoiding the Frankenstein problem of losing control of their creature "is to impose more demanding voting requirements, thereby prohibiting the IO from making decisions over the objections of member states."[77] In that sense, unanimity requirements are deliberately put in place to weaken the independence of the organization and its governing bodies. To a certain extent, this also holds true for situations where consensus is required for all matters. While in such a case a proposal may be approved if a voting member of a governing body abstains from voting, the proposal is deemed to be rejected if one member objects. In case of organizations with a small and homogeneous membership base, such as the Nordic Development Fund,[78] this may be a suitable decision-making paradigm. In organizations with a large and heterogeneous membership base, a consensus requirement for all decisions generally is not conducive to effective decision-making as it risks to cement to lowest common denominator among members.

While, as the example of the GEF shows, non-consensus decision-making procedures are generally not used, they guarantee that neither a single member nor a very small minority of a governing body can block a proposal, which otherwise meets with the overwhelming support of all other members. This is the major benefit of introducing such procedures. The case of the Green Climate Fund shows that it is a formidable task to introduce non-consensus decision-making procedures by consensus.[79] While the Board of the Green Climate Fund is mandated by its Governing Instrument to introduce such procedures, it has not yet been able to agree on the criteria to be applied in this regard.

International organizations' decision-making procedures and the differences between weighted voting systems and the traditional one-country-on-paradigm applicable to the United Nations and its specialized agencies in relation to international financial institutions have been extensively been analyzed in literature,[80] and in relation to international financial institutions, by this author.[81] Both systems

---

[77] Guzman 2013, p. 1005.

[78] See Droesse 2011c, p. 149.

[79] Paragraph 14 of the Governing Instrument provides: "Decisions of the Board will be taken by consensus of the Board members. The Board will develop procedures for adopting decisions in the event that all efforts at reaching consensus have been exhausted." As no agreement on this matter could be reached, the "additional rules of procedure of the Board to supplement the procedural rules contained in the Governing Instrument" were not adopted. See introductory remarks of GCF. Rules of Procedure. https://www.greenclimate.fund/documents/20182/574763/GCF_policy_-_Rules_of_Procedure.pdf/9d55fae7-f4df-45fe-a3f3-754bc0d98e67.

[80] See, with further references: Posner and Sykes 2014, pp. 195–228.

[81] See Droesse 2011c, pp. 149–161, with detailed further references.

are increasingly viewed with a critical eye. One of the shortcomings of the traditional one-country-one-vote paradigm is that it separates voting rights from capital contributions, and other relevant factors (e.g., size of population). This does not encourage donors to contribute resources and often prompts them to establish new organizations where they can impose the voting structures conducive to their interests rather than navigating the difficult and length process of institutional reform. Weighted voting systems, on the other hand, are criticized for not giving sufficient consideration and weight to smaller and pourer developing countries.

Thus, new paradigms of decision-making procedures are sought. There is a "increasing trend to softer decision-making procedures"[82] which may involve double-weighted, or possibly even triple-weighted, voting rights.

The voting power of members and qualified majorities and quorum provisions define the equilibrium of power between the different actors for each organization. Generally, in traditional international financial institutions such as the World Bank and the Asian Development Bank, only the voting power and qualified majorities and quorum requirements are defined. However, some organizations like the IADB apply two sets of criteria, i.e., for certain decisions a majority of regional Board members is required in addition to a (qualified) majority of Board members, as was already shown in Chap. 3 above.

The Multilateral Fund for the Montreal Protocol and the GEF pioneered the introduction of a double weighted voting system.

Article 2, para 9(c) of the Montreal Protocol provides:

> In taking such decisions,[83] the Parties shall make every effort to reach agreement by consensus. If all efforts at consensus have been exhausted, and no agreement reached, such decisions shall, as a last resort, be adopted by a two-thirds majority vote of the Parties present and voting representing a majority of the Parties operating under Paragraph 1 of Article 5[84] present and voting and a majority of the Parties not so operating present and voting;

As regards the GEF, if, in the consideration of any matter of substance, all practicable efforts by the Council and its Chairperson have been made and no consensus appears attainable,

> Unless otherwise provided in this Instrument, decisions requiring a formal vote by the Council shall be taken by a double weighted majority; that is, an affirmative vote representing both a 60 percent majority of the total number of Participants and a 60 percent majority of the total contributions.[85]

---

[82] Ibid., 149.

[83] Relating to adjustments as specified in Article 2, para 9(a) of the Montreal Protocol.

[84] This refers to: "Any Party that is a developing country and whose annual calculated level of consumption of the controlled substances is less than 0.3 kilograms per capita on the date of the entry into force of the Protocol for it, or any time thereafter within ten years of the date of entry into force of the Protocol [....]".

[85] Instrument for the Establishment of the Restructured Global Environment Facility, para 25(c) (i).

This double-weighted voting system is considered for wider application in international financial institutions, e.g. for the election of the executive head of the organization.[86]

While the Climate Investment Funds did not provide for non-consensual decision-making procedures, the Governing Instrument of the Green Climate Fund did so but left it to the Board to implement such procedures. The discussion on the criteria to be applied is interesting as four double-weighted and triple-weighted options were considered.[87]

There is no reason why thematic criteria should not be considered for allocating voting rights.

It would make perfect sense that an institution engaged in climate change activities allocates voting rights based on the reduction of CO_2 emissions of participating countries and that an organization dealing with maritime matters allocates voting rights based on the size of the shipping services provided by countries. However, in practice, such thematic criteria are difficult to implement as any establishment of a new institution is driven, to substantial extent, by the donor countries supporting the initiative and allocating financial resources for it. These countries generally attach greater importance to criteria linked to their financial contributions than to thematic criteria. So far, there is no major institution allocating voting rights based on reduction of CO_2 emissions or other thematic criteria. While in the case of the International Maritime Organization, the interest which countries may have in international shipping services or seaborne trade is considered in relation to the composition of the Council,[88] it is not taken as the basis for countries' voting rights.[89]

---

[86] Droesse 2011c, p. 158.

[87] GCF. 2015. Decision-making Procedures for the Board in the Absence of Consensus (GCF/B.10/11, 12 June). https://www.greenclimate.fund/documents/20182/24952/GCF_B.10_11_-_Decision-making_Procedures_for_the_Board_in_the_Absence_of_Consensus.pdf/579fee8b-2000-4258-bd62-f2bacbc49344.

[88] In accordance with Article 17, the IMO Convention epitomizes a composition of governing bodies based on the interest which governments have in the work of the organization. It provides:

In electing the Members of the Council, the Assembly shall observe the following criteria: (a) Eight shall be States with the largest interest in providing international shipping services; (b) Eight shall be other States with the largest interest in international seaborne trade; (c) Sixteen shall be States not elected under (a) or (b) above which have special interests in maritime transport or navigation, and whose election to the Council will ensure the representation of all major geographic areas of the world. See with detailed references on the status of the Convention: United Nations Treaty Collection. https://treaties.un.org/pages/viewdetails.aspx?src=treaty&mtdsg_no=xii-1&chapter=12&lang=en.

[89] Each member has one vote in the IMO Assembly, Council and Safety Committee, see IMO Convention, Article 57(a).

9.2.7 Design Options and Policy Issues

The above shows the many legal and policy ramifications which representation in governing bodies may have. It underlines that representation and membership—to the extent that an organization has members—are intrinsically interlinked. It also underlines, however, also the need to open governance structures to representation by a variety of stakeholders.

The above discussion on the inclusiveness, legitimacy and functionality of governing bodies has ramifications at several levels.

First, at least for organizations producing global public goods and relying on country-driven processes and interaction with a variety of stakeholders, current state-centric composition of governing bodies entails serious constraints to their effectiveness. Thus, for new organizations to be established, it would be advisable to either allow representation of non-state actors in governing bodies or move to a two-tier structure by transforming the plenary body into a forum for advocacy, policy advice and coordination of policies attended by a variety of stakeholders.

Second, a two-tier structure comprising a governing body of limited membership, a secretariat and an accountability and guidance mechanism may be seen as a functional equivalent of a traditional three-tier structure.

Third, the question as to the composition and functions of governing bodies of limited membership is intrinsically related to manner how such bodies conduct their business. In this context, there is increasing recognition that governing bodies of international organizations need to sharpen their strategic focus. This may open the opportunity for secondary governance structures to be established.

Fourth, there is an increasing trend to softer (double or triple-weighted) decision-making procedures. Moreover, also decision-making procedures based on thematic criteria may be considered.

9.3 Funding Mechanisms, Organizational and Capital Structures and Modalities of Financing of International Organizations

9.3.1 Constraints of Current Funding Structures

Current concepts of membership in international organizations are based on the correlation of benefits and obligations resulting from membership. One of the main advantages of membership is that it allows members to participate in the governance of the institution by being represented in its governing bodies and having a say in the formulation of policies and procedures and in the approval of operations and other activities. Other benefits, in addition to eligibility for financing and procurement, include the right to serve as the source of the organization's borrowings. As a corollary to these benefits, membership comes with obligations, notably the obligation to contribute to the financing of the organization. Hence, international organizations look to their members as their major source of funding.

Schermers and Blokker give a good and detailed overview of the budgetary and funding mechanisms of the United Nations and certain other traditional international organizations. They have shown that only few organizations levy contributions from member states in equal shares, and in most cases, distinctions are made based on optional classes of contribution, scales of assessment, the capacity of donors to pay, interest in the work of the organization, or other factors. In all such cases, traditional official development assistance (ODA) donors organized in the Development Assistance Committee (DAC) are the major source of funding. The same applies to contributions to the operational activities of organizations which are made either based on certain assessment criteria, or as voluntary contributions, or as trust funds or through other co-financing arrangements.[90]

There are only a few United Nations organizations that can substantially fund their administrative expenses or even realize surpluses. The World Intellectual Property Organization (WIPO) is almost self-financing, as under its 2016–2017 biennium budget, about 94% of approved budget expenditure was generated by the fee-paid services provided to users of the international registration systems through the Patent Cooperation Treaty (PCT), Madrid and Hague Systems.[91] Other organizations, such as the International Atomic Energy Agency (IAEA), also can rely on their own resources.

However, for many other organizations, internally-generated resources are very limited and do not cover the cost of administrative expenses (including the cost of staff, buildings, travel and logistical arrangements), let alone the cost of their assistance to their member countries. Their dependence on external resources is further exacerbated by the fact that most organizations have only very limited means to make savings as members usually commit "to pay their share of the agreed expenses" based on certain assessment criteria and hence "expenditure follows income."[92] Thus, while any "increase in agreed expenditure will be met by a commensurate increase in the contributions of the members", the system implies that any "savings will only lead to decrease in the contributions."[93]

In the view of the above, members often hold the United Nations and other traditional international organizations to tight financial strings, which gives them greater leverage to influence these organizations. In effect, organizations often use the major part of their resources to fund administrative expenses, and consequently, only very limited resources are available for financial assistance to their members. This constrains their effectiveness.

For this reason, some UN organizations are seeking to mobilize new sources of funding to overcome their resource constraints, such as by strengthening their

---

[90] Schermers and Blokker 2011, §§925–1138.

[91] WIPO. Results, Budget and Performance. http://www.wipo.int/about-wipo/en/budget/.

[92] Schermers and Blokker 2011, §926.

[93] Ibid.

collaboration with global funds and philanthropic institutions, but their legal and institutional structures and the inflexibility of their procedures often entail problems for such enhancement.

Multilateral development banks (MDBs) and other financial institutions, on the other hand, generally do not need to rely on direct donor contributions to cover their administrative expenses. Such administrative expenses are normally funded by their internal resources, notably by the return on capital investments and income from their operational activities. However, MDBs and other international financial institutions require financial inputs from donors to fund their concessional operations. While so far most financial institutions have only looked to governments as their main source of funding, collaboration with the private sector, foundations and other transnational actors has the potential to enable international financial institutions to leverage substantial additional resources, and, thereby, alleviate their dependence from official development assistance (ODA).

In this context, three issues will be raised:

- First, to enhance their effectiveness and impact, international organizations should explore alternative sources of funding, including the private sector, philanthropy, civil society, foundations, and crowd sourcing.
- Second, new funding mechanisms need to be designed for organizations producing global public goods.
- Third, special issues apply in the case of international financial institutions, whose organizational, capital structures and governance structures are intrinsically linked with membership concepts as they involve the members in their quality of shareholders. The legal structures of concessional windows of international financial institutions, on the other hand, are based on membership concepts only in those cases where they were established as international organizations with international legal personality and legal capacity under national law, but not in those instances where concessional resources are administered under one legal personality together with ordinary capital resources, or through other arrangements (e.g. trust funds). Depending on the legal structure of concessional windows, different constraints and challenges apply for enhancing their effectiveness by leveraging resources on capital markets.

9.3.2 Engagement with the Private Sector, Philanthropy and Civil Society

So far, generally international organizations receive their funding from their member states. Currently, most of the funding for international organizations, including for both administrative and operational expenses was, and still is, provided by states organized in the Development Assistance Committee of OECD.

This is the case for UN organizations and MDBs and other international financial institutions, alike. There are only few international organizations which rely to a substantial extent on funding from philanthropy, civil society or the private sector. The World Health Organization (WHO), and the Global Fund which both count the Bill and Melinda Gates Foundation as one of their biggest donors, fall into this category. However, most other organizations have only engaged such stakeholders half-heartedly, if at all, as a source of contributions.

> However, such funding structures are no longer in accord with the fact that private sector flows to developing member countries have increased dramatically since the establishment of the MFDIs studied here and that philanthropy has become a major source of development financing.[94]

Considering that ODA and public funds, in general, increasingly are getting scarce, organizations need to explore additional sources of financing, including financing from the private sector, foundations, pension funds and crowd sourcing, to enhance their impact.

Private sector entities may provide important contributions to international organizations, either in the form of direct donations to international organizations, or by facilitating donations by their clients. For example, some of the clients of commercial banks may be interested in making donations for specific purposes. Banks may support international organizations by facilitating a contact with their clients and international organizations which promote the purposes which their clients wish to support.

As the experience of the WHO shows, engagement with philanthropic organizations and global funds has the potential of substantially enhancing the financial support of traditional international organizations. However, traditional UN organizations and global funds often have very different organizational structures, corporate cultures and operational priorities and procedures. As shown by a UNDP study, unless organizations "engage more explicitly and consistently with global funds and philanthropic foundations in order to establish common ground and develop mutual approaches to development challenges" and take action "to find solutions to operational and procedural bottlenecks, including issues relating to transparency and oversight, that hamper relationships with global funds and philanthropic foundations", such attempts will often remain ineffective.[95] Hence, collaboration with global funds, private sector entities and philanthropic foundations often requires a change in organizations' procedures and practices.

[94] Droesse 2011a, p. 35.

[95] UNDP. 2012. "Evaluation of UNDP Partnership with Global Funds and Philanthropic Foundation, Recommendations 2 and 5", xxiii and xxiv.

9.3.3 *Global Funding Mechanisms for Organizations Producing Global Public Goods*

As discussed in Chap. 5, international organizations, particularly those producing global public goods, do not need to have members, and there are effectively some international organizations such as the Global Fund and Green Climate Fund which do not have formal membership structures. In the case of organizations without any formal membership structure, the traditional logic of benefits and obligations on which funding structures of international organizations are based, does not apply.

Moreover, even to the extent that organizations have members, there is an increasing tendency to delink certain benefits (e.g., procurement eligibility) from membership. The absence of any tangible benefits attached to membership, normally seen as an incentive for new members to join an organization, may make it more difficult to fund an organization through the traditional schemes of legally binding assessments or fixed-burden sharing arrangements; donors may often only be prepared to provide voluntary contributions which do not allow predictability as to when financing will be available.

Ideally, an organization producing global public goods should also be funded at the global level through appropriate mechanisms. The Adaptation Fund is an interesting example such a global funding mechanism:

> The primary revenue source of the Adaptation Fund is a 2 percent share of proceeds levied from projects registered under Kyoto's Clean Development Mechanism (CDM). This peculiar feature is among the major challenges of the Fund, as the heavily oversupplied market of Certified Emission Reductions (CERs) has progressively shrunk in volume and value, with the price of CERs steadily floating below EUR 1 per tonne since 2013 (from EUR20/t in 2008). In the past years, the resulting revenue crunch has been partially covered by contributions from donor countries.[96]

While currently no substantial income accrued to the Adaptation Fund after the collapse of the carbon markets, the approach to fund international organizations producing global public goods or fighting global wrongs through new types of funding mechanisms at a global scale continues to be conceptually sound. Hence, similar funding schemes for international organization should be considered for any new carbon pricing scheme that is put in place. Attempts should be made to create also in other areas new funding mechanisms for international organization at the global scale.

Moreover, as has already been shown by this author in his book "Funds for Development" there has been a range of innovative financing mechanisms[97] and of proposals for global taxes and levies which could be used to fund global public goods. Global levies and taxes may be an effective way of funding international organizations. France and other countries pioneered an airline solidarity

[96] Climate Policy Observer. In-Depth: The Adaptation Fund From Kyoto To Paris. http://climateobserver.org/depth-adaptation-fund-kyoto-paris/.

[97] Droesse 2011d, pp. 206–207.

contribution (US$1 of the ticket price) as a funding mechanism of UNITAID.[98] "Of the US $2.5 billion in contributions that UNITAID received from 2006 to 2015, 63 per cent come from air ticket levies."[99] Because of this funding mechanism, "UNITAID, is truly additional to the existing agents in the global health financing landscape."[100]

Similar contributions might be levied on shipping. Moreover, a carbon tax or climate change tax might be considered. The challenge is to allow international organization to have direct access to the resources allocated in that manner.

9.3.4 Funding Mechanisms Based Exclusively or Predominantly of Private Sector Funding

The examples in the two sections above relate to new ways of ensuring contributions of private sector entities and other stakeholders to organization which continue to be funded predominantly by governments. However, in certain cases this may not be sufficient and a fundamental paradigm shift of funding structures may be required to the extent that the main funding for operational activities of international organizations needs to come from the private sector and other non-state stakeholders. One of these cases relates to the transition of countries to a "thriving global green economy [….] that is 'low carbon, climate-resilient, resource-efficient and socially-inclusive'."[101] The amounts required for such a transition to a green economy are so enormous that they cannot even predominantly be covered by governments. Also, such transition cannot be facilitated by states alone but requires the involvement of a variety of stakeholders. Investments in the green economy increasing are viable and promising from an economic point of view, given, in particular "the sharply falling generation cost" of renewable power.[102] The great potential of such a funding mechanism is epitomized by the proposal of the Solar Impulse Foundation[103] that has identified 1000 profitable solutions for the

[98] Brookings. Global Health Financing Initiative. Snapshot Series. Airline Solidarity Contribution. https://www.brookings.edu/wp-content/uploads/2016/07/airline.pdf. See also Innovative Financing for Development. The I-8 group Leading Innovative Financing for Equity [L.I.F.E.]. (Douste-Blazy, Coordinator). Cited as I-8 group Innovative Financing for Development. http://www.un.org/esa/ffd/documents/InnovativeFinForDev.pdf.

[99] UNITAID. 2016. UNITAID at 10, Accelerating Innovation in Global Health, 10. https://unitaid.eu/assets/Unitaid-at-10-booklet-EN.pdf.

[100] Bermudez and Douste-Blazy 2009, p. 15.

[101] University of Cambridge and World Green Economy Organization. 2018. 2018 World Green Economy Report, p. 9.

[102] IRENA. 2017. Renewable Power: Sharply Falling Generation Costs. https://www.irena.org/-/media/Files/IRENA/Agency/Publication/2017/Nov/%20IRENA_Sharply_falling_costs_2017.pdf.

[103] https://solarimpulse.com/.

environment. Moreover, there is "a strong and growing business case" for individual businesses to act on the green economy:

> The upside of a sustainability agenda is clear [….]. Regardless of your views on the who, what, when, and why of climate change, the pursuit[104] of sustainable processes up and down supply chains can translate into immediate savings — and opportunities for innovation. Firms as diverse as Walmart and KKR are finding that reducing energy use and embracing renewable energy can be immediately profitable. Moreover, global challenges like water scarcity, severe weather events, and ecosystem degradation — coupled with a growing interest from consumers and investors in whether companies have a 'green' agenda — signal that the environment will have an increasingly direct impact on companies' earnings and risk profiles.

Under the circumstances, one of the main challenges of our time is to show that investments in the green economy are not only viable from a societal point of view, but are also beneficial from an economic point of view for the entities that engage in them, by matching the need of states and other entities for funding of green projects with the need of the private sector and other stakeholders for viable and bankable projects. Under such a model, international organization may obtain the entire or bulk of their funding for operational activities from the private sector. They can do so *inter alia* by organizing each year various pledging or matchmaking conferences which serve for mobilizing funding for projects from the private sector.

9.3.5 Membership and Capital Structures

In the case of international financial institutions, their membership, organizational and capital structures are intrinsically related. This will be discussed in the following in relation to capital structures of MDBs which differ from the legal structures of their concessional windows. The relevance of membership concepts to such differences and the inherent constraints and limitations of current structures of market-based and concessional windows and will be reviewed in this section.

9.3.5.1 Differences Between Capital Structures of MDBs and Legal Structures of Their Concessional Windows

In the case of MDBs, there is a direct correlation between the shareholdings of members, which are determined during the membership process, and their voting rights. Moreover, in the World Bank and other MDBs, members' shareholdings have many other implications, e.g. for representation arrangements in the Executive Boards of these two institutions.

---

[104] Future Economy. Harvard Business Review. https://hbr.org/2017/08/future-economy?referral=03759&cm_vc=rr_item_page.bottom.

The case of MDBs is special as they have a "dual character" as "intergovernmental organizations that are created by states for a public purpose" and as "subjects of international law", while engaging "in financial transactions, which, despite their public purpose, are, by nature, similar to market-based transactions."[105] They "are structured financially as corporations with a capital held in the form of shares by their members, and capital markets are their most important source of funds."[106] As has been analyzed by this author in great detail, traditionally there has been a fundamental difference between the legal structures of concessional and non-concessional funding windows.

> The capital structures of hard and soft windows are fundamentally different. Hard windows relate to the core function of development banks as financial intermediaries and are substantially funded by organizations' own borrowings from capital markets. They are designed to mobilize their resources through shareholder capital and borrowings on capital markets, which are guaranteed by shareholders. Organization members make available only a small portion of their capital (in cash as "paid-in" capital); the remaining portion is subscribed and guaranteed by members ("callable" capital). What Mistry described as the "figment of confidence underlying the capital structure of the MDBs is embedded in the notion of callable capital" and ensures that shareholder equity fully backs MFDI [multilateral financial development institution] borrowings, even though the actual resources members make available in the form of cash or promissory notes are very limited. Shareholder guarantees enable organizations to maintain high credit ratings and borrow on preferential (AAA) terms to support projects in developing countries. Thus, MFDIs can offer preferential market-based terms for loans, along with long-term maturities not generally offered by commercial banks. Since loan repayments enable MFDIs to repay investors, they must provide financing of hard windows on market-based terms.
>
> On the other hand, MFDIs provide concessional financing either on terms considerably lower than regular market rates or on a grant basis. Their soft windows are designed as revolving funds rather than for mobilizing resources directly from capital markets. In organizations such as the AfDF and IDA, which have proper legal personality under international law, members contribute to the capitalization of the organization. Unlike hard windows, these organizations do not use an equity base to support borrowings in capital markets. Rather, organizations pass the resources they receive from donors in the form of subscriptions and contributions directly to the recipients at a rate of 1:1. Thus, their financial structure is similar to the special funds administered by organizations under one legal personality and with nonconcessional resources. The financial architecture of both types of soft windows "is based on the concept of multilateral clubs of donors who collaborate in providing permanent grant resources to these respective funds." Such resources are used for concessional loans and other modalities of concessional financing.[107]

This is not the place to discuss in detail the many legal facets of constitutional and legal frameworks of MDB's capital structures, nor is there a need to repeat the detailed indications contained in the book of this author titled "Funds for Development: Multilateral Channels of Concessional Financing". Rather, this work will focus on some of the links which exist between membership and capital

---

[105] Bradlow 2010, p. 1.

[106] Sureda 2004, p. 219.

[107] Droesse 2011d, pp. 196–197.

structure, on the one hand, and membership and the legal structures of concessional windows, on the other hand, as well to highlight the inherent constraints which are currently applicable to both concessional and non-concessional windows. In addition, it will identify new approaches which may enhance the effectiveness and impact of concessional and non-concessional windows in pursuit of their statuary objectives.

9.3.5.2 Main Principles and Inherent Constraints of Capital Structures of MDBs

As regards MDBs and other international financial institutions, their ability to function effectively as financial intermediaries channeling funds to developing countries on market-based terms is intrinsically related to their organizational structures, institutional structures and capital structures which involve members as shareholders and contributors of funds. Currently, multilateral development banks or related institutions provide the bulk of their financing through their ordinary capital resources. The business model of MDBs is that they leverage resources by "using their capital base to multiply funds several times and to put them to use for development – so 'a dollar in' managed by MDBs results in more than 'a dollar out' in financing for development, maximizing the impact of scarce resources."[108]

As shown by Mistry, "[t]he conceptual architecture common to the equity (i.e. ownership) capital construction of all the MDBs was established with the formation of the IBRD - i.e. the core of the World Bank. From the outset the IBRD was designed to be an institution which would be owned, and whose capital would be provided, by governments and not by private sources."[109] The other MDBs and international financial institutions generally have adopted a similar approach. Overall, MDB's and other financial institutions were successful as financial intermediaries in leveraging resources on capital markets. Nevertheless, their current structures and legal frameworks have not been exempt from criticism, which is voiced, inter alia, (i) regarding the lack of representativeness of universal organizations such as the World Bank and the IMF. Moreover, it may also be questioned (ii) whether it is still appropriate that MDBs are exclusively owned by their member countries, and (iii) whether the correlation of shareholdings and voting rights in MDBs strikes an appropriate balance between the interests of developing and developed member countries.

---

108 See World Bank Group. 2016. "Multilateral Development Banks". http://www.un.org/esa/ffd/wp-content/uploads/2016/01/Multilateral-Development-Banks_WBG_IATF-Issue-Brief.pdf.
109 Mistry 1995.

Representativeness

One core problem of global organizations such the IMF and World Bank is that the shareholdings of some members no longer reflect their weight in the world economy. This has not substantially been altered by the voice reform,[110] which was initiated in 2010, after many years of discussions and deliberations, in the IBRD and IFC and entailed a very limited realignment of capital subscriptions and voting powers of their members and other institutional reforms.[111] The changes which eventually became effective in 2016 were implemented too late and provided too little to alleviate the concerns of countries like China and India. This is underlined by the fact that in the IBRD, despite the voice reform, the capital subscriptions and voting rights of China relate to one fourth of those of the United States, while the capital subscriptions of Belgium, Netherland and Switzerland combined exceed those of China, and those of the Netherlands and Switzerland are higher than the capital subscription of India.[112] The slow progress which was made in the voice reform of the World Bank was one of the reasons for the establishment of a new infrastructure of international organizations in Asia, including the AIIB, New Development Bank and Silk Road Fund.

Ownership

The question is whether only governments should be allowed to own the shares of MDBs. As argued above, there is a strong argument that institutionalized forms of participation of the private sector and other stakeholders involving full, partial, affiliate or sector membership may enhance the effectiveness of international financial institutions. There are no intrinsic constraints allowing private sector entities to own the shares of an international financial institution. From a design perspective, consideration should be given to allowing institutionalized forms of participation of private sector entities for any new international financial institutions to be established. As in the case of the CAF discussed above, special types of shares might be offered to commercial entities for that purpose.

For the MDBs, on the other hand, allowing such participation would require amendment to their constituent agreements. As shown by this author, any such amendment is very difficult, given the qualified majorities required for any

[110] A similar reform was implemented in the IMF. See Press Release: IMF Executive Board Approves Major Overhaul of Quotas and Governance. 5 Nov. 2010, https://www.imf.org/external/np/sec/pr/2010/pr10418.htm.

[111] See World Bank Group. 2010. "Voice Reform: Enhancing Voice and Participation of Developing and Transition Countries in 2010 and Beyond". Development Committee (Joint Ministerial Committee of the Boards of Governors of the Bank and the Fund on the Transfer of Real Resources to Developing Countries), DC2010-0, 19 April.

[112] See IBRD. "Subscriptions and Voting Rights of Member Countries". http://siteresources.worldbank.org/BODINT/Resources/278027-1215524804501/IBRDCountryVotingTable.pdf.

amendment of constituent instrument, which are a formidable obstacle for any institutional reform.

Shareholdings and Voting Rights

Third, there is a direct correlation between MDB's capital structure and voting rights of members. In MDBs, voting rights are generally proportionate to the shareholdings, except that a certain number of votes are allocated to members on an equal basis. The relationship of basic votes distributed equally among all members and proportionate votes allocated based on members' shareholdings is an indication of the extent to which international financial institutions take account of the interest of small members and developing country member with limited capital subscriptions.

ADB is the epitome of an international financial institution which allocates a high percentage of basic votes on an equal basis to all members. Basic votes amount in ADB to 25% of proportionate votes which are allocated based on members' shareholdings.[113] Moreover, as in the case of ADB, the basic votes are defined through a formula, and hence, the total percentage of votes allocated as basic votes remains unchanged in the case of capital increases. However, this was not the case for the World Bank and IMF where the number of basic votes allocated to each member was defined in the Articles of Agreement in numeric terms. Hence, the institutional reform in the IMF and World Bank adopted a formula-driven approach for the allocation of basic votes, consistent with that of ADB. Nevertheless, the percentage of votes allocated on equal terms as basic votes remained in IBRD and IFC far below the 25% ratio of ADB.[114]

9.3.5.3 Legal Structures of Concessional Windows

Membership Structures

Concessional resources are made available either through (i) organizations established for that purpose, either established by a treaty (e.g. International Fund for Agricultural Development),[115] or without treaty foundation (e.g. Green Climate Fund); (ii) organizational groups with affiliated organizations providing concessional financing (e.g. IDA, AfDF, Nordic Development Fund);[116] (iii) through organizations with built-in soft loan facilities (e.g. IADB and the Caribbean

---

[113] The formula for the allocation of basic votes is reproduced in Droesse 2011b, p. 339.

[114] See Development Committee. World Bank Group Voice Reform: Enhancing Voice and Participation of Developing and Transition Countries in 2010 and Beyond (DC2010-0006, 19 April 2010). http://siteresources.worldbank.org/DEVCOMMINT/Documentation/22553921/DC2010-006(E)Voice.pdf.

[115] Droesse 2011c, pp. 61–62.

[116] Ibid.

Development Bank),[117] (iv) special funds or special programs administered by organizations under one juridical personality jointly with ordinary capital resources (e.g. the Asian Development Fund of ADB);[118] through (v) trust funds (e.g. GEF and Climate Investment Funds), or (vi) organizations incorporated under national law (e.g. Global Fund). As has been shown by this author in great detail, the organizational structures mentioned above have multiple implications for governance structures, voting rights, resource mobilization arrangements and modalities of financing. In particular, they are intrinsically related to organizations' membership structures.

The case under (i) is epitomized by the International Fund for Agricultural Development (IFAD). In the case of IFAD, the Agreement establishing IFAD (AEI) defines the membership structure and classifies IFAD members in three categories. Prior to the fourth replenishment, each category was allocated 600 votes which were distributed among individual members based on a formula. As this system did not provide an incentive for donors to make contributions, a link between contributions and voting rights was introduced by resolution of IFAD governing council in the context of the fourth replenishment of IFAD.[119] Hence, IFAD may be seen as a "hybrid organization that combines the features of a specialized agency of the United Nations [....] with those of MDBs with respect to its operating model and governance structure."[120]

Moreover, as have been argued above, there are international organizations providing concessional financing which do not have a treaty foundation. Hence, an organization providing concessional financing, in principle, can be established through any of the non-treaty based mechanisms discussed in Chap. 7. The GCF, which is a major source of financing for climate change adaption and mitigations provided on concessional terms, also falls in this category. As shown, it is a distinguishing feature of the Green Climate Fund that it does not have a formal membership structure.

As regards (ii), the concessional arms of MDBs (e.g. IDA and AfDB) have a treaty foundation and their constituent agreements define their membership and governance structures. In the case of IDA and AfDB, such structures depend on, or are coordinated with, those of the IBRD and African Development Bank, respectively.[121] However, the example of the Nordic Development Fund (NDF) shows that such coordination may not take place in all cases in organizational groups. The membership structure of the NDF is different from that of the Nordic Development

---

[117] Ibid., 66–69.

[118] Droesse 2011b, pp. 299–398.

[119] See Weill-Hallé et al. 2011, pp. 464–465, with further references.

[120] Independent Evaluation Office of IFAD. 2013. "IFAD's institutional efficiency and efficiency of IFAD-funded operations. Corporate-Level Evaluation". https://www.ifad.org/evaluation/reports/cle/tags/operations/y2013/2589509.

[121] See Droesse 2011c, pp. 93, 95–96, 120–121.

Bank and the governance structure of both institutions are for all practical effects separate and not coordinated.[122]

Under (iii) and (iv), a separate membership in concessional windows is not possible as these are not endowed with either international legal personality or legal capacity under national law and are administrated by the MDB concerned under one legal personality.

The Fund for Special Operations of the IADB and the Special Development Fund of the Caribbean Development Bank are two examples of concessional windows provided for under the constituent agreements establishing the aforementioned organizations. In the case of the ADB, on the other hand, the ADF was created based on the powers conferred to ADB to establish special funds as parts of its own resources. Hence, the ADF relates to the case under (iv). Where concessional and non-concessional resources are administered by an organization under one legal personality, generally the same voting rights apply to both financing windows. However, unless expressly precluded by the constituent agreement, in principle special voting rights and governance structures may apply to special funds, as shown by the Islamic Solidarity Fund for Development.[123]

As regards (v), trust funds may or may not have membership structures, depending on their functions and purpose. As the relations between an organization and its members are of an internal nature, it is not a requirement for an organization established as a trust fund to have international legal personality or legal capacity under local law for it to have members. The membership structure and institutional and governance structure of the trust fund can be entirely different from that of the organization acting as trustee.

Finally, (vi) corporations established under local law may have a membership structure depending on their purpose and functions. In this regard, there is a similarity with organizations established as trust funds. Unlike organizations established as trust funds without legal personality, dual and hybrid organizations incorporated under national law are generally endowed with international legal personality (in relation to their host country and other countries) and legal capacity under national law. Hence, such organizations may issue bonds and may be the subject of legal obligations. The same is not applicable to trust funds without legal personality.

Innovative Funding Structures of Concessional Windows

One rare initiative involving the issue of bonds for concessional financing relates to the International Finance Facility for Immunisation (IFFIm),[124] which is the funding vehicle of the Gavi Alliance. As shown by this author, IFFIm

122 Ibid., 121.

123 Ibid., 152.

124 http://www.iffim.org/.

whose institutional structure was partially modeled on the Global Fund, since it was established as a charity with the Charity Commission for England and Wales and registered as a company in England and Wales. To prevent massive loss of life from preventable diseases, the IFFIm was designed to accelerate the availability of funds for health and immunization programs through the Global Alliance for Vaccines and Immunisation (Gavi Alliance) by frontloading resources. For that purpose, several states entered into long-term grant and guarantee agreements under which they agreed to make scheduled payments for as long as 20 years. The IFFIm converts such long-term government pledges into immediately available cash resources by issuing IFFIm bonds. The proceeds of the assigned grant payments are used to repay the principal and interest of the bonds issued by the IFFIm.[125]

The approach pioneered by IFFIm, which originated from a proposal made by the then Chancellor of the Exchequer, Gordon Brown, may "reduce uncertainty about the flow of aid by capturing the costly, up-front investments that otherwise would be inadequately financed."[126] This approach is justified and particularly appropriate for providing urgently needed funding for the activities funded by the Gavi Vaccine Alliance. In other cases, however, it needs to be assessed whether the costs attached to the issuance of bonds are justified and whether a scheme of this kind may erode future assistance by donors.

As regards, the concessional windows of MDBs, irrespective of their legal structures, these have been traditionally rather inefficient financial structures. While under their market-based windows, MDBs have a lot of leeway in leveraging resources through borrowings on capital markets and in offering a wide of range of financial products (e.g., loan products, grants, equity investments, risk mitigation instruments), including a range of innovative schemes of financing, MDBs were constrained, irrespective of the legal structures of their concessional windows, from mobilizing on similar terms resources for their concessional windows, by the legal and policy frameworks governing such windows.

Concessional windows such as the ADF[127] and the FSO do not possess a proper legal personality and cannot issue bonds for that reason as a matter of principle. The same constraint is not applicable to concessional arms of organizational groups, such as IDA and the AfDF which have a treaty foundation and, therefore, possess international legal personality and legal capacity under national law. While their legal personality could have been the basis for issuing bonds, they did not do so in the past. Rather, their legal and policy frameworks were designed, similar to those of ADF and FSO, as revolving funds. This, in essence, meant that they pass on the resources they receive from donors to recipients at the rate of 1:1, after charging a small service or interest fee and with some enhancement of commitment authority resulting from the financial management of concessional resources.

As regards special funds such as the ADF, which are administered by international financial institutions under one legal personality with their ordinary capital

[125] Droesse 2011d, pp. 201–202.

[126] Brookings. "Snapshot Series". *International Finance Facility for Immunization*. https://www.brookings.edu/wp-content/uploads/2016/07/iffim-1.pdf.

[127] For the ADF, see: Droesse 2011b, pp. 299–398; Droesse 2012, pp. 265–314.

resources, the issuance of bonds on account of the ADF is not possible as a matter of principle. As, unlike IDA and AfDB, the ADF neither possesses international legal personality nor legal capacity under national law, only ADB potentially could issue bonds on account of the ADF. However, leveraging resources on capital markets for the ADF meets in the case of ADB with constraints under Article 10 of the ADB Charter which enshrines the principle of separation of operations.[128]

While the rather inefficient financial structures of concessional windows were acceptable at the time when they were created in the 1960 and 1970, the legal and policy frameworks of concessional windows have now become a constraint to their effectiveness and the ability of organizations to their member the required level of concessional financing. As Erquiaga states with regard to the ADF:

> When the ADF was created, this inability to issue debt was not considered problematic as the low creditworthiness of ADF borrowers would have proved to be a constraint in convincing capital market investors to purchase bonds issued by a new entity for lending to these borrowers. This absence of financial leverage was now deemed suboptimal, particularly given the strong track record of regular ADF loan service payments.[129]

Therefore, there is widespread agreement on the need to enhance the legal and policy frameworks of concessional windows. While this concern is applicable to the concessional arms of organizational groups such as IDA and the African Development Fund and special funds like the ADF alike, each of these concessional windows meets different challenges and legal constraints for leveraging resources on capital markets.

Merger of Concessional and Non-concessional Resources

In view of the legal constraints highlighted above, ADB pioneered a merger of ADF and ADB's ordinary capital resources which entailed fundamental changes and the legal framework governing ADF resources. The rationale for such a merger was straightforward, as highlighted by Erquiaga:[130]

> While ADF equity capital is about double the size of the equity capital of OCR [ordinary capital resources], ADF outstanding loans of $29.1 billion were only about 54% the size of

---

[128] Article 10 of the ADB Charter provides:

1. The ordinary capital resources and the Special Funds resources of the Bank shall at all times and in all respects be held, used, committed, invested or otherwise disposed of entirely separate from each other. The financial statements of the Bank shall show the ordinary operations and special operations separately.

2. The ordinary capital resources of the Bank shall under no circumstances be charged with, or used to discharge, losses or liabilities arising out of special operations or other activities for which Special Funds resources were originally used or committed.

3. Expenses appertaining directly to ordinary operations shall be charged to the ordinary capital resources of the Bank. Expenses appertaining directly to special operations shall be charged to the Special Funds resources. Any other expenses shall be charged as the Bank shall determine.

[129] Erquiaga 2016, p. 69.

[130] Ibid.

OCR outstanding loans ($54.2 billion). This translated into a mobilization (leverage) ratio of loans and guarantees to equity capital of 3.1 for OCR, but only 0.9 for the ADF. The divergence in mobilization ratios was attributable to the fact that the ADF, which does not have a separate legal identity as a structured special window of ADB, is not able to issue bonds to support its lending

The figures mentioned above clearly show that the ADF previously was not an efficient financial instrument. Hence, the Board of Governors authorized ADB "to terminate the loan operations of ADF [....], and to continue the operations of ADF as grant operations only", and to "transfer the loan assets of ADF, resources originally set-aside from OCR and other ADF assets as may be determined by the Board of Directors, to OCR", while allocating the corresponding income recognized in OCR "to ordinary reserves."[131] While such approval entailed far-reaching changes to ADB's legal and policy frameworks governing the provision of concessional resources, it did not entail any changes to members' shareholdings and voting rights.

The Board of the Governors gave their approval based on the understanding that donors would continue to be consulted and ADB would continue to lend on concessional terms to the developing member countries that were previously eligible for concessional loans from ADF. Hence, the situation of recipient of ADF concessional loans did not change. However, the concessional loans given to recipients were henceforth to be funded by ADB's OCR resources rather than by the Asian Development Fund. Hence, the situation in ADB is currently as follows. Market-based loans are, in essence, funded by borrowings on capital markets, concessional loans are funded by the equity of ADB's OCR window, while ADF grants for projects and programs are provided by the ADF, i.e. by special fund resources, and are substantially funded by contributions of donors and OCR net income transfers from the ADB.

Project Galaxy, as the merger of ADB and OCR is called in ADB, increased "OCR equity from $18.3 billion to $53 billion,"[132] thereby tripling ADB's equity base. As explained by Erquiaga, it "would allow the use of leverage on the combined resources by significantly expanding ADB's equity base" and "support the transition of ADF-only countries to blend status, and their graduation from blend status to OCR-only status", while also "allowing for an increase in ADB private sector lending operations."[133]

---

[131] ADB Board of Governors. Resolution No. 372: Enhancing ADB's Financial Capacity For Reducing Poverty in Asia and the Pacific. https://www.adb.org/sites/default/files/institutional-document/160051/bog-resolution-372.pdf.

[132] Erquiaga 2016, p. 69.

[133] See, with detailed explanations: Erquiaga 2016, p. 70.

Leveraging of Resources on Capital Markets for Concessional Windows

IDA and AfDF are unable to follow the approach pioneered by ADB because they are international organizations in their own right with treaty foundation and endowed with international legal personality which isolates these two concessional windows from the IBRD and African Development Bank, respectively. Also, they each possess a membership structure which is different from the non-concessional arms of their group. Hence, a course of action similar to the one pioneered by ADB could, if at all possible, only be taken if it was decided to terminate these two concessional windows. While the suggestion to integrate the resources of the AfDB and AfDF has been made by a High Level Panel of the African Development Bank[134] and Shihata did not discard the option of merging IBRD, IFC and the Multilateral Investment Guarantee Agency (MIGA), and restructuring IDA "as an international trust fund administered by the resulting mega institution,"[135] any such course of action would be excruciatingly difficult and is unlikely to succeed; vested interests, the resilience of all international organizations to annihilation, the qualified majorities required for termination, and the complexities of the financial frameworks of the referenced institutions, are daunting obstacles for any such action.

Nevertheless, there are other options available to institutions such as IDA and AfDF for enhancing their impact. In organizational groups like the World Bank Group and the African Development Bank Group, one solution is to enhance the cooperation between the concessional and non-concessional arms of the Group. This is the logic which prompted the proposal made during the IDA 18 replenishment negotiations to create an IFC-MIGA private sector window in IDA 18.[136] The other potential solution is to explore the possibility of transforming the financial frameworks of concessional arms such as IDA and AfDB to leverage resources on capital markets. While giving IDA a formal equity structure equivalent to IBRD involving their members as shareholders, based on concepts of paid-in and callable capital, would require amendment to their constituent agreements, the fact that IDA and AfDB are endowed with international legal personality and legal capacity under national law, allows, as a matter of principle, the issuance of debt

134 AfDB. *Investing in Africa's Future*, 27–28.

135 Shihata 2001, p. 119.

136 IDA. "WBG Collaboration: Proposal for an IFC-MIGA Private Sector Window in IDA 18 (8 June 2016)." http://documents.worldbank.org/curated/en/251611468198009717/pdf/106374-BR-Box396267B-OUO-9-IDA-SecM2016-0120.pdf. See IDA 18. Report from the Executive Directors of the International Development Association to the Board of Governors. Additions to IDA Resources: Eighteenth Replenishment [cited IDA 18 Deputies Report], para 128: "**Private Sector Window**. To support private sector development in IDA countries, Participants endorsed the creation of a SDR1.8 billion IFC-MIGA PSW in IDA18. The PSW will draw on IFC's and MIGA's long-standing experience in emerging markets, and further step up their support to IDA-only countries while also providing greater attention to FCS (Section III.A. 'Creating Opportunities for the Private Sector')." http://documents.worldbank.org/curated/en/348661486654455091/pdf/112728-correct-file-PUBLIC-Rpt-from-EDs-Additions-to-IDA-Resources-2-9-17-For-Disclosure.pdf.

instruments. However, doing so will required substantial changes to their legal and financial frameworks.

It is an important development that during the 18th IDA replenishment:

> 135. **Deputies supported the introduction of a new, integrated financing framework for IDA18 that includes issuance of market debt by IDA as a means to significantly scale up replenishment resources.** This new hybrid model combines partner contributions – in the form of IDA18 contributions and reflows from earlier contributions – with external debt funding, complementing the existing CPL program with access to capital markets [....]. The transformative package will greatly increase efficiency in the use of shareholder contributions and capital, significantly enhancing IDA's Value for Money proposition. [....].[137]

It will be interesting to see whether other MDBs and international financial institutions follow this lead of the World Bank Group. IFAD has so far has only allowed borrowing from concessional partners but is also considering other options, including "[b]orrowing from sovereign and market sources."[138] Given the approach taken during the IDA's 18 negotiations, it can be expected that the discussion on external debt funding will also intensify in IFAD. Hence, we are witnessing a potential far-reaching transformation of the financial structures of concessional windows.

9.4 Membership and Borrowings of International Organizations

The link between borrowings and membership is epitomized by the legal frameworks of international financial institutions which are an important source of financing, particularly for developing countries. Such link, relates, in particular, to the consent requirements that may exist in relation to borrowing in member countries, and conversion of the proceeds in another currency.

Generally, borrowing by an international financial institution in the currency of a member country requires approval of the country where funds are raised and the member country in whose currency the financing is denominated. Moreover, for swapping the proceeds of a borrowing in another currency, the approval of these countries may be required.

This approach is epitomized by Article VII, Section 1(i) of the Agreement Establishing the Inter-American Development Bank (IADB Charter) in relation to borrowings of the IADB:

> before making a sale of its obligations in the markets of a country, the Bank shall have obtained the approval of that country and of the member in whose currency the obligations

[137] IDA. IDA 18 Deputies Report, para 135.

[138] IFAD. 2014. "Financing Options for IFAD Beyond 2015", 5. https://webapps.ifad.org/members/repl/10/3/docs/IFAD10-3-R-5.pdf.

are denominated. In addition, in the case of borrowings of funds to be included in the Bank's ordinary capital resources, the Bank shall obtain agreement of such countries that the proceeds may be exchanged for the currency of any other country without restriction.

Article IV, Section 1(b) of the Articles of Agreement of IBRD provides:

The Bank may borrow funds under (a) (ii) above or guarantee loans under (a) (iii) above only with the approval of the member in whose markets the funds are raised and the member in whose currency the loan is denominated, and only if those members agree that the proceeds may be exchanged for the currency of any other member without consent of members.[139]

There exists a difference regarding the requirements for borrowings under Article IV, Section 1(b) cited above made for the purpose of providing loans and guarantees and borrowings under Article IV, Section 8(iii) which are made for other purposes, and for that reason do not require member agreement of unrestricted convertibility.[140] However, in practice, the distinction between the aforementioned provisions is of limited relevance, as generally "the Bank does not distinguish between its borrowings as to their respective purpose" and, hence, "it is reasonable to view the entire Bank's borrowing activity as supporting its lending operations."[141]

The IBRD uses "the criterion of where each counterparty to the borrowing contract is a resident" for requiring "the consent of each member in whose territories a counterparty to the borrowing contract resides."[142]

While consistent with the wording of Article IV, Section 2(b) of the IBRD Articles of Agreement, which generally require approval of the members concerned for currency swap transactions, the IBRD nevertheless enjoys considerable liberty in the conversion of currencies in accordance with Article IV, Section 2(c) of its Articles of Agreement; this Section provides for freedom of restrictions regarding "[c]urrencies received by the Bank from borrowers or guarantors in payment on account of principal of direct loans."

As interpreted by the Executive Directors, the provisions of Section (c) do not prohibit the Bank from using any currencies received in repayment for any other purpose for which the borrowed funds could have been used, including the making of loans [...].[143]

Thus, based on an interpretation of Article IV, 2(c) of the IBRD Articles of Agreement, the currency holdings derived from IBRD borrowings are freely usable and convertible in IBRD operations.

---

139 Shihata 2001, p. 100.

140 See Shihata 2000, p. 99.

141 Ibid., 100.

142 Ibid.

143 Shihata 1990, p. 30.

The EBRD Articles of Agreement also contain in para 1 of Article 20 approval requirements for borrowings in member countries and elsewhere,[144] however do not contain restrictions regarding the investment of borrowed funds. Article 21, para 2 of the EBRD Articles of Agreement, provides:

> Members shall not impose any restrictions on the receipt, holding, use or transfer by the Bank of the following: [….] ii) currencies obtained by the Bank by borrowing;

This straightforward prohibition on members restricting the EBRD's use of borrowed funds may seem quite different from the more complex provisions of the IBRD Articles. It reflects, however, the understanding in practice of these latter provisions.[145]

Borrowings in nonmember countries are permitted in the IBRD and by all regional development banks. As indicated by Shihata:

> The IBRD and IFC Articles require approval from the members in whose markets IBRD and IFC borrowing are made and in whose currencies the loans are denominated, but these provisions do not prevent them from borrowing in non-member countries (as for example in Switzerland). The inclusion of the words 'or elsewhere' in EBRD Article 20, Paragraph 1 explicitly permits borrowing in any country, with the approval of the country concerned. This is also the case of the ADB, IDB and AfDB. The broad scope of the borrowing markets is particularly appropriate in institutions with a limited membership such as the regional MDBs which may need to provide access to capital markets outside that membership.[146]

While the issue of borrowing in nonmember countries is of limited relevance for universal organizations such as the IBRD, it continues to be very important for regional development banks, in particular. This relates to the fact that in case of regional development banks, there is only a limited number of highly-rated investment opportunities available in their member countries. Therefore, they are looking to non-member countries for suitable investments. Thus, for example, "ADB seeks to diversify its borrowings in a broad range of currencies, instruments, markets and maturities,"[147] including currencies of non-member countries. Hence, ADB has made, inter alia, borrowings in South African rand, Mexican peso and Brazilian real,[148] all currencies on non-member countries.

---

[144] EBRD Articles of Agreement, Article 20 provides: "**General powers** 1. The Bank shall have, in addition to the powers specified elsewhere in the Agreement, the power to; (i) borrow funds in member countries or elsewhere, provided always that (a) before making a sale of its obligations in the territory of a country, the Bank shall have obtained its approval; and (b) where the obligations of the Bank are to be denominated in the currency of a member, the Bank shall have obtained its approvals."

[145] Shihata 1990, p. 30.

[146] Ibid., 27.

[147] ADB Debt Instruments. https://www.adb.org/site/investors/adb-debt-products.

[148] Erquiaga 2016, p. 63.

The AfDB, ADB, IADB and EBRD, are all authorized to borrow in non-member countries. Article 23(a) of the Agreement establishing the African Development Bank states:

> In addition to the powers provided elsewhere in this Agreement, the Bank shall have power to:
>
> a. Borrow funds in member countries **or elsewhere**, and in that connection to furnish such collateral or other security as it shall determine provided always that:
>
> i. Before making a sale of its obligations in the market of a member, the Bank shall have obtained its approval;
> ii. Where the obligations of the Bank are to be denominated in the currency of a member, the Bank shall have obtained its approval; and
> iii. Where the funds to be borrowed are to be included in its ordinary capital resources, the Bank shall have obtained, where appropriate, the approval of the members referred to in sub-para (i) and (ii) of this paragraph that the proceeds may be exchanged for any other currency without any restrictions; (emphasis added)

Very similar provisions are contained in Article 21(i) of the ADB Charter and Article VII, Section 1(i) of the IADB Charter.

Nevertheless, there is one substantial difference between the ADB Charter and the constituent agreement of AfDB, IADB and EBRD. While all four regional development banks are allowed to borrow in non-member countries, the ADB Charter constrains ADB's ability to administer the proceeds of borrowings in non-member countries in the currencies of these countries. This may be derived from Article 21(v) which authorizes ADB to "invest funds, not needed in its operations, in the territories of members in such **obligations of members or nationals thereof** as it may determine [….]." It may be seen as rather peculiar that the constituent agreement of a financial institution would allow it to borrow in nonmember countries, but not permit it to invest the proceeds of the borrowings in nonmember countries. Also, it may be argued that under the residual powers that ADB has under Article 21(vii) of the ADB Charter, ADB may conduct limited investments in currencies of non-member countries. However, the wording of Article 21(v) is quite specific and, in principle, also covers also the case mentioned above. Hence, ADB regularly took action to swap the proceeds of borrowings in nonmember countries in the currencies of ADB members. Similar requirements as in Article 21(v) of the ADB Charter are not contained in the constituent agreements of AfDB,[149] EBRD (see above) or IADB.[150]

---

[149] Article 23(d) of the Agreement establishing the African Development Bank provides that the AfDB shall have power to: "Invest funds not needed in its operations in such obligations as it may determine and invest funds held by the Bank for pensions or similar purposes in marketable securities." No reference is made as to the currency of investments.

[150] Article VII, Section 1(iii) of the IADB Charter shall have the power "with the approval of a three-fourths majority of the total voting power of the member countries, invest funds not needed in its operations in such obligations as it may determine." It is not mentioned that the investment has to be in the currency of a member country.

9.5 Membership, Operational Activities and Procurement

Membership and organizations operational activities are intrinsically linked in many ways. This has already been shown in detail by this author in the book "Funds for Development: Multilateral Channels of Concessional Financing" in relation to international financial institutions. Such institutions have a "dual character" as they are "intergovernmental organizations created by states for a public purpose" and "subjects of international law", while "they engage in financial transactions which, despite their public purpose, are, by nature, similar to market-based financial transactions."[151] In view of the breadth of the modalities of financing used by international financial institutions and the fact that they use market-based transactions and engage in other activities which may be qualified in spite their public purposes as of a commercial nature, the linkages between membership in international organizations and organizations' operational activities can be shown with particular clarity in the case of such institutions.

9.5.1 Membership and Eligibility to Receive Financing

Among the many linkages between membership and operational activities, perhaps the most important one is that between membership and members' eligibility to receive financing and other operational support from an international financial institution. This has been shown by this author in great detail given the example of the MDBs and other international financial institutions and does not need to be duplicated here for that reason.[152]

The Nordic Development Fund and the OPEC Fund for International Development only provide assistance to non-member countries. There are other cases where international financial institutions provide financial assistance to non-members, such as in the case of the Central American Bank for Economic Integration where a special form of institutionalized participation of beneficiary countries has been established. Moreover, organizations may provide financing to non-members through trust funds. Notwithstanding the above, in most cases, eligibility to financing is limited to the members of the organizations, or to certain categories or groups of the members (e.g. regional countries or developing countries).[153] This is due to the fact that based on the club theory, the legal frameworks of international organizations are based on a correlation between the benefits of membership and the obligations of membership. However, as has been shown above, such correlation between is not warranted and appropriate in certain cases, in

[151] Bradlow 2010, p. 1.

[152] See Droesse 2011d, p. 207.

[153] See the section entitled: "Financing Limited to Member Countries". In Droesse 2011d, pp. 191–194.

particular, in the case of international organizations producing global public goods or fighting global public bads. Thus, there are international organizations without a formal membership structure. Moreover, even in the case of traditional organizations which rely on membership benefits as an incentive for attracting new members, there is an increasing realization that the costs of reserving membership benefits to members may exceed the benefit in certain cases. Thus, providing that only member countries can be the source of procuring goods and services may substantially increase transaction costs and confining recruitment of staff to nationals of member countries may entail that the most qualified and suitable individual cannot be recruited.

9.5.2 Country Ownership, Private Sector and No-Objection Procedure

Another important linkage relates to the fact that the governments of organizations' member countries are now widely seen to be in the driver seat of operational activities in their countries funded by an international organization. The Paris Declaration of 1995 marked an important development as it emphasized inter alia:

> **Ownership:** Developing countries set their own strategies for poverty reduction, improve their institutions and tackle corruption.
>
> **Alignment:** Donor countries align behind these objectives and use local systems.

Consistent with the Paris Declaration and the Accra Agenda for Action,[154] country ownership and country driven approaches are now widely recognized and accepted, to the extent that reference to these principles was expressly incorporated in the Governing Instrument of the Green Climate Fund,[155] which also provides:

> The Fund will pursue a country-driven approach and promote and strengthen engagement at the country level through effective involvement of relevant institutions and stakeholders.

One of the core questions is whether, respectively, to what extent, international financial institutions require government approval for conducting private sector operations in a given country. This is not only a procedural issue but has substantial implications for defining the private sector operations of international organizations.

As regards the public-sector operations of international financial institutions, generally the project pipeline is defined in agreement between the governments of member countries and the IFI concerned. The situation is different in case of private

---

[154] Paris Declaration and Accra Agenda for Action. http://www.oecd.org/dac/effectiveness/parisdeclarationandaccraagendaforaction.htm.

[155] The GCF Governing Instrument, para 3 provides: "The Fund will pursue a country-driven approach and promote and strengthen engagement at the country level through effective involvement of relevant institutions and stakeholders."

sector operations as in such a case project proposal may directly emanate from a private sector entity.

Generally, MDBs and other IFIs have taken the position that Government approval/no-objection is required also in private sector operations.[156] However, it has been discussed whether such no-objection may be assumed based on time-lapse. The discussion on the no-objection procedure in the GCF epitomizes such discussion.

One of the core issues discussed throughout the development of the GCF was to what extent private sector entities should be required to clear their activities with national climate agencies or bring projects directly to the GCF Board. In this context, the objective of mobilizing large-scale resources for the GCF through a streamlined procedure had to be considered in line with the need highlighted by developing countries to ensure that all actions are in line with national priorities. When the Governing Instrument of the Green Climate Fund was approved at Durban in 2011, "a compromise was struck" by enabling the Fund through its private sector facility "to directly and indirectly finance private sector mitigation and adaptation activities at the national, regional and international levels,"[157] while requesting

> the Board to develop a transparent no-objection procedure to be conducted through national designated authorities referred to in paragraph 46 of the governing instrument annexed to this decision, in order to ensure consistency with national climate strategies and plans and a country driven approach and to provide for effective direct and indirect public and private sector financing by the Green Climate Fund.[158]

Under the procedure eventually approved by the Board of the Fund, private sector projects are also subject to the no-objection procedure. Unlike proposed by developed countries, such approval cannot be assumed if no objection is received within a certain period. However, the compromise reached for the benefit of speedy processing of projects is that the approval is deemed having been declined if it is not granted during a certain period.

9.5.3 *State-Sector Bias in Project Implementation*

Finally, in addition to their other roles mentioned above, governments are also substantially involved in project implementation. Under the traditional model of

---

[156] Thus, the Operations Manual of the Asian Development Bank provides: "ADB finances a project in a DMC only if the government has no objection. Accordingly, the government's no-objection for each financing must be obtained before the first disbursement by ADB of such financing, and preferably before the financing is submitted to the Board of Directors for approval." ADB. Operations Manual Bank Policies (OM). OM Section D10/BP issued on 2 Jan. 2013.

[157] GCF Governing Instrument, para 41.

[158] Decision 3/CP.17, para 7 http://unfccc.int/resource/docs/2011/cop17/eng/09a01.pdf#page=55.

project financing, both the implementing agency and any executing agency are government institutions. All this translates into a government focus in project design and a state-sector bias in project and program implementation. As indicated in the executive summary of a recent IFAD study:

> There is a state-sector bias. Usually too much is expected from the government lead agencies in terms of project intervention delivery, despite the fact that they often have limited capacity. Less attention is given to building relations (at all levels) with other organizations that could be involved in co-implementation and partnership-building with the private sector in the delivery of private goods.
>
> There is only a partial assessment of the potential of non-state, in-country partners to collaborate with IFAD programmes, and influence existing power relationships and/or imbalances.[159]

It would be appropriate for organizations to discontinue their state-sector bias in project implementation. While there continues to be a need and demand for traditional state-sector projects implemented and executed by governments, new forms of implementation arrangements involving the private sector and other stakeholders need to be developed if organizations wish to enhance their effectiveness. This does not mean giving the private sector an untrammeled freedom to do whatever it deems fit. It is important to define the accountability of private sector entities in project implementation as well as the parameters in which they can operate. Doing so is first and foremost the role of the state. It means, however, that implementation arrangements need to become more diversified.

Similar to funding modalities, the operational modalities of organizations also have to become more diversified. While initially, organizations predominantly provided sovereign loans guaranteed by governments to fund projects, private-sector operations without a sovereign guarantee are now recognized as an integral part of organizations modalities. However, private sector involvement is something which needs to be mainstreamed in organizations activities and involve all sector and operations. While straightforward grants or concessional loans are still justified and may serve a purpose, organizations operational modalitics need to become more sophisticated. Thus, grants may be approved with a contingent repayment obligation or upon performance of certain parameters. Moreover, there is wide recognition that there may a better use of grants than using them for loans, such as funding first loss tranches of financial facilities. In some areas, as in the health sector or climate change adaptation and mitigation, new initiatives abound, as can be shown by even a cursory look at the projects of the Global Fund, Gavi Alliance, the climate-change related initiatives of organizations and by new initiatives such as the Climate Innovation Lab.

---

[159] IFAD. 2013. Synthesis report: Strengthening Institutions and Organizations. An Analysis of Lessons Learnt from Field Application of IFAD's Sourcebook on Institutional and Organizational Analysis for Pro-Poor Change, 7. https://www.ifad.org/documents/10180/a4c30900-e274-4c97-81e7-595256b3441c.

9.5.4 Membership and Procurement

One of the tangible incentives of becoming a member of an organization is to be eligible to participate in procurement by the organization. This is relevant, in particular, for membership in international financial institutions. The principles which are applicable in this regard have been analyzed in detail by this author.[160] While there are still a number of organizations which link procurement eligibility to membership, restrictions to procurement eligibility which are made on that basis clearly come with a cost, as they may imply that goods and services cannot be procured from the most cost-effective source. Thus, there is an increasing trend to global procurement, i.e. to delinking membership and procurement eligibility. Moreover, also in institutions which still adhere to procurement restrictions, such restrictions are increasingly waived.

However, while procurement conditionality relating to membership in international organizations is losing importance, other types of conditionality are gaining in importance. This relates, in particular, to climate-change related conditionality. The EU already

> has embraced the use of procurement to protect the environment and made it easier for governments to buy sustainably. Costs over the lifecycle of a product (like energy use) can now be better integrated into buyers' decision-making. Buyers are encouraged to avoid automatically choosing the cheapest option; instead there is a clear message that lifetime environmental performance is an important factor.[161]

As public procurement is increasingly seen as the "next weapon to fight climate change",[162] other international organizations need to follow suit by incorporating climate-change related concerns in all their operational activities. International organizations already have made substantial progress in this regard. Thus, the World Bank perceives sustainable procurement as "a process which incorporates sustainability considerations throughout the procurement process in order to achieve optimal VfM [value for money] in delivering development objectives."[163] Sustainability considerations are considered "at various stages throughout the procurement process",[164] i.e. in identifying and analyzing sustainability needs, developing sustainability requirements and evaluation methodology, and in

---

160 See Droesse 2011d.

161 Formosa, A. and Weller, C. Public procurement: the next weapon to fight climate change? The Guardian. 21 Jan. 2014. https://www.theguardian.com/public-leaders-network/2014/jan/21/public-procurement-weapon-climate-change.

162 Ibid.

163 World Bank. 2016. Procurement Guidance: Sustainable Procurement. An introduction for practitioners for practitioners to sustainable procurement in World Bank IPF projects, 3. http://pubdocs.worldbank.org/en/788731479395390605/Sustainable-Procurement-Guidance-FINAL.pdf.

164 Ibid., 5.

selecting supplier and contract award.[165] Similarly, also various other organization have adopted green procurement policies.[166] In future, procurement teams will have a "big role" by analyzing carbon footprints of supply chains,[167] "understanding where emissions hotspots are located in their operations, identifying which commodities are affected by the shift to a low carbon economy and knowing which suppliers are heavily impacted by climate change and rising global temperatures, procurement can proactively limit their contribution to greenhouse gas emissions and ensure their suppliers are equipped to do the same."

9.6 Conclusions

As has been shown above, there are many links and ramifications between membership in international organizations and representation in governing bodies, organizations' funding mechanisms, capital structures and borrowings, and the operational and procurement activities of international organizations. Overall the importance of membership is diminishing, in the context of representation mechanisms, because international organization need to open themselves to the outside and give a voice to a variety of stakeholders, and in the context of eligibility to financing and operational frameworks, because it is no longer justified in a number of instances to exclude the populations of certain countries and territories from access to financing or other benefits for the only reason that these are not members of an international organization. International organizations should not only look to their members as their main or only source of funding, but should diversify their funding mechanisms by attracting contributions from the private sector, philanthropy and civil society. Capital structures of international organizations are intrinsically linked to membership concepts. As regards their operational frameworks, international organizations should reconsider their state-bias in project implementation. In procurement, there is a move towards global procurement, however, other conditionalities gain importance, among those relating to climate-change related concerns.

[165] Ibid., 9 ss.

[166] See *inter alia*: EU, 2016. Buying Green, Third edition. file:///C:/Users/WGEO_Org/Documents/Buying-Green-Handbook-3rd-Edition.pdf; EIB, 2009. EIB Green Procurement Guidelines and Objectives. http://www.eib.org/attachments/documents/eib_green_procurement_guidelines_and_objectives_2009_en.pdf; EBRD. Green Building Investment Factsheet: Public Buildings. file:///C:/Users/WGEO_Org/Documents/Green%20Procurement/EBRD%20green%20buildings%20factsheet.pdf. See also the Green Procurement Guidelines (For Suppliers), Ver. 5, 2010 of NEC Display Solutions, Ltd. file:///C:/Users/WGEO_Org/Documents/Green%20Procurement/NEC%20Procurement%20Guidelines.pdf.

[167] Spend Matters Network 2016.

References

Bailin A (2001) From traditional to institutionalized hegemony. http://www.g8.utoronto.ca/scholar/bailin/bailin2000.pdf

Bradlow DD (2010) International Law and the operations of International Financial Institutions. In: Bradlow DD, Hunter DB (eds) International Financial Institutions. Kluwer Law International, Alphen aan den Rijn, pp 1–30

Bermudez J, Douste-Blazy P (2009) Innovative financing for development. UNITAID, pp 13–23

Conforti B, Focarelli C (2016) The law and practice of the United Nations, 5th edn. Brill Nijhoff, Leiden, pp 34–36

Droesse G (2011a) Introductory remarks and overview of publication: proliferation, fragmentation, and earmarking of Concessional Financing. In: Droesse G (ed) Funds for development: multilateral channels of Concessional Financing. Asian Development Bank, Manila, pp 1–37

Droesse G (2011b) Concessional Financing of the Asian Development Bank: the Asian Development Fund and other channels of ADB Concessional Financing. In: Droesse G (ed) Funds for development: multilateral channels of Concessional Financing. ADB, Manila, pp 299–398

Droesse G (2011c) Organizational structures, institutional frameworks, and decision-making procedures of Multilateral Concessional Financing. In: Funds for development: multilateral channels of Concessional Financing. ADB, Manila, pp 59–177

Droesse G (2011d) Modalities of Multilateral Concessional Financing. In: Droesse G (ed) Funds for development: Multilateral Channels of Concessional Financing. ADB, Manila, pp 179–297

Droesse G (2012) The replenishments of the Asian Development Fund: institutional development in the Asian Development Bank and the role of the legal counsel in resource mobilization. In: Quereshi AH, Gao X (eds) International Economic Organizations and Law. The perspective and role of the legal counsel. Wolters Kluwer, Alphen aan den Rijn, pp 265–314

Droesse G (2017) Green climate fund and its role in promoting and funding sustainable investment. In: Dispute resolution and climate change. The Paris Agreement and beyond. International Chamber of Commerce, Paris, pp 52–55

Droesse G (2020) Governance changes in International Organisations: new trends and developments. In: de Cooker C (ed) Governance: International Organizations adapting to changing environments. Bruylant/Larcier, Brussels (forthcoming)

Erquiaga P (2016) A history of financial management at the Asian Development Bank: engineering financial innovation and impact on an emerging Asia. ADB, Manila, p 69. https://www.adb.org/sites/default/files/publication/216736/history-financial-mgt-adb.pdf

Foch A (2013) Explaining the G7 and G10's influence on World Bank decisions: the role of formal and informal rules of governance. ftp://mse.univ-paris1.fr/pub/mse/CES2013/13035.pdf

Guzman A (2013) International Organizations and the Frankenstein problem. Eur J Int Law 24:999–1025

Kharas H (2009) Non-G-20 developing countries and the G-20 summit: perspectives on global leadership. https://www.brookings.edu/opinions/non-g-20-developing-countries-and-the-g-20-summit-perspectives-on-global-leadership/

Martinez-Diaz L (2009) Boards of Directors in International Organizations: a framework for understanding the dilemmas of institutional design. Rev Int Organ 4:383–406

Mistry PS (1995) Multilateral Development Banks: an assessment of their financial structures, policies and practices. FONDAD, The Hague

Posner EA, Sykes AO (2014) Voting rules in International Organizations. Chicago J Int Law 15:195–228

Ragazzi M (2011) The Global Environment Facility: institutional and operational aspects. In: Droesse G (ed) Funds for development: Multilateral Channels of Concessional Financing. ADB, Manila, pp 485–500

Rocabert F, Schimmelfennig T, Winzen T (2014) The rise of International Parliamentary Institutions? Conceptualization and first empirical illustrations, 1. https://www.agora-parl.org/sites/default/files/rise_of_ipis.pdf
Schermers HG, Blokker NM (eds) (2011) International Institutional Law: unity within diversity, 5th edn. Martinus Nijhoff, Boston
Shihata IFI (1990) The European Bank for reconstruction and development. A comparative analysis of the constituent agreement. Graham & Trotman/Martinus Nijhoff, London, p 30
Shihata IFI (2000) The World Bank legal papers. Martinus Nijhoff, The Hague, p 99
Shihata IFI (2001) Techniques to avoid proliferation of international organizations—the experience of the World Bank. In: Blokker NM, Schermers HG (eds) Proliferation of International Organizations: legal issues. Kluwer Law International, The Hague, pp 111–134
Spend Matters Network (2016) A look back at COP21: what the new climate change agreement means for procurement. http://spendmatters.com/2016/01/13/a-look-back-at-cop21-what-the-new-climate-change-agreement-means-for-procurement/
Sureda AR (2004) The law applicable to the activities of International Development Banks. In: Collected Courses of the Hague Academy of International Law, vol 308. Brill/Nijhoff, Leiden/Boston, pp 9–252
Sverdrup U, Nahem J (2017) The G20: inclusivity and legitimacy, a Nordic perspective. Security Policy Working Paper, No. 12/2017, 1. Federal Academy for Security Policy. https://www.baks.bund.de/sites/baks010/files/working_paper_2017_12.pdf
Vogel-Polsky E (1966) Du Tripartitisme à l'Organisation Internationale du Travail. de l'Institut de Sociologie de l'Université Libre de Bruxelles.
Warren B (2017) G20 International Financial Institution reform commitments and compliance. http://www.g20.utoronto.ca/analysis/170105-ifi-reform-research.html#b
Weill-Hallé VP, Licul C, Villanueva IG (2011) Multilateral Concessional Financing of the international fund for agricultural development. In: Droesse G (ed) Funds for development: multilateral channels of Concessional Financing, pp 457–484
Wessel RA, Dekker IF (2015) Identities of states in International Organizations. Int Organ Law Rev 12:293–318

Chapter 10
New Concept of International Organization

Contents

10.1 Theses

Based on the discussion in the previous chapters, *inter alia* the following conclusions may be drawn:

1. (i) There is no need for membership structures to be established by a treaty. Also, international organizations do not need to have members because (ii) the parties to the organization's constituent agreement do not need to become members and (iii) there are effectively international organizations without a formal membership structure.
2. Membership concepts are based on the club theory and are predicated on the correlation of benefits and obligations resulting from membership. This correlation is only suitable to a very limited extent for organizations producing global public goods or fighting global public bads.
3. Membership in international organizations does not need to be confined to states and international organizations. Private sector entities can be full members of international organizations and it is conceivable that an international

All weblinks are updated as of 28 February 2018.

G. Droesse, *Membership in International Organizations*,
https://doi.org/10.1007/978-94-6265-327-6_10

organization exclusively has private sector entities as members. Sub-state actors, including regulatory agencies, can also be members of international organizations. Dual and hybrid organizations incorporated under national law may have membership structures, depending on their purpose and functions. Moreover, as the relation of an international organization with its members is an internal one, also entities without legal personality, such as trust funds, may have membership structures.

4. As the concept of "subject of international law" is broader than "international legal personality", it is not necessary to show that an organization possesses international legal personality for it to be classified as a subject of international law. Hence, organizations established as trust funds without international legal personality and organizations characterized by "institutional ambivalence by design" may be recognized as subjects of international law if it can be established that they operate on the international plane and/or have responsibilities under international law. The detour of affirmation of international legal personality is not required in such a case.
5. The International Committee of the Red Cross (ICRC) should be taken out of the niche of "atypical" subjects of international law and be recognized as the predecessor of a new class of dual and hybrid organizations, incorporated under national law, but with recognition of international legal personality in their host country and certain other countries. These may qualify both for recognition as subjects of international law and as international organizations.
6. Whether an international organization possesses international legal personality does not depend on the will of its founders but on its functions and powers and the position of recognized subjects of international law.
7. An organization may acquire international legal personality subsequent to its establishment based on recognition of its international legal personality in a multilateral agreement, or in a headquarters agreement or in bilateral agreements or arrangements which recognize the international legal personality of the organization and extend to it privileges and immunities.
8. In the case of organizations incorporated under national law or characterized by "institutional ambivalence by design" such agreements have the potential of transforming the character of the organization.
9. Whether subsidiary bodies of an organization, financial mechanisms of multilateral agreements, or EU agencies possess or acquire international legal personality does not depend on their status but on their functions and powers and the positions which recognized subjects of international law have taken in their regard.
10. The concepts and definition of "international organization" and "intergovernmental organization", which are currently influenced by state-centric concepts, need to be interpreted in a broader manner, taking account of the evolution of international law.
11. Use of the term "intergovernmental organization" should not be limited to public international organizations or organizations endowed with international legal personality. Unless expressly mandated otherwise by a convention or

legal act, also dual or hybrid organizations incorporated under national law and organizations established as trust funds without international legal personality may be qualified as intergovernmental.

12. Classification of an organization as "intergovernmental" does not require that the governing bodies of the organization are exclusively composed of state representatives.
13. The classification of organizations as "intergovernmental" is intrinsically problematic for the very reason that this definition seeks to exclude all organizations not established by governments. It should only be used if expressly warranted, and, then, generally be interpreted to include organizations without treaty basis and dual and hybrid organizations.
14. The criteria traditionally used to define "international organization" are too "hard" in the sense that they focus on formal elements (such as treaty foundation, membership structure and international legal personality) rather than on the organization's functions and recognized legal status. Hence, the current criteria need to be revised. Designating certain organizations as "soft organizations" is not an appropriate solution.
15. While treaties are a very important, and perhaps still the most important mode of establishing international forms of cooperation, the relevance of treaties is diminishing. Treaties are only suitable to a limited extent for dealing with economic matters and for creating new funding structures. Also, traditional concepts of treaty-making do not fit well agreements between central banks, ministries of finance, or other national authorities establishing institutionalized forms of cooperation, or the fact that international organizations may have multiple legal personalities. The legal act adopting the governance structure of an international organization may be different from the act establishing the organization. The constitution of an international organization may be contained in an agreement between central banks, ministries of finance or other authorities which does not meet the traditional criteria of a treaty. Also, a constitution of an organization which was not ratified may regulate membership on very similar terms as a ratified constitution. Moreover, it may also be the basis for international action of the organization.
16. The focus on the "establishment" of international organizations gives insufficient weight to the dynamic character of international organizations. The status of an organization at the time of its establishment is only a snapshot of its functions and powers at that time. Organizations may change beyond recognition due to mission creep and progressive institutionalization. Also attempts to associate any legal act establishing an international organization, however remote, with a treaty (e.g. in the case of the Nordic Council) are questionable at best and futile at large and completely fail in some cases.
17. The classification of entities as "international organization" can no longer be reduced to the dichotomies of public and private and governmental and non-governmental. Hence, the term "international organization" needs to be interpreted to comprise dual and hybrid organizations incorporated under national

law but with recognition of international legal personality, such as the Global Fund and the Gavi Alliance.

18. A nongovernmental organization or corporation may convert to a dual and hybrid organization if responsibilities under international law are assigned to it. Conversion to a dual and hybrid organization may also take place based on the adoption of a multilateral agreement on privileges and immunities or the adoption of a headquarters agreement or other bilateral agreements which recognize the international legal personality of an entity incorporated under national law and extend to it privileges and immunities.
19. In certain cases, international organizations have been privatized or been replaced by nongovernmental organizations. Hence, the road between non-governmental organizations and corporations and international organizations is a two-way road. The functions of international organizations and international nongovernmental organizations are interchangeable to a large extent.
20. Whether QABs may be qualified as international organizations does not depend on the act establishing them but, on their powers and functions and the position which recognized subjects of international law have adopted in their regard. QABs may convert to an international organization based on a treaty or due to progressive institutionalization.
21. The term "international organization is wider than the term "intergovernmental organization. Hence, also organization of Parliamentary cooperation, and, potentially, organizations involving sub-state actors and national regulators may be recognized as international organizations. Establishment by international agreement should not be part of the definition of international organization.
22. It does not matter how an international organization is established. What matters are its powers and functions and the position which recognized subjects of international law have adopted vis-à-vis the organization.
23. Also, the autonomy of an international organization is not necessarily a corollary of its international legal personality. Entities without international legal personality may also enjoy autonomy. Their institutional independence needs to be assessed to determine whether they may be regarded as international organizations.
24. Institutionalized participation of non-state actors in international organizations requires that that they meet core standards of good governance. Also, international organization cannot dissociate themselves from the values they preaching to their members. Hence, they need to guarantee due process in all matters, including for claims based on tort. By doing so, they may also ensure certainty of the law in non-member countries.
25. There is a benefit of transforming international organizations into multi-actor institutions that give a voice to a great variety of stakeholders and rely on non-state actors for implementation of operational modalities.
26. While international organizations have shown limited ability and inclination to include transactional actors in their decision-making processes, their ability to incorporate external and even extra-constitutional processes has proved quite remarkable. Situations where international organizations only have the option

to rubberstamp decisions taken in external fora are intrinsically problematic and have adverse implications for the legitimacy of the organization concerned. It is also intrinsically problematic if the "operational constitution" deviates from the constituent agreement to the extent that the authority provided by the constituent agreement is ignored or redefined by unwritten practice. An unwritten practice must not be allowed to outright redefine, beyond any limits of an acceptable interpretation of the constituent instrument, fundamental provisions of the constituent instrument, because by doing so they would change the structure of, and the balance of power enshrined in, the constituent instrument.

27. The traditional three-tier system comprising a plenary body such as a Board of Governors or Assembly, bodies such as a board of directors or council and a secretariat is increasingly questioned regarding its inclusiveness and functionality. There is also a trend toward two-tier structures and a trend towards softer decision-making procedures.
28. New funding mechanisms, including global taxes and levies, need to be developed. An organization producing global public goods or fighting global public bads should be funded wherever feasible by global levies or taxes. Such levies and taxes should be an integral part of any carbon pricing regime that may be designed.
29. International organizations may derive their entire operational funding from institutional investors and private sector entities.
30. The relationship of the terms "international organization", "subject of international law", and "international legal personality" is as follows:

    (i) An entity which possesses international legal personality necessarily qualifies as a subject of international law.
    (ii) However, as the concept of "subject of international law" is broader than "international legal personality", there may be subjects of international law which do not possess international legal personality. Organizations characterized by "institutional ambivalence of design" and organizations established as trust funds without international legal personality may qualify for recognition as subjects of international law.
    (iii) International organizations need to operate on the international plane. Therefore, for an entity to qualify as an international organization, it needs to be the subject of international law in the sense that it can be the subject of duties and responsibilities under international law. Recognition as an international organization generally implies recognition as a subject of international law.
    (iv) However, the term "international organization" is wider than that of "subject of international law". Thus, as a matter of principle, there may be subjects of international law (e.g. a conference or meeting of the parties to a multilateral environmental agreement) that do not qualify for recognition as an international organization.

10.2 New Analytical Framework for International Organization

Taking account of the above, it is necessary to refocus and re-conceptualize the concept of international organization. The position advocated by this book is likely to entail a substantial increase in the number of recognized international organizations, possibly to the thousands. This is an adjustment which merely reflects changed realities and has been overdue for a long time. In some cases, the legal status of an entity may not be apparent at first sight. Therefore, in the view of this author, rather than looking for a straightforward definition, it is more appropriate to define an analytical framework to determine whether an entity qualifies as an international organization.

10.2.1 Requirements for Classification as "Organization"

First, it needs to be determined whether a cooperative undertaking is institutionalized to the extent that it can classified as an "organization". Such classification generally requires that the purpose and functions of the organization have been defined and that it has organs through which it can act. Hence, an analysis of the organization's institutional structure is required. As has been extensively argued above, the fact that the organs of an organization include transnational actors as members does not preclude its classification as an international organization, nor is it necessary that the staff of the organization's secretariat are directly employed by the organization. As the experience of the GEF shows, the staff of the secretariat may have the status of staff of the trustee, or they may have the status of staff of another organization, as previously in the case of the Global Fund.[1]

However, generally it is required that an organization is governed by the rule of law. The criteria mentioned above distinguish international organizations from "elusive" forms of cooperation such as G-20, which cannot be recognized as international organization as its "structure is informal, its lack of clear competences requires little limitation and its activities are largely conducted by government departments or existing international organisations."[2] However, the OSCE qualifies for recognition as international organization under this respect (and other respects) as it has an elaborate organizational structure with organs.

---

[1] This was the case prior to the "termination of the 24 May 2004 service agreement between the Global Fund and the World Health Organization (WHO)—under which WHO provided administrative services to the Global Fund and the staff of the Global Fund enjoyed the privileges and immunities of WHO staff (e.g., under the CPISA)". Droesse 2011a, p. 183.

[2] Henley and Blokker 2013, p. 555.

10.2.2 Political Autonomy and Institutional Independence

Second, an international organization must possess political autonomy and institutional independence.

Gazzini recalls that "autonomy was treated as a matter of degree by the International Court of Justice, holding [in the Advisory Opinion on *Legality of the Use by a State of Nuclear Weapons in Armed Conflict*][3] that '[t]he constituent instruments of international organizations are also treaties of a particular type; their object is to create new subjects of law endowed with a *certain autonomy,* to which the parties entrust the task of realizing common goals'."[4] This author agrees with Gazzini that "autonomy is a matter of degree, not a yes or no question as it is for international legal personality."[5] In particular, in the case of an organization not established by a treaty, it is necessary to assess the degree of autonomy of that organization to determine whether it may be qualified as an international organization.

Autonomy is frequently analyzed "from the point of view of the member-organization relationship" in relation to the organization's capacity "to express a will separate from the will of its members" and to describe "the extent to which the members of the organization can influence its functioning or prevent it from functioning."[6] In this context, the autonomy of international organizations is often viewed as a corollary of their international legal personality established by treaty. However, the autonomy of international organizations should not only be viewed under the aspects of the member-organization relationship and international legal personality, as both aspects are too narrow to fully capture the characteristics of all international organizations, including those without a treaty foundation.

It is important to note that an organization may possess institutional autonomy even if it has not been established by a treaty and does not have international legal personality. This has been discussed in detail in relation to international organizations established as trust funds. Also, an organization may possess autonomy even if it does not have a formal membership structure. This is shown, *inter alia*, by dual or hybrid organizations such as the Global Fund.

Finally, an organization's autonomy must be defined in more general terms, taking account of the fact that also entities created as a subsidiary body of an international organization or as the financial mechanism of a multilateral convention may qualify for recognition as "international organization". The Multilateral Fund and Green Climate Fund are interesting examples of entities established as financial mechanisms of multilateral conventions which, in the view of this author, need to be classified as international organizations. However, as the comparison between the

---

[3] Legality of the Use by a State of Nuclear Weapons in Armed Conflict, Advisory Opinion, ICJ Reports 1996, 66. http://www.icj-cij.org/files/case-related/93/093-19960708-ADV-01-00-EN.pdf.

[4] Gazzini 2011, p. 200.

[5] Ibid., 200.

[6] Ibid., 199–200.

Green Climate Fund and the Adaptation Fund has shown, it was not the fact that the Green Climate Fund was designated "an operating entity of the financial mechanism under Article 11 of the Convention" that qualified it for recognition as an international organization. Rather, this derives from its functions and powers, and the fact that the Green Climate Fund is recognized to be able operating on the international plane. Similar considerations also apply to subsidiary bodies, in general. QABs are not disqualified from recognition as international organizations because they were not established by a treaty or because they were established as subsidiary bodies, but because they are still tied to the UN by many strings and because there is no consistent recognition of their capacity to act on the international plane as an independent organization. Hence, it is necessary in all cases to consider the institutional set-up of an organization, in particular, in the case of organizations which are established as a financial mechanism by an organization or a conference or meeting of the parties to a Convention, or which were established as a subsidiary body or agency with a large degree of autonomy. In this context, it is not the mode of establishment but the actual powers of the organization which are relevant.

While it has been asserted that autonomy is a "nebulous" concept,[7] such concept gains greater focus and clarity if it is viewed from the angles of political and institutional independence, "which do not constitute two completely watertight dimensions of autonomy, for they are inevitably intertwined."[8] Therefore, an entity needs to possess both political and institutional autonomy to be considered an international organization.

The "political autonomy" referred to above relates to the classical notion of "*volonté distincte*", or the organization's autonomy in its internal affairs and its ability to take legally binding decisions pursuant to established procedures. However, as d'Aspremont highlights, "an account of autonomy restricted to the political independence of the organization would certainly be too narrow. Indeed, autonomy can also refer to the degree of institutional independence possessed by the organization; that is, the impermeability of the organization to external institutional interferences."[9]

On the other hand, D'Aspremont relates institutional independence to the "extent to which international organizations constitute a legal order distinct from the general international legal order." This is indeed an important criterion. As has been discussed, constitutions which have not been adopted by a treaty may also create an internal legal order and a hierarchy of laws.

In addition, institutional independence is also intrinsically related to the powers which an organization possesses and exercises, both in relation to its members or in the overall context of the institutional set-up which led to its establishment. Thus, another important criterion is whether an organization is competent to perform

---

7 Gazzini 2011, p. 196.

8 d'Aspremont 2011, p. 64.

9 Ibid., 93.

some of the core functions which any international organization needs to perform, such as the such as the power to approve a budget, appoint the head of the Secretariat and decide on policies, procedures and operational activities.

10.2.3 Ability to Act on the International Plane

Finally, an international organization must act on the international plane. Whether this is the case is an institutional fact and depends on the organization's functions and the position which recognized subjects of international law have adopted in its regard. As indicated above, international organizations necessarily need to be subjects of international law, but they do not need to possess international legal personality in all cases.

10.3 The Power of Creation Has Passed Over to International Organizations and Other Actors

The main objection to international organizations creating new international organizations derive from the principle of "*competence d'attribution*" or the principle of specialty whereby international organizations, unlike states, have no general authority to take actions. The argument that international organizations cannot confer more powers than they possess themselves, appears to be compelling at first sight. Nevertheless, this author believes that the power of creation—to use this quasi-metaphysical concept—has passed over to international organizations and other international actors such as a Conference of the Parties to a multilateral convention, due to the following reasons.

(i) First, the creation of institutionalized forms of cooperation is no longer necessarily based on a treaty between states. As has been extensively argued, many new paradigms for creating such forms of cooperation that have emerged, some of which may involve action by one or more international organizations. As a matter of principle, institutionalized forms of cooperation may also be created by an agreement between international organizations, or by the resolution of one, or parallel resolutions of several international organizations, or through other similar arrangements.

(ii) Second, an entity providing public goods does not need to have all trappings of an international organization and does not need to be endowed with international legal personality at the time it is created. The status of such entity is only a snapshot of its powers at the time it is created. Hence, it is sufficient for an international organization to lay the foundation for an entity which may subsequently acquire the status of an international organization through progressive institutionalization and recognition of its international legal personality, or based on the assignment of international responsibilities by a treaty or other legal act.

(iii) Third, there is a wide range of entities which may convert into an international organization based on progressive institutionalization. In addition to organizations without treaty foundation such as INTERPOL and IPU, dual and hybrid international organizations such as the Global Fund and the Gavi Alliance, organizations characterized by "institutional ambivalence by design" (e.g. OSCE), and cooperative undertakings of sub-state actors and national regulators, in principle also subsidiary bodies and secondary agencies of international organizations may convert to an international organization based on progressive institutionalization and recognition of their international legal personality.

(iv) Fourth, an international organization may be established based on the decision of a conference or meeting of the parties to a convention (e.g., the Multilateral Fund for the Montreal Protocol, the Preparatory Commission of the Nuclear Test-Ban Treaty Organization, and the Green Climate Fund). This is an important new paradigm of establishing an international organization which is more akin to a living treaty regime than to the creation of a traditional international organization.

(iv) Fifth, international organizations may sponsor the establishment of new international organizations established as trust funds with or without international legal personality. Potentially, this might become the area where most new international organizations are created, the reason being that the relationship between the sponsoring organization and the organization established as a trust fund does not involve a delegation of powers by the sponsoring organization. Hence, the limits to delegation of authority discussed in relation to the European Agencies and quasi-autonomous bodies do not apply. Possessing international legal personality is not a requirement for a trust fund with institutional independence and its own governance structure that acts the international plane to be recognized as an international organization. The example of the CGIF shows that a fund created in that manner may have a quasi-equity structure. Moreover, CGIF also shows that, in essence, most powers of the trustee, with the sole exception of the competence of the trustee for the financial management of the assets, may be delegated by the trustee to the governing bodies of the organization established as a trust fund. This also includes the power to sign and execute financial agreements with third parties. Hence, the difference between organizations established as trust funds with legal personality and those without legal personality is less important than would appear at first sight.

10.4 Future Challenges for International Organizations

10.4.1 Opening of International Organizations

International organizations have amply shown their resilience and ability to adapt to changed circumstances. They will remain a prominent feature of the international future landscape, probably to an even greater extent than at present.

However, for them to perform the new tasks which will be requested from them, international organizations will need to meet a series of challenges.

One of these relates to enhancing their inclusiveness. Many international organizations already operate now in a drastically changed environment compared with the time when they were founded. It is expected that to remain relevant, international organizations will need to open themselves to the outside by becoming forums not only for states but also for sub-state actors, the private sector, civil society organizations, philanthropy and other interested parties. This would have far-reaching implications for their institutional and governance structures and operational modalities.

As regards membership, it would require that institutionalized forms of participation of transnational actors involving full, associate, partial, sector membership are encouraged.

At the institutional level, it would entail the transformation of international organizations to multi-faceted and multi-layered structures which involve a great variety of stakeholder in different platforms and umbrella operational frameworks. International organizations may be catalyzers for advanced networking solutions, as well as forums not only for states but also for sub-state actors, the private sector, civil society organizations, philanthropy and other interested parties.

Structuring international organizations in that manner should be considered a design option for any new international organization to be established. However, in principle, it is often also possible as a matter of policy to transform existing international organizations in that manner, as has been shown by this author, giving the example of international financial institutions.[10]

The opening of international organizations may imply in relation to the governance structure their transformation into multi-actor institutions which give a voice to a great variety of stakeholders. Moreover, it can be expected that the trend towards softer forms of decision making will continue, involving double or triple weighted voting or thematic voting mechanisms. Also, international organizations may create secondary governance structure under umbrella arrangements or platforms for certain areas of their activities, which may involve a great variety of stakeholders, including the private sector, philanthropy and civil society.

As regards funding, the opening of international organizations would entail that they explore new sources of funding. Moreover, substantial changes to traditional funding mechanisms of international organizations will become necessary.

[10] Droesse 2011b, pp. 164–166.

The current mechanisms which rely on the members of international organizations as their main source of funding increasing have become strained and are not sufficient to respond to all needs. Hence, international organizations will need to explore new sources of funding, including cooperation with the private sector, foundations and civil society, as well as crowd sourcing and other innovative funding solutions. In principle, international organizations may derive their entire operational funding from institutional investors and private-sector entities.

Finally, to the extent that international organizations conduct operational activities, it will be necessary that they enhance their cooperation with the private sector and other transnational actors and explore innovative operational modalities and promote innovative modalities of financing.

International organizations which undergo transformations as indicated above will look quite different from most current international organizations.

10.4.2 The Evolution of the Architecture of International Organizations

Necessary changes to legal and policy frameworks do not only concern individual organizations. The entire architecture of international organizations will need to change as well. As shown in detail in this study, new paradigms of international organizations are emerging, including organizations without treaty foundation and without international legal personality. The creation of international organizations is no longer the exclusive prerogative of states, as they may also be created by other international organizations or by a conference or meeting of the parties to a multilateral convention. Moreover, organizations may transform their status and be classified as international organizations based on progressive institutionalization. Finally, there may be international organizations which do not have any members. All this adds to an architecture of international organizations of an ever-growing complexity.

While there is an architecture of international organizations, there is "no single architect", as international organizations evolve without a specific blueprint in response to the needs of the international community.[11] The traditional way of creating an international organization with treaty foundation is too slow and, is, in particular, often not suitable for dealing with economic issues or for responding quickly to newly emerging needs. Moreover, states find it generally easier to create

[11] A paper prepared for the 15th replenishment negotiations of IDA stated: "While aid has an architecture, it has no single architect. It has evolved over time much of it without a pre-defined blueprint. Most of today's aid principles and institutions are the result of over half a century of debate and joint decision making. IDA 15. Aid Architecture: An Overview of the Main Trends in Official Development Assistance Flows, para 3. http://documents.worldbank.org/curated/en/745221468313781790/pdf/387500idasecm200710103core.pdf. Similar considerations apply to the architecture of international organizations in general.

new international organizations where they can impose voting rights and other policy and institutional requirements which they view as conducive to their needs rather than navigating the difficult process of conducting an institutional reform of existing organizations. Hence, the current trends toward proliferation of international organizations and fragmentation of the architecture of international organizations is likely to continue and will probably further accelerate.

This poses challenges for defining the relations of international organizations. There are many authors who deplore the inherent risks and adverse effects of proliferation and fragmentation of legal and institutional frameworks. This is not to deny that such risks exist. Proliferation and fragmentation may indeed lead to duplication of efforts and result in scarce resources being wasted. However, as previously discussed by this author, short of a major health or security crisis, any plan for a grand new design of the architecture of international organizations, including the merger of institutions or major changes to their institutional structures, is unlikely to succeed, given vested interests and the qualified majorities and other the statutory requirements which are formidable obstacles for any far-reaching institutional reform.[12] Hence, efforts need to be made to maximize the benefits and minimize the adverse effects of proliferation and fragmentation. Fragmentation may also provide the chance to experiment with new solutions. This should be further explored.

In the book "Funds for Development: Multilateral Channels of Concessional Financing", this author has proposed airline alliances and "cooptition" (i.e. cooperative competition) as new paradigms for the relationship of international organizations.

> Airline alliances may represent a possible paradigm for the relationship of international organizations and other concessional windows in the (possibly extended) interim phase until substantial institutional reforms can be implemented. Airlines that have joined an alliance have largely harmonized their administrative procedures in order to transport passengers and freight effectively to all destinations. Moreover, by cooperating in certain areas (check-in, lounges, etc.), they have not only reduced cost but also streamlined and aligned their operational procedures. However, each airline maintains its own character and competes in providing the best standards of service.
>
> In the same way, MDFIs should try to find new and innovative solutions in responding to the needs of their targets and continue to enhance their development impact, develop new instruments, and provide excellent service while keeping faithful to the purpose for which they were established [....].[13]

"Cooptition" may be a paradigm for the relation of international organizations, in general. Organizations should be encouraged to compete based on excellence of their services while cooperating wherever feasible to reduce transaction costs.

In the future, we may have to deal with thousands of international organizations. To remain relevant to the demands of their members and stakeholders, individual

---

[12] Droesse 2011b, p. 164.

[13] Droesse 2011c, p. 37.

organizations will need to change to enhance their effectiveness and impact. If competition between international organizations based on excellence is encouraged, states and other donors will be in a much better position than at present to decide which organization are most efficient and effective. Such assessment may be taken into consideration when decisions are taken on the allocations of resources to specific organizations. However, to allow such an assessment, evaluation of specific organizations should no longer be conducted on an organization-specific basis, but across international organization of a specific type or located in a specific region. New institutions to conduct such an assessment should be established.

References

D'Aspremont J (2011) A multifaceted concept of the autonomy of International Organizations and International Legal Discourse. In: Collins R, White N (eds) International Organizations and the idea of autonomy: institutional independence in the International Legal Order. Routledge, London, pp 63–86

Droesse G (2011a) Modalities of Multilateral Concessional Financing. In: Droesse G (ed) Funds for development: Multilateral Channels of Concessional Financing. ADB, Manila, pp 179–297

Droesse G (2011b) Organizational structures, institutional frameworks, and decision-making procedures of Multilateral Concessional Financing. In: Funds for development: Multilateral Channels of Concessional Financing. ADB, Manila, pp 59–177

Droesse G (2011c) Introductory remarks and overview of publication: proliferation, fragmentation, and earmarking of Concessional Financing. In: Droesse G (ed) Funds for development: Multilateral Channels of Concessional Financing. Asian Development Bank, Manila, pp 1–37

Gazzini T (2011) The relationship between International Legal Personality and the Autonomy of International Organizations. In: Collins R, White ND (eds) International Organizations and the idea of autonomy: institutional independence in the International Legal Order. Routledge, London, pp 196–212

Henley PH, Blokker NM (2013) The group of 20: a short legal anatomy from the perspective of International Institutional Law. Melb J Int Law 14:550–607

Index

G. Droesse, *Membership in International Organizations*,
https://doi.org/10.1007/978-94-6265-327-6

E

F

G

H

I

W

Y

Z

MIX
Papier aus verantwortungsvollen Quellen
Paper from responsible sources
FSC® C105338

If you have any concerns about our products,
you can contact us on
ProductSafety@springernature.com

In case Publisher is established outside the EU,
the EU authorized representative is:
Springer Nature Customer Service Center GmbH
Europaplatz 3, 69115 Heidelberg, Germany

Printed by Libri Plureos GmbH
in Hamburg, Germany